Early Modern Englisl

# Early Modern English Poetry
## *A Critical Companion*

Edited by

**Patrick Cheney**
*The Pennsylvania State University*

**Andrew Hadfield**
*University of Sussex*

**Garrett A. Sullivan, Jr.**
*The Pennsylvania State University*

New York    Oxford
OXFORD UNIVERSITY PRESS
2007

Oxford University Press, Inc., publishes works that further Oxford University's
objective of excellence in research, scholarship, and education.

Oxford   New York
Auckland   Cape Town   Dar es Salaam   Hong Kong   Karachi
Kuala Lumpur   Madrid   Melbourne   Mexico City   Nairobi
New Delhi   Shanghai   Taipei   Toronto

With offices in
Argentina   Austria   Brazil   Chile   Czech Republic   France   Greece
Guatemala   Hungary   Italy   Japan   Poland   Portugal   Singapore
South Korea   Switzerland   Thailand   Turkey   Ukraine   Vietnam

Copyright © 2007 by Oxford University Press, Inc.

Published by Oxford University Press, Inc.
198 Madison Avenue, New York, New York 10016
http://www.oup.com

Oxford is a registered trademark of Oxford University Press

**Library of Congress Cataloging-in-Publication Data**

Early modern English poetry : a critical companion / edited by Patrick Cheney, Andrew
     Hadfield, Garrett Sullivan.
         p. cm.
     Includes bibliographical references and index.
     ISBN 13: 978-0-19-515387-3
     ISBN 0-19-515387-1 (alk. paper)
         1. English poetry—Early modern, 1500-1700—History and criticism.
     I. Cheney, Patrick Gerard, 1949– II. Hadfield, Andrew. III. Sullivan, Garrett A.

PR533 E17 2006
821'.09003—dc22                                                         2006040034

Printing number: 9 8 7 6 5 4 3 2 1

Printed in the United States of America
on acid-free paper

# Contents

# Contents:
# Thematic and Generic

## Politics

## Printing

## Religion

# Preface

The editors intend this volume to serve as a complementary text in a college or university course in Renaissance poetry, undergraduate or graduate. Whereas most "companion" texts divide material according to topics, ours begins with a slightly different structural principle: authors and their works. In its broadest contour, we have designed the volume to address an imagined classroom model: students will read poems, typically by known authors, and they will benefit from reading informed commentary, geared to their needs and representing important topics of recent critical inquiry. For each work, an expert academic addresses not only a poem or group of poems, but also a specific cultural or literary topic, from religion to Petrarchism, pastoral to the apocalypse, artistic identity to politics of the town. Through this design, we hope that students will read most of the great poems and authors of the period, at the same time that students acquire familiarity with various topics vital for understanding a particular area of investigation.

The first three chapters provide general material that helps to contextualize the rest of the volume. The first chapter (by Susanne Woods) examines the sixteenth-century invention of verse; the second (by Arthur F. Marotti), print and manuscript culture in early modern England and a particular kind of work that emerged from both, the miscellany; and the third (by Peter C. Herman), Renaissance treatises on the art of poetry.

The remaining chapters examine as many poems or groups of poems that we have space for in a single volume. We have endeavored to include essays on works that are commonly anthologized and taught in universities. We have organized this larger set of chapters according to a general chronology of dates for composition or publication, from Wyatt early in the sixteenth century to Milton in the middle of the seventeenth.[1] Three especially important poets appear centrally in more than a single chapter: Spenser, in four chapters; Shakespeare, in three; and Donne, in three. Other poets included, men as well as women, are Surrey, Dyer, Oxford, Gascoigne, Philip Sidney, Raleigh, Marlowe, Mary Sidney Herbert, Wroth, Lanyer, Jonson, George Herbert, Crashaw, Carew, Suckling, Lovelace, Marvell, and the young Milton. Some of these will be familiar names to readers of this volume; others have been included because they deserve to be better known than they are, having had an influence on the history of English poetry or demonstrating an important aspect of English Renaissance culture. We have also tried to balance these principles with the need to include those poets and poems most often taught in college and university courses. Nevertheless, we have been forced to omit a number of important writers, including John Skelton, Thomas Lodge, George Turbeville, and Thomas Herrick. Our hope is that the flexible and innovative design of the volume will not only encourage readers to explore such major poets, but also enable readers to appreciate the poets' work more fully, through the application of the subjects discussed in the chapters to other writers. For this reason, we have included an alternative contents page listing the chapters by subject rather than author.

We would hope that teachers and students will find opportunities to use the volume in a variety of ways. Most obviously, they may read an individual chapter on a poet or poem assigned on a particular class day. But they might also like to *transport* topics from one work or author to another. Most of the chapters provide "background" or "contextual" material on the designated topic. Yet many of the topics pertain directly to many of the poets. As a result, readers can easily consider the topic taken up in conjunction with one poem in relation to another. For instance, readers could transport the topic of "Petrarchism" from *Astrophil and Stella* (in William J. Kennedy's chapter) to any number of poets or poems, such as Shakespeare's *Sonnets*. Similarly, readers might find the chapter on Spenserian pastoral (from Bart van Es's chapter) or Marvellian pastoral (from Thomas Healy's chapter) portable to many other poems, such as Milton's *Lycidas*. Moreover, if teachers and students are reading a poem or poet not covered in the volume, they may nonetheless find some information relevant to it. Thus, if the class is reading Herrick, readers might take a look at the chapter on Cavalier poetry and the English Civil War (by Laura Lunger Knoppers). There are many such possibilities, and we encourage teachers and students to experiment in ways that might prove fruitful. Even though we have had to make choices, we hope our design affords a comprehensive approach to an expansive and complex field.

To augment our design, we have had contributors include a reading list at the end of each chapter, so that teachers and students can follow up their work through a recommended set of secondary works. A chronology of Renaissance poetry precedes the introduction and is related to the contents of the volume.

*A note:* Throughout this volume, we shall be using the terms "Renaissance" and "early modern" as synonyms, as we have done in this preface. Each term has its advantages and disadvantages, which readers ought to note for future reference. "Renaissance" became a means of defining the period, circa 1450–circa 1650, in the nineteenth century.[2] The term was heavily indebted to the high value that nineteenth-century historians and art historians placed on Italian art and to the belief that culture spread throughout Europe from Italy (hence terms such as the "Northern Renaissance," which assumes that the less advanced areas of Europe finally only belatedly caught up with their Mediterranean masters). There was, predictably, a reaction to this loaded term, which placed more emphasis on high culture and southern Europe than on popular culture—especially the impact of the Reformation—and northern Europe. Many now prefer to use the description "early modern period," derived from the usage of historians, which can refer either to the period 1500–1700, or to 1500–1800, when it is used more inclusively. However, there is a major objection to this usage. It denigrates the period before 1500 as premodern and effectively primitive, more so even than the use of "Renaissance," which, meaning "the rebirth" (of learning), also indicated that a glorious dawn had come after a dark, cultureless night (and, in defining 1500–1700 or 1800 as "early modern," it implies that we are now modern or "postmodern" and that mankind has been evolving toward the present). Defining literary texts in terms of the monarchical reigns—for example, Elizabethan, Jacobean—or dynasties—Tudor, Stuart—in which they were written offsets such problems. Yet it does so at the expense of defining the literature in terms of the monarch, which often tends to concentrate the reader's attention on the court established by the monarch or monarchy in question, which may not be intended. In short, we make no distinction between the terms because there is no neutral way of describing the years 1500–1700. All have implications that users may not wish to support. Nevertheless, we offer "early modern" and "Renaissance" as a useful shorthand, rather than as ideologically loaded descriptions.[3]

## Acknowledgments

Like *Early Modern English Drama: A Critical Companion* (Oxford, 2006), this volume began with Tony English, our former editor at Oxford University Press in New York. We are grateful to Tony, as well as to our current editor, Jan Beatty, and to her former assistant editor, Talia Krohn, and her current assistant editor, Jackie Ardam, for helping us with the volume. We also thank Christine D'Antonio, for ushering the volume through production, and Michele Kornegay, for copyediting the manuscript.

We are indebted to OUP's readers—Elizabeth Fowler, University of Virginia; Sean Keilen, University of Pennsylvania; Willy Maley, University of Glasgow—for their support and insightful advice.

The contributors have not only provided us with terrific essays but also have been scrupulous in writing and revising their essays in a timely fashion. We have greatly enjoyed working with all of them.

At Penn State, we would like to thank Julie Noblick, who helped with formatting the twenty-eight essays that make up the volume.

Finally, we once more would like to thank our families for their support during the project: Debora, Alison, Marie, Lucy, Patrick, Evan, Maud, and Kelton.

## NOTES

1. We do not include Milton's later work, such as *Paradise Lost,* because many programs have separate courses in Milton.
2. See J. B. Bullen, *The Myth of the Renaissance in Nineteenth-Century Writing* (Oxford: Clarendon P, 1994).
3. For discussion, see Philippa Berry, "Renewing the Concept of Renaissance: The Cultural Influence of Paganism Reconsidered," *Textures of Renaissance Knowledge,* ed. Philippa Berry and Margaret Tudeau-Clayton (Manchester: Manchester UP, 2003) 17–34.

# Select Chronology, 1503–1681

Literary events are placed first and historical events afterward. We have tried to keep dates to a minimum to give readers a clear outline of the history of English poetry and its place within a wider world. Dates of works indicate publication unless otherwise noted. References to the history of drama can be found in *Early Modern English Drama: A Critical Companion*.

**1503**   Wyatt b.

**1504**   Skelton writes *Philip Sparrow*.

**1509**   Henry VII d. and accession of Henry VIII.

**1510**   Erasmus in England, lecturing at Oxford.

**1513**   Wars between England and Scotland and England and France. The English are victorious at the Battle of Flodden in the former war, but are defeated by the French in the latter.

**1515**   Thomas Wolsey becomes cardinal.

**1517**   Surrey b. (?). The Reformation begins when Martin Luther nails his ninety-five theses to the door of Wittenberg Cathedral, Germany.

**1520**   Field of the Cloth of Gold when Henry VIII and Francis I of France meet near Calais.

**1521**   Skelton writes *Speke Parrot*. Henry VIII named "Defender of the Faith" by Pope Leo X for his attacks on Luther.

**1525**   William Tyndale completes his translation of the New Testament in Germany. Gascoigne b. (?).

**1529**   Skelton d. Disgrace of Cardinal Wolsey (d. 1530).

**1532**   Henry VIII divorces Catherine of Aragon.

**1533**   Wyatt writing his satires (?).

**1534**   Act of Supremacy in England, affirming the independence of the English Church.

**1535**   Sir Thomas More executed. Publication of first complete English Bible.

**1536**   Execution of Anne Boleyn. Pilgrimage of Grace, the most serious threat to the Tudors, as rebels demand restoration of the old church. Sackville b.

**1537**   Leaders of Pilgrimage of Grace executed.

**1540**   Thomas Cromwell, chief architect of Henry's administrative reforms, executed. Turberville b. (?).

**1542**   Wyatt d.

**1543**   Dyer b.

**1547**   Execution of Surrey. Henry VIII d. and accession of Edward VI.

**1549**   First Book of Common Prayer. Kett's Rebellion against enclosures and Protestantism.

**1550**   Earl of Oxford b.

**1552**   Spenser b. (?); Raleigh b. (?).

**1553**   Edward VI d. and accession of Mary I.

**1554**   Sidney b.; Greville b. Wyatt's Rebellion against Catholicism. Mary marries Philip II of Spain.

**1555**   Bishops Latimer and Ridley burned at the stake in Oxford during persecution of Protestants.

**1557**   Tottel's *Miscellany.*

**1558**   Calais, the last English possession in France, is reclaimed by the French. Mary I d. and accession of Elizabeth I.

**1559**   Complete edition of *A Mirror for Magistrates.* Chapman b. (?).

**1561**   John Stowe's edition of Chaucer. Francis Bacon b.; Southwell b. (?).

**1562**   Daniel b.

**1563**   *Mirror for Magistrates,* including Sackville's Induction; Barnaby Googe, *Eclogues, Epitaphs and Sonnets.* Drayton b.

**1564**   Marlowe b.; Shakespeare b.; Mary Sidney b.

**1567**   Campion b.; Nashe b. Mary Stuart abdicates the throne of Scotland in favor of her son, James VI.

**1569**   Googe b.; Lanyer b.

**1569–70**   Northern Rebellion.

**1571**   Donne b. Every cathedral and collegiate church ordered to possess John Foxe's *Acts and Monuments of the Christian Church.*

**1572**   Jonson b. Duke of Norfolk executed for treason. Massacre of Saint Bartholomew's Day in France.

**1573**   Gascoigne, *A Hundred Sundry Flowers;* Whitney, *A Sweet Nosgay.*

**1574**   Barnfield b.

**1576**   Marston b.

**1577**   Gascoigne d.

**1579**   Spenser, *The Shepheardes Calender;* Sidney, *A Defence of Poetry* (written).

**1580**   Sidney, *Astrophil and Stella* (written, published in 1591).

**1581**   Parliament makes it a treasonable offense to convert anyone to Catholicism.

**1582**  Raleigh's poems written and circulated in manuscript at court (1592). French Duke of Alençon leaves England after failure of marriage negotiations with Elizabeth I.

**1583**  Throckmorton Plot to assassinate Elizabeth exposed.

**1585**  Drummond of Hawthornden b.

**1586**  Sidney d. at Zutphen. Mary Wroth b. (?).

**1587**  Execution of Mary Stuart (Queen of Scots).

**1588**  Wither b. Defeat of Spanish Armada.

**1589**  George Puttenham (?), *The Arte of English Poesie.*

**1589–91**  Martin Marprelate Tracts cause a major scandal.

**1590**  First edition of Spenser's *The Faerie Queene,* containing Books 1–3.

**1591**  Herrick b.

**1593**  Shakespeare, *Venus and Adonis;* Marlowe, *Hero and Leander* and *Lucan's First Book* (entered in Stationers' Register); Daniel, *Delia;* Drayton, *Idea.* Marlowe d. at Deptford. George Herbert b.

**1594**  Spenser, *Amoretti* and *Epithalamion;* Shakespeare, *The Rape of Lucrece;* Barnfield, *The Affectionate Shepherd;* Nashe, *The Unfortunate Traveller.* Start of Nine Years War in Ireland. Shakespeare's *Sonnets* first written (?).

**1595**  Donne's early poetry circulating in manuscript; Sidney's *Defence of Poetry;* Spenser, *Colin Clouts Come Home Againe.* Carew b. (?). Southwell executed.

**1596**  Spenser, *Fowre Hymnes* and *Prothalamion;* second edition of *The Faerie Queene,* containing Books 1–6.

**1597**  Turberville d. by this year. Drayton, *England's Heroical Epistles;* Bacon, *Essays* (first edition).

**1598**  Chapman-Marlowe, *Hero and Leander;* Marston, *Scourge of Villainy.*

**1599**  *The Passionate Pilgrim;* includes first printed versions of Marlowe's "The Passionate Shepherd to His Love" and Raleigh's "The Nymph's Reply." Bishops' Ban on satires; Marlowe's *Ovid's Elegies* and Davies's *Epigrams* publicly burned. Spenser d.

**1601**  Shakespeare, "The Phoenix and the Turtle"; Campion, *Book of Airs.* Nashe d. (?). Execution of the Earl of Essex after his failed uprising against Elizabeth.

**1602**  Campion, *Observations on the Art of English Poesie.*

**1603**  Daniel, *A Defence of Ryme.* Elizabeth d. and accession of James I. End of Nine Years War.

**1604**  Peace Treaty with Spain. Earl of Oxford d.

**1605**  Bacon, *The Advancement of Learning.*

**1606**  Waller b.

**1607**  Dyer d.

**1608** Sackville d. Milton b.

**1609** Googe d. Suckling b. Shakespeare, *Sonnets,* and *A Lover's Complaint.*

**1610** Galileo observes the moons of Jupiter using the telescope.

**1611** Donne, *First Anniversary;* Lanyer, *Salve deus rex Judaeorum.* Authorized Version of the Bible.

**1612** Donne, *Second Anniversary;* Drayton, *PolyOlbion* (first edition). Crashaw b. (1612/13). Prince Henry d.; Charles now heir to the throne.

**1616** Jonson, *Workes.* Shakespeare d.

**1618** Execution of Raleigh. Lovelace b.; Cowley b. Thirty Years War begins.

**1619** Daniel d.

**1620** Barnfield d.; Campion d.

**1621** Marvell b.; Vaughan b. Mary Sidney Herbert d.

**1622** Drayton, *PolyOlbion* (second edition). First English newspaper appears.

**1623** Prince Charles and Buckingham travel to Spain to pursue Spanish marriage.

**1625** James d. and accession of Charles I.

**1626** Francis Bacon d.

**1628** William Harvey, *De Motu Cordis,* reveals circulation of the blood. Greville d. Duke of Buckingham assassinated.

**1629** Charles dissolves Parliament and rules alone for next eleven years.

**1630** Future Charles II b.

**1631** Donne d.; Drayton d. John Dryden b.

**1632** Katherine Phillips b.

**1633** Donne, *Poems.* Herbert d.; *The Temple* published. Laud made archbishop of Canterbury.

**1634** Milton, *Comus.* Chapman d.; Marston d.

**1637** Jonson d.

**1638** Milton, *Lycidas.*

**1640** Carew d.; *Poems* published.

**1641** Suckling d.

**1642** Civil War begins when Charles I raises his standard at Nottingham.

**1645** Lanyer d. Milton, *Poems.*

**1646** Suckling, *Fragmenta Aurea.*

**1648** Herrick, *Hesperides.* Lovelace d.

**1649** Crashaw d.; Drummond d. Execution of Charles I. Republic established in England until 1653.

**1650** Vaughan, *Silex Scintillans.*

**1651**  Hobbes, *Leviathan*. Phillips poems circulating in manuscript. Mary Wroth d. (?).

**1652**  Crashaw, *Sacred Poems;* Greville, *Life of the Renowned Sir Philip Sidney.*

**1653**  Cromwell becomes protector.

**1656**  Cromwell assumes title of lord protector, having declined that of king. Cromwell d. Richard Cromwell made lord protector.

**1659**  Suckling, *Last Remains.*

**1660**  Restoration of Charles II.

**1667**  Milton, *Paradise Lost* (Books 1–10).

**1671**  Milton, *Paradise Regained* and *Samson Agonistes.*

**1674**  Milton, *Paradise Lost* (Books 1-12).

**1681**  Marvell's poems published.

# Introduction

## Reading Renaissance Poetry

Most readers are aware that the poetry of the English Renaissance is thought to be among the finest achievements in world literature. This period produced the great national epics of Edmund Spenser and John Milton, the haunting sonnet sequences of Sir Philip Sidney and William Shakespeare, and the exquisite lyrics of Christopher Marlowe, John Donne, Ben Jonson, George Herbert, and Andrew Marvell, among many others. But how exactly should we try to read it? How did Renaissance readers read poetry? What expectations did they have of a poem? And how did their responses tend to differ—if at all—from ours? These are central questions that this volume is designed to help answer.

After all, poetry is not necessarily a vital part of most people's reading today. Far more people read novels—a form of literature that started to dominate literary production in the eighteenth century—if they wish to read fiction. Very few writers can make a living out of writing poetry alone: most either have a day job or exist through giving lectures or readings, writing journalism, or producing other forms of literature. In England, it is well known that the two or three best-selling poets sell more copies of their works than the rest of the poetry community put together. Contemporary poetry is dominated by the lyric, a short poem in which the writer usually recollects something he or she has observed and then reflects on its significance, describing the event in memorable and often startling language, using figurative language to help the reader appreciate the significance of his or her thoughts.

We are, of course, indulging in overgeneralization. There is still a place for other forms of poetry—satire, the dramatic monologue, the verse letter, the sonnet (itself a type of lyric), poetic sequences, and so on. But most schoolchildren when taught poetry will be asked to read works such as Philip Larkin's "An Arundel Tomb," Dylan Thomas's "Do Not Go Gentle into That Good Night," or W. B. Yeats's "An Irish Airman Foresees His Death," all examples of poems that describe a situation, then either draw conclusions from the lyric experience directly or ask the reader to infer what the poem might mean to them. Reading, even when performed in groups in institutions such as secondary schools or universities, is regarded as an intensely private experience, a direct communication between author and reader.

It would be a mistake to imagine that this sort of reading did not take place in the Renaissance and that, as is sometimes suggested, it is a purely post-Romantic phenomenon. Evidence does not always survive, and often when it does, in the form of annotations in the margins of books or published responses to poems, we cannot always be certain that what we have is a private, individual response to a work. However, readers did often copy out striking verses into commonplace books, designed to be read for their own edification and instruction, a practice that suggests that many did read poetry as we usually do today. Moreover, given the wealth of material that circulated in manuscript, often privately, or even surreptitiously, it is hard not to imagine that individual readers conceived the lyric poems of Sir Thomas Wyatt or Donne in ways that we would recognize.

The point that needs to be made is that while there may be much overlap between the ways that people read verse in the early modern period and today, poetry was a far more important way of communicating then than it is now, and it could take a much greater variety of forms. In the Renaissance, poetry was usually defined, following Aristotle, as an art of "imitation" or "making," the poet having the ability and power to shape material from the natural or social world and to make something that was useful, beautiful, and relevant for his or her readers. We often think of literature as an art of the "imagination," but the imagination was thought by Renaissance thinkers to be a part of the mind that led people away from the truth. Rather, the poet's duty was to make something out of the raw materials that he or she encountered, whether that was through observation, reading books, or other means. Poetry was not always conceived in terms of its formal existence as verse, but in terms of what it achieved: the representation of the "truth," produced through the subtle art of imitation, so that the best history, visual art, or philosophy could also be classified as poetry (for further discussion on this point, see chapter 3). When reading poetry written in the early modern period, we have to bear in mind these very different—but not mutually exclusive—definitions.

Poetry was regarded as the most important form of literature, with prose fiction lagging far behind and many not sure whether drama was anything other than popular entertainment. This last fact is something of an irony given Shakespeare's preeminence as a dramatist since the eighteenth century, a reputation that was overshadowed for many of his contemporary readers by his fame as the author of *Venus and Adonis* and *The Rape of Lucrece*, narrative poems that went through a number of editions in his lifetime and sold far more copies than printed copies of his plays did. As these examples indicate, poetry was often used as a vehicle for narrative exposition, a literary mode that in the second half of the twentieth century virtually became extinct as a form that can support a sizable readership and has been declining since the rise of the novel. A work such as Spenser's *The Faerie Queene* seems obscure to many readers today, who resist its verse structure and who feel that it requires too much labor to be an enjoyable work. Yet, it clearly had a considerable impact soon after it was published and became a canonical work in the history of English poetry, read and imitated by most major poets.[1] Most serious writers aspired to be narrative poets as well as lyric poets, imitating, sometimes translating, the great classical poems: Virgil's *Aeneid*, Homer's *Odyssey*, Lucan's *Pharsalia*, and Ovid's *Metamorphoses*, which provided a number of styles and registers for telling stories in verse.

Accordingly, readers in the sixteenth and seventeenth centuries were used to a variety of forms of poetry, as the chapters in this volume will demonstrate. Anyone who went to a grammar school would have learned how to write poetry as well as read it, a skill that played a central role in lessons.[2] The difficulty that we face as contemporary readers of Renaissance poetry is that what may seem like a direct expression of a writer's inner feelings may actually be a skilful piece of writing that follows a pattern the audience would have recognized and appreciated. What seems to us a moving lyric or passage may really be a writer demonstrating his ability to write fluently and use a difficult medium with apparent ease. The poems in question may not be quite what they seem to be, and the more help we can get in trying to de-code them—in itself a fascinating and enjoyable task—the better. A particularly sophisticated sequence of poems, such as Sir Philip Sidney's *Astrophil and Stella* (c. 1582, published 1591), makes use of such potential ambiguity, referring to the poet's own relationship with Penelope Devereux, but also hinting that the speaker—whether Sidney or Astrophil is not always clear—is really more interested in worldly, political issues than a failed love match. Trying to gauge how sincere the poet's passion for his lady really is proves to be part of the game that *Astrophil and Stella* encourages the reader to play. Moreover, poets were acutely aware of the different ways in which their work could be read because they were active readers themselves. All the poetry represented in this volume exists as part of a tradition of writing that responds and reacts to similar forms that were produced by predecessors and contemporaries.

## Kinds of Poetry and Types of Poet

Poetry, then, performed a number of crucially important functions.[3] Poems were regularly written for important occasions of state. Monarchs often employed a poet at court for this reason, and there was a loose tradition in England of there being a royal poet, or poet laureate. John Skelton represented himself as one, but whether the reality matched his sense of his own worth is an unresolved question of literary history. Spenser was awarded a £50 pension from Queen Elizabeth for his poetry, but does not seem to have been required to write to order. A few decades later Jonson was given an official pension and assumed the role in a more serious and organized form, one that still exists in England today. Conversely, poetry was also used as a vehicle for scurrilous satire, as practiced by Donne, John Marston, and Joseph Hall, whose work became so virulent, polemical, and insulting that satire was banned in 1599.

Poetry was also used as a means of narrating epic and heroic subjects, from Michael Drayton's description of the British Isles in *PolyOlbion* (1612, 1622) to Milton's account of the fall in *Paradise Lost* (1667, 1674). Religious subjects were explored in a whole variety of poems. Wyatt's translations of the psalms are a meditation on the problematic nature of translation itself in an age when a mistaken interpretation could lead to an accusation of heresy or even treason, which could lead to the execution of the poet/translator in question. Mary Sidney Herbert's translations of the same works, written some years later when biblical translation was undoubtedly a less controversial activity in England, provided a relatively safe outlet for women writers when it was prudent to be silent and obedient. There was a wealth of religious poetry written in the sixteenth century, but such verse undoubtedly became more complex and ambiguous in the seventeenth century, often providing clues for the reader who knew about the poet's religious affiliation, which remained opaque to the uninitiated reader.

Such sophisticated hermeneutic games and disguises are part of the main tradition of Renaissance English poetry, which demanded an active involvement from the reader eager to understand the literary work in question, but they pose particular problems for readers today, who often struggle with religious themes. Even the celebrated lyrics of George Herbert are complicated and hard to interpret, although they seem straightforward enough. Do they express a particular religious affiliation or allegiance? More importantly, are they a means of exploring the nature of the pious Christian life, as has often been thought, or an agonized exploration of the awful majesty of God? Access to some relevant knowledge should help readers reach a more informed assessment of the purpose and value of such poetry and increase their understanding and enjoyment of a major body of interrelated literary works.

On the other hand, some verse was often occasional, written for a specific event, and not always designed to live on afterward as a literary monument (which does not, of course, mean that it cannot be worth reading now). Many writers explored the tension between ephemerality and permanence, notably Jonson, whose verse assumes a classical style and importance while commenting on subjects the significance of which the writer obviously knows will soon have passed. Verse translation was extremely important and evidently absorbed the energies of many writers. Translations were either relatively faithful renditions of the original, such as Sir Arthur Gorges's translation of Lucan's great anti-epic of civil war, the *Pharsalia* (1614), or creative reinterpretations of well-known poems, such as Jonson's brilliant adaptations of Catullus's Latin poems to his mistress, Celia.

Perhaps the most important point to be made is that many writers, principally those who lived long enough to have substantial careers as writers, turned their hands to a wide variety of types of poetry, exhibiting their interest in the different forms of poetry, confidence in their own powers of expression, and ability to respond to the needs and desires of their patrons. Spenser wrote pastoral poetry, complaints, sonnets, a marriage hymn, verse satire, as well as an epic-romance, showing that he was keen to adapt and invent new forms of writing, as well as to prove his skill by producing a wealth of familiar literary forms. Drayton was equally prolific and diverse, producing sonnets, pastorals, satire, lyrics, verse epistles, historical poetry, and a geographical, Ovidian poem for which he is now best remembered (although it sold badly at the time).[4] Donne wrote lengthy religious poetry, lyrics, sonnets (secular and religious), verse epistles, and satires, as well as a host of occasional poems. Poets could expect to write a variety of forms for a variety of occasions and purposes. The readership may have been relatively small, but it was eager to experience a number of types of verse.

We also need to understand that there were also different types of poets who saw themselves in very different ways.[5] Aristocratic writers, such as Wyatt, Sidney, and Sir Walter Raleigh, would probably never have deigned to publish their poetry—although it is possible that they might have been happy enough for someone else to publish it for them. At the opposite end of the spectrum were commercial writers such as Thomas Churchyard, who labored away for over half a century, publishing a variety of types of writing, from pamphlets on topical subjects to poems for patrons who may never have responded to his overtures, eking out a miserable living and largely forgotten after his death (his one poetic triumph being the "Legend of Shore's Wife," which appeared in the 1563 edition of *A Mirror for Magistrates*). In between these extremes were poets such as Spenser, who was keen to publish his verse but also made a good living as a civil servant and landowner in Ireland.[6] Poets such as Daniel and Drayton carved out careers as professional poets, publishing their works, having plays performed, and being supported by a variety of patrons. Jonson undoubtedly enjoyed the most successful career of all, publishing his collected poetry and plays in an expensive folio edition in 1616, the same year that King James I produced his collected works—a statement of his sense of self-worth, to be sure, but also of the importance of poetry in early modern England.

## NOTES

1. Colin Burrow, *Epic Romance: Homer to Milton* (Oxford: Clarendon P, 1993).
2. For discussion of Tudor education, see Rebecca Bushnell, *A Culture of Teaching: Early Modern Humanism in Theory and Practice* (Ithaca: Cornell UP, 1996); T. W. Baldwin, *William Shakspere's Small Latine and Lesse Greeke,* 2 vols. (Urbana: U of Illinois P, 1944).
3. For a convenient recent overview, see Arthur F. Kinney, ed., *The Cambridge Companion to English Literature, 1500–1600* (Cambridge: Cambridge UP, 2000).
4. Andrew Hadfield, "Michael Drayton and the Burden of History," Chatterton Lecture on Poetry, *Proceedings of the British Academy* 125 (2004): 119–47.
5. Richard Helgerson, *Self-Crowned Laureates: Spenser, Jonson, Milton and the Literary System* (Berkeley: U of California P, 1983); Patrick Cheney, *Shakespeare, National Poet-Playwright* (Cambridge: Cambridge UP, 2004).
6. Richard Rambuss, *Spenser's Secret Career* (Cambridge: Cambridge UP, 1993).

# Early Modern English Poetry

# 1

# Inventing English Verse

## Susanne Woods

In 1575, in the first book of early modern English poetics, George Gascoigne cited "invention" as the principal element of a poem: "The first and most necessarie poynt that ever I founde meete to be considered in making of a delectable poem is this, to grounde it upon some fine invention."[1] By this Gascoigne meant a creative idea or metaphor, but he was less sanguine about the potential for inventiveness when it came to verse. About poetic form he exclaimed disparagingly "that commonly now a days in English rimes (for I dare not cal them English verses) we use none other order but a foote of two syllables, wherof the first is depressed or made short, and the second is elevate or made long: and that sound or scanning continueth throughout the verse" (Gascoigne 1.49). By the time he published his *Certayne Notes,* Gascoigne's England had a solid formal base through which to create poetry, but it was recent and did not seem as revolutionary as in fact it was. It remained for later poets to take that base and show its power and flexibility; "rime" and "verse" were concepts that evolved through the century. How to put colors and invention into a readable and effective English verse was by no means clear at the beginning of the sixteenth century, with uncertainties about models, traditions, and even the language itself still current.[2]

Versification is a system for setting up expectations of rhythmic patterns in order to fulfill or surprise them, controlling the movement of language through time. Today we take for granted that iambic pentameter, one such system, was pervasive in Renaissance English verse. Chaucer, writing two hundred years earlier, is commonly taught as if he, too, were writing in familiar iambic pentameter lines. Chaucer's line was by no means so clear to his sixteenth-century followers. The more-or-less ten-syllable or decasyllabic lines of *The Canterbury Tales* seldom move like the lines of Shakespeare's *Sonnets,* and Chaucer's followers were even more difficult to decipher. The popular and prolific fifteenth-century poet John Lydgate, for example, humbly presents his translation of *The Fall of Princes:*

Thouh that I have lak off eloquence
I shal procede in this translacioun,
Fro me avoiding all presumpcioun
Lowli submyttyng everi hour & space
Mi reud language to my lordis grace.[3]

It is difficult to be sure what rhythms this poet expected his readers to find in lines such as these, to see what patterns of expectation he was seeking to create.

Verse is, first of all, language ordered in measured lines, often put together in groups of lines or stanzas. The meter or measure of those lines will vary from language to language but will usually be based on linguistic features such as number of syllables, number of certain kinds of syllable (accented, alliterating, or long), or the relationship of kinds of syllables (accented-unaccented, long-short). In this last instance, a group of syllables seen in relation to each other is commonly referred to as a metrical foot. In English stress-accent meter a foot consists of a pair or three syllables where one of the syllables is stressed relative to the other or others. Borrowing terminology from classical meters (as they did in the sixteenth century), the normal stress-accent pattern of "today" would be called an iamb, "daily" a trochee, "yesterday" a dactyl, and "in a day" an anapest.

The poetic line as it emerged into modern English was an uneasy inheritance from three traditions: Romance vernacular (and medieval Latin) syllabics influenced by the French-speaking Norman English court, the Germanic Anglo-Saxon four-accent line, and the classical principles of foot meter and equivalence.[4] Chaucer, the English vernacular poet whom the Tudor poets most admired, was probably seeking to imitate the continental decasyllabic line in *The Canterbury Tales,* but with lingering rhythms of four major accents among the ten or so syllables, as in the opening to the "General Prologue":

Whan that Áprill with his shoures sóote
The dróughte of Márch hath pérced to the róote
And bathed évery véyne in swich licóur
Of which vertue engéndred is the flóur.

[When April with its sweet showers
the drought of March has pierced to the root
And bathed every vine in that liquid
From which power the flower is engendered.][5]

Notice the pull toward a fifth major accent on "swich" ("such") in line 3, and possibly toward "is" in line 4. Since the nineteenth century, Chaucer's editors and historians of versification have tried to read Chaucer as if he were writing something more like an Elizabethan iambic pentameter, but that is probably anachronistic.[6] In any case, Chaucer's sixteenth-century readers and editors realized that their language had changed sufficiently in a little more than a hundred years so that Chaucer's verse was sometimes difficult to read. Gascoigne called the verse of the *Canterbury Tales* "ryding ryme," which "serveth most aptly to wryte a merie tale" (1.56).

Though Gascoigne may have misread Chaucer's versification as cruder and more rollicking than it was, there is a reason why Chaucer's roughly ten-syllable lines pulled toward a fifth major accent and later editors and critics thought he was reaching for an Elizabethan iambic pentameter. Since rhythmic emphasis in English is based on stress-accent, not "length," as English developed from Old and Middle versions into early modern English, stress-accent seems increasingly to be a function of the position of a syllable within its context. Given any two or three syllables, no matter what they are, one of those syllables will tend to receive more stress accent than the other or others. If this is true for Chaucer's English, then the relatively unimportant word "swich" in line 3 of the "General Prologue" finds itself with relatively more stress-accent than its surrounding syllables, "in" and the first syllable of "licour" (pronounced in the French manner with emphasis on the second syllable). Similarly, a spondee (two long syllables in Latin, and presumably two accented syllables in English) would become almost impossible in English. Just as a group of less emphatic syllables will nonetheless pull one of them to greater prominence than the others, so a group of more emphatic syllables will tend to downplay one or two in relation to the most heavily accented syllable. Modern translations of the *Aeneid* usually make no effort to imitate the dactylic hexameters, but presume that blank verse accentual iambic pentameter is the English heroic line, as John Milton was to argue in his note on "The Verse" prefacing *Paradise Lost* in 1667: "The measure is *English* Heroic Verse without Rime, as that of *Homer* in *Greek,* and of *Virgil* in *Latin* [. . .] which consists only in apt Numbers, fit quantity of Syllables, and the sense variously drawn out from one verse into another, not in the jingling sound of like endings, a fault avoided by the learned Ancients both in Poetry and all good Oratory."[7]

By Milton's time the English language and English versification were secure because one hundred years earlier, in the midst of linguistic change and in the face of models such as Lydgate, verse in modern English had been invented by a series of talented poets reacting to three major cultural forces in sixteenth-century England: the Italian model of Petrarch, education reform spurred by a renewed interest in classical Greek and Latin texts (the "Renaissance"), and the printing press, which appeared in England around 1480. This confluence helped to develop the versatile iambic pentameter line, blank verse, and numerous stanzaic forms including variations on the sonnet. The origin of English verse is complex and controversial, but it is possible to trace some major trends from the poets associated with the court of Henry VIII (1509–47) to those who flourished at the end of the reign of Queen Elizabeth I (1558–1603). Central to understanding that development is an anthology of lyrics commonly known as Tottel's *Miscellany* (1557).

The actual title of Tottel's *Miscellany* is *Songs and Sonnets, written by the right honorable Lord Henry Howard late Earl of Surrey, and other,* the principal other being Sir Thomas Wyatt. Both Wyatt and Surrey had been luminaries in the court of Henry VIII, with Wyatt an ambassador, musician, and poet and the talented Surrey the heir to the Howard family, one of the most powerful in England (for more on their stories, see chapter 4 in this volume, "Wyatt, Surrey, and the Henrican Court"). A little over ten years later, in 1557, an entrepreneurial publisher named Richard Tottel published the *Songs and Sonnets,* which went through at least seven editions in thirty years. This quarto volume contained 40 poems by Surrey, about 95 by Wyatt, and about 150 by other authors (the number varied by edition), most of them unknown. While manuscript collections of verse were common among the higher classes during this period (see chapter 2 in this volume, "Print, Manuscripts, and Miscellanies"), Tottel's printed book made widely available the best two poets of the first half of the sixteenth century and the work was enormously influential.[8]

Tottel's brief introduction, "To the Reader," invokes and promotes cultural attitudes toward poetry in mid-century. It first situates the poems in relation to the Italian and classical influences that had begun to permeate English culture, asserts the value of writing short verse (not just the epics and tragedies valued in Aristotle's *Poetics*), and elevates the more contemporary Italian vernacular model to the level of the classical Latin poets: "That to have written well in verse, and yea in small parcels, deserveth great praise, the workers of divers Latins, Italians, and other do prove sufficiently." Not only the Italians can write as beautifully as their classical predecessors, Tottel continues: "that our tongue is able in that kind to do as praise worthily as the rest, the honorable style of the noble Earl of Surrey, and the weightiness of the deep witted sir Thomas Wyatt the elders' verse, with several graces in sundry good English writers, do show abundantly." Tottel was best known as a publisher of law books, and the young men who studied at the Inns of Court were often ambitious for the kind of cultural panache provided by knowledge of the classics and of the most fashionable European writers. Now successful English courtiers who preceded them were made widely available by their friendly publisher: "It resteth now (gentle reader) that thou think it not evil done, to publish, to the honor of the English tongue, and for profit of the studious of English eloquence, those works which the ungentle hoarders up of such treasure have heretofore envied thee [that is, those who had the manuscripts have until now denied you]."

Eloquence was a principal value of the educational reform called "the new learning," what we call Renaissance humanism. The new learning placed great emphasis on the study of humanities—history, philosophy, and literature—through classical texts. As European rulers sought to redefine nationhood and consolidate their political and economic advantages, eloquent ambassadors such as Sir Thomas More and Sir Thomas Wyatt were of great value to the court. Speaking well in fine Latin (and with an ability to converse in Greek when called on) signified a cultural advantage reminiscent of the great ages of Athens and Rome. Petrarch, who in 1347 had himself crowned poet laureate on the steps of the Roman senate in order to assert his classical inheritance, was a generator and popularizer of the new learning but also the great model for vernacular love poetry through his sonnet sequence dedicated to a fictive beauty name Laura. By invoking the "Latins and Italians," Tottel conflates classical eloquence with love poems in a modern language.

Many of the poems in the *Miscellany* are translations or imitations of Petrarch's sonnets. Others are courtly songs that might be (some certainly had been) set to music. Still others, following both an earlier English tradition and at the same time seeking to imitate the gravitas of great classical models, are moral lyrics with titles such as "Of the Wretchedness of This World." The book was a compendium of topics of great use to aspiring courtiers who might want to display their own erudition and sophistication through writing verse. It also displayed, for the first time, consistent metrical smoothness in a variety of verse forms and is a triumphant assertion that by 1557 English verse had a stable base on which subsequent writers could build.

In the early sixteenth century it was not altogether clear how English verse was to be measured: By the number of syllables? By the number of accented syllables, and, if so, how would we define those that are accented? By some imitation of classical foot meter, with its offer of considerable syllabic variety over recognizable metrical patterns? Until Gascoigne we do not know exactly how poets of the period thought about the issues, but we do know that poets of the earlier half of the century, notably Wyatt and Surrey, imitated and translated both continental and classical models and were apparently searching within their own vernacular for a robust and flexible way to versify their language. By Tottel's time, ten years after Surrey's death, Surrey especially had given him and mid-century poets the primacy of an accentual-syllabic iambic pattern. Gascoigne may have complained of a regular iambic movement in "rimes," a common term for the syllabic tradition of (rhyming) Romance verse, as opposed to the syllabic and rhythmic variations of (nonrhyming) foot-measure "verse" on the classical model, but at least this new versification was clear, suited to English, and easy to imitate.

Gascoigne's response is to the initial and sometimes excessively regularized English versification celebrated and promoted by Tottel, who very likely also edited or allowed to be edited Surrey and especially Wyatt into the rigorous regularity that became the foundation of the new English verse. If we look at reliable manuscript versions, we can see Wyatt's poems smoothed out by Tottel and even Surrey's poems more relentlessly iambic.

Consider the famous translations of Petrarch's *Rime* 140. The Egerton manuscript, which Wyatt himself oversaw, has the following first stanza:

> The longe love that in my thought doeth harbar
> And in myn hert doeth kepe his residence
> Into my face preseth with bold pretence
> And therein campeth spreding his baner.[9]

Tottel changes the first line slightly, the fourth somewhat more:

> The long love, that in my thought I harber
> [. . .]
> And there campeth, displaying his banner. (Tottel 1.32)

The fifth line is a more substantial change, clearly intended to make Wyatt a smoother poet. The Egerton manuscript has "She that me lerneth to love and suffer," while Tottel has "She that me learns to love, and to suffer."

Still, these are nothing compared to the changes Tottel made to one of Wyatt's most famous poems, "They Flee from Me." Three stanzas of what was called rhyme royal (ababbcc) in protest over the inconstancy of courtly women, the poem is notable for denying some of the distancing elements of the Petrarchan erotic fantasy. This lady was real, no dream. Unlike the convention of the lover as hunter and the lady as the hunted deer, the roles are reversed. The wildness mentioned in the poem suggests that the particular lady of the poem deserves what predators deserve—an unusually sharp response within the tradition of the abandoned lover. The Egerton manuscript gives us an authoritative version, while the Tottel variant not only smoothes out some complex lines of uncertain syllabification and accent but also changes the whole ending. First the authoritative Egerton manuscript version (Harrier 131–32):

> They fle from me / that sometyme did me seke
>     with naked fote stalking in my chamber
>     I have sene theim gentill tame and meke
>     that nowe are wyld and do not remember
>     that sometyme they put theimsself in daunger     5
>     to take bred at my hand & nowe they raunge
>     besely seeking with a continuell chaunge.
> Thancked be fortune it hath ben otherwise
>     twenty tymes better but ons [once] in speciall
>     in thyn arraye after a pleasaunt gyse     10
>     when her lose gowne from her shoulders did fall

and she me caught in her armes long & small
therewithal sweetly did me kysse
and softely saide dere hertr how like you this
It was no dreme I lay brode waking                              15
but all is torned torough my gentilnes
into a straunge fashion of forsaking
and I have leve to goo of her goodenes
and she also to use new fangilnes
but syns that I so kyndely ame served                          20
I would fain knowe what she hath deserved.

The lines are mostly decasyllabic, though after the clearly iambic first line, the ten syllables are not often arranged in an easy accentual iambic pentameter. Syllable counts vary, with line 7 having as many as twelve (depending on whether you elide the last two syllables of "continuell") and line 13 having eight.

Tottel or his editor takes the same poem, keeps the principal imagery and the pun on the hunter and the deer ("deer hart" as "dear heart"), but smoothes out both syllabic number and the placement of stress accents, concluding with a milder and more Socratic question (Tottel 1.39):

They flee from me, that somtime did me seke
    With naked fote stalking within my chamber.
Once have I seen them gentle, tame, and meke,
That now are wild, and do not once remember
That sometyme they have put them selves in danger,          5
To take bread at my hand, and now they range,
Busily sekyng in continuall change.
    Thanked be fortune, it hath bene otherwise
Twenty tymes better: but once especiall,
In thinne aray, after a pleasant gyse,                         10
When her loose gowne did from her shoulders fall,
And she me caught in her armes long and small,
And therewithal, so sweetly did me kysse,
And softly sayd: deare hart, how like you this?
    It was no dreame: for I lay broad awaking.                  15
But all is turned now through my gentlenesse.
Into a bitter fashion of forsakying:
And I have leave to go of her goodnesse,
And she also to use newfanglenesse.
How like you this, what hath she now deserved?                20

Some of the changes appear minor: from "I have sene" to "Once have I seen" in line 3; from "seeking with a" to "sekyng in" in line 7; from "therewithal sweetly" to "And therewithal, so sweetly" in line 13. The last perhaps shows best what Tottel is doing: he has brought the eight-syllable line into a match with the majority of ten-syllable lines, regularizing and smoothing out to a more nearly iambic rhythm. The same process can be seen in line 15, from "It was no dreme I lay brode waking," with its forceful insistence, to the more lyrical, and less emphatic, "It was no dreame: for I lay broad awaking." Similarly, in line 17 "straunge," meaning foreign, gives way to "bitter" in Tottel. The major change is in the last couplet, where the ironic "kyndely," with its overtones of womankind as predatory kind, becomes instead "unkindly," a more one-dimensional assumption about proper womankindly behavior. But the poem does not say that; it says that these women were once tame, but are now wild; they pursued but now flee. The trope suggests an alien being, separate from humanity. Some sophisticated readers (including John Hollander) prefer the Tottel version, in part out of preference for the Tottel conclusion, and in part because Tottel has made a fine iambic pentameter poem out of a more complex original.

Wyatt gets credit for introducing into the Henrican court, and then through Tottel to English culture more generally, a great many of the elements that would support the development of verse in modern English: attention to syllabification but with enough freedom to play with accentual effects within a line; importation of the sonnet through translations and imitations of Petrarch and the innovation of a concluding couplet (Italian and French sonnets followed the octave-sestet model, in which the last six lines typically rhyme cdccdc or cdecde); and explicit importation of classical forms, including the epigram and Horatian satire. Courtiers and university men had imitated these forms in the past (particularly in the Scottish court), but Wyatt's popularity along with his direct influence on the even more influential Surrey gives him pride of place in the invention of verse for early modern English.

Surrey, however, had the most immediate and enduring importance for establishing English verse. He smoothed out the decasyllabic line, creating iambic pentameter as we know it; invented the English sonnet that Shakespeare would later use (ababcdcdefefgg); and saw the utility of the iambic pentameter blank verse line for heroic poetry more than a hundred years before Milton famously affirmed it.

Surrey's version of Petrarch's *Rime* 140 illustrates the success with which he transformed the continental sonnet form. It is easier to sustain a single rhyme sound in Italian and French than it is in English, so the move to ababcdcdefefgg makes the sonnet easier than if English poets felt constrained to follow a typical Petrarchan form such as ab-baabbacdcdcd. Surrey also capitalized on Wyatt's invention of a concluding couplet, which allows for an epigrammatic or summary conclusion. From British Library Additional Manuscript 36529:

> Love that doth raine and live within my thought,
> And buylt his seat within my captive brest,
> Clad in the armes wherein with me he fowghth,
> Oft in my face he doth his banner rest.
> But she that tawght me love and suffer pain,       5
> My doubtful hope & eke [also] my hot desire
> With shamfast looke to shadoo and refrayne,
> Her smyling face convertyth straight to yre.
> And cowarde Love, then, to the hart apace
> Taketh his flight, where he doth lurke and playne [complain]     10
> His purpose lost, and dare not shew his face.
> For my lordes gilt thus fawtles byde I payine;
> Yet from my lorde shall not my foote remove:
> Sweet is the death that taketh end by love.[10]

Tottel's version shows the editor still at work trying to improve even the smoother iambic lines of Surrey. It begins "Love that liveth and reigneth in my thought," presumably to remove the more emphatic and presumably more clumsy "doth." Tottel's fifth line, "She, that me taught to love, and suffer payne," replaces the initial iamb with a trochee—a common substitution in Surrey, and adopted generally by subsequent poets (think of such Shakespeare lines as "When to the sessions of sweet silent thought"). The change may be inconsequential, though "taught me" puts more emphasis on the lady's agency, while "me taught" keeps the focus on the suffering poet. For line 10, Tottel has "Taketh his flight, whereas he lurkes, and plaines," again eliminating the construction with "doth," but "he doth lurke and playne" seems a stronger statement than Tottel's version. It is as if Tottel were after a more rollicking, polysyllabic movement, perhaps in imitation of the elegance and variety of classical verse, or perhaps in an effort to make the rhythms of the decasyllabic line sound more like the increasingly popular and often monotonous verse types known as poulter's measure and fourteeners.

These two verse forms appear to have derived from extending ballad measures, quatrains composed of various combinations of four- and three-accent lines, perhaps in an effort to develop a long line such as Virgil (and before him Homer and others) used for serious verse. But poulter's measure, couplets comprised of a line of six accents followed by a line of seven, and fourteeners, couplets of seven-accent lines, were no dactylic hexameters. Here are the first four of forty-eight lines of one of Surrey's better-known poems in poulter's measure, in which the speaker bemoans the pain of unrequited love:

Suche waywarde wais hath love, that moste parte in discorde.
Our willes do stand, wherby our hartes but seldom dooth accorde.
Disceyte [deceit] is his delight, and to begyle and mocke
The simple hertes which he doth stryke with froward, dyvers stroke. (Surrey 73)

Poulter's measure and fourteeners produced a few successful poems, such as Fulke Greville's elegy on Sir Philip Sidney beginning "Silence augmenteth grief," but the later Elizabethan poets moved away from their insistent rhythms. In this their model again was Surrey, whose development of a versatile iambic pentameter blank verse modified the relentless iambic movement that Gascoigne decried. English iambic pentameter blank verse originally appears in Surrey's translation of books two and four of Virgil's *Aeneid,* also published by Tottel in 1557 but apparently written somewhere in the late 1530s (Surrey 233–34). Surrey's translations owe something to an earlier one in rhyming couplets by the Scottish poet Gavin Douglas (1475–1522), but Surrey apparently recognized that the suppleness of blank verse would be a truer imitation of the dactylic hexameter. The absence of rhyme seems particularly effective for high speech. Christopher Marlowe and then other playwrights (including of course Shakespeare) took this rhetorically powerful blank verse and made it the primary vehicle for English poetic drama. It continues to be a rich resource for English poets, the longest-lasting of Surrey's many formal contributions.

Casting aside rhyme, and learning to play with run-on lines to keep variety in rhetorical pacing across line endings (what Milton meant by "sense variously drawn out"), paved the way for an effort to reproduce quantitative verse in English. Sidney and Spenser both tried to imitate classical verse forms, and Spenser and his friend Gabriel

Harvey discussed its aptness for English verse in a series of letters published in 1580.[11] Sidney's experiments with quantitative verse, set among the eclogues of the *Old Arcadia*, were in general more successful than Spenser's, but neither poet is remembered for these efforts.

While quantitative experiments are not the most successful of Sidney or Spenser's poems, occasionally a lyric coming out of the quantitative verse movement has real charm. Thomas Campion included a fine one in his treatise arguing for the quantitative model, *Observations in the Art of English Poesy* (1602). Campion was a musician as well as a poet, and his musician's sensibility led him to reject the metronomic implications of the rigid iambics associated with rhyming verse:

> Rose-cheekt Laura, come,
> Sing thou smoothly with thy beawties
> Silent musick, either other
> Sweetly gracing. (310, ll. 1–4)

Campion is able to keep the poem moving through a combination of run-on lines and falling rhythms, many lines ending with unaccented syllables and so pulling the motion of the line forward.

Nonetheless, "rhyme" understood as a system of versification in contrast to classical "verse" was to prove the better system for English versification. Samuel Daniel's *Defense of Rhyme* (1603), a response to Campion, effectively puts the end to two generations of experimentation with a classical model for English verse. Daniel argues sensibly for what we would call accentual-syllabic verse and makes it clear that the feature we call rhyme is fine in itself but the larger issue is a commitment to the system that was called rhyme, which is based on traditional romance language syllabic systems but with the accentual patterns and variety native to English.

This triumph of an English over an imported system would not have been possible without the fascination and experimentation with stanzaic forms and with the limits of metrical tension in iambic lines during the last third of the sixteenth century. Among the admired and imitated poets who focused attention on formal variety were Spenser, Sidney, and Sidney's sister, the countess of Pembroke. Spenser's versification, especially, is among the most subtle and accomplished of any in English and can only be suggested here, while Sidney and Pembroke appeared to be jointly interested in testing the limits of stanzaic form in English.

Spenser's *Shepheardes Calender* (1579) was an audacious announcement of poetic ambition and the most influential collection of verse after Tottel. The *Calender* offered a stunningly new set of lyric possibilities that Spenser's archaisms and choice of a native pastoral sought to make boldly English. His twelve "eglogues" seemed to assert both a new poet on the Virgilian model (according to the tradition that Virgil's low-style *Eclogues* were an apprenticeship to his high style *Aeneid*) and a new English poetry as inventive as any Italian sonnet or French virelay. Instead of trying to imitate classical sapphics or anacreontics, Spenser begins with some traditional rhyming forms. *Januarye* and *December* frame the twelve thematic pastoral eclogues with the pentameter ballade stanza (ababcc). *Februarye* offers a rough four-accent (tetrameter) couplet, while *March* through *November* become more complex, with Spenser inventing new verse forms in *Aprill*'s elegant "laye/ Of fayre *Elisa,* Queene of Shepheardes all" and the pastoral elegy of *November*. The former is one of the finest pastoral blazons in English, not least because of the complex stanza with its contrasting line lengths and pivoting central couplet.

The blazon stanzas in *Aprill* anticipate another invention, the Spenserian stanza the poet used throughout *The Faerie Queene* (ababbcbcc). Like the *Aprill* stanza, the Spenserian stanza is nine lines with a pivoting rhyme, but its pivoting center is at lines 4 and 5 rather than 5 and 6, and it is a discursive rather than lyric stanza. In iambic pentameter with a concluding iambic hexameter line (known as an alexandrine), the Spenserian stanza is derived from, and extends, the eight-line ottava rime of Spenser's Italian romance models. Its remarkable flexibility as a narrative stanza shows that English versification has reached tremendous sophistication in the three generations since Surrey. The famous opening stanza of Book 1, for example, uses the pivoting rhyme to shift expectations about the knight it describes, while the concluding alexandrine summarizes what we might anticipate from his appearance:

> A Gentle Knight was pricking on the plaine,
> > Ycladd in mightie armes and silver shielde,
> > Wherein old dints of deepe wounds did remaine,
> > The cruell markes of many' a bloudy fielde;
> > Yet armes till that time did he never wield:
> > His angry steede did chide his foming bitt,
> > As much disdaining to the curbe to yield:
> > Full jolly knight he seemd, and faire did sitt,
> As one for knightly giusts and fierce encounters fit. (1.1.1)

The Red Cross Knight, as we come to know him, is clad in the well-dinted armor of St. Paul, but he has yet to experience those jousts and fierce encounters. The stanza form helps to set up the contrasts between appearance and reality, potential and experience that drive much of Book 1. This is even more clear in the second stanza, where the paradoxes of life and death come at the pivotal rhyme, where "dead as living" resonates with several potential meanings, and the concluding alexandrine reinforces the portrait of seriousness and power:

> But on his brest a bloudie Crosse he bore,
> > The deare remembrance of his dying Lord,
> > For whose sweete sake that glorious badge he wore,
> > And dead as living ever him ador'd:
> > Upon his shield the like was also scor'd,
> > For soveraine hope, which in his helpe he had:
> > Right faithfull true he was in deede and word,
> > But of his cheere did seeme too solemne sad;
> Yet nothing did he dread, but ever was ydrad. (1.1.2)

At other points in the narrative the summarizing alexandrine becomes itself a pivotal device for a variety of effects. At the end of canto 2, for example, when Red Cross Knight has been fooled into abandoning his true love, Una, and has taken up with the wicked Duessa, appearance and reality are suspended between stanzas. Red Cross and Duessa have just heard a terrible story of seduction and betrayal which, unknown to him, is actually a story about her:

Then turning to his Lady, dead with feare her found.

Her seeming dead he found with feigned feare,
    As all unweeting of that well she knew. (1.2.44–45)

Not only is this an excellent use of transition from one stanza to another, the very regular iambics of the first two of these three lines set up a contrast that makes the last part of the third line all the more emphatic. If the third line were to follow the simple iambic pattern, "of" would receive more accent than "that":

As áll unwéeting óf that well she knew.

The pull of syntax tends to emphasize the whole second half of the line: *of that well she knew.* In case you missed it, this lady is bad.

   Sir Philip Sidney, to whom Spenser dedicated *The Sheapheardes Calender,* was the Renaissance ideal of Castiglione's perfect courtier: a young man of high birth whose skills include horsemanship and poetry and who handles himself with an easy grace, a certain nonchalance, that ineffable quality called *sprezzatura.*[12] Sidney was the first in English to take seriously not just the Petrarchan sonnet but the Petrarchan idea of the sonnet sequence, and his example was powerful. The popularity of *Astrophil and Stella,* published in 1591 five years after his death, sparked the sonnet craze of the 1590s, which led to Shakespeare's *Sonnets,* which in turn led to the lasting influence of the sonnet as a staple of English poetry. Most immediately notable in Sidney's sequence is the variety of sonnet forms. Sidney accepts the challenge of the game, that a sonnet is fourteen lines of iambic pentameter, and pushes the possibilities. Among the first eight sonnets, no two are in exactly the same form, and three of these (1, 6, and 8) even move past pentameter to iambic hexameter. Throughout, Sidney feigns to reject all previous models and the rules of art ("Let daintie wits crie on the Sisters nine," 3.1; "I never drank of *Aganippe* well," 74.1), relying instead on his contemplation of Stella: "'Foole,' said my Muse to me, 'looke in thy hearrt and write'" (1.14).

   Sidney's disingenuous claim of artlessness was part of the charm of this extraordinarily artful set of verses. In addition to the sheer variety of verse forms, the versification of individual lines are models of variety across an iambic base. The first line of sonnet 31, for example, begins with a sequence of syllables that are iambic if you look at the relative stress within each foot, but show a pattern of increasing emphasis across the four syllables:

With hów sad stéps, o Móone, thou clímb'st the skíes
    1    2    3    4

Sidney shifts from the ponderous climb of monosyllabic words in the next line just enough to avoid monotony, returning to them at the end of the line:

How silently, and with how wanne a face.

This sure and easy control of line movement is typical of Sidney and a triumph with and over relentless iambics.

As interesting as his rich array of sonnets is the project that Sidney began and his sister continued: the imitation and versification of the psalms, of which Sidney wrote the first forty-three and Pembroke the rest. Although this breathtaking compendium of complex and inventive versification circulated only in manuscript until the twentieth century, it was well known from the seventeenth through the nineteenth centuries, influencing Ben Jonson, Aemilia Lanyer, George Herbert, and Gerard Manly Hopkins, among others. For sheer variety of verse forms there is nothing like it in English.[13] To illustrate something of the range from among Pembroke's poems, here is the first stanza of Psalm 67, a sophisticated invocation asking God's blessing:

> God on us thy mercy show,
> Make on us thy blessings flow:
>> Thy faces beames
> From heav'n uppon us show'r
>> In shining streames:
> That all may see
> The way of thee,
> And know thy saving pow'r.[14]

By contrast in lineation and tone, here is the first stanza of Psalm 94:

> God of revenge, revenging God appeare:
>> To recompence the proud, Earthes judge arise.
> How longe, O Lord, how long, unpunisht, beare
>> Shall these vile men their joyes, their jolities?
>> How long thus talk, and talking tiranize?
> Cursedly doe, and doing, proudly boast;
> This people crush, by thee affected most?
>> This land afflict, where thy possession lies?

And for yet a third sort of versification and tone (simple, straightforward, almost child-like), here is the first stanza of Psalm 133:

> How good, and how beseeming well
>> It is that wee,
>> Who brethren be,
> As brethren, should in concord dwell.

Sidney and then Pembroke employ no two verse forms exactly alike across all 150 psalms. The lineation, mostly iambic, is sure and full of variety. Pembroke fittingly concludes with a sonnet version of Psalm 150, the movement of its final couplet both clear and complex:

> Conclud: by all that aire, or life enfold
> Lett high Jehova highly be extold.

English versification has been fully and richly invented.

## NOTES

1. George Gascoigne, *Certayne Notes of Instruction, Elizabethan Critical Essays,* ed. G. Gregory Smith (Oxford: Oxford UP, 1904) 1.47.
2. John Thompson, *The Founding of English Metre* (New York: Columbia UP, 1961) 2, 156.
3. John Lydgate, *Fall of Princes,* ed. Henry Bergen, 3 vols. (London: EETS, 1924) 1.ll 437–41.
4. Susanne Woods, *Natural Emphasis: English Versification from Chaucer to Dryden* (San Marino: Huntington Library P, 1985) 21–34 and *passim.*
5. John M. Manly and Edith Rickert, *The Text of the Canterbury Tales,* vol. 3, pt. 1, "Text and Critical Notes" (Chicago: U of Chicago P, 1940) 3. My translation.
6. George Saintsbury, *History of English Prosody* (London: Macmillan, 1906) 1.169–76; F. N. Robinson, ed., *The Works of Geoffrey Chaucer,* 2d ed. (Boston: Houghton Mifflin, 1957) xxxv–xxxvi; Woods 32–50; Norman Davis, "Versification," *The Riverside Chaucer,* 3d ed., gen. ed. Larry D. Benson (Boston: Houghton Mifflin, 1987) xlii–xlv.
7. *John Milton: Complete Poetry and Major Prose,* ed. Merrit Y. Hughes (Indianapolis: Odyssey P, 1957) 210.
8. *Tottel's Miscellany,* ed. Hyder Edward Rollins, 2 vols. (Cambridge, MA: Harvard UP, 2d ed., 1965) 2: 107–21. Selections from Tottel are from this edition, except for "To the Reader," which I have modernized from the second 1557 edition (Huntington Library copy).
9. Richard Harrier, *The Canon of Sir Thomas Wyatt's Poetry* (Cambridge, MA: Harvard UP, 1975) 101.
10. *The Poems of Henry Howard, Earl of Surrey,* ed. Frederick Morgan Padelford (Seattle: U of Washington P, 1928) 57.
11. *Three Proper, and wittie, familiar Letters: lately passed between two Universitie men: touching the Earthquake in Aprill last, and our English refourmed Versifying* (London, 1580).
12. Baldassare Castiglione, *The Book of the Courtier* (1527), provided the Renaissance model for courtly wit and behavior; it was translated into English by Thomas Hoby in 1561 as *The courtyer of Count Baldessar Castilio divided into foure bookes. Very necessary and profitatable [sic] for yonge gentilmen and gentilwomen abiding in court, palaice or place.*
13. See in Woods 287–302 (Appendix, "Verse Forms in the Sidney/Pembroke Psalms").
14. *The Psalms of Sir Philip Sidney and the Countess of Pembroke,* ed. J. C. A. Rathmell (New York: New York UP, 1963) 152.

## READING LIST

Attridge, Derek. *Well-Weighed Syllables: Elizabethan Verse in Classical Metres.* Cambridge: Cambridge UP, 1974.

Brogan, T. V. F. *English Versification, 1570–1980: A Reference Guide with a Global Appendix.* Baltimore: Johns Hopkins UP, 1981.

Carper, Tomas, and Derek Attridge. *Meter and Meaning: An Introduction to Rhythm in Poetry.* New York: Routledge, 2003.

Duckworth, George E. *Vergil and Classical Hexameter Poetry: A Study in Metrical Variety.* Ann Arbor: U of Michigan P, 1969.

Fabb, Nigel. *Language and Literary Structure: The Linguistic Analysis of Form in Verse and Narrative.* Cambridge: Cambridge UP, 2002.

Hardison, O. B., Jr. *Prosody and Purpose in the English Renaissance.* Baltimore: Johns Hopkins UP, 1989.

Halle, Morris, and S. Jay Keyser. *English Stress: Its Form, Its Growth, and Its Role in Verse.* New York: Harper & Row, 1971.

Hollander, John. *Vision and Resonance: Two Senses of Poetic Form.* New York: Oxford UP, 1975.

Johnson, Paula. *Form and Transformation in Music and Poetry of the English Renaissance.* New Haven: Yale UP, 1972.

Raffel, Burton. *From Stress to Stress: An Autobiography of English Prosody.* Hamden, CT: Archon, 1992.

Rollins, Hyder Edward, ed. *Tottel's Miscellany.* 2 vols. 2d ed. Cambridge, MA: Harvard UP, 1965.

Saintsbury, George. *A History of English Prosody.* 3 vols. London: Macmillan, 1906–10.

Thompson, John, *The Founding of English Metre.* New York: Columbia UP, 1961.

Woods, Susanne. *Natural Emphasis: English Verse from Chaucer to Dryden.* San Marino: Huntington Library P, 1985.

Wright, George T. *Shakespeare's Metrical Art.* Berkeley: University of California P, 1988.

# 2

# Print, Manuscripts, and Miscellanies

## Arthur F. Marotti

Although the modern reader is used to perceiving poems from earlier eras in isolation from their place in larger collections and as the work of known, canonical authors, the first context for verse for most early modern readers was the poetical anthology, one in which pieces by several authors were presented together. The first substantial poetical anthology of verse printed in sixteenth-century England is known to us as *Tottel's Miscellany*, a title designating the publisher, Richard Tottel, and the type of collection, an anthology of work by multiple authors.[1] First published in 1557, with at least nine editions (plus other reprintings) through the rest of the century, this book actually appeared as *Songes and Sonettes, written by the right honorable Lorde Henry Haward late Earle of Surrey, and other.*[2] Although Surrey, whose execution for treason enhanced his notoriety, was responsible for only forty of the poems contained in the book, the publisher obviously thought it useful to use his name on the title page to promote sales of the volume (title pages of books were normally used separately as advertising posters). The "other" of the book's title included Sir Thomas Wyatt (the author of ninety-seven of the selections), as well as such other early and mid-Tudor poets as Nicholas Grimald, John Harington of Stepney, John Heywood, Lord Vaux, Thomas Norton, and Thomas Churchyard—whose work amounted to 220 of the 265 poems of the first edition.

Tottel's volume, which stimulated the publication of other anthologies through the Elizabethan period,[3] redirected poems originally circulated and compiled in manuscript into the world of print, where individual authorship came to assume higher cultural visibility. Whereas in the manuscript system of literary transmission poems were not usually ascribed to authors and individual collectors could appropriate and revise the texts they received, in print authors' names took on greater importance (if only for commercial reasons), and intellectual property was being reconceived in terms of modern notions of possessive individualism. The publisher, as social agent, could assume cultural importance: Tottel defends his commercial venture as an act of public service, telling his readers that he has rescued for their "profit and pleasure" "those workes which the ungentle horders up of such treasure have heretofore envied thee."[4] His book highlights the relationship of two media and the different conceptions of authorship, author-reader relationships, and textuality proper to manuscript and print in a transitional era in which the two systems of literary transmission interacted.

Gutenberg's invention did not eradicate script as a medium for preserving and transmitting texts. Just as, in our own day, electronic and digital technology has not destroyed the book, print did not substantially reduce the reliance on manuscript documents in various fields of human endeavor. In the case of poetry, there was, as J. W. Saunders pointed out, a "stigma of print" inhibiting genteel, aristocratic, or upwardly mobile individuals from publishing their work,[5] so the normal method of circulating poetical texts (particularly lyric poems, which were conceived as ephemeral artifacts) was in manuscript—usually to restricted readerships. Thus, Wyatt's verse circulated in the Henrician court, gathered, for example, with the work of other individuals in British Library MS Additional 17492, a manuscript associated with five courtly women and their lovers.[6] Later in the century, Sir Philip Sidney handed his verse to such close friends as Sir Fulke Greville and Sir Edward Dyer, but did not let it travel far from his restricted social circle.[7] John Donne, whose collected verse only reached print two years after his death, was a coterie poet, circulating his compositions to restricted audiences in the various social environments in which he functioned through his secular and ecclesiastical careers.[8]

Between 1557 and 1660, anthologies of verse were produced both in manuscript and print, but the story of the relationship of the two media is not one of the steady diminution of the former as the latter grew in importance.[9] On the contrary, judging from the surviving documentary evidence, the seventeenth century witnessed an exponential growth in the production of poetical collections in manuscript—in both freestanding anthologies of verse and in the incorporation of substantial numbers of poems in commonplace books that included other material. There was steady interest in poetical collections; it is just that the print market for them fluctuated greatly and the personal anthologizing of verse in manuscript accelerated as a practice, especially after 1620.

Tottel's collection of verse, published at the end of the reign of Queen Mary, was a publishing success. It was followed in the Elizabethan period by a number of printed poetical miscellanies as well as by "augumented editions" of individual poets' work, which contained the verse of other writers. The range of tastes to which the anthologies appealed ran from the popular to the elite. The first of these is a book whose first two editions have not survived, a collection of broadside ballads compiled by someone named Clement Robinson that, in its 1584 edition, is entitled *A Handful of Pleasant Delights*.[10] This was followed by the a collection that, judging from its ten editions, was the most well received of the poetical miscellanies after Tottel's, a collection based on the compilation of the court poet and dramatist Richard Edwards, *The Paradise of Dainty Devices* (1576).[11] This anthology grew from the 99 pieces of the first edition to 127 poems, by at least thirty authors, including such early to mid-Elizabethan poets as Edwards, Churchyard, Jasper Heywood, William Hunnis, Francis Kinwelmarsh, the earl of Oxford, Barnabe Rich, Lord Vaux, and George Whetstone. Whereas Tottel's collection contains a large number of amatory lyrics, this anthology is dominated by pious and didactic verse, testifying to the low esteem in which erotic poetry was held by Protestant humanists and, generally, by serious, mature individuals in the early to mid-Elizabethan period. In fact, the experience of George Gascoigne demonstrates the difficulty of printing certain types of secular literature: he had published a collection of his poetry, prose, and dramatic translations as a counterfeit miscellany in 1573, *An Hundreth Sundrie Flowres*, but then was forced by the negative response to the collection to reissue it two years later in his own name with an apology and the claim of extensive revision. He had used the form of the literary anthology to hide his identity, but not really, since the table of contents attaches his, and no other, name to several of the pieces in the collection.

In both Tottel's and Edwards's anthologies, the authorship of particular poems is usually indicated either by initials or abbreviations or by full names. Except for two poems attributed to "sir. T[homas]. w[yatt]. the elder," the first thirty-six poems in

Tottel are followed, at the end of this section, by the name "Surrey." The next ninety-one poem section is followed by the attribution "T. Wyate the elder." The following section is announced as "Songs written by Nicolas Grimald" and concludes with his initials. In the next section of poems by other writers, there are no ascriptions, save in the case of one piece, "An epitaph written by w[illiam]. G[ray]."[12] The first edition ends with two appended sections of poems attributed to Surrey and Wyatt. In *The Paradise of Dainty Devices* the authors of almost all the poems are identified by name or initials. In fact, the full title of the work includes the following, "*aptly furnished, with sundry pithie and learned inventions:/ devised and written for the most part, by M. Edwards,/ sometimes of her Majesties Chappel: the rest by/ sundry learned Gentlemen, both of honor,/ and worship./ viz. S. Barnarde./ E. O./ L. Vaux./ D. S./ Jasper Heywood./ F. K../ M. Bewe./ R. Hill./ M. Yloop, with others.*" Aside from the awkwardness of including the name of St. Bernard, a translation of whose poem begins the anthology, the publisher Henry Disle, in naming contributors, obviously thought to attract buyers by offering them literary access to a courtly elite. This practice contrasts sharply with that of manuscript compilation, where authorship was generally left in anonymity.

Chronologically, the next published miscellany after *Paradise* was *A Gorgeous Gallery of Gallant Inventions* (1578).[13] According to Hyder Rollins, Thomas Proctor, its editor, "simply collected from various sources poems that appealed to him, perhaps changing or supplying words and lines at his fancy, and to the whole adding original compositions of his own."[14] Proctor purloined texts from the earlier published miscellanies, but apparently the book was not well received, only appearing in one edition. Its publisher, the entrepreneurial Richard Jones, subsequently published two more miscellanies, *Brittons Bowre of Delights* (1591) (with fifty-six poems) and *The Arbor of Amorous Devices* (1597) (with forty-four poems, ten of which are repeated from *Bowre*).[15] In both, he used the name of one of the authors, Nicholas Breton, to help sell a collection of work by many authors. He thus reversed Gascoigne's trick of passing off a single author's work as an anthology. In *The Arbor of Amorous Devices*, the printer assured the envisioned "Gentlemen Readers" of the book of the quality of the verse and the social probity of the writers, "most [. . .] not the meanest in estate and degree."[16] Both anthologies look to courtly culture and print texts alluding to particular courtly women. The authors represented include Surrey, Edwards, Breton, Sidney, Raleigh, and Oxford.

Emphasizing the gentility of its contributors, but refraining from identifying them except by initials, *The Phoenix Nest* (1593) registers the changes in the styles, tastes, and social receptiveness for lyric poetry in the late Elizabethan period.[17] There was a market for amorous writing, the sonnet and other lyric forms were replacing the clunky rhythms of mid-Tudor verse (especially "poulter's measure" and "fourteeners"),[18] and the "stigma" associated with publishing poetry was lessened, certainly, by the posthumous appearance in print of Sir Philip Sidney's sonnet collection, *Astrophil and Stella*, in 1591 and 1592.[19] Edited by a gentleman from the Inner Temple, one of the Inns of Court and, therefore, part of an environment of avant-garde literary and cultural tastes in late-Elizabethan London, this sophisticated anthology responds to the cultural impact of Sidney as both a writer and a political actor, beginning with prose defending the militantly Protestant uncle of the poet, the (deceased) earl of Leicester, and with poems dedicated to Sidney's memory. What follows is a collection of verse aimed at an elite readership by writers supposedly known to the gentleman-editor, with love poems by "sundry gentlemen" occupying the second half of the book.[20] The selections comprise both old-fashioned forms such as complaints, dream-vision verse, and moral allegories and newer Ovidian, Anacreontic, and courtly verse. The authors include (among others) George Peele, Breton, Thomas Lodge, the earl of Oxford, Dyer, Robert Greene, Matthew Roydon, Sir Arthur Gorges, and Raleigh.

With *England's Helicon* (1600) the Elizabethan poetical miscellany reaches a higher level of fashion and sophistication.[21] Printing 150 poems by some thirty known, plus other anonymous, authors, this collection is a pastoral one. At a time at which some of the best contemporary authors depicted pastoral settings and themes in lyrics, longer poems, and the drama, this anthology satisfied a markedly contemporary literary taste. It proclaims connoisseurship as a cultural value.[22]

Although it is not presented as a poetical miscellany, William Jaggard's *The Passionate Pilgrim by W. Shakespeare* (1599) is a twenty-poem anthology rather than a edition of a single author's work or even, as is the case with the 1591 edition of Sidney's *Astrophil and Stella* (which has, at the end, twenty-eight poems by other poets), an augmented edition. Jaggard attempted to market a poetical collection under the commercially valuable name of the poet-dramatist, including, in addition to five poems by Shakespeare, four poems by Richard Barnfield, Bartholomew Griffin, and Christopher Marlowe and eleven by writers who have not been identified. The third (1612) edition of the work added eleven poems by Thomas Heywood, who subsequently objected to their attribution to another writer (Shakespeare).[23]

The last and largest of the Elizabethan miscellanies is Francis Davison's *A Poetical Rhapsody* (1602), a work that, like *The Phoenix Nest,* exploits Sidney's name for cultural authorization. Dedicated to Sidney's nephew, William Herbert, earl of Pembroke, and prefaced with remarks alluding to Sidney's composition of lyric "Toyes,"[24] the collection opens with "Two Pastoralls, made by Sir Philip Sidney, never yet published."[25] Defending lyric poetry against the traditional prejudice against the form, Davison included his own, his brother's, and an anonymous friend's youthful verse in an anthology of 176 poems by (in addition to Sidney) such authors as Henry Constable, Sir John Davies, Robert Greene, Raleigh, the countess of Pembroke (Sidney's sister), Thomas Spilman, Edmund Spenser, Sir Henry Wotton, and Thomas Watson. Although Davison professed a modest aim in compiling his anthology, he deflects responsibility for the presentation and size of the work to the printer, who supposedly wished "either to grace the forefront with Sir Philip Sidney's and others' names, or to make the book grow to a competent volume [by adding many other poems to the core collection]."[26] Published in three subsequent editions (1608, 1611, 1621), *A Poetical Rhapsody* grew to a collection of 250 poems, the largest printed miscellany of the era.

If one turns to the manuscript remains of the Tudor period, one finds a number of rich and interesting poetical collections done by individuals in different social environments. In fact, some of these easily rival the printed miscellanies in scope and variety. For example, the Arundel Harington manuscript kept by John Harington of Stepney and his son, Sir John Harington of Kelston (the author of the satiric *Metamorphosis of Ajax*), contains 324 poems from the late Henrician through the Elizabethan periods, a collection considerably larger than the most compendious printed miscellany.[27] With poems by Wyatt, Surrey, and other poets also found in *Tottel's Miscellany,* this manuscript has affiliations with the collection that was the basis of that printed volume.[28] It contains poems by the elder Harington and his contemporaries, who include, in addition to Wyatt (his friend) and Surrey, Lord Vaux, Sir John Cheke, Churchyard, Edmund Knevet, John Astley, Admiral Sir Thomas Seymour, Sir Thomas Smith, Sir George Blage, Sir William Cordall, John Dudley (earl of Warwick), Robert Dudley (who became earl of Leicester), and Richard Edwards (among others).[29] The later contents include verse by Sidney, Raleigh, Constable, Greville, Spenser, Daniel, Dyer, Oxford, and the younger Harington. This manuscript is unusual in its chronological scope: the compilation began in the 1550s and ran through the 1590s. Most other sixteenth-century manuscript anthologies were more restricted in time and place.

Among the notable late Elizabethan manuscript poetry collections, some have interesting overlaps in their contents: for example, Humphrey Coningsby's anthology (British Library MS Harley 7392), Anne Cornwallis's miscellany (Folger MS V.a.89), John Finet's collection (Bodleian MS Rawlinson Poetical 85), and Marsh's Library Dublin MS Z3.5.21, all collections with their gaze directed at the court and its fashions, share a number of poems by such authors as Oxford, Sidney, and Dyer.[30] They demonstrate the same interest in courtier poetry as some of the printed miscellanies and suggest the sociopolitical encoding of amorous poetry in the courtly environment. Coningsby's anthology is the second part of a composite manuscript that is preceded by a collection of epigrammatic poems (Morris's "Wasps") and followed by a section of Italian burlesque poetry. It has 152 poems, 127 of them numbered. We can assign some of the pieces to Sidney, Dyer, Raleigh, Oxford, Gorges, Anthony Munday, Barnaby Rich, Churchyard, Thomas Campion, Breton, Peele, Queen Elizabeth, and such minor authors as Thomas Whythorne, Humfrey Gifford, John Thorn, Catherine Killigrew, and Robert Allott, in addition to the compiler himself. The largest number of poems found also in a contemporary printed volume is six (*The Paradise of Dainty Devices*), but there are over twenty that appear in other printed volumes. What is remarkable about the contents of this anthology, however, is the large percentage of apparently unique copies of poems found in it—some 37 percent, or 56 out of 152 items.[31] These would seem to be high numbers, but they are really not so unusual in collections of this kind: for example, one-third of the miscellaneous poems in Anne Cornwallis's miscellany (nine of the twenty-seven pieces) are also apparently unique copies, and some 91 of the 515 poems in the seventeenth-century Christ Church, Oxford, collection (Folger MS V.a.345) discussed later are also apparently unique.

Some of the manuscript anthologies bear the marks of the social environments in which they were compiled. Finet's collection, like Coningsby's, began at the university (at St. John's College, Cambridge) and has occasional writing by fellow students mixed with the poetry of courtly authors. The obscene and misogynistic humor of the student poetry contrasts with the polite amorousness of the courtly verse. The verse miscellany of John Lilliat, an Elizabethan cathedral musician, Bodleian MS Rawlinson Poetical 148,[32] has poems by the compiler and his academic and ecclesiastical associates as well as pieces by Sidney, Dyer, Sir John Davies, Thomas Watson, Thomas Campion, and the earl of Essex. Henry Stanford, who compiled his collection (Cambridge University Library MS Dd.5.75)[33] while he served as a tutor in aristocratic households, included both his own verse and poems he taught his young pupils to compose in a large collection that recorded some of the best manuscript and printed verse of Sidney, Breton,

Spenser, Gorges, Raleigh, and others. The anthology has an interesting variety of contents: politically topical verse (such as poems on Mary, Queen of Scots, and the earl of Leicester), courtly verse, and riddles, satires, libels, and obscene epigrams.

There was a marked drop-off in the production of printed anthologies after the end of Queen Elizabeth's reign. Some Elizabethan miscellanies, such as *A Poetical Rhapsody,* continued to be reprinted or appeared in new editions, but such volumes were obviously seen as belonging to the earlier era.[34] By contrast, the compilation of verse in manuscript was widespread. Students at the university, members of the Inns of Court, individuals in the aristocratic and gentry households, politically and socially active Londoners, and others circulated and collected verse, sometimes assembling very large anthologies of poems. Although there are some manuscript collections that straddle the line separating Elizabethan from Jacobean or belong to the early years of King James's reign—for example, Rosenbach Library MS 1083/15, compiled at the Inns of Court[35]— most of the surviving collections of note belong to the period from 1620 through 1660. Among these are some notable poetical anthologies that give some sense of the vitality of the practice of manuscript anthologizing in the period: for example, British Library MSS Additional 25707 and Harley 6917–18, Huntington Library MS 198 (Part 1), Folger MS V.a.345, and Bodleian MS Ashmole 38.

British Library MS Additional 25707 is a 186-folio Jacobean and Caroline compilation of separate verse collections assembled within the Skipwith family of Cotes (and Prestwold), Leicestershire—mainly by Sir William Skipwith and his son Sir Henry Skipwith.[36] Used by editors of John Donne's poetry, this manuscript contains a large number of poems by that author, transcribed before their printing in the first edition (1633). The collection also has many poems by Henry King, Donne's literary executor. There are other seventeenth-century poets represented (such as Jonson, Sir John Harington, Corbett, Strode, Carew, Francis Beaumont, John Beaumont, Dudley North, Sir Robert Ayton, Thomas Cary, Owen Felltham, and Herrick), but the collection also has many pieces by both the elder Skipwith and his son, as well as a very large number of anonymous poems that exist here in apparently unique copies. This collection bears the marks of its familial and wider social context[37] and demonstrates the degree to which compilers indulged their inclination to add their own verse to the anthologies they assembled. The two-part collection assembled by the Londoner Peter Calfe and his son of the same name (British Library MSS Harley 6917–18), which belongs largely to the era of the Civil Wars and Interregnum, contains over four hundred poems, mostly with a royalist orientation. Huntington Library MS 198, Part 1, is a handsome folio collection with 205 numbered pages and approximately that many poems, transcribed for Edward Denny, earl of Norwich, before 1630. It has, in addition to sixty-five poems by Donne, pieces by many other authors (such as Jonson, Beaumont, Carew, Herrick, Corbett, Strode, and Randolph) working in or before the 1620s, including many political pieces. Folger MS V.a.345 is a 337-page manuscript written by or for an anonymous compiler with Christ Church, Oxford, connections. With over five hundred poems, this is one of the largest poetical anthologies of the era, but it has affiliations with many other collections associated with that Oxford College, where the presence of Richard Corbett and William Strode encouraged students to collect and circulate groups of poems that were merged in large collections. The work included reflects both local, university interests and events and personages in the larger world.[38] Bod. MS Ashmole 38, compiled by Nicholas Burghe, a royalist captain in the Civil Wars, is another large folio manuscript (with 243 leaves), with poems transcribed from around 1630 to 1660. One of the richest collections of mid-seventeenth-century verse, this anthology contains hundreds of poems by a large variety of poets of the age. In fact, it looks like Burghe tried to avoid inserting too many pieces by any one author (the largest number is about ten), so that there are probably more poets represented in this collection than in almost any other seventeenth-century manuscript collection. All these manuscripts (and others like them) demonstrate the widespread character of manuscript anthologizing of verse in the period.

During the Jacobean and Caroline periods, there were few printed poetry anthologies,[39] for, especially after the publication of Sidney's, Spenser's, Daniel's, and Jonson's works,[40] and with the landmark publication of Donne's and Herbert's poetry in 1633, the publication emphasis shifted to single-author editions. This is especially evident in the activities of Humphrey Moseley, who printed verse by John Milton (1645), Edmund Waller (1645), Richard Crashaw (1646 and 1648), James Shirley (1646), Sir John Suckling (1646, 1648, and 1658), Abraham Cowley (1647, 1655), William Cartwright (1651), Thomas Stanley (1651), and Henry Vaughan (1651, 1654).[41] There are, however, in the seventeenth century, some printed works that are or contain poetical anthologies. John Benson's *Poems: Written by Wil. Shakespeare. Gent.* (1640), for example, includes "An Addition of some Excellent Poems, to those precedent, of Renowned *Shakespeare,* By other Gentlemen" (sig. L2)—twenty-one pages of poems by such authors as Jonson, John Beaumont, Herrick, Strode, Cartwright, and Carew.[42] The 1660 volume of *Poems of* [William Herbert, earl of] *Pembroke and* [Benjamin] *Ruddier* contains pieces composed by these two friends, but the majority of poems in the collection are by other authors writing in the Elizabethan through the Caroline periods.[43]

Beginning in the 1640s, a series of poetical miscellanies and books containing both poems and other forms of writing began to appear. Some of these had a long publication life, republished and/or expanded through many editions over an extended period of time. *The Academy of Complements: or the Lover's Secretary* (1640) and *Wits Recreations* (1640) initiated this new fashion, both collections running through many editions.[44] *The Academy* is a courtesy book (for the lower and middling classes) that includes "Complemental and Amorous Poems" (129) along with models of speech and writing; *Wits Recreations* is an anthology of hundreds of short, witty poems—mostly epigrams, riddles, and epitaphs. The latter work has pieces by such poets as Jonson, Beaumont and Fletcher, Chapman, Shirley, Massinger, Drayton, Carew, Strode, Corbett, and others. Its courtly, misogynistic, anti-Puritan, and encomiastic pieces associate it with the many royalist anthologies of this politically turbulent era.

Partly because of the disruption of the English Civil Wars, and partly because of the royalist, courtly orientation of *Academy* and *Wits Recreations,* despite the appearance of single-author collections, there were no new poetry anthologies published until well into the Interregnum period. The most significant collections to appear first are *The Harmony of the Muses* (1654), *Musarum Deliciae: or the Muses Recreation* (1655), and *Parnassus Biceps* (1656).[45] The first is mainly a collection of love poetry, largely of the libertine and bawdy kind;[46] the title page names nine authors from the previous half-century or so, Donne, King, Strode, Sir Kenelm Digby, Jonson, Beaumont, Cleveland, Randolph, and Carew, all of whom are well represented in the manuscript collections of the previous decades.[47] It also contains verse by such other authors as Walton Poole, Richard Clerke, John Grange, Sir John Mennes, James Shirley, William Skipwith, Dr. John Sprint, Sir Simeon Steward, and Josuah Sylvester.[48] This anthology and others like it reveal a conservative political nostalgia for earlier (Stuart) times, when, supposedly, poetry and learning were held in greater esteem.[49] *Musarum Deliciae,* the first of the mid-century "drolleries,"[50] prints, among its general (Caroline) contents, poetry associated with a royalist literary coterie that included John Mennes and James Smith, many of whom were in continental exile.[51] *Parnassus Biceps* includes poems found repeatedly in mid-century manuscript collections. These, and such other collections as *Wits Interpreter* (1655) and *Wit Restor'd* (1658), address a social and intellectual elite, mocking sometimes the self-improvement books aimed at the lower classes. Such printed collections extended into the Restoration era—with either new editions or new publications of the same sort. After 1660, however, as Adam Smyth points out, the new collections showed much less interest in the work of the past and more in that of contemporary times.[52]

Long before the kinds of literary-historical anthologizing that characterize the nineteenth century and later, individuals in the manuscript system of literary transmission and publishers interested in the commercial value of printed poetry assembled poetical collections of various kinds. Although, in the long run, the press eclipsed handwriting as a public communicative technology, it is surprising how long the manuscript transmission and compilation continued as culturally vital activities. When Richard Tottel redirected into print material he found in a manuscript collection, he contributed greatly to a process that was unstoppable, but it took a long time for print culture to capture poetry for its almost exclusive use.

## NOTES

1. Tottel's volume was preceded by *The Court of Venus,* but only a few fragments from three separate editions of this work survive. See Russell Fraser, ed., *The Court of Venus* (Durham: Duke UP, 1955).
2. See Hyder Edward Rollins, ed., *Tottel's Miscellany (1557–1587),* 2 vols., rev. ed. (Cambridge, MA: Harvard UP, 1966).
3. See Elizabeth Pomeroy, *The Elizabethan Miscellanies: Their Development and Conventions* (Berkeley: U of California P, 1973).
4. *Tottel's Miscellany* 1: 2.
5. See J. W. Saunders, "The Stigma of Print: A Note on the Social Bases of Tudor Poetry," *Essays in Criticism* 1 (1951): 139–64.
6. See Richard Harrier, *The Canon of Sir Thomas Wyatt's Poetry* (Cambridge, MA: Harvard UP, 1975) 1–15.
7. See H. R. Woudhuysen, *Sir Philip Sidney and the Circulation of Manuscripts 1558–1640* (Oxford: Clarendon P, 1996).
8. See Arthur F. Marotti, *John Donne, Coterie Poet* (Madison: U of Wisconsin P, 1986).
9. See Arthur F. Marotti, *Manuscript, Print, and the English Renaissance Lyric* (Ithaca: Cornell UP, 1995). In this essay, I use material from several sections of this study.
10. This was first published in 1566. See the facsimile of the 1584 edition: Clement Robinson, *A Handful of Pleasant Delights* (Ilkley, Eng.: Scolar P, 1973).

11. See Hyder Edward Rollins, ed., *The Paradise of Dainty Devices (1577–1606)* (Cambridge, MA: Harvard UP, 1927).
12. See Rollins, *Tottel's Miscellany* 1: 200–201 and commentary on 2: 306–08.
13. See Hyder E. Rollins, ed., *A Gorgeous Gallery of Gallant Inventions [1578]* (Cambridge, MA: Harvard UP, 1926).
14. Rollins, *Gorgeous Gallery* xxi.
15. See Hyder Rollins, ed., *Brittons Bowre of Delights 1591* (Cambridge, MA: Harvard UP, 1933) and ibid., ed., *The Arbor of Amorous Devices* (1936; rpt. New York: Russell & Russell, 1968). The earliest surviving edition of the latter is that of 1597.
16. Rollins, *Arbor* 3.
17. See Hyder Edward Rollins, ed., *The Phoenix Nest 1593* (Cambridge, MA: Harvard UP, 1931). Rollins xvi–xvii observes that this anthology is the first, after Tottel, to emphasize the gentility of the contributors and the only one, other than *A Poetical Rhapsody* (1602), to be edited by a gentleman.
18. The former consists of pairing lines of six and seven beats (sometimes split into quatrains of 3-3-4-3), the latter of seven beat lines in couplets (sometimes split into quatrains of 4-3-4-3).
19. See the argument I make in "'Love is not love': Elizabethan Sonnet Sequences and the Social Order," *ELH* 49 (1982): 396–428.
20. Rollins, *Phoenix Nest* xxxi–xxxvi.
21. See Hyder Edward Rollins, ed., *England's Helicon, 1600, 1614* (Cambridge, MA: Harvard UP, 1935).
22. This project was brought to print under the patronage of John Bodenhan along with three other collections of writing: *Politeuphia: Wits Commonwealth* (1598), *Wit's Theater of the Little World* (1599), and *Bel-vedere: or the Garden of the Muses* (1600) (Rollins, *England's Helicon*, 60). *Politeuphia* and (Robert Allott's) *Wits Theater of the Little World* are compilations of memorable prose citations such as one might record in a commonplace book; *Bel-vedere* is a poetical dictionary, comprising over four thousand short citations of verse. Robert Allott's compilation of poetical treasures, *Englands Parnassus; or the Choysest Flowers of Our Modern Poet,* appeared in 1600.
23. See the discussion of *The Passionate Pilgrim* in William Shakespeare, *The Complete Sonnets and Poems,* ed. Colin Burrow (Oxford: Oxford UP, 2002) 74–82, and in the facsimile edition of the 1612 edition by Hyder Edward Rollins (New York and London: Scribner's, 1940).
24. *A Poetical Rhapsody 1602–1621,* ed. Hyder Edward Rollins, 2 vols. (Cambridge, MA: Harvard UP, 1931) 1: 6.
25. *Poetical Rhapsody* 1: 7–12.
26. *Poetical Rhapsody* 1: 5.
27. See Ruth Hughey, ed., *The Arundel Harington Manuscript of Tudor Poetry,* 2 vols. (Columbus: Ohio State UP, 1960). The original collection was even larger, for, as Hughey (1: 11) points out, some eighty-three leaves of poetry were removed when the Harington family collection, *Nugae Antiquae* (1769), was being assembled for print.
28. Arundel Harington has affiliations, at least in its older contents, with other surviving manuscripts—particularly British Library MS Egerton 2711 (a Wyatt manuscript) and British Library MS Additional 17492 (mentioned earlier).
29. Hughey 1: 27.
30. For a discussion of the first of these manuscripts, see Woudhuysen 278–86; for the second, see Arthur F. Marotti, "The Cultural and Textual Importance of Folger MS V.a.89," *English Manuscript Studies 1100–1700* 11 (2002): 70–92; for the third, see Laurence Cummings, "John Finet's Miscellany" (Ph.D. Diss., Washington U, St. Louis, 1960); for the fourth, see George Martin, "Marsh's Library MS z 3.5.21: An Edition of the English Poems" (M.A. Thesis, U of Waterloo, 1971). See also Marotti, *Manuscript* 63–67, 139–41, 176–81, and Randall

Anderson, "'The Merit of a Manuscript Poem': The Case for Bodleian MS Rawlinson Poet. 85," *Print, Manuscript, and Performance: The Changing Relations of the Media in Early Modern England,* ed. Arthur F. Marotti and Michael D. Bristol (Columbus: Ohio State UP, 2000) 127–71. Anderson (154–59) has a chart showing the overlap of contents of all these manuscripts, plus British Library MS Harley 6910, another ample collection (but one with a large percentage of its poems copied from printed sources). Coningsby's collection, for example, shares forty-five poems with Finet's.

31. I have checked first lines against the database found in Steven W. May and William A. Riagler, Jr., eds., *Elizabethan Poetry: A Bibliography and First-line Index of English Verse, 1558–1603,* 3 vols. (London: Thoemmes Continuum, 2004).

32. See Edward Doughtie, ed., *Liber Lilliati: Elizabethan Verse and Song (Bodleian MS Rawlinson Poetry 148)* (Newark: U of Delaware P; London: Associated U Presses, 1985).

33. See Steven W. May, *Henry Stanford's Anthology: An Edition of Cambridge University Library Manuscript Dd. 5.75* (New York: Garland, 1988).

34. New editions of *A Poetical Rhapsody* appeared in 1608, 1611, and 1621; a new edition of *Englands Helicon* appeared in 1614; one of *Bel-vedere: or the Garden of the Muses* in 1610. Pomeroy 106 suggests that songbooks replaced poetical miscellanies in popularity from the end of the Elizabethan era to about 1630.

35. See James Sanderson, "An Edition of an Early Seventeenth-Century Manuscript Collection of Poems (Rosenbach MS. 186 [1083/15])" (Ph.D. Diss., U of Pennsylvania, 1960).

36. See Mary Hobbs, *Early Seventeenth-Century Miscellany Manuscripts* (Aldershot, Eng.: Scolar P, 1992) 62–67.

37. Hobbs 62–86 connects this manuscript with a number of others with affiliations to the "Stoughton manuscript" (in private hands, but presented in a facsimile edition by Hobbs: *The Stoughton Manuscript: a Manuscript Miscellany of Poems by Henry King and His Circle, circa 1636* [Aldershot, Eng.: Scolar P, 1990]).

38. See Arthur F. Marotti, "Folger MSS V.a.89 and V.a.345: Reading Lyric Poetry in Manuscript," *The Reader Revealed,* ed. Sabrina Alcorn Baron, with Elizabeth Walsh and Susan Scola (Washington, DC: The Folger Shakespeare Library and Seattle and London: U of Washington P, 2001) 45–57.

39. There were some short poetical pamphlets with poems by various authors such as *Certain Elegies Done by Sundrie Excellent Wits with Satyrs and Epigrams* (1618) and *Loves Garland; or Posies for Rings, Handkerchers, and Gloves* (1624), but no large, ambitious anthologies.

40. The folio edition of Sidney's work, which incorporated his lyric poetry along with his other writing, appeared in 1598; prestigious folio editions of Spenser appeared in 1611 and 1617; of Daniel in 1601; and of Jonson in 1616.

41. See John Curtis Reed, "Humphrey Mosely, Publisher," *Oxford Bibliographical Society Proceedings and Papers* 2, pt. 1 (1927–30): 57–142.

42. Benson also reproduces non-Shakespearean poems from Jaggard's *The Passionate Pilgrim.* For a discussion of Benson's book, see Arthur F. Marotti, "Shakespeare's Sonnets as Literary Property," *Soliciting Interpretation: Literary Theory and Seventeenth-Century English Poetry,* ed. Elizabeth D. Harvey and Katharine Eisaman Maus (Chicago: U of Chicago P, 1990) 158–63, and David Baker, "Cavalier Shakespeare: The 1640 *Poems* of John Benson," *Studies in Philology* 95 (1998): 152–73.

43. These include Dyer, Raleigh, Sir Henry Wotton, Dudley North, Walton Poole, William Browne of Tavistock, Carew, King, and Strode.

44. The former had three editions in 1640 and was reprinted or re-edited in 1654, 1658, 1663, 1664, 1670, 1684, 1705, 1727, 1750, 1760, 1790, and 1795; the latter in 1645 (as *Recreations for Ingenious Head-Pieces*), 1650, 1654, 1663, 1667, 1683, greatly expanded in the process.

45. See *"The Harmony of the Muses" by Robert Chamberlain,* introd. Ernest W. Sullivan II (Aldershot, Eng.: Scolar P, 1990); *"Musarum Deliciae" and "Wit Restor'd" (1658),* introd. Tim Raylor (Delmar, NY: Scholars' Facsimiles and Reprints, 1985); and *"Parnassus Biceps, or Severall Select Pieces of Poetry" by Abraham Wright (1656),* introd. Peter Beal (Aldershot, Eng.: Scolar P, 1990).

46. It prints for the first time the whole of Donne's "Elegy 19" ("Going to Bed"), as well as lines 29–46 of the elegy "Loves Warre," along with lines 1–48 and 53–96 of "Loves Progress," pieces censored from the 1633 edition of Donne.

47. Sullivan xi–xii points out affiliations of this collection with Bodleian MS Ashmole 38 and Corpus Christi (Oxford) College MS 328.

48. Sullivan xiii.

49. In the prefatory material to *Harmony,* we read "Poetry in their days [those of the poets represented in the anthology] flourished, and they flourished with it, and gave a crown unto that which hath crowned them with Honor, and perpetual Fame. The Genius of those times produced many incomparable Witts [. . .]" (A3r). On the politics of nostalgia, see Timothy Raylor, *Cavaliers, Clubs, and Literary Culture: Sir John Mennes, James Smith, and the Order of the Fancy* (Newark: U of Delaware P; London: Associated U Presses, 1994) 204–05. For a study of the seventeenth-century miscellanies, see Adam Smyth, *"Profit and Delight": Printed Miscellanies in England, 1640–1682* (Detroit: Wayne State UP, 2004).

50. See Courtney Craig Smith, "The Seventeenth-Century Drolleries," *Harvard Library Bulletin* 6 (1951): 40–51. Other collections of royalist wit include *Choyce Drollery* (1656), *Sportive Wit* (1656), *Wit and Drollery* (1656), and *Wit Restor'd* (1658)—the first two of which were burned by order of the authorities.

51. Raylor, *Cavaliers* 203–05.

52. Smyth 169. He offers a full list of the miscellanies in the appendix to his book (178–82).

## READING LIST

*The Arundel Harington Manuscript of Tudor Poetry.* 2 vols. Ed. Ruth Hughey. Columbus: Ohio State UP, 1960.

*England's Helicon, 1600, 1614.* Ed. Hyder Edward Rollins. Cambridge, MA: Harvard UP, 1935.

Helgerson, Richard. *Self-Crowned Laureates: Spenser, Jonson, Milton, and the Literary System.* Berkeley: U of California P, 1983.

Hobbs, Mary. *Early Seventeenth-Century Verse Miscellany Manuscripts.* Aldershot, Eng.: Scolar P, 1992.

Love, Harold. *Scribal Publication in Seventeenth-Century England.* Oxford: Clarendon P, 1993.

Marotti, Arthur F. *Manuscript, Print, and the English Renaissance Lyric.* Ithaca: Cornell UP, 1995.

May, Steven W. *Henry Stanford's Anthology: An Edition of Cambridge University Library Manuscript Dd. 5.75.* New York: Garland, 1988.

*The Phoenix Nest 1593.* Ed. Hyder Edward Rollins. Cambridge, MA: Harvard UP, 1931.

*A Poetical Rhapsody 1602–1621.* Ed. Hyder Edward Rollins. 2 vols. Cambridge, MA: Harvard UP, 1931.

Pomeroy, Elizabeth. *The Elizabethan Miscellanies: Their Development and Conventions.* Berkeley: U of California P, 1973.

Saunders, J. W. "From Manuscript to Print: A Note on the Circulation of Poetic MSS. In the Sixteenth Century." *Proceedings of the Leeds Philosophical and Literary Society* 6, no. 8 (1951): 507–28.

————. "The Stigma of Print: A Note on the Social Bases of Tudor Poetry." *Essays in Criticism* 1 (1951): 139–64.

Smyth, Adam. *"Profit and Delight": Printed Miscellanies in England, 1640–1682.* Detroit: Wayne State UP, 2004.

*Tottel's Miscellany (1557–1587).* 2 vols. Rev. ed. Ed. Hyder Edward Rollins. Cambridge, MA: Harvard UP, 1966.

Woudhuysen, H. R. *Sir Philip Sidney and the Circulation of Manuscripts 1558–1640.* Oxford: Clarendon P, 1996.

# 3

# Tudor and Stuart Defenses of Poetry

*Peter C. Herman*

In July 1579, Stephen Gosson published, at the behest of London's civic authorities, a little book called *The School of Abuse, Containing a Pleasant Invective Against Poets, Pipers, Players, Jesters, and such like Caterpillars of the Commonwealth.*[1] While the public theater, which had been drawing enthusiastic if unruly crowds since the first playhouse opened in 1567, constituted the primary target of Gosson's "invective," his focus includes all forms of fiction. Gosson's objection is simple enough: poetry in all its guises encourages corruption and leads to the damnation of its consumers:

> You are no sooner entered [the school of abuse] but liberty looseth the reins, and gives you head, placing you with poetry in the lowest form: when his skill is shown to make his scholar as good as ever twanged, he prefers you to piping, from piping to playing, from play to pleasure, from pleasure to sloth, from sloth to sleep, from sleep to sin, from sin to death, from death to the devil. (81)

Gosson's *The School of Abuse* occasioned an immediate riposte from Edmund Spenser, who would publish his own announcement of poetic ambition, *The Shepheardes Calender,* later that year. In December 1579, Spenser and his friend, Gabriel Harvey, printed their correspondence on reforming English verse, and Gosson's perhaps foolish dedication of the *School* to Sir Philip Sidney gave Spenser the opportunity for this nasty jab: "New books I hear of none, but only of one, that writing a certain book, called *The School of Abuse,* and dedicating it to Master Sidney, was for his labor scorned, if at least it be in the goodness of that nature to scorn. Such folly is it not to regard aforehand the inclination and quality of him to whom we dedicate our books" (89).[2]

The print encounter between Spenser and Gosson is part of a larger debate over the morality of verse that flared up in the 1570s, and while the defenses of poetry are well-known today, at the time they were significantly outnumbered. Gosson would write two more books (*An Apology of the School of Abuse* [1579] and *Plays Confuted in Five Actions* [1579]),[3] and at least five more works published between 1579 and 1587 take Gosson's side. Furthermore, these books represent an intensification of the steady stream of antipoetic comments one finds throughout the sixteenth century in texts as various as a humanist defense of women, sermons, devotional manuals, and an early encyclopedia.

Nor were poetry's defenders idle. The Cambridge academic Richard Willes published in 1573 a little Latin treatise, *A Disputation Concerning Poetry (De Re Poetica),*[4] which is the first extended response to English antipoetic sentiment. Thomas Lodge responded to Gosson with *A Defense of Poetry.* Sidney himself, as we shall see, wrote a rebuttal (although that would not see print until 1595; more on this later). We also have William Webbe's *A Discourse of English Poetry* (1586), George Puttenham's

*The Art of English Poesy* (1589), and Sir John Harington's *Brief Apology of Poetry* (1591).[5] In addition, we have references to two defenses that are no longer extant.[6]

What was it about poetry that made so many rational, presumably intelligent people so upset? And how did Elizabethan defenders of poetry, equally rational and intelligent, counter the charges? First, it is important to remember that there are local reasons for why the controversy over poetry flared up in the 1570s. The amount of poetry available for consumption very significantly increased thanks to London's thriving book trade. *Tottel's Miscellany,* first published in 1557, went through three editions in seven weeks, and seven more editions appeared between 1557 and 1587.[7] And in direct reaction to the massive sales of such texts as *Tottel's,* attacks on poetry also proliferated. In 1562, for example, Thomas Brice published a one-page jeremiad, *Against Filthy Writing / and Such Like Delighting,* that begins: "What mean the rhymes that run thus large in every Shop to sell; With wanton sound, and filthy sense." The discomfort of London's authorities with large numbers of young people going to see plays rather than working also played a large part in reviving the dispute between poetry's attackers, or Muse-haters, as Sidney called them, and poetry's defenders.

But the arguments over fiction have their roots in classical antiquity. Famously, in Book 10 of *The Republic,* Plato banished the poets from his ideal state. At first, Plato's objections to poetry seem more philosophical than political. Poetry is an "imitative" art (595a)[8] and, therefore, at least three times removed from the truth (597e). Rather than portraying the truth, the poet gives us "only a dim adumbration" (597b). This distance from the truth, however, has very practical consequences. Because the poet "leads us to dwell in memory on our suffering and impels us to lamentation" (604d) rather than appealing to "the intelligent and temperate disposition" (604e), he appeals "to the inferior part of the soul," and by doing so, he "tends to destroy the rational part" of the soul. Plato then makes the key analogy: allowing the poet to dominate the soul is equivalent to "when in a state one puts bad men in power and turns the city over to them and ruins the better sort" (605b). Plato, however, means this political analogy literally: poetry poses a danger to the state because if the poet is allowed to produce his "inferior works," "pleasure and pain will be lords of your city instead of law" (607a). Poetry's threat, in sum, is not abstract, but actual. Poetry causes political unrest and moral corruption. Ergo, Socrates concludes, and Glaucon, his interlocutor in this book, agrees: poetry must go.

These are exactly the arguments one hears from poetry's enemies (and even, as we will see, some of its friends). Poetry, in their view, directly causes its consumers to act badly. For example, in *The Poor Man's Library* (1571), William Alley included an entry on "Wanton Books." Alley's point is that hearing leads to doing: "In deed that which is willingly and gladly heard, is soon embraced and put in use, nor it can be far set from will which is seen with pleasure" (sig. Liii). Gosson also directly echoes Plato's charge that poets appeal to humanity's worst instincts when he writes that they "turn reasonable creatures into brute beasts" (77), and like Plato, Gosson charges poetry with supplanting the higher faculty of reason: "by the privy entries of the ear, [they] slip down into the heart, and with gunshot of affection gall the mind, where reason and virtue should rule the roost" (89). Poetry "draws the mind from virtue and confoundeth wit" (79), and therefore, writes Gosson, "no marvel though Plato shut them out of his school and banished them quite from his commonwealth as effeminate writers, unprofitable members, and utter enemies to virtue" (77).

The early modern defense of poetry was further complicated by the appropriation of antipoetic rhetoric by the earliest English Protestants, who regularly attacked Catholic dogma as fictions, and it did not take very long for this theological dispute to morph into an attack on fiction itself. For example, in his passage from William Tyndale's *An Answer to Thomas More* (1531) Tyndale refutes More by calling him a "poet":[9]

> *More:* What good will he do, that believeth Martin, how
>     that we have no free-will to do any good with the
>     Help of grace?"
> *Tyndale:* O poet, without shame!

Most of poetry's defenders acknowledge the strength and the depth of the opposition. Willes begins his *Disputation Concerning Poetry* by admitting that "in our age certain men who are evidently barbarous and enemies of the Muses despite and hold in contempt [. . .] those most noble sciences, rhetoric and poetry" (246–47). Sir Philip Sidney similarly begins *An Apology for Poetry* by noting that poetry "from almost the highest estimation of learning is fallen to be the laughing stock of children" (57);[10] and George Puttenham also testifies to how poetry's reputation has plummeted: "But in these days, although some learned princes may take delight in them [poets], yet universally it is not so. For as well poets as poesy are despised, and the name become of honorable infamous, subject to scorn and derision, and rather a reproach than a praise to any that useth it" (2: 19).

To answer the charges of the Muse-haters, Tudor and Stuart defenders also turned to the classical tradition for ammunition. If poetry's enemies ransacked the classics for denigrating comments by ancient Greeks and Romans, poetry's friends did the same to find an equal number of comments in praise of poetry. Willes, for example, cites the legend that Aristotle educated the future Alexander the Great using Homer (254–55), and Lodge counters Gosson's charge that poets are universally despised by asking "Why did Alexander give praise to Achilles, but for the praises which he found written of him by Homer?" (Smith 1: 70), whose body, Lodge also notes, multiple cities fought over for the honor of claiming him for their own (1: 70). And if Plato disliked poets, "yet the wisest had not all that same opinion. [. . . Seneca, for example,] sayeth that the study of poets is to make children ready to the understanding of wisdom" (1: 70).

Furthermore, poetry's defenders repeated the claim that poetry constitutes the source of civil society, a defense that also originates in ancient Rome. Lodge, for instance, cites his translation of Horace's *Art of Poetry* to prove that poetry, contra Plato, is the cause, not the enemy, of political stability: Orpheus "Did drive the savage men from woods, / And made them live aright." The poets, Lodge asserts through Horace, laid the foundation for all laws, both moral and civil, as well as religion:

> This wisdom this was it of old
> All strife for to allay;
> To give to every man his own;
> To make the Gods be known
> To drive each lecher from the bed
> That never was his own;
> To teach the law of marriage;

The way to build a town;
For to engrave these laws in woods—
This was these men's renown. (1: 74)

But most importantly, poetry's defenders counter the charge that poetry corrupts by emphasizing that poetry teaches virtue, not vice. As Willes writes, poetry's goal is "the moral education of the minds of the citizens through poetical harmony" (253). More often, however, poetry's defenders turned to Horace's formulation in the *Art of Poetry* that poetry achieves its didactic aim by appealing to the higher and the lower simultaneously. Poetry's goal, Horace writes, is to mingle "profit with pleasure by delighting the reader at once and instructing him." Lodge repeats exactly this claim: "what so they wrote, it was to this purpose, in the way of pleasure to draw men to wisdom" (66), and so does William Webbe: "All poets desire either by their works to profit or delight men, or else to join both profitable and pleasant lessons together for the instruction of life" (1: 250–51).

While the defenses of poetry by Willes, Lodge, Webbe, and Puttenham are all important, the best-known Elizabethan defender of poetry today is Sir Philip Sidney, the man to whom Stephen Gosson dedicated *The School of Abuse*. But while Sidney likely penned his rebuttal of Gosson's arguments soon after the *School's* publication in 1579, his response would not be published until 1595, when it appeared in two editions, and was frequently reprinted during the seventeenth century in Sidney's collected works.[11]

Sidney begins by rehearsing some of the more common arguments in poetry's favor. Poetry, Sidney writes, "hath been the first light-giver to ignorance and first nurse, whose whole milk little and little enabled them to feed afterwards of tougher knowledges" (57). Furthermore, poets were honored in antiquity and throughout the world. "In Turkey," Sidney informs us, "they have no other writers but poets" (61), and among "the Romans a poet was called *vates,* which is as much as a diviner, a forseer or prophet" (61). Sidney's argument, however, starts to become more original when he turns to the poet's relationship to nature. All other arts, Sidney writes, derive from nature and have nature as their object. The astronomer, for example, looks "upon the stars"; "the natural philosopher "standeth upon the natural virtues, vices, or passions of man" (64), and so on. The poet's relationship to nature, on the other hand, is fundamentally different:

> Only the poet, disdaining to be tied to any such subjection, lifted up with the vigor of his own invention, doth grow in effect another nature in making things either better than nature bringeth forth, or quite anew, forms such as never were in nature, as the heroes, demigods, Cyclops, Chimeras, Furies, and such like. So as he goeth hand in hand with nature, not enclosed within the narrow warrant of her gifts, but freely ranging only within the zodiac of his own wit. (64–65)

Having created this "idea," which he also calls a "fore-conceit," the poet then couples it with an image which he delivers "forth in such excellency as he had imagined them" (65).

Sidney's defense of poetry, however, does not lie in poetry's abstract superiority, even less in the glories of the imagination. Sidney's argument is a fundamentally practical one. If the Muse-haters charge that poetry causes immorality, and if Plato boots the poets out of the ideal republic because of the threat they pose to political stability,

Sidney counters by emphasizing that poetry leads to virtuous *acts,* not just virtuous ideals: "it is not *gnosis* [knowledge, theory] but *praxis* [practice] must be the fruit" (83). Consequently, the centerpiece of Sidney's argument against the Muse-haters is his version of the competition among the three chief sciences: poetry, philosophy, and history. Since, as Sidney puts it, "the ending end of all earthly learning being virtuous action" (71), whoever best accomplishes this task wins the prize, and so Sidney sets out to "show the poet's nobleness by setting him before his other competitors," specifically, the "moral philosophers and the historians" (71). Sidney argues that both are fundamentally flawed:

> For the philosopher setting down with thorny arguments the bare rule, is so hard of utterance and so misty to be conceived that one that hath no other guide but him shall wade in him till he be old before he shall find sufficient cause to be honest. For his knowledge standeth so upon the abstract and general that happy is that man who may understand him, and more happy that can apply what he doth understand. On the other side, the historian, wanting the precept, is so tied, not to what should be, but to what is, to the particular truth of things, and not to the general reason of things, that his example draweth no necessary consequence, and therefore a less fruitful doctrine. (73–74)

The philosopher, in other words, is less effective in inspiring virtuous action because he is too difficult to comprehend: "happy is that man who may understand him, and more happy that can apply what he doth understand" (74). As for the historian, he is bound to report what happened, not what should have happened: he "is so tied, not to what should be, but to what is," and so, "his example draweth no necessary consequence" (74). History does not always present the lessons one might wish.

The poet, on the other hand, can combine the strengths of both with none of their weaknesses: "Now doth the peerless poet perform both, for whatsoever the philosopher saith should be done, he giveth a perfect picture of it in someone by whom he presupposeth it was done, so as he coupleth the general notion with the particular example" (74). As for the historian, "captived," as Sidney writes, "to the truth of a foolish world" (81), the poet surpasses him "not only in furnishing the mind with knowledge, but in setting it forward to that which deserves to be called and accounted good, which setting forward and moving to well doing indeed setteth the laurel crown upon the poets as victorious, not only of the historian, but over the philosopher" (82). Consequently, "Of all sciences [. . .] is our poet the monarch. For he doth not only show the way, but giveth so sweet a prospect into the way as will entice any man to enter into it" (83). Reading poetry is not an act of idleness but a preparation for action:

> Truly I have known men that even with reading *Amadis de Gaul,* which, God knoweth, wanteth much of a perfect poesy, have found their hearts moved to the exercise of courtesy, liberality, and especially courage. Who readeth Aeneas carrying old Anchises on his back that wisheth not it were his fortune to perform so excellent an act? (84–85)

Yet despite these claims, Sidney is remarkably hesitant and conflicted about the claims he makes in poetry's defense in the *Apology.*[12] After his emphatic and spectacular description of the poet's freedom, Sidney brackets these concepts as a kind of thought-experiment—"But these arguments will by few be understood, and by fewer granted" (66)—and he restarts his argument with a definition of poetry that is the *opposite* of

what he has just proposed: "Poesy, therefore, is an art of imitation, for so Aristotle ter-
meth it in this word *mimesis,* that is to say, a representing, counterfeiting, or figuring
forth, to speak metaphorically" (66). To re-present, or to figure forth, or to imitate,
means that the poet is no longer "freely ranging only within the zodiac of his own wit"
but is now *subject* to Nature. Another example: Sidney praises mixing genres in one
passage ("some have mingled matters heroical and pastoral, but that cometh all to one
in this question, for if severed they be good, the conjunction cannot be hurtful" [87])
only to condemn this practice in another ("mongrel tragicomedy" [116]).

These seemingly minor contradictions signal deeper conflicts, for in many respects,
Sidney agrees with Gosson. Both, for example, denounce contemporary poets. After
noting that poetry's reputation in England is so low that only "base men with servile
wits undertake it" (110), he complains that there are so many bad poets publishing away
that it seems as if "all the Muses were got with child to bring forth bastard poets" (111).
To be sure, Sidney asserts toward the beginning of the *Apology* that his claims pertain
only to the "Right Poets" (67), and that he distinguishes between the art and its abuse:
he will "not say that poetry abuseth man's wit, but that man's wit abuseth poetry" (100).
But Sidney never identifies any "Right Poets," and in a book littered with allusions, the
reticence is notable. Allowing that most contemporary poets "abuse" their art also does
not help poetry's defense.

Sidney's doubts are shared by poetry's other defenders, who agree with their
antagonists more often than one might imagine. First, both the Musophiles and the
Musophobes agree that poetry can significantly affect the behavior of its consumers.
The disagreement, of course, is over whether that effect is for good or for ill, but even
here, the two sides seem to concur almost as much as they differ. Richard Willes fully
supports the bowdlerization (or censorship) of certain writers. We must, Willes writes,
"read Virgil *in safety;* let us read Horace—*but purged of vices;* and let us read Martial,
*but gelded by Augerius"* [13] (255; my emphasis). He agrees with Plato that certain works
should not be read by the young (Terence), and Willes "would not venture to advise
anyone to read the poems of Catullus" (256). Thomas Lodge betrays a similar insecu-
rity. While "poetry is a heavenly gift," Lodge admits that not "all poets are holy" (1: 75).
The Muse-haters' denunciation of contemporary poets is not, Lodge admits, entirely
wrong: "And surely, if I may speak my mind, I think we shall find but few poets, if it
were exactly weighed, what they ought to be" (1: 75). Lodge even sides with poetry's
enemies in some cases. "I abhor those poets that savor of ribaldry: I will with the zealous admit the expulsion of such enormities" (1: 76).

Elizabethan defenders of poetry, in sum, are oddly hobbled by their partial agreement
with the people they are ostensibly arguing against. Having argued that poetry can affect
behavior, it seems that Sidney, Lodge, and the others felt compelled to grant poetry's
potential for good and for bad, whereas poetry's enemies only allowed for the bad.

As Elizabeth's reign ended and James's reign began, the intensity of the argument
over poetry started to wane, and while one could attribute this development to the usual
ebb and flow of popular controversy, one can again point to local reasons for this development. While the fact that Elizabeth wrote verse was common knowledge, she restricted the audience to the Court, while James published two books of poetry and a
short statement on poetics while king of Scotland.[14] James also had his mini-epic,
*Lepanto,* reprinted in England in 1603. Doubtless, the king's very public poetic leanings

had a dampening effect on the Muse-haters, since attacking one perforce meant attacking the other. (The obverse is also true, as Ben Jonson used his first epigram to celebrate both: "How, best of Kings, dost thou a scepter beare! / How, best of Poets, dost thou laurel wear!"[15]) In addition, the constitutional crisis that originated in James's absolutism and would eventually result in the English Revolution put into perspective the dangers verse posed to the state.

Yet if the numbers of books pro- and contra-poetry declined as the Elizabethan age segued into the Stuart era, the issue did not disappear altogether. Francis Meres, for example, in his *Palladis Tamia, Wit's Treasury* (1598), notes the continuing association of antipoetic sentiment with the harder-shell forms of Protestantism: "As the Anabaptists abhor the liberal arts and humane sciences, so puritans and precisians detest poetry and poems" (Smith 2: 310). The dramatist, Thomas Heywood, would publish his own rebuttal of Stephen Gosson's *The School of Abuse, An Apology for Actors* (1612) that repeats the standard argument against the Muse-haters, that is, that poetry's goal is to "persuade men to humanity and good life, to instruct them in civility and good manners, showing them the fruits of honesty and the end of villainy."[16] Ben Jonson also lampooned the Muse-haters in his plays (in particular, the character Zeal-of-the-Land Busy in *Bartholomew Fair,* who in the final act gets into an argument—which he loses—with a puppet over the morality of the theater [V.v.]).

Yet the controversy over poetry did not simply keep going over the same ground, for two new developments occurred in the seventeenth century. The first is the stamp of approval to antipoetic, anti-imagination sentiment given by Francis Bacon. Bacon's project in *The Advancement of Learning* was to place knowledge on firmer foundation, to understand nature through inductive experiments, through concrete details, and thus build a true understanding of the world, "such as it is in facts," rather than on received opinions or, worse, figments of the imagination. Bacon seems to follow Sidney in granting the poet's freedom to create independent of nature: "Poesy is a part of learning in measure words for the most part restrained, but in all other points extremely licensed, and doth truly refer to the Imagination; which, being not tied to the laws of matter, may at pleasure join that which nature hath severed, and sever that which nature hath joined."[17] Bacon thus seems to agree with Sidney that the poet "doth grow in effect another nature in making things either better than nature bringeth forth, or quite anew, forms such as never were in nature" (64). But while Sidney celebrates the poet's ability to alter nature, Bacon condemns it. By joining the severed, and severing the joined, the poet makes *"unlawful* matches and divorces of things" (my emphasis). Bacon does not, as do so many Muse-haters, claim that poetry leads to immorality. He allows that for the "expressing of affections, passions, corruptions, and customs, we are beholding to poets more than to the philosophers' works" (344). But in a sense, Bacon's view is even more threatening to poetry's stature, since he reduces poetry to insignificance, to a mere diversion. After perfunctorily discussing and classifying the different types of poetry, Bacon moves on to the description of reason in terms that make clear his impatience with lesser matters: "But it is not good to stay too long in the theatre. Let us now pass on to the judicial place or palace of the mind, which we are to approach and view with more reverence and attention" (346). Poetry, as he writes later, is "a pleasure or play of imagination, than a work or duty thereof" (382).

If Bacon marginalizes poetry, and in so doing creates the opposition between the humanities and the hard sciences, John Milton defends poetry by elevating the poet to the highest position imaginable. Milton, however, does not accomplish this task in ignorance of the antipoetic tradition. He could even play the Muse-hater himself when it suited his purposes. In *Eikonoklastes* (1650), Milton uses Charles's taste for verse to further undermine the executed king's political credibility: "The simile wherewith he [Charles] begins I was about to have found fault with, as in a garb somewhat more poetical then for a statist [statesman]."[18] Milton thus appropriates the fairly common charge of the Muse-haters that poetry is incompatible with politics for his own, republican use, and by doing, testifies to the continuing presence and cultural power of antipoetic sentiment.

But more often, Milton defends the Muses. In "Ad patrem," a verse letter to his father, Milton confronts John Milton, Sr.'s, antipoetic leanings, which originate more from practicality than morality (you can't make money from poetry). Even so, Milton commands his father, "Do not despise divine poetry" (l. 17), although later he softens the command to a request: "Please, do not scorn the holy Muses; don't think that they are idle or unprofitable" (ll. 56–57).[19] Recalling the earlier defenses of poetry, Milton reminds his father of poetry's previous greatness and its didactic function: "Songs used to adorn noble feasts of kings. [. . .] In those days, the bard, [. . .] his flowing hair wreathed with oak leaves, sang of the achievements of heroes worthy of emulation" (ll. 41–46).

In the biographical digression to *The Reason of Church Government* (1642), Milton takes this defense one step further by elevating the poet to a previously unheard-of status. Along with Sidney and the others, Milton does not think much of contemporary poetry, condemning "the corruption and bane which [England's youth] suck in daily from the writings and interludes of libidinous and ignorant poetasters" (923–24). But while earlier defenses of poetry asserted that the poet has the potential to inspire virtuous actions, nobody asserted that poets, especially contemporary poets, were in fact divinely inspired. Sidney even distances himself from such a claim: "[Plato, in the *Ion*] attributeth unto poesy more than myself do, namely, to be a very inspiring of a divine force, far above man's wit" (107). But in *RCG,* Milton conflates poetry and divinely inspired prophecy by styling himself the future poet-prophet of the English nation. After describing the poetic virtues of classical tragedy and the Book of Revelations, Milton states that "These abilities, wheresoever they be found, are the inspired gift of God rarely bestowed, but yet to some (though most abuse) in every nation and are of power beside the office of a pulpit to inbreed and cherish in a great people the seeds of virtue and public civility" (923). Even further, after promising his reader that he will write a national epic, Milton asserts that this great work will not originate in "the vapors of wine, like that which flows at waste from the pen of some vulgar amorist," or from study alone, but "by devout prayer to that eternal Spirit who can enrich with all utterance and knowledge, and sends out his Seraphim with the hallowed fire of his altar to touch and purify the lips of whom he pleases" (924). The allusion is to Isaiah 6:1–7, in which God sends an angel to purify Isaiah's lips, so that he can denounce Israel's sinfulness. Milton, in other words, declares that he will be the new Isaiah, and his epic be the word of God itself. That work would, of course, be *Paradise Lost,* which Milton would not complete until 1667.[20]

But until then, Milton's answer to the Muse-haters, his answer to Plato's charge that poetry should be banned from the state, is not to simply assert proper poetry's divine origins, but to conflate epic virtue with the English Revolution and Milton's defense of it. Thus at the end of *A Second Defense of the English People* (1654), Milton compares the method of his defense of Charles's execution to that of "the epic poet," who celebrates "one event" in the life of the epic hero, "the exploits of Achilles at Troy, let us say, or the return of Ulysses, or the arrival of Aeneas in Italy." The overthrowing of monarchy, Milton asserts, constitutes the "heroic achievement of my countrymen," and he, their epic bard, the "one who could rightly counsel, encourage, and inspire, who could honor both the noble deeds and those who had done them, and make both deeds and doers illustrious with praises that will never die."[21] If for many courtier poets earlier in the Tudor-Stuart era (including Sidney), poetry was often a covert form of commenting on politics, for Milton, politics itself becomes a form of poetry. The virtuous act and the inspiration for it have become one.

## NOTES

1. *The School of Abuse, Markets of Bawdrie: The Dramatic Criticism of Stephen Gosson*, ed. Arthur F. Kinney (Salzburg, Austria: Salzburg Studies in English Literature, 1974). All further references will be parenthetical. For ease of reference, I have silently modernized the spelling and expanded contractions for all early modern texts.
2. Spenser and Gabriel Harvey, *Two Other Very Commendable Letters* (1579), *Elizabethan Critical Essays*, ed. G. Gregory Smith, 2 vols. (Oxford: Clarendon P, 1904), vol. 1.
3. For a very useful compilation of attacks on the stage, see Tanya Pollard, *Shakespeare's Theater: A Sourcebook* (Malden, MA: Blackwell, 2004). For a broad selection of classical and early modern attacks on poetry, see *Sir Philip Sidney's An Apology for Poetry and Astrophil and Stella: Texts and Contexts*, ed. Peter C. Herman (Glen Allen, VA: College Publishing, 2001) 218–76.
4. *De Re Poetica,* trans. and ed. A. D. S. Fowler (Oxford: Luttrell Society, 1958). All citations to this text will be to my slightly modified and annotated selection in *Sir Philip Sidney's "An Apology for Poetry" and "Astrophil and Stella."*
5. All references to Tudor and Stuart defenses of poetry, unless otherwise noted, will be to *Elizabethan Critical Essays*, ed. Smith.
6. See Smith 1: 62.
7. Wendy Wall, *The Imprint of Gender: Authorship and Publication in the English Renaissance* (Ithaca: Cornell UP, 1994) 24.
8. *The Republic,* trans. Paul Shorey, *The Collected Dialogues of Plato,* ed. Edith Hamilton and Huntington Cairns, Bollingen Series 71 (New York: Pantheon Books, 1961). All further references will be parenthetical and by Stefanus number.
9. *An Answer to Sir Thomas More's Dialogue,* ed. Henry Walter (Cambridge, 1850) 188.
10. All references to Sidney's writings will be to the Herman edition, and cited parenthetically.
11. Sidney's importance, however, does not lie in the originality of his ideas. He draws much of what he has to say in poetry's defense from Italian literary criticism—Julius Caesar Scaliger in particular, whose *Poetics* Sidney had read deeply and carefully. Sidney's contribution, therefore, lies in his injecting these ideas into English literary discourse and in his bringing together an extraordinary mosaic of earlier Renaissance thought about the nature and purpose of poetry. On Scaliger and the Italian tradition generally, see Baxter Hathaway, *The Age of Criticism: The Late Renaissance in Italy* (Ithaca: Cornell UP, 1962).

12. Nor is the *Apology* Sidney's only assessment of the relationship between poetry, history, and moral philosophy. In a letter to his friend Edward Denny, dated May 22, 1580—exactly the time Sidney was composing the *Apology*—Sidney responded to his friend's request for a list of books an educated man should have read by recommending moral philosophy (ranking Cicero's *De Officiis* "next to the foundation of scripture" [213]) and history. Not only does Sidney not even mention poetry, but his justification for recommending moral philosophy is the same one he uses for elevating poetry in the *Apology,* and his reason for recommending history is the same reason he criticizes the historians: "The first shows what should be done, the other what hath been done" (213). Next, in a letter Sidney wrote to his brother Robert on October 18, 1580, Sidney gives yet another version of poetry's status. After recommending that his brother read historians, Sidney says that "the historian makes himself a discourser, for profit, and an orator, yea, a poet sometimes, for ornament" (217). Therefore, the best one can say is that the *Apology* is not Sidney's final word on poetics, but one statement among three, and it is not clear which, if any, has priority.

13. Emond Auger (Augerius; no dates available), editor of an expurgated edition of Martial's epigrams published in 1585.

14. "A Short Treatise, Containing Some Rules and [Devices] to be Observed and Eschewed in Scottish Poesy," appended to James's first book of verse, *The Essays of a Prentice* (1584). The second, *His Majesty's Poetical Exercises,* appeared in 1591.

15. Quoted in Jonathan Goldberg, *James I and the Politics of Literature* (Stanford: Stanford UP, 1989) 17.

16. Heywood, "A Defence of Drama," *English Renaissance Literary Criticism,* ed. Brian Vickers (Oxford: Clarendon P, 1999) 495.

17. *The Advancement of Learning, The Works of Francis Bacon,* ed. James Spedding et al. (London, 1887) 3: 343.

18. *Complete Prose Works of John Milton,* ed. Don M. Wolfe et al. (New Haven: Yale UP, 1962) 3: 406. I have modernized the spelling and punctuation.

19. All references to Milton's works, except when noted otherwise, are to *The Riverside Milton,* ed. Roy Flannagan (Boston: Houghton Mifflin, 1998).

20. Nonetheless, Milton's epic is far from unconflicted about the problem of poetry, as shown by the many parallels between the poet and Satan. See William G. Riggs, *The Christian Poet in Paradise Lost* (Berkeley: U of California P, 1972).

21. *Complete Prose Works of John Milton,* vol. 4, pt. 1, 685–86.

## READING LIST

Barish, Jonas. *The Antitheatrical Prejudice.* Berkeley: U of California P, 1981.

Bundy, Murray W. "Bacon's True Opinion of Poetry." *Studies in Philology* 27 (1930): 244–64.

————. "The Theory of Imagination in Classical and Mediaeval Thought." *University of Illinois Studies in Language and Literature* 12 (1927): 1–28.

Ferguson, Margaret W. *Trials of Desire: Renaissance Defenses of Poetry.* New Haven: Yale UP, 1983.

Hathaway, Baxter. *The Age of Criticism: The Late Renaissance in Italy.* Ithaca: Cornell UP, 1962.

Havelock, Eric. A. *Preface to Plato.* Cambridge, MA: Belknap P of Harvard UP, 1963.

Herman, Peter C. *Squitter-wits and Muse-haters: Sidney, Spenser, Milton and Renaissance Antipoetic Sentiment.* Detroit: Wayne State UP, 1996.

Huntley, John F. "The Images of Poet and Poetry in Milton's *The Reason of Church Government.*" *Achievements of the Left Hand: Essays on the Prose of John Milton.* Ed. Michael Lieb and John T. Shawcross. Amherst: U of Massachusetts P, 1974. 142–59.

Javitch, Daniel. *Poetry and Courtliness in Renaissance England*. Princeton: Princeton UP, 1978.

Lamb, Mary Ellen. "Apologizing for Pleasure in Sidney's *Apology for Poetry:* The Nurse of Abuse Meets the Tudor Grammar School." *Criticism* 36.4 (1994): 499–519.

Levao, Ronald. *Renaissance Minds and Their Fictions: Cusanus, Sidney, Shakespeare*. Berkeley: U of California P, 1985.

Riggs, William G. *The Christian Poet in Paradise Lost*. Berkeley: U of California P, 1972.

Rossky, William. "Imagination in the English Renaissance: Psychology and Poetic." *Studies in the Renaissance* 5 (1958): 49–73.

Smith, G. Gregory. "Introduction." *Elizabethan Critical Essays*. Oxford: Clarendon P, 1904. 1: xi–xcii.

Vickers, Brian, ed. *English Renaissance Literary Criticism*. Oxford: Clarendon P, 1999.

# 4

# Wyatt, Surrey, and the Henrician Court

## Catherine Bates

A little play. Act 1: a scene at court. Sir Thomas Wyatt coming upon Anne Boleyn while she was "earnest at worke," "in sportinge wise" snatched a small jewel that was hanging by a lace from her pocket and thrust it into his bosom, refusing all entreaties to give it back. Henry VIII, not witnessing this particular scene yet keeping "a watchful eie upon the Knight" since he seemed "more to hover about the lady," was "whetted the more to discover to her his affection," and, taking her aside, "in the end fel to win her by treatie of marriage," in token of which he received from her a ring. "Yet al this with such a se-cresie was carried," the narrator continues, "as none or verie few esteemed this other then an ordinarie cours of dalliance."[1] Act 2: a few days later; a game of bowls. The king "sportinge himselfe" and being "more then ordinarily pleasantly disposed," jokingly claimed as his own a throw that was plainly someone else's, and when the surrounding group of courtiers, including Wyatt, respectfully demurred, Henry "pointinge with his finger whereon he ware her ringe, replied often it was his, and especialy to the Knight he said, 'Wiat, I tel thee it is mine,' smilinge upon him withal." Wyatt, "castinge his eye upon the King's finger, perceived that the Kinge ment the Lady whose ring that was," and, finding Henry "bent to pleasure," replied: "'And if it may like your Majestie to give me leave to measure it, I hope it will be mine,'" whereupon he took from his bosom the lace that Henry, "espiinge," knew to be Anne's, and used it to measure the throw. The episode was not perceived "of many," the narrator tells us, "but of some few it was."

So much is here: the teasing blend of jest and earnest (mapped, interestingly, onto a distinction between male play and female work); the ruthless competition of this mas-culine "sport" in which the woman is quarry in the sexual chase and circulates as an object of homosocial desire;[2] the courtly "game of love"[3] in which not only material objects (jewels, laces, rings) but a whole field of action becomes a tableau of encrypted signs to be read, but where the point of the game is to keep everyone guessing, and where the question of whether and what things mean is ultimately in the arbitration of the woman; and finally the calculated visibility, the dramatic interplay of hiding, seeing, showing that is the playwright's stock in trade (and as easily turned, as Shakespeare would show, to comic as to tragic effect), the play of looks in which the actors are sub-ordinated to the viewer's gaze (the reader is not only put in the position of those privi-leged "few," but privy to scenes that neither king nor courtier see) and where the woman is, for all her eyes cast demurely down on her sewing, again, no passive pawn (Anne rejected Wyatt's advances, the narrator tells us a few sentences earlier, but in such a way as "might the rather occasion others to turn their looks to that which a man of his worth was brought to gaze at in her, as indeed after happened").

This little anecdote is impossible to authenticate, but that, precisely, is why I cite it. Supposedly originating with Anne Gainsford, one of Anne Boleyn's former maids, the

eck Out Receipt

rmington Hills Library

esday, May  7 2013 10:33AM
627

em: 30036009498807
tle: Early modern English poetry : a c
tical companion
terial: Book
e: 05/28/2013

em: 30036010910923
tle: The complete works
terial: Book
e: 05/28/2013

tal items: 2

LIBRARY HOURS **
nday-Thursday 9:00 - 9:00
iday-Saturday 10:00 - 6:00
nday 1:00 - 5:00

RENEWALS **
line: http://www.farmlib.org/renew
one: 248-553-0300

story is retold some fifty or sixty years after the event by Wyatt's grandson, George Wyatt, himself born twelve years after the poet's death. As we sift first through these layers of second- and third-hand report, and then through the various motivations—late-Elizabethan nostalgia, Protestant zeal, a vindication of family honour—that led George Wyatt in the 1590s to answer the recusant Nicholas Sander's hostile Catholic tract *De origine ac progressu Schismatis Anglicani liber* (1585) by defending the English Reformation in the persons of Queen Elizabeth's mother and the grandfather he never knew, so we realize that, in trying to read the signs and to evaluate the shifting evidence before us, we are caught up in exactly the same game, and that the answers we seek—did it "really" happen, does it contain a "grain" of truth?—are no less elusive for us than they are for the characters involved. In what might have been Act 3 of our little play Henry, mortified, stalks off to seek clarification from Anne who, explaining "with good and evident proofe" how Wyatt came by the jewel, mollifies the king so effectively that he was more confirmed in her "truith" than ever before. A happy ending, then. But there is no such "truth" for us, any more than we would look for documentary evidence in *Othello* or *Love's Labour's Lost* ("what child is there," wrote Sidney, "that, coming to a play, and seeing *Thebes* written in great letters upon an old door, doth believe that it is Thebes?").[4]

That George Wyatt's text can in the end invite nothing but speculation is entirely appropriate given that what we are looking at is a piece of dramatic writing—and a rather masterful one at that, whether crafted by George himself (undeservedly criticized for the dullness of his prose) or, more pleasingly, perhaps (and continuing the theme of female work), by the maidservant, Anne Gainsford. Over the last twenty or thirty years critics and historians have cautioned us against trivializing courtly literature and ritual, against treating it as mere play and games—"a little music after supper" as C. S. Lewis once characterized it—since, as Stephen Greenblatt pointed out, conversation with Henry VIII "must have been like small talk with Stalin."[5] Let us have "no more pretty pictures of gallants and galliards" in our studies of the Tudor court, pleaded G. R. Elton, but "painful studies of Acatery and Pantry," and the result of such correctives has been an investigation into the workings of power that has rightly revolutionized our understanding of Tudor Court texts.[6] But there is a danger of going too far in the other direction: for to dismiss play in favor of "hard" fact can, as Marguerite Waller has warned, run the risk of turning literature back into history—and not a "new" history in which the historian's own position as knower is understood to be as historical and textual as the material in hand, but the old kind in which the texts of the past are once more treated as ocular proof and the critic expected to deliver "knowledge" if not truth about them.[7] But to read courtly texts as play—in all the senses of that word—is not necessarily to trivialize them. On the contrary, it has the advantage, first, of following through the new historicist injunction to read history as literature and, second, of matching our reading practice to the practice of these texts, so that the very way we read—no longer detached or separate but involved and playing the same game—can be drafted in as a way of understanding and appreciating how these texts work. As readers we ourselves learn the art of *sprezzatura*—the ability to balance play and earnest and to cultivate an intellectual openness, a willingness to hold alternatives in mind—that a light rather than a heavy touch can allow for.

It is especially important to bear this in mind since the period in question was one in which the claim to read meaning into such courtly words and actions and to "know" what they signified became one of the most deadly weapons in the assertion and exercise of state power. When in July 1536, for example, Surrey's young uncle, Lord Thomas Howard, and his sister's close friend, Lady Margaret Douglas, were taken in for questioning regarding a supposed love affair if not clandestine marriage between them, it was exactly the same "play"—of gifts exchanged and intimate scenes hidden from or spied by prying eyes—that became the object of inquisitorial scrutiny. When examined, Lord Thomas was asked what tokens he had given the lady ("none but a crampring") and received from her ("none but her 'phisnamye,' painted, and a diamond"); and when questioned as to whether he had ever "seen him [. . .] resort unto her," a servant, one Thomas Smyth, answered that Lord Thomas would "watch till my lady Boleyn was gone" (Margaret Douglas had been among her train), "and then steal into her chamber."[8] The context of the episode is the jitteriness that followed Ann Boleyn's execution on May 19, an event that had left the succession more unresolved than ever. With Henry's two daughters now bastardized, and his only son—the illegitimate Henry Fitzroy, duke of Richmond, married to Surrey's sister—far from well (he was to die on July 22), Margaret Douglas was, as the king's niece, daughter of his sister Mary, the queen of Scotland, too close to the throne for comfort. In the circumstances, behavior that might otherwise have been deemed the "ordinarie cours of dalliance" was judged high treason and Thomas Howard was indicted and charged (he died in the Tower in October 1537).

With such a model of critical interpretation in mind, then, how do we approach those poems that are associated with the couple and that find themselves inscribed in that quintessential example of Tudor courtly literature, the Devonshire manuscript? At various intervals throughout the manuscript (an anthology of verses and love songs, many of them attributed to Wyatt, that belonged to Surrey's sister and her circle), and written out in the same hand (though precisely whose remains the subject of debate), are a series of poems that correspond closely to Thomas and Margaret's predicament: "Alas that euer pryson stronge / Sholde such too louers separate!" the first poem in the sequence laments. What follows largely presents itself as an epistolary exchange ("To yowr gentyll letters an answere to resyte, / Both I and my penne there to wyll aply," the lover writes, assuring his beloved that "I take god to record whych knowyth my hart") and proceeds to detail the trials of love—separation, secrecy, renewed vows of faithfulness in the face of adversity, and so forth—all of them familiar from the annals of courtly love, and, indeed, for the most part copied out directly from William Thynne's edition of Chaucer (published in 1532). At one point in the manuscript, for example, four stanzas from Book 4 of *Troilus and Criseyde* have been inscribed with Criseyde's name omitted and space left for Margaret's to be written in (so it has been speculated), and in any case clearly allowing the lover to present himself as a latter-day Troilus: "O very lord, O loue! O god, alas! / That knowest best myn hert and al my thowght."[9] But to historicize these poems as "actual" love letters penned by the two and passed surreptitiously between them or to romanticize them as evidence of "real" love (as many critics have done): is this not to assume the position of the state interrogator who could claim, on the basis of such actions or words, to understand exactly what they signified and, like the god of love evoked here, to "knowyth" the contents of the heart? Is it not preferable in literary historical terms, and closer to the spirit of Renaissance Court practice, to suspend critical judgment, to delay pronouncing the fatal "meaning," and to sustain the play of enigmatic signification, since to do this leaves open the whole range of possibilities that such play-acting allows for: namely, that Thomas Howard and Margaret Douglas dramatized themselves as tragic lovers (or were so dramatized by their friends) either because such role-play did indeed correspond to their inner feelings, or because it allowed them to dissemble feelings that were quite different, or because the whole thing was a joke or game in which no feelings were involved at all, or because it provided an idealized model for feelings to which they aspired?

Reading Wyatt calls for the same spirit of caution and open-mindedness. Early in May 1536 (only weeks before the incarceration of the star-crossed lovers) Wyatt found himself in the Tower along with five other men who were accused of having been intimate with the queen. Once again, conduct that might otherwise have been deemed but the "ordinarie cours of dalliance" became the subject of state scrutiny and "pastime in the queen's chamber" (which included, according to the indictments, flirtatious conversations, dancing, and the exchange of kisses, jokes, and gifts among Anne and her admirers and friends) could, under that hostile and pre-determined glare, all too easily lend itself to unfavorable interpretation.[10] This is not to suggest that Wyatt's poems were used as evidence against him, but rather to ask whether those editors, critics, biographers, and historians who identify the so-called Anne Boleyn poems—including "What word is that that changeth not / Though it be turned and made in twain" ("anna," someone has helpfully written over the poem in the Egerton manuscript), "Sometime I fled the fire that me brent" (seemingly written when Wyatt, along with most of the rest of the Court, accompanied Henry and Anne to Calais in October 1532), and "If waker care," which refers to "Brunet that set my wealth in such a roar" (a discreet alteration of "Her that did set our country in a roar")—are not, in reading such references as documentary and in building upon them a whole history of emotional relations between Wyatt and Anne, putting themselves in the position of inquisitor?[11] In one of his elegies on Wyatt, "Dyvers thy death doo dyverslye bemone," Surrey claimed truly to "knowe what harbourd in that hedd," but the posture surely suits a mourning friend better than a literary historian.[12] As John Kerrigan has suggested, "Wyatt's reticence makes all his poems, to some degree, riddles," and while some seem to dangle their answers easily (like "A lady gave me a gift she had not" or "What means this when I lie alone?"), others play with the reader's desire for meaning like shaggy-dog stories (like "Perdie, I said it not" and "Me list no more to sing"), and others still (like "What vaileth truth") problematize their own status as meaningful utterance as effectively as the Cretan liar.[13]

It is because such playfulness undermines the critic's claim to "know," perhaps, that the general tendency in Wyatt criticism has been to restore the elusive signified and to extrapolate intention, agency, and above all *power* as lying behind the poet's crafty mask. In Greenblatt's celebrated reading in *Renaissance Self-Fashioning,* for example, Wyatt's poems are said to conceal—behind diplomatic chicanery or postures of submission—a ruthless will to power. For Greenblatt, "the poems only make sense in a society of competing players" (137) and Wyatt is the "superior performer" (120), the "master" of the game (137). Wyatt's riddling is here seen as tactical, as strategic—as the author's way of asserting his integrity and of critiquing a tyrannical regime with what (in Greenblatt's words) "government spokesmen now call 'deniability'" (121). This reading is difficult to resist since, as with any conspiracy theory, it is difficult to deny "deniability." But playing does not have to mean playing to win, and to equate the two, as here, can have serious consequences for our understanding of Wyatt's poetry. Take, for example, that most anthologized of "Anne Boleyn poems," "Whoso list to hunt," a text in which the themes of our opening anecdote (the predatory circulations of homosocial desire, the question of sexual possession, the enigmatic meaning of a ring) once more present themselves. The poem enacts the failure to capture or seize hold of meaning, the signified proving to be as elusive for us as the lady/hind is for the speaker: "in a net I seek to hold the wind." This failure, moreover, is universal, for although the poem appears to be one of renunciation—with the speaker relinquishing the object of desire to the more powerful male—in fact Caesar/Henry is, for all his proprietary ownership of the deer, no more guaranteed of knowing her "truith" than any jealous husband (there is no reason why the text on the animal's collar, "And wild for to hold though I seem tame," should not apply as much to him as to other men). It is not to mystify the "Eternal Feminine" to say that the inability to know for certain the contents of the female heart and womb was a classic site of masculine anxiety (the fact that Henry was married to Anne, after all, would not prevent him, Othello-like, from accusing her of having slept with a hundred men).[14] Greenblatt, however, reads this failure to "know" as a mask for the more effective assertion of power. The delicacy, restraint, and suggestiveness of the poem are turned around, "translated," into an "immense power of implication" (146), and the ambiguous play of meanings and identifications becomes a "dangerous game of power" (149)—one that Wyatt wins. The same thing happens in Greenblatt's interpretation of "They flee from me," where an exquisite moment of masculine sexual surrender is bizarrely read as "a mask for a more potent aggression" (153). The potency that is so confidently posited as being what "really" lies behind the mask corresponds to the power the critic claims for himself (that is, his ability to "know" both that the poem is a mask and what the mask conceals): the effect being not only to perpetuate, at the level of literary criticism, the competitive and explicitly masculinist circulations of power but, more seriously, to misrepresent the multivalency if not sheer unknowability that is the chief characteristic of Renaissance courtly texts.

Consider another "Anne Boleyn poem"—"Who list his wealth and ease retain"—a text almost universally cited as evidence for the fact that Wyatt witnessed the execution of Anne and her "lovers" from his cell in the Tower: "The bell tower showed me such a sight / That in my head sticks day and night." In a particularly bad case of circular reasoning, a poem that may or may not be by Wyatt (it exists in only a single manuscript) is used to corroborate an unreliable contemporary source in order, first, to prove that Wyatt is the author and then to build on this a whole biography of traumatized reaction: "These bloody days have broken my heart. / My lust, my youth did then depart." We do not need to say that the poem is by Wyatt, however, or that he witnessed anything from his cell, to say that whoever did write the poem knew all about the state's calculated use of dramatic device in its exercise of power. As Thomas More (who had lost his head on the same spot less than a year before) had presciently written in his *History of Richard III*: "these matters bee Kynges games, as it were stage playes, and for the more part plaied vpon scafoldes."[15] Nor do we need to affirm that the poem is Wyatt's in order to say that its author, understanding this very well, answered in kind—play for play—for the poem's refrain, "*circa Regna tonat,*" is a direct quotation from, and its first two stanzas a translation of, the Chorus from Act 4 of Seneca's play, *Phaedra*. These allusions, which refer to Jove, who "thunders around thrones," and to the perils that afflict those who aspire too high, are generally read as advice given by a speaker who is all too visibly the victim of brutal state power. In the context of Seneca's play, however, the menace of Jove's power does not refer to an aspirant courtier but rather to the *king*, Theseus (another monarch, incidentally, with a dubious marital past), and it relates specifically to the anguish—later, the agonized remorse—that he suffers at having violently destroyed the beautiful and innocent youth, Hippolytus, falsely accused, as it turns out, of having slept with the queen. Identifying with Hippolytus—if that is what he is doing—allows the poet to adopt the classic posture of Stoic withdrawal (one adopted in numerous anti-Court satires of the period, including Wyatt's "Mine own John Poyntz") since the youth's love of hunting and of the wild forests is explicitly an escape from the corrupt and oversexualized Court. Moreover, in myth, although killed and horribly dismembered by Theseus's wrath, Hippolytus is miraculously resurrected by the healer Asclepius and reborn as Virbius ("twice-man"). So a poem that at first seems a statement of helplessness before a crushing state power can also be seen not only to reassert the speaker's innocence and survival but to predict the terrible suffering that will surely come to the king when he bitterly regrets his abuse of power.

None of this, however, is "proof" of Wyatt's authorship or of what the person who wrote the poem may have seen, thought, felt, or meant. To take the next step and to affirm that the poet is hiding behind "deniability" in order to criticize a despotic regime, however obvious, is still to pass literature off as history and to treat as evidence what would be inadmissible in anything but the most corrupt of courts. The only thing we can say for certain is that the poem matches play for play, a "king's game" with Senecan drama. Everything else is speculation. For the critic to go any further would be to act like the commissioners who, when sifting through the papers of the by then disgraced and fallen Thomas Cromwell some five years later—and coming upon a series of accusations that had been levelled against Wyatt by Edmund Bonner back in 1538, among them the charge that he "dooth often call to his remembrance his emprisonement in the Towere, which semeth soo to sticke in his stomacke that he can not forget it"—used this to implicate Wyatt in a Catholic plot against the king and to throw him in the Tower again on suspicion of treason. Crafty or innocent, Wyatt's words in his own defense might be directed at all those, including literary critics, who take it upon themselves to read Tudor courtly texts. That he regretted his incarceration in May 1536 Wyatt does not deny, but that this signified "a desyer to revenge," who is to say?—neither "theie nor anye other man cane ether prof that or mayke a lykelyhoode of a prof therof."[16]

For another fiction taken as supposed "evidence" for a traumatic prison experience, consider two poems, this time by the earl of Surrey: "When Windesor walles sustained my wearied arme" and "So crewell prison howe could betyde, alas." As Surrey's most recent biographer has pointed out, it is a paucity of "hard" evidence that (whether in colorful sixteenth- or seventeenth-century retellings of Surrey's story by Thomas Nashe, Michael Drayton, or Lord Herbert of Cherbury, or in more modern historical accounts) has been largely responsible for the development of a "myth-like narrative" or "cult-memory" of an event in Surrey's life for which there is not much more evidence than the poems themselves.[17] In the summer of 1537 Surrey seems to have been accused of some offense, not recorded (possibly striking another courtier within the precincts of the Court) the penalty for which—loss of the right hand—was commuted to temporary incarceration in Windsor Castle. It may or may not have been then that he wrote the sonnet and the longer elegy in heroic quatrains, both of which are set there and both of which mourn the death the previous summer of his friend, confidant, and brother-in-law, the duke of Richmond. As William Sessions argues, however, the point is not that the poems document anything but rather that they *dramatize* the event, that is, they authenticate the speaker's experience only insofar as—using naturalistic imagery, a contemporary and native setting (the parapet on which he rests his "wearied arme" can still be seen to this day), and, through caesura and enjambement, a recognizably conversational idiom—they command audience assent in a probable history and thus re-create, if not an actual event, then a "poetic" truth (remember Thebes). It is in the nature of prison poems to stress the speaker's isolation, but the inspiration of combining this form with personal elegy is what allows Surrey to emphasize this condition to the point of an almost existential aloneness: "Thus I alone, where all my fredome grew, / In pryson pyne with bondage and restraynt." As the place where the two young friends had once sported and played, Windsor is not just a prison but a place now hauntingly derelict and empty, the speaker not just alone but positively *deprived* of the friend who should properly have been his poems' recipient and addressee. The sense of palpable loss that is opened up by the death of his companion goes well beyond the old cliché of the cell walls echoing back the prisoner's laments: it powerfully interpellates the reader as a new addressee—as necessary witness to the tragic scene—a dramatization of the "turn inwards" that, as Sessions rightly notes, was in 1537 a whole new departure in the representation of the subjective voice.

In the sixteenth century, introspection was (as Anne Ferry has shown) most commonly depicted as a withdrawal into some enclosed, internal space—a chamber, closet, or, paradigmatically here, a cell—where the mind could be both alone, communing privately with itself, and in company, turned outward to unknown eyes and ears: the paradox of the dramatic soliloquy.[18] The result is the so-called subjectivity effect: the illusion, created purely on the page, of an individual working mind, of a living human self, that is as opaque and mysterious as any other, yet, vulnerable and exposed in all its intimacy, something with which every audience and reader can identify.[19] When, in another poem, Surrey sets his speaker in a secluded space and dramatizes his train of thought—"Laid in my quyett bedd, in study as I weare"—he creates the same sense of subjective realism. But this impression of a core, centered self, of an "I" who thinks and feels, is an entirely literary invention; and the most forceful assertions of a sincere and truthful self can often, for Surrey as well as for Wyatt, be the product of borrowing somebody else's words: the "quiet mind" in which both poets take refuge, for example, that famed resort of the honest man, is a quotation, in Surrey's case from Martial, and in Wyatt's from Plutarch.[20] When, this time as the locus for a specifically Reformation spirituality, the two poets depict the soul as withdrawing into the same inner sanctum—a "deep," "dark cave" for Wyatt, "In humble spritte [where] is sett the temple of the Lorde" for Surrey, a place for devotional exercises, private meditations, and prayerful examinations of conscience—even there where, in unmediated communion with God, the self is at its most vulnerable and exposed, both poets make the same move, again dramatizing the psychology, assuming the role, and ventriloquizing the voice of another: the psalmist David or his son Solomon.[21] It was round the turn of 1546/1547—in prison once again and this time facing execution for treason—that Surrey produced his own translations of this Wisdom literature, adopting an alien voice at this most critical juncture of his young life not because his own had failed him but because doing so allowed him, as Sessions puts it, to "textualize the scream" (385), that is, to depict a crisis that was all the more intense, compelling, and "real" for being a dramatization. When, in an earlier sonnet, Surrey had commended Wyatt's translations of the psalms, what he singled out for praise was not that they were a direct utterance of the poet's mind but rather that they were, precisely, an *artistic* representation: Wyatt, he wrote, "dothe paynte the lyvely faythe and pure."[22] It was this that made them personal, sincere, and "true."

The world, wrote Surrey, translating Ecclesiastes 1, "But sarves us for a place too play our tragedes uppon," a citation of that ancient metaphor that might stand as one of many examples from the period to illustrate what Alistair Fox has identified as "the distinctive early Tudor tendency to represent thought in the form of dramatized situations."[23] But perhaps Surrey's greatest achievement—certainly his most enduring legacy—was the invention of what, though announced by its first publisher in 1554 as a "straunge metre" would, within a couple of generations, have become the standard line in English drama: blank verse.[24] Translating Books 2 and 4 of Virgil's *Aeneid,* Surrey needed an English line that was weighty, noble, yet fast-paced enough to match epic's dactylic hexameter, and he found it in the unrhymed, stress-driven, iambic pentameter that—from out of Aeneas's great account of the fall of Troy and Dido's operatic speeches on love and death—would come to resonate across the English stage for centuries and become dramatic soliloquy's most favored form. As in the Windsor elegies, the experience of loss—exile and abandonment—leads to an exercise in literature, and the presentation of human beings at their most vulnerable, weak, and alone dramatizes their subjectivity in the most specific way. For the fact that the people who *should* have been present to see and hear are absent (a family and people destroyed, in Aeneas's case, and, in Dido's, a lover fled and gone) requires the audience/reader to take their place all the more urgently, so that instead of being mere spectators, passive and detached, we find ourselves made active respondents: hailed, summoned, addressed, pressed to react, and called to account. Indeed, it is almost as if Surrey were anticipating the power his new invention would come to have over theater audiences of the future, for translating Books 2 and 4 allowed him, quite apart from anything else, to dramatize the drama of his own line: that is, to show the sheer impact it has on the story's internal audience, both the rapt Carthaginian Court that Aeneas holds captive with his tale ("They whisted all, with fixed face attent, / When prince Aeneas from the royal seat / Thus gan to speak" [2.1–3]) and, of course, Dido, who is driven to desperation by his words:

> But now the wounded quene with hevy care,
> Throughout the veines she norisheth the playe,
> Surprised with blind flame; and to hir mind
> Gan eke resort the prowesse of the man
> And honour of his race; while in her brest
> Imprinted stack his wordes and pictures forme. (4.1–6)

Moreover, it is specifically Aeneas's *dramatic* rendering of the Troy story that enflames the queen here, for where Virgil has Dido feeding the wound of love with her life-blood ("*volnus alit venis*", *Aeneid* 4.2), Surrey—in a startling departure from his source— renders this "Throughout the veines she norisheth the playe": an alteration of the sense that, in equating *wound* with *play,* not only neatly brings together our themes of pathos and drama but, in demonstrating the power of play so forcefully to move those who read and hear it, promotes what Sidney (who largely saw himself as following in Surrey's footsteps) would come to defend as literature's superior power over history, the ability of its mere probabilities to convey a higher, golden, more "poetic" truth.

The cue for how best to approach the poetry of Wyatt, Surrey, and the Henrician Court, however, might come not from Sidney but from Shakespeare (arguably the greatest inheritor of Surrey's blank verse line), above all at the moment when, in 1613, he turned his eyes back to that period in what was probably the last play he ever wrote: *Henry VIII*. For this play not only subjects the chronicle accounts to a degree of compression and poetic "licence" that is unusual even for a Shakespearean history play, but, as Bill Readings suggests, it positively relinquishes history in favor of theater, sacrificing causality in order to present as iconic tableaux of tragedy's *de casibus* tradition the three great structural moments of the play: the falls of Buckingham, Wolsey, and Katherine of Aragon.[25] The truth of what "really" happened during that turbulent time is pointedly subordinated to form—history to literature—and to look behind this for "hard" fact or for a "grain" of truth is to seek the enigmatic signified that, as this literature repeatedly demonstrates, will always elude us. As readers or audience we are not aloof, objective, or detached, looking down on history for meaning or as something we can "know." As historical subjects ourselves, we are involved, caught up in the same play, and necessarily playing the same game. We can do no more than speculate (*to theorize* means to look, and comes from the same root as *theater*, after all), for history is literature; and this, perhaps, is what Shakespeare was suggesting when he chose for his play its enigmatic subtitle—"All Is True."

## NOTES

1. From George Wyatt, "The Life of Queen Anne Boleigne," cited in Kenneth Muir, *Life and Letters of Sir Thomas Wyatt* (Liverpool: Liverpool UP, 1963) 15–19. My title alludes to Joel B. Altman's *The Tudor Play of Mind* (Berkeley: U of California P, 1978).

2. See Eve Kosofsky Sedgwick, *Between Men: English Literature and Male Homosocial Desire* (New York: Columbia UP, 1985).

3. See John Stevens, *Music and Poetry in the Early Tudor Court* (London: Methuen, 1961) esp. 154–202.

4. Sir Philip Sidney, *An Apology for Poetry*, ed. Geoffrey Shepherd (Manchester: Manchester UP, 1973) 124.

5. C. S. Lewis, *English Literature in the Sixteenth Century, Excluding Drama* (Oxford: Clarendon P, 1954) 230; Stephen Greenblatt, *Renaissance Self-Fashioning* (Chicago: U of Chicago P, 1980) 136–37.

6. G. R. Elton, *Studies in Tudor and Stuart Politics and Government*, 3 vols. (Cambridge: Cambridge UP, 1983) 3: 53.

7. Marguerite Waller, "The Empire's New Clothes: Refashioning the Renaissance," *Seeking the Woman in Late Medieval and Renaissance Writings*, ed. Sheila Fisher and Janet E. Halley (Knoxville: U of Tennessee P, 1989) 160–83.

8. *Letters and Papers, Foreign and Domestic, of the Reign of Henry VIII*, ed. J. S. Brewer et al., 23 vols. (London: HMSO, 1862–1932) 11: 48.

9. Citations from poems numbered 7, 13, 14 (the latter quoting *Troilus and Criseyde* 4.288–89) in Kenneth Muir, "Unpublished Poems in the Devonshire Manuscript," *Proceedings of the Leeds Philosophical and Literary Society* 6 (1947): 253–82.

10. See E. W. Ives, *Anne Boleyn* (Oxford: Blackwell, 1986) 398.
11. *Sir Thomas Wyatt: The Complete Poems,* ed. R. A. Rebholz (Harmondsworth: Penguin, 1978).
12. *Henry Howard, Earl of Surrey: Poems,* ed. Emrys Jones (Oxford: Clarendon P, 1964).
13. John Kerrigan, "Wyatt's Selfish Style," *Essays and Studies* 34 (1981): 1–18: 9.
14. *Letters and Papers* 10: 909.
15. *The Complete Works of St Thomas More,* ed. Louis L. Martz et al., 15 vols. (New Haven: Yale UP, 1963–97) 2: 81.
16. Muir, *Life and Letters* 66, 200.
17. W. A. Sessions, *Henry Howard, The Poet Earl of Surrey* (Oxford: Oxford UP, 1999) 129.
18. Anne Ferry, *The "Inward" Language* (Chicago: U of Chicago P, 1983).
19. See Joel Fineman, *The Subjectivity Effect in Western Literary Tradition* (Cambridge, MA: MIT P, 1991).
20. See Surrey's "Marshall, the thinges for to attayne" (a translation of Martial's epigram, "Vitam quae faciunt beatiorem"), and Wyatt's *The Quyete of Mynde* (a translation of Plutarch's *De tranquillitate et securitate animi*).
21. Wyatt, "dark cave," "deep cave" from *Paraphrase of the Penitential Psalms,* ll. 60, 666; Surrey, "In humble spritte" from "When I be thought me well," l. 51.
22. Surrey, "The great Macedon that out of Perse chasyd," l. 7.
23. Alistair Fox, *Politics and Literature in the Reigns of Henry VII and Henry VIII* (Oxford: Blackwell, 1989) 212; Surrey, "I Salamon, Davids sonne, King of Jerusalem," l. 10.
24. *Surrey's "Fourth Boke of Virgill,"* ed. Henry Hartman (New York: Purchase, 1933) xv.
25. Bill Readings, "When Did the Renaissance Begin? The Henrician Court and the Shakespearean Stage," *Rethinking the Henrician Era,* ed. Peter C. Herman (Urbana: U of Illinois Press, 1994) 283–302.

## READING LIST

Anglo, Sydney. *Images of Tudor Kingship.* London: Seaby, 1992.
Boffey, Julia. *Manuscripts of English Courtly Love Lyrics in the Later Middle Ages.* Woodbridge: D. S. Brewer, 1985.
Crewe, Jonathan. *Trials of Authorship: Anterior Forms and Poetic Reconstruction from Wyatt to Shakespeare.* Berkeley: U of California P, 1990.
Foley, Stephen Merriam. *Sir Thomas Wyatt.* Boston: Twayne, 1990.
Fox, Alistair. *Politics and Literature in the Reigns of Henry VII and Henry VIII.* Oxford: Blackwell, 1989.
Greenblatt, Stephen. *Renaissance Self-Fashioning.* Chicago: U of Chicago P, 1980.
Heale, Elizabeth. *Wyatt, Surrey and Early Tudor Poetry.* London: Longman, 1998.
Herman, Peter C., ed. *Rethinking the Henrician Era.* Urbana: U of Illinois P, 1994.
Ives, E. W. *Anne Boleyn.* Oxford: Blackwell, 1986.
Lerer, Seth. *Courtly Letters in the Age of Henry VIII.* Cambridge: Cambridge UP, 1997.
Loades, David. *The Tudor Court.* London: Batsford, 1986.
Mason, H. A. *Humanism and Poetry in the Early Tudor Period.* London: Routledge and Kegan Paul, 1959.
Sessions, W. A. *Henry Howard, The Poet Earl of Surrey.* Oxford: Oxford UP, 1999.
Starkey, David, et al., eds. *The English Court: From the Wars of the Roses to the Civil War.* London: Longman, 1987.
Walker, Greg. *Plays of Persuasion: Drama and Politics at the Court of Henry VIII.* Cambridge: Cambridge UP, 1991.

# 5

# Spenser's *May* Eclogue and Mid-Tudor Religious Poetry

*John N. King*

By praising Immerito (a pseudonym for Edmund Spenser) as "the new Poet" in the dedicatory epistle to *The Shepheardes Calender* (1579), E. K. asserts that this great Elizabethan author breaks away from previous poetic tradition. As E. K. indicates, the *Calender*'s amalgamation of imported Italianate and neoclassical conventions with a virtuoso array of metrical and stanzaic patterns lacks precedent in English verse. Nevertheless, Spenser assumes not only the Virgilian pose of pastoral apprenticeship, but also humble voices that recall the language of mid-Tudor religious poets whose verse satires attacked alleged abuses of the Church of Rome. The stylistic plainness of *May* and the other ecclesiastical eclogues in the *Calender* (*July* and *September*) is a hallmark of the native tradition of vernacular poetry.[1] It is true that these poems, in which E. K. identifies "some Satyrical bitternesse" (Spenser 23), draw considerable energy from a tradition of continental pastoral satire that goes back to Petrarch (Francesco Petrarca) and Mantuan (Baptista Mantuanus Spagnuoli), notable Italian humanistic poets of the fourteenth and fifteenth centuries. Spenser extends this tradition by employing English vernacular language and poetic effects in speeches attributed to Piers, the shepherd who attacks ecclesiastic abuses in the *May* eclogue. This plain idiom is very different from the more ornamental style and dense rhetorical complexity that we encounter in verse by seventeenth-century poets such as John Donne, George Herbert, and John Milton. Examination of how *May* exemplifies stylistic and satirical practices that we encounter in English religious verse composed during the second and third quarters of the sixteenth century opens a window into our understanding of Tudor religious verse.

In comparison with the high style of *April* and *October, May* conforms to the rougher native style typical of late medieval verse. Although E. K.'s sense of poetic decorum leads him to condone Spenser's employment of archaic language, he acknowledges that this vernacular practice will disappoint more sophisticated readers when he declares: "Other some not so wel seene in the English tonge as perhaps in other languages, if them happen to here an olde word albeit very naturall and significant, crye out streight way, that we speak no English, but gibberish" (Spenser 16). Neoclassical assumptions thus led critics such as Sir Philip Sidney and George Puttenham to exclude humble vernacular language as a model for stylistic imitation. Although Sidney's *Apology for Poetry* acknowledges Chaucer's "reverent antiquity," the Elizabethan poet finds that his medieval progenitor had "great wants" and that full appreciation of his verse is lost "in that misty time." Sidney similarly qualifies his judgment that *The Shepheardes Calender* is the only collection by a contemporary poet that is "worthy the reading, if I be not deceived" by declaring that no precedent exists for Spenser's imitation of archaic language: "That same framing of his style to an old rustic language I dare not allow."[2] George Puttenham concurs with Sidney's criticism in *The Art of English Poesy:* "Our maker therefore at these days shall not follow Piers plowman nor Gower nor Lydgate nor yet Chaucer, for their language is now out of use with us." Although Puttenham argues that the English vernacular is a suitable medium for sophisticated verse, he rejects the "terms hard and obscure" (i.e., archaic language) of *Piers Plowman* as a model for stylistic imitation because "in them is little pleasure to be taken" (Smith 2: 65; 2: 150).

Sidney's complaint against "rustic language" to the contrary, he does adopt archaic language akin to that of the *May* eclogue in his own Ister Bank eclogue. Sung in the *Old Arcadia* by Philisides, a persona for Sidney as a shepherd-poet, this beast fable employs the gathering of a parliament of animals to satirize the increasingly authoritarian reign of Elizabeth I. It may date from 1579–80, at which time Protestant militants like Sidney agitated against the proposed marriage between the queen and François, duc d'Alençon, the brother of the king of France. The prospect of this union evoked Protestant fears of a Roman Catholic succession should the queen give birth to a child. Insofar as religion and politics were inseparable in early modern England, the yearning of the parliament of beasts for replacement of republican government with monarchy suggests covert criticism of Elizabeth's perceived endangerment of English Protestantism. Indeed Jove, a figure for divine wisdom in the Ister Bank eclogue, criticizes the proposed institution of monarchy:

> O beasts, take heed of what you of me desire.
> Rulers will think all things made them to please
> And soon forget the swink [i.e., work] due to their hire.[3]

Sidney modeled this fable on the antiregal strand in the Old Testament, in which the prophet, Samuel, views the Israelite appeal for him to "make us now a king to judge us" so that "we also will be like all other nations" as a rejection of divine authority (1 Sam. 8:5, 8:20).[4]

The *May* eclogue involves a versified debate between two shepherds, who respectively personify different conceptions of clerical vocation. The use of shepherds to personify alternative approaches to ministerial life hinges upon the longstanding use of *pastor,* which means "shepherd" in Latin, to denote a member of the clergy. Piers articulates a reformist vision of clerical life whereby shepherd-pastors must dedicate themselves strictly to the needs of their "flocks" (i.e., church congregations). He is uncomfortable with the retention of formalistic ceremonies, in contrast to the more worldly Palinode ("counter-song"), who embraces religious formalism and believes that members of the clergy may enjoy themselves in the manner of laypeople. The woodcut printed with the eclogue portrays a traditional May celebration of the kind that Palinode endorses when he asks:

> Is not thilke the mery moneth of May,
> When love lads masken in fresh aray?
> How falles it then, we no merrier bene,
> Ylike as others, girt in gawdy greene? (ll. 1–4)[5]

Palinode condones the merriment and frivolity with which youths traditionally greeted the arrival of springtime. These springtime celebrations involved the gathering of greenery, dressing in green costume, dancing around maypoles, sexual promiscuity, and the crowning of peasants who ruled as the king and queen of May. Piers's curt response cuts down his interlocutor for not acting his age and for sanctioning transgressive behavior that Piers associates with the colorful ritualistic ceremonies and cult practices of the Roman Catholicism:

> For Younkers *Palinode* such follies fitte,
> But we tway bene men of elder witt. (ll. 17–18)

They continue to speak at cross-purposes until Piers interrupts their conversation with an allegorical beast fable that serves as a warning against clerical laxity.

The poem as a whole is framed by an introductory argument and a concluding emblem (i.e., a moralistic epigram), which precedes a "gloss" that comments on particular words and passages in the poem. This annotation and others, in addition to "The generall argument [i.e., introduction] of the whole booke," were presumably written by a mysterious figure known as E. K., whose initials appear as a signature for the poem's dedicatory epistle. He addresses it to Gabriel Harvey, a friend of Spenser who was a scholar at Cambridge University (Spenser 13–25). Although the identity of E. K. is unknown, it seems likely that the initials conceal the sentiments of Spenser himself or someone close to him. This elaborate apparatus, which lacked precedent in collections of verse published in the English vernacular, presents Spenser as a budding pastoral poet who is the peer to great classical and continental predecessors such as Virgil, Petrarch, Mantuan, and Pierre de Ronsard.

The introductory "Argument" of *May* invites the reader to interpret this eclogue in terms of the general conflict between "two formes of pastoures or Ministers, or the protestant and the Catholique." That is, it identifies the chief speaker, Piers, and his antagonist, Palinode, respectively as personifications of Protestantism and Catholicism. This interpretation is in keeping with the incessant religious controversy that followed England's schism from the Church of Rome during the reign of Henry VIII. Piers's speeches are filled with scriptural metaphors concerning sheep and their vulnerability to wolves (see Jer. 5:6; Matt. 10:16; Luke 10:3), as in this instance.

> Tho under colour of shepeheards, somewhile
> There crept in Wolves, ful of fraude and guile,
> That often devoured their owne sheepe,
> And often the shepheards, that did hem keepe. (ll. 126–29)

Models for Piers's reformist vision of the clerical vocation include the Parable of the Good Shepherd (John 10:1–16), which affords a precedent for the belief that clergy should follow Gospel prototypes for spiritual husbandry. Sheep and lambs provide enduring symbols both for Christ as a sheep led "to the slaughter" (Acts 8:32) and for individual Christians. Paradoxically, Christ as the Lamb of God functions as the *shepherd* of those who are saved (Rev. 7:17). Related scriptural tropes concern dangers posed to flocks by rapacious wolves, who function as figures for "false" pastors in accordance with wording from the Sermon on the Mount: "Beware of false prophets, which come to you in sheep's clothing, but inwardly they are ravening wolves" (Matt. 7:15). Piers's diatribe against hireling shepherds and those who abandon their flock by putting them out for hire (i.e., nonresident holders of clerical appointments) is set against the background of Christ's Parable of the Lost Sheep and the history of the unworthy servant in Christ's Parable of the Talents (Matt. 18:12–14, 25:14–30):

> I muse, what account both these will make,
> The one for the hire, which he doth take,
> And thother for leaving his Lords taske,
> When great *Pan* account of shepeherdes shall aske. (ll. 51–54)

In worrying about the fate of a solitary sheep that has lost its way, the Good Shepherd affords a figure for Christ as a spiritual savior. The contrasting failure of the servant to invest a sum of money entrusted to him functions as a figure for one who is damned. The gloss on Pan as "Christ, the very God of all shepheards, which calleth himselfe the greate and good shepherd" (gloss on l. 54) acknowledges Spenser's intermingling of biblical and classical pastoral. Piers does not actually argue in favor of clerical celibacy, as some critics believe, but he does oppose the acquisition of wealth by clerics for the sake of their offspring:

> The sonne of his loines why should he regard
> To leave enriched with that he hath spard? (ll. 83–84)

Ministers may father children, but they ought not attempt to bequeath inheritances to them.

Although long-standing tradition identifies the conflict between Piers and Palinode as an allegory for Puritan hostility to semi-papists,[6] opposition to "popery" was not distinctively Puritan. (*Puritan* is a highly flexible term that originally denoted an orthodox Protestant commitment to the total eradication of religious practices not based on the Bible.) This position was widespread in the Elizabethan church. Prior to the accession of Charles I in 1625 and the ascendancy of William Laud as archbishop of Canterbury and primate of the Church of England (1633–41), which brought to an end a broad Protestant consensus that prevailed in the Church of England during the reigns of both Elizabeth I and James I, early readers tended to emphasize the presence of antipapal satire, rather than Puritan sentiment, in Spenser's verse. Puritans could have found confirmation for their zeal in the *May* eclogue's satire against Wolves and Foxes, but E. K.'s more literal interpretation justifiably interprets these shepherds as Protestant and Catholic sympathizers. He explicitly guides the reader to interpret this eclogue as commentary on Reformation conflicts. The immediate religiopolitical context of *The Shepheardes Calender* supports this view because the organization of the English Mission (a Jesuit effort to minister to recusants and reclaim converts to Protestantism) during the year of publication made Catholic priests and laity conventional subjects for Protestant satire. Not only are Spenser's other writings devoid of outright Puritan propaganda, but the prominence of the Fox in *Mother Hubberds Tale* (1591), whose date of composition might have been close to that of the *Calender,* also suggests that Spenser harbored little sympathy for religious nonconformity. The variety of disguises that the hypocritical beast assumes makes it difficult to reduce it to a stock Puritan type for a crypto-papist cleric. On the contrary, the Priest's recommendation that the Fox "fashion eke a godly zeale" in order to curry favor with a noble patron of "a zealous disposition" sounds very much like a stab against hypocritical sectarians.[7]

Piers engages in a railing attack that links clerical transgression with indulgence in traditional May celebrations. In attacking Palinode, who believes in these practices, Piers articulates fundamental questions concerning the laxity of clerics who "playen, while their flockes be unfedde":

> Perdie so farre am I from envie,
> That their fondnesse inly I pitie.
> Those faytours little regarden their charge,
> While they letting their sheepe runne at large. (ll. 37–40, 44)

This alliterative barrage of bilabial consonants—*f* and *p*—explodes with scorn for the negligence of "false" ministers who deprive parishioners of spiritual nurturance. (Alliteration was a favorite device of nativist poets.) Favoring the proliferation of holidays and veneration of the saints in the sacred calendar of the Roman church (*May* ll. 15, 310), Palinode lodges a counterattack against his opponent as an irrational zealot:

> Thou raylest on right withouten reason,
> And blamest hem much, for small encheason. (ll. 146–47)

The negative position taken by Piers on Maying customs reflects the emergence of the Sabbatarian movement to observe Sunday strictly as a day of worship, Bible reading, and rest. Rigorous Sabbatarians emphasized the keeping of the Fourth Commandment ("Remember the Sabbath day, to keep it holy") (Exod. 20:8), rather than the outright prohibition of Maying, playgoing, and other pastimes. Their goal was to prevent profanation of Sunday. Of course, medieval authorities also attempted to enforce sober conduct on Sundays. Piers's views may resemble the Puritan attack against May games, but he is a proponent of clerical reform rather than a Sabbatarian as such. He cites Algrind as his authority for imposing a higher moral standard on clergy than laity: "But shepheards (as Algrind used to say,) / Mought not live ylike, as men of the laye" (*May* ll. 75–76). This name provides a thinly veiled anagram for Edmund Grindal, the reformist archbishop of Canterbury (1576–83) who had offended Elizabeth I with his desire to promote Bible study among zealous ministers. She suspended him from his duties as leader of the Church of England when he challenged her power as the final authority in religious affairs.[8]

At the center of Piers's attack against allegedly false religious practices is the fable that he tells concerning the Fox and the Kid. Despite the mother Goat's warning that her son avoid the treacherous Fox, who is a "maister of collusion" (l. 219), the foolish Kid admits the predator into their home when he wanders by in disguise as a decrepit tradesman:

> Not as a Foxe, for then he had be kend,
> But all as a poore pedler he did wend,
> Bearing a trusse of tryfles at hys backe,
> As bells, and babes, and glasses in hys packe. (ll. 237–40)

The gullible youth is taken in by this merchandise (bells, religious images, and paxes), but E. K. attacks it as "reliques and ragges of popish superstition, which put no smal religion in Belles: and Babies .s. Idoles: and glasses .s. Paxes, and such lyke trumperies" (gloss on l. 240). This kind of antiritualistic jargon was a standard feature of contemporary

Protestant propaganda. After the Kid unwaringly gazes at his image in a mirror (a symbol of worldly vanity), the Fox succeeds at kidnapping the youth by luring him with a bauble that he leaves at the bottom of his pack:

> Tho shewed his ware, and opened his packe,
> All save a bell, which he left behind
> In the basket for the Kidde to fynd.
> Which when the Kidde stooped downe to catch,
> He popt him in, and his basket did latch,
> Ne stayed he once, the dore to make fast,
> But ranne awaye with him in all hast. (ll. 287–93)

No sooner does the unsuspecting youth reach into the pack to take hold of the bait, a bell, than the Fox shuts him in and runs away. The gloss claims that this capture provides an allegory for how Roman Catholics trick naive individuals into espousing "false" religion: "By the Kidde may be understoode the simple sorte of the faythfull and true Christians. By hys dame Christe, that hath alreadie with carefull watchewords (as heere doth the gote) warned his little ones, to beware of such doubling deceit. By the Foxe, the false and faithlesse Papistes, to whom is no credit to be given, not felowshippe to be used" (gloss on ll. 174–305). In the opinion of E. K., the moral of this fable "is to warne the protestaunt beware, howe he geveth credit to the unfaythfull Catholique" (gloss on l. 304). Spenser thus applies a frequently used set of figures familiar from biblical pastoral—shepherds, sheep, wolves, and foxes—to controversial issues concerning faith, spiritual regeneration, and salvation.

Spenser's acquaintance with religious satire would have dated back to the time when he enrolled as a poor student at Merchant Taylors School in London. He joined the other boys (if girls received education, they were tutored at home) in studying the humanistic curriculum, which entailed the study of Latin and Greek texts, in addition to some Hebrew. Their studies included Latin verse on religious topics, including Mantuan's vigorous attacks on ecclesiastical abuses. Pedagogical treatises written by the headmaster of this grammar school, Richard Mulcaster, also took the novel step of advocating the study of reading and writing in the vernacular. It was during the course of instruction in his mother tongue that Spenser joined the other boys in composing English vernacular poetry. It may be that the young poet began to compose religious satire under the influence of Mulcaster, who was not only the foremost educational theorist of the Elizabethan era, but also a zealous Protestant ideologue. Indeed, this pedagogical reformer incorporated religious polemics into a narrative account of pageantry in celebration of the precoronation entry by Elizabeth I into the city of London. The following verses from that account, which were published in 1559, celebrate the imposition of a Protestant settlement in religion at the outset of the reign of Elizabeth I as the virgin queen of England:

> While that Religion true shall Ignorance suppress
> And with her weighty foot break Superstition's head,
> While Love of Subjects shall Rebellion distress
> And with Zeal to the Prince Insolency down tread.[9]

Elizabeth's accession marked a radical change in policy from that followed during the reign of her late sister, Mary I, under whom hundreds of Protestants were persecuted and burnt alive as heretics. Nevertheless, the new queen disappointed militant Protestants by favoring an ambiguous combination of Protestant theology with Roman Catholic ceremonialism. In juxtaposing Protestantism and Catholicism as "true" versus "false" religions, this propagandistic allegory affords a prototype for Spenser's allegorization of religious controversy in the *May* eclogue in addition to Book 1 of *The Faerie Queene* (1590).

Combination of stylistic plainness with highly charged biblical imagery was common in mid-Tudor religious verse that argues that sincere worship should be based upon the scriptures and that ministerial integrity should avoid pride, avarice, and ignorance. English poems of the 1560s and 1570s accordingly apply poetic language from the Bible in a manner reminiscent to the *May* eclogue. For example, Barnaby Googe's *Eclogues, Epitaphs, and Sonnets* (1563) affords a precedent for Spenser's combination of plain vernacular style with Protestant religious allegory. In Googe's third eclogue, in particular, Coridon laments the persecution of good shepherds (i.e., preachers) by a herdsman who leads "silly sheep" into error:

> O cruel clownish [i.e., rustic] Coridon,
> O cursed carlish [i.e., churlish] head,
> Thy simple sheep, constrained he,
> Their pasture sweet to leave. (sig. B1ʳ)

This account of the martyrdoms of "good shepherds" and deception of their "flock" (i.e., Protestant believers) alludes to Mary Tudor's effort to dismantle Protestantism in England. Although George Turberville fails to add an overtly Protestant edge to his translation of Mantuan's *Eclogues* (1567), pastoral decorum does lead him to imitate rustic dialect in the manner of the *May* eclogue: "So have I shaped my style and tempered it with such common and ordinary phrase of speech as countrymen do use in their affairs" (sig. A3ᵛ).

E. K.'s invocation of *The Canterbury Tales* by Geoffrey Chaucer and of *Piers Plowman,* a late medieval religious allegory often attributed to William Langland, indicates that Spenser's departure from English literary tradition is not as great as it may at first appear to be. Indeed, Piers Plowman is the namesake of Piers, the chief speaker in *May.* Even though these pre-Reformation writings were theologically orthodox, Tudor editors and readers interpreted them as proto-Protestant appeals for the correction of ecclesiastical abuses and social ills. Other additions to this ever-expanding canon of radical poetry included genuinely heretical compositions by followers of John Wyclif known as Lollards, who opposed "papistry" and the Roman-rite Mass. They included pseudo-Chaucerian satires such as *Jack Upland,* which John Foxe assimilated into the *Book of Martyrs* (first published in 1563) as an "ancient treatise compiled by Geoffrey Chaucer by the way of a dialogue or questions moved in the person of a certain uplandish and simple plowman of the country."[10] The addition of lexical notes and glossaries to these texts suggests that contemporary readers would have recognized both the archaism of *The Shepheardes Calender* and E. K.'s explanatory notes on word meanings as constituent elements of Protestant satire.[11] The printing of *The Plowman's Tale* exemplifies how early modern Protestants embraced this apocryphal tradition in a debate between a Protestant Pelican and Roman Catholic Griffin that supplies a vehicle for Reformation controversy. During the aftermath of the Gunpowder Plot, a Roman Catholic conspiracy to blow up James I and Parliament on November 5, 1605, the title page of the 1606 edition of this work claimed that this poem reveals "by the doctrine and lives of the Romish clergy, that the Pope is Antichrist and they his ministers." Indeed, a marginal note concerning avaricious clergy links these texts by noting: "Of such shepherds speaks Master Spenser in his *Calender*" (sig. A3ᵛ). Texts in the Epistles of John (1 John 2:18–29, 4:1–6; 2 John 1:7–11) identify Antichrist as the demonic archenemy of Christ.

The humble plowman who exemplifies Christian social ideals—poverty, hard work, piety, and humility—affords a prototype for the flat plain style, archaic diction, and alliteration that we encounter in Piers's attack against prideful clergy in the *May* eclogue:

> Some gan to gape for greedie governaunce,
> And match them selfe with mighty potentates,
> Lovers of Lordship and troublers of states. (ll. 121–23)

He criticizes the aggrandizement of haughty clerics who disturb society by acting as if they were powerful princes. The commentary observes that this passage opposes "the Pope, and his Antichristian prelates, which usurpe a tyrannical dominion in the Churche, and with Peters counterfet keys, open a wide gate to al wickednesse and insolent government" (gloss on ll. 121–31). (The keys of St. Peter, whom Roman Catholics revered as the first pope, are a well-known papal symbol.) This attack on clerical corruption contradicts Palinode's approval of shepherds who neglect hard work in favor of the pleasures of singing, dancing, and maying:

> Ah *Piers*, bene not thy teeth on edge, to thinke,
> How great sport they gaynen with little swinck? (ll. 35–36)

Palinode seems to suggest that his opponent is driven by envy.

In constructing the character of Piers, Spenser aligns himself with the sixteenth-century Protestant authors who continued the Lollard tradition of articulating appeals for reform in the voice of a blunt, truth-telling character named Piers Plowman. The force of this plowman conceit during this age of religious renewal and reform is manifest in the popular evangelical sermons of Hugh Latimer, a Protestant reformer who advocated a preaching ministry and adopted alliteration and archaic vernacular diction associated with the *Piers Plowman* tradition. Although he originally preached his *Sermon on the Plowers* during the reign of Edward VI (1547–53), this popular sermon remained in print during Spenser's lifetime. It applies a text from Christ's Parable of the Sower, "He that soweth, the husbandman, the plowman, went forth to sow his seed" (Luke 8:5), as an allegorical figure for the fulfillment of clerical vocation.[12] Within Latimer's analysis of the Protestant ministry, seed functions as a figure for biblical teaching, the plowman represents the "true" preacher, and sown fields represent the congregation of believers. Latimer sees clergy and laity as common laborers in the Reformation plowland.

On the model of works such as *Piers Plowman* and *The Plowman's Tale,* Protestant satirists constructed their own appeals for ecclesiastical and social reform. A distinct subgenre of Reformation satire emerged in a prolific series of conventional debates between a bluntly honest Protestant peasant and a Catholic cleric whose ignorant attempts at sophisticated eloquence cannot mask his spiritual ignorance. Typical of this convention is the humble laborer's stubborn skepticism about transubstantiation in

Luke Shepherd's *John Bon and Mast[er] Person* (1547) because it can be neither tasted nor seen:

> Yea but, Mast Parson, think ye it were right
> That if I desired you to make my black ox white
> And you say it is dun, and still is black in sight,
> Ye might me deem a fool for to believe so light. (King, *Voices* no. 4.1, ll. 128–31)

Drawing upon his folk wisdom, this dissenting layperson mocks the idea that the sacramental elements of bread and wine undergo transformation into the body and blood of Christ as a violation of common sense.

The presence in the *May* eclogue of the pose of the plain-spoken truth-teller looks backward to mid-Tudor religious verse of this kind. The "honest" peasant would soon disappear from popular religious propaganda, to be replaced by a view of the unlettered countryman as an obstinate opponent of true religion whom the preacher must try to convert. Although George Gascoigne's *The Steele Glass* (1576) resembles *May* by paying homage to "good *Pierce*, thou plowman by thy name,"[13] Thomas Nashe transforms the Protestant plowman into a malcontent rogue who rails against vices of which he is himself guilty in *Pierce Penniless His Supplication to the Devil* (1592). Most authors following Spenser would in the future see the religion of the common people as "ungodly" and anticlerical (i.e., anti-Puritan), in contrast to views of "godly" laity who side with the clergy. This generic shift comes at a time when aspiring satirists like John Marston, John Donne, and Ben Jonson were abandoning the conventions of native satire to embrace neoclassical standards of formal verse satire modeled on the works of Juvenal, Horace, and Persius.

Spenser's conversion of the biblical Wolf into the Fox of *May* alludes to the satirical tradition that Wolves who could prey openly during a Roman Catholic regime conceal themselves as Foxes under Protestant monarchs. E. K.'s interpretation of the Fox as a crypto-Catholic belongs to a tradition initiated by polemical hunting dialogues in which William Turner and John Bale applied the imagery of Romish Foxes and Wolves to the broad outlines of Reformation controversy during the reigns of Henry VIII, Edward VI, and Mary I. These authors originally designed their series of polemical beast fables to attack Stephen Gardiner, bishop of Winchester, as a Henrician Fox who thwarted religious reform through cunning concealment of his "papist" sympathies. Turner then claimed that the bishop revealed himself openly as a Roman Wolf under the aegis of Mary Tudor. Although a prefatory attack against "popish" vestments added to the revised second edition of Turner's *Hunting of the Romish Foxe* (c. 1565) stresses its relevance to the contemporary controversy concerning the wearing of clerical vestments, it should be noted that its composition predated the emergence of the Puritan movement under Elizabeth I. From the 1560s onward, Puritans expressed outrage at the retention of elaborate priestly robes as a vestige of Roman Catholicism.

A contemporary satirical broadside attests to the depth of Protestant hatred for Gardiner when it vilifies this prelate as a predator and slaughterer of Christ, who is portrayed as a sacrificial Lamb who protests: "Why do you crucify me again For with one oblation have I for ever made perfect those that are sanctified." In the guise of the "Winchester Wolfe," Gardiner replies:

Whilome in youth a fox that have been
In age am a Wolf more valiant in sin
A fox when I was, the lamb and the hen
Did them me content, but nowe I feed on men. (King, *Spenser's Poetry* 37–39)

He boasts about transforming himself from a cunningly concealed fox into a more insidiously disguised wolf in sheep's clothing. John Bale interpolates a slur of this kind into *Three Laws,* the Protestant moral interlude that he wrote in 1538 under the patronage of Thomas Cromwell. The Catholic Vice known as Infidelity provides a cue to Ambition, who is costumed "like a bishop," to demonstrate to the audience the resemblance between his miter and the "mouth of a wolf":

If thou stoop downward, lo, se how the wolf doth gape.
Ready to devour the lambs, lest any escape.[14]

In its application of the beast fable as a genre appropriate for satire, the *May* eclogue emulates versifications of the story of Reynard the Fox. Medieval poets exploited the craftiness and deceitfulness of this sly trickster, whose cunning behavior ignores conventional standards of behavior, as a means of submitting social behavior to a searching critique. Spenser's poem also joins Sidney's Ister Bank eclogue in its concurrence with Sidney's moralistic interpretation of Aesop's fables in *An Apology for Poetry:* "whose pretty allegories, stealing under the formal tales of beasts, make many, more beastly than beasts, begin to hear the sound of virtue from these dumb speakers" (Smith 1: 167). Sidney may well allude to Spenser's inclusion of beast fables within eclogues when he lists animal tales among the variations of pastoral: "Is the poor pipe disdained, which [. . .] sometimes, under the pretty tales of wolves and sheep, can include the whole considerations of wrong doing and patience" (Smith 1: 175). Referring to the playing of music on the shepherd's pipe as a metaphor for the composition of pastoral poetry, he argues that pastoral verse is not confined to light poetry concerning the loves of shepherds and shepherdesses. It also embraces the rough harshness of satire. The fable that Piers tells concerning the Fox and the Kid is akin to contemporary Protestant tracts, such as William Turner's dialogue, which identify stealthy predators as allegorical types for crypto-Catholic clergy within the Church of England, who prey upon their innocent "flock." This fiction builds upon tropes of scriptural pastoral, in addition to Jesus' application of the unruly behavior of young goats as a figure of damnation when he speaks of the Last Judgment as a time when the Son of Man will judge souls "as a shepherd separates the sheep from the goats, and shall set the sheep on his right hand, and the goats on the left" (Matt. 25:32–33). E. K.'s commentary leaves it open to question whether the Kid in *May* will undergo damnation.

Because Spenser structures the *May* eclogue as a genuine debate rather than a one-sided pamphlet, reduction of its artistry to mere argumentation loses sight of the dramatic interplay and dialectical tension within the various months of the *Calender.* E. K.'s biases may weight our interpretation of *May* in favor of Piers's strident attack, but the poet himself takes no explicit stand. The poem attacks "papist" vestiges, but it also calls into question forms of extreme piety and devotion that alienate this shepherd-pastor from more moderate and humane forms of conduct and belief. Palinode's call for tolerance is not altogether lacking in sympathy. Furthermore, Piers's attack on Maying customs is associated with attacks on drama and fiction because they "lie" or exert a morally corrupting influence (see *King, Voices* no. 5.3). Palinode's tolerance for dancing and entertainment does mirror Spenser's evident approval of fictionality and artistry, however, as it is embodied in the complex interplay of narrative and dramatic structures in the *Calender.* The work as a whole contains pastoral dialogues that are genuine discussions in which speakers disagree and valid arguments may be brought forward on both sides. We need to take seriously E. K.'s interpretation of the debate in *May* in Piers's favor, but this shepherd is neither flawless nor a simple mouthpiece for Spenser's religious opinions. The issues that Piers raises are, nevertheless, staple Protestant concerns.

Spenser's *May* harnesses the powerful energy of mid-Tudor religious verse. During an era marked by pendulum shifts in religious policy, mid-sixteenth-century English poets resorted to verse as a means of articulating uncompromising convictions concerning burning ecclesiastical issues. Protestants in particular utilized poetry in their attempts to convert English people from older religious practices with which they had grown up. Pastoral verse provided a powerful tool for combining controversial argument with ludicrous entertainment. The *May* eclogue constitutes a tribute to Spenser's masterful virtuosity in drawing upon the plain-spoken eloquence of native traditions deeply rooted in the late Middle Ages at the same time that he assimilates Italianate and neoclassical modes that his contemporaries had begun to import from continental Europe.

## NOTES

1. Ivor Winters, "The 16th Century Lyric in England: A Critical and Historical Reinterpretation," *Poetry* 53 (1939): 258–72, 320–35; 54 (1939): 35–51.
2. G. Gregory Smith, ed., *Elizabethan Critical Essays,* 2 vols. (London: Oxford UP, 1904) 1: 196.
3. David Norbrook and H. R. Woudhuysen, eds., *The Penguin Book of Renaissance Verse, 1509–1659* (London: Penguin, 1992) no. 14, ll. 30–32.
4. Scriptural texts are cited from a facsimile of the 1560 *The Geneva Bible,* introd. Lloyd E. Berry (Madison: U of Wisconsin P, 1969).
5. Edmund Spenser, *The Yale Edition of the Shorter Poems of Edmund Spenser,* ed. William A. Oram et al. (New Haven: Yale UP, 1989) 85–108. For references to books that lack pagination, I refer to signatures (abbreviated as sig.) that follow the order of the alphabet.
6. See Frederick M. Padelford, "Spenser and Puritan Propaganda," *Modern Philology* 11 (1913): 85–106.
7. Edwin Greenlaw et al., eds., *The Works of Edmund Spenser: A Variorum Edition* (Baltimore: Johns Hopkins P, 1932–57) 8: 119, ll. 491–93.
8. David Norbrook, *Poetry and Politics in the English Renaissance,* Rev. ed (Oxford: Oxford UP, 2002) 61–62.
9. John N. King, ed., *Voices of the English Reformation: A Sourcebook* (Philadelphia: U of Pennsylvania P, 2004) 336.
10. This quotation is from the second edition (1570) 341. See 965–66 for additional information concerning Chaucer's status as a proto-Protestant. John Day published this work under the formal title of *Acts and Monuments of These Latter and Perilous Days.*
11. John N. King, *Spenser's Poetry and the Reformation Tradition* (Princeton: Princeton UP, 1990) 15–30.

12. King, *Voices* no. 2.3. The scriptural text quoted by Latimer comes from neither the Tyndale nor the Geneva translation.
13. Richard S. Sylvester, ed., *The Anchor Anthology of Sixteenth-Century Verse* (New York: Anchor, 1974) 311, l. 1017.
14. Peter Happé, ed., *The Complete Plays of John Bale,* 2 vols. (Cambridge: D. S. Brewer, 1985–86) 2: 99, 3.1184–86; 2: 121, stage direction.

## READING LIST

Gilman, Ernest. *Iconoclasm and Poetry in the English Reformation: "Down Went Dagon."* Chicago: U of Chicago P, 1986.
Hadfield, Andrew. *Literature, Politics, and National Identity: Reformation to Renaissance.* Cambridge: Cambridge UP, 1994.
Johnson, Lynn Staley. *The Shepheardes Calender: An Introduction.* University Park: Pennsylvania State UP, 1990.
King, John N. *Spenser's Poetry and the Reformation Tradition.* Princeton: Princeton UP, 1990.
———. "Spenser's Religion." *The Cambridge Companion to Spenser.* Ed. Andrew Hadfield. Cambridge: Cambridge UP, 2001. 200–16.
———, ed. *Voices of the English Reformation: A Sourcebook.* Philadelphia: U of Pennsylvania P, 2004.
Norbrook, David. *Poetry and Politics in the English Renaissance.* Rev. ed. Oxford: Oxford UP, 2002.
Norbrook, David, and H. R. Woudhuysen, eds. *The Penguin Book of Renaissance Verse, 1509–1659.* London: Penguin, 1992.
Spenser, Edmund. *The Yale Edition of the Shorter Poems of Edmund Spenser.* Ed. William A. Oram et al. New Haven: Yale UP, 1989.

# 6

# Early Courtier Verse: Oxford, Dyer, and Gascoigne

## Steven May

What role did poetry play in the scramble for recognition and royal patronage at the Elizabethan Court? Was the ability to write love sonnets or any other kind of verse a mandatory attainment of the successful courtier, as our received notions of the all-accomplished Renaissance man would suggest? Could a professional, out-of-Court writer gain a place at Court by virtue of poetry alone? The careers of two courtiers, the seventeenth earl of Oxford and Sir Edward Dyer, contrasted with that of the professional writer George Gascoigne, answer these questions in ways that qualify and revise the romantic myth of Tudor courtiership.

The structure of Elizabethan society evolved directly from the feudal pattern that had defined European culture for more than a thousand years. Except for the queen herself, everyone in the social hierarchy owed allegiance to someone of higher status; and, except for the lowest of the working poor, everyone received tribute of one kind or another from at least one social subordinate. The basic unit of social organization was the individual household, the center of nearly everyone's livelihood and social life.[1] Queen Elizabeth's Court was the center of the largest household in the realm. It employed more than one thousand ordinary servants, yet the numbers who daily crowded its halls and chambers were more numerous than that, for the queen's attendant courtiers were not necessarily on the Court payroll, while both courtiers and most of the household servants employed servants of their own.[2]

The Court was necessarily the center of national patronage because Elizabeth could dispense offices and bounty far beyond the confines of her own household. She controlled major appointments throughout the realm, from wardenships of royal palaces and forests, to offices of tax collection at the various ports, monopolies, including licenses to print certain types of books, to appointments of her ambassadors abroad. Her control of the exchequer and royal estates also allowed her to grant a variety of other lucrative rewards including pensions, annuities, leases, and gifts of cash outright. In order to benefit from this largesse it was necessary to gain the personal, favorable attention of the sovereign or, barring that, the favor of a courtier who could prefer a suit by virtue of his or her personal access to Elizabeth. The royal household was under continuous assault by seekers of patronage who thronged to the Court in hopes of attracting the attention of Elizabeth and her chief courtiers. For anyone of genteel social status (superficially identifiable by one's dress, speech, and bearing) it was easy enough to penetrate the fringes of the household as far as the presence chamber. But the social center of the Court was located a gallery or two further on in a suite of rooms termed, cumulatively, the Privy Chamber. And access to the Privy Chamber was strictly regulated.[3]

Here, Elizabeth and her courtiers socialized or conducted business in isolation from the household at large. The Privy Chamber *was* the Court if by Court we mean the physical location of the nation's patronage and power.

Queen Elizabeth was herself a poet, and during her reign a small but ever-increasing minority of her courtiers turned to composing English verses. Their example no doubt inspired would-be courtiers to display their intellectual attainments, including poetry, in their efforts to ingratiate themselves with the queen. But did any aspiring courtier gain regular access to the Privy Chamber by virtue of his or her writings? The role of poetry at the Elizabethan court of the 1570s is well represented in the works of Edward De Vere, seventeenth earl of Oxford (1550–1604), and Sir Edward Dyer (1543–1606). Both were courtiers who enjoyed, intermittently at least, Elizabeth's favor and patronage as early as the 1560s. Both wrote lyrics expressing their devotion to her, and both profited in different ways from the royal bounty. George Gascoigne's verse, on the other hand, exemplifies the varied ways in which an out-of-Court poet attempted to cultivate poetry in a bid for royal patronage that was ultimately unsuccessful.

Gascoigne (c. 1535–77) was undeniably the most talented and ambitious creative writer of the three, indeed, the foremost English poet from the death of Henry Howard, earl of Surrey, in 1547 to the emergence of Sir Philip Sidney as an author shortly after Gascoigne's death. Gascoigne dedicated a number of his works to Elizabeth and spent most of his active writing career during the 1560s until his death clamoring for her patronage or for that of various noblemen in her entourage. Yet his success was limited to a modest degree of temporary support from some of the queen's retainers. Nothing that he accomplished by either pen or sword (for Gascogine followed a military career as well) earned him a bare living, much less the income required for a gaudy life of display as a courtier. Why did Gascoigne's talent fail to attract significant patronage while both Oxford and Dyer were widely acclaimed poets as well as successful courtiers?

For Edward De Vere a place at Court was virtually a birthright. He was heir to the second oldest continuously inherited earldom in England and, as a royal ward, received an excellent education in the household of Sir William Cecil, the queen's principal secretary and lord treasurer. Oxford began participating in the life of the Court while still in his teens. He wrote his earliest datable poem to commend a book published in 1572 by his fellow courtier, Thomas Bedingfield, one of the queen's gentleman pensioners. Bedingfield's translation of Girolamo Cardano's *Comfort* included as well a commendatory letter from the earl stressing the value of Cardano's work and his own role in bringing it to the press. The title page proclaims that it was "Published by commaundement of the righte Honourable the Earle of Oxenforde." De Vere had reached his majority only the year before but was already a highly favored courtier. His bold publication of both prose and verse calls into question the long-standing belief that Elizabethans recognized a "stigma of print."[4] According to this hypothesis, it was beneath the dignity of a gentleman, much less a nobleman, to publish his own work as if he were a common pamphleteer. Yet Oxford was by no means the first English nobleman to see his own creative writing into print,[5] and it seems doubtful that he would have jeopardized his career as a royal favorite by violating any widely recognized standard of behavior. Moreover, another eight lyrics were published under his name or initials in the first edition of the *Paradise of Dainty Devices* (1576). Six of these works appeared as Oxford's in eight subsequent Elizabethan editions of the *Paradise,* nor were his initials removed from the

list of authors whose works appeared in these reprints.[6] Had any of this publicity compromised the earl's reputation, Elizabeth certainly had the power to revoke it if Oxford
himself did not.

For Edward Dyer, eldest son of a genteel Somersetshire family, courtier status was
perhaps less likely than it was for Gascoigne, and we do not know exactly how Dyer
gained the queen's favor. By 1565 he was a follower of Robert Dudley, earl of Leicester.
In 1568 he was described as a sworn servant of the queen and the beneficiary of a roy-
ally sanctioned export patent. In 1570 Elizabeth appointed him steward of the manor
and ranger of the woods of Woodstock Palace. Other offices and rewards would follow,
but despite all the royal favor he received, Dyer sank ever deeper in debt to the end of
his life. His close friendship with Sir Philip Sidney enabled him to participate in the innovative upgrading of English verse pioneered by Sidney and copied by poets in and out
of Court circles during the late 1580s and thereafter. Dyer's earliest poems, however,
show little evidence of Sidney's influence and were probably composed before 1578.[7]

George Gascoigne's birth and social status seemingly offered him more opportunity than Dyer to become a successful courtier. Gascoigne's father, Sir John, was a justice of the peace in Bedfordshire and had served as a member of Parliament. George
gained a fleeting entree to Elizabeth's Court in January 1559 when he served as almoner
at her coronation. The Gascoigne family owned land that allowed them to claim this
honorary post, and George performed the office in place of his father. On November 23,
1561, he married the widowed Elizabeth Breton, who had, however, previously remar-
ried a gentleman named Edward Boyes. Gascoigne was charged with bigamy, and violent street brawls between his servants and Boyes's men erupted in the streets of
London. In several poems, including his "Woodmanship" (*Flowres* 72),[8] Gascoigne
explains that he attempted the life of a courtier at about this time yet never found means
for advancement or patronage. Although he was left with an adequate if modest income
at his father's death in 1568, a series of lawsuits left George increasingly destitute.

By the early 1570s, Oxford and Dyer were among the first of Elizabeth's courtiers to
introduce the writing of vernacular verse at her Court. Their example seemed to demonstrate that writing poetry could be as much an attribute of successful courtiership as good
looks, personal charm, and witty conversation. Their verse circulated widely in contemporary manuscripts for decades to come but, aside from Oxford's commendatory poem for
Bedingfield's book, neither poet made any effort to publish his verse. Both, however,
turned out lyrics that might have been interpreted at court as declarations of love for their
sovereign. Dyer's Poem 3, for example, pledges eternal love to an aloof mistress:

It was a World of Joyes for me, to live within thy sighte,
  Thy Sacred presence unto me did give so greate delighte.
It was a Heaven to me to view thy face Devine,
  Wherin besides Dame Venus' stayne great Majesty did shine. (ll. 15–18)

These lines necessarily evoke the "sacred majesty" of the queen. Similarly, Oxford
describes the charms and virtues of Juno, Pallas, and Venus, then attributes all these
qualities to "her alone, who yet on yearth doeth reigne/ Whose beauties' stryng no Gods
can well destraine" (Poem 6, ll. 11–12). Again, the poetic vocabulary points to Elizabeth
as the superlative woman in this poem, while its traditional, despairing lover's lament
fits perfectly with her unobtainable status as the poet's sovereign.

Gascoigne was probably writing poetry by the 1560s but, unlike Oxford and Dyer, his verse saw very little circulation in manuscript, and there is no evidence that it circulated in courtly anthologies.[9] Instead, he published a substantial collection of his work in 1573, the *Hundreth Sundrie Flowres.* This book is, however, disguised as an anthology of works by various poets. True, parts of *Jocasta,* one of two plays included in the volume, are attributed by name to other writers, yet most of the *Flowres* are ascribed outright to Gascoigne. The work was reissued in 1575 as *The Posies of George Gascoigne Esquire.*[10] In 1576 he published *The Steele Glas,* a broad social satire in nearly twelve hundred lines of blank verse. Gascoigne meanwhile found several opportunities to attract the queen's attention directly. He collaborated with other out-of-Court poets on the elaborate entertainment that the earl of Leicester staged for Elizabeth during her visit to his Kenilworth estate in July 1575. That September, Gascoigne recited his "Tale of Hemetes the Heremyte" before the queen during her sojourn at Woodstock Palace; in the course of this entertainment, Dyer too performed, perhaps by virtue of his office as steward of the manor. "The songe in the Oke" (Poem 1), which he sang to Elizabeth on this occasion, is his earliest datable verse.

Gascoigne followed up his appearances before the queen during her summer progress by sending her poetic gifts in manuscript for the New Years celebrations of 1576 and 1577. Elizabeth accepted them both, for these attractively written pamphlets are still preserved in the royal collection at the British Library.[11] But Gascoigne's name appears on none of Elizabeth's New Years gift rolls, the official records of those who were allowed to exchange gifts with the queen. In fact, the elaborate illustration that prefaces the work he gave her in 1576, "The Tale of Hemetes the Heremyte," portrays a wholly fictional gift-exchange scene.[12] In it, the poet kneels before his enthroned sovereign in the Presence Chamber. Spear in hand and with a laureate wreath hovering above his head, he offers the manuscript to her. But this was not the way Elizabeth received her New Years gifts. The exchange etiquette required that the donors' servants deliver the gifts to the queen's servants; the reception of each gift by a crown servant is carefully recorded on the extant gift rolls. The same practice of servant-to-servant gift exchange was observed in upper-class society at large. Elizabeth accepted Gascoigne's offerings, yet there is no record that she gave him anything in return, nor did she admit him to a place at her Court in any capacity. Did Gascoigne fail to attract the queen's favor because his poetry lacked something in style or theme, some aura of a "courtly aesthetic," that Oxford and Dyer conveyed successfully in their verse? In most respects, style and content in the works of these three poets were very similar.

While no one subject typifies Elizabethan courtly verse, poems about love in all its manifestations dominate the canon of her courtier poets. Aside from his elegy for Sir Philip Sidney (Poem 12), Dyer's certain poems deal exclusively with amorous subjects and always from the standpoint of the disappointed, absent, or rejected lover. Oxford treated a more diverse array of poetic subjects: twelve of his sixteen canonical poems concern love, but Poem 16 is a philosophical speculation in verse on the nature of contentment, while Poems 4 and 10 are explosive temper tantrums that rail against unspecified wrongs. This genre of complaint is all but unknown in the work of other Elizabethan poets whether courtiers or not. Gascoigne's nonamatory laments fall short of Oxford's intensity, yet the subjects of his verse overlap in some detail with those of the two courtiers. Gascoigne nevertheless attempted a far more varied repertoire of poetic genres and topics than either of the courtiers. His canon includes *Jocasta,* a collaborative verse drama translated from Euripides; a wedding masque; his full-dress satire, *The Steele Glas* (1576); moral and religious poems; and poems commending books by several of his friends including, with Oxford, Thomas Bedingfield's translation of Cardanus. But Gascoigne's output is also dominated by love lyrics of all kinds. These include approaches to the subject equivalent to those used by Oxford and Dyer. Dyer's despairing love laments, Poems 2 and 3, for example, are matched in technical form and tone by Gascoigne's "I cannot wish thy grief" (*Flowres* 8), and "Nowe must I needes recant" (*Flowres* 57). Oxford's verse dialogue between personified Love (Cupid) and an interrogator (Poem 11) resembles the dialogue beginning "I sigh. Why so?," the single poem attributed to Gascoigne in the *Paradise of Dainty Devices* (1576). Gascoigne's "Complaynt of Phylomene," published with *The Steele Glas,* is an elaborate variation on the dream vision genre represented by Oxford's Poem 8. And Oxford's rejection of the lady in Poem 9 balances a similar rejection in Gascoigne's "An uncurteous farewell to an unconstant Dame" (*Flowres* 45). Gascoigne wrote in a broader range of genres and on a wider array of topics than did Oxford or Dyer, yet amorous lyrics in modes similar to theirs are well represented in his canon as well.

Although pastoralism is often considered a trademark genre of Renaissance courtly art, it is represented among these three poets' works only in Dyer's narrative of a disastrous rural love triangle (Poem 8) and the lovelorn shepherd's lament of his Poem 11. Neither Oxford nor Gascoigne attempted the pastoral mode in any well-defined manner. Granted, Oxford's Poem 8 takes place in a rural setting that is superficially pastoral. Its speaker, however, encounters a knight who personifies amorous desire; the poem then ignores its outdoor setting to concentrate on the discourse of its upper-class speakers. Gascoigne's "Woodmanship" (*Flowres* 72) concerns hunting, but only as a background for the autobiographical narrative that is its true subject. No pastoral atmosphere emerges in this poem, and, in fact, only a handful of Elizabeth's courtier poets wrote pastoral verse,[13] most of it in the wake of Sir Philip Sidney's cultivation of the subject after 1580. Clearly, Gascoigne's neglect of this genre had nothing to do with his failure to gain royal patronage.

All three poets wrote at least one love lyric that expresses a mysterious love dilemma never fully explained. Dyer's Poem 10 describes "A man in Joy, that lyveth still in woe" (l. 6); Oxford complains that "With faygned joye I hyde my secret greefe" (Poem 12, l. 16); and Gascoigne, "I laugh sometimes with little lust,/ So jest I oft and feele no joye" (*Flowres* 30, ll. 7–8). The contradictory emotional states set forth in these lyrics differ from the standard Petrarchan and neo-Petrarchan oxymorons as exemplified by Romeo's "bright smoke, feather of lead, cold fire" in Shakespeare's *Romeo and Juliet.*[14] This rhetorical device uses contradictions to express the conflicting emotions induced by being in love. The contradictions in the three poems by Oxford, Dyer, and Gascogine allude instead to unusual external situations the lovers must endure. Gascoigne observes that "I have and misse the thing I crave./ These things seeme straunge, yit ar they trew" (ll. 12–13); Oxford laments that "I would possesse yet needs must flee the place/ Where I do seek to wyn my cheefest grace" (ll. 17–18); and Dyer concludes, "What discontent to live in suche desyre,/ To have his will and ever to requyre" (ll. 11–12). All three poets describe in verse riddles their unique and unresolved quandaries in love.

From a technical standpoint, too, these three poets composed similar verse, but we must remember that its regularity was still something of a novelty even as late as the 1570s. Accentual-syllabic English poetry was well-established by the middle of the fourteenth century as evidenced by the works of Chaucer, John Gower, and lesser poets of the age. During the fifteenth century, however, English poets lost the ability to forge rhythmic lines of poetry through the regular alternation of stressed and unstressed syllables. For more than a century English verse was characterized by rough and irregular accentual prosody. Iambic rhythms were very gradually rediscovered during the second quarter of the sixteenth century. In his "Certayne notes of Instruction concerning the making of verse," published at the end of the *Hundreth Sundrie Flowres,* Gascoigne became the first English critic to explain how to create a line of regular iambic verse. By this time, of course, a second generation of English poets had developed an ear for the effect produced by the regular alternation of stressed and unstressed syllables. These writers had rediscovered rhythm, and they made the most, at times too much, of what they heard. Gascoigne, Oxford, and Dyer composed metrically similar lines of verse of the kind that typified mid-sixteenth-century poetry. With other poets of the age, they amplified the metrical beat by avoiding runover lines (enjambment). The popularity of long-line verse forms also emphasized the regularity of their technique. Among the most commonly used meters were "poulter's measure" (alternating iambic hexameter and heptameter lines) as in Dyer's Poem 2 and Gascoigne's *Flowres* 54,[15] and "fourteener" couplets, metrical units in iambic heptameter (thus fourteen syllables per line) as represented, for example, by Gascoigne's *Flowres* 65 and Oxford's Poem 13. In these meters, too, the rhythms were amplified by the alternation of strongly stressed and unstressed syllables. Poets tended as well to emphasize the beat with a fondness for strong caesuras (pauses) in the middle of lines, especially between the third and fourth feet of hexameter lines, as in these poulter's measure couplets from Dyer's Poem 2:

> My sense my passions' spie, my thoughtes like ruins old
> Of famous Carthage or the towne which Synon bought and sold,
> Which still before myn eyes my mortall fall dothe lay,
> Whom love and fortune once advanced but now have cast away. (ll. 19–20)

Among the larger rhetorical patterns in the mid-century tradition, copiousness or amplification of types is perhaps the most common device. This figure was a standard part of the teaching of composition in Renaissance grammar schools. Copiousness generates content by multiplying examples that illustrate a given theme. The trope often takes the form of a simple listing, as with the entities Oxford invokes in Poem 4 to help him bewail the loss of his good name: "Helpe gods, helpe saintes, helpe sprites and powers, that in the heaven doo dwell/ Helpe ye that are to waile aye woont, ye howling hounds of hell" (ll. 13–14); Dyer similarly lists the "pangues" that afflict the abandoned lover: "Now love, now feare, now playnt, now spight, long sorow mixt with short delight" (Poem 6, l. 21); and Gascoigne catalogues feminine adornments in *Flowres* 13:

> The garments gay, the glittring golden gite,
> The tysing talk which floweth from Pallas pooles:
> The painted pale, the (too much) red made white,
> Are smyling baytes to fishe for loving fooles. (ll. 5–8)

These poets frequently produced copious effects by using examples from classical mythology or history, especially ancient history. In Poem 6, for instance, Oxford cites a series of mortals whom various gods and goddesses deigned to love:

> Yet Phebe faire disdainde the heavens above
> To joye on yearth her poore Endimions love.
> [. . .]
> A happie starre made Giges joye attaine
> A slavishe Smith of rude and rascall race,
> Founde means in tyme to gaine a Goddess' grace. (ll. 17–18, 22–24)

In Poem 2, Dyer compares his suffering to that of Niobe and Sisyphus (ll. 67, 72), while Gascoigne cites Troy, Priam, Caesar Augustus, Apelles, and Phoebus Apollo in just fourteen lines of his sonnet "in commendation of the said house of Fountaine bel'eaü" (*Flowres* 6).

Another rhetorical device pervasive in mid-century verse is its alliterative phrasing. Two different repeated sounds often balance out a single line, as in Dyer's "To nettles now my Corne, my feild is turned to flint" (Poem 2, l. 27), or Oxford's "Nowe crazed with Care, than haled up with Hope" (Poem 12, l. 11). Occasional alliterative triplets can be found in mid-century verse, such as Gascoigne's "My stagring stepps eke tell the truth, that nature fadeth fast" (*Flowres* 54, l. 16). More often, a single initial sound alliterates across the line, as in Oxford's "As death shall daunte my deadly dolors longe" (Poem 10, l. 4) or Dyer's "The firmest faith is in the fewest words" (Poem 9, l. 9). In Gascoigne's love lament beginning "Content thy selfe with patience perforce" the poet complains of absence in love: "Beleve me now it is a pinching payne" (*Flowres* 40, ll. 1, 21). Oxford works both of these alliterative tags into a single line: "Pacience perforce is such a pinchinge payne" (Poem 10, l. 5), and later complains that "froward Fate defers my happy hower" (l. 24). It is not surprizing that these poets sometimes employ very similar or even identical alliterative phrases, nor do such overlaps suggest plagiarism or even direct influences among them. As with copiousness, alliteration was everywhere in mid-century verse. Poets simply helped themselves to the common stock of alliterating phrases as they did to the store of well-known mythological and historical examples. Personification of abstractions such as hope, dread, and despair and the weaving of proverbial sayings into their verse are two further hallmarks of early Elizabethan lyrics that characterize the poems of Oxford, Dyer, and Gascoigne.

Despite Gascoigne's skillful culitivation of poetry and its wide dissemination, he attracted no patronage beyond a few commissions from the nobility. Elizabeth ignored him. The royal neglect cannot be attributed to lack of skill, for Gascoigne's verse, as we have seen, resembled that of his successful courtier competitors Oxford and Dyer. Indeed, had creative writing been a viable means of gaining royal patronage, Gascoigne's work in many genres would surely have won him a place in Elizabeth's entourage. The inescapable conclusion is that poetry was deemed too trivial a pursuit to warrant more than passing attention by Court patrons. Oxford and Dyer had learned to use vernacular poetry as one, but only one, of several accomplishments that displayed their qualifications as courtiers. Oxford endeared himself to the queen as a champion jouster and outstanding dancer. Although several of his poems were meant to be sung, there is no record that the earl ever sang them at Court. Dyer did sing at least one of his poems before the queen, but he was most often praised for his learning and good judgment. As we have seen, both poets wrote lyrics that seem to address Elizabeth, yet there is no explicit evidence that she recognized their poetic talents or responded to the verses they sent to her.

During the last two decades of the reign there is some evidence that a few of the queen's courtiers, notably Sir Walter Raleigh and Robert, second earl of Essex, used verse to enhance their rapport with the queen. But Elizabeth never promoted any of her subjects to courtier status wholly or even primarily because of their skills at versification. Poetry was not, in short, a courtly commodity, least of all during the first two decades of Elizabeth's reign. Accordingly, much in the way Gascoigne presented his writings in print seems consciously designed to elevate poetry's esteem. His *Hundreth Sundrie Flowres* characterized verse not only as an art worthy of study and acquisition by the leisure class but also as the kind of "good letters" that people of the upper classes did in fact analyze with great seriousness. Thus the lyrics embedded in his *Adventures of Master F. J.*, a significant work of early prose fiction that he included in the *Flowres* volume, receive considerable attention. The editor of this tale (Gascoigne himself, no doubt) intervenes after one of its sonnets to note that this lyric "was highly commended, and in my judgement it deserveth no lesse, I have heard *F. J.* saye, that he borowed th'invention of an *Italian:* but were it a translation or invention (if I be Judge) it is both prety and pithy" (*Flowres* 156). Of another poem we are told, "This is but a rough meeter, and reason, for it was devised in great disquiet of mynd [. . .] yet have I seene much worse passe the musters" (*Flowres* 162). And a third poem receives the following verdict: "This Ballade, or howsoeuer I shall terme it, percase you will not like, and yet in my iudgement it hath great good store of deepe invention, and for the order of the verse, it is not common" (*Flowres* 171). In the poems that follow *Master F. J.* in the *Flowres* Gascoigne used titles that sometimes expand into prose links between the poems. Through these prose titles, Gascoigne likewise attempted to coach into existence an appreciative readership. Most of the age's secular verse was set forth in print under titles that simply explained the subjects treated in the following lines. Tottel's *Songs and Sonnets* (1557) for instance, entitles poems in straightforward, descriptive terms: "The complaint of a hot woer, delayed with doutfull cold answers"; "Of the vanitie of mans lyfe."[16] Similarly, George Turberville's titles in his *Epitaphes, Epigrams, Songs and Sonets* (1567) sum up the theme of the poems that follow: "The Louer against one that compared his Mistresse with his Ladie"; "The Louer abused renownceth Loue."[17] But in the *Flowres,* Gascoigne provides full contexts for the composition of his lyrics, with some titles reaching paragraph length. We learn, for instance, that the poem beginning "To binde a bushe of thornes [· ·]" (*Flowres* 68) was written for a lady who owned "a booke wherein she had collected sundry good ditties of divers mens doings, in which booke she would needes entreate him to write some verses." Several poems are introduced as written in response to various "themes" supplied by named friends, and a set of verse riddles with their responses is introduced as the ordinary pastime after a dinner party in polite society (*Flowres* 17–20). Gascoigne insinuates in these evaluations a widespread audience of connoisseurs who evaluate poetic expression and study technical forms with avid interest and discriminating taste. He thus seems bent on calling into existence the kind of audience by whom his own poetry would be well received.

Gascoigne's poetically sophisticated associates were not wholly fictitious, of course. Scores of manuscript anthologies of verse that survive from Elizabeth's reign testify to the fact that hundreds if not thousands of poems circulated in coteries at all levels of literate society. There was a great deal of interest in poetry, but the concern for it tended to be rather cavalier. At Court, Sir Nicholas Bacon entitled the manuscript of his own poems "The Recreacons of his age." The queen's gentleman pensioner Sir Arthur Gorges termed his collected poems the "vannetyes and toyes of yowth."[18] Among courtiers, reading and writing verse was a hobby, not the serious avocation Gascoigne needed for it to be if he were to rise to favor through poetry. Moreover, Oxford, Dyer, and their fellow courtiers nurtured poetry without devising a "courtly aesthetic" that identified their lyrics in any distinctive way with the elite and restricted social atmosphere of the Court. Instead, they often imported the subjects and norms of contemporary out-of-Court verse into the courtly settings of their poetry. This common poetic stock belonged alike to courtiers and to the age's professional writers such as George Gascoigne. It is ironic, however, that despite his superiority as a practitioner, Gascoigne's original verse was forgotten by the end of Elizabeth's reign. Overshadowed by the brilliant works of Sidney, Spenser, Shakespeare, and many more, his contribution to English verse lay dormant, awaiting its rediscovery in the twentieth century. Yet his courtier rivals managed somehow to produce a few lyrics that remained popular for generations. Oxford's Poem 13, which compares the state of being in love to a game of tennis, reached print in 1655 and was reprinted well into the eighteenth century. Dyer's "He that his mirth hath lost" (Poem 2) was first published in 1660, but by then it had circulated in manuscript for nearly a century. As the quintessential lover's lament, moreover, it was imitated by poets as diverse as King James VI, Fulke Greville, Robert Southwell, and Sir Francis Drake. And whether Oxford or Dyer wrote "My mind to me a kingdom is" (Oxford's Possible Poem II), this smug reflection in verse, a perennially popular lyric, has been almost continuously in print since 1588. Nor can we attribute the popularity of these poems to their authors' status as courtiers, for after Elizabeth's reign their texts were disseminated anonymously. A number of Gascoigne's poems are quite as interesting and well executed as these three works, yet his rivals' creations triumphed in their posthumous renown just as they had prevailed at Court during the lifetimes of all three poets.

## NOTES

1. Peter Laslett, *The World We Have Lost,* 2d ed. (New York: Charles Scribner's Sons, 1973) chap. 1, "English Society Before and After the Coming of Industry"; Penry Williams, *The Later Tudors: England 1547–1603* (Oxford: Clarendon P, 1995) 124–31.
2. Wallace MacCaffrey, "Place and Patronage in Elizabethan Politics," *Elizabethan Government and Society: Essays Presented to Sir John Neale,* ed. S. T. Bindoff et al. (London: Athlone, 1961) 95–126.
3. Steven W. May, *The Elizabethan Courtier Poets* (Columbia: University of Missouri P., 1991) chap. 1, "The Social Organization of the Court"; Pam Wright, "A Change in Direction: The Ramifications of a Female Household, 1558–1603," *The English Court: From the Wars of the Roses to the Civil War,* ed. David Starkey (London: Longman, 1987).
4. J. W. Saunders, "The Stigma of Print," *Essays in Criticism* 1 (1951): 139–64.
5. Steven W. May, "Tudor Aristocrats and the Mythical 'Stigma of Print,'" *Renaissance Papers* (Durham, NC: Southeastern Renaissance Conference, 1981 for 1980): 11–18.
6. For the disposition of Oxford's poems and their indications of authorship in all but the 1577 edition of this anthology, see the summary table between pages xiv and xv in *The Paradise*

*of Dainty Devices* (1576–1606), ed. Hyder Edward Rollins (Cambridge: Harvard UP, 1927).

7. May, *The Elizabethan Courtier Poets* 54. I cite Oxford's and Dyer's poems by their numbers as edited here, pages 269–86, 287–316.

8. Citations to the 1573 collection of Gascoigne's works refer to *A Hundreth Sundrie Flowres*, ed. G. W. Pigman III (Oxford: Clarendon, 2000).

9. See Peter Beal, *Index of English Literary Manuscripts 1475–1625*, vol. 1, pt. 2 (London: Mansell, 1980), for the preservation of Gascoigne's verse in manuscript.

10. Edited in *The Complete Works of George Gascoigne*, ed. John W. Cunliffe, 2 vols. (1907; rpt. New York: Greenwood, 1969), vol. 1.

11. "The tale of Hemetes the heremyte" (1576), British Library, Royal MS. 18.A.48; "The Grief of Joye. Certeyne Elegies: Wherein the doubtfull delightes of manes lyfe are displayed" (1577), British Library, Royal MS. 18.A.61.

12. The drawing is reproduced in Cunliffe 2: 472.

13. Of thirty-three identifiable Elizabethan courtier poets, only eight wrote well-defined pastorals: Dyer; Sir Arthur Gorges; Fulke Greville; Mary Herbert, countess of Pembroke; Henry Noel; Sir Philip Sidney; Sir Robert Sidney; and Ferdinando Stanley, fifth earl of Derby (May, *The Elizabethan Courtier Poets,* "Part II: The Courtier Poets, Canons and Texts").

14. *The Riverside Shakespeare,* ed. G. Blakemore Evans (Boston: Houghton Mifflin, 1974) 1.1.180.

15. The six stresses of the hexameter line and seven of the heptameter produce thirteen beats in each "poulter's measure" couplet, named for the custom of Renaissance poultry merchants who added an extra egg to the purchase of a full dozen.

16. *Tottel's Miscellany,* ed. Hyder E. Rollins, Rev. ed. (Cambridge, MA: Harvard UP, 1966), vol. 1: 235, 245.

17. *Epitaphes, Epigrams, Songs and Sonets,* STC: 24326, sig. C3v, Q2v.

18. *The Recreations of His Age by Sir Nicholas Bacon,* ed. C. H. O. Daniel (Oxford: Clarendon P, 1919); *The Poems of Sir Arthur Gorges,* ed. Helen Estabrook Sandison (Oxford: Clarendon P, 1953).

# READING LIST

Bell, Ilona. *Elizabethan Women and the Poetry of Courtship.* Cambridge: Cambridge UP, 1998.

Eriksen, Roy T. "Typological Form in Gascoigne's 'De Profundis.'" *English Studies* 66 (1985): 300–09.

———. "Two into One: The Unity of George Gascoigne's Companion Poems." *Studies in Philology* 81 (1984): 275–98.

Gibson, Jonathan. "Remapping Elizabethan Court Poetry." *The Anatomy of Tudor Literature: Proceedings of the First International Conference of the Tudor Symposium.* Aldershot: Ashgate, 2001. 98–111.

Hughes, Felicity. "Gascoigne's Poses." *Studies in English Literature* 37 (1997): 1–19.

May, Steven W. "The Authorship of 'My Mind to Me a Kingdom Is.'" *Review of English Studies* 26 (1975): 385–94.

Nelson, Alan. *Monstrous Adversary: The Life of Edward de Vere, 17th Earl of Oxford.* Liverpool: Liverpool UP, 2003.

Prouty, C. T . *George Gascoigne: Elizabethan Courtier, Soldier, and Poet.* New York: Columbia UP, 1942.

Sargent, Ralph M. *The Life and Lyrics of Sir Edward Dyer.* Oxford: Clarendon P, 1968.

Stephens, John. "George Gascoigne's Posies and the Persona in Sixteenth-Century Poetry." *Neophilologus* 70 (1986): 130–41.

# 7

# Sidney's *Astrophil and Stella* and Petrarchism

## *William J. Kennedy*

Be glad that you're studying the sonnet sequence *Astrophil and Stella* by Philip Sidney (1554–86) in the twenty-first century. If you had done so in, say, the 1960s, the classroom emphasis would have focused on close textual reading (I happen to believe that's a good thing), but with special effort directed to explaining the harmony, unity, and dramatic irony of individual poems. In a study typical of that time, one critic wrote at length about Sidney's "energetic attempt to disentangle what is and what is not satisfactory in Petrarchan love."[1] Such an approach summons the formal concerns and stylistic figurations of the fourteenth-century Italian poet Francesco Petrarch (1304–74), whose *Rime sparse* "Scattered Rhymes" assemble 366 poems (comprising 317 sonnets, twenty-nine songs, nine sestinas, seven ballads, and four madrigals) on the poet's anguished, idealized, forever unrequited love of a woman named Laura.[2] In the full sweep of Sidney's sequence, however, a more concrete understanding of the poetry (comprising 108 sonnets and eleven songs) derives from what we know about its historical context. Few poets are more witty, direct, and un-self-conscious than Sidney. But to appreciate how much so, so much depends on being able to re-imagine conditions of the poetry's original performance and the real-life situations that spurred its imitation of Petrarchan forms.

Here's an example. Sidney's sonnet 71 clearly echoes sonnet 248 from Petrarch's *Rime sparse*. Both poems address readers who would estimate the beloved's excellence: in Petrarch, "Chi vuol veder quantunque pò Natura / e 'l Ciel tra noi, venga a mirar costei" ["Whoever wishes to see all that Nature and Heaven can do among us, let him come gaze on her"]; in Sidney, "Who will in fairest booke of Nature know, / How Vertue may best lodg'd in beautie be."[3] Both direct their readers to the beloved: in Petrarch, "Vedrà, s' arriva a tempo, ogni vertute" ["He will see, if he comes in time, every virtue"]; in Sidney, "There shall he find all vices' overthrow." And both conclude that the beholder might remain unsatisfied: in Petrarch, "Ma se più tarda, avrà da pianger sempre" ["But if he delays too long, he shall have reason to weep forever"]; in Sidney, "'But ah,' Desire still cries, 'give me some food.'" This last line betrays Astrophil's sensual nature. In earlier sonnets Stella has chastely refused his sexual advances. Here, signaling his clumsy efforts to seduce her, the lover transposes his iambic meter into a trochaic beat: "Lét him but leárne of *Lóve* to reáde in thée, / *Stélla*, those fáire lines, which trúe goódnesse shów," and limps through a series of off-rhymes with *flie* (for 'fly')/*soveraigntie, move*/*love,* and *good*/*food.* Like Petrarch's poem, Sidney's concerns the act of reading, and specifically the reader's ability to decipher meanings through a thicket of conflicting meters and off-rhymes. But Petrarch's poem emphasizes a moral dimension wrought by the passage of fleeting time and the approach of the beloved's death, which the *Rime sparse* announces at sonnet 267. Petrarch's speaker has loved Laura chastely until then—she is in fact married to another man—and after her death (during the Bubonic Plague of 1348), he comes to reconceptualize his love as a sort of Divine *caritas.*

Such elevated thoughts play no role in Sidney's sequence. In the 119 poems of *Astrophil and Stella,* the speaker loses his beloved not through her mortality, but because of his own amorous folly. Two poems after sonnet 71, he kisses Stella while she sleeps (narrated in song 2: "Have I caught my heav'nly jewell / Teaching sleepe most faire to be? [. . .] / Oh sweet kisse, but ah she is waking"). She expresses anger at his rashness ("She makes her wrath appeare / In Beautie's throne," sonnet 73), but he persists in asking for more: "Stop you my mouth with still still kissing me" (sonnet 81). By sonnet 86, Stella is no longer receptive to him ("Alas, whence came this change of lookes?") and she begins a withdrawal that leads to her disappearance in sonnet 106 ("O absent presence Stella is not here"). In view of these developments, we might subdivide Sidney's sequence not as Petrarch did his according to poems "In Laura's Life" and those "After Her Death," but according to poems "Before Astrophil's Kiss" and those "After His Kiss." Just as Petrarch's sonnet 248 radiates a premonition of Laura's death announced nineteen poems later, so Sidney's sonnet 71 offers an ironic forecast of the lover's impulsive kiss narrated two poems later (in song 2) that undermines his relationship with the beloved.

In the context of Sidney's life and the circumstances in which he wrote *Astrophil and Stella,* the poem has a lot more to be ironic about. Petrarch's Laura refers to a real woman (likely one who lived near the papal court of Avignon in southern France, where Petrarch spent most of his life—until 1353—in service to the exiled papacy). She was probably the wife of the minor lord Hughes de Sade (an ancestor of the notorious eighteenth-century marquis), but the poet's treatment of her name functions homonymously with the "poetic laurel" to figure the writer's artistic aspirations and his professional commitment to stylistic excellence. Sidney's Stella likewise refers to a real woman, but in ways that are both more direct and less obvious. She was a daughter of the earl of Essex, Penelope Devereux, who at the age of eighteen became engaged to Lord Rich in March 1581 and married him the following November.[4] *Astrophil and Stella* abounds in puns on the bridegroom's name (see sonnets 35, 37, 78, and 79), not the least of which portray him ("Riche fools there be," sonnet 24) as sublimely unaware of his wife's potential to commit adultery. (As it happened in a sensational scandal twenty years later, Penelope Rich divorced her husband to marry her paramour, Charles Blount; by then Philip Sidney had been dead for fifteen years.)

The poet had been implicated with Penelope Devereux early on, as in 1576 their fathers had brokered a marriage arrangement to end a long-standing political rivalry between their families. Sidney reneged upon the deal, however, probably because he was hoping for a yet more prestigious marriage with continental royalty (at one time he apparently considered marriage with a German princess), but he no doubt came to regret his decision as the Essex family fortunes later rose.[5] Sonnet 33 intimates as much on sexual if not political grounds, as Astrophil complains: "I might, unhappie word, o me, I might, / And then would not, or could not see my blisse: [. . .] / But to my selfe my selfe did give the blow."

In any case, Sidney composed his sonnets not for printed publication or broad dissemination. They were printed only after his death in a 1591 pirated version, to which his sister Mary, married since 1577 to the influential earl of Pembroke, reacted by supervising the authoritative edition of his belletristic works, including *Astrophil and*

*Stella,* his other poetry, and his revised *Arcadia,* in 1598.[6] Sidney's first audience, then, was a coterie readership of family, friends, associates, and acquaintances who knew him and his personal tribulations. They could laugh with him, not at him, as he recounts in poetic form the missteps and reversals on his road to maturity (he was only twenty-seven years old in 1581), and the wiser among them could admire his capacity for witty self-criticism and his potential for growth. To represent himself as a green-eared Astrophil might seem a calculated risk, but it could only pay off in multiple dividends invested with a readership who knew the contours of his life and aspirations.

Why? The wordplay associated with Sidney's fictional names for his Petrarchan lover and beloved suggests a few possibilities. "Astrophil" means "lover (Greek *philos*) of stars (Greek *astra*)," incorporating the author's given name Philip (given because his godfather was King Philip II of Spain, married to England's Queen Mary; his father Henry belonged to the entourage that brought the Spanish monarch to England a few months before the poet's birth).[7] Stella's name also means "star" (Latin *stella*), and Sidney's play on this meaning evokes his own family name in yet another Latin word, *sidereus,* "starry." Philip's marriage to Penelope Devereux would have raised his family's political fortunes considerably. His father Henry Sidney, son of a counselor to Henry VII, was an untitled gentleman who had been companion and counselor to Henry VIII's son and heir, Edward VI, and had been appointed president of Wales and lord deputy of Ireland in 1579. His mother, Mary Dudley, was the daughter of one of England's leading peers, the duke of Northumberland, who had been executed by Queen Mary in 1553 for plotting to supplant her with Lady Jane Grey, daughter of the duke of Suffolk and wife of his son Guildford.[8] Mary Dudley's brother Robert, earl of Leicester, was Queen Elizabeth's one-time favorite as well as Philip Sidney's patron and protector. Elizabeth rankled the family by not granting noble title to Henry Sidney. Philip, Leicester's presumptive heir, expected elevation but received from the queen only an honorary knighthood (with the accompanying "Sir") in order to serve as proxy for the Polish prince's installation into the Order of the Garter in 1583. (Leicester's title eventually acceded to Philip's younger brother Robert in 1618.) Frustrated in his aspirations for advancement, Philip Sidney already cut a slightly comic figure among the courtly coterie of lords and ladies whom he asked to listen "with good eare to me, / For of my life I must a riddle tell" (sonnet 37).[9]

Besides his broken engagement to Penelope Devereux, another major incident subtended the composition of *Astrophil and Stella.* In August 1579, Queen Elizabeth had renewed negotiations to marry the duc d'Anjou, brother of the Catholic king of France. This prospect displeased the earl of Leicester and his allies who led a "radical Protestant" faction among some members of the aristocracy. The term refers not to their religious beliefs or theological commitments, but rather to their political conviction that England's national interests would best be served by joining a continental Protestant insurgence against the Catholic powers of Spain, France, and the papacy.[10] In September 1579, Leicester's group appointed Philip Sidney to write a letter denouncing the marriage plan, for which he then suffered the queen's displeasure. The following spring and summer, and occasionally during the next few years, he sought respite at his sister Mary's estate at Wilton, the site of a brilliant gathering of intellectuals, writers, artists, and musicians, where he likely began his *Defence of Poetry* and finished the first version of his prose romance, *Arcadia.*

At both Wilton and the queen's Court at Whitehall, the earliest audience of *Astrophil and Stella* in the winter of 1581–82 would have understood this sequence in the light not just of Penelope Devereux's recent engagement and marriage, but also of Philip's fall from grace with Elizabeth. So much it would have gathered from references to the speaker as "a banckrout [. . .] / Of all those goods, which heav'n to me hath lent" and to "Nature's rent, / Which unto it by birthright I do ow" (sonnet 18); to his now dashed "great promise" and that "to my birth I owe / Nobler desires, least else that friendly foe, / Great expectation, weare a traine of shame" (sonnet 21); to suppositions "that I thinke state errours to redresse" because of "ambition's rage, / Scourge of itselfe, still climbing slipprie place" (sonnet 23); to "discourse of courtly tides, / Of cunningst fishers in most troubled streames" (sonnet 51); and finally to his plea that his alienated beloved might charge him to perform some "great cause, which needs both use and art" (sonnet 107). How better for Philip Sidney to redeem himself from Elizabeth's displeasure than by assuming the abject position of the defeated Astrophil?

But if we might better understand the poetry through these amatory and political contexts, we can still ask why Philip Sidney embedded them in the Petrarchan sonnet form. Is Petrarchism particularly hospitable to representing the courtier-poet as a bungling amatory and political fool? To some extent the *Rime sparse* had already made their mark on English literature in this way since Chaucer (around 1400) had interpolated his translation of Petrarch's sonnet 132 into *rhyme royale* stanzas as a *Cantus Troili* in *Troilus and Creseide* (1.400–20).[11] At the court of Henry VIII, Sir Thomas Wyatt (likely after his diplomatic visit to Italy in 1526–27) and Henry Howard, earl of Surrey (probably around 1541), translated some two dozen of Petrarch's sonnets.[12] Both earned the king's displeasure indirectly through their work, the former because the object of his amatory attention might have been Anne Boleyn, the latter because his literary posturing might have increased royal suspicion about his potential to usurp Edward VI's claim to the throne (he was the son of England's leading peer and a descendant of Edward III). By the time their poems were published in Richard Tottel's innovative anthology *Songes and Sonnettes* in 1557, their political reputations had already preceded them as evidence of the risks associated with life in high places, heated in a potent brew of sex and politics that offered readers a cautionary glimpse into the aristocratic world and its real-life temptations.[13]

Sidney drew deeply from the examples of Wyatt and Surrey, but he did so through a direct encounter with Petrarch's *Rime sparse*. From June 1572 through May 1575, he had traveled through Europe, with long sojourns in France (where he witnessed the St. Bartholomew's Day massacre at Paris in August 1572), Germany, Austria, Hungary, and Poland, and with an extended residence in Venice and at the University of Padua from November 1773 to October 1574. His knowledge of Petrarch's Italian poetry deeply imbues his imitative efforts throughout *Astrophil and Stella*. Sonnet 1, for example, proposes Astrophil's reason for writing sonnets so that Stella's reading them "might make her know, / Knowledge might pitie winne, and pitie grace obtaine." The repetition of "pitie" reaches back to Petrarch's first sonnet, which explicitly summons a reader in whom "spero trovar pietà, non che perdona" ["I hope to find pity, not only pardon"]. The moral difference is striking because Petrarch's speaker seeks from his reader a pity that will mitigate harsh judgment upon his cupidinous love, and especially upon his choice of another man's wife as the object of his amatory devotion. Astrophil on the other hand wants his beloved to pity him so that she will yield to his seduction. In sonnet 2 Astrophil avows that he fell into love "not at first sight," but "by degrees" until "it had full conquest got." His avowal inverts Petrarch's proclamation in his second sonnet that his *virtute,* "strength," was "turbata nel primiero assalto" ["confused in the first assault (of Cupid)"]. Again the moral difference is striking because it locates the Italian poet as the victim of a sudden force beyond his control, while Astrophil exults in his gradual—one might say willing and conspiratorial—descent into lust and darkly corrupted passion.

Other resemblances suggest Astrophil's deliberate appropriation of Petrarchan tropes to enhance his sexual pleasure. His blazon of Stella's features in terms of gold, porphyry, pearl, and marble in sonnet 9 draws upon similar figurations from Petrarch's sonnet 157. His attempt to distance himself from Stella collapses the moment he sees her in sonnet 47, recalling Petrarch's sonnet 169. His declaration in sonnet 64 of remaining constant to Stella in the face of any adversity recalls Petrarch's similar declaration in sonnet 145. His apology in sonnet 91 for casting an occasional glance upon other attractive women because they remind him of Stella follows the profane argument of Petrarch's sonnet 16. His apostrophe in sonnet 98 to his empty bed evokes Petrarch's sonnet 234. His account of sleepless nights in sonnet 99 parallels the one in Petrarch's sonnet 164. His depiction of Stella sailing down the Thames in sonnet 103 brings to mind Petrarch's address to the Rhone river in sonnet 208. But consistently Astrophil shifts reminders of spiritual gravity from Petrarch's poetry on to self-absorbed expressions of his own delight or despair. In sonnets 66 and 67 he vaunts his belief in Stella's reciprocal feelings for him. In sonnet 70 he prompts his muse to rejoice in his success: "Sonets be not bound prentice to annoy." In sonnet 74 he celebrates his independence from Petrarchan misery: "I am no pick-purse of another's wit." All of this is supremely premature. Through Sidney's artful manipulation of genre codes, Astrophil iterates wholly conventional Petrarchan figurations of contrariety in the teeth of his own denials, revealing better than he knows the artificial posturing of his erotic sentiment and the recklessness of his promiscuity.[14]

Current criticism finds *Astrophil and Sella* an ironic representation of amatory naivete and moral folly, with some precedent for the latter in sixteenth-century moralized interpretations of Petrarch's poetry written by Italian and English literary commentators. In this fashion University Wit Thomas Nashe, who was Philip Sidney's contemporary, introduced the work in its original pirated edition as a "tragicommody of loue."[15] The majority of Italian and English commentators, however, focused their attention less on Petrarch's moral issues (which in any event they might have taken for granted) and more upon his stylistic virtuosity. Early in the age of the printed book, Petrarch was acknowledged as the supreme master of Italian poetic form, exceeding even Dante, whose occasional vulgarity seemed a breach of decorum.[16] The key text was an enormously influential dialogue on language and style, *Prose della volgar lingua* [*Writing About the Vernacular*] (1525), by the Venetian humanist Pietro Bembo, Castiglione's real-life interlocutor for Platonic love at the end of the *Book of the Courtier* (1528). Bembo's endorsement of Petrarch spurred further sixteenth-century editions of the *Rime sparse,* many of them accompanied by commentaries that represent the poet alternatively as an idealized lover, a compromised lover, a failure in love, or a slave to love. Philip Sidney would have read the *Rime sparse* in contemporaneous editions with such commentaries, and their effect on his representation would be decisive.

Seen in this light, Sidney's choice of Petrarch as a model for English poetry is fraught with ideological implications for England's self-consciousness as a cultural entity. As Sidney wrote in semi-retreat following his political discomfiture in promoting Leicester's Protestant cause and his marital setback in rejecting Penelope Devereux, he came to fashion his character of Astrophil as representing a specifically courtly type of failure. Astrophil distances himself from the attitudes and presumptions of his courtly peers even while he indulges in their worst behaviors. In the conflict between his behavior and his critical postulates, he reveals himself to be at the same time both courtly and anticourtly—the latter in the sense of satirizing social pretensions and sexual hypocrisies—just as in his poetry he shows himself to be both Petrarchan and anti-Petrarchan—the latter in the sense of making the lover's idealism appear foolish and self-serving.[17] In these respects Astrophil functions as a spokesperson for his author, who could as well identify with his public and poetic personas as stand apart from them. Both pro and con, *Astrophil and Stella* displays Sidney as a critic of the self-indulgent factionalism to which he adheres as an insider. Both pro and con, it also displays him as a critic of the very Petrarchan poetry that he so brilliantly executes and undermines.

Astrophil bears all the marks of an upper-class aspirant to political office as was common at Elizabeth's Whitehall Court. From a good family and with some university training (his quibbles with grammar and logic in sonnets 34, 52, and 63 exhibit his pseudo-educated skills; Sidney himself attended Oxford from 1569 to 1572, but received no degree), the would-be courtier advertises his attainments in both arms (the traditional preserve of the nobility) and letters (prominently foregrounded by Renaissance humanists). Astrophil takes care to impress Stella with his athletic prowess at chivalric tournaments (sonnet 41) and martial sports (sonnet 53). He laces his discourse with references to diplomatic policy (sonnet 29), current political events (sonnet 30), and past political history (sonnet 75). He promotes himself as a skilled writer, even though he protests the "weake proportion" of his words in relation to Stella as their object (sonnet 50), and he affirms his attentions as an amateur rather than professional poet: "Stella thinke not that I by verse seeke fame" (sonnet 90). He nonetheless enjoys hearing her sing his songs ("so sweet my pains that my paines me rejoyce," sonnet 57) and read his poetry ("most ravishing delight / Even those sad words even in sad me did breed," sonnet 58).

At every turn, in fact, Astrophil proves exceedingly self-conscious about his poetic talents. Right from the start he rejects fashionable modes and current styles of elite poetry.[18] In sonnet 3 he distances himself from "daintie wits" who mask their fantasies in elaborate allegories; from "*Pindare's* Apes" who dignify their thoughts in high-style odes; from those who recycle old ideas in "new found Tropes"; and from those who estrange their writing with exotic figuration. In sonnet 6 he extends his critique to those who obsessively deploy oxymoronic contrarieties, mythological ornament, and pastoral conceit. In sonnet 15 he abjures the topic of "poore *Petrarch's* long deceased woes" as it was often embellished with flowers of classical rhetoric or alliterative method of "rimes, running in ratling rowes." And in sonnet 74 when he disclaims the theft of "another's wit," he disclaims as well the conventional topics of classical invention and the "furie" of divine inspiration. Astrophil's simultaneous criticism and embrace of both courtly and anticourtly forms consequently reveal his contamination of both Petrarchism and anti-Petrarchism and the paradox of the author's grounding his literary success in the speaker's failure.[19] Astrophil is a witty speaker who abuses speech, everywhere signaling his imposition as a lover, his disappointment as an ambitious young gentleman, and his impending political failure in consequence of both.

What then might be the role of poetry in such a courtly society as Philip Sidney envisions and participates in it? Certainly the wit and effervescence of *Astrophil and Stella* imply that its sheer entertainment value ranks high on the list. But its self-deprecatory gestures and its critique of courtly practices also imply a moral purpose embedded within its high-spirited humor. These qualities proved to exercise a popular as well as courtly appeal. Before *Astrophil and Stella,* the Petrarchan poems in Tottel's aforementioned 1557 anthology attracted a broad readership among the rural gentry and urban middle classes as they offered a peek into courtly life. In 1573 George Gascoigne targeted a similar readership when he interpolated eight sonnets into his titillating novella about adulterous love, *The Adventures of Master F. J.*[20] At the height of the sonnet craze in commercial London, Nashe repeated this formula for his novella, *The Unfortunate Traveler* (1593), in an episode that fictionalizes Henry Howard's amorous escapades in Italy. Meanwhile other poets, both courtly and commercial, translated or adapted continental Petrarchan forms in various ways. Sir Arthur Gorges, a friend of Spenser and Raleigh, paraphrased poems by Du Bellay, Ronsard, and Desportes in a coterie manuscript compiled without intent for publication in the mid-1580s.[21] Thomas Watson translated into an eighteen-line form seven poems by Petrarch (four of them into Latin) along with twenty-six others by various Italian and French poets in his *Hekatompathia* (published 1582), appending to each poem a brief commentary identifying its learned sources and sometimes its moral import. Two years later John Soowthern published his lumbering, sometimes incomprehensible translations of twenty-one poems by French Petrarchists in his *Pandora, the Musyque of his Mistresse Diana* (1584).[22]

It was nonetheless the 1591 unauthorized publication of *Astrophil and Stella* (augmented with sonnets from Samuel Daniel's *Delia*) that prompted the Petrarchan craze of the early 1590s. In quick succession there appeared in print dozens of sonnet sequences, including Daniel's authorized *Delia* (1592), Henry Constable's *Diana* (1592, expanded in 1594), Barnabe Barnes's *Pathenope and Parthenophil* (1593), Giles Fletcher's *Licia* (1593), Thomas Lodge's *Phyllis* (1593), Michael Drayton's *Idea's Mirrour* (1594, revised and expanded as *Idea* until 1619), and Spenser's *Amoretti* (1595).[23] Shakespeare's *Sonnets* were published in 1609. Toward the close of this Petrarchan run, there appeared in 1621 the sequence *Pamphilia to Amphilanthus,* a collection of 103 songs and sonnets appended to the prose romance *The Princess of Montgomery's Urania* by Philip Sidney's niece, Mary Wroth. The posthumous publication in 1633 of *Caelica* (though written between 1577 and 1588) by Philip Sidney's friend and early biographer, Fulke Greville, marks its effective end. It is fair to assess Sidney's Petrarchism as the fulcrum of this century of Tudor and Stuart sonnets, just as it is fair to assess Petrarchism as the fulcrum of his *Astrophil and Stella.* Sidney's complex engagement with the Petrarchan legacy invites us to explore his poetry in its formal aspects, its historical context, and its imitative relationship with literary models indebted to Petrarch and international Petrarchism. The thrill of seeing these perspectives converge can only increase our enjoyment of these fascinating poems.

## NOTES

1. David Kalstone, *Sidney's Poetry* (Cambridge, MA: Harvard UP, 1965) 116. A superbly annotated comprehensive survey of scholarship and criticism on Sidney published before 1984 is Donald Stump, Jerome S. Dees, and C. Stuart Hunter, *Sir Philip Sidney: An Annotated Bibliography of Texts and Criticism, 1554–1984* (New York: Garland P, 1994).

2. The title derives from sonnet 1, "Voi ch' ascoltate in rime sparse il suono" ["You Who Hear in Scattered Rhymes the Sound"]. An alternative title is *Canzoniere* [*Song Book*], designating an organized collection, or *Rerum vulgarium fragmenta* [*Fragments of Vernacular Writing*], a Latin inscription that the poet used. Quotations are from *Petrarch's Lyric Poems*, trans. Robert M. Durling (Cambridge, MA: Harvard UP, 1976). A comprehensive introduction is Giuseppe Mazzotta, *The Worlds of Petrarch* (Durham: Duke UP, 1993). The poems were widely imitated in sixteenth-century Italian, Spanish, French, and other European languages. For Petrarch's impact upon Joachim Du Bellay and Pierre de Ronsard in France and Thomas Wyatt in England, see Thomas M. Greene, *The Light in Troy* (New Haven: Yale UP, 1982).

3. All quotations of Sidney's poetry are from *The Poems of Sir Philip Sidney*, ed. William A. Ringler, Jr. (Oxford: Clarendon P, 1962).

4. For a biography of Penelope Devereux, see Sylvia Freedman, *Poor Penelope: Lady Rich, an Elizabethan Woman* (Abbotsbrook, UK: Kensal House, 1983).

5. See Katherine Duncan-Jones, *Sir Philip Sidney: Courtier Poet* (New Haven: Yale UP, 1991) 230–41.

6. See H. R. Woudhuysen, *Sir Philip Sidney and the Circulation of Manuscripts, 1558–1640* (Oxford: Clarendon P, 1996) 224–41 and 357–83.

7. See Duncan-Jones, *passim*, and for Sidney's fiction as an instrument to maximize the family's legacies, see Elizabeth Mazzola, *Favorite Sons: The Politics and Poetics of the Sidney Family* (New York: Palgrave Macmillan, 2003), especially 13–27 for Sidney-Astrophil's attempt to win Queen Elizabeth's maternal love without remaining her child.

8. Yes, these relationships appear confusing, but with a little patience—and perhaps such college-library reference works as the English *Dictionary of National Biography*—you can sort them out. Two useful on-line web sites devoted to the Sidney family provide many background materials: one administered by Dr. Gavin Alexander of Cambridge University at <www.english.cam.ac.uk/sidney/resources> (with fine biographies of Philip and Mary Sidney by Roger Kuin and Margaret Hannay), and the other administered by Prof. Donald Stump of St. Louis University at <www.slu.edu/colleges/AS/ENGLISH/sidney>.

9. For the sequence as a mock encomium of the self, see Alan Hager, *Dazzling Images: The Masks of Sir Philip Sidney* (Newark: U Delaware P, 1991) 103–14.

10. See Blair Worden, *The Sound of Virtue: Sir Philip Sidney's "Arcadia" and English Politics* (New Haven: Yale UP, 1996) 41–124; for Sidney's fantasy of extending this program to the New World, see Roland Greene, *Unrequited Conquests* (Chicago: U of Chicago P, 1999) 171–94.

11. See David Wallace, *Chaucerian Polity: Absolutist Images and Associational Forms in England and Italy* (Stanford: Stanford UP, 1997) 38–62.

12. See Alistair Fox, *The English Renaissance: Identity and Representation in Elizabethan England* (Oxford: Blackwell, 1997) 38–92.

13. See the chapter in this volume, "Wyatt, Surrey, and the Henrician Court," by Catherine Bates.

14. See Roland Greene, *Post-Petrarchism* (Princeton: Princeton UP, 1991) 171–94, and Roger Kuin, *Chamber Music: Elizabethan Sonnet Sequences and the Pleasure of Criticism* (Toronto: U of Toronto P, 1998) 114–49.

15. See Thomas P. Roche, Jr., *Petrarch and the English Sonnet Sequences* (New York: AMS, 1989) 193–242; 194. For Astrophil's concern with social rather than moral consequences, see Edward Berry, *The Making of Sir Philip Sidney* (Toronto: U of Toronto P, 1998) 101–41.

16. See William J. Kennedy, *Authorizing Petrarch* (Ithaca: Cornell UP, 1994) 32–102.

17. See William J. Kennedy, *The Site of Petrarchism: Early Modern National Sentiment in Italy, France, and England* (Baltimore: Johns Hopkins UP, 2003) 163–250.

18. See Heather Dubrow, *Echoes of Desire: English Petrarchism and Its Counterdiscourses* (Ithaca: Cornell UP, 1995) 99–119.

19. Dubrow 106–09.

20. The novella forms part of the author's *A Hundreth Sundry Flowres*, revised as *The Posies* in 1575, an anthology that includes twenty-three other sonnets.

21. Its circulation in unpublished manuscripts may parallel that of Sidney's unpublished manuscripts; see chapter 2 in this volume, "Print, Manuscripts, and Miscellanies," by Arthur F. Marotti. Three of Gorges's poems were published in the 1593 anthology, *The Phoenix Nest*, and in the twentieth century his work appeared in print as *Poems*, ed. Helen Estabrook Sandison (Oxford: Clarendon P, 1953); see Anne Lake Prescott, *French Poets and the English Renaissance* (New Haven: Yale UP, 1978) 52–56, 108–09, 138–42.

22. See *Pandora*, Facsimile of the 1584 edition with notes by George B. Parks (New York: Columbia UP, 1938), and Prescott 105–07.

23. Roche 518–22 lists forty-four separate sonnet sequences published in London between Anne Locke's *A Meditation of a Penitent Sinner* (an expanded paraphrase of Psalm 51 in twenty-six sonnets, 1560) and William Habington's *Castaria* (1634); to them he adds thirty-seven collections of nonsequential songs and sonnets (such as John Donne's posthumously published *Poems*, 1633). He also lists thirty-five reprints of the major sonnet sequences. Among them, *Astrophil and Stella* led the way, beginning with the countess of Pembroke's authorized edition of 1598 and continuing with reprints in 1605, 1613, 1621, 1622, 1623, 1627, 1629, and 1633. Daniel published his authorized *Delia* in 1592, with revised editions in that same year; in 1594 (reprinted in 1595 and 1598); and in 1601 (reprinted in 1602, 1607, 1611, and 1623). Constable published his *Diana* in 1592, but revised and greatly expanded it in 1594, with a reprint in 1598. Drayton published his first sonnets in *Idea's Mirror* in 1594, revised and augmented them through five subsequent editions of *Idea* (1599, 1600, 1602, 1605, and 1619), and reprinted the final version three more times (1620, 1630, and 1637). Manuscripts of undated and unpublished sonnet sequences include ones by William Alabaster, John Davies, and Robert Sidney.

## READING LIST

Berry, Edward. *The Making of Sir Philip Sidney.* Toronto: U of Toronto P, 1998.

Dubrow, Heather. *Echoes of Desire: English Petrarchism and Its Counterdiscourses.* Ithaca: Cornell UP, 1995.

Duncan-Jones, Katherine. *Sir Philip Sidney: Courtier Poet.* New Haven: Yale UP, 1991.

Fox, Alistair. *The English Renaissance: Identity and Representation in Elizabethan England.* Oxford: Blackwell, 1997.

Greene, Roland. *Post-Petrarchism.* Princeton: Princeton UP, 1991.

———. *Unrequited Conquests.* Chicago: U of Chicago P, 1999.

Hager, Alan. *Dazzling Images: The Masks of Sir Philip Sidney.* Newark: U of Delaware P, 1991.

Kennedy, William J. *Authorizing Petrarch.* Ithaca: Cornell UP, 1994.

———. *The Site of Petrarchism: Early Modern National Sentiment in Italy, France, and England.* Baltimore: Johns Hopkins UP, 2003.

Kuin, Roger. *Chamber Music: Elizabethan Sonnet Sequences and the Pleasure of Criticism.* Toronto: U of Toronto P, 1998.

Mazzola, Elizabeth. *Favorite Sons: The Politics and Poetics of the Sidney Family.* New York: Palgrave Macmillan, 2003.

Roche, Thomas P., Jr. *Petrarch and the English Sonnet Sequences.* New York: AMS P, 1989.

Stump, Donald V., Jerome S. Dees, and C. Stuart Hunter, *Sir Philip Sidney: An Annotated Bibliography of Texts and Criticism, 1554–1984.* New York: Garland P, 1994.

Worden, Blair. *The Sound of Virtue: Sir Philip Sidney's "Arcadia" and English Politics.* New Haven: Yale UP, 1996.

Woudhuysen, H. R. *Sir Philip Sidney and the Circulation of Manuscripts, 1558–1640.* Oxford: Clarendon P, 1996.

# 8

# Spenserian Pastoral

*Bart van Es*

The critical eye of Dr. Samuel Johnson did not look kindly upon Spenserian pastoral. Taking the form to be based on the description of nature, he concluded "it will not be found easy to improve upon the pastorals of antiquity."[1] Certainly Spenser had not done so. Johnson deplored the "studied barbarity" of *The Shepheardes Calender*'s language. The mistake of the poem's pseudo-rustic diction was compounded by its mismatch with Spenser's subject matter. Noting that the *Calender* was replete with allusions to contemporary religious controversies, Johnson observed with acidic understatement "surely, at the same time that a shepherd learns theology, he may gain some acquaintance with his native language."[2] Of what is perhaps the greatest poem in the Spenserian pastoral tradition, Milton's *Lycidas,* Johnson tells us:

> It is not to be considered as the effusion of passion; for passion runs not after remote allusions and obscure opinions. Passion plucks no berries from the myrtle and ivy, nor calls upon Arethuse and Micius, nor tells of rough satyrs and fauns with cloven heel. Where there is leisure for fiction, there is little grief.[3]

This mid-eighteenth-century verdict anticipates the Romantic distaste for Renaissance pastoral. For those who experienced the natural world at first hand and expressed their passion directly, Spenserian pastoral could appear safe, derivative, and artificial (and thus inimical to the demands of real poetry).

Those looking for the first time at Spenser's *Calender* may well find themselves attracted to this line of argument. The work is neatly divided into twelve eclogues, one for each month of the year. Intermittently running through the whole are the complaints of the shepherd Colin Clout concerning his unrequited love for Rosalind. In each of the eclogues we also find a formal verse exchange on some established point of controversy. *Julye* gives us a representative example: it features a set-piece discussion between two shepherds on a very artificial topic, the relative merits of dale or hill. The fact that the debate often echoes an earlier eclogue by Jean Baptista of Mantua and that the layout of these pages (featuring a woodcut of a very artificial-looking hill) imitates the *mis en page* of Virgil's *Eclogues* in Renaissance editions could all count as further evidence. A first-time reader might reasonably complain that the work lacks originality; few today would begin to read it for pleasure. Yet the *Calender* was Spenser's most popular work, going through five editions in his lifetime.

A "defence" of Spenserian pastoral (which in some ways is what this essay is) must respond to the accusations that Johnson and many after him laid at the door of this genre. It can do so in three ways. First, it can prove that some of these assumptions are simply unfounded. Pastoral, for example, is very far from being a "safe" form of literature: right from its beginnings it is a mode with strong political investment. In the Middle Ages its political content was joined by religious and satirical elements, making it one of the most politically engaged of Renaissance forms. Second, a defense can acknowledge that while some of these observations are true, they are based on a slanted conception of what should be expected of this mode of literature. Renaissance pastoral is thus not, on the whole, an attempt to convey the everyday life of rural folk or to plumb the emotional depths of shepherds: despite its setting it is a courtly and highly literary genre. Finally and most fundamentally, however, a defense of Spenserian pastoral must work to promote the recognition that it is in fact the characteristics that are held against the form—its artificiality, its conventions, its courtliness—that lie at the heart of its intellectual vibrancy. Spenserian pastoral, in many ways, *is* conventional, but it is in the exploiting, mocking, or twisting of (often contradictory) conventions that the fascination of the form lies.

Spenserian pastoral throws down a gauntlet asserting the difference of Renaissance poetry compared with the modern. In approaching it we need to abandon a search for unmediated access to personal feeling. It is through the exploitation of conventions, and recognition of their multivalency, that an expression of individual experience may be achieved. A love of pastoral, we might say, is a true "moment of arrival" in the appreciation of much of the literature of this period.

How, then, can we define Renaissance pastoral? And, having done so, how do we situate Spenser as the author of a distinct tradition? First, it is helpful to think about pastoral as a *genre:* that is, as a form that gains its stamp from Theocritus and Virgil, is adapted in a Christianized form in the medieval period, and continues as a discernable tradition in Renaissance England. This line of descent gives us not only the world of the shepherd (with its concerns of Arcadian tranquillity, lost love, lost sheep, and the like) but also the forms that come with it (pastoral singing contests, complaints, eclogues, elegies, and an episodic structure lacking a real plot). There are tens of works published in early modern England that follow this format, including Michael Drayton's *Shepheardes Garland* (1593), Richard Barnfield's *Affectionate Shepheard* (1594), and George Wither's *The Shepherd's Hunting* (1614). Almost all these works acknowledge the strong influence of Spenser's *Calender,* a work that is distinctive in its successful fusion of classical and medieval traditions.

Genre is one important way of approaching pastoral. A second is to explore it as a *mode,* that is, as a world—a set of character types, conventions, or expectations—that a writer can engage with even where he or she does not use a specific pastoral genre (such as the eclogue or the elegy). *Colin Clouts Come Home Againe* (1595) might be considered through this characterization, and it is certainly the most productive way of approaching an episode like the pastoral sojourn in cantos 10 and 11 of Book 6 of *The Faerie Queene* (1596). It is more difficult to label work in this tradition as distinctly Spenserian. William Browne's *Britannia's Pastorals* (1613) is one cast iron example, but there are also traces of Spenserian influence in pastoral episodes stretching from Shakespeare's *Winter's Tale* to Milton's *Paradise Lost.* For whether as mode or genre, Spenserian pastoral confronts the writer and reader with a number of exceptionally difficult questions: about the purpose of literature (and the role of the poet), about the competing claims of political power and romantic love, and about the justification or otherwise of escapism (both literary and personal). In relation to these questions the form does after all hold the key to a great many profound, passionate, and *un*conventional concerns in the Renaissance.

To access these debates we need briefly to sketch the roots of Renaissance pastoral. As a form it is one of those useful blind spots in ancient literary criticism. There is no definite classical prescription as to its function. Aristotle does not discuss it (largely because, as a sustained literary practice, it has its roots in Roman rather than Greek literature), and Horace's *Ars Poetica* is likewise silent about the nature of pastoral. It is the practice of Virgil's *Eclogues*—more than any prescription—that is the reference point in relation to which later practitioners build the genre.

The most succinct formulation is to say, in the words of Paul Alpers, that pastoral comes to life "by Virgil out of Theocritus."[4] The *Idylls* of Theocritus are the product of the third century BC (Theocritus is a Helenistic writer, probably born in Sicily and spending some of his life in Alexandria). They do not all have bucolic subject matter, but it is those that do that were of interest to Virgil. In these, shepherds, goatherds, and other rustic folk converse and sing in an artificial version of a Greek dialect (Doric) employing finely tuned hexameters. The artificiality of this situation is part of the point of the *Idylls*. As William Empson's influential work *Some Versions of the Pastoral* (1935) put it: it is the process of "putting the complex into the simple" that is the hallmark of the form.[5] At a basic level this is the mildly comic effect of putting complicated thoughts and meters into the mouths of simple folk. This essential "light" quality of Theocritus's form fits in with the "aesthetic" creed that is often ascribed to him. Against a tradition that expected serious poetry to be morally and politically beneficial, he asserted the claims of a poetry that should be pleasant, clever, and highly wrought. This notion that pastoral contains a defense of poetry for its own sake is important to bear in mind. It is an aspect of the form that conflicts with others and thus one of the elements that makes pastoral morally and intellectually challenging in the Renaissance.

In the *Eclogues* Virgil is imitating Theocritus (a writer who is already highly sophisticated and artificial). He follows many of his themes, produces a Latin version of his diction, and frequently echoes the lines of his model. But in important respects Virgil also transforms his inheritance. The ways in which this happens are multiform, but it is worth highlighting two specific elements. First, Virgil adds to Theocritus a dynamic relationship between town and country. The eclogues are set in the country, but urban concerns intrude. Most importantly these are issues of land sequestration. In eclogue 1 Meliboeus has been driven from his "home place" and Tityrus tells of his successful appeal to a patron in Rome. This is a very different world from the insulated retreat described by Theocritus: real politics—the sequestrations of Octavian under whom Virgil wrote—find their way into the poem.

Politics, then, became a discernible presence in the pastoral of Virgil in a way that was not the case in Theocritus. A second—and more diffuse—element that Virgil adds to pastoral is a quality of moral and poetic gravity. This may be located in numerous areas. The celebrated fourth eclogue, for example, proclaims "Sicilian Muses, let us sing a somewhat loftier strain" (1.1) and goes on to prophesy the birth of a wondrous child. The prophecy was taken by later commentators as a pagan foresight of the birth of Christ. It made the low pastoral voice the subject of a high vatic calling. In eclogue 6, too, the rustic speaker appears possessed of a deeper wisdom. The poet remembers how in the past "kings and wars" possessed him, but that now the teaching of Apollo has directed his muse to concentrate on what is simple and good. The lowly shepherd is thus the recipient of profound truths.

In a number of ways, Virgil fixes a sense of political and poetic seriousness to the pastoral form. He makes it a genre that facilitates allusion to contemporary events, and—poetically—he makes it a literary space from which one might project onward to a grander philosophical vision. The fusion of courtly and rural that was there in Theocritus is made more of a dynamic: Virgil gives us a bucolic world but allows city affairs to change it; he gives us a modest muse but allows the anticipation of greater poetic heights. Both geographically and temporally, then, pastoral projects into other worlds.

All these elements of the pastoral were conspicuously present to Spenser's readers, not least because the editorial machinery of the *Calender* prompted them in the development of an encyclopedic understanding of the genre. The poem, it is made clear, is deeply engaged with Virgilian precedent, both as a work of political engagement and as a poem that strives proleptically for laureateship. That second aspect of pastoral had been made stronger in the light of retrospective readings of the Roman poet's career development. The *genera dicendi* established on the basis of Virgil's movement from the "low" (pastoral) to the "middle" (georgic) and then the "high" style of epic offered a pattern for Renaissance poets to emulate.

Simply in physical terms, *Calender*'s pages (with their woodcut illustrations, preparatory "arguments," and learned annotations) deliberately imitate the way in which Virgil's poem was presented to an Elizabethan readership. The gloss (composed by the mysterious E. K.) points out rhetorical figures, explains obscure words, and—most of all—sets out poetic sources and precedents just as one would find in a scholarly edition of the great Latin model. The accompanying material, moreover, explicitly sets up the expectations that make this most humble form also the most ambitious:

> So flew Theocritus, as you may perceiue he was all ready full fledged. So flew Virgile, as not yet well feeling his winges. So flew Mantuane, as being not full somd. So Petrarque. So Boccace; So Marot, Sanazarus, and also diuers other excellent both Italian and French Poetes, whose foting this Author euery where followeth, yet so as few, but they be wel sented can trace him out. So finally flyeth this our new Poete, as a bird, whose principals be scarce growen out, but yet as that in time shall be hable to keepe wing with the best.[6]

Spenser's *Calender* is a prepackaged classic that instantly launches its author onto an epic trajectory. But it is also calculatedly modest (leaving its author unnamed and being dominated by a poetics that is self-consciously provisional and experimental).

Aspiration is one half of the Virgilian matrix. The other politically allusive one is just as present. And here too E. K.'s notes do the necessary prompting to set the reader off in this direction. In the passage following that quoted earlier we are told that the poet is "him selfe labouring to conceale" the "generall dryft and purpose of his Æglogues," but that the annotator was "made priuie to his counsell and secret meaning in them." Although E. K. does not spell it out, this allegorical aspect of pastoral was also there in the Virgillian tradition, and eclogues like *Februarie* (which features the fable of the Oak and Briar) enthusiastically follow this precedent.

Virgil provided Spenser with an immensely strong and complex model. But it was not the only one. E. K. as we have seen, makes mention of a number of other pastoral poets, notably "Mantuane" (Baptista Spagnuoli of Mantua) and Clément Marot. These authors had not simply traced the path plotted by Virgil—they also represented a significant alternative tradition: that of Christian pastoral. For the pastoral genre created by Virgil collided with an equally powerful religious tradition: the fundamental biblical metaphor that equates the individual believer with a sheep in Christ's flock. Psalm 23 sings of the Lord as "my Shepherd," and Christ (for example, in Matt. 18 or John 10) offers parables of "lost sheep." Matthew 7:15 speaks of prophets who "come to you in sheep's clothing, but inwardly [. . .] are ravening wolves," and throughout the Latin Vulgate there is the unavoidable doubleness of "pastor" in the senses of "shepherd" and "minister."

Biblical pastoral, like the Virgilian, is a conspicuous presence in the *Calender*. In the *Julye* eclogue mentioned at the opening of this chapter, for example, we find that Thomalin and Morrell are announced in the "Argument" as engaged in an exchange concerned with "the commendation of good shepeheardes, and to the shame and disprayse of proude and ambitious Pastours." As well as the work of Virgilian laureateship and politics, then, Spenser's poem is also engaged in religious controversy.

Christian and classical pastoral (also known as the "Mantuanesque" and "Arcadian") are not merely distinct, they are also potentially in conflict. In a Christian tradition reaching back to the Middle Ages we find a pastoral world that (unlike the geographically restricted world of Virgil) encompasses all humanity, and therefore offers very different moral teaching. In the words of Patrick Cullen's influential study, the Arcadian "for the most part takes the pastoral ideal of the *pastor felix* and the soft life of *otium;* correspondingly, it locates its characters in a landscape of varying degrees of idealization, a landscape originating in Theocritus's idylls, named 'Arcadia' by Virgil, and explored by the Renaissance, a landscape lush and pleasant but at the same time almost always vulnerable and precarious." The Mantuanesque, taking its name from Baptista Spagnuoli of Mantua (1448–1516), in contrast "takes as its ideal the Judaeo-Christian *pastor bonus,* the shepherd unwaveringly committed to the flock and to the requirements for eternal salvation, and consequently one largely opposed to the shepherd of worldly felicity."[7] The notion of *retreat,* therefore, while ideal in one pastoral tradition, becomes profoundly questionable in another.

Spenser's *Calender,* as E. K.'s commentary makes clear, is a supremely inclusive example of the genre: alongside the model of Virgil (with its suffering lovers, political intrigue, and literary self-consciousness) we have those of the Bible and the vernacular tradition (a tradition that Spenser, through his archaic language, chose to highlight with equal determination). Helen Cooper calls the poem "the supreme example of the fusion of the mediaeval and Renaissance forms."[8] In the example of the *Julye* eclogue, which can seem poetically moribund if viewed from a Johnsonian perspective, we may thus discover a subtle intertwining of rival strands.

The debate about the rival merits of hill and dale thus operates at numerous levels. On the one hand, from the Mantuan perspective, it sets the life of the isolated, high-church pastor Morrell against that of the lowly hard-working and more stringently Protestant vicar Thomalin. The "low" shepherd reaches back to the tradition of pastors following the example of Moses: "Whilome all these were lowe, and lief, / and loued their flocks to feede, / they neuer strouen to be chiefe / and simple was theyr weede" (*Julye* 165–68). From Spenser's Protestant standpoint the superiority of the "lowly playne" seems incontestable.

From a perspective encompassed by both the Virgilian and the medieval models, however, the debate also contains political allegory. The two shepherds spend a good deal of the eclogue discussing the fate of "old Algrind" (l. 126). As Thomalin explains:

> He is a shepheard great in gree,
>     but hath bene long ypent.
> One daye he sat vpon a hyll,
>     (as now thou wouldest me:
> But I am taught by *Algrins* ill,
>     to loue the lowe degree.) (*Julye* 215–20)

Algrind, we learn, climbed a hill, and by thus making himself an easy target sustained a serious injury. Thomalin's argument for the low dale *here* is not one in support of worldly engagement but rather one of avoiding commitment. "Algrind" is an anagram of Grindal, the name of the strongly reformist cleric who reached the highest ecclesiastical office by becoming archbishop of Canterbury. Once in place he greatly offended Queen Elizabeth and was placed under house arrest (the "lingring payne" of the allegory). Given Spenser's support for the elevated Grindal's low-church politics, the account leaves the choice between hill and dale decidedly ambiguous. In this case classical and medieval traditions are irretrievably enmeshed.

Yet, from a purely Virgilian perspective the juxtaposition of high and low also foregrounds an exchange about literary ambition. Virgil's fourth and sixth eclogues suggest the possibility of movement from pastoral to more exalted forms, and in the light of Renaissance readings of Virgil's generic progression from pastoral to epic that possibility became all the stronger. The *June* eclogue features Hobbinoll attempting to persuade Colin (Spenser's pastoral persona) to progress from singing "lowe in shade of lowly groue" so as to "dwell on *Parnasse* hight" (ll. 71 and 28) thus joining with Calliope, the muse of heroic poetry. Morrell, in the *Julye* debate, likewise insists that "they that con of Muses skill, / sayne most what, that they dwell / (As Goteheards wont) vpon a hill" (ll. 45–47). E. K. glosses that hill as "Parnassus afforesayd." In this context the final juxtaposition of Thomalin and Morell's emblems—"*In medio virtus*" and "*In summo fœlicitas*" ("virtue resides in the middle" and "felicity lies at the summit")—offers a tempting commentary on the poet's own ambitions. In this purely Virgilian sense one might say that the whole impetus behind Spenser's choice of the pastoral is the prospect of progressing beyond it: that he locates himself in the low dale only so as to ascend the high hill of epic.

In *Julye,* then, Spenser is concerned with dramatizing a conflict of pastoral perspectives. The subtlety of this debate depends exactly on the "conventional" nature of the form because it is in this that the allusive power of the work lies. By playing on a form that had changed over the ages the poet was able construct an intellectually complex and morally probing exchange of views. This distillation of pastoral multiplicity is itself distinctly Spenserian. Sukanta Chaudhuri maintains that the work "displays *all* the possibilities of pastoral" and that inclusiveness is one part of Spenser's originality.[9] It is this that makes it possible for Spenser always to be poised between different kinds of pastoral perspective. The juxtaposition of hill and dale in the *Julye* eclogue thus offers a visual emblem for the acute ambivalence that Spenser makes his own in this genre. The combination of the "Argument," "Glosse," and the debate between the shepherds themselves facilitates a dynamic between humility and aspiration, between high and low church theology, between political engagement and retreat, between optimism and melancholy.

This unstable movement between the varying implications of ascent and descent reverberates through almost all of Spenser's pastoral encounters, often through the reappearance of the hill itself. Thus, looking ahead to *Colin Clouts Come Home Againe* we find that Spenser's persona begins by situating himself "Vnder the foote of *Mole* that mountaine hore, / Keeping my sheepe amongst the cooly shade" (ll. 57–58). The shepherd's subsequent move to Cynthia's court is in many ways a welcome elevation, yet it is also the place "Where each one seeks with malice and with strife, / To thrust downe other into foule disgrace, / Himselfe to raise" (ll. 690–92). In a reversed but comparable movement, Calidore in Book 6 of *The Faerie Queene* abandons his heroic quest in order to live in the world of pastoral. He is condemned for having come "From so high step to stoupe vnto so low" (6.10.3.1–2), so that both the knight's and his creator's retreat from epic look at first like straightforward decline.[10] Yet the bucolic world of *The Faerie Queene*'s sixth book is also the place where we find the flawless Pastorella "Vpon a little hillocke [. . .] placed / Higher than all the rest" (8.1–2) and where Colin Clout himself, on "an hill plaste in an open plaine" (6.1), provides the most glorious depiction of poetic order in the entire poem. As in the *Julye* eclogue, the question of what kind of elevation is being considered remains slippery. Poetic, moral, and political ascent again prove dispiritingly incompatible; Spenserian pastoral is the mode in which the anxiety of this condition is most powerfully expressed. Spenser had made pastoral a supremely self-reflexive genre: by channelling into it such a rich range of poetic traditions (including the Theocritan celebration of poetry for its own sake) he made it a superbly adaptable form through which to assess the purpose of his own art. Whenever Spenser uses pastoral the question of artistic purpose is not far behind.

When we examine Spenserian pastoral as a movement that unites writers of the early seventeenth century such as William Browne, George Wither, and Michael Drayton, this notion of the shepherd as the figure through which to examine the function of the poet is one consistent element. A related feature is that of the *fellowship* of shepherds. Again, this is a tradition that may be tracked to the *Julye* eclogue. For while the bulk of its verse presents Thomalin and Morrell as opposing parties in the debate between hill and dale, the concluding section offers a different view of their relationship. When the two discuss "old Algrind" even Morrell accepts this figure as a worthy fellow shepherd. It is he who provides the final quatrain, which expresses concern for "good *Algrin*" and hope for his recovery. The mood at the close of the eclogue is one of a united community, albeit one engaged in vehement debate.

If we look at a Spenserian collection such as *The Shepherd's Pipe*, which was produced under the direction of William Browne in 1614, we find discussions that have much in common with the *Calender*. Eclogue 6 even involves a discussion concerning the decision to leave "the lowly plains" (5.1.54) to travel to "yond mountains" (5.1.71).[11] The mood here is consistently in line with that which we glimpse at the close of the *Julye* eclogue. There is the same sense of pastoral community. Indeed, the community is real as much as fictional: the characters "Cutie" and "Willie" who are presented in dialogue are the pastoral personae of William Browne and Christopher Brooke, who worked together in the construction of the volume. Community and literary ambition are also carefully united: the "mountains" under discussion represent Brooke's ambitious new project *The Ghost of Richard the Third* (1614). For these poets the eclogue is the natural location in which to hold such an exchange.

*The Shepherd's Pipe,* as a collaborative work, is an attempt—at more than one level—to emulate the Spenserian world of the shepherd. In using names such as "Willie" (familiar from the *Calender's March* and *August* eclogues) the poets Browne, Brooke, Wither, and Davies retrospectively write themselves into the literary past. They also project Spenser forward in time, recruiting the older poet as participant in their own literary endeavor. Appropriately enough, that action, and the network of intertextual references it constructs, is itself also typical of Spenserian pastoral.

The *Calender,* in introducing Colin, Cuddie, Piers, and others as participants in a debate about the purpose of the shepherd's life, formed the basis for a pastoral community. Yet it is only with the return to pastoral—in *Colin Clout, Astrophel,* and *The Faerie Queene* Book 6—that Spenser truly declared this mode to be the ground of literary production. This principle of return (comprehensively established by Patrick Cheney) makes Spenser's approach still more distinctive.[12] One might even suggest that in *Colin Clout* and *Astrophel* Spenser fashioned one of the earliest self-conscious literary movements in English history.

The publication of *Colin Clout* together with *Astrophel* in 1595 recast pastoral so as to make it not a staging post toward literary achievement, but rather the center of that achievement itself. The volume is pivotal in the creation of "Spenserian pastoral" as the form would come to be understood by those writing in the seventeenth century. If *The Shepheardes Pipe* posthumously recruits Spenser as part of the Jacobean "Shepherd Nation," then it is a trick picked up from the example of *Astrophel.* This belated collection of pastoral funeral verse for Sir Philip Sidney has attracted little academic criticism, yet it constitutes an extraordinary piece of literary empire building. The dedication of *The Shepheardes Calender* to Sidney had already made an attempt to accommodate a prestigious fellow poet into the Spenserian circle, but that attempt only really succeeded with *Astrophel,* an elegy that turns a courtier poet into a pastoral type.

Sidney never presented himself in this way. (It is true that his *Arcadia* makes use of a pastoral setting, but its princes are shepherds in nothing other than their dress, and the narrator himself remains decidedly aristocratic.) Spenser's 1595 publication transformed Sidney in such as way as to make him part of a collective shepherd-poet tradition. Not only does the first elegy of the *Astrophel* collection cast Sidney as a pastoral persona, in the closing stages it does the same for his sister, the countess of Pembroke. Spenser's poem concludes by telling us how the shepherdess Clorinda mourns her brother's loss and expresses her grief in a "dolefull lay" (l. 214). That "Dolefull Lay" then follows as the next elegy in the collection. This second poem was almost certainly also written by Spenser, rather than by countess herself. The fact that there is still some doubt, however, is a mark of the success of the project. For in the other pastoral elegies by contributors that follow we have the first emergence of the Spenserian "Shepherd Nation" that was to come to its full strength after the poet's death.

That community is first introduced in *Colin Clouts Come Home Againe,* which precedes *Astrophel* in the 1595 volume. In it we find the return of the characters familiar from the *Calender:* Colin, Hobbinol, Cuddie, and even Rosalind. What is more remarkable, however, is that the poem also casts the whole company of Elizabethan poets as pastoral figures, starting with Sir Walter Raleigh as "the shepheard of the Ocean."[13] Harpalus, Corydon, Alcyon, and others among the "learned throng" who ring Cynthia/Elizabeth may not all be as readily identifiable today, but they are certainly recognizable as poets. The act of appropriation is a powerful one. Like the *Calender, Colin Clout* and *Astrophel* represent literary composition as a pastoral activity. Much more radical, however, is the way in which the collection envisages the diverse body of England's versifiers as participants in a Spenserian project of which Sidney/Astrophel is made the patron:

> All these, and many others mo remaine,
> Now after *Astrofell* is dead and gone:
> But while as *Astrofell* did liue and raine,
> Amongst all these was none his Paragone.
> All these do florish in their sundry kynd,
> And do their *Cynthia* immortal make:
> Yet found I lyking in her royall mind,
> Not for my skill, but for that shepheards sake. (*Colin Clout* 448–55)

It is worth noting how misleading this picture of the Elizabethan literary scene really is. Sidney and most of the other poets alluded to in *Colin Clout* did not direct their literary work to the queen in anything like this fashion. Nor were they part of a unified literary community. The ideal of this collective literary endeavor is largely a Spenserian one, and it is projected with particular strength by Spenser's pastoral poems.

The community of pastor-poets (and sometimes pastor poet-priests) stands at the heart of the tradition of Spenserian pastoral as it would be understood in the seventeenth century. Spenser offered a vision of the ideal relationship between that body and the sovereign: one of collective praise eliciting both reward and respect from the monarch. Louis Montrose has explored this relationship in cultural materialist terms across a series of deeply influential essays. In his formulation "the shepherd's *gift*—both his *talent* and his *offering*—is the power to create symbolic forms, to create illusions which sanctify political power; his expectation is a reciprocal, material benefit."[14] Yet Spenserian pastoral also has the capacity to depict the breakdown of that system of exchange, through the effects of corruption, neglect, and even the superior claims of private romantic love.

In poets such as Wither, Browne, Drayton, and Milton the form of Spenserian pastoral could work to signal alienation from the established church and state. Wither's *The Shepherd's Hunting* (1614) was completed while its author was imprisoned as a consequence of his satires on the state; Milton's *Lycidas* when republished in 1645 as part of the author's *Poems* was billed as a composition that "foretells the ruin of our corrupted clergy, then in its height."[15] At the same time these works celebrate a unity of purpose, even where that purpose is simply the questioning of the object of literary and religious endeavor. Michelle O'Callaghan's study of the Jacobean "Shepherd Nation" emphasizes the way in which Spenser provided these writers with a model for a print community in which meaning is produced collectively through acts of collaboration.[16] *The Shepherd's Pipe* and *The Shepherd's Hunting,* she notes, even share eclogues—so that both textual fragments and pastoral personae are carried over from one publication to the next. Exploiting the multiplicity of generic strands within Spenser's texts (from Virgilian laureateship to Ovidian exile, from Theocritan greenworld to the darkness of

medieval satire) they managed to encapsulate a distinctly Protestant classicism that figured the role of poet in terms of both national and personal vocation.

It would be reductive to label a work as original as Milton's *Lycidas* "Spenserian."
Yet the poem can be seen as the culmination of the innovative eclecticism that Spenser
brought to the form. *Lycidas* follows in the tradition of *Astrophel* to mourn the loss of a
fellow poet and religionist. (Both Philip Sidney and Edward King died abroad while
supporting the Protestant cause.) In depicting King as the shepherd "Lycidas" Milton
established a complex network of lines of connection:

> For we were nursed upon the self-same hill,
> Fed the same flock, by fountain, shade, and rill.
> > Together both, ere the high lawns appeared
> Under the opening eyelids of the morn,
> We drove a field, and both together heard
> What time the gray-fly winds her sultry horn,
> Batt'ning our flocks with the fresh dews of night. (*Lycidas* 23–29)

Johnson, of course, leveled contempt at this passage, so transparently derivative and un-
connected with nature: "we knew they never drove a field, and that they had no flocks
to batten."[17] For those familiar with the Spenserian tradition, however, this "self-same
hill" is an intellectual and moral location much more than a physical one. Like the high
hill of the *Julye* eclogue or Mount Acidale of *The Faerie Queene* Book 6, this is a place
with complex personal, political, and literary associations, a place that stands as synecdoche for pastoral itself and thus a location whose values will be questioned over the
course of the elegy. Spenserian pastoral is, above all, a literary space through which to
examine the competing demands of poetry, action, and religious vision. There is little
that is straightforwardly "natural" about it, yet it is the form through which a generation
of English poets addressed the nature of their art.

# NOTES

1. *Rambler* 36, 21 June 1750.
2. *Rambler* 37, 24 July 1750.
3. Samuel Johnson, *Lives of the English Poets,* ed. George Birkbeck Hill, 3 vols. (Oxford: Clarendon P, 1905) 1: 163–64.
4. Paul Alpers, *What Is Pastoral?* (Chicago: U of Chicago P, 1996) 174.
5. William Empson, *Some Versions of the Pastoral* (London: Chatto & Windus, 1935) 23.
6. Edmund Spenser, *The Shepheardes Calender, The Shorter Poems,* ed. Richard A. McCabe (London: Penguin, 1999).
7. Patrick Cullen, *Spenser, Marvell, and Renaissance Pastoral* (Cambridge, MA: Harvard UP, 1970) 2–3.
8. Helen Cooper, *Pastoral: Medieval into Renaissance* (Cambridge: D. S. Brewer, 1977) 153.
9. Sukanta Chaudhuri, *Renaissance Pastoral and Its English Developments* (Oxford: Clarendon P, 1989) 132.
10. Edmund Spenser, *The Faerie Queene,* ed. A. C. Hamilton (London: Longman, 2001).
11. William Browne et al., *The Shepherd's Pipe, Early Stuart Pastoral,* ed. James Doelman (Toronto: CRRS P, 1999).

12. Patrick Cheney, *Spenser's Famous Flight: A Renaissance Idea of a Literary Career* (Toronto: U of Toronto P, 1993).

13. Raleigh himself had anticipated this characterization through the use of pastoral in his *Ocean to Cynthia* (composed in 1592).

14. Louis Adrian Montrose, " 'Eliza, Queen of Shepheardes,' and the Pastoral of Power," *English Literary Renaissance* 10 (1980): 153–82; 168.

15. John Milton, *Lycidas, Poetical Works,* ed. Douglas Bush (Oxford: Oxford UP, 1966).

16. Michelle O'Callaghan, *The 'Shepheards Nation': Jacobean Spenserians and Early Stuart Political Culture, 1612–1625* (Oxford: Oxford UP, 2000).

17. Johnson, *Lives* 1: 168.

## READING LIST

Alpers, Paul, *What Is Pastoral?* Chicago: U of Chicago P, 1996.

Chaudhuri, Sukanta, *Renaissance Pastoral and Its English Developments.* Oxford: Clarendon P, 1989.

Cheney, Patrick. "Spenser's Pastorals: *The Shepheardes Calender* and *Colin Clouts Come Home Againe,*" *The Cambridge Companion to Spenser.* Ed. Andrew Hadfield. Cambridge: Cambridge UP, 2001, 79–105.

Cooper, Helen. "Pastoral." *The Spenser Encyclopedia.* Ed. A. C. Hamilton. Toronto: Toronto UP, 1990, 529–32.

_____. *Pastoral: Medieval into Renaissance.* Cambridge: D. S. Brewer, 1977.

Cullen, Patrick. *Spenser, Marvell, and Renaissance Pastoral.* Cambridge, MA: Harvard UP, 1970.

Empson, William. *Some Versions of the Pastoral.* London: Chatto & Windus, 1935.

Grundy, Joan. *The Spenserian Poets: A Study in Elizabethan and Jacobean Poetry.* London: Edward Arnold, 1969.

Montrose, Louis Adrian. " 'Eliza, Queen of Shepheardes,' and the Pastoral of Power." *English Literary Renaissance* 10 (1980): 153–82.

O'Callaghan, Michelle. *The "Shepheards Nation": Jacobean Spenserians and Early Stuart Political Culture, 1612–1625.* Oxford: Oxford UP, 2000.

# 9

# Spenser's Poetry and the Apocalypse

## *John Watkins*

The Christian Bible concludes with an account of God's judgment against a seven-headed Beast, a Dragon, and a woman "araied in purple & skarlat, & guilded with golde, & precious stones, and pearles, and [. . .] a cup of golde in her hand, ful of abominations, and filthines of her fornication" (Rev. 17:4).[1] *The Faerie Queene* opens with one of English literature's most celebrated retellings of this story. Spenser transforms the Whore of Babylon—still riding her seven-headed beast—into the enchantress Duessa and changes the biblical Dragon that drives a virtuous woman into a wilderness into the Dragon that terrorizes Una and her parents. Archimago figures as a type of the False Prophet, yet another infernal character from the Book of Revelation. To round things off as neatly as possible, Redcrosse defeats the Dragon and takes Una's hand in a betrothal ceremony that conspicuously recalls the Wedding Feast of the Lamb in Revelation's final chapter.[2]

By opening *The Faerie Queene* with a retelling of Revelation, Spenser placed himself in a long, often controversial literary and theological tradition. The word "apocalypse" derives from the Greek word *apokalypsis,* which means "an uncovering" or "unveiling." Apocalyptic texts claim to reveal secrets of a world that lies beyond ordinary human perception. They inform their readers, for example, about mysteries unfolding around the throne of God or about events that what will happen at the end of time. The period between 300 BCE and 100 CE witnessed an outpouring of apocalyptic writings in ancient Palestine, but only a handful of these works made it into the canon of Jewish and Christian scriptures. The Hebrew Bible includes only the Book of Daniel, with its haunting visions of monsters representing a succession of Near Eastern empires, and some isolated apocalyptic passages in Ezekiel, Isaiah, and Zechariah. Each of the Christian Gospels includes a version of Jesus' discourse about his Second Coming (or *parousia*), and this theme sometimes figures in the epistles written by Paul and other leaders of the early church. But Revelation is the only extended apocalypse in the New Testament.[3]

The relative sparsity of apocalyptic material in either the Hebrew or Christian canon reflects long-standing ambivalence toward the mode's dualistic view of a corrupt world facing destruction by a righteous God. Works like the Books of Daniel and Revelation tended to be written during periods of heightened ethnic or religious persecution. Jews under foreign domination or Christians forbidden to practice their religion found comfort in texts promising that God would soon overturn the current political order and establish a kingdom of perpetual justice. Apocalyptic discourse was typically hostile to secular rulers, whom it characterized as tyrants usurping divine authority. As a result, it proved especially popular among Hellenistic Jews, Christians in the pagan Roman Empire, and the first Protestants. When persecutions abated, however, apocalyptic rhetoric lost much of its cachet. Identifying Rome as the Whore of Babylon or the Roman emperor as the Beast no longer made much sense after Emperor Constantine legalized Christianity in 312 CE and Emperor Theodosius made it the empire's official religion in 391. In late antiquity, theologians often questioned whether or not Revelation was a divinely inspired text. St. Augustine (354–430 CE), the most influential of the theologians, accepted it as part of the Christian canon, but treated it as an allegory about the present state of the Church rather than as a prediction of the future.[4]

Similar ambivalence toward the Book of Revelation resurfaced in the sixteenth-century Protestant Reformation. The great German reformer Martin Luther (1483–1546) originally denied that it was divinely inspired, but later hailed it as the authentic word of God when he discovered that it could be a useful source for anti-Catholic propaganda.[5] Protestants interpreted Revelation as a history of trials that the Church would undergo between its apostolic foundation and its ultimate redemption at Christ's Second Coming. Multiple sources made this exegesis familiar to Spenser and other sixteenth-century English readers, including the marginal glosses in the Geneva Bibles, tracts like John Bale's *The Image of Both Churches* (1545), John Foxe's popular *Acts and Monuments* (1563), and countless sermons delivered from pulpits throughout the realm (Sandler 157–67).

But as much as Protestants embraced Revelation as an attack on the papacy, the book's antipathy toward secular rulers complicated its reception in countries like England, where monarchs like Henry VIII and Elizabeth saw themselves as agents of godly reform.[6] Not everyone, of course, felt that the reforms initiated by the monarchs were godly enough. Throughout the sixteenth century, radical Protestants who believed that the Church of England retained too many Catholic practices and found themselves openly persecuted by the Tudor establishment rallied behind Revelation's promise of an imminent apocalypse. More moderate English Protestants had good reason to fear these extremist readings of the Book of Revelation as a sanction for resistance to secular authority. The sixteenth century had already witnessed outpourings of apocalyptic frenzy throughout Europe. In 1534 and 1535, for example, radical Protestants believing that they had to prepare the world for the imminent return of Jesus overthrew the government of Münster and established a theocracy under John of Leyden. John's communism appealed to many of the impoverished masses of northern Germany and Holland, but he brutally suppressed all dissent. Catholics and Lutherans were driven from the town and two women were later executed for objecting to forced polygamy.[7] The millenarian kingdom of Münster proved short-lived, but it haunted the European imagination for centuries as an inspiration to some and as a warning to others about the revolutionary potential of apocalyptic speculation. In *The Unfortunate Traveller* (1594), Spenser's contemporary Thomas Nashe concluded a bitter account of John of Leyden's ill-fated career with the observation: "Hear what it is to be Anabaptists, to be Puritans, to be villains. You may be counted botchers for a while, but your end will be 'Good people, pray for us.'"[8]

Scholars have long debated the extent of Spenser's sympathies with the more radical elements of the Reformation.[9] Spenser adopts a staunchly anti-Catholic position in all his writings, but we can probably never know whether or not his highly conventional attacks on Rome mask a critique of the established English Church. One thing is clear: he approached the Book of Revelation with enough ambivalence to distinguish himself from reformers like John of Leyden, who used it to justify attacks on secular leaders. For years, scholars approached Book 1 of *The Faerie Queene* in particular as if it were simply a versification of biblical themes and motifs in the light of Protestant polemic. But Spenser was no mere propagandist. In adapting St. John's Revelation, he transformed it into a medium for reflection not only on Scripture, politics, and religion, but on the nature of poetry, its didactic value, its consolatory powers in the face of death, and its relationship to the mystery of time itself.

The first sign of Spenser's strongly revisionist stance toward the Bible was his decision to retell the Christian apocalypse at the *beginning* rather than at the end of his poem. In a sense, Spenser wrote the New Testament in reverse. The New Testament— at least in the order familiar to sixteenth-century English readers—began not with Revelation, but with the Gospels and their account of a dramatic movement from eternity into time with the Word made flesh. The Book of Acts and the subsequent Epistles recounted the Church's struggles to keep that Word morally and spiritually present in a fallen world. The authors of these middle New Testament works broadened the Gospels' account of Jesus' conflict with the scribes and Pharisees into a story of perpetual struggle against the internal and external enemies of the Church: hostile magistrates, false prophets, apostates, simoniacs, schismatics, and individuals and whole communities charged by Paul with laxness in their pursuit of perfection. These writers present a world in which conflict and setback seem inevitable until Jesus returns to redeem his Elect at the end of time. They thus set the stage for the New Testament's final book, with its visions of struggle between agents of good and evil on a cosmic scale before Jesus returns to announce the end of time itself.

Spenser may have believed in this prophecy of an eventual end to time, but as a poet, he does everything in his power to delay it. In one of Book 1's most conspicuous swerves away from its Biblical subtext, Spenser transforms the *Marriage* of the Lamb— the climax of Revelation and all Christian Scripture—into a *betrothal* ceremony in which Redcrosse and Una promise to marry at a later date. In Revelation, the Marriage of the Lamb marks the end of history itself. With the Beast, the False Prophet, and the Dragon thrown into a lake of fire and brimstone, the Elect no longer face adversity. Time itself passes away, along with the planets and instruments that once marked its course:

> And the citie hathe no nede of the sunne, neither of the moone to shine in it: for the glorie of God did light it: & the Lambe is the light of it.

> [. . .] And there shalbe no night there, and they nede no candle, nether light of the sunne: for the Lord God giueth them light, and they shal reigne for euermore. (21:23, 22:5)

Redeemed from the tribulations of time, the citizens of the New Jerusalem so approximate the serenity of the Godhead that the distinction between the human and the divine diminishes and God becomes all in all.

As scholars have often noted, this end of history is not what happens in *The Faerie Queene*. Acting in the person of the apocalyptic bridegroom, Redcrosse kills the Dragon and wins the Bride who allegorizes Christ's true Church. But he cannot marry her yet because he is obligated to serve for six more years in Gloriana's wars against the Paynim King. The False Prophet reappears in the guise of Archimago and disrupts the joyful occasion with a letter from Duessa-Fidessa accusing Redcrosse of already being affianced to her by a precontract. Even though Una proves the charge false and the guard arrests Archimago, the villain comes back in later books and lays further plots against Redcrosse and the other Knights of Maidenhead. Archimago's temporary imprisonment has Biblical precedent. In Revelation, the Devil is bound for a thousand years but then "loosed a little season [. . .] to deceive the nations" (20:3, 8). But that season soon expires, the devil joins the Beast and False Prophet in the lake of fire, and the New Jerusalem descends. Archimago and Duessa, however, continue on their rampage throughout much of the extant *Faerie Queene,* where they are soon joined by myriad other embodiments of evil.[10]

Spenser's turn away from an apocalyptic embrace of eternity complicates his relationship to two other important aspects of Reformation thought: *predestination* and *solafideism,* the doctrine that salvation was only possible through faith alone (Latin, *sola fide*) in the saving merits of Christ's death. According to Protestant theologians like Luther and John Calvin (1509–64), Adam's original sin in Eden so tainted each of his human descendants that they were incapable of avoiding sin and, on the basis of their merit alone, would be damned. But God in His infinite mercy granted an absolute pardon to certain individuals chosen before the beginning of time without respect to their actual deserts, the so-called Elect. Despite their sinfulness, these specially chosen individuals were *predestined* to an eternity in heaven. The medium of their salvation was the faith that God gave them, an irresistible confidence in the power of Jesus' death to redeem them. The Elect could do nothing to resist this saving faith, and everyone else, the Reprobate, could do nothing to achieve it. Since their sinfulness was unredeemed by faith in Christ, the Reprobate would spend eternity in hell while the Elect enjoyed the pleasures of the heavenly Jerusalem.[11]

Predestination generally reinforced the kind of apocalypticism that Spenser espouses in *The Faerie Queene:* like the redemption of the Elect and the damnation of the Reprobate, Christ's Second Coming, the destruction of the world by fire, and the establishment of the New Jerusalem were inevitable. Nothing could stop the apocalypse from taking place, and nothing could make it happen before God was ready for it. But just as Spenser's poetry continually resists apocalyptic closure, it also resists a complete alignment with the doctrines of predestination and solafideism in their more radical articulations. One canto before Redcrosse's apocalyptic showdown with the Dragon, the narrator seems to preach standard Calvinist doctrine:

> Ne let the man ascribe it to his skill,
> That thorough grace hath gained victory.
> If any strength we have, it is to ill,
> But all the good is Gods, both power and eke will. (1.10.1.8–9)

You could not ask for a more succinct statement of the view that people are saved through faith alone and that they are incapable of working toward their own salvation. The grim assertion that "if any strength we have, it is to ill" captures in all its darkness the Protestant belief that outside a state of grace, one's most noble efforts only redound to one's ultimate damnation. But this is not Spenser's last word on the subject. After Redcrosse defeats the Dragon at the end of the next canto, Una thanks him and also praises God for her rescue: "Then God she praysd, and thankt her faithfull knight, / That had atcheived so great a conquest by his might" (1.11.55.8–9). In characteristic Spenserian fashion, the antecedent of the pronoun "his" is ambiguous. If we take "his" to mean "God's," the line expresses orthodox Protestant opinion: God alone achieves victory over the apocalyptic dragon. But if we take "his" to mean "Redcrosse's," then the line admits a considerable degree of human agency into the story of salvation, one that might even blur the boundaries between Protestant and Catholic opinion as they were defined in the sixteenth century.

Spenser's imagination repeatedly proves itself less at home with eternity than with continuing human struggle in a fallen world.[12] In that sense, his poetry is generally more militant and incarnational in spirit than apocalyptic. It acknowledges eternity as the end of human striving, but it focuses primarily on the manifestation of eternal verities within the fallen temporal order. His moral drama has more in common with those earlier books of Christian Scripture, in which Jesus and his apostles cast out demons, expose hypocrisy, rebuke corruption, champion the oppressed, and comfort the downtrodden. The knights who embody his twelve titular virtues—at least as he imagines them in the poem that he describes in the Letter to Raleigh—share little with the citizens of the New Jerusalem. But they have quite a bit in common with the Twelve Apostles, especially in their medieval legendary identities as preachers and miracle-workers moving out from Jerusalem to all the ends of the earth.

After the conclusion of Book 1, *The Faerie Queene* becomes even more insistent in its prioritization of time over eternity. Almost by definition, the virtue of Book 2— Temperance—cannot be conceived outside a temporal framework. As an Aristotelian virtue that steers a golden mean between extremes, temperance can only manifest itself in a fallen world where errors of excess and deficiency remain possible. At the end of Book 2, Sir Guyon, the Knight of Temperance, defeats his antagonist, the enchantress Acrasia, whose name means Intemperance. But unlike Redcrosse, Guyon does not kill her, in part because his own identity is so closely bound up with hers that her annihilation might undermine the terms of his own existence. Both in Book 3's Gardens of Adonis (3.6) and Book 4's River Marriage (4.11), Spenser temporalizes and even naturalizes moments of vision that a more orthodox poet might treat as adumbrations of the Christian apocalypse. In both instances, the answer to a world infected by death is not the collapse of time into eternity, but an exalted vision of cyclical natural process itself "by succession made perpetuall" (3.6.47.6).

In some of the poem's strangest moments, Spenser condemns efforts to hasten either the individual's or the world's passage into the eternity. Redcrosse eventually learns that he has been numbered among the Elect, catches a glimpse of the New Jerusalem from the Mount of Contemplation, and longs to go there immediately:

> O let me not (quoth he) then turne againe
> Backe to the world, whose ioyes so fruitlesse are,
> But let me heare for aie in peace remaine. (1.10.63.1–3)

Reminding him of his commitments to Gloriana, Contemplation denies his request. Within the chivalric conventions that govern the poem, Redcrosse's longing constitutes a potential dereliction of duty. On an even more disturbing level of interpretation, the contempt for the world that follows his vision of the New Jerusalem suggests a kind of death-longing that bears a suspicious resemblance to his earlier brush with Despaire. Redcrosse's attitude, which Contemplation urges him to resist, recalls the pathos of

St. Paul's pledge to persevere in his service to the Church, despite his personal desire to die and be with Christ: "For I am in a strait betwixt two, having a desire to depart, and to be with Christ; which is far better" (Phili. 1:23). Almost paradoxically, the promise of eternity that inspires the Apostle and Spenser's Knight alike threatens to become an object of obsession that jeopardizes their Christian calling.[13]

An impatience with life that borders on despair is only one of the dangers that Spenser associates with the Book of Revelation and its promise of a perfect society awaiting Christians at the end of time. In Book 5 of *The Faerie Queene,* Spenser's ambivalence about the apocalypse manifests itself in one of the poem's most memorable episodes. When the Knight of Justice, Sir Arthegall, encounters a Giant holding a pair of scales and promising to restore all things to an original state of equality, the latter's arguments recall the egalitarian ideals of many sixteenth-century millenarians:

> Tyrants that make men subiect to their law,
> I will suppresse, that they no more may raine;
> And Lordings curbe, that commons ouer-aw;
> And all the wealth of rich men to the poore will draw. (5.2.38.6–9)

Like John of Leyden's promise to restore an apostolic common ownership of property in preparation for the millenium, the Giant's communism appeals to masses who "did about him flocke / And cluster thicke" (5.2.33.1–2).[14] But Arthegall rejects his arguments wholesale and condemns his plan to create a new heaven and a new earth in advance of the actual Second Coming as presumption. However out of balance the current age may seem to those who suffer its apparent injustices, Arthegall argues that we must accept them as part of a divinely ordained plan: "All in the powre of their great Maker lie: / All creatures must obey the voice of the most hie" (5.2.40.8–9).

The violence with which Arthegall, or, more precisely, his henchman Talus, quells the Giant has long disturbed readers of *The Faerie Queene,* many of whom feel that the Giant makes a better case.[15] After all, Spenser himself is a social ameliorist whose entire poem sets out to make the world a better place by fashioning its individual readers "in vertuous and gentle discipline." But if his poetry aspires, at least on one level, to make the world better, it repeatedly draws back from making the world perfect. Spenser rejects the utopianism that fired the political imaginations of radical millenarians in part because the establishment of a truly egalitarian society would eliminate the temptation, failure, conflict, and struggle that he saw as fundamental to the perfection of the individual character (Fletcher 64, 72–76).

Some readers have found Arthegall's repudiation of the Giant's arguments troubling because they echo the narrator's own remarks on the world's decline from a pristine state of justice in Book 5's Proem:

> For that which men did vertue call,
> Is now cald vice; and that which vice was hight,
> Is now hight vertue, and so vs'd of all. [. . .]
> Ne wonder: for the heauens reuolution
> Is wandred farre from, where it first was pight,
> And so doe make contrarie constitution
> Of all this lower world, toward his dissolution. (5.Proem.4)

Contemplating the apparent disorder in the heavens detected by astronomical observations as a metaphor for the seemingly perennial experience of injustice in human affairs, Spenser's narrator begins to think in apocalyptic terms of the world's final consummation. A bit like Redcrosse after his glimpse of the New Jerusalem, he sees the current natural and political order in the most negative possible light. Throughout this proem, the apocalypticist's vision of a world sinking ever deeper into chaos intersects an equally pessimistic interpretation of history that Spenser borrows from the first book of Ovid's *Metamorphoses,* the story of humanity's descent from a golden period of moral perfection through ages of silver, bronze, and iron before its destruction in a great flood.

Despite the power of Spenser's writing in this particular passage, and its tendency to be excerpted as a classic statement of late Elizabethan pessimism, it should not be read out of context as Spenser's own judgment on the world. No more than Redcrosse's desire to die and enter the New Jerusalem, it marks a passing mood in a poem whose presentation of divergent and even antithetical attitudes is too complex to give lasting authority to any one. Like any other apocalyptic statement in *The Faerie Queene,* it must be read as an expression of Spenser's narrator, a figure who sometimes voices positions we might reasonably associate with the poet's own, but at other times does not. The tone of the passage itself famously undercuts its avowed pessimism with its witty descriptions of the constellations crashing into each other in a moment of cosmic slapstick. Readers who come to *The Faerie Queene* with a knowledge of Ovid, moreover, know that the Iron Age destruction of the world marked not the end of the current human order, but its beginning. Pleased by the goodness of one human couple, Deucalion and Pyrrha, the gods decide to repeople the planet. Spenser's myth proves just as resilient. Astraea's departure may mark the end of the Golden Age, but it also signals the coming of Arthegall as her surrogate, who keeps open the possibility of justice in world that is still not ready to be destroyed.

The dialogue that Spenser creates between Christian and Ovidian subtexts resonates far beyond the limits of this particular passage. As a meditation on the end of the world, Book 5's opening image of the heavens collapsing into chaos finds its fullest answer in the *Mutabilitie Cantos,* in Nature's vision of apparent chaos masking a divinely ordained underlying pattern:

> [. . .] all things stedfastnes doe hate
> And changed be: yet being rightly wayd
> They are not changed from their first estate;
> But by their change their being doe dilate:
> And turning to themselues at length againe,
> Doe worke their owne perfection so by fate:
> Then ouer them Change doth not rule and raigne;
> But they raigne ouer change, and doe their states maintaine. (7.7.58.2–9)

The pronouncement comes at the end of the *Mutabilitie Cantos,* a fragment that Spenser probably planned to use as the core of a projected seventh book of *The Faerie Queene* and that has appeared as the poem's implicit conclusion in every major edition published since it first appeared in 1609. In the fiction of this final, profoundly Ovidian fragment, the rebellious Titaness Mutabilitie introduces a procession of the months and seasons in Nature's court to prove that she has a greater right than the Olympian gods to rule the heavens. As Nature "weighs" the evidence, the scene recalls the Giant's efforts to fill his scales with proof of an imbalance in the world's present order that he was ordained to correct. Like Arthegall, Nature rejects the argument that seeming imbalances in the constitution of the universe justify cataclysmic remediation. When seen from the right perspective, the changes that may strike us as random are in fact part of a larger pattern whose design is both rational and benevolent.

As scholars have long recognized, Spenser's celebration of order within apparent change owes as much to Pythagoras's sermon at the end of the *Metamorphoses*, in which the pre-Socratic sage voices Ovid's belief in change as the paradoxical constant of cosmic existence. Pythagoras's speech is a profoundly anti-apocalyptic statement that subsumes the myth of the four ages that opened the poem. The story of a world that grows so degenerate that the gods decide to destroy it once and for all turns out to be only part of a much longer story, one that never really ends. From an Ovidian perspective, all apparent ends mask new beginnings in a universe founded on an eternal principle of cosmic renewal. For Ovid, there is no apocalypse, or at least not one imagined as an escape from time into eternity.

Spenser's vision in *Mutabilitie* is profoundly indebted to Pythagoras's sermon, but it differs from it in two important ways. In Ovid, change is an inevitable, sublimely impersonal, morally neutral fact. Spenser, at least in *Mutabilitie,* sees change as part of an ultimately benevolent plan orchestrated by a God who finally exists outside time, even though He is profoundly engaged with what happens in time. Unlike Ovid, moreover, who never acknowledges that change—or time as the medium in which change takes place—might cease, Spenser's Nature anticipates a genuine apocalypse. Having ruled against Mutabilitie's claim that change governs all things, Nature urges her to put her ambitions on hold lest she hasten the moment when all things will change, including the temporal grounds of change itself: "But time shall come that all shall changed bee, / And from thenceforth, none no more change shall see" (7.7.59.4–5). Nature's discourse finally moves entirely beyond classical typologies to echo one of the oldest apocalyptic passages in the New Testament—one that in fact predates the Revelation by over a half century—from St. Paul's epistle to the Corinthians:

> Beholde, I shewe you a secret thing, We shal not all slepe, but we shal all be changed, In a moment, in the twinkling of an eye at the last trumpet: for the trumpet shal blowe, and the dead shal be raised vp incorruptible, and we shalbe changed. For this corruptible must put on incorruption: and this mortal must put on immortalitie. (1 Cor.15:51–53)

Almost at the end of a massive poem that has strayed far from its beginnings in a retelling of St. John's story of a beast, a dragon, a false prophet, and a woman dressed in scarlet, Nature's last words move us back into the familiar landscape of Christian orthodoxy.

But not quite. Once more, *The Faerie Queene* invites us to weigh an apparently decisive pronouncement against the competing claims of other voices. Nature does not have the last word of the poem; Spenser's narrator does. His response to Nature's verdict—one of the poem's most moving and remarkable passages—signals a lingering uneasiness with Christian teaching about the world's consummation:

> When I bethinke me on that speech whyleare,
> Of *Mutability* and well it way:
> Me seemes, that though she all vnworthy were

> Of the Heav'ns Rule; yet very sooth to say,
> In all things else she beares the greatest sway.
> Which makes me loath this state of life so tickle,
> And loue of things so vaine to cast away;
> Whose flowring pride, so fading and so fikle,
> Short *Time* shall soon cut down with his consuming sickle.
>
> Then gin I thinke on that which Nature sayd
>    Of that same time when no more *Change* shall be,
> But stedfast rest of all things firmely stayd,
>    Vpon the pillours of Eternity,
>    That is contrayr to *Mutabilitie:*
> For, all that moueth, doth in *Change* delight:
> But thence-forth all shall rest eternally
> With Him that is the God of Sabbaoth hight:
> O that great Sabbaoth God, graunt me that Sabaoths sight. (7.8.1–2)

Ostensibly, this is one of the most orthodox moments in *The Faerie Queene.* The last lines engage the longing and expectation with which the narrator of Revelation concludes his vision: "He which testifieth these things, saith, Surely, I come quickely. Amen. Euen so, come, Lord Iesus" (Rev. 22:20). But echoing a prior subtext is not necessarily the same thing as reproducing it. The verse from Revelation incorporates the oldest and simplest apocalyptic prayer of the Christian community, *"marana tha,"* "Come, Lord." This is the cry of the martyrs, those who suffered the persecutions of Domition and other enemies of the early Church. It is an immediate and unambiguous plea for rescue. Spenser's prayer, in contrast, introduces a considerable degree of ambiguity. The second-person urgency of "come, Lord Iesus" yields to the third-person obliqueness of "O that great Sabbaoth God, graunt me that Sabbaoths sight." Spenser does not ask for the coming of the great Sabbath per se, but for its *sight.* "Sight" can be read as a synecdoche suggesting the speaker's desire for total incorporation in the New Jerusalem, but it can also be taken literally as a request not for the end itself, but for a glimpse of it. The narrator may be asking for nothing more than Redcrosse's vision on the Mount of Contemplation.

As one of the greatest visionary poets in the English language, Spenser aligns himself more with the distant perspective than with the immediate experience of Eternity. As Harry Berger has noted, the stanzas leading up to this final ambiguous prayer constitute some of the most linguistically and syntactically equivocal in the poem.[16] The word "Sabbaoth," for instance, puns on two different Hebrew words, *"shabat,"* or *"sabbath,"* and *"tsevaot,"* or "armies." Thus far, I have been reading the passage exclusively as an anticipation of the eternal sabbath marking the end of time. But it is characteristic of Spenser's ambivalence toward the New Jerusalem that he shadows its ultimate evocation in the poem with recollections of strife. The lines can still be read in apocalyptic terms, with images of a militant Christ coming with troops of angels to purge the world of evil before establishing His eternal kingdom. But they can also be read more generally as an affirmation of God's captaincy of the Church militant throughout human history.

That history of human struggle in time is precisely what Spenser is reluctant to abandon. In the passage's most tellingly ambiguous lines, the narrator voices nostalgia for the view of history as an endless process that has no beginning or end. When he asserts that Nature's judgment against Mutabilitie "makes me loath this state of life so tickle, / And loue of things so vaine to cast away," he presumably means that it fills him with a contempt for the world akin to Redcrosse's response to the vision of the New Jerusalem. Anticipating a "time when no more *Change* shall be," Nature makes him loathe this fragile life and also makes him abandon his love of vain things that are ultimately to be cast away. But a syntactical ambiguity over the precise object of the infinitive "loath" introduces a counterargument reaffirming the mortal existence that apocalyptic discourse traditionally discredits (Berger 269). In this sense, Nature's reminder of the coming end makes him loath *to cast away* this present life with all the pleasures that a darker theology discounts as vanities. The passage ends up regretting the projected apocalypse as much as it affirms it as the ultimate object of human longing.[17]

Many early modern writers viewed their craft as a means of hastening the apocalypse. Milton, for example, thought of his poetry and political prose alike as instruments inspiring the saints to godly reformation in advance of Christ's Second Coming. Nothing could be more foreign to Spenser, who repeatedly corrects his characters' attempts to accelerate God's plans as manifestations of either hubris or, in some cases, despair. One might plausibly argue that his poetry works to forestall the apocalypse by keeping it always somewhere beyond his story's narrative present. Perhaps there is no greater confirmation of this tendency than the uncertain textual situation of his prayer for a mere sight of the great eschatological sabbath. Most approach that prayer as the concluding lines of *The Faerie Queene.* But that approach derives from editorial conventions that have governed the printing of Spenser's poem since the early seventeenth century. Presumably Spenser himself planned to place them just past the middle of a seventh book, at the beginning of the eighth of twelve cantos. We have printed them at the end of the poem for the last four hundred years because their echoes of Revelation satisfies our sense of what constitutes a fitting end, but not necessarily Spenser's. Like the *Cantoes of Mutabilitie, The Faerie Queene* is one massive fragment whose unfinished state resists an apocalyptic sense of history and affirms instead the universe as a site of endless new creation.

Some historians of religious thought have suggested that speculation about the end of the world began in human resentment over the apparent fact that we all have to die, while the world itself goes on forever. Apocalyptic theologies thus mark a projection of human finitude onto the cosmos itself. As the writer of one of the longest extant poems in any language, Spenser provides a very different response to the brevity of "this state of life so tickle." He offers *The Faerie Queene* itself, in all its "endless worke" of tangled plots and suspended storylines, as a sublime defiance not only of death, but of an eschaton imagined primarily as a kind of static death-in-life.

It may just be that Spenser draws back from the conventional Christian apocalypse, with its New Jerusalem where the sun and moon never shine and where night never falls, as something finally too sterile. That vision clearly moved the author of the medieval dream vision *Pearl,* a poem that concludes with an extended description of the New Jerusalem and all its jeweled surfaces that is heavily indebted to the final chapters of Revelation. That author casts *Pearl* itself as a fitting monument to eternity, with alliterative stanzas circling back on each other in a perfectly concatenated structure in which the last line brings the poem itself back full circle by repeating its opening line. In salient contrast, *The Faerie Queene* rambles here and there until it breaks off somewhere—at the end of Book 6, or two stanzas into the eighth canto of Book 7—with an ellipsis. As much as *Pearl*'s formal precision gestures beyond a mutable world to the stability of eternity, *The Faerie Queene*'s endless generation of interrupted, disjointed, and asymmetrical narratives mimes its author's attachment to the present temporal order in all its mutable vitality.

## NOTES

1. All Biblical quotations are from the 1560 edition of the Geneva Bible, an annotated version favored by Spenser and other English Protestants.

2. Numerous scholars have written on Spenser's adaptation of Revelation, and I am indebted to their work throughout this essay. See especially Andrew Escobedo, *Nationalism and Historical Loss in Renaissance England: Foxe, Dee, Spenser, Milton* (Ithaca: Cornell UP, 2004) 81–140; Daryl Gless, *Interpretation and Theology in Spenser* (Cambridge: Cambridge UP, 1994) 118–26; John King, *Spenser's Poetry and the Reformation Tradition* (Princeton: Princeton UP, 1990) 72–75, 82–87; Richard Mallette, *Spenser and the Discourses of Reformation England* (Lincoln: U of Nebraska P, 1997) 142–68; Florence Sandler, *"The Faerie Queene:* An Elizabethan Apocalypse," *The Apocalypse in English Thought and Literature,* ed. C. A. Patrides and Joseph Wittreich (Ithaca: Cornell UP, 1984) 148–74.

3. Norman Cohn, *Cosmos, Chaos, and the World to Come: The Ancient Roots of Apocalyptic Faith* (New Haven: Yale UP, 1993) 141–93.

4. Bernard McGinn, *Visions of the End: Apocalyptic Traditions in the Middle Ages* (New York: Columbia UP, 1979) 25–27; Kenneth Gross, *Spenserian Poetics: Idolatry, Iconoclasm, and Magic* (Ithaca: Cornell UP) 70.

5. Jaroslav Pelikan, "Some Uses of Apocalypse in the Magisterial Reformers," Patrides and Wittreich 74–92.

6. Bernard Capp, "The Political Dimension of Apocalyptic Thought," Patrides and Wittreich 93–124.

7. Cohn, *The Pursuit of the Millennium: Revolutionary Millenarians and Mystical Anarchists of the Middle Ages,* Rev. ed. (1961; rpt. New York: Oxford UP, 1974) 253–80.

8. Thomas Nashe, *The Unfortunate Traveller and Other Works,* ed. J. B. Steane (1972; rpt. Harmondsworth: Penguin, 1984) 286.

9. For a convenient summary and discussion of the controversy, see John King, "Was Spenser a Puritan?" *Spenser Studies* 6 (1985): 1–31.

10. For an alternative discussion of the episode's theological and historiographical significance, see Escobedo 136–40.

11. For a more extensive discussion of these doctrines and their historical context, see James D. Tracy, *Europe's Reformations, 1450–1650* (Lanham, MD: Rowman and Littlefield, 1999).

12. For previous discussion of Spenser's ambivalence toward apocalyptic thought, see Angus Fletcher, *The Prophetic Moment: An Essay on Spenser* (Chicago: Chicago UP, 1971) 3–4, 59–76; Gross 57–58, 125–31, 198–99; Escobedo 134–40. See also Gless's reminder that apocalyptic writing entails more than eschatology (118–26).

13. For complementary discussion, see Mallette 46–49; Escobedo 130–34.

14. For further discussion of the Giant's relationship to John of Leyden and sixteenth-century millenarianism, see Fletcher 242–46; Frederick Pandelford, "Spenser's Arraignment of the Anabaptists," *Journal of English and Germanic Philology* 12 (1913): 434–43.

15. Andrew Hadfield, "Was Spenser a Republican," *English* 47 (1998): 169–82.
16. Harry Berger, *Revisionary Play: Studies in the Spenserian Dynamics* (Berkeley: U California P, 1988) 268–71.
17. See Gross's discussion of *Mutabiltie* as "a last vision written 'in lieu of' the Book of Revelation" (236).

# READING LIST

Arthur, Anthony. *The Rise and Fall of the Anabaptist Kingdom of Münster.* New York: St. Martin's, 1999.

Bauckham, Richard. *Tudor Apocalypse.* Oxford: Sutton Courtenay P, 1978.

Escobedo, Andrew. *Nationalism and Historical Loss in Renaissance England: Foxe, Dee, Spenser, Milton.* Ithaca: Cornell UP, 2004.

Fletcher, Angus. *The Prophetic Moment: An Essay on Spenser.* Chicago: U of Chicago P, 1971.

Gless, Darryl. *Interpretation and Theology in Spenser.* Cambridge: Cambridge UP, 1994.

Hume, Anthea. *Edmund Spenser: Protestant Poet.* Cambridge: Cambridge UP, 1984.

Kaske, Carol V. *Spenser and Biblical Poetics.* Ithaca: Cornell UP, 1999.

King, John. *Spenser's Poetry and the Reformation Tradition.* Princeton: Princeton UP, 1990.

Mallette, Richard. *Spenser and the Discourses of Reformation England.* Lincoln: U of Nebraska P, 1997.

McGinn, Bernard. *Visions of the End: Apocalyptic Traditions in the Middle Ages.* New York: Columbia UP, 1979.

Patrides, C. A., and Joseph Wittreich, eds. *The Apocalypse in English Thought and Literature.* Ithaca: Cornell UP, 1984.

Watkins, John. "'And yet the end was not': Apocalyptic Deferral and Spenser's Literary After-life." *Worldmaking Spenser: Explorations in the Early Modern Age.* Ed. Patrick Cheney and Lauren Silberman. Lexington: UP of Kentucky, 2000. 156–73.

Wittreich, Joseph. "Apocalypse." *The Spenser Encyclopedia.* Ed. A. C. Hamilton et al. Toronto: U of Toronto P, 1990. 46–48.

# 10

# Spenser, Virginity, and Sexuality

### Elizabeth D. Harvey

Sexuality figured prominently in the cultural imagination of early modern England because the survival of the family and patriarchal society itself depended on its regulation. Traditional sexual norms were simultaneously reinforced and turned upside-down during Elizabeth I's reign, for as a Tudor monarch and especially as a female ruler, her decisions about marriage and her use of her virginity as political capital were intertwined with the sexual and obstetrical history of past Tudor sovereigns. Her parents' reproductive histories shaped hers: Henry VIII's desire for a male heir permanently altered England's religious destiny, and Anne Boleyn's inability to produce a son ultimately led to her execution. Elizabeth's half-sister, Mary I, had widely publicized false pregnancies that brought public embarrassment and linked her in her subject's eyes and her own to Henry VIII's procreative vulnerabilities.[1]

Many historians have emphasized Elizabeth I's brilliantly adroit political maneuvering that allowed her to transmute the potential liability of her unwedded state into a source of strength. Elizabethan images linked the impermeability of the queen's virgin body with the integrity of England's political and geographical boundaries, suggesting by implication that England's ability to repel such threats as the armada was tied to the sexual closure of the sovereign's body.[2] At other moments, Queen Elizabeth emphasized the hermaphroditic component of her identity, especially as she aged, thus directing attention away from her female and reproductive nature. But her rhetoric and strategizing could not assuage the anxiety her subjects harbored about the succession, particularly as it became clear that she would not produce an heir. Their speculations ranged from the many comments about her potential marriages, to rumors about illegitimate children, to the penetrability of her body: it is recorded in Ben Jonson's conversations with William Drummond, for instance, that the queen "had a membrana on her, which made her uncapable of man, though for her delight she tried many."[3]

Edmund Spenser's depictions of virginity, sexual desire, and birth can be usefully contextualized both in relation to the Tudor politics of begetting—or not begetting—heirs and to the central role these topics had in the imaginative, cultural, medical, legal, political, and economic discourses of the time. Spenser's representations of sexualized or virginal bodies reflect the larger cultural problematic of female power, of human generation, and of the politics of patronage. He is an important voice for his time, at once articulating the culture's general understanding of sexuality and providing one of the most forceful interventions into those portrayals of intimate bodily knowledge and sexual subjectivity.

The representation of early modern sexuality was not symmetrically gendered. Although male sexuality was codified and disciplined through social norms, the erotic was disproportionately associated with women. It tended to be displaced onto the female body, where it could be scrutinized, castigated, celebrated, and controlled. This asymmetry was partly a function of power relations, but it was also the result of reproductive differences; although both men and women participated in the generational act, women displayed the visible signs because they became pregnant and bore the offspring. The male role was both relatively confined in time and also proportionately invisible. In a patriarchal society in which familial lineage—which sometimes included not only a family name, but also land and property—depended upon ensuring that the child was descended from the father, it was crucial to regulate a female sexuality upon which genealogical purity depended. This disciplining was accomplished overtly through such social institutions as the family, the law, and the church, but cultural forces such as literature also exerted powerful formative influences. The imaginative role that pamphlets, sermons, poems, plays, and essays had in early modern culture can be compared to the place that the media occupies in Western society in the early twenty-first century; like television, film, and popular music, early modern writing had a formative capacity to shape individuals, to mold their sense of who they were and how they should behave. Spenser describes his epic-romance, *The Faerie Queene,* as a courtesy book that has the capacity to "fashion a gentleman," to form his readers through their engagement with his text.[4] Early modern readers identified with the characters and episodes in his poem in ways that we might now designate as interactive because it encouraged them imaginatively to encounter their fears and desires and to learn from the characters' encounters with danger and temptation. Book 3, which features Britomart, the knight of chastity, treats eroticism, sexuality, and reproduction as its central topics, and these ideas expatiate in narrative form the depictions of love and sexuality that are encapsulated in Spenser's shorter poems on desire and marriage.

Spenser's *Amoretti,* his sequence of eighty-nine sonnets, records his courtship of Elizabeth Boyle, and his *Epithalamion,* which was published together with the *Amoretti* in 1595, is the hymn of celebration that he wrote for his wedding to her.[5] The *Amoretti* participate in a mode of sonnet writing that was wildly popular in England in the 1590s. For Spenser and his contemporaries the sonnet was a primary vehicle for the expression of male sexual passion and subjectivity. It codified sexual relations in a specific configuration (male desire, female indifference, disdain, or unavailability), and it not only became the fashionable idiom of amorous exchange, but also provided a dominant pattern of political relations in the English Court, where Elizabeth I was the idealized Petrarchan lady: always desired but perpetually unobtainable, perennially flattered by her aspiring courtiers but ultimately unable to requite their desire. Spenser revises this paradigm in significant ways even as he echoes it because his sonnets are written to a woman who ultimately becomes his wife. Although he invokes such Petrarchan tropes and conventions as the blazon—the itemized praise of the beloved's body parts (eyes, hairs, cheeks, lips)—Spenser also departs from the convention in his portrayal of a developing relationship (sonnets 52 and 73), which includes his depiction of the lovers' kiss (sonnet 64) and both lovers' awareness, and even mockery, of the contrived vocabularies of erotic love (sonnet 54). Sonnet 74 gathers together Spenser's mother, his beloved, and his queen through their shared name, Elizabeth, a conceit that illuminates the way genealogy and the family, court politics and patronage, and a private love relationship overlap and inform one another.

Spenser invokes the Petrarchan tradition in *The Faerie Queene* in sustained and sometimes mordantly critical ways. Belphoebe, the twin who embodies virginal love and chastity and who shadows forth the private rather than the public person of Queen Elizabeth, is, for example, portrayed in an extended blazon that draws on the language of the sonnet tradition (2.3.22–30). While this praise of the female body idealizes Belphoebe in conventionally Petrarchan terms, the celebratory rhetoric is undermined by the leering voyeurism of Braggadocchio, who watches Belphoebe from the bushes. That Braggadocchio subsequently takes the false Florimell (3.8.6–8)—a hideous parody of a sonnet lady concocted by the witch from snow and "virgin" wax—for the real thing suggests that his eyes (*occhio* means "eye" in Italian) are infected with and distorted by the bragging hyperbole of Petrarchan rhetoric.

If the false Florimell demonstrates the vacuity of the amorous idiom, the house of Busirane illustrates the anguish of erotic desire. The evil enchanter Busirane is allied with the figure of the poet though his book of spells, which are "pend" (3.11.11) with Amoret's heart's blood, a pun that elicits both Amoret's amorous captivity and Busirane's sado-masochistic control of erotic passion through writing. The first room in Busirane's house is hung with tapestries depicting scenes of love and rape from Ovid's *Metamorphoses*. The second room is equally literary in its staging of the masque of Cupid, a procession of allegorical figures who embody the psychic torment that love engenders. In the third chamber Amoret, Belphoebe's twin and the exemplar of sexualized or married chastity, is chained to a pillar (3.12.30). Her naked breast is cut open, and her "trembling hart" has been lifted out of her body, where it lies, "transfixed with a deadly dart" in a silver basin (3.12.21). Harry Berger, Jr., describes the house of Busirane as a male psychomachia, a portrait of "the male mind wounded first by desire and then by jealousy and envy,"[6] but it is important to recognize that Amoret's plight and the theatrical displays that Britomart witnesses also represent female sexual experience. The chambers and the masque are focalized through Britomart's gaze, and that she is herself wounded in her struggle with Busirane suggests that the house is a landscape saturated with female, as well as male, erotic fantasy and anxiety.

Busirane abducts Amoret just after her marriage to Scudamour. Spenser is precise about the timing: she is still at her own wedding feast, and although the guests are "[s]urcharg'd with wine," the bride has yet to be "bedded" (4.1.3). Amoret is kidnapped during the "mask of love," a theatrical display that precedes and ritually presages the withdrawal of the bride and groom to the wedding chamber. The masque of Cupid that Britomart watches in horrified fascination in Busirane's house thus poetically replicates the scene of Amoret's original abduction, and the vision of the orifice that Busirane cuts in Amoret's body calls up, among other things, the potential psychic and physical violence that sometimes attended the bride's passage into marriage. In his *Epithalamion* Spenser alludes to the ancient fertility rites that are encoded in the form of the marriage hymn. The god of marriage, Hymen, is also the name of the anatomical part that designates virginity, the hymen. The epithalamion was a poem that celebrated not just marriage, then, but the defloration of the bride, her transformation from a virginal girl to a woman who would bear children. "Epithalamium" means "around the bridal chamber," and it is metaphorically and ritually associated with the bride's rite of passage. In anthropological ritual, such transitions are often dangerous, and the ominous signs that Spenser catalogues in stanza 19 of the *Epithalamion* signal the perils that attend this liminal moment. Customs such as carrying the bride over the threshold of the bridal chamber or house preserve the vestigial cultural memory of practices designed to protect the bride in this moment of passage. Spenser's language in response to the imaginary threats that might menace his own wedding night works analogically in some of the same ways, for it functions like an incantation: the stanza is structured around the repetition of "Let no," as if the anaphora (the repetition of those words in successive lines) could magically ward off all of the evils Spenser lists (19). The mixture of religious description and classical allusion in the *Epithalamion* evokes the pagan roots of the poem with its fertility rituals, and it celebrates the transposition of that sexual act—with its attendant connotations of familial continuity—into early modern culture. Where we can read the flowers that adorn the bridal bed in stanza 17 as a symbol of natural fecundity, they also point to the defloration of the bride, the rupturing of the hymenal membrane that will presage the flowering of her body in pregnancy.

If Spenser's poem is a personal and poetic celebration of his marriage to Elizabeth Boyle, which is suffused with nationalism and a sense of the importance of lineage through the generation of offspring, Amoret's relationship with Scudamour is suspended through Amoret's abduction and further deferred by Spenser's rewriting of the ending of Book 3 in his edition of 1596. In the 1590 edition of *The Faerie Queene,* Amoret and Scudamour are reunited, and when Scudamour clasps his beloved in his arms, Amoret "did in pleasure melt,/ And in sweete rauishment pourd out her spright" (3.12.45a). The lovers "like two senceles stocks in long embracement dwelt" (3.12.46a), fused together, Spenser tells us, like the lovers from Ovid's *Metamorphoses,* Hermaphroditus and Salmacis, whose merging was so complete that they became one body. The allusion is complex, referring as it does both to the desired imaginary plenitude of Aristophanes's myth in Plato's *Symposium* and to Ovid's poem with its monitory message about the dangers of the loss of self. The hermaphrodite is itself a figure of ambiguity, and just as it unites male and female sexual characteristics in a single body, so it is simultaneously a symbol of power—like Elizabeth I, who claimed to "have the body but of a weak and feeble woman, but [. . .] the heart and stomach of a king"[7] —and an image of dangerous indulgence that leads to the loss of a distinct gendered identity. This latter fear about the perils of erotic dissipation also informs the depiction of the seductive enchantress Acrasia in the Bower of Bliss, where when Guyon, the knight of temperance, sees the sexually enervated Verdant, languorously resting with his head in Acrasia's lap, he confronts an early modern warning about the dangers of emasculation that attend excessive sexual indulgence (2.12). Britomart, herself a spectator of Amoret and Scudamour's sexual ecstasy, looks on, "halfe enuying their blesse" (3.12.46a). Her sense of melancholy one-ness, or half-ness, is reiterated in Spenser's famous pun about Amoret's heart: when Britomart rescues her from Busirane, Amoret's heart is healed and becomes a "perfect hole" (3.12.38). Both Amoret, and Britomart, with whom she is closely linked, yearn for a complete union that would fill their longing and make them "whole." Spenser's erasure of the 1590 ending of Book 3 underscores forcefully the complexity of the ideal sexual union he envisions; although we as readers glimpse the fleeting and effaced portrayal of Scudamour and Amoret's embrace, it is an erotic closure more deferred than offered.

Florimell, who appears at the beginning of Book 3, is the embodiment of the Petrarchan lady, distinguished as she is by her crystal-clear complexion and her golden

hair. She enters the poem in flight, chased by a "griesly Foster" (3.1.17) who is attempting to rape her, and she functions throughout the middle books of the poem as a kind of
emblematic object of desire, always pursued, always elusive. When she escapes from
the monstrous hyena that feeds on women's flesh and is itself a figure of lust, she leaves
her golden girdle behind (3.7.22–31). This cestus, which was fashioned by Vulcan for
Venus, symbolized chaste married love and had the power to give the "virtue of chast
loue" (4.5.3), but if an unchaste woman attempted to wear the belt, it would slip from
her middle. The word that Spenser uses to describe the girdle's untying is "loose," a
term that suggests not only the belt's judgment of the woman's virtue but also gestures
to her "loose" sexual behavior. When Sir Satyrane binds the hyena with the cestus, the
lascivious, ravenous beast becomes a "lambe," obediently following the knight as a dog
on a leash might (3.7.36). Florimell's golden belt stands, then, as the sign for the way
potentially bestial or monstrous sexual desire can be restrained by the domesticating
powers of chastity or moral purity.

Britomart, Spenser's transvestite embodiment of chastity, is in some respects a prisoner of her gynecological urges. At least one critic has defined Britomart's task as sexual
heroism, "whose quest is to find the fitting husband to father her child through whom
the heroic line will continue."[8] We can see this assertion in starker physiological terms,
since she functions not so much like a knight errant as an errant womb. Although
Renaissance gynecological theory tended to refute Plato's description in the *Timaeus* of
the womb as an animal that is motivated by the desire to bear children and that if left
unfruitful is aggrieved and wanders throughout the body, blocking channels and respi-
ration and bringing disorder,[9] the metaphor of the migratory uterus continued to haunt
both medical and literary texts.[10] Richard Halpern suggests that the withholding of
sexuality—commonly expressed in the figure of the fierce virgin, the Amazon, Diana
and her followers, or the maenad—is often seen as strange and threatening, especially
because of its capacity to overturn domestic rule.[11] Maenadism, which Halpern
describes as a revolt against the constrictions of the household and the Attic state,
involved a reversion from culture to nature.[12] In the figure of the wandering womb, we
can see a related rebellion against domesticity in the sense that the uterus is unhoused
from its proper sphere, and its wandering brings the disorder of an unstructured and
potentially dangerous desire. Britomart seems to combine the attributes of Diana, or
Belphoebe, a militant virginity, with the desire and desirability of Venus or Amoret, so
that she unites the potential or lure of sexuality with the unassailability of virginity. Of
course, she never fulfills the maenadic threat of disruption, as her encounters with her
sexual antitypes, Malecasta and Radigund, makes clear, but that she is wounded in each
of these encounters suggests the perils they pose as versions of herself.

Patricia Parker memorably argued in *Inescapable Romance* that the structure of
romance as a mode is bound up with the pleasure of the female body. She drew attention
to the common etymological roots of dilation and deferral, arguing that delay produced
the expansion and opening that is the generative nature of romance.[13] Associated with
deferral in its operations is error, not only as a description of the knights' wandering
(*errare*), but also as embodied in the dragon Error. Linked through its name to the wandering womb, it is perhaps not surprising to see Error as an image of monstrous birth, a
creature who incarnates the womb as a site of chaotic generation. Indeed, the simile that
Spenser uses to describe the vomit she brings forth—since her mouth and womb are

curiously conflated—is the familiar trope of the flooding Nile, a figure that is reiterated in Spenser's description of Chrysogone's impregnation. But if Error and the dark cave she both inhabits and embodies stand for a monstrous version of the wandering womb, Britomart figures a more positive and ideologically useful one.

As an unhoused womb, Britomart wanders, seeking her lover, Arthegall, who will impregnate her. When this happens, according to Merlin's prophecy, she will be housed again, not only in the domestic space her future husband will provide, but in the royal house of the prophesied lineage, which begins with Troy and ends with Elizabeth I's Troynovant. Although we never see Britomart's marriage with Arthegall, or their child, the prophetic vision inhabits the poem proleptically in its metaphors. When Britomart first reveals her destiny to the Redcrosse Knight, for instance, she is so pleased to hear her future husband praised by Redcrosse that she rejoices, we are told, just as a "loving mother" does who sees her baby "safe appeare" after bearing it for nine months "In the deare closet of her painefull side" (3.2.11). This image points forward in the poem and backward in time to the first moment Britomart glimpses her lover; in that scene, she is cloistered in her father's closet, where she looks in his magic mirror. For Britomart, the access is through vision, a function not of—in Merlin's phrase—her "wandring eye," but of destiny (3.3.24). The image of Arthegall that Britomart sees causes her to be pierced with love's arrow (3.2.26), and although she does not initially feel the wound, its symptoms soon manifest themselves. While her complaints are the classic afflictions of heroic love, they also share the cluster of ailments associated with wandering wombs, hysteria, or, as it was commonly known in the early modern period, the "suffocation of the mother." As Robert Burton says of the disease in *The Anatomy of Melancholy,* the best remedy is to be married to good husbands so that afflicted women may satisfy their desires.[14] Britomart's destiny unites the private and public, since her own erotic satisfaction will bring about a crucial political goal, the production of an heir. Merlin's recounting of England's genealogical future to Britomart and her nurse thus perhaps inevitably culminates in a prophetic portrait of Elizabeth I, the "royall virgin," who will stretch her "white rod over the *Belgicke* shore" and make the "great Castle" of Spain shake and fall. Yet the triumph of this vision is infected with the anxiety about the succession that Elizabeth's subjects must have felt increasingly as she aged. After the prophetic glimpse of Elizabeth, Merlin grows silent, "As overcomen of the spirites powre,/Or other ghastly spectacle dismay,/That secretly he saw, yet note discour" (3.3.50). This moment introduces a note of doubt about Elizabeth's own political, genealogical, and perhaps gynecological destiny at the precise moment that Spenser is asserting a stable future and a glorious progeny for Britomart through her "enwombment" of Britain's heir.

Britomart's desire and the conception and future pregnancy toward which it directs itself is assaulted by versions of false desire (Malacasta) or images of womanhood that threaten her quest (the Amazonian Radigund), and it is by subduing these threats that Britomart can domesticate the urges of her womb. In doing so, she reaffirms the lessons of patriarchy, overcoming alternative eroticisms and forms of female power in order to assert the primacy of patrilineal generation. The fulfilment of her gynecological destiny would thus mark the confinement of the uterus within the body, and the woman within the sphere of domesticity, signaling an end to the freedom of disguise and her relative power of self-determination. Merlin forecasts that Britomart will bear arms with

Arthegall until her "wombes burden" (3.3.28) calls her away from martial exploits. Thereafter, she is relegated to a private sphere, synecdochized in the house; this movement is expressive of a concept that Mark Wigley has described in his analysis of the architecture of gender in Xenophon's *Oeconomicus* and Leon Battista Albert's fifteenth-century treatises on architecture and the family. The primary role of the house, he asserts, is to protect the father's genealogical claims by isolating the wife from other men.[15] Just as the wandering womb is anchored in the body through intercourse, conception, and pregnancy, so too is the woman who houses the matrix enclosed within an architecture designed to protect and perpetuate a lineage or house that is the major building block of patriarchal culture. The vicissitudes of conception thus would seem to encapsulate the dynastic imperative at the level of biology, for in 1596, when Spenser published the last three books of *The Faerie Queene,* it was now abundantly clear to her subjects that Elizabeth's powerful virginity had a cost, for her successor would have more in common with the foundling children of Spenser's poem than with the mighty lion "enwombed" in Britomart's body.

Chrysogone would seem to offer the ideal poetic solution to the problem of succession posed by Elizabeth I's virginity. Like the Virgin Mary, on whom she is partly modeled, Chrysogone retains her virgin state and yet gives birth to twins. She is related to Elizabeth I obliquely through this birth narrative and explicitly in her connection to one of the twins, Belphoebe, whom Spenser tells us in *The Letter to Ralegh* "shadows" one version of his queen. Spenser does not name Chrysogone's male parent, and given that her mother is Amphisa, whose name means "double nature," the elision of a paternal origin points to Amphisa's self-creating or androgynous capacity. There are strong associative and structural links between Chrysogone's impregnation and birth narratives, which take place in pastoral settings, and the Garden of Adonis, as if Chrysogone's sleepy trances themselves imaginatively generate the psychic landscape of that "wide womb."

Chrysogone's story begins with her withdrawal into nature; on a hot summer day, she goes into the forest, "farre from all mens vew," to bathe. Immersing herself in a fountain, she anoints herself with the sweetest flowers of the forest—violets and roses. Afterward, overcome with weariness, she lies down on a grassy bank to rest. As she sleeps, the sun-beams play upon her body, which, Spenser tells us, is "mollified" by her bath; the rays "pierst into" her womb with "so sweet sence and secret power unspide" that in her "pregnant flesh they shortly fructifide" (3.6.7). This tale is filiated with the myth of Danaë's insemination by Zeus. Danaë was locked in a bronze subterranean chamber by her father because of a prophecy that she would bear a son who would kill him. Zeus fell in love with her and visited her in a golden shower; by these means she conceived a son. Chrysogone's name means "golden race" or "gold begetting," and despite the absence of a Zeus figure in Spenser's account, the landscape is not emptied of volition or desire. Indeed, the slumber into which Chrysogone falls has a magical quality: "a gentle slombering swowne/Upon her fell all naked bare displayd" (3.6.7). The syntactical strangeness of the line "Upon her fell all naked bare displayd" derives from its elision of agency, for although her nakedness is voyeuristically enjoyed, not least by the sun-beams that "play" upon her body and pierce it, the eyes that see are invisible. Even the flowers that perfumed her bath seem to collude, transmuting into "sweet sence" within her womb, where they ripen into the fruit of her children, "fructifying,"

Spenser tells us, in her pregnant flesh. What is outside the female body (sun, flowers, water) has been mysteriously incorporated into it, just as Danaë's seemingly impregnable prison—and by extension, her womb—has been secretly infiltrated. Even though Spenser's account draws some of its resonance of the miraculous from myth, the enigmatic nature of conception, which is much discussed in medical texts of the period, shares this sense of a mystery whose origins can never quite be captured by the eye.

In late sixteenth-century England, there were two prevalent explanations of conception, one that was derived from Aristotle, and one from Hippocrates, via Galen. The Galenic model held that in order for conception to occur, both the man and the woman had to contribute seed, and when the semen joined and mixed, if the circumstances were favorable, conception occurred. Because male and female sexual organs were identical, except that men's genitalia were on the outside and women's were on the inside, a homology of function was supposed. Therefore, just as men needed to climax and ejaculate in order to produce semen, so too was it assumed that women must have an orgasm in order to contribute seed. In other words, according to the Galenic model, female pleasure was essential to conception, and as Thomas Laqueur has argued, conception remained linked to female orgasm until the eighteenth century.[16] Spenser is clearly not relying on Galenic theory for his account of Belphoebe and Amoret's conception, of course, since he is careful not only to leave out the human male principle, but also to assert that Chrysogone was unaware of her impregnation, and that "she conceived/ Withouten pleasure" (3.6.27). Spenser's account, if it can be assimilated to a medical model at all, has more in common with Aristotle than with Galen. Aristotle claimed—in a surprisingly modern series of metaphors that still inform medical accounts of conception—that male material is active and that females supply the passive matter that is acted upon.[17] Spenser grafts the Aristotelian theory onto a classical theory of spontaneous generation, which was frequently associated with the Nile and the overflowing of its banks, and which Spenser, following Ovid, invokes.

Even when Spenser transforms her into the synecdoche of her generative organs, Chrysogone retains a human and a social dimension. It is important to notice in this spontaneous conception that the body of a woman is inserted as the "fertile ground" between sun and water, and although Spenser's description of Chrysogone intermingles metaphors of nature, she still has a link to society. As her pregnancy becomes visible to herself and to others, Chrysogone is overcome with fear, wonder, and shame "to see her belly so upblone" (3.6.9). The secret of conception apparent, she flees the censure that society visits on illegitimate pregnancy. Having reached the wilderness—the space outside the law—and worn out from her flight, she is overcome with a "sad cloud of sleepe" (3.6.10). It is in this "slombry traunce" that Chrysogone "unwares" bears her "two babes, faire as springing day" (3.6.26). As Spenser summarizes, "Unwares she them conceiv'd, unwares she bore:/She bore withouten paine, that she conceived/ Withouten pleasure: ne her need implore/*Lucinaes* aide" (3.6.27). Chrysogone is thus simultaneously present and absent; her body houses a matrix that operates independently of her knowledge, volition, and even sensation. Although much early modern writing on women assimilates them to their sexual and procreative functions, Chrysogone is a woman who seems not to have been touched by Eve's curse. While she receives no sexual pleasure, neither does she suffer the pain of childbirth. Diana and Venus come upon her shortly after she has given birth and when she is still sleeping, and each takes one of the twin daughters as a foster child. Diana brings Belphoebe to a nymph, who will bring her up in "perfect Maydenhed," and Venus takes Amoret to be raised in the Garden of Adonis (3.6.28), thus enacting Spenser's separation of virginal and married chastity.

Chrysogone represents most clearly the partitioning of desire from conception and pain from parturition. In this figuration, Spenser seeks to purge human desire from generation, thus offering the closest human analogue to his Neoplatonic allegory of the generation of souls in the Garden of Adonis. Set in obvious opposition to the begetting of Argante and Olliphant, which imprints lust and perversion in the monstrous flesh of the twin giants, the birth of Amoret and Belphoebe marks its offspring with an ethereal chastity, for though born of woman, they are purified of the desire that stands at the origin of most human conception and are seemingly untainted by the genitality and corollary mortality (signaled in metonymic form by the pain of childbirth) associated with the body of the human mother. Sexuality as a social manifestation is always complicated and ambiguous for Spenser, and this may be one reason why he omits the genitalia from his allegory of the body in Book 2. Although *The Faerie Queene* provides an extraordinary abundance of sexual excess, perversion, and violence that ranges from allegorical figures like Lust, whose monstrous body is shaped like a giant male sexual organ, a kind of walking penis, to Hellenore's orgy with the priapic satyrs, the representations of ideal human sexual love are few.

Indeed, perhaps the most exuberant expression of human generation occurs not in a social context, but in a landscape, the Garden of Adonis, the centerpoint or imaginative matrix of Book 3. If Petrarchism supplies the lexicon of desire, Platonism and Neoplatonism furnish the most complete philosophical systems for joining the ideal and material realms, and it is this conceptual underpinning that shapes the allegory of generation. The Garden of Adonis is both a natural paradise and a topographical description of the female body. It is guarded by a porter, Genius, whose name is derived from the Latin *gignere*, to give birth. At its center stands the Mount of Venus crowned with its grove of "mirtle trees" that drop "sweet gum" from their "fruitfull sides," exuding "dainty odours" and "most sweet delight" (3.6.43), a description that can be as erotically explicit as it is because it has been transposed into landscape, into a natural form. Beneath the mount lies a rocky cave in which Venus has imprisoned the boar, slayer of her lover Adonis, and symbol of death. The incarceration of the mortality that is linked to human birth suspends sexual love in an ideal world where only Time with his "flaggy wings" (3.6.39) disrupts the imaginative plenitude of sexuality and generation. The ideal union flourishes here precisely because it stands apart from the mundane world in which ordinary human beings must desire and couple, a world in which erotic exchange is continually besieged by forces it cannot control and often distorted by the very social fabric that gives it being. If the Garden of Adonis stands as an interlude that is out of time, Spenser's genius in *The Faerie Queene,* the *Amoretti,* and the *Epithalamion* lies in his ability to situate an array of philosophical, psychological, and medical theories about sexuality and generation within political and social contexts. He not only offers powerful representations of early modern sexuality but also invites his readers into his poems in order to confront the dark counterparts of their own urges, to explore the full complexity of their own desires, and to work imaginatively toward the ideals of virtue that he provides.

# NOTES

1. Leah S. Marcus, "Erasing the Stigma of Daughterhood: Mary I, Elizabeth I, and Henry VIII," *Daughters and Fathers,* ed. Lynda E. Boose and Betty S. Flowers (Baltimore: Johns Hopkins UP, 1989) 400–417; 402.
2. Louis Montrose, "The Elizabethan Subject and the Spenserian Text," *Literary Theory/ Renaissance Texts,* ed. Patricia Parker and David Quint (Baltimore: Johns Hopkins UP, 1986) 303–40; 312–15.
3. *Ben Jonson: The Complete Poems,* ed. George Parfitt (1975; New Haven: Yale UP, 1982) 471.
4. Spenser, *The Faerie Queene,* ed. Thomas P. Roche, Jr. (Harmondsworth: Penguin, 1978). All references are to this text.
5. All citations from the *Amoretti* and the *Epithalamion* are from *Spenser's Poetical Works,* ed. J. C. Smith and Ernest de Selincourt (Oxford: Oxford UP, 1912).
6. Harry Berger, Jr., "Busirane and the War Between the Sexes," *Revisionary Play: Studies in the Spenserian Dynamic* (Berkeley: U of California P, 1988) 172–94; 172.
7. Elizabeth I, *Selected Works,* ed. Leah Marcus, Janel Mueller, and Mary Beth Rose (Chicago: U of Chicago P, 2000) 326.
8. Maurice Evans, "Hero," *The Spenser Encyclopedia,* ed. A. C. Hamilton et al. (Toronto: U of Toronto P, 1990) 362a.
9. Plato, *Plato's Cosmology,* trans. Francis MacDonald Cornford (1937; Indianapolis: Bobbs-Merrill Company, 1975) 357.
10. Ian Maclean, *The Renaissance Notion of Woman: A Study in the Fortunes of Scholasticism and Medical Science in European Intellectual Life* (Cambridge: Cambridge UP, 1980) 40.
11. Richard Halpern, "Puritanism and Maenadism in 'A Mask,'" *Rewriting the Renaissance: The Discourses of Sexual Difference in Early Modern Europe,* ed. Margaret W. Ferguson, Maureen Quilligan, and Nancy J. Vickers (Chicago: U of Chicago P, 1986) 94.
12. Halpern 90.
13. Patricia Parker, *Inescapable Romance: Studies in the Poetics of a Mode* (Princeton: Princeton UP, 1979) 54–77.
14. Robert Burton, *Anatomy of Melancholy,* ed. Holbrook Jackson (London: Vintage Books, 1977) 417.
15. Mark Wigley, "Untitled: The Housing of Gender," *Sexuality and Space,* ed. Beatriz Colomina (Princeton: Princeton Architectural Press, 1992) 327–89; 336.
16. Thomas Laqueur, *Making Sex: Body and Gender from the Greeks to Freud* (Boston: Harvard UP, 1990) 25–62.
17. Aristotle, *De Generatione Animalium, The Basic Works,* ed. Richard McKeon (New York: Random House, 1941) 676; Laqueur 47.

# READING LIST

Berger, Harry, Jr. *Revisionary Play: Studies in the Spenserian Dynamic.* Berkeley: U of California P, 1988.
Berry, Philippa. *Of Chastity and Power: Elizabethan Literature and the Unmarried Queen.* London: Routledge, 1989.
Eggert, Katherine. "Spenser's Ravishment: Rape and Rapture in *The Faerie Queene.*" *Representing Rape in Medieval and Early Modern Literature.* Ed. Elizabeth Robertson and Christine M. Rose. New York: Palgrave, 2001. 381–409.

Gregerson, Linda. *The Reformation of the Subject: Spenser, Milton, and the English Protestant Epic.* Cambridge: Cambridge UP, 1995.

Krier, Theresa M. *Gazing on Secret Sights: Spenser, Classical Imitation, and the Decorums of Vision.* Ithaca: Cornell UP, 1990.

—————. "Mother's Sorrow, Mother's Joy: Mourning Birth in Edmund Spenser's Garden of Adonis." *Grief and Gender: 700–1700.* Ed. Jennifer C. Vaught and Lynne Dickson Bruckner. New York: Palgrave Macmillan, 2003. 133–47.

Miller, David Lee. *The Poem's Two Bodies: The Poetics of the 1590 "Faerie Queene."* Princeton: Princeton UP, 1988.

Montrose, Louis. "The Elizabethan Subject and the Spenserian Text." *Literary Theory/ Renaissance Texts.* Ed. Patricia Parker and David Quint. Baltimore: Johns Hopkins UP, 1986. 303–40.

—————. "Spenser and the Elizabethan Political Imaginary." *ELH* 69 (2002): 907–46.

Parker, Patricia. *Literary Fat Ladies: Rhetoric, Gender, Property.* London: Methuen, 1987.

Schwarz, Kathryn. *Tough Love: Amazon Encounters in the English Renaissance.* Durham: Duke UP, 2000.

Stallybrass, Peter. "Patriarchal Territories: The Body Enclosed." *Rewriting the Renaissance: The Discourse of Sexual Difference in Early Modern Europe.* Ed. Margaret W. Ferguson, Maureen Quilligan, and Nancy J. Vickers. Chicago: U of Chicago P, 1986. 123–42.

# 11

# Raleigh, the Queen, and Elizabethan Court Poetry

### William A. Oram

In *Colin Clouts Come Home Againe,* Edmund Spenser's retrospective account of his 1590 trip to the English Court, the poet pictures Sir Walter Raleigh as the Shepherd of the Ocean singing a lament meant for Elizabeth I:

> His song was all a lamentable lay,
> Of great unkindnesse, and of usage hard,
> Of *Cynthia* the Ladie of the sea,
> Which from her presence faultlesse him debard. (164–67)[1]

The poem is a *complaint,* a song of grievance, sung to the queen, who is treated as both a deity—Cynthia, the moon-goddess—and as a cruel mistress who has exiled the Shepherd of the Ocean from her presence. The poet, a suitor, engages in a Court ritual, playing the part of the faithful lover, and his poetry is meant to restore him to the queen's presence and her favor. We do not know if Spenser's poem refers to one of Raleigh's actual complaints, but in *Colin Clout* the song seems to have succeeded: a shepherdess later remarks: "Right well he sure did plaine: / That could great *Cynthiaes* sore displeasure breake, / And move to take him to her grace againe" (173–75).

As Spenser's portrait suggests, Raleigh's poetry was entangled with his life at Court. It was written with a courtier audience in mind, often the queen herself. Yet his relation to the Court was complex. Raleigh stands apart from Elizabeth's other highly placed courtiers as one of the very few who belonged neither to the traditional nobility nor to the class of administrators who had grown up around the Tudor dynasty. The youngest son of a Devonshire gentry family, he had to make his way on his own: his extraordinary rise depended entirely on his personal relation to the queen. That grandly exposed position intensified other ways in which Raleigh stood out, as an innovator in ship-design and naval tactics, an advocate for English colonies in the New World, a man whose curiosity and freedom of conversation gave him an unsavory reputation for unconventional religious beliefs. While his poems often promote his Court career, they also turn a sardonic gaze on the Court world.

## Raleigh and the Court of Elizabeth I

The Court of Elizabeth I differed from that of her father, Henry VIII, in many ways, but the differences center in the fact that the prince was a woman. If Henry, with his six wives, his desire to distinguish himself in war, and his willingness to send his courtiers to the block emphasized his manhood, the virgin Elizabeth, with her surrounding ladies, her dislike of warfare, and her erotically charged relation to her male courtiers, staged herself as female. She did so to make a strength out of what her subjects saw as an obvious weakness. It was felt to be unnatural, as John Knox had written in attacking Mary Tudor, for a queen to govern a nation. "To promote a woman to bear rule, superiority, domination of empire above any realm, nation or city, is repugnant to nature, contumely [an insult] to God [. . .] and finally it is the subversion of good order, of all equity and justice."[2] Women were less rational than men, and government by a woman was bound to bring disaster—a belief that Elizabeth's subjects could support by instancing the unfortunate reign of her sister Mary. During the early years of Elizabeth's rule, everyone expected her to marry and successive Parliaments pleaded with her to do so. Elizabeth remained, however, single and dominant.

She used the fact that she was a woman in many ways. During the first half of the reign her marriage negotiations with various royal suitors, Catholic and Protestant, strengthened her hand internationally and neutralized the threat of invasion from France or Spain. As her reign progressed she emphasized her "marriage" to her people. The summer "progresses" during which Elizabeth and her Court journeyed through southern England and the midlands enabled her to see her subjects and be seen by them. The day of her accession, November 17, came increasingly to be celebrated throughout the kingdom by bell-ringing and bonfires, and at Court by ritualized tilting matches and masques—festivities that, it has been argued, put the Protestant queen in the space left by the discredited Catholic worship of the saints.[3]

Especially during the second half of her reign she encouraged what has come to be called "the cult of Elizabeth." She was celebrated as Astrea, goddess of Justice, or as Flora, goddess of Spring, who was bringing a new Golden Age to the earth. The poetry of the second half of her reign insists on her agelessness, and the faces of her late portraits—the faces that her subjects outside the London were likely to see—remain young. One of Raleigh's poems from the 1590s exemplifies the rhetoric celebrating this goddess-queen. The poem, which seems to originate in a gift-giving ceremony, may have been sung.

> Now we have present made
> To Cynthia, Phoebe, Flora,
> Diana and Aurora,
> Beauty that cannot fade.
>
> A flower of love's own planting,
> A pattern kept by nature
> For beauty, form and stature,
> When she would frame a darling.
>
> She as the valley of Peru,
> Whose summer ever lasteth,
> Time conquering all she mastereth
> By being always new. (1–12)[4]

The poem sets the queen above the mutable world. Its opening lines associate her with a list of classical goddesses, each one an aspect of her divine nature, while the appositional phrases that follow insist on her timelessness. As "a pattern kept by nature" she becomes the equivalent of a Platonic form, source of all "beauty, form and stature" in the world. Yet the very extremity of the praise suggests the importance of what is being denied. Elizabeth's courtiers knew perfectly well that "Time conquering all" was not to be mastered by any human ruler, and so the poem is an exercise in wishing, a turning-aside from truth in ritual celebration. Raleigh's poetry elsewhere insists on the force of time that this poem denies, and during the second half of Elizabeth's reign the disjunction between the aging body of the monarch and the idealized language describing her was a fact of Court life.

With her favorites Elizabeth played the Petrarchan mistress, an unreachable lady whom her courtiers worship and desire. This wooing of the queen was serious play, a game in which both Elizabeth and courtiers assumed roles creating personal ties. The game afforded ground-rules by which the courtier might approach his sovereign, and ask for what he desired, while simultaneously demonstrating his personal loyalty. As Leonard Tennenhouse among others has pointed out, the language of love and the language of political appeal overlapped. "The language of love, particularly of Petrarchanism, was exploited for the terms it had in common with the social and economic vocabulary of patronage. Such words as 'service,' 'suit,' 'suitor,' 'love,' 'favor,' 'envy,' 'scorn,' 'hope,' and 'despair' could be used at the same time to create a romantic fiction and to characterize the dynamics of a real client-patron relationship."[5] This game of courtship informed the chivalric tournaments with which the queen was entertained. If she could not, as her father had, stage herself as a warrior king, triumphant in the tilting yard, she could make herself the central attractive figure for whom the tournament was fought.

A minority of Elizabeth's courtiers wrote poetry, especially in the latter part of Elizabeth's reign, and a number of those wrote, like Raleigh, poems wooing the queen. But as Stephen May has pointed out, courtiers wrote many kinds of verse, from the occasional poems on deaths or marriages written throughout the reign, to the satiric epigrams of Sir John Harington, the sonnet-sequences of Sir Philip Sidney and his circle, and the translations of the psalms begun by him and finished by his sister, Mary, countess of Pembroke.[6] That poetry includes Harington's brilliant translation of Ariosto's *Orlando Furioso* and Fulke Greville's Senecan dramas. May argues that much of the best court poetry can be traced to a small group of courtiers from the circle around the Sidney family—Philip himself, his sister Mary, his brother Robert, his friends Fulke Greville and Edward Dyer, and Harington, who associated himself with the group.

These courtier poets were what Richard Helgerson has called "amateurs": their poetry was incidental to the main business of their lives, which was administrative, military, or diplomatic.[7] The best of them, Sir Philip Sidney, wrote his fictions in the interstices of his public career, and his work went unpublished until after his death. Although the idea that courtiers scrupulously avoided the "stigma of print" has been overstated (in 1595 Harington published his translation of Ariosto with an elaborate introduction), most courtiers chose to circulate their poems in manuscript (May, *Courtier Poets* 157–58). Printed work was addressed to the world at large, available to anyone able to purchase the book. By contrast poetry circulating in manuscript belonged to an elite often related by ties of blood: one was writing for one's own class. As often happens with Raleigh, two courtiers will oppose poems in a courtly game, as statement and counterstatement. When a courtier wrote a poem for print, it was often an act of public commemoration or commendation. Only four of the lyrics that we know Raleigh wrote were printed during the Elizabeth's reign, three of which were commendatory poems for other works and one an elegy for Sir Philip Sidney. The uncertainties of manuscript transmission obscure the authorship of individual poems, and several of "Raleigh's" most famous poems were attributed to him on very slim evidence.[8]

Elizabeth's reign was already halfway over when Raleigh came to Court in late 1581: he was twenty-nine and the queen was nearly fifty. He had spent time at Oxford, had fought for the Huguenots against Catholic forces in France, and had served in Ireland. According to John Aubrey, the seventeenth-century collector of biographical information, "He went into Ireland, where he served in the Wars, and showed much courage and conduct, but he would be perpetually differing with [. . .] Lord Grey, then Lord Deputy, so that at last the Hearing was to be at council table before the Queen, and with so good a Grace and Presence, that the Queen took especial notice of him, and presently preferred him."[9] There was probably no confrontation at the counsel table, but Aubrey is right about Raleigh's characteristic willingness to differ with his commander. If he originally came to Court as an expert on Irish policy, his looks, his intelligence, and his abilities soon recommended themselves to the queen. Sir Robert Naunton, who later came to know him, wrote that she soon "began to be taken with his elocution and loved to hear his reasons to her demands [questions]."[10]

Over the next decade Raleigh rose startlingly in wealth and importance. He gained a series of patents and licenses along with extensive gifts of lands (the thrifty Elizabeth used lands in the gift of the church and the universities as well as lands of attainted traitors). He was knighted in 1585, and in the same year was made vice-admiral for Devon and Cornwall, steward of the Duchy of Cornwall, and warden of the Stanneries, the Cornish tin mines. In 1587 he succeeded Sir Christopher Hatton as captain of the Queen's Guard, which guaranteed him access to his royal mistress. In 1592 he received the ninety-nine-year lease of the manor of Sherborne, in Dorset, which gave him a family seat. Yet he spent money as fast as it came to him, not only on his famously extravagant clothing, but in outfitting ships for exploration and attack on Spanish commerce. Raleigh was one of the militant Protestant faction at Court. He advocated contesting the Spanish claim to the new world by creating English colonies in the Americas, and between 1585 and 1590 he attempted to found a new colony—"Virginia," for the virgin queen—on the coast of what is now North Carolina.

Much of Raleigh's poetry is political. While it often wooed the queen directly, it could do so indirectly, as in a sonnet he published commending Spenser's epic, *The Faerie Queene*.

Me thought I saw the grave, where *Laura* lay,
Within that Temple, where the vestal flame
Was wont to burn, and passing by that way,
To see that buried dust of living fame,
Whose tomb faire love, and fairer virtue kept,
All suddenly I saw the Faery Queene:
At whose approach the soul of *Petrarch* wept,
And from thenceforth those graces were not seen.

For they this Queene attended, in whose steed
Oblivion laid him down on *Laura's* hearse:
Hereat the hardest stones were seen to bleed,
And groans of buried ghosts the heavens did pierce.
Where *Homers* spright did tremble all for grief,
And curst th'access of that celestial thief.

Here Spenser's poem furnishes an excuse for praising Elizabeth. By the sixth line it is she, not the epic, who becomes "the Faery Queen" and she who as a "celestial thief" steals the Graces from Petrarch's Laura.

Raleigh's extraordinary success upset Elizabethan beliefs in inherited rank and made him envied and often hated by others he had displaced. "Truth it is," Naughton writes, the queen "took him for a kind of oracle, which nettled them all."[11] Sir John Harington wrote several epigrams about him as "Paulus":

No man more servile, no man more submis
Than to our Sovereign Lady *Paulus* is.
He doth extol her speech, admire her feature,
He calls himself her vassal, and her creature.
Thus while he daubs his speech with flattery's plaster
And calls himself her slave, he grows our Master.
    Still getting what he list without control
    By singing this old song *re me fa sol.*[12]

Yet Raleigh was never admitted to the privy council—perhaps his militant Protestant agenda made the queen hesitate—and his position with Elizabeth was soon challenged. In 1587 the queen advanced a new favorite, Robert Devereux, earl of Essex, who had come to Court several years earlier, and was, at twenty-two, thirteen years younger than Raleigh. Essex could be charming and charismatic. As an earl he viewed Raleigh as an upstart and on at least one occasion said so to the queen in Raleigh's hearing.

The rivalry informs several of Raleigh's poems, including this complaint to Elizabeth.

Fortune hath taken thee away, my Love
My life's Joy and my soul's heaven above;
Fortune hath taken the away my princess,
My world's delight and my true fancy's mistress.

Fortune hath taken all away from me,
Fortune hath taken all by taking thee,
Dead to all Joys, I only live to woe,
So Fortune now becomes my fancy's foe. (1–8)

This seems a conventional, if intense, opening. Raleigh's histrionic sorrow proclaims his utter dependence on his mistress's love—a love that Fortune has removed. Fortune here seems the traditional medieval goddess ruling capriciously over earthly events. We know that the six-stanza poem was addressed to the queen because in one manuscript we find it paired with her six-stanza reply in the same pentameter couplets.

Ah silly pug, wert thou sore afraid?
Mourn not my Wat, nor be thou so dismayed;
It passeth fickle fortune's power and skill
To force my heart to think thee any ill.[13]

The mournful histrionics yield to an intimate, colloquial comforting. The affectionate nicknames—"silly pug," "my Wat"—insist on the enduring personal relationship.

Yet the context of the earl of Essex's rivalry suggests more in the exchange. Stephen May has argued shrewdly that "Fortune" in Raleigh's poem refers not only to the goddess but also to the earl, whom Fortune has favored and who has attacked him contemptuously as a parvenu.[14] Raleigh is accusing the queen of having favored the earl. Elizabeth's poem, with considerable tact, both accepts and avoids this identification of the earl with Fortune. In speaking of "fickle fortune" she associates Fortune with the traditional Goddess and nowhere does her treatment of Fortune's title suggest anything else. Yet in mentioning that Fortune has not "power or skill / To force" her heart to think badly of him, she addresses the earl's insults, asserting that nothing he can say will alter her affection. Raleigh's complaint has, however, a further dimension. In associating the earl with Fortune Raleigh touches on the opposition, common in Renaissance treatises on honor, between *birth* and *merit* and implies that the earl, whose birth Fortune has favored, in fact lacks merit.[15] Raleigh's rise at Court depended on his abilities, not his birth, and this fact necessarily finds its way into the rivalry. To attack the earl as Fortune is, implicitly, to downgrade the importance of his hereditary rank. The queen's response refuses to notice this dimension of the complaint.

## Raleigh's Ironies

Raleigh's poetry offers evidence, however, that he felt some uneasiness in his role as Court suitor. Court life involved a compromise between two opposing imperatives: the need to stay at the center of power and the need to distinguish oneself in action. It is hard to remember, in an age of cell phones and email, how essential personal presence was in the Renaissance. One exerted influence in person, by argument, insistence, charm. This was especially true in the eroticized interchange between Elizabeth and her favorites. The letters of courtiers away on missions—to France, Ireland, the Low Countries—repeatedly worry that their advice is being disregarded and that their enemies are attacking them at home. To influence the queen successfully, one had to stay at Court. Further, Elizabeth was notoriously reluctant to let her favorites leave the Court to incur danger, and her reluctance may have included the fear that, once away, they would act contrary to her orders.

At the same time, the traditional code of nobility insisted that an aristocrat prove his worth in battle. The history of the Elizabethan Court is full of accounts of Elizabeth's younger courtiers—Sidney, Greville, Essex—sneaking away in order to take ship and fight only to be brought back at the queen's insistence. For a man who took this view of honor seriously, an extended flirtation with an aging queen must have seemed time spent ingloriously. In his long complaint, *The Ocean to Cynthia,* Raleigh looks back on the queen's recalling him from the voyage in 1592 to intercept the Spanish treasure fleet.

To seek new worlds, for gold, for praise, for glory,
To try desire, to try love severed far,
When I was gone she sent her memory
More strong than were ten thousand ships of war,
To call me back, to leave great honor's thought,
To leave my friends, my fortune, my attempt,
To leave the purpose I so long had sought,
And hold both cares and comforts in contempt. (61–68)

The ambitions imaged in the opening lines include not only seeking new worlds but try-ing "love severed far"—a separation from the queen's presence. When she recalls him she forces him to leave everything he values and to "hold both cares and comforts in contempt." Return to the Court means that both the "cares" of the voyage and its "comforts"—its joys of achievement—must be sacrificed for this female ruler.

Elizabeth's favor held a second problem for her courtiers. The queen, who had not married, did not wish her favorites to marry either. Yet the begetting of offspring to con-tinue the family line depended on legal matrimony. Sir Christopher Hatton never mar-ried, but her other favorites—Leicester, Essex, Raleigh—each wed secretly and were afterward forced abjectly to beg the queen's pardon. While each fell temporarily into disfavor, Raleigh received especially harsh treatment, first being imprisoned, then forced to give up his part in the richest prize his privateers had taken, and then banished for five years from Court. The queen eventually restored Raleigh to favor, but her sever-ity suggests that his betrayal was particularly hurtful as, indeed, the evidence suggests. Raleigh may have married Elizabeth Throckmorton, one of the queen's ladies in wait-ing, as early as 1588, but the queen seems not to have learned until 1592.[16] Raleigh and his wife continued to play their parts at court and when, on March 29, 1592, Lady Raleigh gave birth to a child, she returned to Court as if nothing had occurred. When the queen angrily sent both Raleigh and his wife to the Tower in August 1592, she may have realized that Raleigh had continued to court her for months and, possibly for years, after being married.

The so-called Cynthia poems come from this period of disgrace, and they suggest how Raleigh's poetic wooing of the queen can, almost despite itself, transcend its initial purposes. The poems exist in a single manuscript and consist of two short lyrics and a work of more than five hundred lines called *The 21st (and last) Book of the Ocean to Cynthia* followed by a fragment of twenty-two lines, *The beginning of the 22nd Book of the Ocean to Cynthia, entreating of sorrow.* Most critics believe that Raleigh sent them to his sometime ally Robert Cecil to show to the queen but, despite bursts of extraordi-nary eloquence, they would not have done their writer much good. *The Ocean to Cynthia* displays too much self-assertion, too much injured pride and insistent accusa-tion to have pleased its royal audience. Describing the devastating effect of the queen's "marvelous perfections" upon him, Raleigh remarks sardonically:

Yet have these wounders want, which want compassion,
Yet hath her mind some marks of human race,
Yet she will be a woman for a fashion,
So doth she please her virtues to deface. (201–04)

The queen's "wonders" are also "wounders," lacking the virtue of mercy, and the divine Elizabeth is no more than "a woman for a fashion." The passage typifies the poem in its tendency, not to address the queen, but to talk *about* her.

*The Ocean to Cynthia* differs from Raleigh's other poems. It is long where they are short, chaotic and obscure where they are elegantly controlled. While it probably began as an attempt to influence the queen it became a dramatization of self-division, an argument between Raleigh's pride in his loyalty to the queen and his rage at her turning against him. Where one might expect an apology for the marriage, Raleigh stresses the intensity of his suffering and the injustice of his punishment. As May has suggested, the poem proceeds from memory of earlier wooing, to awareness of present bereavement, to declaration of continuing fidelity (*Ralegh* 49). But the line-to-line movement of the work obscures this pattern, insisting throughout on the speaker's present suffering and on the gap between the queen's imagined perfection and her cruel abandonment of her poet-lover.

The poem repeatedly undermines its assertions, contradictions appearing between or even within sentences.[17] Toward the end of the triumphant concluding passage in which Raleigh insists on the unchangeableness of his love, he moves into simile:

> Yet as the air in deep caves under ground
> Is strongly drawn when violent heat hath rent
> Great clefts therein, till moisture do abound,
> And then the same, imprisoned and up-pent,
> Breaks out in earthquakes, tearing all asunder,
> So in the center of my cloven heart—
> My heart, to whom her beauties were such wonder—
> Lies the sharp poisoned heat of that love's dart,
> Which till all break and all dissolve to dust,
> Thence drawn it cannot be, or therein known.
> There, mixed with my heart blood, the fretting rust
> The better part hath eaten, and outgrown. (450–61)

The main *point* of the passage comparing the heat causing the earthquake with the heat of love's dart is the speaker's fidelity: he will never cease to love. But the simile's *effect* is to stress that love's destructive power. The "fretting rust" of the dart, with its associations of dirt and decay, has "eaten and outgrown" the lover's "better part." This is powerful writing, but its energy undermines its intended appeal to the queen's love.

While *The Ocean to Cynthia* is a profoundly ambivalent poem, caught up in the world of courtship, other lyrics by Raleigh take a stance apart from the Court, anatomizing its limitations. In "The Lie" Raleigh looks sardonically at the whole world in which he was so invested. The poem's immediate predecessors are Skelton's and Wyatt's satires against the Court, and perhaps Gascoigne's long satiric complaint, *The Steel Glass*. But Raleigh's opening suggests his wider focus.

> Go soul, the body's guest,
> Upon a thankless errand,
> Fear not to touch the best,
> The truth shall be thy warrant:

Go, since I needs must die,
   And give the world the lie. (1–6)

The speaker prepares himself to die by speaking the truth to the world. "World" here opposes "Soul" because traditional Christian discourse associates "the world" with the temptations that turn one aside from salvation. Preparing for heaven, the speaker "give[s] the world the lie," calling it a liar and, by implication, challenging it to a duel. Yet in repudiating the world the speaker also repudiates the values that others would have identified with Raleigh himself.

The subsequent attack is necessarily miscellaneous, asserting in terse and often paradoxical epigrams the worthlessness of everything that "worldly" men value. Seemingly powerful potentates (including Raleigh's queen) are in fact helplessly forced to do what others want. They "live / Acting but others action / Not loved unless they give, / Not strong but by a faction" (13–16). Occasionally Raleigh seems to refer to his enemy the earl of Essex:

Tell men of high condition
   That rule affairs of state,
Their purpose is ambition,
   Their practice only hate. (19–22)

But this attack is followed by another that is more personal:

Tell them that brave it most
   They beg for more by spending,
Who in their greatest cost
   Like nothing but commending. (25–28)

Those that "brave it most" include Raleigh himself, for the image of a man "braving it" is quite specific. To *brave it* is to act aggressively, but it is also to wear costly clothes. This conspicuous consumption, for which Raleigh was famous, involves the courtier in a self-defeating cycle of extravagance and neediness as he begs for more by spending. Yet all this effort arises from the desire for "nothing but commending"—nothing but the queen's praise.

The poem thus asserts the vanity of all those things that Raleigh prided himself on—wit, honor, favor, wisdom, learning. The directions to the soul end with a final irony:

So when thou hast, as I
   Commanded thee, done blabbing,
Although to give the lie
   Deserves no less than stabbing,
Stab at thee he that will,
   No stab thy soul can kill. (73–78)

To speak thus is to "blab," an ugly colloquialism, to expose the emperor's (or the World's) new clothes as illusion. While we cannot know whether or not Raleigh actually believed in a conventional Christian God, he here invokes Christian standards to attack the world's vanity.

"The Lie's" subversiveness registers in the ferocity of the attacks on it. There were a number of these, including two angry poems, probably by the earl of Essex, attacking Raleigh *ad hominem:* "The lie's descent is over base to tell; / To us it came from Italy, to them it came from hell" (3–4).[18] The reference to the poem's "base" descent suggests Raleigh's gentry origins. The rest of the response insists that "The Lie's" condemnation is too general: "You argue from particulars, your reason is not good" (16). The Court has both good and bad inhabitants: "Confess in glittering court all are not gold that shine / Yet say one pearl and much fine gold grows in that princely mine" (7–8). The queen, of course, is the pearl that Raleigh's poem has implicitly dismissed. This answer thus avoids the real target of "The Lie," which is the emptiness of the values that the Court holds dear.

One of Raleigh's most brilliant poems suggests this emptiness without the support of a Christian standard. "Nature that Washed her hands in Milk" begins as a sardonic parody of the language of Petrarchan compliment—the language with which one addresses the queen—and turns into something quite different.

> Nature, that washed her hands in milk
>     And had forgot to dry them,
> Instead of earth took snow and silk
>     At Love's request to try them
> If she a mistress could compose
> To please Love's fancy out of those. (1–6)

Love (or a lover) asks for woman and Nature obliges, using the stock clichés of Petrarchan poetry—hair like gold, complexion like snow. What "Love's fancy" (his *fantasy* or imagination) wants is a Petrarchan pinup, a doll with the physical beauty of the traditional poet's lady. But the imagination is a suspect faculty, easily swayed by the desire that appears unmistakably in the second stanza.

> Her eyes he would should be of light
>     A violet breath and lips of jelly,
> Her hair not black, nor over-bright,
>     And of the softest down her belly;
> As for her inside he'll have it
> Only of wantonness and wit. (7–12)

The first line of the stanza draws on the cliché that mistress' eyes are suns, but the following images descend from sight to touch. "Lips of jelly" suggest an edible woman, and this stress on sensuous appetite reappears in the softness of the lady's "belly." Love wants his lady's "inside" to match her outward appearance, limiting it to "wantonness and wit." The third verse brings this satiric portrait to a close as erring Love is hoist on his own petard. Because he forgot to give the lady a capacity to love, she possesses the traditional heart of stone, frustrating him while perhaps playing him false. At this point the poem seems to mock the short-sightedness of the lover's fantasies.

The poem could end here, and perhaps at one stage in its composition it did. For the next verse—a second act—comes as a surprise. Time appears on the scene turning "snow and silk and milk to dust" (24). The brilliant, playful ironies of the first three stanzas abruptly encounter a grimmer and less manageable truth. Love is not only frustrated but mortal, and with the new awareness of Time's power, the poem's values shift.

> The light, the belly, lips and breath
>     He dims, discovers, and destroys;
> With those he feeds, but fills not, Death,
>     Which sometimes were the food of joys;
> Yea, Time doth dull each lively wit,
> And dries all wantonness with it. (25–30)

Earlier the poem treats the Lady's fantasy-body contemptuously: the comic rhymes of "jelly" and "belly" underline the lust behind the portrait. Now, however, "the light, the belly, lips and breath" become "the food of joys," affirmations of life, to be lost and mourned. The final stanza is a desolate apostrophe:

> O cruel Time, which takes in trust
>     Our youth, our joys, and all we have,
> And pays us but with age and dust;
>     Who in the dark and silent grave,
> When we have wandered all our ways,
> Shuts up the story of our days. (31–36)

The stanza's power comes partly from the absence of the command or request that usually follows an apostrophe. The whole stanza simply describes Time, suggesting that all the speaker can do is call it cruel and describe what it does. The dominant metaphor of the stanza is financial: Time is a fraudulent banker who "takes in trust" all that we have and returns to us nothing more than the dust into which our bodies decay. Time is also a reader who "shuts up the story of our days" between the covers of the grave. The poem has no silver lining, no conventional emphasis on the immortal soul. Instead we wander our uncertain ways in this world and expire.

Although "Nature, that washed her Hands in Milk" may not seem to address the Court world, it responds to Raleigh's awareness of the difference between the fantasies of wishing so evident in the praises of an immortal Elizabeth and the actuality of time. Yet Raleigh's years at Elizabeth's Court were, for all their uncertainties, the high point in his career. Shortly after the accession of James I in 1603 he would be imprisoned on a charge of treason and, after fifteen years, beheaded. Naughton writes, "Sir Walter Ralegh was one that it seems fortune had picked out of purpose of whom to make an example or to use as her tennis ball thereby, to show what she could do, for she tossed him up of nothing, and to and fro and from thence down to little more than that wherein she found him, a bare gentleman" (71). While the poetry that he wrote during this earlier period often promotes his relations with the queen, it also comments sardonically on the evanescence of the success for which he and other courtiers were striving.

## NOTES

1. Quotation from *The Yale Edition of the Shorter Poems of Edmund Spenser*, ed. William A. Oram et al. (New Haven: Yale UP, 1989).
2. John Knox, *The First Blast of the Trumpet against the monstrous regiment of Women*, ed. Edward Arber (London, 1878) 11.
3. Roy Strong, *The Cult of Elizabeth: Elizabethan Portraiture and Pageantry* (London: Thames and Hudson, 1977) 125–28, 164–85.

4. Quotations from Raleigh's poetry follow Michael Rudick, ed., *The Poems of Sir Walter Ralegh: A Historical Edition* (Tempe, AZ : Renaissance English Text Society, 1999). Spelling and punctuation have been modernized.
5. Leonard Tennenhouse, "Sir Walter Ralegh and the Culture of Cliantage," *Patronage in the Renaissance*, ed. Guy Fitch Lytle and Stephen Orgel (Princeton: Princeton UP, 1982) 238.
6. Stephen W. May, *Elizabethan Courtier Poets* (1991; Ashville, NC: Pagasus P, 1999) 225.
7. Richard Helgerson, *Self-Crowned Laureates: Spenser, Jonson, Milton and the Literary System* (Berkeley: U California P, 1983) 25–34.
8. In *The Poems of Sir Walter Ralegh* xxxix, lxv, and lxxix–lxxiv, Ruddick doubts Raleigh's authorship of "Walsingham," "The Nymph's Reply to the Shepherd," and "The Passionate Man's Pilgrimage."
9. John Aubrey, *Aubrey's Brief Lives,* ed. Oliver Lawson Dick (1949; Ann Arbor: Michigan UP, 1962) 253.
10. Sir Robert Naughton, *Fragmenta Regalia or Observations of Queen Elizabeth, Her Times and Favorites*, ed. John S. Cerovski (Cranbury, NJ: Associated UP, 1985) 73.
11. Naughton 73.
12. *Re fa me sol* (macaronic): "the king makes me [a] sun." Text from Norman Egbert McLure, ed., *The Epigrams of Sir John Harington* (Philadelphia, 1926) 183.
13. Quoted from May, *Courtier Poets* 319.
14. Stephen W. May, *Sir Walter Ralegh* (Boston: G.K. Hall [Twayne Publishers], 1989) 31–33; see also *Courtier Poets* 119–21.
15. See, for instance, the debate in Giovanni Battista Nenna, *A discourse whether a noble man by birth or a gentleman by desert is greater in nobilitie,* trans. Sir William Jones (London, 1600).
16. The fullest account of Raleigh's marriage occurs in A. L. Rowse, *Ralegh and the Throckmortons* (London: Macmillan, 1962), but for the date of 1588 see Pierre Lafranc, "La Date du Mariage de Sir Walter Ralegh: un Document Inédit," *Ètudes Anglaises* 9 (1956): 193–212.
17. Stephen Greenblatt analyzes these contradictions in *Sir Walter Ralegh: The Renaissance Man and His Roles* (New Haven: Yale UP, 1973) 80–93.
18. Qtd. from May, *Courtier Poets,* 265.

## READING LIST

Greenblatt, Stephen. *Sir Walter Ralegh: The Renaissance Man and His Roles.* New Haven: Yale UP, 1973.

Lacey, Robert. *Sir Walter Ralegh.* New York: Atheneum, 1974.

Lefranc, Pierre. *Sir Walter Ralegh, Ècrivain, L'oevere et les idées.* Paris: Librarie Armond Colin, 1968.

Marotti, Arthur F. *Manuscript, Print and the English Renaissance Lyric.* Ithica: Cornell UP, 1995.

May, Stephen W. *Sir Walter Ralegh.* Boston: G.K. Hall (Twayne Publishers), 1989.

————. *The Elizabethan Courtier Poets.* Ashville: U of North Carolina at Ashville (Pegasus P), 1999.

Montrose, Louis. "Eliza, Queen of shepheardes' and the Pastoral of Power." *English Literary Renaissance* 10 (1980): 153–82.

Rowse, Alfred Leslie. *Ralegh and the Throckmortons.* London: Macmillan, 1962.

Ruddick, Michael, ed. *The Poems of Sir Walter Ralegh: A Historical Edition.* Tempe, AZ: Renaissance English Text Society, 1999.

Somerset, Anne. *Elizabeth I.* New York: Knopf, 1991.

Strong, Roy. *The Cult of Elizabeth: Elizabethan Portraiture and Pageantry.* London: Thames and Hudson, 1977.

————. *Gloriana: The Portraits of Elizabeth I.* New York: Thames and Hudson, 1987.

Wallace, Willard M. *Sir Walter Raleigh.* Princeton: Princeton UP, 1959.

# 12

# Marlowe's Erotic Verse

## *Alan Sinfield*

Christopher Marlowe was probably a student at Cambridge when he chose to translate the love elegies of the renowned Roman poet Ovid: the *Amores*. By allowing them to circulate, Marlowe made a typically controversial intervention in current ideas about sex, gender, love, marriage, and power. Smart young gentlemen at the universities and the Inns of Court in the 1590s acclaimed the elegies for their relaxed, sophisticated, and illuminating approach to love and sexuality. The authorities responded differently, however. When ten of the poems were printed in 1599, bound up with the satiric *Epigrams* of Sir John Davies, they were called in by the bishops to be burnt. This was six years after Marlowe's violent death in 1593.

Ovid, too, was controversial in his lifetime (43 BCE–17 CE). The emperor Caesar Augustus (Octavius in Shakespeare's *Julius Caesar* and *Antony and Cleopatra*) banished him from Rome in 8 CE for unidentified misdeeds. The story is told by Ben Jonson in his play *Poetaster* (1601–02), where Ovid's offenses are disrespect toward the gods and sleeping with the emperor's daughter. These offenses, in fact, correlate with the two aspects of classical culture that embarrassed Elizabethan Christianity: the representation of the gods, who were multiple and often written of slightingly; and ideas about sexuality, which were far more casual about sex outside marriage, including same-sex liaisons.

There was no prospect of banishing Ovid and the classics from early modern England, however; their writing was so fluent and confident that it could not but impress. Translations, such as Marlowe's, were a major resource through which Elizabethans sought to deepen and broaden their culture. Some strove to contain Ovid's influence by strenuous interpretation. Arthur Golding's translation of the *Metamorphoses* was published with a moralizing epistle in 1567. For instance, the passionately erotic merging of Salmacis and her beloved Hermaphroditus (of whom more shortly) is said, by Golding, to demonstrate that idleness is the nurse of voluptuousness, making men effeminate and weak.[1]

The three books of poems which make up the *Amores* are, rather loosely, about the poet's wooing of Corinna (some of them are written to her, others are about their situation). Although Corinna is not a consistent character and the narrative is not continuous, we do get a set of interlocking ideas and attitudes, amounting to a model of intimate relations; a scenario, we might say. The lover, his mistress, the husband, the slave girl, and the eunuch are, we shall see, offered as particular figures in particular situations.

The poet opens with the standard theme of innumerable poems and songs of courtship, a vow of everlasting fidelity:

I love but one, and her I love change never,
If men have faith, I'll live with thee for ever.

The years that fatal destiny shall give
I'll live with thee, and die, ere thou shalt grieve. (1:3, 15–18)[2]

This ideal is maintained by the poet through to the end. Yet Corinna suddenly complicates the scenario: the poet reports that an old bawd has been teaching her the tricks of
a prostitute (1:8), and now she has asked him for payment (1:10). The poet wants to
view sexual love as something they share—"the pleasure / Which man and woman reap
in equal measure"—and promises to eternize Corinna by his art (1:10, 35–36, 60). But
she regards the liaison as a mercenary opportunity.

To work out what is happening here we need to know something about the Roman
sex/gender system. Marriage was scarcely regulated by the state; women had considerable independence in choice of a partner, and in the household; divorce was not difficult
to obtain. In 18 BCE, when Ovid was twenty-five, Augustus introduced laws making
adultery a crime and penalizing celibacy and childless marriages.[3] At the same time, historians detect in Ovid's time a new emphasis on the personal relationship between husband and wife. Though passionate sexuality might be thought out of place in marriage,
reciprocal commitment was commended.[4] This picture is drawn from notably high-
minded texts, which may explain why it is at odds with the Ovidian image of the husband as suspicious, tyrannical, foolish, and deserving to be betrayed.

This unstable mixture of fidelity and exploitation, liberty and restraint, may begin
to account for the co-presence of the idealism that inspires the poet, and the cynicism
that allows Corinna to ask for money. The further factor is slavery: Roman expansion
overseas led to the accumulation of innumerable slaves. Accomplished freed women,
attached only loosely to the social system, found opportunities as high-class courte-
sans; meanwhile many tied slaves afforded scope for bribed or enforced sex. Female
and male slaves, including eunuchs, figure continually in the *Amores*—tempting and
resisting the lovers, spying and informing on them, passing messages and opening
doors. When he is obliged to deny Corinna's accusation that he has seduced her maid,
the poet pretends to resent the idea that he might desire a slave: "With Venus' game
who will a servant grace? / Or any back made rough with stripes embrace?" (2:7,
21–22). Would he make love with a slave who has been flogged by his mistress? It
transpires in the next elegy that the answer is yes. Indeed, if the maid refuses to
accommodate him again, the poet threatens to procure her punishment by betraying the
liaison to Corinna. Marlowe replanted this scenario of violence, deceit, and exaltation
in Elizabethan England—which was, as we shall see in a moment, partly similar and
partly different.

Ovid places his commitment to love and poetry in an incessant standoff with the
expectations of society and the state for a man of his class. He intended to sing of military matters, he says at the beginning, but Cupid compels him to deal with love (1:1).
He is accused of being idle, refusing the responsibilities of warfare and the law. He re-
sponds with a dissident love ethic and an alternative system of rewards. He seeks eter-
nal fame: "To verse let kings give place, and kingly shows" (1:15, 33). That is why
Corinna should not expect payment: "So likewise we will through the world be rung, /
And with my name shall thine be always sung" (1:3, 25–6). Corinna is not persuaded.
Later on in the sequence she prefers a soldier, and the wealth he has gained by fighting.
The poet is not just disappointed, he is baffled and repulsed by the disjunction in

values: "Canst touch that hand wherewith someone lie dead? / Ah whither is thy breast's soft nature fled?" (3:7, 17–18). He is back where he was, singing outside the door, while Corinna seems unconcerned about her new suitor's murderous complicity with the state.

The poet's assertion of alternative values is undermined by his inability to forsake the imagery of military conquest. It suits so well the scenario of tormented love: whatever the outcome, someone is defeated and humiliated—the lover, the mistress, the husband, the slave. The poet is led in triumph by Cupid:

> Lo, I confess, I am thy captive I,
> And hold my conquer'd hands for thee to tie.
> What need'st thou war? I sue to thee for grace;
> With arms to conquer armless men is base. (1:2, 19–22)

Correspondingly, when Corinna accepts him it is a conquest, paralleling infamous rapes in mythology (2:12). The poet means to eternize his art, but mediates into personal life the violence and exploitation of the warfare state. It is because of these internal contradictions, we may suppose, that the poet's dissident love ethic doesn't work. Corinna asks for money and prefers a soldier because she is not persuaded that poetry offers a viable alternative currency.

In his moments of highest aspiration, the poet looks for love to transform society. At other times, perhaps, he is saying something else. Despite his repudiation of the warfare state, the poet seems aware that sexual passion is involved with power. He complains that being in love with two women doubles the grief, but really he enjoys the challenge. "He's happy who love's mutual skirmish slays, / And to the gods for that death Ovid prays" (2:10, 29–30). Passion thrives on power; the most intimate and sexy incidents involve an element of violence. He beats his mistress, and in return offers himself for punishment: "Bind fast my hands, they have deserved chains" (1:7, 1). Danger is stimulating. When the poet, Corinna, and her husband are at a banquet, he urges her to operate an elaborate system of signals, so that they can enjoy their intimacy even in the husband's presence (1:4).

In the most celebrated elegy, on Corinna coming to bed, power-play is titillating. The poet sets an idyllic bedroom scene, with light twinkling through the shutters as in a leafy wood. Corinna's show of resistance is thrilling:

> I snatch'd her gown; being thin, the harm [concealment]
>      was small,
> Yet striv'd she to be cover'd therewithall,
> And striving thus as one that would be cast [overcome],
> Betray'd herself, and yielded at the last. (1:5, 13–16)

Though the thin gown scarcely impedes the poet's view, it is sexy to snatch it, so that she can surrender. As well as a representation of the sex/gender system, Ovid and Marlowe supply an awareness of its fantasy structure and its potential to excite. "Jove send me more such afternoons as this" (1:5, 26).

It should be no surprise that the Ovidian scenario spoke so effectively to Elizabethans. They did not have slaves or eunuchs (generally speaking) or perpetual warfare, but, like the Romans, they had arbitrary arrest, torture, and public executions. Both states employed informers and spies (Marlowe, for instance). The Elizabethan government was less autocratic; its limited and frail parliamentary system was more like that which had been overthrown in Rome when Augustus established the empire. In both societies some women were demanding to be taken seriously, and there were moves to make marriage more of a personal and loving relation. In both there was scandal, satire, and legislation about (supposed) sexual immorality. Marlowe's contemporaries had a religion that absorbed emotional commitment and encouraged the development of a conscience.

These inexact correspondences allowed Elizabethans to recognize much of the scenario of the *Amores,* while finding also compelling representations of thoughts and images that they might otherwise have only dreamt of. The Petrarchan tradition prizes chaste worship; the *Amores* depict passion unconfined, and noble aspirations tangled in with lust and selfishness. The exploitative, commercial, and flippant aspects of Ovid's elegies were unsurprising in ancient Rome, whereas in Tudor England they offered new ways of thinking about sexual expression. Elizabethans found in them a vision of love and, in the same breath, a recipe for abuse. What is so striking about Marlowe is the rapidity with which he assimilated all this. In *Hero and Leander* he finds further potential in Ovid, and a more confident and individual voice.

The main source for *Hero and Leander,* which Marlowe wrote probably in the year of his death, is Musaeus's popular fifth-century Greek version of the story, but the main influence is Ovid.[5] As in the *Amores,* the young man is the wooer; the impediment, rather than a husband, is Hero's vow to be Venus's nun. The idealism of love at first sight and "equal balance" is again offered (1:176; 2:32), alongside an element of manipulation in Leander's approach. Both Corinna's lover and Leander's love thrive on resistance, as a proud horse becomes more spirited when it is reined in (3:4, 13–16; 2:141–45).

What is much diminished in *Hero and Leander* is the language of conquest. The gods contribute an air of "heady riot, incest, rapes" (1:144), but the current deities are not hostile. Cupid is disruptive, but not in a vaunting way. Hero and Leander dwell in a picturesque world of beautiful humans, capricious mythological personages, and animated natural elements, in which love is fun. The ambiance is quite different from George Chapman's moralizing continuation of the story, which is sometimes published with it. Marlowe's poem takes its tone from Ovid's *Metamorphoses:* a sequence of stories featuring transformations into animals, birds, trees, flowers, springs, and stones, which come about mainly as ways of rescuing or punishing nymphs, maidens, and boys who have attracted the lascivious attentions of gods and heroes. The manner is part folklore, part cautionary tale, part fairy tale. The overall impression is of human and divine beings as shape-changing, mobile, and fleeting, unable to stabilize even the individual body.

Hero and Leander do not appear in the *Metamorphoses,* but in Marlowe's poem their characters are strangely inconstant (subject to metamorphosis), especially around gender roles. Leander is an eager suitor, yet he doesn't know what to do with Hero when he gets her into bed. His ignorance about manly behavior belies any notion that it is simply natural for a boy to want genital intercourse with a girl. Hero is confused in another way: she wants to defend her honor, but takes the initiative by allowing Leander to know her thoughts: "'Were I the saint he worships, I would hear him'" (1, 179). Again: "'Come thither,'" she says, after a sequence of incitements and discouragements: "As she spake this, her tongue tripp'd, / For unawares 'Come thither' from her slipp'd" (1:357–8). Is this the first Freudian slip in English poetry?

The naivety of Leander and the forwardness of Hero amount to a transposition of conventional gender roles. Indeed, Leander is taken for a girl by some of his admirers. "Some swore he was a maid in man's attire, / For in his looks were all that men desire" (1:82–3). The narration colludes with the feminization of Leander by portraying his physical appearance as fully as Hero's. Indeed, more so; Gregory Bredbeck remarks: "Hero is all clothing and words, but Leander is a *presence* to be dealt with."[6]

> I could tell ye
> How smooth his breast was, and how white his belly,
> And whose immortal fingers did imprint
> That heavenly path with many a curious dint,
> That runs along his back. (1:65–69)

Yet other observers know Leander to be a man and urge him on to "amorous play" (1:88). In a long and dogged speech he tries to talk Hero into compliance, using aggressive arguments such as were attributed to the old bawd in the *Amores* (brass shines with handling, good clothes ask to be worn, houses keep better when they are occupied; 1:8, 51–52; 1:231–40).

Marlowe's ambivalent gendering of Leander prompts two scenarios. One involves his relations with Hero. As in the *Amores,* Marlowe broaches the entrancing thought that an equal love may transcend worldly conditions:

> Sweet are the kisses, the embracements sweet
> When like desires and affections meet,
> For from the earth to heaven is Cupid rais'd,
> When fancy is in equal balance peis'd [weighed]. (2:29–32)

The main impediment to this exalted, symmetrical vision is male dominance. In *Hero and Leander* Marlowe evades this by merging the two youngsters into an ideal androgyny. Hero, when she is most decisive in her approach to Leander, is compared to Salmacis:

> Therefore unto him hastily she goes,
> And, like light Salmacis, her body throws
> Upon his bosom. (2:45–47)

In the *Metamorphoses* Salmacis is the Ovidian nymph who entwines her body with that of the reluctant Hermaphroditus, to the extent that they merge into an androgynous figure:

> [A]s they lay together, their bodies were united and from being two persons they became one. As when a gardener grafts a branch on to a tree, and sees the two unite as they grow, and come to maturity together, so when their limbs met in that clinging embrace the nymph and the boy were no longer two, but a single form, possessed of a dual nature, which could not be called male or female, but seemed to be at once both and neither.[7]

In this fantasmatic amalgamation gender difference is rejected. It is at this point that Leander proves himself most spectacularly uninterested in genital sex:

> And as a brother with his sister toyed,
> Supposing nothing else was to be done,

Now he her favour and good will had won.
But know you not that creatures wanting sense
By nature have a mutual appetence [. . .]? (2:52–56)

Animals are drawn spontaneously to mate, but not Leander; he only "suspected / Some amorous rites or other were neglected" (2:63–64). It is Hero accidentally rubbing against him that awakens his desire.

Despite his naivety, Leander's eventual congress with Hero reverts to imagery of conquest and rape:

Love is not full of pity (as men say)
But deaf and cruel where he means to prey.
Even as a bird, which in our hands we wring,
Forth plungeth, and oft flutters with her wing,
She trembling strove. (2:287–91)

This violent image is tempered by more slapstick, as Leander fumbles his way into Hero's bed, and by her acquiescence ("In such wars women use but half their strength," 2:296). But in the scenario of Hero and Leander gender assertion triumphs eventually over androgynous harmony.

A second scenario concerns Leander's relations with the sea god, Neptune. Because he is girlish, we are told, men perceive him as a sex object. Bredbeck compares Michael Drayton's *Endymion and Phoebe* (1595):

And Jove oft-times bent to lascivious sport,
And coming where Endymion did resort,
Hath courted him, inflamed with desire,
Thinking some nymph was cloth'd in boy's attire.[8]

In *Dido Queen of Carthage* Venus complains that Jupiter is toying with his cup-bearer, Ganymede, "that female wanton boy," instead of attending to the founding of Rome.[9]

Neptune takes Leander initially for Ganymede: "The lusty god embrac'd him, call'd him love, / And swore he never should return to Jove" (2:167–68). Neptune's lovemaking uses delightfully the idea of the waves lapping through and around the swimming body:

He watch'd his arms, and as they open'd wide
At every stroke, betwixt them would he slide
And steal a kiss, and then run out and dance,
And as he turn'd, cast many a lustful glance,
And threw him gaudy toys to please his eye,
And dive into the water, and there pry
Upon his breast, his thighs, and every limb,
And up again, and close beside him swim,
And talk of love. (2:183–91)

Leander's response is characteristically naive: "'You are deceiv'd, I am no woman, I'" (2:192). But it is not a female that Neptune wants, but a female wanton boy—which

Leander is for some of the time. Leander extricates himself only when Neptune goes to find gifts for him. Compare Corinna's demand for payment in elegy 1:10: inequality may encourage a mercenary attitude. Ovid's friend Tibullus comments: "Unfortunately our age has grown used to some miserable practices—/ Nowadays a tender young boy will expect a present."[10] Ganymede bargains with Jupiter in *Dido:*

> I would have a jewel for mine ear,
> And a fine brooch to put in my hat,
> And then I'll hug with you an hundred times.[11]

We should observe that Marlowe's two scenarios for Leander—his relations with Hero and with Neptune—may not be regarded as embodying a progressive politics today.[12] We may prefer to believe that heterosexuality can be fun and nongenital without being ridiculous; that a boy can be attractive when he is masculine, feminine, or neither in particular; and that power disparity in a relationship need not mean that everything comes down to money.

Ovid is remarkable for his lack of interest in same-sex love, unlike other poets of his time—Virgil, Catullus, Horace, Tibullus—for whom the loves of women and boys appear equally exciting and equally acceptable. However, this is true only as long as the man retains his dignity and command. If same-sex passion was far more legitimate in Rome than it has generally been in the Christian centuries, that was true only of the "active" partner. To subject oneself to another male was deeply shaming. In this context, we may wonder at the representation of Cupid as a conquering young man in the *Amores,* and in other classical and Renaissance writing. Why was it through imagined submission to a tyrannical master that impressionable youths were supposed to approach manly sexual love? The poet of the *Amores* surrenders to Cupid:

> I, lately caught, will have a new-made wound,
> And captive-like be manacled and bound;
> Good Meaning, Shame, and such as seek love's wrack
> Shall follow thee, their hands tied at their back. (1:2, 29–32)

Perhaps this illustrates that, while manliness may appear to be about impressing women, actually it is asserted through measuring up to other men. Actually, Cupid is not always imperious. In *Hero and Leander* he is an infant, as befits the more playful tone of that poem. At one point in the *Amores* he appears surprisingly accessible: opposing Corinna's attempt to charge for her favors, the poet declares: "Love is a naked boy, his years sans stain, / And hath no clothes, but open doth remain" (1:10, 15–16). This version of Cupid is submissive, rather than dominating. Perhaps the conventional categories, active/passive, were not so invariably distinct as the prevailing ideology of gender suggested. There were rumors that both Julius Caesar and Augustus Caesar had taken the passive role with men at some time.[13]

In an interesting analysis of the ten Marlovian elegies published initially in 1599, Ian Frederick Moulton argues that these poems spoke to an Elizabethan anxiety about effeminate weakness in men—which could mean a man devoting himself too blindly to women, as well as assuming a passive role with men. Opponents of love poetry, such as Stephen Gosson (*The Schoole of Abuse,* 1579) and Philip Stubbes (*The Anatomie of Abuses,* 1583), blamed it for effeminate weakness, undermining manhood and the state. Moulton sees a narrative pattern in which love is "a fall into impotence and powerlessness, a loss of manly strength, and even of identity."[14] The culmination of this theme is elegy 3:6, where the poet finds himself unwontedly impotent: despite his mistress' efforts, he droops like a wilting rose (3:6, 66).

Effeminate weakness is certainly a preoccupation in many texts of the time. Tamburlaine (in Marlowe's play), when he conceives a passion for Zenocrate, exclaims:

> But how unseemly is it for my sex,
> My discipline of arms and chivalry,
> My nature, and the terror of my name,
> To harbour thoughts effeminate and faint![15]

He reassures himself that his behavior is that of a warrior. Tamburlaine finds it intolerable when his oldest son, Calyphas, announces his dislike for warfare and preference for residing with his mother (2, I.iii.65–73). An "effeminate brat," Tamburlaine calls him as he kills him (2, IV.i.160).

As Jonathan Goldberg suggests elsewhere in this book, same-sex passions were not so foreign to Elizabethans as might be supposed. What is striking in *Hero and Leander* is how casually same-sex passion is mentioned. "For in his looks were all that men desire" (1:84), the narrator remarks of Leander, as though it were taken for granted that men desire boys. Even the most reluctant men may be attracted; Hippolytus, for instance, who resisted the advances of his stepmother, Phaedra, would have been enamored of Leander's beauty (1:77–78). The seductiveness of boys was, in fact, a key objection of antitheater campaigners, such as Stubbes and Gosson. Both women and men, they alleged, would be attracted sexually by cross-dressed boy actors; this is why they had to be stopped. In Shakespeare's *Midsummer Night's Dream* both Oberon and Titania desire the lovely Indian boy.[16]

Generally, though, same-sex passion drew little attention. The preoccupation, in writing of this period, is with women disturbing the system—resisting arranged marriages, running off with the wrong man, not bearing (male) children, committing adultery, producing illegitimate offspring, becoming widows and exercising the power of that position.[17] Relations between men and women affected the regulation of lineage, alliance, and property, and hence might profoundly disrupt the social order and the male psyche. Same-sex passion became threatening if, as in the instance of Marlowe's *Edward II,* it was allowed to interfere with other responsibilities.

In Bruce Smith's reading, *Hero and Leander* amounts to an opportunity for a lustful male reader to fantasize. The protagonists' experience is inconclusive and frustrating; the desire between the reader and the characters is more important. Noting that the story appears unfinished, Smith wonders: "Did Marlowe lose interest because there were no more opportunities for homoerotic titillation?"[18] This is well observed, but perhaps rather austerely framed. It does seem likely that Marlowe composed the part of the story that engaged his imagination and that the writing is designed to implicate the reader by arousing his or her sexual interest. But this is not unusual in literature and art; many of the great classical paintings may be regarded as soft pornography for the upper classes. Engaging with such depictions may lead the reader into unaccustomed identifications. When Neptune accosts the swimming boy, for instance, do you see yourself as Leander, Neptune, Hero, the waves, the narrator, or none of these?

In fact, seduction is what Marlowe's poetry is all about. "The Passionate Shepherd to His Love" ("Come live with me, and be my love") was first printed in 1599 as a poem of four stanzas, in the collection *The Passionate Pilgrim*. The six-stanza version usually printed today appeared in another collection, *England's Helicon,* in 1600. In a simple verse movement, the poem evokes a charming rural scene of "valleys, groves, hills and fields, / Woods, or steepy mountain"; the beloved will lie on "beds of roses," and be showered with "a thousand fragrant posies." The simplicity is only at first sight, however. There is another classical model here—pastoral: nature and the rural scene are viewed through a lens of urban refinement, knowingness, and artificiality. The birds will sing madrigals (generally a rather elaborate kind of composition); slippers will be fitted "With buckles of the purest gold"; a rustic belt will fasten "With coral clasps and amber studs." Pastoral is city poets cultivating a fantasy about the country, in which labor is effaced and sexual desire is unencumbered by social pressures.

Pastoral also points us, once more, toward the classical ethos in sexuality—in which the love object was as likely to be a boy as a girl (in the pastoral poetry of Virgil and Theocritus, preeminently). In Virgil's second eclogue the shepherd Corydon offers gifts to a boy, Alexis. The addressee of Marlowe's shepherd may be of either gender (Hero wears a "kirtle" [1, 15], but it was also a man's tunic). Further, it is not entirely fanciful to imagine the passionate shepherd's song as the seductive tale Neptune begins to tell in *Hero and Leander*—"How that a shepherd, sitting in a vale, / Play'd with a boy so fair and kind" (2:194–95). Notice that the second line there is shorter than in the rest of *Hero and Leander;* in fact, the same length as the lines of "The Passionate Shepherd." Look at them together:

Play'd with a boy so fair and kind

Come live with me, and be my love.

There is another familiar theme in "The Passionate Shepherd": the split between two kinds of love. One posits an ideal, symmetrical passion, which may be figured as androgynous—beyond gender difference. The poem's amiable manner and the indeterminacy of gender in the love object perhaps suggest this motif. However, another kind of love expects girls and boys to be available for the erotic attentions of older, wealthier, and more experienced men. "The Passionate Shepherd," while surely a delightful lyric, is all about the speaker's promised offerings. "And if these pleasures may thee move, / Come live with me, and be my love." As Neptune put it, "'Tis wisdom to give much, a gift prevails, / When deep persuading oratory fails" (2:225–26).

Finally, "The Passionate Shepherd" cannot be pinned down to one scenario; it is available for diverse readings in diverse circumstances. Explicit appropriations followed soon upon its publication. In Marlowe's *Jew of Malta* the Turkish slave Ithamore appropriates the opening line for his wooing of the courtesan, Bellamira.[19] The poem is used comically in Shakespeare's *Merry Wives of Windsor,* where a Welsh parson sings it, jumbled incongruously with a psalm, to keep up his spirits as he waits to fight a duel.[20] In an anonymous play, *Choice, Chance and Change,* Arnofilo invites Tidero to live with him since he is without heirs; Tidero backs away—"Why how now? Do you take me for a woman, that you come upon me with a ballad, of Come live with me and be my Love?"[21] Poets wrote imitations and additional stanzas; John Donne contributed an exuberant version transposed into the imagery of fishing: "The Bait."[22] Sir Walter Raleigh penned a skeptical reply for Marlowe's addressee:

> But could youth last, and love still breed,
> Had joys no date, nor age no need,
> Then these delights my mind might move,
> To live with thee, and be thy love.[23]

So why not give the proposal a try?

# NOTES

1. Ovid, *The Metamorphoses: The Arthur Golding Translation,* ed. John Frederick Nims (New York: Macmillan, 1965) 408. See Raphael Lyne, *Ovid's Changing Worlds* (Oxford: Oxford UP, 2001) 27–79.
2. The translated elegies, and other poems by Marlowe, are quoted from Christopher Marlowe, *The Poems,* ed. Millar MacLure (London: Methuen, 1968). The *Amores* are cited by book and poem, or book, poem, and line. *Hero and Leander* is cited by book and line.
3. See Pat Southern, *Augustus* (London: Routledge, 1998) 144–50.
4. Michel Foucault, *The Care of the Self: The History of Sexuality,* vol. 3, trans. Robert Hurley (London: Allen Lane, 1988) 71–80, 145–85.
5. See Roma Gill, "General Introduction" to "Hero and Leander," *The Complete Works of Christopher Marlowe,* vol. 1, ed. Gill (Oxford: Clarendon, 1987) 177–86.
6. Gregory W. Bredbeck, *Sodomy and Interpretation* (Ithaca: Cornell UP, 1991) 112.
7. Ovid, *The Metamorphoses,* trans. Mary M. Innes (Harmondsworth: Penguin, 1955) 104.
8. Bredbeck, *Sodomy and Interpretation* 109–10; Michael Drayton, *Endymion and Phoebe: Idea's Latmus, Elizabethan Verse Romances,* ed. M. M. Reese (London: Routledge, 1968) 161.
9. Marlowe's plays are quoted from Christopher Marlowe, *The Plays,* ed. Roma Gill (Oxford: Oxford UP, 1971): *Dido Queen of Carthage* I.i.51.
10. Tibullus, *The Poems,* trans. Philip Dunlop (Harmondsworth: Penguin, 1972) 1:4: 57–58.
11. Marlowe, *Dido Queen of Carthage* I.i.46–48.
12. See Jonathan Goldberg, "'Play the Sodomites, or Worse': *Dido Queen of Carthage,*" *Sodometries: Renaissance Texts, Modern Sexualities,* ed. Goldberg (Stanford: Stanford UP, 1992) 105–43.
13. Eva Cantarella, *Bisexuality in the Ancient World,* trans. Cormac Ó Cuilleanáin (New Haven: Yale UP, 1992) 155–64. The role of Cupid is broached by Catherine Belsey, "Cleopatra's Seduction," *Alternative Shakespeares 2,* ed. John Drakakis (London: Routledge, 2002).
14. Ian Frederick Moulton, "'Printed Abroad and Uncastrated': Marlowe's *Elegies* with Davies' *Epigrams,*" *Marlowe, History, and Sexuality,* ed. Paul Whitfield White (New York: AMS P, 1998) 82.
15. Marlowe, *Tamburlaine 1* V.i.174–77.
16. See Alan Sinfield, "Cultural Materialism and Intertextuality: The Limits of Queer Reading in *A Midsummer Night's Dream* and *The Two Noble Kinsmen,*" *Shakespeare Survey* 56 (2003): 67–78.
17. See Stephen Orgel, *Impersonations: The Performance of Gender in Shakespeare's England* (Cambridge: Cambridge UP, 1996).

18. Bruce R. Smith, *Homosexual Desire in Shakespeare's England* (Chicago: Chicago UP, 1991) 132–36.
19. Marlowe, *Jew of Malta* IV.ii.93.
20. William Shakespeare, *The Merry Wives of Windsor*, ed. H. J. Oliver (London: Methuen, 1971) III.i.16–29.
21. Quoted in Rictor Norton, "Pastoral Homoeroticism and Barnfield, the Affectionate Shepherd," *The Affectionate Shepherd*, ed. Kenneth Boris and George Klawitter (Selinsgrove: Susquehanna UP, 2001) 127–28.
22. Marlowe, *Poems*, ed. Maclure xxxvii–xxxviii and 258.
23. Hugh Macdonald, ed., *England's Helicon* (London: Routledge, 1962) 193.

## READING LIST

Bartels, Emily C., ed. *Critical Essays on Christopher Marlowe*. New York: G.K. Hall, 1997. Includes Miller, David Lee. "The Death of the Modern: Gender and Desire in Marlowe's *Hero and Leander*." 71–94.

Bredbeck, Gregory W. *Sodomy and Interpretation*. Ithaca: Cornell UP, 1991.

Callaghan, Dympna. "Comedy and Epyllion in Post-Reformation England." *Shakespeare Survey 56: Shakespeare and Comedy*. Ed. Peter Holland. Cambridge: Cambridge UP, 2003.

Cheney, Patrick. *Marlowe's Counterfeit Profession: Ovid, Spenser, Counter-Nationhood*. Toronto: U of Toronto P, 1997.

Downie, J. A., and J. T. Parnell, eds. *Constructing Christopher Marlowe*. Cambridge: Cambridge UP, 2000. Includes Summers, Claude J. "*Hero and Leander:* the Arbitrariness of Desire." 133–47.

Gill, Roma. "General Introduction" to "Hero and Leander." *The Complete Works of Christopher Marlowe*, vol 1. Ed. Roma Gill. Oxford: Clarendon P, 1987. 177–86.

Goldberg, Jonathan. " 'Play the Sodomites, or Worse': *Dido Queen of Carthage*." *Sodometries: Renaissance Texts, Modern Sexualities*. Ed. Jonathan Goldberg. Stanford: Stanford UP, 1992: 105–43. Excerpted in Wilson, Richard, ed. *Christopher Marlowe*. London: Longman, 1999: 83–94.

Keach, William. *Elizabethan Erotic Narratives*. Hassocks: Harvester, 1977.

Kelsall, Malcolm. *Christopher Marlowe*. Leiden: E.J. Brill, 1981.

Koppenfels, Werner von. "Dis-Covering the Female Body: Erotic Exploration in Elizabethan Poetry." *Shakespeare Survey 47: Places for Shakespeare*. Ed. Stanley Wells. Cambridge: Cambridge UP, 1994.

Sinfield, Alan. *Faultlines: Cultural Materialism and the Politics of Dissident Reading*. Berkeley: U of California P; and Oxford: Oxford UP, 1992.

Smith, Bruce. *Homosexual Desire in Shakespeare's England*. Chicago: U of Chicago P, 1991.

Taylor, A. B., ed. *Shakespeare's Ovid: The "Metamorphoses" in the Plays and the Poems*. Cambridge: Cambridge UP, 2000.

White, Paul Whitfield, ed. *Marlowe, History, and Sexuality*. New York: AMS P, 1998. Includes Moulton, Ian Frederick. " 'Printed Abroad and Uncastrated': Marlowe's *Elegies* with Davies' *Epigrams*." 77–90; Brown, Georgia E. "Breaking the Canon: Marlowe's Challenge to the Literary Status Quo in *Hero and Leander*." 59–76.

Wilson, Richard, ed. *Christopher Marlowe*. London: Longman, 1999. Includes excerpts from Goldberg, Jonathan. " 'Play the Sodomites, or Worse': *Dido Queen of Carthage*." 83–94.

# 13

# Literary Criticism, Literary History, and the Place of Homoeroticism

## Jonathan Goldberg

Literary history often is told in stories of pairs.[1] Sometimes the couple collaborates on writing projects: Beaumont and Fletcher, Wordsworth and Coleridge. Although the paired writers may have known each other and worked together, more often they are contemporaries who literary historians take to conveniently epitomize a moment in literary history.

Nothing intrinsic to gender may necessitate that these pairs be male couples, nothing, that is, except for the general absence of women from the kind of canonical discussions that mark these pairings; hence, cross-gendered couples are rare (Whitman and Dickinson), pairs of women even more so. Nonetheless, in examining how these male couples are imagined, it is not unusual to find that gendered differences, and with them sexualized difference, come to mark literary history. When, for example, the history of the novel is told through the initiatory figures of Richardson and Fielding, the axis of gender crosses these writers insofar as Richardson's psychological realism cannot be separated from female interiority. Is one member of this couple more masculine than the other? Or is the function of such pairing—by virtue of the couple form, by virtue of a gendering of the members even of a same-sex couple—somehow meant to guarantee that literary generation serves a heterosexual plot?

These are questions for the Renaissance, as might be most economically indicated by recalling Joel Fineman's claim that in his sonnets Shakespeare "invents the poetics of heterosexuality."[2] Fineman's arguments are complex, but one thing his statement clearly means to suggest is that all poetry before Shakespeare addresses an idealized other who is nothing but a version of the sonneteer. For Fineman, Shakespeare's poems to the young man thereby reveal the logic of all previous love poetry—that it is homoerotic, and, at the same time, insofar as an ideal simulacrum is involved, that love poetry before Shakespeare, albeit definitionally homoerotic, is nonetheless fantasmatic, spiritual, nonsexual. Shakespeare, resolutely uncoupled from anyone else in Fineman's account, slips into the role he usually plays in canonizing histories, as the repository for the most socially conservative values. In inventing a heterosexual poetics, Shakespeare for Fineman also for the first time puts real sex into poetry—real sex being definitionally heterosexually directed at an other of the so-called opposite sex. Fineman's arguments thus might lead us to assume that Renaissance pairs are likely to be homoerotic and that such a revelation would also be inconsequential: an erotics that is desexualized, pairings that do not produce anything since poetry begins its modern epoch only with Shakespeare's decisive invention, his singular break.[3]

To get some leverage on Fineman's claims, and to go on thinking about the homoerotic in relationship to literary history, one might turn to the work of Eve Kosofsky Sedgwick, in particular her argument throughout *Epistemology of the Closet* that among the binarisms that structure questions of knowledge in modernity there is always to be found the diacritical difference between supposedly opposing forms of sexuality.[4] Fineman's argument is as much a demonstration of a certain modern form of knowledge as it is a historical claim about the Renaissance. In fact, it is arguable that Fineman's homo/heteroerotic distinction is itself a product of modernity and that early modern texts are not structured by that modern binarism. That is the guiding supposition here as it has been in work largely subsequent to Fineman's that has explored the question of sexuality in early modern representation.[5] Certainly neither the sonneteer nor the young man confines his desire to his own sex, while the lady is morally dark because her promiscuity respects no marital limits. This suggests, at least, that it may be a misnomer to imagine that Shakespeare invents a heterosexual poetics and a mistake to assume that nonheteronormative desire is inconsequential, immaterial. My aim in the pages that follow is not to go further with an account of Shakespeare's sonnets, however, not wishing to privilege those poems, but to summon up a couple of couples in early modern literary history in order to ask how and where questions of sexuality—in particular the sexual field that is somewhat euphemized in the word homoerotic—comes to figure in critical accounts of such relations. I'm interested in these pages to look a bit at one way that literary history in early modernity is made, to treat same-sex pairing as consequential. I begin with the ur-couple in English literary history, Wyatt and Surrey.

There is no evidence of any great intimacy or friendship between Sir Thomas Wyatt and Henry Howard, styled earl of Surrey, although critics with different agendas like to suppose or to deny such a relationship.[6] The two writers have been linked from the start, however, thanks to Surrey's elegy for Wyatt, along with several sonnets (one of them similarly elegiac) in which Wyatt figures, as well as a love poem the initial letters of whose stanzas spell out WIATT.[7] This coupling, however, only occurs in one direction; there is no definitive allusion to Surrey anywhere in Wyatt's oeuvre.[8] When the two first appeared significantly in print, in Richard Tottel's 1557 miscellany, it was Surrey's name that was advertised on the title page. The proper title of the volume is *Songes and Sonettes, written by the Right Honorable Lorde Henry Haward late Earle of Surrey, and other*. The only "other" named in Tottel's prefatory address to the reader that follows the title page was Sir Thomas Wyatt—there are, in fact, more poems by Wyatt than by anyone else in Tottel. Nonetheless, it was for Tottel important to gather all the verse in his collection under the authorizing name of Surrey, perhaps because his execution for treason at the very end of Henry VIII's reign made him a kind of political-religious martyr; or perhaps for the aristocratic glamour that the name possessed (Tottel aims to make available for readers he calls swinelike some of the refinements of courtly writing). It is certainly something akin to these latter motives that lead Sir Philip Sidney, in the brief paragraphs he devotes to contemporary English literary production in his *Defence of Poetry*, to find "in the Earl of Surrey's lyrics many things tasting of noble birth, and worthy of a noble mind."[9] Sidney only mentions four sixteenth-century precedents and only one of them by name, Surrey. George Puttenham, writing at more or less the same time as Sidney, and with something of Tottel's aim to extend a knowledge of courtly production beyond courtly confines, offers a much more generous survey of writers of his age. His habit of pairing leads him to begin English literary history with "*Chaucer* and *Gower* both of them I suppose Knights," a coupled history repeated in the sixteenth century when there appeared "a new company of courtly makers, of whom Sir *Thomas Wyat* th'elder and *Henry* Earle of Surrey were the two chieftaines."[10] Two pages later, when Puttenham recaps his history, he says that between Surrey and Wyatt he finds "litle difference": "their conceits were loftie, their stiles stately, thir conveyance cleanly, their termes proper, their meetre sweete and well proportioned" (76). In this lack of difference Wyatt acquires all the qualities associated with Surrey in literary history. One reason for this indistinction lies with Tottel, who had not merely absorbed Wyatt as "other" into Surrey on the title page, but had, in his editing of both poets, made them seem as much like each other as he could, which meant, in effect, as much like Surrey as possible.

When modern commentators wish to make Surrey and Wyatt close friends and seek the proximity of identification, they continue the drive of this coupling impulse, but usually in the opposite direction. Although Surrey maintained precedence in this pairing through the opening years of the twentieth century, modernist revaluations of literary value reversed the judgment and, ever since, Wyatt has been assumed to be the more accomplished poet.[11]

To take a measure of where the comparisons stand at present there is no better guide than the latest edition of *The Norton Anthology of English Literature* (2000), and I will be treating it as symptomatic of the current critical consensus in the pages that follow.[12] The Surrey headnote offers the prevailing estimation of Wyatt even as it seeks somewhat to correct it: "Though his historical importance continues to be acknowledged, Surrey's poetry, harmonious, musical, and metrically regular, is now often compared unfavorably to Wyatt's more vigorous, knotty, and idiosyncratic verse" (570). Trying to be historically correct, the sentence cited does not really retract the favorable judgment about Wyatt's verse. Indeed, the headnote to Wyatt admires the craft of his performance "as a plain-speaking and steadfast man," and responds, while hardly missing a beat, to the "tinge" of misogyny in Wyatt's poems, by unabashedly endorsing their "blend of passion, anger, cynicism, longing and pain" (526). Part of the hesitation about according Surrey an entirely secondary position in the pair lies in the fact that while the Norton wishes to credit Wyatt with introducing Petrarchan sonnets into English, it acknowledges that "Surrey established a form for these that was used by Shakespeare and that has become known as the English sonnet"—and "even more significant, he was the first English poet to publish in blank verse" (570), once again pointing ahead to Shakespeare (the Norton appears to assume that canonical value equals Shakespeare, which is why it is forced to admit Surrey's historical significance). Wyatt's accomplishments as a literary technician do not point so readily to Shakespeare, yet Surrey's literary historical value pales beside the praise of Wyatt. "As a conventional love poet he is not very convincing," the headnote on Surrey proclaims, adding, however, that there is "power and grace" in his epitaph for Wyatt, that "his verse comes alive when he writes about his deep male friendships or imagines himself in a chorus of women longing for their men or savagely attacks the 'womanish dotage' of an unmanly king" (570). What uncoupling story is being told here as the Norton tells its readers what Surrey does well?

Fineman's story, I think; if Surrey brings literary form to Shakespeare, Shakespeare surpasses this inheritance in all the ways he resembles Wyatt. Behind the Norton's parsing of literary value lies perhaps Jonathan Crewe's *Trials of Authorship,* which summarizes the difference between Surrey and Wyatt by invoking Fineman's thesis, claiming that Surrey's poems—especially his elegies—call up "homosexual love, eventually unmasked in Shakespeare's sonnet sequence as the hidden topic of all hitherto known Petrarchan sonneteering."[13] The Norton couples Surrey and Wyatt in a similar way; Surrey is clearly not much good at a real heterosexuality—that is Wyatt's domain; Surrey merely makes formal contributions to literary history, a formalism that is at the same time devalued for its motivating homoerotics. However, since the Norton does not wish simply to devalue Surrey utterly (if only because of his legacy to Shakespeare), it attributes to him the devaluation of unmanliness, thereby keeping the Norton from seeming to attribute unmanliness to him—despite his deep relations with men or his ability to join the chorus of pining women. This involuted and convoluted story at the very least suggests something very fraught in the initiating couple in sixteenth-century literary history.

The Norton offers Surrey's "So cruel prison how could betide" as evidence of his ability to write about male friendship, a presumably autobiographical poem occasioned by Surrey's 1537 imprisonment in Windsor for striking another courtier at court, an offense for which he could have lost his hand, and one that anticipates his later challenges to royal authority, for which he lost his head. In the poem, Surrey recalls a happier earlier time at Windsor palace, when he was the companion of Henry Fitzroy, the illegitimate son of Henry VIII, and a possible heir. As part of Howard strategies to assume what they considered, on the basis of their birth, rightful proximity to the king, Fitzroy was first joined to Surrey and then married to Surrey's sister in what W. A. Sessions describes in his recent biography of Surrey as "a *ménage à trois*" (64); Fitzroy died in 1536, and Surrey's father reported him inconsolable. Sessions picks up on what has been, since Crewe's account of the poem, the assumption that Surrey's relationship with Fitzroy was an erotic one. As Crewe sees it, however, this is a love "doubly doomed" (73) from the start: doomed as a stage in sexual development that must be surpassed, and doomed as well because based on Surrey's hopeless fantasy that he might actually become the heir apparent by identifying himself with and as the royal scion (Surrey was in fact descended from kings of England; moreover, both Anne Boleyn and Katherine Howard were his first cousins).

Crewe's reading of a fatal homosexual desire in Surrey also extends to another elegy (this one not included in the Norton), the poem on the 1545 death of Thomas Clere, Surrey's "companion and squire" (as Emrys Jones parses the relation in his note to "Norfolk sprang thee, Lambeth holds thee dead"). In "outing" Surrey's desire in this poem, Crewe counters a reading offered by S. P. Zitner, and in his recent *Homoerotic Space,* Stephen Guy-Bray applauds Crewe for noting the intense male-male relation in the poem compared to the couples' perfunctory wooing of a woman, and bristles at Zitner's pronouncement that whatever is to be made of the male-male relation in the poem it poses "no problem" since Surrey's marriage to Lady Frances de Vere was quite "regular" (i.e., they had a number of children). "Zitner's uses of 'problem' as a synonym for homoeroticism is revealing," Guy-Bray comments, and the notion that a married man could not be interested in another man "sexually or romantically" he dismisses as "untenable now" and nonsensical in the sixteenth century.[14] Guy-Bray gives a positive spin to a relationship that Crewe sees as marked by puerility and fatality. Recognizing that homo- and heteroerotic desire are not incompatible certainly demands that one not treat same-sex desire as a stage to be overcome, but valuable in its own right, and it is moreover crucial not to suppose that the parsing of homo- and heterosexual is a transhistorical phenomenon. But beyond realizing the significant differences that mark the history of sexuality, what might be the relationship between the form of same-sex desire in Surrey and literary history?

The answer might lie in noting that the qualities that the Norton assigns to Wyatt— both as a poetic innovator (if not a polisher) and as the embodiment of all kinds of gendered values (vigor, intellectual depth, crafty calculation, personality, emotional rawness)—are precisely those that Surrey assigns to him in his elegy, "Wyatt resteth here, that quick could never rest" (I will be citing it from the Norton). The kind of identification with a monarch that Crewe notes as a sign of the pathos of Surrey's doomed desire for the king's son is also how Surrey identifies Wyatt's supremacy. Wyatt is represented as a master of both/and and neither/nor, of hiddenness and overtness; looked at whole his is a body "where force and beauty met" (29), although the meeting so beneficial for everyone is nonetheless a site of envy and of his own mortality and, after thirty-two lines commending Wyatt's embodied virtues in all their complexity, the poem buries the body and imagines the soul flying to heaven. In effect, Wyatt is delivered in the poem, but otherwise remains unavailable to those who are left behind in a state of collective guilt: "Thus for our guilt, this jewel have we lost" (37). Somehow, the poem that preserves Wyatt also announces that "we" killed him. Or, rather, the poem seems to demonstrate that it both makes this Wyatt even as it undoes him—the body it delivers is a "valiant corpse" (29). The ambivalences and duplicities that structure the poem, and are said to structure Wyatt, are Surrey's double doings. Hence the poem delivers a man of virtue, the man, in fact, who sums up for Surrey the very quality "of manhood's shape" (32). After Wyatt, the poem proclaims, there will be no other; just as, it affirms, after Wyatt "reft Chaucer the glory of his wit" (16) there can be no further literary accomplishment— except, that is, the accomplishment of writing this poem about Wyatt in which Wyatt is said to be in every respect unsurpassable. And in every respect dead and buried by the guilty lesser and yet knowing survivor who makes Wyatt what he is—and what he will be said to be in subsequent literary history. Makes him, it needs to be added, in a poem that is formally an anatomy, or a blazon, that is typically used, as Nancy Vickers argued persuasively of the form in Petrarch's hands, to extol and eviscerate the beloved.[15]

Frederic Tromly describes this poem as an act of "fidelity" to Wyatt, one in which Surrey so completely identifies with Wyatt and writes so much like Wyatt that the effect of the poem is, Tromly declares, as if Wyatt were writing his own epitaph. What fantasy is this, if not Surrey's own motivating fantasy, the one in which he manages to survive everyone by beating them first to an inevitable death? The game of loser wins, which Wyatt wins first by dying in Surrey's poem to a life that Surrey also gives him—indeed, as I have been suggesting, the life that guarantees his place and gives the terms of it in subsequent literary history. If so, the question that might remain to be asked is whether this can be said to be the effect of a fatal homosexual love or of a homoerotic desire that knows no bounds. The echo of Surrey's estimation of Wyatt in the Norton is merely the latest instance of a process that can be seen as early as Tottel's address to the reader in which "the honorable stile of the noble earle of Surrey" is juxtaposed to "the weightinesse of the depewitted sir Thomas Wyat the elders verse," a juxtaposition that owes everything to Surrey's elegy.

If Surrey gives Wyatt the manhood and depth that he supposedly lacks, does this really put Surrey into the female position of endowing her beloved, or is this the male position of aggressive endowment that makes the blazon a loving assault and defense? Can hetero- and homo-desire be sorted out, sorted, for example, when Surrey's claim that Wyatt "Lived and ran the race that Nature set" (31) echoes the line Surrey provided in his translation to sum up Dido's position in the *Aeneid* 4.653 just before she commits suicide, "Lived and ranne the course fortune did graunt." This is not the only time that Wyatt, paradigm of manhood, is feminized; in "Dyvers thy death doo dyverslye bemone" (Jones no. 29), Surrey's elegiac sonnet on Wyatt, the speaker ends likening himself to Pyramus unleashing a flood of tears "on Thisbes brest." Editors throw up their hands here—Jones declares the comparison "inapt," while Richard Sylvester explains it by getting Ovid's story wrong, reversing the deaths of Pyramus and Thisbe, while Seth Lerer reads this arsyversy allusion as a motivated error that must be reversed to be gotten right—that is, to realign gender properly.[16] But can gender be stabilized in a syntax of heterosexual difference? And, since the relation between Surrey and Wyatt also is a fundamental literary relation, what does it say about how Renaissance poets conceived each other, or how modern critics position themselves, about their identifications and their desires in relationship to texts that they, in some fashion, love?

These are questions to be asked, too, in relationship to "O happy dames, that may embrace," the poem included in the Norton as the example of Surrey joining the chorus of pining women wishing the return of their men. In a note to the poem, the reader is told this: "The speaker is a woman. The poem was probably written for Surrey's wife, from whom he was separated on military duty in France in the 1540s." The reader needs to be told that the speaker is a woman because, in fact, nowhere is the gender of the speaker in the poem marked, although the desire of the speaker for the return of a male beloved is unmistakable.[17] The Norton wouldn't want the reader to think that the speaker is male, it seems. And what of the notion that the poem was written "for Surrey's wife"? That explanation was first offered I believe in Frederick Padelford's 1928 edition of Surrey's poems (still the only complete one).[18] It's a handy explanation in so many respects; one almost forgets Surrey was a poet, since he is on military duty. If Surrey writes it for his wife, then he can't be writing it for himself, or for (i.e., to) one of the male beloveds with whom he identified. And if it is for Frances de Vere, I suppose Padelford's point—or that of the Norton—is that it is the position of a wife to voice her husband's self-love, or express the kind of "fidelity" Tromly sees in Surrey's ventriloquizing Wyatt.[19] The reader, it seems, ought not to suppose that the countess of Surrey was able, had she wished, to write a poem herself.

This editorial imposition is complicated, however, by the fact that the only authoritative manuscript version of this poem is in a woman's hand—a hand most recently said to be that of Surrey's sister, wife of Fitzroy; for a long time before, the hand seen in this poem was said to have belonged to Mary Shelton, the beloved of another Surrey companion, Thomas Clere. Whoever wrote this poem (and I put it that way to keep the question of authorship in question), it is a fact that it appears in a manuscript in which a number of women's hands are to be found, a manuscript that serves to remind us that while literary history often may be written as a story of male-male relations, many of the texts we ascribe to men were preserved, transmitted, possibly even composed by women who have remained unnoticed, recognized at best only in the workings of hands that are themselves barely recognizable as individualizing property, let alone for the role they play in literary history.[20]

For beside this unrecognized possibility of a genuinely other hand must be put the story of this couple in which, as I have been retelling the story, the two unstably change places with each other, and in which the modern estimation of Wyatt can be seen as the latest effect of the supposed loser in the pair, the earl of Surrey. Congruently, I would point to the challenge to the current version of literary history and its relationship to sexual history offered in an essay by Daniel Juan Gil that finds in Wyatt a strong example of the possibility that sexuality was a domain unto itself as early as the sixteenth century.[21] Gil is not interested in labeling this emergent form under the modern rubrics of hetero- or homosexuality as much as to imagine sexuality as not simply an effect of pre-existing social forms of hierarchy and difference. Rather than being its master, sexuality is experienced as mastering, and by new and unaccountable forces; sexuality is experienced as loss, self-division, pain. It is not in the Wyatt swagger that Gil locates the site of sexuality; rather those moments when he is virtually indistinguishable from Surrey: "Wyatt's poetry celebrates suicidal despair, murderous hatred, fear, and contempt of self and other as the luxuriant signs of a new form of pleasure that combines a profound turn away from others with a brazen disregard for the limits of the self," his essay all but concludes (882).

Gil's characterization of sexuality works a reversal of the usual Wyatt/Surrey pairing without invoking Surrey at all, and thereby without invoking the hetero-homo distinction that has underpinned the comparison. Nonetheless, in associating Wyatt with traits more often used to characterize Surrey, Gil also prompts us to consider that Surrey's poetic stance is a consequential one, not simply to be equated with modernity and with heterosexuality, and can serve to introduce the second pair to which I turn now in what will stand as a brief coda to this essay. I will be concerned in the pages that follow with two episodes from *The Faerie Queene* that are conventionally paired—with some warrant from the poem itself—the Bower of Bliss episode that concludes Book 2 and the Garden of Adonis that comes in the middle of Book 3.

Ever since C. S. Lewis joined these episodes in his 1936 *The Allegory of Love*—in order to point a difference between them that he claimed previous critics had not seen—the terms for understanding this pair have been set: "The one is artifice, sterility, death: the other, nature, fecundity, life."[22] Lewis's terms could easily translate into homo/hetero difference; however, what he guards against is the misunderstanding that the contrast is between "lawless, that is, unwedded, love, as opposed to lawful love. It is a picture," he continues, "one of the most powerful ever painted, of the whole sexual nature in disease. There is not a kiss or an embrace in the island: only male prurience and female provocation" (332). Again, these terms are amenable to invidious distinctions between homo- and heterosexuality, but Lewis appears to know only about the latter, and the difference he points, between titillation and actual performance. Hence, for him, "the good Venus" of the Garden "is a picture of fruition," while Acrasia is anything but. Oddly enough, when one looks at the descriptions, one sees almost the same picture: Verdant is "sleeping by" Acrasia (2.12.79.1), while Adonis is said to "ly, Lapped in flowres and precious spycery" (3.6.46.4–5). Lewis somehow misses the clear fact that the scene with Acrasia is postcoital—that is, that there is sex in the Bower. That Lewis continues to provide the groundwork for readings of the paired cantos can be seen succinctly in a note to 3.6.43 to be found in the 1993 Norton critical edition of Spenser's poetry: "The Garden's healthy fruitfulness contrasts with the Bower's infertile voyeurism and artifice."[23] What is most extraordinary here is the fact that it is impossible to figure out what in Spenser motivates it. Are Venus and Adonis married? Since the answer obviously is no, in what sense does their sex represent marriage? And, since they have no children either, in what sense does their coupling represent procreation? Granted, there are babies in the Garden, but they are not made by this couple; also, they are not actually babies, but baby forms of existence. Spenser, it is true, uses images of procreation to suggest processes of creation, but these just don't happen to be invested in human beings or in human sex (the closest to that in the canto is the impregnation of Crysogonee; she is penetrated by the sun and bears Amoret and Belphoebe as a result).

Moreover, when we look at Venus and Adonis, it's not only that they look remarkably like Acrasia and Verdant; it's also the fact that there is some kind of ménage à trois here. Adonis is possessed by Venus—she "takes her fill" (3.6.46.3) of him, reaping "pleasure of the wanton boy" (46.3); he, in turn, or at the same time, sports with "the winged boy" Cupid "in safe felicity" (49.3, 4). Critics who have noticed this pederastic dalliance take two opposing but fully congruent tacks. Richard Neuse, for instance, claims that whatever Adonis is doing with Cupid it's necessarily not sexual (an extraordinary thing to say, but motivated by the belief that we saw in Fineman as well, that homoerotics just can't be sex; in this case one of the male figures is Eros). Neuse insists that however Adonis "playes his wanton parts" (49.9) it can't be the same way that Cupid "playes" with Psyche in the next line (50.1): "Adonis's playing is different from Psyche's, since hers is sexual and hence involves the (possible) motive of reproduction."[24] Jon Quitsland, on the other hand, allows that Cupid and Adonis have sex, but only because "homoerotic pleasure keeps Venus's consort ready for her" (208)—and for marriage, Quitsland adds. Sex with Cupid warms up Adonis for the real thing, sex with Venus (this is the maturity plot that Crewe foisted onto Surrey's love to make it fated not to have a future). The remarkable thing about Quitsland's reading is that it grants that same-sex sex and heterosexual sex might not be regarded as necessarily antithetic even as it tries to draw a distinction between the two. But when the distinction is made in the name of marriage, and in the supposition that the only point in having sex is procreation, it flounders precisely when put beside the scene it parallels: the "play" of Cupid and Psyche. Granted, this is procreative: they have a child called Pleasure. This procreative act reverses the supposition that the only point in having sex is to procreate by making the fruit of procreative sex Pleasure itself, thereby making pleasure the point of sex, not procreation.

Finally, to throw into question the supposition that human purposiveness only is found in or matched by marriage—or that male heroic activity in Spenser is tied to procreation—one might recall the narrator's relation to Verdant, his loving lingering over the young man's face and the bit of downy hair above his lip:

> A sweet regard, and amiable grace,
> Mixed with manly sternnesse did appeare
> Yet sleeping, in his well proportioned face,
> And on his tender lips the downy heare
> Did now but freshly spring, and silken blossomes beare. (2.12.79.5–9)

Or remember the scene of male bonding that follows, as Verdant is released and sent on his way with the blessings of the Palmer and Guyon. Which is only to say that, in the purposive conclusion to the Bower, as in the coupling of Adonis and Cupid, forms of male-male attraction are acknowledged. It just might be that marital sex is not where one finds sexuality in *The Faerie Queene,* but rather in couples, whether of the same sex or not, whose sex is not bound to its institutionally valid form.

## NOTES

My thanks to Meredith Evans for her research assistance and to Michael Moon for reading this essay in draft.

1. For a psychoanalytically inflected account of the phenomenon in the nineteenth and twentieth centuries, see Wayne Koestenbaum, *Double Talk* (New York: Routledge, 1989). For a study of collaboration in Renaissance drama attuned to the materiality of textual and (homo)sexual production, see Jeffrey Masten, *Textual Intercourse* (Cambridge: Cambridge UP, 1997).
2. Joel Fineman, *Shakespeare's Perjured Eye* (Berkeley: U of California P, 1986) 18.
3. It is worth noting that when Shakespeare does get coupled in literary history, it is most often with Marlowe, a coupling that further secures Shakespeare's place in the heterosexual column—this despite the fact that the 126 sonnets to the young man are the most sustained homoerotic poems of the era.
4. See Eve Kosofsky Sedgwick, *Epistemology of the Closet* (Berkeley: U of California P, 1990).
5. This is an argument that I make in *Sodometries* (Stanford: Stanford UP, 1992). Eve Kosofsky Sedgwick in her chapter on Shakespeare in *Between Men* (New York: Columbia UP, 1985) offers a reading of Shakespeare's *Sonnets* that could valuably be compared with Fineman's contemporaneous account.
6. Edwin Cassady, *Henry Howard, Earl of Surrey* (New York: Modern Language Association of America, 1938), in what has been the standard biography, devotes the first appendix of his book to a discussion that seeks to disentangle Surrey from Wyatt in every respect—both biographically and also to allow for Surrey's poetic independence. See Patricia Thomson, ed., *Wyatt: The Critical Heritage* (London: Routledge & Kegan Paul, 1974) for an anthology of texts from the sixteenth through the early twentieth centuries that conveniently provides materials for the history of the Wyatt/Surrey relation as a critical topic.
7. The love poem is the first in the Emrys Jones edition of Surrey's *Poems* (Oxford: Clarendon P, 1964), "When raging love with extreme payne"; the elegy, "W. resteth here, that quick could never rest," is no. 28, followed by the elegiac sonnet, "Dyvers thy death doo dyverslye bemone," and two sonnets in which Wyatt's psalms are praised, "In the rude age when science was not so rife" (no. 30) and "The great Macedon that out of Perse chasyd" (no. 31); Wyatt is also quoted in the final line of no. 34, "My Ratclif, when thy rechlesse youth offendes."
8. One poem, "Sometime the pride of my assured truth," that addresses "Mine Earl" in its sixth line, is assumed addressed to Surrey by W. A. Sessions, *Henry Howard the Poet Earl of Surrey: A Life* (Oxford: Oxford UP, 1999) 243–45. R. A. Rebholz doubts this identification in his note to the poem in his edition of Sir Thomas Wyatt, *The Complete Poems* (London: Penguin, 1978) 544. Kenneth Muir assumes the identification in his *Life and Letters of Sir Thomas Wyatt* (Liverpool: Liverpool UP, 1963) 173, only later to doubt the supposition (215).
9. Sir Philip Sidney, *A Defence of Poetry,* ed. J. A. Van Dorsten (Oxford: Oxford UP, 1966) 64. Sidney begins his literary history with Chaucer's *Troilus and Criseyde* and then names the *Mirror for Magistrates, The Shepheardes Calender* and, on page. 65, *Gorboduc* as the only exemplary sixteenth-century English texts beside Surrey's. William J. Kennedy, *The Site of*

*Petrarchism* (Baltimore: Johns Hopkins UP, 2003), notes Sidney's professed admiration for Surrey but insists (presumably because he finds the modern estimation of Wyatt inescapable) that Sidney follows Wyatt in *Astrophil and Stella* (203, 207).

10. *The Arte of English Poesie* (1589), cited from the Edward Arber, 1906 facsimile edition (Kent State: Kent State UP, 1970) ) 74.

11. For a rapid summary of this history, see the opening pages to Dennis Keene's introduction to his edition of *Selected Poems* of Henry Howard, earl of Surrey (Manchester: Fyfield, 1985) 7–9. Modern commentators who wish to elevate Surrey back to the status he once held seek to decouple him, as can be seen, for example, in Frederic B. Tromly, "Surrey's Fidelity to Wyatt in 'Wyatt Resteth Here,'" *Studies in Philology* 77 (1980): 376–87, or attempt to return to the ur-story, as Sessions does in his recent biography.

12. All citations from the seventh edition of vol. 1 of *The Norton Anthology of English Literature*, 2 vols. (New York: Norton, 2000).

13. Jonathan Crewe, *Trials of Authorship* (Berkeley: U of California P, 1990) 65. As co-editor, Stephen Greenblatt was, I presume, involved in writing the Norton headnotes, presumably drawing on his own discussion of Wyatt in *Renaissance Self-Fashioning*, chapter 3 (Chicago: U of Chicago P, 1980). His reading and feminist critiques of it, as well as Crewe's intervention, are among the topics I take up in *Sodometries* 56–60.

14. Stephen Guy-Bray, *Homoerotic Space* (Toronto: U of Toronto P, 2002) 105. Guy-Bray's endorsement of Crewe (112) is an addition to the discussion as it first appeared as "'We Two Boys Together Clinging': The Earl of Surrey and the Duke of Richmond," *English Studies in Canada* 21 (1995): 138–50. Zitner's essay is "Truth and Mourning in a Sonnet by Surrey," *ELH* 50 (1983): 509–29.

15. See Nancy J. Vickers, "Diana Described: Scattered Woman and Scattered Rhyme," *Critical Inquiry* 8 (1981): 265–79.

16. See Richard S. Sylvester, ed., *English Sixteenth-Century Verse* (New York: Norton, 1984) 189, n14: "*Pyramus*: Thisbe slew herself, thinking her lover Pyramus was dead. He then committed suicide"; Seth Lerer, *Courtly Letters in the Age of Henry VIII* (Cambridge: Cambridge UP, 1997) 204–05.

17. I discussed this poem briefly in *Sodometries* (60), and at greater length in *Desiring Women Writing* (Stanford: Stanford UP, 1997) 142–63.

18. Frederick Morgan Padelford, ed., *The Poems of Henry Howard Earl of Surrey* (Seattle: U of Washington P, 1928). Padelford titles the poem "A Ladys Lament for her Lover Overseas" and comments that the poem "may have been written [. . .] for the Countess of Surrey, to voice her impatience at the separation from her husband, during his absence on military duty in France" (215).

19. It is precisely this way that W. A. Sessions understands Surrey's performances in drag: "Surrey inverts gender for his deeper penetration into the life of the beloved. He writes poems in his wife's voice, a ventriloquism of utter love" (212).

20. For more on this point see my discussion in *Desiring Women Writing*. There I assumed that Mary Shelton wrote the poem in the Devonshire manuscript. Mary Fitzroy is now said to be the writer, by Raymond Southall, "Mary Fitzroy and 'O Happy Dames' in the Devonshire Manuscript," *Review of English Studies* n.s. 45 (1994): 316–17; and, in the same issue, by Helen Baron, "Mary (Howard) Fitzroy's Hand in the Devonshire Manuscript," 318–35, a finding accepted by Elizabeth Heale, "Women and the Courtly Love Lyric: The Devonshire MS (BL Additional 17492)," *MLR* 90, no. 2 (1995): 296–313. Baron attempts to prove the identification by noting that certain features of spelling and certain habits of correction can also be found in Mary Fitzroy's holographs; somehow, she takes these compositional habits to prove the authenticity of what she nonetheless supposes to be a copy. As to why Mary Fitzroy should have copied this poem into the manuscript—it is the only instance of her hand found there—Baron opines it might have been written for Margaret Douglas, "as a gesture of

celebration, commiseration, and valediction" (329), for a woman who suffered the loss of her Howard husband—an explanation that is distinctly odd, considering that Margaret Douglas's hand, indeed poems by her, about and arising from the relationship, are in the Devonshire manuscript. Heale, similarly "cautious" (313) in attributing authorship to the many women whose hands she finds in the manuscript, assumes that Surrey's sister entered the poem in the manuscript "as a gesture of commiseration with a wider group of women, of whom Surrey's own wife was one" (309). That is, she generalizes Padelford's notion that Surrey wrote it for his wife to a community of women writing for each other, a view that does not, to my mind, prove the "centrality" (313) of women in the Devonshire manuscript and in the circulation and composition of love poetry that Heale wishes to argue.

21. Daniel Juan Gil, "Before Intimacy: Modernity and Emotion in the Early Modern Discourse of Sexuality," *ELH* 69 (2002): 861–87.

22. C. S. Lewis, *The Allegory of Love* (New York: Oxford UP, 1958) 326. The legacy of Lewis is continued in Harry Berger's 1961 essay "*The Faerie Queene*, Book III: A General Description," rpt. in Berger, *Revisionary Play* (Berkeley: U Of California P, 1988), with its stress on married love as an antidote to the "confusion and ambiguity" (98) of sexual relations that fall under the labels of the "auto-erotic and homosexual" (98); in Stephen Greenblatt's *Renaissance Self-Fashioning*, in which the excessive sexuality of the Bower is contrasted with more purposive sex that has "the sanctification of marriage" and culminates in "the generation of offspring" (176); or in David Lee Miller's *The Poem's Two Bodies* (Princeton: Princeton UP, 1988), where the Garden is said to be the ideal locus where "orgasm and insemination cohabit like spring and harvest meeting at one time" (277); "the Garden of Adonis idealizes wedded love" (281).

23. Hugh Maclean and Anne Lake Prescott, eds., *Edmund Spenser's Poetry* (New York: Norton, 1993) 316n3.

24. Richard T. Neuse, "Planting Words in the Soul: Spenser's Socratic Garden of Adonis," *Spenser Studies* 8 (1990): 94. A similar collapse of sex and procreation can be found in Ronald A. Horton, "The Argument of Spenser's *Garden of Adonis*," *Love and Death in the Renaissance*, ed. K. R. Bartlett (Ottawa: Dovehouse, 1991), so that the safety of male-male sex, he argues, "render[s] service to sexual purity" (69), a view matched by Jon A. Quitsland, *Spenser's Supreme Fiction* (Toronto: U of Toronto P, 2001).

## READING LIST

Bray, Alan. *Homosexuality in Renaissance England*. London: Gay Men's P, 1982; rpt. New York: Columbia UP, 1995).

Gil, Daniel Juan. "Before Intimacy: Modernity and Emotion in the Early Modern Discourse of Sexuality." *ELH* 69 (2002): 861–87.

Goldberg, Jonathan. *Desiring Women Writing*. Stanford: Stanford UP, 1997.

———, ed. *Queering the Renaissance*. Durham: Duke UP, 1994.

———. *Sodometries*. Stanford: Stanford UP, 1992.

Masten, Jeffrey. *Textual Intercourse*. Cambridge: Cambridge UP, 1997.

Rambuss, Richard. *Closet Devotions*. Durham: Duke UP, 1998.

———. "Sacred Subjects and the Aversive Metaphysical Conceit; Crashaw, Serrano, Ofili." *ELH* 71 (2004): 497–530.

Sedgwick, Eve Kosofsky. *Between Men*. New York: Columbia UP, 1985.

Traub, Valerie. "Recent Studies in Homoeroticism." *English Literary Renaissance* 30 (2000): 284–329.

# 14

# "The Phoenix and the Turtle," Renaissance Elegies, and the Language of Grief

*Lynn Enterline*

This essay explores Shakespeare's much admired yet enigmatic poem, "The Phoenix and the Turtle" (1601), in light of the emergent connection in the English Renaissance between the genre of elegy and the process of mourning. We now think of elegy as the name for a "song of lamentation," but it was only over the course of the seventeenth century that the exclusive connection between this genre and grief emerged as a signif-icant phenomenon in English literary history. Greek and Roman elegies covered a wide variety of subjects, from drinking songs and songs for soldiers to love lyrics and epi-taphs. As late as the 1590s Michael Drayton could lament "My Lives complaint in dole-ful Elegies" while John Donne wrote erotic poems called "elegies" bearing such titles as "Love's Progress" and "To His Mistress Going to Bed." But by 1645, when Milton wrote "Lycidas," English elegy had taken a decisive turn toward an exclusive associa-tion with the vicissitudes of mourning.

Yet neither the story of the seventeenth century elegy, nor the place of Shakespeare's poem in that tradition, can be told within an exclusively national context. Readers also require some sense of its writers' deep involvement with classical literature, art, rhetoric, and culture. English poets borrowed many of elegy's chief features from their classical forbears. Among the most important of these for "The Phoenix and the Turtle" are a tendency toward poetic self-reflection, direct addresses from narrator to reader, sections devoted to praising the deceased, an overall movement from mourning to con-solation, and a tendency to offer the poem itself as a form of recompense for loss. For modern readers, borrowing others' words seems to belie authentic feeling, but such was not the case in the Renaissance. Perhaps the best way to understand this rich tradition of poetic borrowing, as well as what such habits of revision and rewriting have to do with the intensity of human feeling, is to remember the words of Erasmus, the humanist scholar whose theories of imitation decisively influenced the course of English educa-tion and, by that route, the nature of literary production during the sixteenth and seven-teenth centuries. In a theory about language's primacy, Erasmus observed that "all knowledge falls into one of two divisions: the knowledge of 'truths' and the knowledge of 'words'; and if the former is first in importance, the latter is acquired first in order of time."[1] Putting words before truth, at least chronologically, Erasmus inaugurated a shift in English pedagogy. Following Erasmus's precepts, humanist schoolmasters instituted a program of teaching based on the belief that language training preceded and shaped character. Virtually every schoolmaster who commented on the matter claimed that rig-orous drilling in the language and texts of the classical, Latin past would produce proper "gentlemen" for the good of the English commonwealth.

Largely because of humanist pedagogy, imitation of classical precursors soon became a hallmark of literary invention. Poets imitated Roman precursors and expected their audience to appreciate even the subtlest manipulations of precedent Latin texts. Renaissance authors laid claim to innovation as well as social standing, in other words, as something achieved *in relation* to classical literary models. In such an educational context, allusion to past texts became much more than mere exercise because the art of imitation was deeply rooted in the dramas of childhood—in the practices, rituals, habits, and interpersonal hierarchies at school that gave young boys their place in the world and their sense of social meaning. An English Renaissance schoolboy learned to find his own voice, and gained the approval of both teacher and peers, by first turning to the words and voices of others. He became part of his social milieu by paying close attention to language, precedent, and form as a necessary step to any eloquent expression of thought or emotion. And eloquence, schoolmasters told them, was all.

Grammar school students who became poets turned the humanist tenet of language's foundational importance into an art: their poems often reflect deeply on the relationship between literary form and nuances of personal feeling. From a very early age, young orators were trained to think about the work and effects of language on the emotions (both the speaker's and the audience's). This rhetorical self-reflection is, of course, evident in myriad sixteenth- and seventeenth-century poems and plays. But poems about death make the task of finding words adequate to the occasion particularly difficult: elegies operate by trying to find an "accommodation between the mourning self on the one hand and the very words of grief [and] consolation on the other."[2] Renaissance elegies were written by former Latin students schooled to think daily about their own verbal performance and power. Whether to evoke a sense of grief or to console, Renaissance elegies do more than represent a loss. Rather, they often suggest that they are a form of symbolic action, that the poem itself has a kind of emotional work to perform for both speaker and reader.

Reading Renaissance elegies also requires some familiarity with the history of grief. Ways of feeling (as well as ways of describing, understanding, and dealing with emotion) vary across time and cultures; notions about mourning are no different. While the vast ancient and Renaissance commentary on melancholia lies beyond the scope of this essay, a few prominent strands distinguishing early modern conceptions of grief from our own are particularly important for "The Phoenix and the Turtle."[3] Right alongside a medical tradition that treated melancholia as a debilitating, morbid sorrow caused by the humor of "black bile," another popular one saw an intimate connection between grief and love. The idea of "love-melancholy" had enormous currency in all kinds of ancient, medieval, and Renaissance writing; an elegy on the death of two "Co-Supremes and stares of Loue" (51) is a logical extension of this convention.[4] Indeed, one can trace the influence of love-melancholy right across Shakespeare's texts. Readers often notice that Shakespeare's vision of the birds' ecstatic union and death—"the essence but in one" (26), "Either was the others mine" (36), "Neither two nor one was called" (40)—characterizes his tragic couples: Juliet and Romeo, Cleopatra and Antony, Desdemona and Othello all recall the "mutall flame" (24) at the heart of the elegy's "Tragique Scene" (52).

Another, perhaps more influential, philosophical tradition represented melancholia as a prominent characteristic of intellectuals and artistic genius. Passed down from Florentine

Neoplatonists and well known in England, this tradition associated melancholia "with intellectual acumen and profundity, with artistic ability, sometimes with divine inspiration." There arose a "persistent vogue of melancholy" among English intellectuals; such suffering, though painful, was generally thought to be "an attribute of superior minds."[5] In Italy, several philosophers, painters, and poets claimed to be melancholic. The best known literary example in England is, of course, Hamlet. Most important for our purpose, however, is that combined with melancholia's association with artistic genius, elegy's tendency to reflect on its own verbal power meant that Renaissance poems on death could also become particularly important occasions for poetic self-display. The poet's medium and technical skill, far from being either distraction or intrusion, might instead play a crucial role in the work of mourning.

## Classical Precursors

A history of the ancient elegiac forms so well known among English poets must start with form in its strictest sense: in contrast to our own understanding of genres, Greek and Roman poetic modes were based on *meter* rather than subject or theme. In ancient Greek poetry, elegiac meter was a development of epic hexameter. Ancient derivations for the Greek word, *elegos,* were several: it was popularly associated with lament, some saying it came from the god of poetry's grief-stricken cry over the death of his beloved Hyacinthus; others said that it came from a non-Greek word for the *aulos,* or double-piped flute that accompanied songs in elegiac meter.[6] While Greek poets used elegiacs for a wide variety of topics, the Latin poets best known in English grammar schools increasingly used elegiac couplets to explore just one subject: love. Under Augustus, Roman love-elegy flourished as Tibullus, Propertius, and Ovid (among others) tried their hand at it. Elegy became increasingly associated with expressions of deep personal attachment which carried within the immanent possibility of loss or disappointment.

In the *Metamorphoses,* one of Shakespeare's favorite poems, Ovid brings together the various strands of Roman elegy—love, loss, and poetry—in his story of Pan and Syrinx. The story imbeds loss and the activity of writing verse in the psychology of love, sexuality, and desire; this entanglement is one that his Renaissance inheritors continued to expand and explore. Indeed, Ovid turns the very instrument associated with Pan's poetry—the reed pipe—into a relic of lost love. In Book 1, Pan falls in love with Syrinx but she runs from him, refusing his desire; she pleads with her "sisters of the stream" to change her form before he catches her. When Pan does finally touch Syrinx, he finds a reed rather than a nymph in his hands. He "sighs" in disappointment and the wind from his breath "stirs in the reed, making a low sound like a complaint." The "sweet" sound of this "new art for the voice" (1.709) pleases the god so much that he fashions the reed into a pipe and consoles himself that he can still have some kind of "union" with her.[7] When Pan appears later in the epic, he is still playing those pipes in a poetry contest with Apollo. At once a poetic instrument and a relic of lost love whose very sound preserves a sense of that loss, the flute is Pan's only consolation. The substitute allows him to deflect his passion for a nymph into poetry, but the flute's "complaining" sound reminds Pan that his instrument is not, in fact, the woman he wanted. In an equivocal resolution that anticipates the complexities Shakespeare elaborates in his elegy's story of love—"To themselues yet either neither, / Simple were so well compounded" (43–44)—Ovid leaves unclear whose "voice" Pan hears in the reed's complaint. Is it his own or Syrinx's?[8] The two characters' distress merge into one "low sound" to memorialize their loss (Pan's of Syrinx, hers of life) while holding out the possibility that poetic invention itself provides some form of solace.

Ovid became one of Rome's most resourceful practitioners of elegiac couplets. English grammar schools helped make Ovid's poetry extremely popular, but the *Amores,* his cycle of elegiac love poems, remained so controversial that it was never part of the school curriculum and was the last of his major works to be translated. When an English version finally was published, however, the translator was no lesser a poet than Christopher Marlowe.[9] And it is from two funeral elegies in this notorious cycle that Shakespeare borrows several fundamental elements of "The Phoenix and the Turtle."[10] We'll examine the most obvious source, Ovid's poem on the death of Corinna's parrot (*Amores* 2.6), in some detail in the next section. But the only other death poem in the *Amores* may also anticipate Shakespeare's elegy (and many other Renaissance poems of grief), lamenting, as it does, over the funeral pyre and death-urn of a fellow poet. As Marlowe translates it, Ovid stops writing about Corinna to lament that Tibullus's "dead body" "burnes [. . .] in the funerall flame" (3.8.6).[11] Like "The Phoenix and the Turtle," Ovid's elegy moves from flame to urn and ash. And like Shakespeare's narrator, Ovid's ends with a prayer over that urn:

> Thy bones I pray may in the urne safe rest
> And may th'earths weight thy ashes nought molest. (3.8.67–68)

The elegy also depicts contemporary Roman poets gathering around Tibullus's shade in Elysium, suggesting that such a gathering is a noble kind of survival beyond death. Both Ovid's version of Tibullus's funeral and the origin of Pan's flute rely on, and develop, a venerable ancient tradition of thinking about poetry as a way of making some kind of amends for loss and death. As we shall see, this Ovidian attention to poetry as consolation characterizes Shakespeare's elegiac narrator, presiding over the "flame," "cinders," and "urne" of another, far more mysterious funeral.

## Language and Death

Young students trained in the grammar school's Latin curriculum were familiar with the ancient commonplace that poetry has the power to endure against time. From Greek tombs and epitaphs to Roman lyric poems, ancient writers and mourners looked to words as a monument that would survive the body's decay.[12] Horace, capable of a bleak vision of death ("everyone comes to same end, everyone is tossed in the same urn," 2.3.25–26), nonetheless claims that poetry is a "monument more lasting than bronze" that "neither wasting rain nor raging wind nor the countless series of years nor time's flight can destroy" (3.30.1–5).[13] Ovid followed suit, ending the *Metamorphoses* by boasting that though his body might be destroyed, his "better part" will "live" as long as readers' lips pronounce his poem's words out loud. Horace and Ovid are both drawing on a common burial practice in the ancient world: tombstones often called upon passersby to read their engraved words aloud as a way of giving the deceased renewed life.

Thus Ennius's epitaph read, "Living I fly through the mouths of men." Evoking the sound and breath of a collective human voice, such epitaphs look for permanence beyond bodily decay in the rites and customs of a community of speakers.[14]

Renaissance writers often took up the classical notion that verbal monuments could provide a bulwark against time. They did so not merely because of its obvious imaginative appeal for speaking beings but because questions about the power of words became newly vexing in a period of deep religious controversy that called traditional language and rituals into question. The Reformation did more than challenge a culturally important religious institution. It simultaneously eroded conviction in the usefulness of the Catholic church's ritual language. At the end of the sixteenth century, for example, John Marston (who published elegies alongside Shakespeare's in *Loves Martyr*) derides "papists" as "chattering." By the end of the seventeenth century, one writer surmised that the Latin words of transubstantiation, *hoc est corpus,* gave rise to the words of a juggling trickster, *hocus pocus.*[15] Such satires of Catholicism tell us that crises of belief were understood, as well, to be a failure of traditional language; only phrases emptied of conviction and institutional power "chatter" and produce nonsense.

Even more to the point for elegiac verse, funeral services changed rapidly and significantly during the Reformation. The Catholic belief in purgatory sustained prayers and masses for interceding on behalf of the deceased, but purgatory was "one of the first [. . .] tenets that the Church of England abandoned." The belief that the living can actually help souls in purgatory with their prayers "channeled personal and communal religious practice" in the middle ages and fuelled "an enormous investment in prayer, masses, and multifarious charitable works."[16] The enforced abolition of purgatory, "perhaps the most sweeping [. . .] uncompromising" and "traumatic" change in the Reformation, tore apart a long-standing sense of "communal solidarity between the living and the dead."[17] Perhaps most important for Renaissance poems on death is the fact that this change eroded faith in the efficacy of symbolic action that made such communal solidarity possible. In the 1540s, the crown confiscated endowments left to fund lights and intercessory masses; by 1563, a churchman condemned prayers for the dead as useless. Though some funeral rituals were allowed to stand, their meaning shifted as they became ceremonial rather than directly functional. As Ralph Houlbrooke remarks, the change from Catholic requiem Mass to Protestant funeral marked a shift from "intercession to commemoration."[18]

Such confusion over the usefulness of intercessory prayers could not help but turn the form of elegy itself—as a lament for the dead—into a matter of renewed importance. Moreover, it can hardly surprise that when sectarian controversy challenged the value of traditional words and rituals, poets might find new appeal in the ancient commonplace that poetry created a "monument" against the ravages of time, oblivion, and death. Or to put it another way, boys from a culture deeply divided about the efficacy of religious language were also trained at school to think about their own verbal power on a daily basis; such students might well find some consolation in, or affinity for, ancient rhetoric's central claim that words have power to act, perhaps even against time. As young orators, Renaissance schoolboys imbibed a discipline that stressed language's power to persuade and to act rather than simply to represent. A revealing index of the period's interest in rhetorical power is the fact that Orpheus became one of the most popular classical figures for the poet. As Ovid tells it in the *Metamorphoses,* his voice was so beautiful that he persuaded even the god of death to change his mind. Though Orpheus fails in the end, the dream remains: his song still had the power to animate the natural world as trees and stones "moved" to hear him. In other words, Ovid's stories of Orpheus, Pan and Syrinx, and Tibullus's afterlife suggest that the compensations of poetic language, though perhaps limited, are better than none at all.

## Two Dead Birds?

Sudden Reformation changes in funeral rituals, the culturally significant connection between grief and artistic genius, and elegy's tendency toward poetic self-reflection may all help shed some light on "The Phoenix and the Turtle." But something about this lovely, famously enigmatic "wonder" (32) nonetheless evades the grasp of contextual explanations. The critical tradition is full of controversy, particularly about the poem's reference. Readers continue to pursue questions that will doubtless never be solved to everyone's satisfaction. To whom do the phoenix and the turtle refer? The historical candidates are several, but generally the phoenix is taken to signify Queen Elizabeth and the turtle, more tentatively, the earl of Essex.[19] Then again, is the allegory's chief significance politically topical? Perhaps it is more broadly religious, philosophical, and spiritual? Or perhaps it has more to do with the occasion of its publication in *Loves Martyr*, a collection of poems "by the best and chiefest of our moderne writers" about the mysterious "Turtle and Phoenix."[20] Could the lovers' fate have something to do with the volume's dedicatee? One reason for the critical controversy, of course, is the sense that such an "exalted" poem, concerned with the paradoxes of love and the self, "Beautie" and "Truth" (53), must be about something more than two dead birds.[21] But whatever external reference the poem has, critics frequently note that it also makes several self-reflexive comments on poetry: some take "The Phoenix and the Turtle" to be a kind of portrait of the poet's own self-perpetuating imagination. Perhaps it is a comment on the relationship between lyric and emblem? Or perhaps between lyric and theater, particularly from a dramatist who ends his elegy with a tragic "chorus"?[22]

I see no end to the controversy, nor do I propose to adjudicate a solution. Rather, I'll take a cue from the elegiac tradition itself and ask, instead, what kind of *work* the poem represents itself as performing. We've already seen that elegy, particularly in Ovid's hands, is intensely engaged with the relationship between death and the power of poetry. As such, individual elegies frequently comment upon the emotional, literary, rhetorical, communal, or authorial labor they hope to perform. Shakespeare's poem is no exception. Richard McCoy approaches the elegy's sense of its own work by reading it in light of the "liturgical irresolution" that characterized an era fractured by sectarian controversy. Comparing "The Phoenix and the Turtle" to the "maimed rites" for Ophelia in *Hamlet,* he interprets both alongside the period's failed funerary rituals: for him, a "sense of inefficacy pervades" the elegy because "nothing happens" in the poem.[23] On his argument, the transcendent moment of the birds' fiery love-death remains resolutely past; the poem's present is merely commemorative. The elegy becomes a poem conscious of its own status as mere summons, anthem, and lament that can do nothing after the fact. For McCoy, the narrator ends on a note without future: the lovers' death leads only to "cinders" and leaves "no posteritie" (55, 59).

Clearly it is important to keep religious controversy in mind while reading this elegy's sense of its own labor, especially since much of the debate revolved around language's potential to *do* something for the dead. But McCoy's account of the poem's work depends on interpreting its final lines in a way that excludes another, equally possible reading:

> To this urne let those repaire,
> That are either true or faire,
> For these dead Birds, sigh a prayer. (65–67)

"This urne": we might understand the "this" not to refer outside the poem (to a funerary object somewhere outside, in the world) but rather to the words of the poem itself. The poem-as-funerary-urn may not seem to offer much consolation. But understood in light of the ancient tradition in which both poems and epitaphs are monuments against time (where future readers speak engraved words out loud and so give the deceased new life), it is not "nothing," either.[24] In the ancient tradition, to "sigh a prayer" would not indicate despair, but would, instead, conjure a collective kind of animation (a word derived from the Greek *anemos* signifying both external "wind" and interior "breath").[25] Taking poetic words as objects whose impersonal, communal persistence defies the body's decay is a Greco-Roman version of what we might now call an "aesthetic" impulse. Certainly the late Shakespeare was taken with the idea that the "rich and strange" world of what we now call the aesthetic does, indeed, oppose death's leveling work: "Of his bones are coral made / Those are pearls that were his eyes."[26] "The Phoenix and the Turtle" offers itself as another such beautiful object, the one thing that persists after "flame" and "cinders" as an "urne" to hold them. The birds may leave no "posteritie" in the form of children, yet "this urne" of a poem is still "Here" (55).

Once we read "this urne" as an invitation to take the elegy as itself a funerary object, we notice that the poem's narrator keeps using what linguists call "deictics"— "this" or "that," "here," "now"—to draw attention to his own words. Deictics are local and concrete while at the same time strangely floating. "This" is a shifting word that can be employed on completely different occasions to signify utterly singular events. "Here" and "this" refer ambiguously: they depend on the particular moment of speech, the context, and the parties addressed while also carrying the reminder that they can be endlessly repeated, emptied of specific significance. Over the course of "The Phoenix and the Turtle," the narrator uses several deictics. He points to *this* Session" (9); notes that "*Here* the Antheme doth commence" (21); singles out "*this* troupe" (8), "*this* Threne" (49), "*this* urne" (65), "*these* dead Birds" (67); and, more generally still, directs our attention to a "Here" where the lovers' cinders lie "enclosde" (55). Each "this" and "here" anchors the poem in a specific context and at the same time detaches it from such reference. The same, of course, might be said for "the phoenix" and "the turtle," enigmatic allegorical signs that appear to refer to particular historical figures while also transcending their specific occasion. This movement between general and particular is intrinsic to allegory, a poetic mode that creates the sense that there must be a specific, hidden meaning while also suggesting that the "dark conceit" signifies something still more than that. Allegories therefore tend to generate, as does this poem, endless interpretations and controversies about which particular meaning is the "real" one.

From such interpretive effects, certain kinds of permanence are born. Shakespeare's elegiac narrator has a gift for exploiting the ambiguity's potential. If we take the narrator's deictics to signify in only one way (to a particular funeral service outside the poem), then, indeed, nothing happens. "The Phoenix and the Turtle" leaves us with a glorious, past "flame" and "no posteritie." But if we take these pointers to refer to the poem's own words—to an iterative present of a "here" and a "this" that repeatedly signifies the poem itself whenever it is read—then the narrator is advancing an important claim about his elegy's power to become a rite or monument *by virtue of its successive readings.* It is not only the swan, but the narrator himself, who vies with the missing "Priest in Surples white" (11) whose rituals, at the moment of the poem's writing, were declared to have neither meaning nor power.

Shakespeare's last command, "sigh a prayer" (67), asks mourners to lend the poem the kind of animating breath and voice invoked by Ennius, Horace, Ovid, and innumerable ancient tombstones. And indeed, Shakespeare signals his sense that the poem's symbolic labor derives from ancient tradition when he gives the elegy's final lines the unusual name, "threnos" (a Greek word for death-song).[27] Other early modern poems of mourning keep a similar double focus on the period's religious debates *and* its institutionally sustained impulse to invoke classical precedent. One contemporary collection of verses juxtaposes three "epitaphs" to a final "threnodia" on the death of the earl of Essex. The epitaphs all begin with a version of "here lies," taking a poetic "threnodia" and "tombstone" to be virtually synonymous.[28] Several years after the publication of *Loves Martyr,* a less exalted and little known collection of English elegies, also called a "threnodia," invokes an animating breath more plainly than "The Phoenix and the Turtle." It suggests that the idea acquired a certain persuasive currency among England's classically educated elite. The poet addresses his departed subject, claiming that "tears" and "verse" are "the things which may adorne thy death/ And give thy name an everliving breath."[29]

Shakespeare, of course, is quite capable of bringing this ancient idea of the poem-as-epitaph to bear on other occasions. In the sonnet that begins, "Or I shall live your Epitaph to make," he expands the notion implicit in "The Phoenix and the Turtle":

Your monument shall be my gentle verse,
Which eyes not yet created shall o'er-read,
And tongues to be your being shall rehearse,
When all the breathers of this world are dead;
    You still shall live (such virtue hath my pen)
    Where breath most breathes, even in the mouths of men. (81.9–14)[30]

If the efficacy of prayer waned in the wake of anti-Catholic polemic, there were still other nonreligious discourses available in the schools—ancient tropes to which writers could turn to conduct their own kind of poetic rituals: "tongues to be your being shall rehearse." By way of such rhetorical and institutional crossings, more secular discourses of the aesthetic could emerge.[31] Read in light of its classical lineage, the narrator's call to "sigh a prayer" over "this urne" of his elegy constitutes a symbolic, vocal act that the period's classical curriculum proclaimed could outlast death. Shakespeare's tendency to invoke aesthetic objects, including words *as* objects, as things that resist decay is most obvious in his romances but is also implicit throughout "The Phoenix and the Turtle."

The elegy's self-designation as a funeral "obsequie" (12) and "Requiem" (16) invites us to read this tendency as, in part, a rhetorically trained poet's response to the "liturgical indeterminacy" surrounding the abolition of purgatory and the enforced suspension of prayers for the dead. Built on the ancient orator's claim for the performative power of eloquent speech, such a proto-secular move away from the realm of religious doctrine into the realm of art was made possible because of the discursive and material practices of contemporary grammar schools.

If we read "The Phoenix and the Turtle" as a poet's Latinate endeavor to negotiate a way around the impasse arising from Reformation controversy, the obvious question—why birds?—offers an intriguing glimpse into Shakespeare's habits of invention and sense of poetic vocation. First, in writing about the phoenix, Shakespeare is following the lead of other poets in *Loves Martyr*. Writing variations on a theme set out in advance, all the volume's authors respond according to school training: boys were asked on a daily basis to write exercises on a given theme as preparation for full-fledged orations. Second, critics often take the poem's call to a procession of birds as homage to Chaucer's *Parlement of Fowles*. This literary genealogy has merit, especially since Chaucer's poem concerns love. But Chaucer's parliament may derive from the same classical source as Shakespeare's flock: Ovid's elegy on his lover's dead parrot in the *Amores* (2.6). And it is Ovid's elegy, not Chaucer's dream vision, that narrates a bird's death and funeral as part of a love story. Ovid's poem also begins and ends like Shakespeare's, opening with a call for other birds to mourn with him and concluding with the dead bird's funeral monument.

Shakespeare's and Ovid's elegies share other important details. The only bird Ovid's narrator names specifically in the opening group of mourners is *turtur amice,* the "Loving turtle-dove": "Full concord all your lives was you betwixt,/ And to the end your constant faith stood fixt" ("concordia vita," 2.6.13). When he describes the birds' after-life in Elysium, we learn that other, "uncleane fowles" are "forbidden" from the spot ("obscenae [. . .] aves," 2.6.52), anticipating Shakespeare's initial attempt to banish certain birds from "this troupe" (8). The birds' eternal grove, moreover, echoes Ovid's verses about the poets who gather around Tibullus's shade in Elysium. Both the love-elegist and the parrot find companionship after death. Ovid names just two of the parrot's cohorts: swans (associated with Apollo, song, and poetry) and the "lively phoenix, a bird always unique" ("vivax phoenix, unica semper avis," my translation).

Most important for Shakespeare's elegy, Ovid's vision of the afterlife lays heavy emphasis on the parrot's vocal power: his voice brings other "faithful birds" around to hear "his words" ("convertit volucres in sua verba pias," 58, my translation). We are to mourn because the parrot belonged to Ovid's beloved *and* because he was gifted in speech: in Marlowe's translation, "no such voyce-feigning bird was ever on the ground" (23). The poem's final lines quote the "verses" engraved on the parrot's tombstone: "This tombe approves, I pleasde my mistresse well, / My mouth in speaking did all birds excel" (61–62). The epitaph stresses what the narrator repeats throughout: this parrot was a skilled "imitator" ("imitatrix," 1), was "talkative" ("garrulus," 26), had a voice with a "genius for changing sounds" ("vox mutandis ingeniosa sonis," 18), and excelled all others in "simulating" the human voice, returning "words" with his own "throaty sound" (my translations, 23–24). In fact, the narrator tells us, the parrot had such a "love of talke" (29) he could scarcely eat. The poet mourns this loquacious bird, in sum, because he was the "speaking image of mans voyce" ("humane vocis imago," 37). Shakespeare, deeply attuned to Ovid's meta-poetic representations of vocal skill, could hardly have missed the fact that the only two poems in the *Amores* dedicated to funerals were as much about the medium of poetry as death. The first mourns a fellow poet, the second a bird whose vocal talent makes him the poet's surrogate. Indeed, the word on the epitaph for the parrot's mouth—"docta," or "learned"—was a favorite among Augustan poets for designating their own technical skill. And so Ovid's final description of the parrot resembles his story of Orpheus in two ways. Orpheus gathers trees and animals to hear him in a woody glade and his dying act is to call out the name of his beloved Eurydice. So, too, does Corinna's parrot gather Elysium's other birds to him "by the sound of his words" (58, my translation); and his final moments were similarly Orphic: "Yet words in thy benummed palate rung, / Farewell Corinna cryed thy dying tongue" (48).

When Shakespeare blends the poet's and the parrot's funerals from the *Amores,* he reminds us that Ovid was making a claim about the eternizing and compensatory power of poetic language in both. But instead of writing about the death of a "voice-feigner," he expands Ovid's phrase for the phoenix—"unica semper"—by stressing his bird's uniqueness. The phoenix's singularity allows Shakespeare's narrator to reflect upon a necessary component of a funeral "obsequie" (12): the gesture of praise.[32] In ancient and Renaissance nomenclature, words of praise are "epideictic" (a word derived from the same Greek root as "deictics," meaning "to point," "show," or "tell"). To find words adequate to praising such a singular creature, and a singular death, is no small task. And so the poem's chief paradox—what is the nature of the "selfe" (38) when love makes "Two distincts, Diuision none" (27)?—also tells us something about the poet's predicament:

Propertie was thus appalled,
That the selfe was not the same:
Single Natures double name,
*Neither two nor one was called.* (37–40)

The birds' "simplicitie" (54) is not, in fact, so simple: understood according to the elegy's central enigma, in which "Simple" can be "so well compounded" (44), such "simplicitie" resists the division between word and thing on which language operates. Rather like Shakespeare's narrator in the sonnets, constantly "thematizing" the difficulty of writing poems adequate to his beloved, this elegy's narrator stresses how far his avian subjects escape the grasp of "names."[33] Such a predicament tells us that his task is more difficult than Ovid's: this death robs such words as "Beautie, Truth," "Raritie" and "Grace" of their meaning (53–54). The birds to whom these words once referred "Here enclosed, in cinders lie" (55)—and so, by implication, do those words. What can an elegiac poet say when the lovers' death has brought such words to ruin? "Beautie" may "bragge, but tis not she" (63).

The answer to such a question is the elegy itself: the poet manages to praise their wondrous, sublime death precisely by pointing out his own verbal quandary. The birds' "mutuall flame" appalls property, defies reason, robs traditional elegiac language of its significance. Yet by describing his dilemma, the narrator substitutes his "threnos" for the ashes of "Beautie" and "Truth" and creates a poem by meditating on whether or not his words are equal to their unique subject. Shakespeare's narrator points to the dead birds and to the words with which he honors them, engaging in what Joel Fineman aptly describes as an "indicative speech that [. . .] works by showing its own showing, by pointing to its pointing": epideictic rhetoric is therefore an "objective showing that is essentially a subjective showing off."[34] Working with the possibilities for poetic self-reflection afforded by the ancient elegiac tradition as well as the vogue for associating grief and genius, Shakespeare turns a poem of death into one that makes large claims for his own verbal power. The phoenix's uniqueness enables him to recall Ovid's poetic parrot and raise the stakes, signaling to his community of rhetorically trained readers that his skill makes him as singular among poets as the phoenix and the turtle were among their kind. Such readers would understand that fulfilling an elegiac task more difficult than Ovid's (who himself made a career of competing with Virgil) was no mean feat. But the elegy's work extends beyond the poet's individual skill: the narrator's concluding call to "sigh a prayer" over "this urne" relies on an ancient funerary commonplace to turn the elegy's symbolic labor over to its readers.[35] Shakespeare's last three lines invite us to become part of a chorus, to join an ongoing, shared act of speaking that revivifies an ancient claim for verbal efficacy and permanence. The elegy's final, collective act inaugurates a tradition of successive reading and speaking that allows a very different kind of afterlife to be born from the ashes of contemporary religious controversy.

## NOTES

1. As quoted in T. W. Baldwin, *William Shakespeare's Small Latine and Lesse Greeke* (Urbana: U of Illinois P, 1944) 79.
2. See Peter M. Sacks, *The English Elegy: Studies in the Genre from Spenser to Yeats* (Baltimore: Johns Hopkins UP, 1985) 2.
3. See Stanley W. Jackson, *Melancholia and Depression from Hippocratic Times to Modern Times* (New Haven: Yale UP, 1987).
4. Quotations from *Loves Martyr Or, Rosalins Complaint* (London: 1601) 170–72.
5. Lawrence Babb, *Elizabethan Malady: A Study of Melancholia in English Literature from 1580 to 1642* (East Lansing: Michigan State UP, 1951) 175, 184. On melancholia's masculinist bias, see Juliana Schiesari, *The Gendering of Melancholia: Feminism, Psychoanalysis, and the Symbolics of Loss in Renaissance Literature* (Ithaca: Cornell UP, 1992). In *The Tears of Narcissus: Melancholia and Masculinity in Early Modern Writing* (Stanford: Stanford UP, 1995), I argue that melancholia's figural language disrupts gender categories.
6. Margaret Alexiou, *The Ritual Lament in Greek Tradition* (Cambridge: Cambridge UP, 1974) 104. See also Sacks, *English Elegy*.
7. Citations are from Frank Justus Miller, ed., *Metamorphoses* (Cambridge, MA: Harvard UP, 1984). Translations mine.
8. I explore the blended "complaint" issuing from Pan's pipe as an extension of Ovid's habit of exploring his own poetic predicaments through ventriloquized female voices in *The Rhetoric of the Body from Ovid to Shakespeare* (Cambridge: Cambridge UP, 2000).
9. On the importance of the *Amores* in shaping Marlowe's conception of his own career and the cycle's "dubious distinction" of being "a cultural taboo," see Patrick Cheney, *Marlowe's Counterfeit Profession: Ovid, Spenser, Counter-Nationhood* (Toronto: U of Toronto P, 1997) 31–67.
10. For the *Amores'* influence on the narrator of Shakespeare's sonnets, see M. L. Stapleton, *Harmful Eloquence: Ovid's Amores from Antiquity to Shakespeare* (Ann Arbor: U of Michigan P, 1996).

11. Unless otherwise indicated, translations are Marlowe's, *All Ouids elegies* (Middlebourgh, n.d.). The Latin text is from Grant Showerman, ed., *Ovid: Heroides and Amores* (Cambridge, MA: Harvard UP, 1977).

12. See Jesper Svenbro, *Phrasiklea: anthropologie de la lecture en grèce ancienne* (Paris: Editions la Découverte, 1988); Sheila Murnaghan, "Body and Voice in Greek Tragedy," *Yale Journal of Criticism* 1, no. 2 (1988).

13. Horace, *Odes and Epodes*, ed. C. E. Bennet (Cambridge, Mass.: Harvard UP, 1914). Translations modified.

14. This paragraph draws upon *The Rhetoric of the Body*.

15. *The Metamorphosis of Pigmalion's Image, Elizabethan Minor Epics,* Elizabeth Story Donno (London: Routledge, 1963). *The Compact Edition of the Oxford English Dictionary* (Glasgow, New York: Oxford UP, 1971). In *Hamlet in Purgatory* (Princeton: Princeton UP, 2001), Stephen Greenblatt details Protestant attacks on Catholic writing as "fable" and "mere rhetoric"—as William Fulke put it in 1577, "more of garrulity than eloquence" (32–40).

16. Quotations from Ralph Houlbrooke, *Death, Religion, and the Family in England, 1480–1750* (Oxford: Clarendon P, 1998) 37. On the institutional, economic, and social upheavals surrounding the abolition of purgatory, see Greenblatt 10–46.

17. Anthony Low, "*Hamlet* and the Ghost of Purgatory: Intimations of Killing the Father," *English Literary Renaissance* 29 (1999): 447.

18. Houlbrooke 265–68.

19. See Patrick Cheney, *Shakespeare, National Poet-Playwright* (Cambridge: Cambridge UP, 2004) 174–76.

20. The title page to *Loves Martyr*.

21. William Empson, "The Narrative Poems," *Essays in Shakespeare*, ed. David B. Pirie (Cambridge: Cambridge UP, 1986) 1–26.

22. For Cheney, the narrator modulates between singular and collective voices: by "displac[ing] himself," he marks "the boundary between lyric and tragedy" (*Shakespeare, National Poet-Playwright* 176–96).

23. McCoy, "Love's Martyrs: Shakespeare's 'Phoenix and Turtle' and the Sacrificial Sonnets," *Religion and Culture in Renaissance England*, ed. Claire McEachern and Debora Shuger (Cambridge: Cambridge UP, 1997) 195.

24. A classicizing alternative for the newly abolished prayers for the dead occurred in 1551: a group of Oxford scholars honored another's tomb with Greek and Latin verses. See J. W. Binns, *Intellectual Culture in Elizabethan and Jacobean England, the Latin Writings of the Age* (Leeds: Francis Cairns, 1990) 38–40.

25. The lyric by "Ignoto" preceding Shakespeare's opens with a similar idea: "Suppose here burnes this wonder of a breath/ In righteous flames." (1–2).

26. *The Tempest* (1.2.397–99), *The Riverside Shakespeare*, 2d ed., ed. G. Blakemore Evans (Boston: Houghton Mifflin, 1997).

27. Shakespeare used a Greek word only twice. Of the nine publications in England in which "threnos" or "threnodia" appear in the title, only two appeared before *Loves Martyr*. See Binns, *Intellectual Culture* 480–81.

28. John Kendall, *Flowers of Epigrammes* (John Shepperd: London, 1577). See also *A Booke of Epitaphes made upon the death of the Right worshipfull Sir William Buttes Knight* (London, 1583).

29. *Threnodia in obitum d. Edouardi Lewkenor Equitis [. . .]* (London, 1606) 35.

30. From *The Riverside Shakespeare*.

31. See Michael Neill on the proliferation of funeral monuments as secular displays that emerged in place of abolished prayers for the dead (*Issues of Death: Mortality in English Renaissance Tragedy* [New York: Oxford UP, 1997] 38–42). Neill stresses the strictly retrospective

function of memorial shrines—which is, I believe, precisely the problem that Shakespeare's call for readers to "sigh a prayer" over the urn of his poem is trying to remedy.

32. Richard Wills's *Scholia* (1573) calls the part of an obsequy devoted to praise an "epicedium" (Binns, *Intellectual Culture* 60). Marston follows Shakespeare in *Loves Martyr*, interpreting his predecessor's poem as "a moving Epicedium!" before contending with him over which poet praises best.

33. See Joel Fineman, *Shakespeare's Perjured Eye: The Invention of Poetic Subjectivity in the Sonnets* (Berkeley: U of California P, 1986) 5–6.

34. Fineman 5.

35. Anthony Low's analysis of fraternities, guilds, and burial societies disbanded during the Reformation—groups "from the middling or poorer sort" who "hired priests to say masses on their behalf and for the dead"—suggests the kind of collectivities for which Shakespeare's "troupe" of sighing readers offers a classicizing substitute (448–49).

## READING LIST

Cheney, Patrick. *Shakespeare, National Poet-Playwright*. Cambridge: Cambridge UP, 2004.

Enterline, Lynn. *The Tears of Narcissus: Melancholia and Masculinity in Early Modern Writing*. Stanford: Stanford UP, 1995.

Fineman, Joel. *Shakespeare's Perjured Eye: The Invention of Poetic Subjectivity in the Sonnets*. Berkeley: U of California P, 1986.

Houlbrooke, Ralph. *Death, Religion, and the Family in England, 1480–1750*. Oxford: Clarendon P, 1998.

Jackson, Stanley W. *Melancholia and Depression from Hippocratic Times to Modern Times*. New Haven: Yale UP, 1987.

Kay, Dennis. *Melodious Tears: The English Funeral Elegy from Spenser to Milton*. New York: Oxford UP, 1990.

Neill, Michael. *Issues of Death: Mortality and Identity in English Renaissance Tragedy*. New York: Oxford UP, 1997.

Pigman, G. W. *Grief and English Renaissance Elegy*. Cambridge: Cambridge UP, 1985.

Sacks, Peter M. *The English Elegy: Studies in the Genre from Spenser to Yeats*. Baltimore: Johns Hopkins UP, 1985.

# 15

## Shakespeare's Literary Career
## and Narrative Poetry

### *Patrick Cheney*

Today, critics do not often consider William Shakespeare an author with a literary career. Most often, they consider him a "man of the theatre": a playwright, actor, and shareholder of an acting company (the Lord Chamberlain's Men during the reign of Queen Elizabeth I [1558–1603]), renamed the King's Men during the reign of James I [1603–1625]). In fact, twentieth-century scholarship worked hard to establish this very classification. In an important 1986 essay, Harry Levin writes, "Our century has restored our perception of him to his genre, the drama, enhanced by increasing historical knowledge alongside the live tradition of the performing arts."[1] Levin is reacting to the Restoration, Augustan, Romantic, and Victorian reduction of Shakespeare's theatrical genre to what John Dryden called in 1668 "Dramatick Poesy."[2] If critics from the late-seventeenth century through the nineteenth usually read Shakespearean drama as poetry, critics in the twentieth century finally detached the drama from poetry, viewing it primarily as theater. In 1997, *The Norton Shakespeare: Based on the Oxford Edition* virtually institutionalized this performative classification, with Stephen Greenblatt presenting "Shakespeare" as "the working dramatist."[3]

In addition to plays, however, Shakespeare composed three valuable narrative poems: *Venus and Adonis, The Rape of Lucrece,* and *A Lover's Complaint.*[4] These "nondramatic" works join the *Sonnets* and "The Phoenix and Turtle" in challenging the twentieth-century project announced by Levin and confirmed by Greenblatt. The occasion to capitalize on this challenge arises because several new books present Shakespeare as a "literary dramatist," even if they do not extend their project to his poems.[5]

In this chapter, we will look into the terms of the challenge. We will see that *Venus, Lucrece,* and *A Lover's Complaint* reveal the famed theatrical man to have more interest in the authorship of a literary career than we might be used to thinking. In the first section, we will look into the problem that Shakespeare's authorship of poems creates for his otherwise theatrical career. In the second section, we will discover a historical model for viewing that problem. In the next three sections, we will turn to *Venus* to see in outline how Shakespeare introduces the model, to *Lucrece* to see more fully how he develops it, and to *A Lover's Complaint* to see briefly how toward the end of his career he crystallizes the model. We will conclude with some summarizing remarks on Shakespeare as an early modern author. Because all three poems are complex, and the space brief, students are invited to supplement (or interrogate) the few details provided.

## The Critical Problem

In 1593, when the theaters close due to plague, Shakespeare makes his well-known turn from stage to page. He publishes his first narrative poem, *Venus and Adonis,* in 1194 lines of iambic pentameter verse, written in a sixain stanza (six lines rhyming ababcc), on an erotic topic in imitation of the Roman poet Ovid. As preface, he attaches a two-line Latin quotation from Ovid's *Amores* and a dedicatory epistle, addressed to the earl of Southampton and signed "William Shakespeare." In the epistle, the print-author asks Southampton to accept the "first heir" of his "invention" until he can produce a work of "graver labor."[6] Then, in 1594, Shakespeare publishes a poem that most scholars believe fulfills this promise. *The Rape of Lucrece* consists of 1855 verse lines, in a rhyme royal stanza (seven lines rhyming ababbcc), on a topic both erotic and political, in imitation of Ovid's *Fasti [Rituals]* and Livy's *History of Rome.* Again, Shakespeare pens a dedication to Southampton and signs his name; instead of a Latin epigraph, he includes a prose "Argument," narrating events leading up to his plot. Finally, in 1609, Thomas Thorpe prints a quarto volume titled *Shake-speares Sonnets,* which includes the 154 sonnets in the Petrarchan mode and *A Lover's Complaint.* This latter work consists of 329 verse lines, in the rhyme royal stanza, in another popular genre with ties to Ovid, the complaint. Scholars now believe that Shakespeare composed this poem between 1602 and 1605, and that he may have refined it as late as 1609. Although this volume contains no prefatory material by the author, Shakespeare's third narrative poem is valuable for showing his authorial project late in his career.

When critics remember Shakespeare's poems at all, they tend to assume that Shakespeare "cease[d] in his efforts to combine the professions of courting poet and dramatist, and turn[ed] more exclusively to the world of the theater"; and that his poems function as a "a proto-sketch for [. . . the] drama."[7] These formulations are anachronistic because they view the poems through the achievement of the plays. Significantly, the formulation originates in the nineteenth century, when Coleridge refers to "our *myriad-minded* Shakspear": "I mean the 'Venus and Adonis' and the 'Lucrece'; works which give at once strong promises of the strength, and yet obvious proofs of the immaturity, of his genius."[8] While Coleridge helped recuperate the poems in a culture that was then finding poetry largely in the plays, this Romantic genius consolidated a misguided model so strong it persists today.

For instance, in our most important study of literary careers, Richard Helgerson classifies Shakespeare as simply a "professional" writer because he "made [. . . his] living from the public theater."[9] For Helgerson, professionals differ from "amateur" poets, such as Sir Philip Sidney, who write poetry during their youth, see their art as a pastime, and do not publish their work. Eventually, amateurs repent of their folly and turn to serving the state, whether in church, government, or university. In contrast, "laureates" such as Edmund Spenser and Ben Jonson write serious literature throughout their adult lives to serve the state and eternity (8, 12). According to Helgerson, Spenser is Renaissance England's first "laureate" (100) because he uses strategies of *self-crowning* to present himself as a poet who will shape national destiny. Helgerson's distinction between the laureate Spenser and the professional Shakespeare (10) continues to inform criticism today.[10] In our received narrative about the Renaissance invention of modern authorship, Spenser and Jonson receive the role of founder while Shakespeare fails to find a part.[11] Evidently, critics remain uncomfortable thinking about Shakespeare as a self-crowned author with a literary career. Yet such discomfort is worth scrutinizing, especially since we have recently acquired enough evidence to see Shakespeare as more than simply a man of the theater.

## A New Historical Model

If we return to the material writing conditions of the late sixteenth and early seventeenth centuries, we discover a more accurate historical model than the theatrical classification allows. For starters, we see that Shakespeare did not abandon poetry for the stage but wrote poems during the whole of his professional life: his "concern with the writing of narrative poems did not abort with *Venus and Adonis* (1593) and *Lucrece* (1594) but extended through the time of *The Phoenix and Turtle* (1601) to within four years of the end of his career as a dramatist [through *A Lover's Complaint*]: he was occupied with writing non-dramatic poetry for a much longer time than we have imagined."[12] Since this account is factually true, we might re-imagine Shakespeare as an author who interleaves poems with plays from beginning to end.

Shakespeare's contemporaries understood this interleaving well enough. At the midpoint of his career, Gabriel Harvey writes: "The younger sort take much delight in Shakespeare's Venus and Adonis; but his Lucrece, and his tragedy of Hamlet [. . .] have it in them to please the wiser sort."[13] Harvey divides Shakespeare's works by audience appeal or moral effect. He conjoins *Lucrece* with *Hamlet,* a printed poem with a stage tragedy, and he contrasts both with another printed poem, *Venus.*

The combination of poems and plays within a single career is fundamentally a sixteenth-century phenomenon, so much so that we might claim it as a historic legacy of the "Renaissance." English precursors to Shakespeare include John Skelton, George Gascoigne, and Thomas Watson, while precursors on the Continent include Marguerite de Navarre in France, Lope de Vega in Spain, and Torquato Tasso in Italy. The simultaneous emergence of both a print culture and a theater culture no doubt undergirded the authorship of the new English and European poet-playwright. While print had been invented in the fifteenth century, it became a veritable institution in England only late in the sixteenth. Similarly, the first commercial theaters were built in the 1570s.

A classical precedent exists in Shakespeare's favorite author. Ovid pens amorous elegies, represented by his *Amores,* and epic, his *Metamorphoses.* But he also wrote a tragedy, *Medea,* extant in two lines. Ben Jonson, in his 1601 *Poetaster,* puts this "Ovid" on the stage. Ovid's genres here counter the famous Virgilian model of pastoral, georgic, and epic—the standard for Western literary careers.[14] In the *Amores,* Ovid counters this Virgilian standard by telling a story about his attempt to write epic and tragedy, his failure and turn to love elegy, and then his final turn to tragedy.[15]

Christopher Marlowe is the first author in any European vernacular to translate the *Amores.* He makes the Ovidian *cursus* (or career) available to Renaissance culture and adopts it as his own career path. In doing so, he builds on the common practice of emulating or contesting an authoritative classical source. *Ovid's Elegies* and Marlowe's famous lyric "The Passionate Shepherd to His Love" form a phase of amorous Ovidian poetry; his plays, a phase of tragedy; and his minor epics, *Lucan's First Book* and *Hero and Leander*, a phase of proto-epic. Although Marlowe's *cursus* remains truncated, he produces a canon right on the cusp of a literary career, and he does so in opposition to Spenser, known as the "Virgil of England."[16] Before the English nation, Marlowe and Spenser replay the Roman rivalry of Ovid and Virgil, establishing the very benchmark for English authorship and literary careers.

Shakespeare's poems and plays recall Marlowe's practice more than that of Spenser, who published poems but eschewed the popular theater. Like Marlowe, Shakespeare produced amorous poetry (*Venus, Sonnets*), one work of graver labor (*Lucrece*), and the greatest tragedies since antiquity (*Hamlet, King Lear*). But he overgoes Marlowe by extending his dramatic production beyond tragedy, to pen masterpieces in comedy (*A Midsummer Night's Dream*), history (*1 Henry IV*), and "romance" (*The Tempest*). Shakespeare's overarching genius was to produce sustained and enduring masterpieces in both poetry and theater, for both the nascent printing press and the new commercial theater. While his literary combination follows no set pattern, he still works from Marlowe's "Ovidian" foundation and from Marlowe's subversive counterpoint to the Virgilian Spenser.

We need to take this foundation and counterpoint seriously because Shakespeare tends to organize his fictions as an erotic, political, and religious conflict between two literary aesthetics that look conspicuously like those of the Ovidian Marlowe and the Virgilian Spenser. Among English and European poet-playwrights, Shakespeare is arguably the first to use a literary conflict as the main frame of his art. While we can discern this frame in his plays, it more clearly structures the plots of his narrative poems. Nominally, all three narrate a sexual conflict between male and female: Venus courts Adonis; Tarquin rapes Lucrece; and the young courtier seduces the country maid. Virginity and chastity lie at the heart of all three, in part because they process the Protestant queen's Cult of the Virgin. Perhaps curiously by modern standards, Shakespeare maps an aesthetic opposition between rival career models onto this erotic, political, and religious conflict. In particular, his engagement with the premier authors of his day in the writing of nationhood marks William Shakespeare as an author with a literary career.

## *Venus and Adonis*

The prefatory items to Shakespeare's first narrative poem encourage us to view his fiction through the lens of a literary career. In Marlowe's translation, the Ovidian epigraph from the *Amores* reads:

> Let base-conceited wits admire vilde things,
> Fair Phoebus lead me to the Muses springs.[17]

Here Ovid asserts the higher value of his poetry over a lower art practiced by others. Yet long ago Muriel Bradbrook found Shakespeare using the epigraph to "dissociat[e . . .] himself from [the] baseness [. . .] of popular playwrighting" and to turn to "courtly poetry."[18] In *Venus and Adonis,* Shakespeare uses the Ovidian epigraph as a career announcement for his turn from stage to page.

Correspondingly, the *Dedicatory Epistle* to Southampton introduces a Virgilian lens of pastoral/georgic and epic:

I know not how I shall offend in dedicating my unpolished lines to your Lordship, nor how the world will censure me for choosing so strong a prop to support so weak a burden. Only if your Honour seem but pleased, I account myself highly praised, and vow to take advantage of all idle houres, till I have honoured you with some graver labour. But if the first heir of my invention prove deformed, I shall be sorry it had so noble a godfather: and never after ear so barren a land, for fear it yield me still so bad a harvest. (*Riverside* 1799)

Shakespeare relies on a European discourse originating in Virgil's *Eclogues* (6.10), through which a young writer acknowledges the lowness of his work and prophesies his progression to a higher form.[19] Hence Shakespeare uses terms of georgic husbandry ("labour," "barren a land," "harvest") but then promises "some graver labour."[20]

The two-part structure of *Venus* fulfills the prefatory career advertisement. Lines 1–810 occur in the pastoral setting of the "primrose bank" (151), where Venus attempts to seduce Adonis; then lines 811–1194 move to the locale of the hunt, where the Boar kills Adonis—a locale associated with warfare.[21] Through this structure, Shakespeare narrates a Virgilian/Spenserian progression from pastoral to epic. Then he superimposes on to this structure a Marlovian/Ovidian narrative of poetry and theater. Initially, Venus uses poetry to court the idyllic young hunter: "Bewitching" him with a "tempting tune" sung "like the wanton mermaids' songs" (777–78), she "sings" "extemporally a woeful ditty" (836), evocative of the poet Orpheus, for it records "echoes" from "the neighbor caves" (830–34).[22] As the theatrical term "extemporally" implies (cf. *1 Henry IV* 2.4.280), Venus also coerces Adonis into her erotic theater: "And all this dumb play had his acts made plain / With tears which chorus-like her eyes did rain" (359–60). The theatrical metaphor shows the couple's inability to enact reciprocity: they appear on stage together, but Adonis is a silent speaker of a dumb show, while Venus performs the chorus using tears to comment on his tragic action.

Venus's songs and plays critique the popular invitational mode of Marlowe's "The Passionate Shepherd": "Come live with me, and be my love, / And we will all the pleasures prove" (1–2). Similarly, Adonis's commitment to what Venus calls "fruitless chastity" (751) critiques Spenserian chastity, as Shakespeare's imitation of Spenser's sixain stanza from the 1579 *Shepheardes Calender* indicates (*Januarye* and *December* eclogues). Thus, at the end Venus fails to protect Adonis from the Boar and he metamorphoses into a flower.

Yet, when the goddess bends to "crop [. . .] the stalk" (1175) and bears it away to Paphos in her "chariot" (1192), Shakespeare constructs a new icon of authorship. According to Jonathan Crewe, "The only 'progeny' resulting from the relationship is the flower Venus maternally cherishes in the end; since flowers traditionally stand for poetic creations, the poem becomes the sole 'offspring' of this ill-fated love."[23] Effectively, Shakespeare grafts the career models of Spenser and Marlowe, producing a new hybrid art of dramatic poetry. When Coleridge observed that "'Venus and Adonis' seem at once the characters themselves, and the whole representation of those characters by the most consummate actors" (rpt. Kolin 70), he intuited the fusion of poetry and theater that here the author depicts iconographically.

## *The Rape of Lucrece*

Even more than *Venus, Lucrece* is imbued with the discourse of an author's literary career, as its borrowing of Chaucer's rhyme royal stanza from *Troilus and Criseyde* hints. Certainly, Tarquin and Lucrece remain the legendary Roman prince and ravished matron from Livy and Ovid, in a narrative about government change: after her suicide, Lucrece's husband, Collatine, and kinsman, Lucius Junius Brutus, expel the Tarquins from Rome, ending the Roman Empire and giving birth to the Roman Republic. Consequently, critics read *Lucrece* productively for its dynamics of rape and republicanism.[24] Yet critics also note something else: Shakespeare suffuses his retelling of the West's arch-myth of sexual violation and political formation with a Petrarchan discourse from the profession of printed poetry.[25] Extending this criticism, we may say that here the author processes his career as an English author—and not simply of printed poems, but also of staged theater.[26]

Shakespeare underwrites the conflict between Lucrece and Tarquin with authorial discourse. In the first half of the poem, Tarquin emerges as an author who both writes a book and plays the part of an actor. When Lucrece first greets him, she

> Could pick no meaning from their parling looks,
> Nor read the subtle shining secrecies
> Writ in the glassy margents of such books.
> [. . .]
> He stories to her ears her husband's fame,
> Won in the fields of fruitful Italy;
> And decks with praises Collatine's high name,
> Made glorious by his manly chivalry. (*Rape of Lucrece* 100–09)

The discourse of printed books reveals what Lucrece recognizes only unconsciously: the need to read a printed copy of concealed truth. Since she "never cop'd with stranger eyes" (99), she reads the book without comprehending its marginal glosses, which reveal the truth of the inner-text. In his scripted book, Tarquin presents himself to Lucrece as the author of a romance epic about her husband's glorious chivalry.

The contents of Tarquin's "book" are formally Spenserian. Inventorying the central words of *The Faerie Queene,* Tarquin tells Lucrece a story about her husband's standing as an epic hero. Yet, since Tarquin merely plays a part, he hypocritically appropriates England's Virgil for erotic purposes. His strategy reproduces that of Marlowe, who had used it to de-authorize Spenser's Virgilian authority (Cheney, *Profession* 116–17).[27]

The presence of Marlowe helps account for subsequent theatrical discourse in Tarquin's introspection:

> "Then childish fear avaunt, debating die!
> [. . .]
> Sad pause and deep regard beseems the sage;
> My part is youth, and beats these from the stage." (*Rape of Lucrece* 274–78)

A man about to rape a woman imagines himself as an actor on the stage. Significantly, Tarquin's metaphor identifies theater as a dangerous instrument targeting female chastity.

If in the first half of the poem Tarquin appears as a Marlovian poet-playwright violating chastity, in the second half Lucrece emerges as a Spenserian figure of chastity associated with Spenser's two arch-myths of national authorship: Orpheus and Philomela.[28] At lines 547–53, Shakespeare concludes a metaphorical description of the clouding sky with a seemingly gratuitous reference: "And moody Pluto winks while Orpheus plays" (553). Yet here Shakespeare anticipates what a second Orphic allusion clarifies: that his story of rape and republicanism is also a story about authorship. Lines 1142–48 allude to Orpheus during Lucrece's apostrophe to the nightingale Philomela: "'And for, poor bird, thou sing'st not in the day, [. . .] / [. . .] we will unfold / [. . .] sad tunes to change their kinds; / Since men prove beasts, let beasts bear gentle minds."

Shakespeare unfolds his representation of the violated Orphic author in three principal stages: Lucrece's complaint to Night, Opportunity, and Time (764–1036); her identification with Philomela (1079–1211); and her viewing of the Troy painting (1366–1582). These self-reflexive moments correspond to complaint, pastoral, and epic. For Elizabethans, these genres were practiced most famously by Spenser, who had published his pastoral *Calender* in 1579, his epic *Faerie Queene* in 1590, and his *Complaints* in 1591. While Shakespeare's order of the three genres progresses from lower to higher, it disrupts Spenser's publishing chronology, perhaps to signal a critique.

Hence, after her complaint and her pastoral song to Philomela fail to console her, Lucrece searches out a painting that depicts the enterprise of Western epic: the fall of Troy. For Spenser, as for Virgil, the Troy story begins as a tragedy—Paris *rapes* (seizes) Helen from her husband to create international war—but by the end the story gives birth to a new nation: Aeneas leaves Troy to found Rome; and his descendent, Brute, founds London. Marlowe attacks this imperial mythology in translating the Roman poet Lucan's *Pharsalia,* a counter-Virgilian epic about the death of the Roman Republic.[29] By narrating the birth of the Republic from the rape of Lucrece, Shakespeare overgoes Spenser, with his Virgilian imperial myth, as well as Marlowe, with his Lucanian republican myth. In *The Rape of Lucrece,* the "print–epicist" creates a new foundational myth for the Elizabethan nation.[30]

Lucrece's turn to the Troy painting supports this interauthor interpretation. Since the tragic painting hangs in Lucrece's own house, it reveals that she is doomed from within: her own domestic ideology licenses Tarquin's "rape" of a beautiful woman in a national setting.[31] Specifically, the Troy painting reveals that Lucrece's home has been infiltrated by an intruder who represents the state.[32] That intruder is not simply Tarquin but Virgilian art, and especially the Virgilian art of Spenser, now impersonated by the art of Marlowe. Hence Lucrece learns to locate Tarquin in the false theatrical face of the Trojan traitor Sinon (1536), who strolls through the pastoral fields outside Troy to enter the epic city (1501–05): "He entertained a show of seeming just" (1514).

Although Lucrece's "newer way" of reading epic succeeds in consoling her momentarily, in the end the graver genre fails as sadly as do the lower genres of complaint and pastoral: "none it ever cured" (1581). Here Shakespeare discards one of the West's most enduring ideas, the very heart of Spenser's Virgilian enterprise: that art can redeem tragic suffering.

Yet when Lucrece concludes, "I am the mistress of my fate" (1069), she appears to link poetry and theater in a new way, channeling art into political action through religious sanction. After writing a letter to call her husband home, she moves to the marketplace to perform her suicide. Now the ravished woman appears as "the pale swan on her wat'ry nest" singing "the sad dirge of her certain ending" (1611–12)—an ancient topos for the divine birth of lyric poetry (Cheney, *Shakespeare,* ch. 4). But Lucrece also meets Collatine and Brutus as an actor, wearing a "mask" (1602) of "mourning black" (1585) that anticipates Hamlet. When Brutus, himself wearing an "antic disposition" (*Hamlet* 1.5.172) to protect himself from the Tarquins, "pluck'd the knife from Lucrece' side" (1807) and "throws that shallow habit by, / Wherein deep policy did him disguise" (1814–15), we witness a remarkable form of succession: not only "from kings to consuls" (Argument)—or monarchy to republic—but from a dead-end opposition between the aesthetics of Spenser and Marlowe to a new hybrid aesthetics of the Shakespearean author: a theatrical epic for the nation.

Thus, in the poem's final stanza we witness the very conjunction of poetry and theater organizing the poem, as well as the author's literary career: the men

> show her bleeding body thorough Rome,
> And so to publish Tarquin's foul offense;
> Which being done with speedy diligence,
> The Romans plausibly did give consent
> To Tarquin's everlasting banishment. (*Rape of Lucrece* 1851–55)

The word "publish," which appears first in line 33, writes Heather Dubrow, "signals the movement from [. . .] complaint to epic."[33] *The Rape of Lucrece* records a powerful transition from a culture of poetry to a culture of theater, print publication to theatrical show, the Virgilian career model of pastoral and epic to the Ovidian career model of amorous poetry and tragedy.

Moreover, when the men "show" the dead body of the chaste matron in order to "publish" it throughout the nation, the author weds poetry and theater within what Patrick Collinson terms "the monarchical republic of Queen Elizabeth I."[34] At this time, the word "publish" meant both "make public" and *put into print.*[35] Similarly, the word "plausibly" means "with applause" (*Riverside* 1836), indicating that the Romans give their consent by applauding Tarquin's banishment. The printed poem ends with a version of the theatrical convention closing a play, in which the presenter figure steps forward to ask for the audience's applause, as Puck does in *A Midsummer Night's Dream.* Shakespeare gestures to his own reading public, lending consent to the author's republican frame of art within the queen's monarchy, which will be "everlasting." Finally, Shakespeare's "graver labour" is about—and is brought about by—the Marlovian invasion of the Spenserian domain. In this epic venture, we see an etiological narrative not just about the formation of the Roman Republic, or a strong female voice, but also about the printing of the Shakespearean poet-playwright in Renaissance England.

## A Lover's Complaint

We cannot identify *Lucrece* and *Venus* simply as youthful forays abandoned by the mature dramatist in part because of *A Lover's Complaint.* Within a few years of retirement, Shakespeare constructs a narrative poem that makes his earlier authorial template the main frame of his fiction. A young courtier "daff[s]" the "white stole of [the country maid's . . .] chastity" (297) by deploying two kinds of literary art: "deep brain'd sonnets" (209) and "tragic shows" (308). He is at once a manipulator of the Petrarchan idiom (with roots in Ovid) and a playwright-actor with a dark script to play on and against women.

Shakespeare again situates this "Ovidian" fiction in a Virgilian landscape of court and country. Amid hills and riverbanks, cattle graze and conventional pastoral figures preside, including an old cowherd, who "graz'd his cattle nigh, / Sometime a blusterer that the ruffle knew / Of court, of city" (57–59). As John Kerrigan notes, the cowherd's life-pattern resembles old Melibee's in Book 6 of Spenser's *Faerie Queene*. Both pastoral figures act out what Isabel G. MacCaffrey calls Spenser's "formula of out-and-back," which begins in the country, moves to court, then comes home again.[36]

In Shakespeare's fiction, the old cowherd tries to use counsel to "assuage" the country maid's "suffering ecstasy" after she loses her virginity (69). His status as a "reverend man" (57) evokes a Spenserian figure of wisdom. Thus, the old man voices a central tenet of Spenser's national epic: "counsell mittigates the greatest smart" (*Faerie Queene* 1.7.40). Yet the word "blusterer" and the image of the "grained bat" (64) suggest dubious motives—as with Spenser's Archimago, the enchanter who disguises himself as a hermit (*Faerie Queene* 1.1–2).[37] Correspondingly, the young courtier, who has left court for the country to deploy his sonnets and shows, resembles Christopher Marlowe, the "Dead shepherd" (*As You Like It* 3.5.81) who wrote amorous verse and tragedic shows to attack the "fruitless chastity" in Spenser's "Legend of Chastity" (*Faerie Queene* 3).[38]

Yet *A Lover's Complaint* is notorious for not resolving its plot. The poem ends with the country maid's complaint against the artistic deceptions of the young courtier: "'O, that infected moisture of his eye, / [. . .] Would [. . .] / [. . .] new pervert a reconciled maid'" (213–29). Instead of recording the maid's consolation through the reverend cowherd, the poem crystallizes the form of Shakespearean art itself: a competition between Marlovian and Spenserian career models over the rights to represent the national virtue of chastity.

## Shakespeare's Counter-Laureate Career

Some might be uncomfortable thinking about Shakespeare as an author with a literary career, but Shakespeare's poems lend us a genuine opportunity. Initially, some might speculate: If Spenser invents English notions of authorship and career, and Shakespeare is not Spenser, then the famed theatrical man cannot be a Spenserian career author.[39] The problem with this logic is that it does not accurately map Shakespeare's singular contribution to English literature, including his status since the eighteenth century as England's "National Poet."[40] Clearly, he does not exhibit Spenser's laureate strategy of authorial self-crowning. Yet Shakespeare's narrative poems, like the *Sonnets* and "The Phoenix and Turtle," join nearly forty extant plays in displaying Shakespeare's clear authorial ambitions to write the Elizabethan nation.[41] Perhaps, then, we might speak about Shakespeare as an author with a *counter-laureate career*. We could then see his narrative poems, not as apprentice work for his plays, but as the one genre that this counter-laureate author returned to as he worked out the main frame of his art, in poems and plays alike: in the genre of the Ovidian narrative poem, this author found a formal fusion of theater to poetry that became his historic signature.

# NOTES

1. Levin, "Critical Approaches to Shakespeare from 1660–1904," *The Cambridge Companion to Shakespeare Studies,* ed. Stanley Wells (Cambridge: Cambridge UP, 1986) 213–29 (228).
2. Rpt. *Shakespeare: The Critical Heritage,* ed. Brian Vickers, 6 vols. (London: Routledge & Kegal Paul, 1974–81) 1: 136.
3. *The Norton Shakespeare: Based on the Oxford Edition,* ed. Stephen Greenblatt et al. (New York: Norton, 1997) 1. The phrase "man of the theatre" comes from the *"Oxford Edition"* itself: *William Shakespeare: The Complete Works,* ed. Stanley Wells and Gary Taylor (Oxford: Clarendon, 1988) xxxvi.
4. The phrase "narrative poems" is a recent invention, useful for identification purposes. A more accurate classification, adopted later, might be "Ovidian minor epic." See Clarke Hulse, *Metamorphic Verse: The Elizabethan Minor Epic* (Princeton: Princeton UP, 1981), esp. 3–34.
5. See Lukas Erne, *Shakespeare as Literary Dramatist* (Cambridge: Cambridge UP, 2003); but also Harry Berger, Jr., *Imaginary Audition: Shakespeare on Stage and Page* (Berkeley: U of California P, 1989); Frank Kermode, *Shakespeare's Language* (London: Allen Lane-Penguin, 2000); Douglas Bruster, *Quoting Shakespeare: Form and Culture in Early Modern Drama* (Lincoln: U of Nebraska P, 2000); James P. Bednarz, *Shakespeare & the Poets' War* (New York: Columbia UP, 2001); Sean Keilen, *Vulgar Eloquence: On the Renaissance Invention of English Literature* (New Haven: Yale UP, 2006), esp. ch. 2. My own *Shakespeare, National Poet-Playwright* (Cambridge: Cambridge UP, 2004) extends the conversation to the poems.
6. Quotations of Shakespeare come from *The Riverside Shakespeare,* ed. G. Blakemore Evans et al. (Boston: Houghton, 1997).
7. Gary Schmidgall, *Shakespeare and the Poet's Life* (Lexington: UP of Kentucky, 1990) 1; Helen Vendler, ed., *The Art of Shakespeare's Sonnets* (Cambridge, MA: Harvard UP, 1997) 3.
8. Rpt. *"Venus and Adonis": Critical Essays,* ed. Philip C. Kolin (New York: Garland, 1997) 69.
9. Helgerson, *Self-Crowned Laureates: Spenser, Jonson, Milton, and the Literary System* (Berkeley: U of California P, 1983) 4–5. Criticism on careers has grown up largely around Edmund Spenser, foregrounded in Helgerson (ch. 1): see Patrick Cheney, *Spenser's Famous Flight: A Renaissance Idea of a Literary Career* (Toronto: U of Toronto P, 1993). On "career criticism" as a recent methodology, see Patrick Cheney, "Introduction," *European Literary Careers: The Author from Antiquity to the Renaissance,* ed. Cheney and Frederick A. de Armas (Toronto: U of Toronto P, 2002) 3–23.
10. Cf. the commonplace in Alvin B. Kernan, *Shakespeare, the King's Playwright: Theater in the Stuart Court, 1603–1613* (New Haven: Yale UP, 1995): "Shakespeare was not an autobiographical poet. [. . .] He remains, in fact, the most anonymous of our great writers" (179).
11. See Wendy Wall, "Authorship and the Material Conditions of Writing," *The Cambridge Companion to English Literature 1500–1600,* ed. Arthur F. Kinney (Cambridge: Cambridge UP, 2000) 64–89, esp. 86. Wall mentions Shakespeare only once in passing (83).
12. A. K. Hieatt, T. G. Bishop, and E. A. Nicholson, "Shakespeare's Rare Words: *A Lover's Complaint, Cymbeline,* and *Sonnets,*" *Notes and Queries* 34 (1987): 219–24 (220). The idea remains neglected.
13. Rpt. *The Shakspere Allusion-Book: A Collection of Allusions to Shakspere from 1591 to 1700,* ed. C. M. Ingleby, L. Toulmin Smith, and F. J. Furnivall; rev. ed. John Munro; pref. Edmund Chambers, 2 vols. (1909; Freeport, NY: Books for Libraries P, 1970) 1: 56.
14. Joseph Farrell, "Greek Lives and Roman Careers in the Classical *Vita* Tradition," Cheney and de Armas, eds. 24–46.
15. This paragraph and the next summarize Patrick Cheney, *Marlowe's Counterfeit Profession: Ovid, Spenser, Counter-Nationhood* (Toronto: U of Toronto P, 1997).

16. Thomas Nashe (1592), *The Works of Thomas Nashe,* ed. Ronald B. McKerrow, rev. ed. F. P. Wilson, 5 vols. (Oxford: Blackwell, 1958) 1: 299.

17. Marlowe, *Ovid's Elegies* 1.15.35–36, *The Collected Poems of Christopher Marlowe,* ed. Patrick Cheney and Brian J. Striar (New York: Oxford, 2006).

18. Bradbrook, "Beasts and Gods: Greene's *Groats-Worth of Witte* and the Social Purpose of *Venus and Adonis,*" *Shakespeare Survey* 15 (1962): 62–72 (62–63).

19. See also Marlowe, *Dedicatory Epistle* to Mary Sidney Herbert, *Poems,* ed. Cheney and Striar.

20. Only Hulse places the minor epic—including Shakespeare's *Venus* and *Lucrece*—along the "Virgilian path" in an author's career (12, 175), but he neglects to find this progression in the fiction of the poems themselves.

21. See Robert P. Merrix, "'Lo, In This Hollow Cradle Take Thy Rest': Sexual Conflict and Resolution in *Venus and Adonis,*" Kolin, ed. 341–58 (350).

22. On echo in the Orpheus myth, see Thomas H. Cain, "Spenser and the Renaissance Orpheus," *University of Toronto Quarterly* 41 (1971): 24–47 (28).

23. Crewe, ed., *William Shakespeare: The Narrative Poems,* Pelican Shakespeare (New York: Penguin, 1999) xxxix.

24. On rape, see Catherine Belsey, "Tarquin Dispossessed: Expropriation and Consent in *The Rape of Lucrece,*" *Shakespeare Quarterly* 52 (2001): 315–35; for republicanism, see Andrew Hadfield, *Shakespeare and Renaissance Politics,* Arden Shakespeare, 3d Ser. (New York: Thomson Learning, 2004), ch. 3.

25. On the Petrarchan discourse, see Nancy J. Vickers, "'The blazon of sweet beauty's best': Shakespeare's *Lucrece,*" *Shakespeare and the Question of Theory,* ed. Patricia Parker and Geoffrey Hartman (New York: Methuen, 1985) 95–115. On intertextuality, see Jonathan Bate, *Shakespeare and Ovid* (Oxford: Clarendon, 1993) 65–82; Lynn Enterline, *The Rhetoric of the Body: From Ovid to Shakespeare* (Cambridge: Cambridge UP, 2000) 152–97. On Shakespeare's worrying about print publication, see Colin Burrow, "Life and Work in Shakespeare's Poems," *Proceedings of the British Academy* 97 (1998): 15–50.

26. Space prohibits discussion of *Lucrece*'s Southampton dedication along this line (see Cheney, *Shakespeare,* ch. 4).

27. Marlowe and Spenser are well known to underlie Shakespeare's poem (Cheney, *Shakespeare,* ch. 4).

28. On Orpheus in Spenser, see Cheney, *Flight* 22–76; on Philomela, 77–110. Orpheus is a founder of poetry who uses music to tame wild animals. When his wife Eurydice dies, he uses his art to retrieve her from the god Pluto in Hades, but he loses her again when he looks back at her. Philomela is raped by Tereus, but the gods turn her into a nightingale, icon of the poet. For superb recent commentary on both myths in English Renaissance literature, see Keilen, esp. ch. 1 and 2.

29. Patrick Cheney, "Introduction," *The Cambridge Companion to Christopher Marlowe* (Cambridge: Cambridge UP, 2004) 3–23.

30. On *Lucrece* and epic, see Joel Fineman, "Shakespeare's Will: The Temporality of Rape," *Representations* 20 (1987): 25–76 (64).

31. On the frescoes in Virgil's *Aeneid,* which depict a Trojan myth important to Aeneas' destiny within Dido's Carthaginian Temple of Juno (Troy's enemy) in order to license the Pax Romana, see Ralph Hexter, "Sidonian Dido," *Innovations of Antiquity,* ed. Hexter and Daniel Selden (New York: Routledge, 1992) 332–84.

32. See Richard Helgerson, *Adulterous Alliances: Home, State, and History in Early Modern European Drama and Painting* (Chicago: U of Chicago P, 2000) 30, 39.

33. Heather Dubrow, *Shakespeare and Domestic Loss: Forms of Deprivation, Mourning, and Recuperation* (Cambridge: Cambridge UP, 1999) 59.

34. Collinson, "The Monarchical Republic of Queen Elizabeth I," *Bulletin of the John Ryland's Library* 69 (1987): 394–424.

35. Colin Burrow, ed., *William Shakespeare: The Complete Sonnets and Poems*, Oxford World's Classics (Oxford: Oxford UP, 2002) 338, 245.
36. Kerrigan, ed., *"The Sonnets" and "A Lover's Complaint"* (1986; New York: Penguin, 1995) 402; MacCaffrey, *Spenser's Allegory: The Anatomy of Imagination* (Princeton: Princeton UP, 1976) 366.
37. On the reverend man's "grained bat" deriving from Spenser's *Mother Hubberds Tale* (217), see Katherine Duncan-Jones, ed., *Shakespeare's Sonnets,* Arden Shakespeare, 3d ser. (London: Thomas Nelson, 1997) 436.
38. See Cheney, *Shakespeare*, ch. 8.
39. See Stephen Greenblatt, *Will in the World: How Shakespeare Became Shakespeare* (New York: Norton, 2004): "In Shakespeare's work there are relatively few signs of the influence of Spenser" (207).
40. See Michael Dobson, *The Making of the National Poet: Shakespeare, Adaptation, and Authorship, 1660–1769* (Oxford: Clarendon, 1992).
41. See Richard Helgerson, *Forms of Nationhood: The Elizabethan Writing of England* (Chicago: U of Chicago P, 1992) 193–245.

## READING LIST

Burrow, Colin. "Life and Work in Shakespeare's Poems." Chatterton Lecture on Poetry. *Proceedings of the British Academy* 97 (1998): 15–50.

Cheney, Patrick. *Shakespeare, National Poet-Playwright*. Cambridge: Cambridge UP, 2004.

———, ed. *The Cambridge Companion to Shakespeare's Poetry*. Cambridge: Cambridge UP, 2006.

Cousins, A. D. *Shakespeare's Sonnets and Narrative Poems*. Harlow, Essex, Eng.: Longman, 2000.

Dubrow, Heather. *Captive Victors: Shakespeare's Narrative Poems and Sonnets*. Ithaca: Cornell UP, 1987.

Duncan-Jones, Katherine, ed. *Shakespeare's Sonnets*. Arden Shakespeare. 3d ser. London: Thomas Nelson, 1997.

Donaldson, Ian. *The Rapes of Lucretia: A Myth and Its Transformations*. Oxford: Clarendon, 1982.

Empson, William. "The Narrative Poems." *Essays in Shakespeare*. Ed. David B. Pirie. Cambridge: Cambridge UP, 1986. 1–28.

Hyland, Peter. *An Introduction to Shakespeare's Poems*. Basingstoke: Palgrave Macmillan, 2003.

Kay, Dennis. "William Shakespeare." *Sixteenth-Century British Nondramatic Writers*. Ed. David A. Richardson. *Dictionary of Literary Biography*. 172. Detroit: Gale Research, 1996. 217–37.

———. *William Shakespeare: Sonnets and Poems*. New York: Twayne, 1998.

Kerrigan, John. *Motives of Woe: Shakespeare and "Female Complaint."* Oxford: Clarendon, 1991.

———. "Shakespeare's Poems." *The Cambridge Companion to Shakespeare*. Ed. Margreta De Grazia and Stanley Wells. Cambridge: Cambridge UP, 2001. 65–81.

Mortimer, Anthony. *Variable Passions: A Reading of Shakespeare's "Venus and Adonis."* New York: AMS, 2000.

Roberts, Sasha. *Reading Shakespeare's Poems in Early Modern England*. Basingstoke: Palgrave Macmillan, 2003.

Roe, John, ed. *The Poems*. By William Shakespeare. New Cambridge Shakespeare. Cambridge: Cambridge UP, 1992.

# 16

## Shakespeare's *Sonnets* and English Sonnet Sequences

### *Sasha Roberts*

In the late sixteenth century the sonnet sequence captured the imagination of poets as a means of exploring desire, service, and the act of writing poetry itself—but by 1609 when *Shake-speares Sonnets* first appeared in print it had fallen out of favor. As Berowne put it in *Love's Labour's Lost* (c. 1596), the sonneteering fashion "makes flesh a deity / A green goose a goddess; pure pure idolatry. / God amend us God amend!" (4.3.74–76). So what encouraged Thomas Thorpe, publisher of *Shake-speares Sonnets,* to take the risk of producing a volume some ten years "out-of-date"? Shakespeare's name alone was not guaranteed to sell among a Jacobean readership, but a new approach to the sonnet sequence might—and *Shake-speares Sonnets* reveled in both novelty and tradition, infusing the sonnet sequence with unexpected skepticism and satire, bawdiness and bitterness. It also traversed a remarkable range of issues, from nature to time, immortality, mutability (change), procreation, death, idolatry, service, friendship, beauty, truth, writing, and, of course, love. But although love brings exhilarating rewards in *Shake-speares Sonnets,* the sequence as a whole takes the reader on an emotional rollercoaster that ends in paradox: while its speaker concludes on a note of disillusion, cynicism, and exhaustion, the sequence itself is an extraordinary testament to the vitality of imaginative writing and the dazzling wit of its author.[1]

### Writing Against Tradition I: The Sonnet Mistress and Sonnet Form

The most striking break *Shake-speares Sonnets* made with tradition was its thorough-going *anti-Petrarchism*—particularly its description of an unattainable *male* beloved (apparently the subject of the first subsequence of Sonnets 1–126), an *attained* female beloved (Sonnets 127–54), and the seeming love-triangle between both beloveds and the (male) speaker (summarized in Sonnets 42, 133–34, and 144). The first English sonnet sequence to be printed was religious in nature, Ann Lock's *A Meditation of a Penitent Sinner* (1560), and spiritual sonnet sequences continued to be published—most famously John Donne's *La Corona, Holy Sonnets* (1633, 1635)—but the English sonnet sequence has generally been regarded as a secular tradition inspired by Petrarch's sonnet sequence *Canzoniere* (c. 1335).[2] Celebrating the ravishing but distant Laura, the *Canzoniere* dwelt upon the poet's conflicted experiences as a lover; "Petrarchism" is consequently characterized as the depiction of a tormented (male) lover's passion for an idealized and unattainable female beloved, generally in sonnet form and using a stan-dard set of tropes or images (such as the poetic "blazon" that itemized the beloved's beautiful features, which Shakespeare parodies in Sonnet 130, "My mistress' eyes are nothing like the sun").

The translation of Petrarch's sonnets into English by the Henrician courtiers Thomas Wyatt and Henry Howard, earl of Surrey (which first appeared in print in Richard Tottel's hugely influential 1557 miscellany of *Songs and Sonnets*), demonstrated the potential of the Petrarchan sonnet as an expression of frustrated desire—in romantic, erotic, and political terms—but it was the Elizabethan courtier Sir Philip Sidney's *Astrophil and Stella* (1591) that really fueled the English vogue for the sonnet sequence. A series of 108 sonnets interspersed with eleven songs, *Astrophil and Stella* both describes the speaker's volatile states of mind as he struggles with his (arguably adulterous) desire for the unattainable Stella and examines the process of writing itself: "Loving in truth, and fain in verse my love to show [. . .] But words came halting forth, wanting Invention's stay" (*A&S* 1.1–9). It was swiftly followed by a spate of sonnet sequences in the 1590s—perhaps most notably Samuel Daniel's *Delia* (1592), an anagram of "Ideal," which aptly characterizes Daniel's disdainful but idealized sonnet mistress ("a Goddess chaste I find," 5.3); Michael Drayton's *Ideas Mirrour* (1594), which used Petrarchism to explore Neoplatonic notions of an elevated "pure idea" of Love (*Ideas Mirrour*, 49.13); and Edmund Spenser's *Amoretti and Epithalamion* (1595), in which the speaker's conflicted "sacred" and "sensual desire" (84.2–3) is redirected toward a Protestant meditation upon marriage. In a literary culture that prized *imitation*—the ability to master and play with convention—many English sonneteers wrote sonnets not out of autobiographical experience but as exercises in literary expression; hence they wrote to nonexistent women, wrote to women they were not in love with, or experimented in Petrarchan complaint when they were happily married. Further, as Arthur Marotti points out, in the context of the charged relations between male courtiers and an intransigent female monarch, "love" in the Elizabethan sonnet could also be turned to political courtship: an attempt to win the favor of that most powerful and unattainable of women, Elizabeth I.[3]

Shakespeare's sonnet mistress, however, is notoriously attainable. Often referred to in criticism as the dark lady on account of her "black" beauty (130–32), she is first praised then condemned by the speaker as "the bay where all men ride," "the wide world's common place," a "false plague" (137.6–14) who "lies" (138.2–7), breaks her "bed-vow" (152.3), and will, in turn, "fire out" the speaker's "friend" (144.14)—an allusion to the burning pain of syphillis.[4] This invective is followed through to the final sonnets of the sequence (153–54), which turn anacreontic fantasy (the personification of Love as the mischievous boy Cupid, a key trope of English sonnet sequences) into a bawdy scene with a bitter ending: the "sick" and "diseased" speaker is unable to find a "cure" in a "seething bath" heated by Cupid's "inflaming brand" (a flaming torch, and here a phallic symbol)—an image reminiscent of the sweating tubs used in Jacobean London to treat venereal disease (see *Measure for Measure* 3.2.57 and *Troilus and Cressida* 5.10.55).

Although Spenser's sonnet mistress tells "false forged lies" (86.7), Shakespeare's promiscuous and potentially pox-ridden mistress utterly broke the mold of the Petrarchan sonnet mistress, bringing a new charge to the old adages that "my love is as a fever" and that "desire is death. [. . .] Past cure I am" (147.1, 8–9). But Shakespeare also innovated in the linguistic register he used to describe her. Petrarchism was often lampooned for its tortuous turns of phrase, but a plain and direct speaking style had long been deployed by English sonneteers—from Wyatt's marvelous "Who so list to hunt I know where is an hind" to Drayton's "Since there's no help, come, let us kiss and part, / Nay, I have done, you get no more of me" (*Ideas Mirrour* 61.1–2). Nor did sonneteers shy away from sensual desire: "Her breast that table was so richly spread, / My thoughts the guests, which would thereon have fed" (Spenser, *Amoretti* 77.13–14). But the bawdiness deployed by Shakespeare's speaker is not only remarkably "saucy" at times (128.9)—as in the speaker's contemplation of his "flesh" (penis) that will "stand," "rise and fall" *in* his mistress' "affairs" (151.8–14)—it can also be harsh and abusive, as in the veiled allusions to her vagina as "hell" ("none knows well / To shun the heaven that leads men to this hell," 129.13–14; "I guess one angel in another's hell," 144.12; see also 119.2, 147.14, and compare *King Lear* 4.6.124–29).

The speaker's vitriol against female duplicity and promiscuity, particularly in Sonnets 137–47, is unmistakeable; what remains at stake is how far we read the *Sonnets* as condoning, promoting, challenging, or condemning such views. For Katherine Duncan-Jones, the "strongly misogynistic bias" hinted at in earlier sonnets—whereby women figure either as chaste phialls for the male beloved's seed (1–17) or as false creatures less worthy than men (the "shifting change" of "false women's fashion," 20.4–5)—is compounded by "the outrageous misogyny of 127–54"; hence the dark lady is aligned with despair, corruption, pride, the plague, hell, evil, a devil, and a fiend (137.12, 152.14). If misogyny reduces women to objects rather than independent subjects, then the *Sonnets* surely objectifies women. In a similar vein Eve Kosovsky Sedgwick stresses the *homosocial* logic of the *Sonnets* that limits women to their strategic use in fostering relations between men (whether eroticized or platonic); thus the dark lady's most decisive impact is precisely upon the speaker's privileged relationship with his friend, not with her ("That she hath thee is of my wailing chief," 42.3).[5] But, crucially, Shakespeare's *Sonnets* invites critical distance: we are not necessarily invited to agree with the speaker or his views; rather, he admits to being a liar (as in 138.8–14 and 147.13–14), questions his own judgment ("where is my judgement fled?," 148.3), and hypocritically complains of his mistress's promiscuity while admitting to his own infidelities ("in my nature reigned / All frailties that besiege all kinds of blood," 109.9–10; "Two loves I have," 144.1).

Moreover, the volume in which *Shake-speares Sonnets* first appeared provides the reader with an alternative point of view. The 1609 quarto printed the sonnets alongside Shakespeare's *A Lover's Complaint*—a deliberate *pairing* of sonnet sequence and complaint (a poem usually written in the voice of a fallen woman who has been betrayed by a lover) that was characteristic of English sonnet sequences after Daniel's *Delia [. . .] with the Complaint of Rosamond* (1592).[6] *A Lover's Complaint,* which tells of a young woman betrayed by a "fair" but "foul" (170) young nobleman, not only includes many verbal echoes of the *Sonnets;* its constructions of male and female desire *counter* those in the *Sonnets,* and the sympathetic voice it gives to the female lover (so often "silenced" in English sonnet sequences) serves to frame the misogynist sentiments of the sonnet speaker. More widely, reading Shakespeare's *Sonnets* alongside his complaint raises the status of the sonnet as *authentic* romantic expression. The young woman of *A Lover's Complaint* tears up the treacherous youth's "deep-brained sonnets" with "wit well-blazoned," condemning their contents as "a register of lies" (see *ALC*

43–56, 209–27): thus while the speaker of the *Sonnets* imagines his poems surviving into posterity, *A Lover's Complaint* characterizes the sonnet as impermanent and untrustworthy. Although this may not make *Shake-speares Sonnets* "a book of lies and lying" (Duncan-Jones 95), it does heighten awareness of its literary artifice and rhetoric (the art of persuasion)—calling attention to the confessional mode as a rhetorical stance not a biographical truth, to both speakers as literary personas with partial points of view and axes to grind, and ultimately to their author's skillful creation of the *effect* of eavesdropping on a heady, passionate, and painful affair. In short, the brilliance of Shakespeare's sonnets is precisely that they are so *persuasive* as deeply personal poems of romantic and erotic love.

At a local level Shakespeare also uses the sonnet form to stage a remarkable series of counterpoints and contradictions. Although in early modern England the term "sonnet" was sometimes used to describe lyric poems of varying lengths, today it is conventionally understood to mean a fourteen-line poem (often, though not always, written in English in iambic pentameter); further, those fourteen lines are organized as a movement from question to answer, problem to resolution, cause to effect. Wyatt deployed the "Petrarchan" two-part structure of octave and sestet; Surrey introduced a four-part structure of three quatrains (a group of four lines) followed by a couplet—an arrangement that allowed the writer to *develop* an idea in three stages and, crucially, to *conclude* with a pithy couplet that could be used to elucidate, summarize, or resolve what has gone before.[7] This structure formed the basis of the "Spenserian" sonnet (with the rhyme scheme ababbcbccdcdee) and the "Shakespearean" sonnet (with the rhyme scheme ababcdcdefefgg), but Shakespeare was especially interested in using the final couplet (or occasionally a turning point in the third quartrain) to disrupt expectations and *undermine* the previous quatrains—and, in so doing, the very authority of the speaker's pronouncements. For instance, in a stunning display of condensed thought, Sonnet 147 ("My love is a fever longing still") moves from the idea of being sick with "longing" (first quartrain) to acting without "reason" (second quatrain) to being "mad" in "thoughts" and "discourse" (third quatrain)—clearly ironic, since the speaker nonetheless pulls off the difficult trick of writing a beautifully constructed sonnet—to the devastating final couplet: "For I have sworn thee fair, and thought thee bright, / Who art as black as hell, as dark as night" (147.13–14). While the trope of being "madly in love" is usually used to suggest the depth of a lover's *devotion to* his beloved, here it leads to his *aversion from* the beloved, to the lover's critical error in mistaking "fair" from "dark," good from "hell." More widely, the speaker's radical about-turn invites the reader to question his judgment and the provisionality of his pronouncements on love and his beloved(s) elsewhere, an invitation made time and again in the sonnets.

Changes of mood and scene were characteristic of sonnet sequences: the sonnet *sequence* allowed writers to shift perspective from one sonnet to the next, to juxtapose images and ideas, to follow a train of thought from one sonnet to another, or, alternatively, to disrupt it and in so doing leave questions unanswered. In this respect the very *form* of the sonnet sequence was especially apt for writers exploring the contrary states of desire. But Shakespeare's *Sonnets* goes further than earlier sonnet sequences in its patterning of *reversal*—as couplet reverses quatrains, as one sonnet reverses the ideas and assumptions of another, as the second subsequence of sonnets (apparently) on the sonnet mistress (127–54) reverses the sentiments of the first subsequence (apparently) on the fair man (1–124), and, finally, as *A Lover's Complaint* reverses the perspective of the *Sonnets*. Although earlier writers were fascinated by the conflicted state of the Petrarchan lover, the artistry of Shakespeare's *Sonnets* is that contradictions are layered so intricately and fundamentally that the reader never quite knows where he or she stands.

## Writing Against Tradition II: The Male Beloved

Although *Shake-speares Sonnets* was not the first sonnet sequence to celebrate male beauty—Richard Barnfield's *Cynthia* (1595) tells of a male speaker's admiration for the gorgeous and effeminate Ganymede (the personal cupbearer to the lascivious Jove in Greek mythology who thence became a figure of homoerotic desire in the Renaissance)— it was innovative in exploring passion between men in such tantalizing depth.

The unconventional nature of the relationship between the male speaker and male beloved of the *Sonnets* is apparent by Sonnet 20 ("A woman's face, with Nature's own hand painted, / Hast thou," 20.1–2). The sonnet hinges on ambiguity: the description of the fair youth as "the master-mistress of my passion" (20.2) is a deliberately ambivalent turn of phrase both hinting at the fair youth's mastery over the speaker and casting him as a conventional female beloved; in addition, the speaker's sexual interest in him remains equivocal. On the one hand the speaker claims that the one "thing" Nature added to the youth (a penis) is "to my purpose nothing," hence Nature "pricked thee out for women's pleasure" (20.11–13); on the other hand to take literally the speaker's suggestion that the youth's "thing" is of no interest or "purpose" to him—especially amidst such punning talk of pricking and when the sonnet sequence as a whole calls attention to the speaker's evasions and vicissitudes—is to "misconstrue teasing inconsequence as unambiguous statement" (Kerrigan 201). But the case for the *Sonnets'* portrayal of homoerotic desire goes beyond Sonnet 20: many sonnets depict the speaker's intense love for his friend and his jealousy of his friend's "sensual" betrayal (35.6), leaving the speaker like "a deceived husband" (93.2). Moreover, the love between the speaker and his friend must remain hidden—"I may not evermore acknowledge thee, / Lest my bewailed guilt should do thee shame" (36.9–10)—and the speaker's continued preoccupation with "shame" and "vulgar scandal" (112.2) is arguably evocative of the controversy surrounding same-sex passion in the early modern period. While Joseph Pequiney's conclusion that the *Sonnets* depicts a consummated "homosexual" love affair is too literal-minded, attempts at explaining the speaker's passion in Neoplatonic terms (in which the speaker aspires toward not earthly desire but a higher love) falter in the face of the sonnet sequence's insistent allusions to sensual desire and use of bawdy innuendo.[8] The point of Sonnet 20 still holds: the speaker's love for his friend remains ambiguous.

It remains vital, however, to be alert to contemporary discourses of service and friendship as a context for the speaker's "love" for his "lord" (26.1) and "dear friend" (30.13). As historian Keith Wrightson points out, relations between masters and servants (including younger members of the aristocracy who served in the great households of their relatives) were "shot through with ambiguities and inconsistencies, if not outright contradictions. [. . .] Authority was besieged with obligations of love and care."[9] Such ambiguities and inconsistencies shape the speaker's relations with the fair youth: thus Sonnet 26 positions the speaker as servant to his "Lord," bound "in vassalage" and by "duty strongly knit" yet hopeful for "thy sweet respect" (26.1–12), while Sonnets 57–58 develop the theme of subjection in service: "Being your slave, what should I do but tend / Upon the hours and times of your desire?" (57.1–2). This pair of sonnets has been seized upon by modern readers for its apparent expression of an eroticized masochism ("O, let me suffer," 58.5), but as David Schalkwyk argues, if we recall the conditions of service they describe—"Being your vassal bound to stay your leisure" (58.4)—we come "closer to the lived, material and ideological conditions of late medieval and early modern England than is suggested by the purely literary, erotic reading" of the sonnets.[10] Hence contemporary discourses of service resonate with the speaker's intense devotion to his "lord," such as William Gouge's account of the idolatrous servant who places his master's will above his duty to God: "to be obsequious to a man, so addicted to please him, and so subiect to his will, as to do whatsoever he will have done: to prefer it before Gods word and will."[11] And indeed the speaker is keenly conscious of the conflict between prosaic love and the love of God: thus the opening line of Sonnet 58, "That God forbid that made me first your slave," echoes Galatians 6:14—"But God forbid that I should rejoice, but in the cross of our Lord"—while Sonnet 105 provocatively demands, "Let not my love be called idolatry" (105.1). However, for early modern readers attuned to contemporary religious discourses idolatry is precisely what the speaker invokes—especially in linking the "holy and obsequious tear / [That] dear religious love stol'd from mine eye" to his beloved: "images I loved I view in thee" (30.5–13).

Similarly, we also need to bear in mind the *conventional* use of romantic and amorous language in early modern discourses of friendship. For instance, Sonnets 30–32 and 46–47 speak of "my lovers" (31.10) and "lover" (32.4), the "inward love of heart" (46.14), and eyes "famished for a look" (47.3), but John Benson, editor of Shakespeare's *Poems* in 1640, nonetheless gave them titles of unambiguous friendship: "The benefit of Friendship" (Sonnets 30–32) and "Two faithfull friends" (Sonnets 46–47; see Roberts 161). For Bruce Smith, however, Benson's edition is "a sign that the cultural moment of Shakespeare's sonnets had passed," that "the ambivalent alliances between male bonding and sexual desire that demanded such sensitive and varied treatment in poetic discourse" were increasingly subject to schematic opposition.[12] But Benson did not perform the thoroughgoing excision of homoerotic desire in the *Sonnets* that is often claimed; rather, the more striking revisions he made to the *Sonnets* was to tone down the most vitriolic of the sonnets addressed to the sonnet mistress (Roberts 165). Yes, Shakespeare's *Sonnets* broke the mold by exploring in delicious detail one man's emotional investment in another, but as Margreta de Grazia has argued, the real "scandal" of Shakespeare's *Sonnets* is not its portrayal of homoerotic passion but its figure of the promiscuous mistress whose adulterate liaisons threaten a "shocking social peril": a dissolution to "the distribution of power and property [which] depended on orderly sexuality"—the chaste, fertile marriage with which the *Sonnets* begins.[13]

## The Problem of Narrative, Speaker, and Wit

One of the games played by English sonnet sequences is that they do not reveal all in the manner of a novel or a play but rather offer *glimpses* into a supposed affair and a lover's state of mind, reveling in the elusive and the tacit. Even so, a provisional narrative can perhaps be traced in Shakespeare's *Sonnets:* (1) the invitation to a fair young man to marry and perpetuate his beauty in a son, a wholly unusual topic for a sonnet sequence (the so-called procreation sonnets, 1–17); (2) the speaker's initial love for his friend (18–32; compare 53–54, 68, 77, 104, 106); (3) the friend's betrayal, including an affair with the speaker's sonnet mistress (34–35, 40–42; compare 69–70, 92–96, 120); (4) the speaker's melancholy and absence from his friend (34, 36, 44–46, 47, 50); (5) the speaker's troubled subjection to his friend (50–51, 57–58, 66); (6) the speaker's immortalization of his friend in verse (54–56, 59–60, 62–65); (7) the appearance of a rival poet (78–86); (8) the friend's rejection of the speaker (89–90); (9) the speaker's betrayal of his friend (109–12, 117–21); (10) the speaker's reiteration of his love (87–92, 97–99, 109–15, 117–21); and (11) the speaker's further immortalization of his friend in verse (100–08, 115–16, 123–25).

Sonnets 56 and 97 both mark turning points with their suggestion of renewed love, and after Sonnet 97 the speaker becomes increasingly retrospective. Writing and Time emerge as dominant themes of the first subsequence, and its concluding poem urging "my lovely boy" to fear "Time's fickle glass" (126.1–2) ends abruptly—the final couplet indicated only by empty parentheses in the 1609 quarto—as if cut short by Time itself or to reiterate that as readers we will never be privy to the underlying narrative of the sonnet sequence (assuming there is one). The second subsequence (Sonnets 127–52) apparently charts (1) the speaker's initial praise for his mistress (127–30); (2) his rebuke of her deceitfulness and promiscuity, including her affair with his friend (129, 131, 137–44); (3) his continued subjection to her in abject and destructive desire (135–36, 146–51); and (4) his final attack on his mistress's treachery (152)—hence the speaker concludes that she turns out to be, like his "perjured" oaths, "so foul a lie" (152.13–14). The final anacreontic sonnets (153–54) argue that "diseased" love cannot be relieved since "Love's fire heats water, water cools not love" (154.12–14): from the lyrical heights of love's "delight" (36.8) through the torment, rejection, subjection, shame, madness, and sickness that love has brought him, the speaker ends without hope of a "cure" (153.13, 154.13) or even of closure.

But there are significant problems in assuming a narrative structure to Shakespeare's *Sonnets;* not only does the sonnet sequence play a game of cat-and-mouse with the reader, never yielding full answers, but so much about the *Sonnets'* production remains a mystery. It is not known whether the sequence was *authorized* by Shakespeare—that is, whether Shakespeare gave the stationer Thomas Thorpe the authority to print the sonnets in the form in which they appeared in 1609—nor do we know *when* the sonnets were written (separately and/or as a sequence?), *who* they were dedicated to (was "Mr W. H.," the dedicatee and "only begetter of these sonnets," William Herbert, third earl of Pembroke, Henry Wriothesley, Shakespeare's dedicatee for *Venus and Adonis* and *Lucrece,* or an unknown other?), *who* ordered the sequence (Shakespeare? Thorpe?), *how* the sonnets were selected for printing, or from *what* copies (like Shakespeare's plays, no manuscript of the complete sequence has survived).[14] It was long assumed that Thorpe's quarto was a "pirated" text (produced without permission) and thus inherently unreliable; more recently Katherine Duncan-Jones has argued that Thorpe's quarto represents an "authorized" version of the sonnet sequence—arguing (among other points) for the deliberate numerical patterning in the sequence and Thorpe's reputation for reliability—while Colin Burrow points out that Thorpe's quarto remains "a radically ambiguous thing," and since we cannot determine whether Shakespeare authorized the *Sonnets* we should instead notice the quarto's physical resemblance to its acclaimed (and "pirated") predecessor, Sidney's *Astrophil and Stella*.[15]

Heather Dubrow takes the uncertainties surrounding the ordering of the sonnets a stage further to argue that the assumption that the *Sonnets* proceeds as two chronologically distinct subsequences addressed to a fair man and a dark lady is fundamentally suspect. Over 120 of the sonnets in the entire sequence do not specify an addressee through a gendered pronoun; thus Sonnet 2, the most popularly transmitted sonnet in manuscript in the seventeenth century, was frequently titled as a poem addressed to a "maid" (Roberts 176). As a consequence we cannot be sure that sonnets that make no reference to a specific lover or relationship—such as 116 ("Let me not to the marriage of true minds") or 129 ("Th'expense of spirit in a waste of shame")—necessarily pertain to the friend or dark lady (or even presume a *male* speaker). Nor can we assume a linear development from Sonnet 1 to 154 (Sonnets 42 and 144, for instance, appear to describe the same scenario). Further, as Dubrow points out, other English sonnet sequences—including Daniel's *Delia* and Mary Wroth's *Pamphilia to Amphilanthus* (1621)—make "no pretense of a coherent plot or a single beloved"; thus an early modern reader was far more likely to expect a "loose and at some points arbitrary" arrangement of sonnets in any given sequence, including Shakespeare's, rather than a "readily discerned narrative."[16]

Narrative in Shakespeare's *Sonnets* is further complicated by the inconsistencies of the speaker. The speaker may best be understood in terms of impersonation: just as in his plays Shakespeare created powerfully vivid characters, the speaker of the *Sonnets* is not Shakespeare the poet describing a historical reality but a literary character articulating an imaginative scene; hence the *Sonnets* deploys "performative language" and "language games" (Schalkwyk 241) and are often described as *dramatic* monologues (and used by actors as audition pieces). It is sometimes objected that Sonnets 135–36, which riddle on six senses of the word "Will," denote William Shakespeare, but we cannot extrapolate from two sonnets the speaker's identity across the whole sequence; the point of the sonnets is rather their teasing (often bawdy) wordplay. Moreover, understanding the speaker of the *Sonnets* in terms of impersonation allows for critical distance: just as we may be invited to take a critical stance toward (for instance) Romeo, Hamlet, or Othello, the *Sonnets* may invite us to take a skeptical view of (for instance) the speaker's treatment of his mistress or abject subjection to his friend. Repeatedly revealed to be unreliable, unfaithful, and subject to profound changes of mind, Shakespeare's speaker is not one from whom we should expect *consistency*—either at the level of character or narrative—nor should we always take him at his word.

The elusive narrative and speaker of Shakespeare's *Sonnets* do not, however, divert from the larger issue at stake in the sequence: the display of poetic wit. "Wit" in the early modern period denoted ingenuity, intelligence, imagination, and verbal prowess and was arguably the most highly valued literary faculty—more so than originality or authenticity, so favored in post-Romantic constructions of poetry. Shakespeare's *Sonnets* demonstrates *wit* in abundance, not least in its deft use of paradox (which Shakespeare repeatedly deploys in both the sonnet sequence and complaint), conceit (an ingenious comparison, often turning on unexpected or contrary states), imagery, and wordplay— including puns and double-entendres (such as "Will will fulfil the treasure of thy love, / Ay, fill it full with wills, and my will one," 136.5–6), coinages and unfamiliar words (as in "The world will waile thee like a *makelesse* wife," 9.4), grammatical transformations

(such as "And thou (all they) hast all the all of me," 31.14), and phrases loaded with ambiguous meaning (as in "I never writ, nor no man ever loved," suggesting both "no man
ever loved" and "I never loved a man," 116.14). Moreover, Shakespeare brilliantly
uses—indeed, almost seems to defy the constraints of—the fourteen-line sonnet to develop complex ideas in condensed form. Thus one of the best-known sonnets, "Shall I
compare thee to a summer's day" (18), widens in scope and gravity from "thee" and a
"day" (18.1–2) to a month ("May," 18.3) and a season ("summer," 18.4) through to the
"changing course" of nature (18.7), finally overcoming "death" with "eternal" art
(18.11–12). As Helen Vendler remarks, "it is a long way from an apparently fanciful natural simile to eternal art, and yet Shakespeare traverses it in twelve lines." Furthermore,
the sonnet connects words through alliteration that in themselves prompt intriguing associations: day, darling, dimmed, declines, death; lovely, lease, lose, lines, long, lives, life.[17]
Ostensibly this sonnet is about a speaker's love for his beloved, but its wider subject is actually the remarkable ability of the author's "lines" to bring "life" to their subject
(18.12–14).

This is not to deny that the sonnets are steeped in (romantic, erotic, platonic, and
spiritual) love—that the speaker's beloved "and love are still my argument" (76.10)—
but rather to observe how the underlying subject becomes writing itself, particularly as
a way of overcoming mortality: "My love looks fresh, and Death to me subscribes, /
Since, spite of him, I'll live in this poor rhyme" (107.10–11). In this respect the title
*Shake-speares Sonnets* is extremely apt: whereas earlier sonnet sequences are typically
titled according to the lovers whose stories they lamented (*Astrophil and Stella, Delia,
Diana, Parthenophil and Parthenophe, Phillis, Licia, Coelia, Fidessa, Chloris, Cynthia, Laura, Alba, Aurora*) *Shake-speares Sonnets* draws attention instead to authorship
and literary form. And although earlier sonnet sequences reveled in reflexivity ("Go,
wailing verse," *Delia* 2.1; "Go you, my lines," *Ideas Mirrour* 72.1) and a keen awareness of the literary field ("Let others sing of knights and paladins," *Delia* 53.1; "Let each
commend as best shall like his mind, / Some Sidney, Constable, some Daniel," *Ideas
Mirrour* 73.3–4), Shakespeare innovated by personifying literary competitiveness in the
figure of the rival poet, whose "wit" and "style" is "admired everywhere" (84.11–12).
Sonnets 78–86 on the rival poet not only function as a meta-commentary upon the *Sonnets* and poetic writing (and as such merit careful reading) but are also gloriously disingenious. On the one hand the speaker claims to be "tongue-tied" (80.4, 85.1) and
"dumb" (85.14) when confronted with the rival poet's "polished form" (85.8) and "great
verse" (86.1); on the other hand he is not only remarkably eloquent but also contrasts
other writers' use of "strained [. . .] rhetoric" to his own "true plain words" (82.10–12),
an assertion complicated by a sequence of sonnets whose sense is often far from "plain."
Perhaps what we witness here is an oblique allusion to "plain style"—a direct, sometimes "rough" mode of speech favored especially by satirists from the late-1590s—and
indeed Shakespeare's *Sonnets* (which are often argued to date from the 1590s) shares
many affinities with late-Elizabethan satire: the use of bawdiness, the abusive tone of
voice, the figure of the morally compromised and ultimately unreliable speaker.

More widely, however, the "rival poet" sonnets speak to contemporary literary culture: the "strained" relations between poet and patron (82.10). While efforts to identify
the rival poet or the *Sonnets'* enigmatic dedicatee, "Mr. W. H.," remain ultimately inconclusive, the scenario depicted in Sonnets 78–86 of competition between writers

for patronage (financial support and prestige) was characteristic of Elizabethan literary production. Thus the speaker's dependence upon his Muse evokes (in part) the dependence of contemporary writers upon their patrons, a relationship complicated in the development of the English sonnet sequence by a transition from manuscript to print. Wyatt's and Surrey's sonnets initially circulated only in manuscript; Sidney, an aristocrat, did not offer his writings for general consumption and even when printed *Astrophil and Stella* communicated the aura of an elite, coterie world.[18] But the very success of *Astrophil and Stella* led to the *popularization* of sonnet sequences by middle-class writers—such as Daniel, Drayton, Barnfield, and of course Shakespeare—all jostling for "place" (79.4) in an increasingly competitive literary marketplace. We perhaps get a sense of this world in Shakespeare's Sonnet 29, in which the speaker laments his "outcast state" in a fiercely competitive social arena where he wishes himself "like to one more rich in hope, / Featured like him, like him with friends possessed, / Desiring this man's art, and that man's scope" (29.2–7). "Verse" thus becomes the nexus of an extraordinary range of issues in Shakespeare's *Sonnets,* from the expression of romantic and erotic desire to the defeat of mortality, from soaring imagination to strained rhetoric, from intimacy between friends to inequalities between poet and patron, from personal expression to professional rivalry. Indeed, "verse" is not simply the form of the *Sonnets* but also its content.

## Coda: Shakespeare Versus Wroth

After Shakespeare's 1609 *Sonnets* few sonnet sequences appeared in print: writers were instead drawn to other poetic modes to explore romantic and erotic love—the metaphysical conceit, the frank "Cavalier" lyric, the acerbic epigram, and the idealizing elegy or epithalamion (marriage poem). However, the last English sonnet sequence to be published in the Elizabethan-Jacobean period, *Pamphilia to Amphilanthus* (1621) by Mary Wroth (Sidney's niece), countered not only Petrarchan convention but also Shakespeare's potent anti-Petrarchism: where Petrarchan convention idealized the sonnet mistress and Shakespeare dealt her a devastating satiric blow, Wroth constructed the female lover as sympathetic; where the Petrarchan sonnet mistress was coy and Shakespeare's dark lady promiscuous, in Wroth's sonnets it is the "false" male beloved (*PA* 40.1) who betrays the female lover's "constancy" (*PA* 103.12); where both Petrarchism and Shakespeare's *Sonnets* dwelt on the male psyche, Wroth explored a woman's experience of desire and, crucially, gave her the central poetic voice: "My muse now happy, lay thyself to rest" (*PA* 103.1–3). Thus a literary tradition that, despite the structural centrality of the female beloved, is so striking for its occlusion of women is curiously framed by two women writers, Ann Lock in 1560 and Mary Wroth in the 1621—both of whom were innovators. Shakespeare's Sonnets are indeed a tour de force and, surely, some of the most evocative love poetry in the English language, but in the best tradition of imitation it was his reworking of convention that produced such dazzling literary experiment. Perhaps the more remarkable literary history to be told of the English sonnet sequence is that it was a woman who laid at least part of the groundwork for that convention and a woman who ultimately departed from its established traditions of poetic voice.

# NOTES

1. For a good overview of criticism of Shakespeare's *Sonnets* see James Schiffer, "Reading New Life into Shakespeare's Sonnets: A Survey of Criticism," *Shakespeare's Sonnets: Critical Essays,* ed. James Schiffer (New York and London: Garland, 1999) 3–71.

2. On the religious sonnet sequence, see Thomas P. Roche, *Petrarch and the English Sonnet Sequences* (New York: AMS P, 1989) 154–92.

3. Arthur Marotti, "'Love is not Love': Elizabethan Sonnet Sequences and the Social Order," *ELH* (1982): 396–428.

4. On the semiotics of color in Shakespeare's dark lady, see Marvin Hunt, "Be Dark but Not Too Dark: Shakespeare's Dark Lady as a Sign of Colour," in Schiffer 368–89.

5. Shakespeare, *The Sonnets and A Lover's Complaint,* ed. Katherine Duncan-Jones (Arden Shakespeare, London: Thomas Nelson, 1999) 49–50; Eve Kosovsky Sedgwick, *Between Men: English Literature and Male Homosocial Desire* (New York: Columbia UP, 1985), ch. 1.

6. See Duncan-Jones 89; Ilona Bell, "That which thou hast done': Shakespeare's Sonnets and *A Lover's Complaint,*" in Schiffer 435–73; and Sasha Roberts, *Reading Shakespeare's Poems in Early Modern England* (Houndmills: Palgrave Macmillan, 2003) 143–53.

7. As Samuel Daniel explained, the art of writing a sonnet was "the apt planting [of] the sentence [the *sententia* or pithy summary, example, or moral] where it may best stand to hit" and thus have greatest impact (*A Defence of Ryme,* 1602, cited in Michael R. G. Spiller, *The Development of the Sonnet: An Introduction* [London: Routledge, 1992] 135).

8. Joseph Pequigney, *Such Is My Love: A Study of Shakespeare's Sonnets* (Chicago: U of Chicago P, 1985). On homoeroticism in Shakespeare's *Sonnets,* see Bruce R. Smith, "I, You, He, She, and We: On the Sexual Politics of Shakespeare's Sonnets," in Schiffer 411–30; and Valerie Traub, "Sex Without Issue: Sodomy, Reproduction, and Signification in Shakespeare's Sonnets," in Schiffer 431–54.

9. Keith Wrightson, *English Society 1580–1680* (London: Hutchinson & Co, 1982).

10. See David Schalkwyk, "Love and Service in *Twelfth Night* and the Sonnets." *Shakespeare Quarterly,* 56, 1 (2005 Spring): 76–100.

11. William Gouge, *Of Domesticall Duties* (1622), cited by Schwalkyk.

12. Bruce Smith, *Homosexuality in Shakespeare's England: A Cultural Poetics* (Chicago: U of Chicago P, 1991) 270; see also Roberts 161–64.

13. Margreta de Grazia, "The Scandal of Shakespeare's Sonnets," *Shakespeare Survey* 46 (1994): 35–49; rpt. in Schiffer 89–112; 106.

14. For a concise overview of arguments about the dating, authorization, order, and dedication of the *Sonnets,* see Schiffer, "Reading New Life into Shakespeare's Sonnets" 5–12.

15. Colin Burrow, ed., *The Oxford Shakespeare: Complete Sonnets and Poems* (Oxford: Oxford UP, 2002) 98.

16. Heather Dubrow, "Incertainties now crown themselves assur'd': The Politics of Plotting Shakespeare's Sonnets," *Shakespeare Quarterly* 47 (1996): 291–305; rpt. in Schiffer 113–33; 122–23.

17. Helen Vendler, *The Art of Shakespeare's Sonnets* (London and Cambridge, MA: The Belknap P of Harvard UP, 1999) 121.

18. Diana E. Henderson, "Love Poetry," *A Companion to English Renaissance Literature and Culture,* ed. Michael Hattaway (Oxford: Blackwell, 2000) 378–91; 384.

# READING LIST

Ferry, Anne. *The "Inward" Language: Sonnets of Wyatt, Sidney, Shakespeare, Donne*. Chicago: Chicago UP, 1983.

Henderson, Diana E. "Love Poetry." *A Companion to English Renaissance Literature and Culture*. Ed. Michael Hattaway. Oxford: Blackwell, 2000. 378–91.

Hyland, Peter. *An Introduction to Shakespeare's Poems*. Houndmills: Palgrave Macmillan, 2003.

Innes, Paul. *Shakespeare and the English Renaissance Sonnet: Verses of Feigning Love*. Houndmills: Macmillan; New York: St Martin's P, 1997.

Leishman, J. B. *Themes and Variations in Shakespeare's Sonnets*. London: Hutchinson, 1961.

Lever, J. W. *The Elizabethan Love Sonnet*. London: Methuen, 1956.

Marotti, Arthur F. "'Love Is Not Love': Elizabethan Sonnet Sequences and the Social Order." *ELH* (1982): 396–428.

Muir, Kenneth. *Shakespeare's Sonnets*. London: Methuen, 1957.

Neely, Carol Thomas. "The Structure of English Renaissance Sonnet Sequences." *ELH* 45 (1978): 359–89.

Roberts, Sasha. *Reading Shakespeare's Poems in Early Modern England*. Houndmills: Palgrave Macmillan, 2003.

Roche, Thomas P. *Petrarch and the English Sonnet Sequences*. New York: AMS P, 1989.

Schalkwyk, David. *Speech and Performance in Shakespeare's Sonnets and Plays*. Cambridge: Cambridge UP, 2002.

Schiffer, James, ed. *Shakespeare's Sonnets: Critical Essays*. New York: Garland, 1999.

———, "Reading New Life into Shakespeare's Sonnets: A Survey of Criticism." Schiffer, ed. 3–71.

Spiller, Michael R. G. *The Development of the Sonnet: An Introduction*. London: Routledge, 1992.

Vendler, Helen. *The Art of Shakespeare's Sonnets*. Cambridge, MA: Belknap P of Harvard UP, 1997.

# 17

# Mary Sidney Herbert and Women's Religious Verse

## Danielle Clarke

Mary Sidney Herbert's Psalm versions are full of cries for attention: "Give heed to what I say," "My people here to you I speech will use," "let not my heavy words be counted light," "hearken what I say," "To highest God I will erect my cry," "To thee I cry / My crying hear," "Lord bend to me Thine ear."[1] Such self-assertion, at first glance, would seem to indicate a powerfully present speaker, a voice that manages to retain its integrity even in the midst of a text that, properly, can be said to belong to everyone and to no one at the same time. How are we to read this voice? Whose voice can it really be said to be? What kinds of authorial traces does the countess of Pembroke leave on this most communal of texts?[2] And how do we "find" Mary Sidney Herbert within the complex matrix of textual reference and deferral inherent to a paraphrased—as opposed to an original—text? The Psalter's modes of articulation are strongly masculine, its speakers and their concerns a long way away from the conventional idea of the early modern woman. The Psalms articulate desire, sin, despair, temptation, exultation, praise, revenge, fury; in short, the full range of emotional and spiritual states. By speaking in, with, and through the Psalmist's voice, the countess of Pembroke is, by definition, a considerable distance from disinterested piety. These versions are full of passion, poetic and spiritual. In this essay we will explore the sources of this passion and outline the ways in which Mary Sidney Herbert disciplines and contains it within the parameters of her sources and, as a consequence, how she negotiates female authorship.

For two decades, Mary Sidney Herbert, the countess of Pembroke (1561–1621), was the foremost literary patronness in England, a figurehead for many of the leading writers of the English Renaissance, bringing the ideals outlined by her brother Philip in his *Defence of Poetry* to fruition. Her role as the literary executor of his work, and the way in which she used Philip's work as the authorizing source for her own writing, is without precedent in this period.[3] Her experience of editing his *Old Arcadia* no doubt taught her to hold in balance the authority of a source text and the need to produce a coherent, "finished" text for public consumption—exactly the process she was to engage in, more ambitiously, when she turned her attention to the Psalter. The Sidney Psalter, as it is usually called, is in every sense a composite text. Sir Philip Sidney had versified Psalms 1–43 before his death, basing his work on the standard English versions (the Geneva Bible, the Book of Common Prayer, and the much derided metrical Psalter compiled by Sternhold and Hopkins), but attempting to write them anew as English poems. It would be reasonable to concur with the countess's own assessment of the full 150 psalms as "this coupled work, by double interest thine," even if her strategically humble claim that "he did warp, I weaved this web to end" significantly underplays the degree to which hers was the shaping hand at work, to the extent that she—cautiously—revised a number of her brother's versions.[4] As if a bi-authored text did not do enough to unsettle our notion of the author as individual, the Psalms themselves pose a challenge to ideas of origin or singularity. Furthermore, the Sidney Psalter is not simply a rewriting, the turning of prose into poetry, of one idiom into another, but a stitching together of fragments, some of them traceable, some of them not. Mary Sidney Herbert's characterization of the text as "the Cloth," "[a] livery robe," is uncannily apt, suggesting that the text is an interwoven tissue of sources, fragments, traces, echoing with words and images from the past and the present ("Even Now," 33; 34).

The countess of Pembroke, by all accounts, was a shrewd, determined, intelligent, and pious woman.[5] Like many women of her age, her idea of her self was dependent in nearly all respects upon her social status and the kinship networks of which she was a part.[6] In the case of Mary Sidney Herbert, this identity provides the key to understanding her literary work, where private individual endeavor produced a public text marked by multiplicity and collectivity. Not only was she born into one of the most influential noble English families, one with extensive lands and a tradition of service to the crown, but she was also the heir to a committed tradition of radical Protestantism. Her three uncles, the earls of Warwick, Leicester, and Huntingdon, were all advocates of the military support of continental Protestantism, an advocacy that her brother Philip was to pay for, first with his political ambition (when he opposed Elizabeth I's marriage to the duke of Alençon on the grounds of Catholicism) and second with his life (when he was hit in the thigh by a musket fighting the Spanish in the Netherlands in 1586). These commitments were not just martial and political; they were integrally bound up with a set of cultural and intellectual ideals that were dashingly embodied by the countess's accomplished, handsome, and headstrong brother, who for many represented the courtly ideal of the soldier-poet—learned, fluent in several languages, conversant with the key thinkers in Europe. He was, simply, the most important influence on her writing life, and the preservation and perpetuation of his memory and his religious and political ideals enabled her to circumvent some of the social conventions that placed women's literary work outside of the rhetorical mainstream. Paradoxically, had he lived, she would probably have left a small legacy of accomplished writing on "private" subjects; in the wake of his death, she produced a poetic corpus that transcends the "domestic" concerns so often associated with women writers in this period. Even to write an elegy on her brother was to adopt a public and political position, especially when, as in the case of "To the Angel spirit" the envisaged reader was Queen Elizabeth. The poet Edmund Spenser might stand in for many when he asserted of Philip's legacy, "who can better sing, / Than thine own sister, peerless lady bright, / Which to thee sings with deep heart's sorrowing, / Sorrowing tempered with dear delight."[7]

## "Divine Translation": The Nature of the Text(s)

Sending poems to Lucy Harington, countess of Bedford, on December 19, 1600, Sir John Harington writes: "I have sent you here the divine, and truly divine translation of three of David's psalms. Done by that Excellent Countess, and in Poesie the mirror of our Age."[8] The three versions that he enclosed were Psalm 51 ("O Lord, whose grace no limits comprehend"), Psalm 104 ("Make oh my Soul, the subject of my song"), and Psalm 137 ("High-seated, where the river flows"). Despite the fact that Mary Sidney Herbert's psalm translations were not printed until 1823 and were not graced with a major scholarly edition until 1998, Harington's circulation of the countess's versions indicates the centrality of the countess, and her poetic work, to early modern culture, but also tells us something about the readership deemed appropriate for these texts.[9] In the first instance, these poems are manuscript versions, which Harington had copied from either the presentation copy or the countess's working copy.[10] In the second instance, all three players in this textual transaction were known to one another; they were related through an extended kin network and shared common cultural and political interests. Sir John was one of the few members of Sir Philip Sidney's circle to have in his possession a manuscript copy of Sidney's *Old Arcadia* (Hannay, *Phoenix* 70). Harington's letter was written shortly before the Essex rebellion and he had himself been knighted by Essex in Ireland; Lucy Harington's husband, the earl of Bedford, was a close associate of Essex and was later fined £10,000 for complicity in the rebellion. The enclosure of these *particular* three psalms with their stress on deliverance and spiritual freedom might have been intended as a coded gesture of comfort and support at what must have been an anxious and stressful time for the countess. These factors point to some key points regarding the psalms and the wider Sidney circle; first, they often carried political meaning, however obliquely; second, manuscript circulation was often carefully nuanced, with texts being sent to those who were broadly in sympathy with the ideas that they represented; and third, the use made of psalm versions did not necessarily carry, or have to carry, the *imprimatur* of their "author." This textual moment is an acknowledgment of the links between divine poetry and the old Protestant ideals of the Sidney circle, and the figure who links all the parts of the chain together, in terms of blood, writing, and politics, is the countess of Pembroke. It is not an accident that Harington marshals the image of the countess as "in Poesie the mirror of our age," as it suggests an elision of the texts that she has produced and the context into which they are here being placed; in other words, through her poems, she reflects and refracts her age, as her brother had done before her.

Harington's gesture suggests that the countess of Pembroke's reputation as a divine poet was assured, and as the succeeding generation of poets was to affirm, not least because she was widely seen as the living embodiment of her brother's legacy. Donne's praise of the Sidney Psalter, "They show us Islanders our joy, our King, / They tell us *why*, and teach us *how* to sing," is justly famous, not least for its emphasis on the fact that the psalms have been rendered into English *poetry*.[11] Equally important, for the purpose of this essay, is Donne's repeated emphasis on the countess's role in the production of the psalms: "Two, by their bloods, and by thy Spirit one; / A Brother and a Sister, made by thee/ The Organ, where thou are the Harmony" (14–16) and his representation of the Sidneys as the living embodiment of the Psalmist's voice, "this *Moses* and this *Miriam*" (46). Lucy Harington, countess of Bedford, the recipient of Psalms 51, 104, and 137, was herself a poet and succeeded the countess as a champion of English poetry, becoming the influential patron of Donne and Jonson (Hannay, *Phoenix* 208). Both Mary Sidney Herbert and Lucy Harington were lauded for their spiritual virtue by Aemilia Lanyer in her *Salve Deus Rex Judaeorum* (1611), in the case of the countess of Pembroke in terms that specifically alluded to her status as a writer of divine poetry, referring to "[t]hose rare sweet songs which *Israels* King did frame / Unto the Father of Eternity," glossed as "The Psalms written newly by the Countess Dowager of Pembroke" (Clarke 217).[12]

Modern readers struggle rather harder to find what is important and distinctive about these poems. A clue to these difficulties can be found in Harington's and Lanyer's terminology; the "text" is both a "translation" and something that has been "written newly." In other words, the countess's versified psalms are *versions,* not original texts, but poems whose authority depends fundamentally on the Old Testament writings that frame them. Behind each text lies another text—or texts—in a succession of palimpsests, behind which ultimately lies the abstract Word of the divine. Neither the Psalter, nor any one individual psalm, can truly be said to be a single text, and the Book of Psalms itself might best be imagined as a chain of linked verses that in their entirety narrate the sufferings of the Israelites in epic form, yet equally each singular psalm comprises the larger sufferings of the sequence as a whole. Each text is both allusively comprehensive in its scope and specific in its representation of an individual state or emotion. Yet neither are the countess's renderings translations in the modern meaning of that term to refer to the process of turning one language into another. The countess of Pembroke's writings are not ultimately free-standing or self-explicating texts in the sense that formalist criticism, or even historicist criticism, has trained us to expect. In this sense the psalm versions must be seen as mobile and dynamic texts, constantly traversing the territory between the ultimate authority of God's word in the Scripture, and the eloquence and beauty of their poetic but fallen manifestation. The difficulty for the modern reader is that, by and large, this intertextual world has to be actively reconstructed, rather than simply being a cultural given. Whatever lyrics we may hold in our heads or store on our mp3 players, they are unlikely to include the full text of the Book of Psalms.

The parallel with lyrics is not as contrived as it might appear, and an exploration of the nature of the psalm tradition in which the countess was intervening may help to explain some characteristics of her text. For Protestants, the Book of Psalms was a foundational text, central to the ideas of selfhood and deliverance that underlay the reformed religion. The Psalms is a heterogeneous body of work, consisting of lyrics, lamentations, prayers, cries for vengeance, and professions of thanks for deliverance from the enemy. They were widely viewed by Protestants as a kind of mini-compendium of the Bible as a whole, and this was one reason why the Book of Psalms was integral to the liturgy, the entire cycle being read through in the course of the church year—as is the case in Anglican churches to this day. Luther called the Psalms "a little Bible, for in it all things that are contained in the whole Bible [. . .] are condensed into a most beautiful manual," and he asserted it as "the Anatomy of all the partes of the Soule."[13] Just as important as this deeply ingrained—and public—acquaintance with the Psalter was the role that the Book of Psalms played in private meditation and prayer. Study of the Psalms was frequently specifically recommended to the believer, in the belief that its constant modulations of mood and voice would bequeath appropriate models for individual prayer.

The tradition that viewed the Psalms as a compendium for the expression of a variety of emotional and moral states easily elided these with broader political and ethical considerations. For most radical Protestants in sixteenth-century Europe, the Psalms were also political, advancing arguments and typologies for the ways in which the oppressed should deal with their oppressors; the Psalms' repeated concern with conflicts between the godly (the Israelites) and their enemies (the Philistines) could be read as an analogy for religious conflicts in early modern Europe. This thinly coded connection was made by Mary Sidney herself in her dedicatory poem to Elizabeth I, "Even Now That Care":

> For even thy Rule is painted in his Reign:
> both clear in right: both nigh by wrong oppressed:
> And each at length (man crossing God in vain)
> Possessed of place, and each in peace possessed.
> proud Philistines did interrupt his rest,
> The foes of heav'n no less have been thy foes;
> He with great conquest, thou with greater blest;
> Thou sure to win, and he secure to lose. (65–72)

David's conflict with the Philistines is explicitly compared to attacks on Elizabeth by Catholic powers (probably the Spanish armada), but the inference is also more critical, suggesting that Elizabeth should aspire to fulfill her role as England's David. Such implications were usually a matter of context and application, and rarely needed to be spelled out. The very act of versifying the Psalms was a politically and theologically charged act; an act that was compounded by the partisan nature of the source texts that the countess used to guide her stylistic and lexical choices.

In the absence of an established text for the Psalms, the countess used a range of English, French, and (scant) Latin sources. These included the Geneva Bible, with commentary; Calvin's commentary on the Psalms, translated by Arthur Golding; the French metrical Psalter produced by Clément Marot and Theodore Bèze; Bèze's commentary, translated by Anthony Gilbie; as well as Miles Coverdale's Bible. Each of these texts was strongly identified with a particular form of continental Protestantism, and all of them display a sustained interest in resistance theory, the notion that monarchs might be deposed in certain circumstances. For this ideological group, that meant apostasy. The Sidney Psalter is thus a composite text, a tissue of textual references, rather than a unidirectional movement from one text to another; it is a translation, but in a rather unusual sense. It is largely *inter*lingual, rather than *intra*lingual, and profoundly intertextual.

The countess of Pembroke focused on the notion of fidelity in multiple ways; she aimed to produced renderings that were true to the content of the text, but also to the spirit as embodied in God's word, which lay both within her source text and beyond it; and finally, she tried to produce poetic versions that were appropriate to the high status of the text that she was paraphrasing, poems that were not simply functional, but resonant with divine eloquence. Despite the apparent humility articulated in the dedicatory poems prefacing the presentation copy created for Elizabeth I, this represents the highest form of poetic ambition for a devout believer:

> [. . .] he did warp, I weaved this web to end;
> the stuff not ours, our work no curious thing,
> Wherein yet well we thought the Psalmist King
> Now English denizened, though Hebrew born. ("Even Now" 27–30)

The very lack of an identifiably "personal" voice that modern readers find so disconcerting is also fundamental to the nature of the countess of Pembroke's literary undertaking. The text, in a sense, cannot be said to be authorial property, "the stuff not ours," and the countess of Pembroke very carefully presents her work through various authorizing frameworks, not least that of the precedent of her brother:

> Then these the Posts of Duty and Goodwill
> shall press to offer what their Senders owe;
> Which once in two, now in one Subject go,
> the poorer left, the richer reft away;
> Who better might (O might ah word of woe,)
> have giv'n for me what I for him defray. ("Even Now" 19–24)

This is not so much modesty—false or otherwise—on her part, but the standard interpretation of the relationship of the individual reader, reciter, or rewriter of the Psalter to the text. The multiple voices of the Psalms (God, David, believers) were understood to be open-ended and not the specific property of any one speaker; this was an integral part of their universal appeal being applicable "indifferently unto all men, of what estate, degree, sex, age, or calling so ever."[14] Voice here is not always clearly marked, and may be internalized by each reader or speaker; the Psalms are the property of a collectivity of individual believers and the whole point is that as the speaker recites, he or she joins a universal chorus: "whosoever take this book in his hand, he reputeth and thinketh all the words he readeth [. . .] to be as his very own words spoken in his own person."[15] Thus any adequate paraphrase has to permit the individual reader to forge his or her own relationship to the text rather than directing or overtly personalizing its meanings.

## "Pen's impressions": The Psalms as Poetry

One of the key aspects of the reception of the Sidney Psalms concerned their quality as poetry; Donne notes that "these Psalms are become / So well attired abroad, so ill at home, / So well in Chambers, in thy Church so ill" (37–39), and the countess of Pembroke herself draws attention to the *poetic* aspiration of the Psalms: "yet well we thought the Psalmist King / Now English denizened, though Hebrew born, / would to thy music undispleased sing, / Oft having worse, without repining worn" ("Even Now" 29–32). These assessments bring together two crucial aspects of thinking about the Psalter in the sixteenth century: on the one hand, the fact that most existing English versions were either in prose or had been versified in a very clumsy way; on the other, the notion that the Book of Psalms was in itself an example of the highest forms of poetry. Sir Philip Sidney had argued "[t]hat the holy David's Psalms are a divine poem [. . .] even the name of Psalms will speak for me, which being interpreted, is nothing but songs; [. . .] it is fully written in metre."[16] For Sidney, and for a host of other commentators, the problem with existing versions was that they attended only to content, and not to style. Existing paraphrases, prior to the eloquent heights of the 1611 ("Authorised Version"), stuck to the sense of the text and failed to capture its poetry or eloquence. It is this stylistic deficit that the countess of Pembroke aimed to counteract.

Although the countess was clearly concerned with fidelity to meaning, her work went considerably beyond this. The effort to convey the truth of the Psalter in all its aspects perhaps accounts for her tendency to continually revise and rewrite, adding phrasing, reshaping stanzas, and bringing Sir Philip Sidney's versions of Psalms 1–43 into stylistic conformity with the text as a whole. This process of poetic reflection cannot readily be distinguished from religious meditation as it marks a profound engagement with the concrete and abstract meanings of the text before her and reflects the open-endedness of spiritual searching. As Gary Waller argues, "in a sense, the countess had no 'final' version of the work."[17] In the first instance this is manifested in the countess's mastery of poetic form and meter; no two psalm paraphrases in the 150-poem sequence use the same meter. The resulting poems are an attempt to re-create the Psalms in English, and this goes some way to accounting for some of the stylistic aspects that modern readers find awkward or disconcerting: for example, the use of repetition and inversion in Psalm 51—"For I alas, acknowledging do know / My Filthy fault, my faulty filthiness" (8–9). Examples like this can be found throughout the Psalter, and they are an attempt to reproduce the dynamic of Hebrew poetry where each verse is divided into two parts, the second of which recapitulates the ideas of the first, using synonym rather than pure repetition. This principle helps to explain the countess's habit of restatement and her stylistic adherence to tropes of repetition, using parallelism, echoing, and variation. These techniques include the use of chiasmus (inverting the order of repeated words, as in the previous example), polyptoton (repetition of words with the same root using different endings), and antimetabole (inversion of words). In Psalm 148, for example, attention is drawn to the materiality of the language (sounds, shapes) when the countess introduces polyptoton: "who bidding into form and frame [. . .] / All formed, framed, founded so" (148.19, 21). The use of inversion and repetition is widespread: "Fountain of pity now with pity flow" (56.1), "hide me, hive me, as thine own" (57.4), "look with ruth upon my woes, / whom ruthless foes, / with long pursuit have chased" (143.11–13). These randomly selected instances can reasonably be asserted as representative of the distinctive poetic idiom of the Sidney Psalter, using wordplay, rhyme, and meter to create coherent emotional patterning. Furthermore, the countess is a keen coiner of new words and new forms of words, often adapting these from hints and suggestions in her sources. For example, the use of compounding in Psalm 104 expands the biblical text's image of bird-song:

> The free-born fowls, which through the empty way
> Of yielding air wafted with wingy speed
> To Art-like notes of nature-tuned lay
> Make earless bushes give attentive heed. (104.37–40)

Although the "lay," or song, is produced by nature, it also shows God's "art"; in the case of the term "earless" Mary Sidney Herbert takes a term only previously applied concretely to wheat and uses it metaphorically. The Psalter as a whole is full of words that predate their earliest citations as recorded by the *Oxford English Dictionary,* words like "prospect" (place with a commanding view, 102.65), "partaged" (divided into parts, 45.62), "upcheer" (encourage, 55.61), "bankless" (69.44), "embosomed" (concealed, 74.60), "abjected" (cast down, 89.97), "spiteful" (92.32), and "sail-winged" (104.85).[18] What this suggests is that the effort to fully represent what the Psalms say at all levels exerts a good deal of pressure on poetic language, leading the countess to use accepted methods to expand the lexicon in order to find appropriate and distinctive language. In these ways, the raw untrammelled passions of the text are shaped into a clear narrative. The effect allows the reader to enter this most familiar of texts anew, to see it from a new perspective and to appreciate the poetic architecture missing from the more functional metrical version designed for singing or reciting in the public context of the church service. To use a modern critical term, the countess of Pembroke's undertaking aims to defamiliarize this text.

The Sidney Psalter reflects its composition and milieu in another key way. While it is clearly a religious undertaking, the countess's choice of imagery and vocabulary is indebted to her own reading and experience. This mixing of discourses often seems incongruous to the modern mind, but it ultimately derives from the perception that the Psalter was poetry (as were the Scriptures more broadly) and that the biblical text had an immediate and contemporary application. It therefore was entirely consistent to attempt to make the text speak with what was a largely contemporary idiom. Many of the versions resonate with references to secular poetry, and not only that of the Sidney circle. Psalm 57, for example, recalls the lyrics of Wyatt, as well as demonstrating the ideas of repetition alluded to earlier:

My heart prepared prepared is my heart
to spread thy praise
with tuned lays:
wake my tongue, my lute awake,
thou my harp the consort make,
my self will bear a part. (31–36)

Her phrasing here comes in a direct line from her sources—"Awake my glory, awake lute and harp" and "Awake my joy, awake I say, / my Lute, my Harp, and strong"—but this is underlined by a courtly image of participatory singing, as the speaker is imagined singing a part (a countermelody) in an accompanied song.[19] The idea of consolation in the psalm is effectively counterpointed by echoes of Wyatt's existential despair in his lyric "My lute awake." The countess often appears to read the Psalms as if they are courtly lyrics.[20]

Such referentiality underlines the oblique political application of the Psalter. This is manifested in a variety of ways: sometimes, this is a question of the countess deploying a particular item of vocabulary that hints at the parallel between the relationship of the believer to God and that between ruler and servant. In other cases, the use of courtly discourse suggests the need for the principles of faith articulated in the Psalter to be applied at Court. In Psalm 45, a marriage song (epithalamion), the queen is described as being attended by "maids of honor" (54); in Psalm 50 the word of God is a "pursevant" (3); God inhabits "Courts" (84.3) and his servant is a "household-man" (84.18); the service of the faithful is compared to the obligations between servants and masters: "lift I my earthy seeing / right as a waiters eye on a graceful master is holden: / as the look of waitress fixed on a lady lieth" (123.2–4). Such examples demonstrate the effort to supply concrete and socially meaningful images through which her audience might apprehend the relationship of the believer to the divine. Asking for God's grace is paralleled with the courtier seeking favor (99.17–20), but sometimes these analogies suggest more targeted critiques. In Psalm 104, for example, courtly imagery is used to draw a pointed parallel between divine and earthly government by emphasizing that pomp and ornament properly belong to the divine realm, not to the human:

> O lord, o god of might,
> to thee, to thee all royal pomps belong,
> clothed art thou in state and glory bright:
> for what else is this Eye-delighting light;
> but unto thee a garment wide and long?
> the vaulted heaven but a Curtain right,
> a Canopy, thou over thee hast hung? (2–8)

It is not only courtly imagery that is added, however. Most frequently the countess builds upon ideas or metaphors found in the Psalms themselves, but gives them a more concrete or precisely contemporary cast. At the same time, much is left for the reader to infer. The Psalter as a whole betrays an intense interest in ideas of justice as a primary means by which rulers reveal their adherence to tenets of faith:

> Teach the kings son, who king himself shall be,
> thy judgements lord, thy justice make him learn:
> to rule thy Realm as justice shall decree,
> and poor men's right in judgment to discern. (72.1–4)

This idea that monarchs should exemplify God's law and that their authority is divinely ordained was central to the thinking of radical protestants, with its corollary that such authority should be rescinded if God's law is broken. Such ideas, however, were not usually directly expressed. Take, for example, the opening lines of Psalm 82:

> Where poor men plead at Princes bar,
> who gods (as gods vicegerents) are:
> the god of gods hath his tribunal pight,
> adjudging right
> both to the judge, and judged wight. (1–5)

The meaning here is to be found through a process of comparative reading; the rest of the psalm in the countess's version emphasizes the monarch's duty as God's deputy. However, it is in what is left *unsaid* that the application of this text is to be found, namely, in the marginal gloss to the Geneva Bible, a key source for Mary Sidney Herbert and one that would have been well known to her readers. This states unequivocally that "[t]he Prophet showeth that if princes and judges do not their duty, God, whose authority is above them, will take vengeance on them."[21] Other key areas where the countess makes specific interventions include the addition of classical references, allusions to music, and a degree of self-consciousness about the process of writing itself.

The Sidney Psalter is a complex and challenging text, or cycle of texts. Its very plurality creates an opportunity both for the countess of Pembroke to be integrally involved in the formation of images, and also for her authorship to be fundamentally dispersed. The version of voice envisaged by the biblical text itself is flexible and collective, yet personal and open-ended, and no psalm versions can be seen as "self-sufficient verbal artefacts" (Davie lii). While the Psalter represents considerable poetic ambition, it is not the case that Mary Sidney Herbert is challenging the parameters of decorum, because her role is that of compiler and versifier, as well as that of literary executor to her brother. Having said this, it would be misleading to suggest that her chosen medium should suggest that there is anything marginal about her undertaking; as we have seen, the central place of the Psalms within early modern Protestant culture, together with the insistence on their status as poetry, means that the Sidney Psalter must be viewed as culturally mainstream. As the poet, critic, and psalm versifier Donald Davie says, "The Countess's poem is a work of literary art, but only in the second place; in the first place it is a work of devotion. To think that its devotional dimension detracts from its status as art is to devalue everything, including art" (Davie 1).

# NOTES

1. All texts by Mary Sidney Herbert are quoted from *Isabella Whitney, Mary Sidney and Aemilia Lanyer: Renaissance Women Poets,* ed. Danielle Clarke (Harmondsworth: Penguin Books, 2000). I have silently modernized spelling of all early modern texts. Psalm 49:1–2; 50:19; 54:4; 55:4; 57:7; 61:1–2; 86:1.
2. Because most of Mary Sidney Herbert's contemporaries used her title, the countess of Pembroke, I use her name and title interchangeably in this essay.
3. My thinking about Mary Sidney Herbert as literary executor is indebted to Marie-Louise Coolahan.
4. "To the Angell spirit" 2; "Even Now That Care" 27.
5. See Margaret P. Hannay, *Philip's Phoenix: Mary Sidney, Countess of Pembroke* (New York: Oxford UP, 1990).
6. For an introduction to these issues, see Sara Mendelson and Patricia Crawford, *Women in Early Modern England* (Oxford: Oxford UP, 1998).
7. *The Ruines of Time* (1591), *The Yale Edition of the Shorter Poems of Edmund Spenser,* ed. William A. Oram et al. (New Haven: Yale UP, 1989) 316–19.
8. Inner Temple Library, Ms Petyt, 538.43, f.303v.
9. The definitive edition is *The Collected Works of Mary Sidney Herbert, Countess of Pembroke,* ed. Margaret P. Hannay, Noel J. Kinnamon, and Michael G. Brennan, 2 vols. (Oxford: Clarendon P, 1998).
10. There were at least two working copies; the presentation copy was prepared for the visit of Queen Elizabeth in 1599 to Penshurst. The visit never took place. For a full account of the complex textual history of the Sidney Psalter, see Hannay, Kinnamon, and Brennan.
11. "Upon the translation of the Psalmes by Sir Philip Sydney, and the Countesse of Pembroke his Sister," *The Divine Poems,* ed. Helen Gardner (Oxford: Clarendon P, 1952) 34–35, ll. 21–22.
12. "Authors Dream," in Clarke ll. 117–18.
13. Qtd. in Barbara K. Lewalski, *Protestant Poetics and the Seventeenth-Century Religious Lyric* (Princeton: Princeton UP, 1979) 42, 43.
14. *The Psalmes of David and Others: With M. John Calvins Commentaries,* trans. Arthur Golding (n.p.: 1571) sig. *iir.
15. Athanasius, quoted in Hannay, *Phoenix* 96.
16. *The Defence of Poesy, Sir Philip Sidney,* ed. Katherine Duncan-Jones (Oxford: Clarendon P, 1994) 104.
17. Gary Waller, "The Countess of Pembroke and Gendered Reading," *The Renaissance Englishwoman in Print: Counterbalancing the Canon,* ed. Anne M. Haselkorn and Betty S. Travitsky (Amherst: U of Massachusetts P, 1990) 327–45; 338.

18. Clarke records these instances in the notes to each psalm.
19. *Book of Common Prayer* 57.9.
20. See Donald Davie, ed., *The Psalms in English* (Harmondsworth: Penguin Books, 1996) xlix.
21. *Geneva Bible* (Geneva, 1560) gloss 82.1a.

## READING LIST

Baroway, Israel. "The Bible as Poetry in the English Renaissance: An Introduction." *Journal of English and Germanic Philology* 32 (1933): 447–80.

Clarke, Danielle. *The Politics of Early Modern Women's Writing.* Harlow: Longman, 2001. ch. 4.

Crawford, Patricia. *Women and Religion in England, 1500–1720.* London: Routledge, 1993.

Hannay, Margaret P. "'Princes You as Men Must Dy': Genevan Advice to Monarchs in the *Psalmes* of Mary Sidney." *English Literary Renaissance* 19 (1989): 22–41.

———. *Philip's Phoenix: Mary Sidney, Countess of Pembroke.* New York: Oxford UP, 1990.

———. "'Wisdome the Wordes': Psalm Translation and Elizabethan Women's Spirituality." *Religion and Spirituality* 23 (1991): 65–82.

——— "'House-confinèd Maids': The Presentation of Woman's Role in the *Psalmes* of the Countess of Pembroke." *English Literary Renaissance* 24 (1994): 44–71.

Rathmell, J. C. A., ed. *The Psalms of Sir Philip Sidney and the Countess of Pembroke.* New York: Anchor Books, 1963.

Steinberg, Theodore L. "The Sidneys and the Psalms." *Studies in Philology* 92 (1995): 1–17.

Trill, Suzanne. "Sixteenth-Century Women's Writing: Mary Sidney's *Psalmes* and the 'Femininity' of Translation." *Writing and the English Renaissance.* Ed. William Zunder and Suzanne Trill. London: Longman, 1996. 140–58.

Zim, Rivkah. *English Metrical Psalms: Poetry as Praise and Prayer 1535–1601.* Cambridge: Cambridge UP, 1987.

# 18

# Lady Mary Wroth and Women's Love Poetry

*Naomi J. Miller*

Women's love poetry in early modern England was a paradox, a forbidden thing of beauty. Indeed, women's love poetry was so terrifying to the "literary police" of the time, or the intelligentsia of the royal Court, that it was frequently censored and condemned, and yet it sprung up repeatedly at unexpected moments and in unpredictable forms. Before considering how this state of affairs came to be, and what its consequences have been for our understanding of love poetry even today, we might consider the paradox of our own relation to the "early modern world," or what we used to call "the Renaissance."

The historical period that has been called "the Renaissance" (roughly A.D. 1500–1700 in England, but over a century earlier than that in Europe) was given that label, looking backward, in recognition of the "rebirth" of attention to classical art and culture that shaped not only art but even politics at that time. The Renaissance was renamed "the early modern period" by recent scholarly consensus, looking ahead with an eye to evaluating its enduring influence upon our own "modern" culture of today. Whether exploring the paintings of Da Vinci or the plays of Shakespeare, students of the early modern period oftentimes uncover the unexpected in considering how our own modern perspectives came to be—or not to be. When we look to the early modern world for precursors of our own modernity as much as for flashbacks to an even earlier period of classical culture, we might recognize that what we find is shaped by *who we are* as much as by *what is "there"* in a hypothetically objective sense. Thus our contemporary awareness of the challenges and triumphs of women poets in the four centuries succeeding the appearance of a Renaissance woman poet named Lady Mary Wroth will legitimately affect the kinds of questions we ask about the topic. I call attention to this conundrum at the start of this essay because it is useful to remember that our own investment in what we study is part of the ongoing challenge, as well as the pleasure, of what we learn as students of literature.

Lady Mary Wroth wrote the first sonnet sequence in English by a woman, *Pamphilia to Amphilanthus* (1621); one of the first plays by a woman, *Love's Victory* (printed for the first time in 1988); and the first published work of fiction by an Englishwoman, *The Countess of Mountgomeries Urania* (1621; first modern edition published in 1995).[1] Wroth is noteworthy not simply for her gender as a woman writer in a period dominated by male voices, but for the range of her authorship as well: where other English women writers at this time are known for single texts or for their work in single genres, the volume and diversity of Wroth's texts amply attest to the complexity of her voice. But the consequences of such courage and creativity on the part of a woman were immediate and oppressive: Wroth was forced by members of King James's court to withdraw *Urania* and *Pamphilia to Amphilanthus* only six months after their publication and to leave the Court herself in disgrace—in part precisely because her authorial choice of a secular romance narrative and sonnet sequence was deemed inappropriate for a woman. These consequences illuminate the gendered perspective of outsider and "other" that invests Wroth's authorial voice with its particular angle on her culture.[2]

The response of some of King James's male courtiers to the publication of Wroth's romance and sonnet sequence in 1621 revealed their deep-seated alarm at the potentially unregulatable power of women's love poetry. Letters that document the Court furor indicate that Wroth's gender, her choice of genres, and her social position outside the inner circle of power rendered her authorship unacceptable. In fact, although the topical allusions to various Court scandals that intermittently mark Wroth's narrative in *Urania* clearly antagonized some of the most powerful males in King James's Court, thus jeopardizing her subsequent standing in courtly circles, it is quite likely that her marginalized political position had already shaped her writing voice rather than vice versa. Moreoever, as far as the problem of women's love poetry was concerned, it was precisely Wroth's disregard for gendered protocol, in daring to write secular love poems that featured a female speaker addressing a male beloved, that was attacked by the most virulent of her critics: Edward, Lord Denny, disparaged her "lascivious tales and amorous toys," by contrast to the religious poetry of her "virtuous and learned aunt," Mary Sidney, the countess of Pembroke.[3] Reading Wroth's sonnets now, we may be hard pressed to identify any such "lascivious tales and amorous toys," but that absence in itself defines the problem, which was not so much the secular (and/or sexual) specificity of this example of women's love poetry as the mere fact of its existence, which was deemed unacceptable and offensive by the ruling authorities.

One of the characteristics of women's love poetry in early modern England was that, in order to appear at all, in many cases it had to go divine. With the exception of Lary Mary Wroth, the handful of English women poets from this period whose work is currently anthologized and reproduced for the twenty-first century classroom are mostly religious poets: for example, Mary Sidney Herbert, countess of Pembroke and translator of the Psalms; Aemilia Lanyer, author of a long and passionate poem celebrating the presence of Christ in women's lives; and Rachel Speght, whose allegorical poetry is grounded in "Christian faith and reason."[4] And yet, as will become apparent in my discussion of the models drawn upon by Mary Wroth, these other women poets can hardly be considered to have been "constrained" by their religious focus. Indeed, some of the most passionate poetry of the period, ranging from John Donne's *Holy Sonnets* to the *Salve Deus Rex Judaeorum* of Aemilia Lanyer, clearly arose from an outpouring of religious faith. One paradox of women's love poetry was that, barred from "amorous" outlets, women poets frequently found that the passion of religious verse offered a liberation from male authority rather than a constraint.

Early modern women writers in England were faced on all sides with masculine parameters, with definitions of female sexuality and subjectivity as "other" in mirror-image relation to masculine standards and assumptions, within male-authored texts ranging from handbooks for women to Petrarchan sonnet sequences. Meanwhile their own discourses, in letters and diaries, poems and plays, represent the potential power of female subjectivity in multiple terms. Instead of accepting masculine definitions of woman simply as "other" in relation to man, some early modern women authors were able to explore versions of the "otherness in themselves."[5]

Whereas women can be mothers and daughters, rulers, writers, and friends in relation to other women as well as to men, conventional Renaissance conceptions of the
beloved, wife, and widow underscore many women's accepted (and typically subordinate) relations to the "other" sex. The underlying connections between the roles can be
glimpsed in their paradoxically oppositional interdependence. Thus Petrarchan poetic
constructions of the female beloved as a potentially unattainable object of desire, seemingly controlled by the male gaze, represent the flip side of the conduct manuals' concern
with wives whose refusal to accept subordination as domestic chattel might suggest the
presence of disquietingly ungovernable sexual passions of their own. Likewise, the social constraints publicly proclaimed appropriate for widows reveal a large measure of the
cultural anxiety generated by the prospect of widows' freedom from husbandly authority.

Moreover, the conventional gendering of responsibilities can be disrupted,
reversed, and further transfigured by women endeavoring to rewrite their positions as
objects of male authority and desire in order to claim some degree of agency as speaking subjects. Thus a female sonneteer might adopt the voice of lover rather than simply
beloved, for example, while a widow might dare to assume the discourse of authority
previously preempted by her husband. Wroth's texts, significantly, represent female
characters in multiple combinations of roles as lover and mother, wife and widow, ruler
and writer, whose voices bespeak both confidence and discouragement, and whose experiences, far from projecting an idealized roster of feminine triumphs, instead span a
gamut of relationships from abandonment to independence that can be seen to reflect the
complex and often conflicting constructions of gender in early modern England.

Examining moral, religious, and dramatic texts, Mary Beth Rose argues that there is
a shift in sixteenth- and early seventeenth-century England from the dualistic conception
of women as either transcendently idealized or physically degraded to the Protestant celebration of marriage as the predominant, authoritative sexual discourse.[6] In both cases,
however, women are represented as objects to be valued or devalued by male-authored
discourse. Early modern conduct books voice consistent concern with the chastity and
decorum not only of unmarried women and of wives, but of widows as well, demonstrating the masculine parameters of culturally approved forms of desire, based upon the
relationship between a desired (female) object and a desiring (male) subject. The other
side of (male) desire is understood to be (female) chastity, which simultaneously elicits
and validates the prescribed direction of that desire. This subject/object dichotomy is per-
petuated in the rhetoric of marriage treatises, which maintain that husbands are to control
wives in practice, no matter how affective their relationship in theory.

Furthermore, a double standard of sexual conduct operated beyond the scope of the
marriage manuals, according to which women, whether married or unmarried, were expected to contain their sexual appetites, while men could and did participate both in conju-
gal relationships for the purpose of procreating male heirs and in extramarital relationships
for love, companionship, and sexual pleasure, although such behavior was condemned in
a number of the manuals. Thus the male courtier William Herbert, for example, suffered
few consequences for his sexual relationships with various women, while the social ostra-
cization endured by his female cousin and lover, Mary Wroth, for the two illegitimate children she bore Herbert during her years of widowhood, has been well documented.[7]

Like her contemporary Anne Clifford, Lady Mary Wroth turned to writing as an expression of autonomy during a difficult marriage and widowhood, in her case producing

a sonnet sequence, a play, and a prose romance that represent women's struggles to become speaking subjects. In turning to her poems, it is important to situate Mary Wroth's exploration of female subjectivity in relation to some of the central images not just in women's love poetry but more extensively in a range of love poems about women in the period. In order to appreciate the transgressive achievements of women's love poetry, we must first look to the standard of male love poetry against which many of the women poets were writing.

The Petrarchan objectification of the beloved that recurs in many Renaissance sonnet sequences, for example, frequently represents a type of "dark lady," however fair in appearance. A distant and unattainable object of desire—beautiful and virtuous on the one hand but proud and cruel on the other—the female beloved is often characterized by a quality of elusiveness that serves both to perpetuate male desire and to allow masculine constructions of her identity that are not limited by any professed subjectivity on her part. While the recipient of voluble praise from the sonneteer, the sonnet lady often remains voiceless herself within male-authored poems, her description serving more to indicate the exclusive nature of the sonneteer's passion and ingenuity in love than to reveal her own character.

Nancy Vickers's well-known explication of Petrarch's use of the blazon indicates how the fragmentation of Laura into different body parts encourages a distorted view of the woman as an assortment of scattered particulars to be assembled by the male sonneteer's governing eye.[8] Central to the representation of "woman viewed" is the issue of sexual difference: Vickers suggests that the encounter between Petrarch's Actaeon and Diana, both hunters, is "a confrontation with difference where similarity might have been desired or even expected," and leads to the man's desire to descriptively dismember the threat posed by this glimpse of female sexuality as "other" than the male norm (Vickers 273). Once again, female subjectivity is erased by masculine inscriptions (Ovid's, Petrarch's, Actaeon's) of the "difference" of female sexuality. Such literary inscriptions of the sexual difference of the beloved are not far removed, in cultural terms, from the anxieties and prohibitions on women's behavior inscribed in the conduct manuals and sermons on marriage, linking the "otherness" of the apparently unattainable beloved and the seemingly attained wife after all.

Potentially even more disturbing to the male Renaissance sonneteer as well as the conduct manual author is not difference alone, but rather the possibility that the objectified sonnet mistress or wife may herself seek to become a speaking subject. Karen Newman has noted how the fragmentation of the female body into parts in both wedding sermons and love poetry focuses not only on the genitals but also on the mouth as source of speech.[9] While the Protestant preacher Henry Smith associates chastity with silence in a good wife ("As the open vessels were counted uncleane; so account that the open mouth hath much uncleannes"), both Philip Sidney (Wroth's uncle) and his brother Robert (Wroth's father) produced lyric sequences in which the lady, albeit briefly, is given a voice.[10] In the Eighth Song of *Astrophil and Stella* and the Sixth Song of Robert Sidney's untitled sequence, the lady speaks her love within a third-person narrative frame that places both lover and beloved at one remove from the first-person frame of the larger sequence. The lady's voice in each case heralds or reflects a further separation from the lover, leaving the sonneteer's song "broken."[11] Moreover, the latter portions of both sequences are devoted to reducing the woman to silence once more, as in the wedding sermons, in order to perpetuate the music of the lover's complaint. By contrast, Mary Wroth transforms the role of the lady in her own sequence from a breaker into a maker of songs. In *Pamphilia to Amphilanthus,* the woman appears not as an object of adoration but as a lover, not as a muse but as a poet.

When the "sonnet mistress" becomes the sonneteer, the conventional rhetoric of the lyrics can serve unexpectedly as a feminine discourse of sexual difference. Wroth's lyrics work even more particularly to encode not simply an oppositional or "mirror-image" discourse in relation to Petrarchan conventions, but a woman poet's voicing of  the "otherness in herself." Heather Dubrow convincingly argues in her analysis of the counterdiscourses of Petrarchism that, just as being silent is not the same as being silenced, so "speech is not necessarily an unqualified source or sign of power." Dubrow goes on to caution that "the voice of the Petrarchan mistress should not invariably be crammed into the category of disempowered silence," citing instances in which some Petrarchan mistresses achieve agency even in silence, while some Petrarchan poets manifest prolific speech without agency.[12] This useful reminder of the complexities and ambiguities in the linkage between speech and agency illuminates the potential signifi-cance of Wroth's lyric sequence as well, not as an unqualified representation of suc-cessful female agency merely because the woman has a voice, but rather as an evolving articulation of competing cultural conceptions of voice and otherness.

Most often, of course, Renaissance sonneteers dwell upon the potential duplicity of the woman neither as voice nor as "other in herself," but as other than the professedly constant male lover. In the twenty-third sonnet of Edmund Spenser's *Amoretti,* for example, the poet counterpoises Penelope's deception of her suitors through the covert unweaving of her "web" with his beloved's destruction (with "one word") of his own "whole years work" of discourse.[13] Spenser's recasting of the tale so that the male poet alone has the power to weave language into artistic creation, his beloved retaining only the power of speech to "undo," exposes the male sonneteer's fear of female speech as competitive with and destructive of his own.

Although Shakespeare alters the polarized constructions of gender that operate in other Renaissance sequences by triangulation incorporating a young man as well as a "dark lady" who are both beloved by the speaker, the presence of the young man does not foster a new treatment of sexual identity and difference as much as it underscores the dominant subjectivity of the poet-speaker. Just as in other male-authored sequences, Shakespeare's "dark lady" is convicted, by implication, of "false women's fashion" and of "fairing the foul with art's false borrowed face."[14] The poet counters the deceptive-ness of the dark lady's discourse, identified in "her false-speaking tongue," with his own ability to "lie with her" likewise (Sonnet 138), producing a conflation of verbal and sexual intercourse that reduces the woman, once again, from a potentially speaking subject to a sexualized physical object. While the young man is represented early in the sequence in notably singular, if physicalized, terms, the dark lady's duality is repeatedly reinscribed in the latter portion of the sequence, emphasizing the speaker's fear that "thy sweet virtue answer not thy show" (Sonnet 93).

Often, indeed, women poets such as Mary Wroth, Aemilia Lanyer, and even Elizabeth I voice the ambivalence and alienation of writing against cultural discourses  that have constructed women's selves as dual, duplicitous, and ever other. At the same time, they themselves work to represent conventional metaphors in unconventional

contexts or voices and strive to change the subject of the metaphors by claiming subjectivity for themselves. Even such an apparently conventional Petrarchan poem as
Queen Elizabeth's "On Monsieur's Departure," with its alternating metaphorical extremes, opens out at the end of the first stanza with the poet's ambiguous construction of
a divided "self": "I am and not, I freeze and yet am burned, / Since from myself another
self I turned."[15] For a woman, and a queen, to declare "I am and not" reads differently
than does the same complaint from the pen of a male Petrarchan lover, given that women
constantly faced the erasure of their potential subjectivity within cultural constructions of
gender, and given that the queen in particular grounded her princely authority in her doubled identity as monarch and woman. In light of this doubled identity, Elizabeth's observation that "from myself another self I turned" may perhaps refer not only to "Monsieur,"
but also to her own alternating celebration and suppression of her femininity, in self-
fashioning such roles as mother to her people and prince to her kingdom.

   In *Salve Deus Rex Judaeorum*, Aemilia Lanyer reconfigures the mirroring potential
of verse, traditionally claimed by male Renaissance poets to depict women as objects in
mirrored opposition to their own subjectivity, in the service of constructing femininity
in female-authored terms. Thus she urges Queen Anne, in the first dedicatory poem, to
"Looke in this Mirrour of a worthy Mind, / Where some of your faire Virtues will appeare," and further urges "all vertuous Ladies in generall" to "let this faire Queene not
unattended bee, / When in my Glasse she daines her selfe to see."[16] The "mirror" of
Lanyer's verse can reflect the multiplicity of female subjectivity, when women "read"
each other rather than suffering themselves to be written and read by men.

   Near the end of *Pamphilia to Amphilanthus*, Mary Wroth's poet-speaker contrasts
the "true forme of love" in her thoughts with those "ancient fictions" that conjure shapes
from the stars (P100). Even as she makes deliberate reference to the "olde fictions" of
*Arcadia* in her prose romance, *Urania*, in order both to relate and to differentiate her narrative from that of Philip Sidney, so she changes the subject of "star-struck" Petrarchan
sequences, from Philip Sidney's *Astrophil and Stella* on, rewriting male-authored
"fictions" to body forth the "true forme" of a woman's desire. At the same time, Wroth's
representations of sexual identity and difference in love become more understandable
when viewed in relation to such examples as Lanyer's feminine revision of the Petrarchan
blazon, cited earlier, than solely in comparison to male-authored discourses. Both as a
woman and a woman poet, Wroth could fashion her voice in relation to the voices of other
women as well as men, writing in response to multiple cultural constructions of gender.

   In *Pamphilia to Amphilanthus*, Wroth counterpoises speech and silence, absence
and presence, in such a way as to decenter the authority of the male beloved, so that it is
the woman, as speaking subject, who commands if not the entirety, then at least the balance, of the discourse. By contrast to the male love poets discussed earlier, Wroth gives
the speaker's voice to the woman, thus silencing the man and simultaneously undermining Renaissance strictures of female silence. Wroth's treatment of constancy may be
regarded less as a self-destructive idealization of a dominant masculinist ideology than
as a manifestation of women poets' potential to transform strictures upon their actions
into enabling grounds for discourse. What is at stake in Wroth's texts, then, is not simply female behavior, but female speech.

   By contrast to many male love poets who periodically blame their personal trials
upon the harshness of their ladies, Wroth's speaker moves beyond blame or self-pity to

celebrate the "true forme of love" apart from the caprice of her male beloved. In structuring her sequence around a woman's voice, Wroth does more than simply reverse the conventional relationship of male lover and female beloved. Instead, Pamphilia speaks not solely as a lover focused upon the beloved but as a woman cognizant of the shared female experience of suffering for love. In her voicing of the inclusive rather than exclusive nature of her passion, Pamphilia refuses to speak from the margins of discourse as an isolated woman in love. Writing at once within and against the gendered constraints of her patriarchal culture, Wroth uses not the egocentrism of masculine rhetoric but Pamphilia's feminine awareness of mutuality to empower her lyric voice.

*Pamphilia to Amphilanthus* opens with a dream vision in the first sonnet that establishes the female speaker's initial loss of identity, when "sleepe deaths Image did my senceses hiere / From knowledg of my self" (P1). Venus and Cupid succeed in "martiring" the dreamer's heart so that Pamphilia awakens as a "lover," a newly acquired role that initiates her discourse. Because the male beloved is absent except for the presence of his name in the title, Wroth from the first emphasizes the speaking voice of the female lover. The evolving dynamic among the central characters soon differentiates Wroth's perspective from that of her male literary predecessors, allying her more clearly with a female poet such as Lanyer, who also worked to transfigure Petrarchan traditions. In Wroth's sequence in particular, the speaker's relation to Cupid shifts when the sonneteer is a woman. For example, whereas Philip Sidney presents the figure of Cupid as both ally and rival to Astrophil in the pursuit of the female beloved (*AS* 11), Wroth's Cupid becomes the female poet's suitor. Thus Pamphilia finds herself in the position of denying Cupid's suit while affirming her constancy toward her male beloved (P8).

Wroth further delineates the altered relation of her female speaker to Cupid in order to revise the conventionally masculine metaphor of battle. The male sonneteers regularly represent the lover's predicament in martial terms, outlining the speaker's attempts on the one hand to conquer the beloved's heart (Philip Sidney, *AS* 61, 69; Robert Sidney, Sonnet 7; Spenser, *Amoretti* 14), or on the other hand to resist captivity himself, when faced with his beloved's arsenal of beauty (Philip Sidney, *AS* 53; Robert Sidney, Sonnets 15, 18, 33). Wroth, however, shifts the focus of the strife, so that her speaker's conflict is with Cupid rather than with her beloved:

> Am I thus conquer'd? have I lost the powers
> That to withstand, which joy's to ruin mee?
> Must I bee still while itt my strength devowres
> And captive leads mee prisoner, bound, unfree? (P16)

Here are encoded the potential victimization and loss of liberty that have focused some previous critical attention upon Wroth. At the same time, Wroth's verse inscribes speech rather than silence, and Pamphilia's question can be read as posing a contestation of agency rather than a loss of identity, suggesting a starting point for resistance rather than simply a concluding point for denied anger.

While the male love poets emphasize the strength of their efforts to preserve their autonomy, surrendering only when "no power is left to strive" (Robert Sidney, Sonnet 18), Wroth's female speaker demonstrates her passion without the masculine emphasis on aggression. All the "powre" and aggressive strife is left to Cupid, while the lady admonishes him that "'tis cowardise, to strive wher none resist" (P8). Asserting that

"I ame thy subject, conquer'd, bound to stand" (P8), Pamphilia paradoxically claims a voice from the very position of subjection. Furthermore, by displacing the focus of the conflict onto Cupid, the female lover maintains the prerogative of choosing her beloved willingly. By acknowledging rather than resisting her passion, she is enabled to reject the authority of Cupid's "boyship" once she has directed her love toward Amphilanthus (P8). Both as a lover and as a poet, Wroth's speaker prefers to take the initiative in offering her affections through song directly to her beloved rather than prolonging a martial engagement with Cupid.

In the crown, or corona, of fourteen sonnets at the heart of the sequence, Wroth explores the challenge of representing subjectivity in a woman poet's voice. One of the first instances of the corona in English occurs in Philip Sidney's prose romance (*Old Arcadia* 72), while Robert Sidney includes an incomplete crown of sonnets in his sequence. By choosing the same form for inclusion in her sequence, Wroth doesn't hesitate to engage head-on with these literally patriarchal precedents, while at the same time fashioning her own crown as a testament to the emerging power of the voice of the lady. Indeed, the pervasive image of a "strang labourinth" (P77), in which the speaker must find "the thread of love"—the opening and governing image of the sequence—can be read in direct relation both to Robert Sidney's description in his sequence of "the saving thread" which "the maze unwound" (Robert Sidney, *Pastoral* 9), and to the background myth of Theseus and Ariadne as well. In Robert Sidney's sequence, the "saving thread" turns out to be the lady's faults, which can bring the lover to his senses so that he can change his mind and relinquish love. There love is described as a "maze" along the lines of the labyrinth housing the Minotaur, from which Theseus escaped with Ariadne's help. According to one version of the myth, Ariadne provided Theseus with the thread, only to be abandoned by him and left alone on the island of Naxos to commit suicide in despair. Embedded in Robert Sidney's use of the thread-and-maze image, therefore, is a trope of masculine abandonment of the feminine other, justified as masculine escape from feminine wiles, with the understated possibility that female sexuality is perceived as the monstrous power lurking at the center of the maze of male desire.

By contrast to this oppositional constitution of the sonnet mistress as "other" in every sense, Wroth reclaims the image of a "labourinth" to explore the possibility of a female subjectivity that can not only endure the male lover's abandonment, but even prevail. The "thread" in Wroth's sequence is not, in simple reversal of Robert Sidney's sequence, a list of male faults, but rather a "thread of love" (P77), which emerges through the power of female discourse to unwind a maze of male inconstancy. As the final line of each sonnet in the corona is repeated in the first line of the successive sonnet, Pamphilia's voice itself becomes her thread of love expressed, revealing her chosen path through the labyrinthine turns of her male beloved's fluctuating behavior, and allowing Wroth to enter into a "dialogue" with her father's and uncle's texts. Read as a trope not simply for masculine abandonment, but for emergent female subjectivity, Wroth's "strang labourinth" becomes at once a trial for the woman lover suffering her beloved's absence, and a testament to the woman poet's ability to view the pattern whole, inclusive of a future time when "I ame my self, and blest" (P52).

Early in the corona, Wroth highlights the issue of constancy from a female point of view. In the third sonnet, the speaker describes the testing ground of true love:

Heere are affections, tri'de by loves just might
As gold by fire, and black desernd by white,
Error by truthe, and darknes knowne by light,
Wher faith is vallwed for love to requite. (P79)

In the trial of affections, faith is valued and true love proves "constant as fate" (P79). The series of similes, from "gold by fire" to "darknes knowne by light," outlines a Petrarchan knowledge based on contrarieties, an identity for the lover based on "difference." When Wroth's diction is viewed as offering a dialogue with the discourse of her male predecessors, however, it becomes apparent that her concern may be less with the oppositional relation between the genders than with different versions of women's subjectivity when constructed by female- as opposed to male-authored discourse. For eight lines of her monorhymed sonnet, Wroth chooses two of the same ending words—"might" and "light"—that Philip Sidney uses for his monorhymed sonnet in the *Old Arcadia.* Sidney's sonnet, significantly, is attributed to Gynecia, who is tormented by her selfish desire to betray her marriage for adulterous love of Pyrocles. In that sonnet, Gynecia invites "clowdie feares" to close her sight (*Old Arcadia* 72), while in Wroth's sonnet, Pamphilia declares that "noe clowde can apeere" to dim the light of true love (P79). The deliberately allusive echoes of the earlier sonnet serve to emphasize the contrast between Sidney's inconstant Gynecia and Wroth's constant Pamphilia, revealing not a gap or a silence erasing female agency but rather an active re-vision of the subjectivity of the female lover.

The third sonnet of Wroth's crown also alludes to the third sonnet of Robert Sidney's crown, in which the speaker professes his faith to his beloved, yet admits that he has loved others before her. In excusing his behavior, he argues that "Love gave me not to them, he did but lend" (Robert Sidney, Sonnet 13), and offers a justification in the following sonnet: "Ah let not me for changing blame endure, / Who only changed, by change to find the best" (Robert Sidney, Sonnet 14). Wroth demonstrates her awareness of that particular justification of change in her own depiction of the relationship between lover and beloved, yet in her case she attributes that position to Amphilanthus. When Pamphilia remarks upon her beloved's inconstancy in *Urania,* he replies that "none can bee accused [. . .] for their change, if it bee but till they know the best, therefore little fault hath yet been in me: but now I know the best, change shall no more know me." Pamphilia's response is simply that "every change brings this thought."[17] Within the corona, Wroth emphasizes not a man's egocentric quest for "the best" object of desire as a justification for change, but rather a woman's assertion of love beyond male inconstancy as a justification for subjectivity. In place of patriarchal Renaissance conceptions of constancy as rare in women and optional for men, Wroth represents constancy as one potentially empowering parameter of female sexual identity.

Later in the corona, Wroth inscribes the possibility of mutual love between the sexes in terms that suggest a response to her contemporary, John Donne. Wroth claims for love the power "to joine two harts as in one frame to move; / Two bodies, butt one soule to rule the minde," adding that love "doth inrich the witts, and make you see / That in yourself, which you knew nott before" (P82). Instead of resorting to a third "other" (whether phoenix, compass, or flea) to define union in terms of obliterated sexual difference, Wroth allows for the "otherness in themselves" of both lovers. Still possessed of "two bodies," the lovers enrich rather than erase each other's subjectivity, each learning to see "that in yourself, which you knew nott before." In Wroth's construction of gender, love is not a substitute for subjectivity, but rather an opportunity for sexual connection that can include difference on both sides, for a union between two equal subjects rather than "container and contained."

As a woman poet, Mary Wroth carves out a discursive space among early modern constructions of gender within which she can configure both sexes anew as mutual agents of passion. The masculine parameters of her culture's dominant discourses can be viewed as providing not so much the boundaries, then, as the starting point for Wroth's assertion of her own voice as a female poet. Finally, if Wroth's articulation of love helping the lover to "see that in yourself which you knew not before" strikes us as a "modern" sentiment, we may find ourselves able to recognize another paradox: while it may have arisen from different circumstances than our own, women's love poetry in early modern England forges a connection with modern readers across time and/or gender when we, as readers, choose to embrace that connection on our own initiative, seeing that in ourselves which we knew not before.

## NOTES

1. Modern published editions include *The Poems of Lady Mary Wroth,* ed. Josephine A. Roberts (Baton Rouge: Louisiana State UP, 1983); *Lady Mary Wroth's "Love's Victory": The Penshurst Manuscript,* ed. Michael G. Brennan (London: The Roxburghe Club, 1988); and Roberts's recent edition of the complete *Urania* (Renaissance English Texts Society, 1995). Only twenty-eight copies of the 1621 edition of *The Countesse of Mountgomeries Urania* and only one copy of the manuscript continuation of the romance (Newberry Library, Case Msfy 1565.W95) survive today. Subsequent citations of Wroth's poems will refer to the modern published editions, using Roberts's numbering scheme for the poems.

2. Much of the material in this essay is adapted from my own book-length study of Lady Mary Wroth, entitled *Changing the Subject: Mary Wroth and Figurations of Gender in Early Modern England* (Lexington: UP of Kentucky, 1996). See also *Reading Mary Wroth: Representing Alternatives in Early Modern England,* ed. Naomi J. Miller and Gary Waller (Knoxville: U of Tennessee P, 1991).

3. For reproductions of the letters and satirical poems associated with the court furor, see Roberts, *Poems* 32–35, 233–45.

4. For examples of the anthologizing of these poets, see *Women Writers in Renaissance England,* ed. Randall Martin (London: Longman, 1997); *Women Poets of the Renaissance,* ed. Marion Wynne-Davies (New York: Routledge, 1999); and *Reading Early Modern Women: An Anthology of Texts in Manuscript and Print, 1550–1700,* ed. Helen Ostovich and Elizabeth Sauer (New York: Routledge, 2004). See also the introductory attention to Mary Sidney, countess of Pembroke, and to Lady Mary Wroth as the only two women poets named in chapter subtitles in Gary Waller, "Gendering the Muse: Women's Poetry, Gay Voices," *English Poetry of the Sixteenth Century* (London: Longman, 1993) 241–58.

5. For further elucidation of the concept of "otherness in themselves," see the analysis of French feminist critic Luce Irigaray, "This Sex Which Is Not One," *This Sex Which Is Not One,* trans. Catherine Porter (Ithaca: Cornell UP, 1985) 26, 28–29.

6. Mary Beth Rose, *The Expense of Spirit: Love and Sexuality in English Renaissance Drama* (Ithaca: Cornell UP, 1988) 3–5.

7. The William Herbert/Mary Wroth affair is only one of many examples; for more extensive discussion of their relationship, see Waller, *The Sidney Family Romance: Mary Wroth,*

*William Herbert, and the Early Modern Construction of Gender* (Detroit: Wayne State UP, 1993).

8. Nancy J. Vickers, "Diana Described: Scattered Woman and Scattered Rhyme," *Critical Inquiry* 8 (1981): 266–67.

9. Karen Newman, *Fashioning Femininity and English Renaissance Drama* (Chicago: U of Chicago P, 1991) 10–11.

10. Henry Smith, *A Preparative to Marriage* (London, 1591), D1v, D2v, cited in Newman, *Fashioning Femininity* 149n12.

11. Astrophil resumes his first-person voice to lament: "With what she had done and spoken / [. . .] therewith my song is broken" (Eighth Song of *Astrophil and Stella*, from *The Poems of Sir Philip Sidney*, ed. William A. Ringler, Jr. [Oxford: Clarendon P, 1962]). In Robert Sidney's poem, the lady's expression of love is an epitaph (Sixth Song of Robert Sidney's sequence, from *The Poems of Robert Sidney*, ed. P. J. Croft [Oxford: Clarendon P, 1984]). The poems of Robert and Philip Sidney (including the *Old Arcadia* poems) will hereafter be cited from these Oxford editions, by poem number in the text.

12. Heather Dubrow, *Echoes of Desire: English Petrarchism and Its Counter-discourses* (Ithaca: Cornell UP, 1995) 274–75.

13. Edmund Spenser, *Amoretti* 23, from *Spenser: Poetical Works*, ed. J. C. Smith and E. de Selincourt (Oxford: Oxford UP, 1989).

14. William Shakespeare, Sonnets 20 and 127, from *Shakespeare's Sonnets*, ed. Stephen Booth (New Haven: Yale UP, 1977). Shakespeare's sonnets will be cited hereafter from this edition by number in the text.

15. Elizabeth I, "On Monsieur's Departure," *Elizabeth I: Collected Works*, ed. Leah S. Marcus, Janel Mueller, and Mary Beth Rose (Chicago: U of Chicago P, 2000) 302–03.

16. Aemilia Lanyer, "To the Queenes most Excellent Majestie" 37–38, and "To all virtuous Ladies in generall" 6–7, *Salve Deus Rex Judaeorum* (London, 1611), *The Poems of Aemelia Lanyer*, ed. Susanne Woods (Oxford: Oxford UP, 1993).

17. *The Countesse of Mountgomeries Urania* (London, 1621), STC 26051, 138.

## READING LIST

Dubrow, Heather. *Echoes of Desire: English Petrarchism and Its Counterdiscourses.* Ithaca: Cornell UP, 1995.

Irigaray, Luce. *This Sex Which Is Not One.* Trans. Catherine Porter. Ithaca: Cornell UP, 1985.

Jones, Ann Rosalind. *Currency of Eros: Women's Love Lyric in Europe, 1540–1620.* Bloomington: Indiana UP, 1990.

Martin, Randall. *Women Writers in Renaissance England.* London: Longman, 1997.

Miller, Naomi J. *Changing the Subject: Mary Wroth and Figurations of Gender in Early Modern England.* Lexington: UP of Kentucky, 1996.

Miller, Naomi J., and Gary Waller, eds. *Reading Mary Wroth: Representing Alternatives in Early Modern England.* Knoxville: U of Tennessee P, 1991.

Newman, Karen. *Fashioning Femininity and English Renaissance Drama.* Chicago: U of Chicago P, 1991.

Ostovich, Helen and Elizabeth Sauer, eds. *Reading Early Modern Women: An Anthology of Texts in Manuscript and Print, 1550–1700.* New York: Routledge, 2004.

Rose, Mary Beth. *The Expense of Spirit: Love and Sexuality in Renaissance Drama.* Ithaca: Cornell UP, 1988.

Vickers, Nancy J. "Diana Described: Scattered Woman and Scattered Rhyme." *Critical Inquiry* 8 (1981): 266–67.

Wynne-Davies, Marion. *Women Poets of the Renaissance.* New York: Routledge, 1999.

# 19

# Donne's *Songs and Sonets* and Artistic Identity

## Andrew Hadfield

John Donne, like many of his contemporaries, published very few poems in his lifetime. He did publish a number of prose works—assorted sermons and a number of lengthy treatises such as *Pseudo-Martyr,* a government sponsored work designed to persuade Catholics that it was better to obey than to rebel against the king.[1] The only published poems of substance that he appears to have authorized were the two *Anniversaries,* works that lamented the death of Elizabeth Drury, the daughter of Donne's principal patron before he took Holy Orders in 1615, Sir Robert Drury.[2] The poems on which his posthumous reputation has rested, with one or two minor exceptions, all appeared in print after his death in 1631. That *Poems, by J. D., with Elegies on the Author's Death* went through six editions between 1633 and 1654, not quite as many as a bestseller such as Shakespeare's *Venus and Adonis,* but more than a popular work such as *The Faerie Queene,* indicates that Donne's poetry struck a chord with readers.

There are many reasons why Donne might not have wanted his poetry to reach a wide audience. He wrote satires in the 1590s when such work came under suspicion and was censored by the Bishops' Ban of 1599, either for its sexual impropriety or for its subversive political content.[3] His poetry was indeed racy and would not necessarily have been how the dean of St. Paul's Cathedral would have wanted to present himself to the world. It is also likely that Donne had a clear conception of his art and that he wrote for a close circle of friends who could read him right and not for the wider public.[4] In doing so he earned the scorn of Michael Drayton, a poet committed to the world of print who felt that Donne was shirking his duties as a writer by retreating into private meanings.[5] Certainly, the nature and meaning of poetry changes when it ceases to circulate in manuscript form and enters the world of print. The nuances of private communication have to surrender to the broader significance of the mass market. When Richard Tottel published the first anthology of English lyric poetry in 1557, *Songes and Sonnettes, written by the ryght honourable Lorde Henry Haward late Earle of Surrey, and other,* the intricate, coded significance of the poetry of Wyatt and Surrey that had circulated in secret at the Court of Henry VIII was transformed into songs and ballads lamenting the fates of unhappy men in love (Hadfield, *Renaissance* 274–76). It is undoubtedly no accident that Donne's love poetry was collected posthumously and given the same title, *Songs and Sonets,* nearly eighty years later.

The result is that we do not know how and why Donne composed his poetry, what order it was written in, and to whom he addressed it. The edition of poems published in 1633 may well bear some relation to Donne's designs or the poems may have been compiled in a purely random manner, a striking contrast to George Herbert's *The Temple,* published in the same year. The relationship between Donne's poetry and his life is equally problematic. Some poems were undoubtedly written in direct response to events in his life, such as "A Nocturnal upon S. Lucy's Day, being the shortest day," a meditation on the death of Ann Donne on August 15, 1617, and such precisely dated religious lyrics such as "Good Friday, 1613. Riding Westward" and "A Hymn to Christ, at the Author's Last going into Germany." Numerous other poems invite the reader to speculate that they have an autobiographical basis, and there is a long tradition, from Izaac Walton onward, of reading Donne's life through the poetry.[6] Donne, it was assumed, lived a dissolute youth, before repenting and entering the church as time caught up with him (Bald ch. 1). This tradition has largely fallen into disrepute. Commentators have become increasingly suspicious of such biographical explanations, arguing, quite rightly, that there need be no correspondence between the life and the art and that Renaissance readers were more than capable of separating the speaker from the poet.[7] Others have pointed to the fact that Donne's secular and religious verse are not poles apart, consisting of similar forms, style, and modes of speech, Donne addressing God as a lover to be cajoled, subdued, persuaded, or forced into submission.[8] Although much erotic verse probably does date from the 1590s, it cannot be read as a separate canon from the sacred works.

Yet it seems as though we ought to be careful of this reaction too. Renaissance poets frequently represented themselves in their poetry, inviting readers to read their work in terms of their lives, while at the same time making readers aware that not everything would be revealed. It is hardly surprising that this should be the case. Wherever writers turned for inspiration they would have found evidence of the poet's life. Ovid wrote about his affairs and exile; Catullus wrote about his sexual exploits; Dante found inspiration for all his significant poetry in Beatrice; and Petrarch had the equally potent muse, Laura. English poets also wrote using their immediate experience—or, at least, were believed to do so. The legend that Wyatt was the lover of Anne Boleyn, was forced to watch her execution, and wrote his most famous lyric, "Whoso list to hunt," for her, was already current in the early seventeenth century; John Skelton wrote vigorous satires against Wolsey using the solidly English persona, Colin Clout; Edmund Spenser then cast himself as Colin Clout in three of his major works; Sir Philip Sidney represented himself as Astrophil, the thwarted lover of Stella, Penelope Devereux, in the work that inaugurated the vogue for sonnet sequences in the late 1580s and early 1590s; and William Shakespeare cast himself as the lover of an unnamed man and an unnamed woman in his sonnets, a literary maneuver that has baffled and frustrated critics ever since. We should not be surprised that Donne followed suit in giving us glimpses of his life in his work. But we should also recognize that what we have probably bears a complicated, often tangential relationship to an external reality. In Sonnet 24 of *Astrophil and Stella* Astrophil quibbles extensively on the word "rich," signaling that Stella is Penelope Devereux, Sidney's erstwhile fiancé, who subsequently married Lord Rich. In Sonnet 30, Astrophil carefully lists all the main events taking place in Europe—the threat of the Turks in the Mediterranean, the French civil wars, the struggle of the Dutch against the Spanish, and so on—before declaring that he only discusses such events at Court out of politeness because all he really thinks of is Stella. The reader of this in manuscript would have known that this was a joke, a way of teasing the reader, simultaneously affirming and denying that Astrophil was Sidney, as the author was widely known to be extremely interested in political events.[9] When Edmund Spenser represented himself as Colin Clout he played similar games with the reader. Colin invariably appears as a disaffected, miserable figure who may or may not bear a close resemblance to the author. In *The Shepheardes Calender* he is a hapless shepherd hopelessly in love with Rosalind, pining away and neglecting his flock; in *Colin Clouts Come Home Againe,* he is a more definite figure of the author, having just returned to the "shepherd's nation" (Ireland) from "Cynthia's land" (England), lamenting the ways in which the queen neglects her loyal subjects overseas; and in *The Faerie Queene,* Book 6, he conjures up the Graces with his pipe, only to see the oafish Knight of Courtesy, Calidore, make them disappear, much to his understandable chagrin.

It is in terms of these sorts of clever literary games that we should read John Donne's poetry, suggesting that we need to pay careful attention to the ways in which Renaissance poets situate themselves in terms of their precursors, as well as the ways in which they "speak." Given that virtually all of Donne's lyrics are addressed to women, we also need to think about how his artistic identity situates the poet within gender relations. Donne has often been celebrated as a persuasive seducer of women, and just as often attacked as a misogynist. However, if we read his work scrupulously, a much more complicated picture of his achievement should emerge, one that suggests that Donne was especially concerned with his writing and his relationship with his readers, and not as interested in asserting his power over women as many have thought.

Like his English predecessors, Donne was conscious that he belonged to a tradition of poetry, but he was also keen to forge an individual identity within it (Roston 18). Donne's rewriting of Marlowe's "The Passionate Shepherd to His Mistress" as the cynical and world-weary "The Bait" makes precisely this point in poetic form. He may owe a great deal to Ovid in particular, but then do so many other English Renaissance poets, and it does less than justice to writers as diverse as Marlowe, Spenser, and Donne to label them all as "Ovidian."[10] Representing himself in his work, along with the development of a highly personal style of writing, Donne's poetry seeks to establish the voice of a "dramatic speaker."[11] Donne, following the great Roman theorist of oratory, Quintillian, makes the trope of "apostrophe" the key feature of his verse.[12] Quintillian defined "apostrophe" as "a diversion of our words to address some person other than the judge."[13] Quintillian is referring to forensic oratory, the art of persuading a jury in a courtroom, suggesting that a successful orator will address different audiences depending on the circumstances involved. Donne applies this lesson to his poetry, leaving us with a series of dramatic monologues that demand that the reader work out who is speaking, who is being addressed, and what this tells us about the poem in question. The poetic voice takes center stage.

The much-anthologized "The Flea" is often taken to be Donne's most characteristic poem, an example of the lecherous and witty young Jack Donne at his most rampant.[14] But the voice in the poem is perhaps more subtle, witty, and personal than has often been realized. The poem begins dramatically *in media res,* forcing the reader to reconstruct the encounter: "Mark but this flea, and mark in this, / How little that which thou deny'st me is."[15] These opening lines make the situation clear enough. The speaker is a man who wishes to persuade a reluctant woman to go to bed with him. He then uses the example of the flea to show her that surrendering her honor to him is not of great consequence so she might as well submit and enjoy the experience. The three stanzas reveal the speaker using a variety of strategies in response to dramatic developments in the situation. In the first stanza he claims that the insect has sucked the blood of both of them, so he argues that mingling their bodily fluids through sexual intercourse is of no greater consequence. In the second she has obviously threatened to kill the flea, so he argues that the flea represents their marriage. Therefore, killing it would be a sacrilege. In the final stanza she has killed the flea, so he argues that as the death of the flea has caused no serious consequences, neither will their making love.

Not only were such seduction poems so common that they formed a recognizable type of literature, but the "flea" poem formed a distinct subgenre within this larger group. As Murray Roston has pointed out, because Ovid was thought to be the author of an erotic "flea" poem, imitations and adaptations were so numerous that an anthology of them was compiled in France in 1582 (Roston 109). Donne's poem is hardly a scandalous departure from the norms and traditions of classical erotic poetry and its later European forms. It is the second stanza, I think, that makes the lyric both interesting and distinctive:

> Oh stay, three lives in one flea spare,
> Where we almost, nay more than married are.
> This flea is you and I, and this
> Our marriage bed, and marriage temple is;
> Though parents grudge, and you, we'are met,
> And cloistered in these living walls of jet.
> Though use make you apt to kill me,
> Let not to this, self murder added be,
> And sacrilege, three sins in killing three.

The second line has invariably been taken as a metaphor, with the poet addressing an unnamed lady—real or fictional—as though she were his wife simply as a means of gratifying his appetites.[16] But it is surely more plausible to read this lyric as a witty marriage poem, one addressed by a fictionalized Donne to Ann. The Donnes were ruined by their secret marriage in December 1601, when their secret union was discovered by Ann's father, who made every effort to block Donne's potential avenues of advancement at Court, a fact that may explain the nature of many of Donne's poems (which is not to seek to reduce his poetry to biography). The wit of the first four lines works best if we imagine that the speaker is addressing someone to whom he is not just pretending to be married. What seems like a hypothesis is actual fact. It is a device Donne employs when his speaker addresses God in "Divine Meditation" 7, "At the round earth's imagined corners," a sonnet that, as the first line indicates, depends on the interplay between the fictional and the real. The last lines rely on the shock of the real: "Teach me how to repent; for that's as good / As if thou hadst sealed my pardon, with thy blood." The conditional "if" is counterfactual because every reader would have known that Jesus had died for man's sins, so making it possible for repentance to save the individual's soul.

The same may well be true of the lines "This flea is you and I, and this / Our marriage bed, and marriage temple is," referring to the poverty that the Donnes had to endure together. If so, then Donne has adapted a prominent form of seduction poem as a humorous and witty comment on his own fate—as well as that of his wife. The reason why the lady will not be shamed by surrendering to him is because there is nothing wrong with a husband and wife making love. Even more to the point perhaps, their marriage has already brought them a great deal of poverty and shame, so advertizing their love life will not make a lot of difference. It is significant that Donne refers to the "parents grudge" when it was Ann's father who objected most to the marriage, having the bridegroom dismissed from his job as sword bearer to his son, and then imprisoned. The description of the lovers "cloistered in these living walls of jet" is one of many images in Donne's poems of small rooms as an escape from a hostile world: again, the reader might infer that this powerful image could well refer to Donne's own life. The last line of the stanza, suggesting that the lady will commit "three sins in killing three" could be taken to refer to her pregnancy, and the need for the couple to make the best of their circumstances.

Donne has often been seen as a misogynistic author, notably by Achsah Guibbory, who suggests that "Donne's *Elegies* represent women, not as idealized creatures, closed and inviolable in their chastity, but as low, impure, sometimes even disgusting creatures."[17] Guibbory is quite right to characterize many of Donne's poems in this way, and *Songs and Sonets* is full of works of typical masculine contempt for women, such as "Air and Angels," which argues that men's love is far purer than that of inconstant women, and "The Apparition," in which the spurned lover threatens to return to haunt his cruel mistress. The problem is that we do not know how these poems were intended to be read, or how they were actually read by contemporaries. It is often assumed that Donne was a male poet writing for male readers.[18] But we should note that he was supported by women patrons, most notably Lucy Harrington, countess of Bedford, with whom he appears to have enjoyed a close friendship (Bald 172–80). Donne wrote a number of verse letters to the countess, and he also set one of his lyrics in her estate, "Twickenham Garden." This spring poem is spoken by another neglected lover who sees his fortune at odds with the traditional rites of spring and so roundly curses all womankind in the final stanza:

> Hither with crystal vials, lovers come,
> And take my tears, which are love's wine,
> And try your mistress' tears at home,
> For all are false, that taste not just like mine;
> Alas, hearts do not in eyes shine,
> Nor can you more judge woman's thoughts by tears,
> Than by her shadow, what she wears.
> O perverse sex, where none is true but she,
> Who's therefore true, because her truth kills me.

Even if this did not appear to be addressed to—or, at the very least, connected with—the countess of Bedford, it is hard not to read this poem as a witty joke, exposing ridiculous male attitudes to women. The paradox that women are so false that the truest woman is a false one is part of the standard misogyny that blamed women's inconstancy on Eve's inability to resist the serpent.[19] A poet who could write a sophisticated pastiche of Neoplatonic beliefs in "The Extasie" could surely not be lapsing into simple-minded anti-feminism elsewhere. Although John Carey thinks otherwise, "Twickenham Garden" would appear to be a poem that was designed to be read by women as well as men, who would have enjoyed the exaggerated role-playing that this absurd monologue involves.[20]

The evidence provided by "Twickenham Garden" suggests that the poems in *Songs and Sonets* were gathered together from different sources, that they were largely occasional poems written for different audiences, and, as a result, that they have widely different meanings. What holds them together as a group is the individual voice that Donne creates, the mark of his artistic identity. We need to be careful to distinguish between the poems in the collection, many of which provide clues as to their meaning, but not always in a straightforward manner. Even the most obvious assaults on women may not have been intended for an exclusive male audience and so may not mean what subsequent commentators have assumed they do.

Another interesting case in point is "The Sunne Rising." As in "The Flea," Donne provides a variation on a traditional form of lyric. Here, he adapts the poem of the lover addressing the dawn after a night spent with his mistress (the alba), having his speaker curse the sun with considerable venom rather than praise the dawn as a life-giving and creative force (although Donne is not entirely without precedent: Chaucer has Troilus curse the day in *Troilus and Criseyde* after his first night in Criseyde's bed). As in "The Flea," the situation is made obvious enough in the opening sentences: "Busy old fool, unruly sun, / Why dost thou thus, / Through windows, and through curtains call on us? / Must to thy motions lovers' seasons run?" Donne employs the familiar staged argument whereby the male lover demands that the rhythms of the natural world obey the dictates of his desires:

> Saucy pedantic wretch, go chide
> Late school-boys, and sour prentices,
> Go tell court-huntsmen, that the King will ride,
> Call country ants to harvest offices;
> Love, all alike, no season knows, nor clime,
> Nor hours, days, months, which are the rags of time.

This complex and startling passage juxtaposes a number of ideas and contexts. Like so many of Donne's poems it demands to be read in terms of a commonly known history of poetry, a current historical situation, intellectual currents operating in the Renaissance, and, most importantly, his own life. Unless we take some or all of these factors into account we may miss the subtle ironies of the stanza.

The lover addresses the sun in irreverent terms as a "saucy pedantic wretch," as though the sun had a choice whether to rise or not and is simply behaving badly in shining so early. Clearly such words place the reader in a mildly ironic position to the speaker, exposing him as a victim of the madness that afflicts those passionately in love. But, as everyone knew, the mad would alternate between speaking nonsense and speaking the truth that no one else dared to say. The following two lines, as has often been noted, are a swipe at the behavior of King James, and his addiction to hunting at the expense of governing the kingdom he claimed he wanted to rule so badly.[21] James and his courtiers are equated with schoolboys and irritable apprentices, suggesting that they all perform equally minor tasks. On the one hand this shows the conceit of the myopic lover; on the other, it suggests how petty public life in England had become. Love may well know no days or seasons, but then neither do those who choose to go out hunting instead of ruling the kingdom. And, if the lover is a figure of Donne himself, then his disastrous marriage to Ann More left him with a great deal of time on his hands to contemplate such matters, as he no longer had a career but spent his time making a series of unsuccessful applications for positions, until he eventually took holy orders and was ordained deacon of St. Paul's Cathedral in 1615, thirteen years after he confessed to his father-in-law that he was married. Donne may well be reflecting on the fact that, unlike the king, who was eager to go out hunting, he had no real need to get out of bed in the morning so had good reason to curse the sun.

As the short narrative continues the ego of the lover reaches ever greater proportions. The second stanza leaves the bed the lovers lie in behind so that they can eclipse the world: "Thy beams, so reverend, and strong / Why shouldst thou think? / I could eclipse and cloud them with a wink, / But that I would not lose her sight so long." The exaggerated compliment to the woman is made partly as a means of exploding the Petrarchan tradition in English poetry, whereby the lover heaped praise upon a silent and impossibly beautiful lady.[22] Philip Sidney in *Astrophil and Stella* had already made this tradition complicated and at least partially ironic in having Astrophil praise Stella in absurdly artificial terms (Sonnet 9) and confuse himself with ridiculous twists of grammar (Sonnet 63) before she explicitly rejects him (ninth song). Sir John Davies had gone further when he satirized Petrarchan love poetry in his manuscript collection, "Gullinge Sonnets" (1590s), which represented the lover transformed into a "patiente burden-bearing Asse" through his devotion in the opening sonnet.[23] Donne makes the reader aware that he can do what he likes in his paper world, unlike the real one where his status has been reduced to that of a supplicant. The lover's celebration of his angry power is, I think, designed to draw our attention to his situation in the real world outside the poem, as the references to the king and the Court make clear. Furthermore, in handing his power over to the woman, he is constructing her as his partner in poverty, a similar maneuver to that undertaken in "The Flea" when she crushes the insect and makes him change his argument, equating the two outcasts with the highest offices in the land. The subtext of the poem is that they must make their love powerful together because they have no choice. It is all they have.

The second stanza ends with the whole world moving into their bed: "Ask for those kings whom thou saw'st yesterday, / And thou shalt hear, All here in one bed lay." The final stanza continues this line of rhetorical exaggeration, confirming the lovers' centrality:

> She'is all states, and all princes, I,
> Nothing else is.
> Princes do but play us; compared to this,
> All honour's mimic; all wealth alchemy.
> Thou sun art half as happy as we,
> In that the world's contracted thus;
> Thine age asks ease, and since thy duties be
> To warm the world, that's done in warming us.
> Shine here to us, and thou art everywhere;
> This bed thy centre is, these walls thy sphere.

Having asserted that all kings exist within their bed, so inviting the supposedly assembled monarchs into the chamber, the lover now banishes them. The change in focus and argument resembles the sudden shift in argument at the end of "The Flea," another personal poem set in a small room. The lovers now blot out the world outside rather than stand for the whole. "Princes do but play us" suggests that the lover is not asserting that they are the equal or superior to kings in significance. Rather, they live a life that is more fulfilling, as the subsequent references to honor and wealth in the following line indicate. Again, if this is about Donne's own situation, the irony is especially pointed, given that his marriage left him without a job or prospects, publicly shamed by his father-in-law, and penniless.

The final lines reaffirm the sense of mutual dependence that the lovers have, that they can only exist in each other so at odds are they with the world outside their little room. The world has indeed contracted and they will have to accept this as a fait accompli. In the fictional world of the poem they can at least make the sun shine for them and control his power. Donne's lover speaks and the lady remains silent, the traditional relationship between the sexes in erotic poetry that women poets such as Mary Wroth sought to confront in her sonnet sequence, *Pamphilia to Amphilanthus,* which has each lover addressing the other. On this score Donne remains a deeply conservative poet, with the prominent exception of the elegy, "Sappho to Philaenis" (Meakin 85–101). Nevertheless, poems such as "The Flea" and "The Sun Rising" demonstrate that Donne not only was acutely aware of the different subject positions he adopted in his poetry and the problematic power relationship between men and women, but also used autobiographical material to affirm a more balanced and mutual relationship between himself and his wife. Of course, the achievement has come partly as a result of failure to achieve worldly success, an irony that could hardly have escaped Donne. It is likely that the two poems analyzed so far were designed for a female audience as well as a male one and that we should be careful of assuming that Donne simply wrote for one type of reader. The poems are undoubtedly more occasional than later printed texts would indicate.

If Donne did little to revise the traditional literary relationship between voluble men and silent women, he does seem to practice his familiar technique of pushing a generic expectation so far that the reader becomes aware of the absurdity of prevailing conventions. The opening stanza of "The Canonization" is a case in point:

> For God's sake hold your tongue, and let me love,
> Or chide my palsy, or my gout,
> My five grey hairs, or ruined fortune flout,
> With wealth your state, your mind with arts improve,
> Take you a course, get you a place,
> Observe his Honour, or his Grace,
> Or the King's real, or his stamped face
> Contemplate; what you will, approve,
> So you will let me love.

Here, the situation of the speaker does not become clear until the end of the stanza and the poem does not fit into any recognizable generic patterns. We realize that we are overhearing a conversation between two men, one of whom, the speaker, is defending his right to love and declaring his indifference to the worldly success that others are pursuing (again, the relationship to Donne's own life is obvious enough). However, the poem would appear to set up other expectations in the reader. When we read the opening line, do we not imagine that this is a man addressing a woman, telling her to keep quiet while he declares that he truly loves her? The subsequent list of his ailments in the next two lines only confirms this impression and it is not until the speaker mentions wealth, arts, honor, the life at the Court and money (significantly here in the form of actual coins) that we realize that we are in a male world, witnessing two equals talking about their prospects at Court. In itself, this is an unusual mode of love poetry, and the signaled discrepancy between the sexes, especially if read in terms of Donne's other poems, is unsettling. The famous opening line of "The Canonization," read this way, becomes an acknowledgment that men silenced women when they wrote poetry. The opening stanza reminds us in virtually every line of Donne's own circumstances and his need to find salvation in love as a counterbalance to his failure in the world. The speaker draws attention to his age, with the onset of ailments such as gout and partial paralysis (palsy), as well as his "ruined fortune." The advantages of life at Court are all available for the addressee, not the speaker, who is acutely aware that such opportunities have passed him by.

The reader's knowledge of Donne's circumstances, which he advertises in the first stanza, are wittily exploited in the second. The speaker complains, "Alas, alas, who's injured by my love?," and then lists some of the many people who will remain unaffected by his liaison—merchants, soldiers, lawyers—and some of the events that will take place whether it takes place or not—wars, trials, the plague. The situation is a fictional inversion of the real, as the answer to the speaker's question is, of course, "John and Ann Donne." The effect is to emphasize that the couple and the world have parted company through their rash decision. In the final two stanzas the speaker argues that they must live and die by their love, and so canonize themselves in poetry. This rhetorical maneuver has had a huge impact on twentieth-century literary criticism, and it is no coincidence that one of the most important works of American new criticism, Cleanth Brooks's *The Well Wrought Urn,* should take its title from a key image in Donne's poem.[24] The speaker, quite deliberately and with the possibility of blasphemy that Donne often courted in his religious verse, argues that this poem elevates their mutual feelings to the most exalted levels:

> We can die by it, if not live by love,
> And if unfit for tombs and hearse
> Our legend be, it will be fit for verse;
> And if no piece of chronicle we prove,
> We'll build in sonnets pretty rooms;
> As well a well wrought urn becomes
> The greater ashes, as half-acre tombs,
> And by these hymns, all shall approve
> Us canonized by love:

The love lyric is elevated to the status of a hymn, making the lovers into saints who are canonized for love. However, the poem is not quite as straightforward as its ostensible meaning implies. The fact that it circulated in manuscript in Donne's lifetime and that he made little attempt to publish it suggests that it was written to be read by a few friends and not a wider public. Hence, if the lovers were canonized, it was only in front of a few people, a fact that makes the speaker's assertions somewhat bathetic. Once again, Donne's poem revolves around an intensely private image of life in a small room—here, explicitly equated with his writing—another reminder of his conspicuous lack of worldly success. The reference to their death from love in the opening line is probably not simply a piece of rhetorical exaggeration, but at least half a real fear. As Donne was undoubtedly acutely aware, this poem might well have remained forgotten after his death. The final stanza suddenly reverses the perspective of the reader, a familiar trick of Donne's, who was keenly interested in new scientific discoveries (Docherty ch. 1). The change inverts that in the final lines of "The Sun Rising." Having confined the lovers to a tiny room that shrinks even further to an urn, the speaker now asserts that the lovers form an example for everyone else to copy so that all who read the poems will "beg from above / A pattern of [their] love."

Donne's sense of his poetic identity in *Songs and Sonets* is complicated and fraught with anxiety. Our ability to read the different tones and modulations of the author's voice is severely compromised by the fact that the volume was clearly not authorized and we do not know how Donne regarded his poetry. Donne's poetry is indeed characterized by his recognizable style, as virtually all commentators have noted.[25] But this does not mean that we have to read all the poems in the same way, or assume that a recognizable voice speaks a universal message. Many of Donne's poems are fiercely misogynistic. Some of these, as I have argued, may have been intended for a female as well as a male audience and so be shrouded in a lively irony that the audience recognized immediately. Others, as Achsah Guibbory has perceptively noted, were probably written as a reaction to Elizabeth's rule, making them part of a series of attacks on Elizabeth in the 1590s.[26] Many of his most famous poems, however, written with an acute and ready awareness of the recent history of English poetry, attempt to establish a more balanced relationship between a man and a woman and to contrast this—albeit, problematic—harmony with the vices and vicissitudes of the world. Then, again, women do not often speak in Donne's poetry.

# NOTES

1. John Donne, *Pseudo-Martyr,* ed. Anthony Raspa (Montreal: McGill-Queen's UP, 1993); John Donne, *Selected Prose,* ed. Neil Rhodes (Harmondsworth: Penguin, 1987).
2. R. C. Bald, *John Donne: A Life* (Oxford: Clarendon P, 1970), ch. 10.
3. Richard A. McCabe, "Elizabethan Satire and the Bishops' Ban of 1599," *Yearbook of English Studies* 11 (1981): 188–93.
4. Arthur F. Marotti, *John Donne, Coterie Poet* (Madison: U of Wisconsin P, 1986).
5. Andrew Hadfield, *The English Renaissance, 1500–1620* (Oxford: Blackwell, 2000); Andrew Hadfield, "Michael Drayton and the Burden of History," Chatterton Lecture on Poetry, *Proceedings of the British Academy* 125 (2004): 119–47.
6. Isaac Walton, *The Lives of John Donne, Sir Henry Wotton, Richard Hooker, George Herbert and Robert Sanderson* (1670), ed. George Saintsbury (London: Oxford UP, 1927).
7. Alan Armstrong, "The Apprenticeship of John Donne: Ovid and the *Elegies,*" *English Literary History* 44 (1977): 419–42.
8. Murray Roston, *The Soul of Wit: A Study of John Donne* (Oxford: Clarendon P, 1974), 8.
9. Katherine Duncan-Jones, *Sir Philip Sidney: Courtier Poet* (New Haven: Yale UP, 1991).
10. Armstrong, "Apprenticeship" 431; Patrick Cheney, *Marlowe's Counterfeit Profession: Ovid, Spenser, Counter-Nationhood* (Toronto: U of Toronto P, 1997).

11. A. LaBranche, "'Blanda Elegeia': The Background to Donne's 'Elegies,'" *Modern Language Review* 61 (1966): 357–68; 359.

12. John O. Ward, "Cicero and Quintillian," *The Cambridge History of Literary Criticism: Vol. 3, The Renaissance*, ed. Glyn P. Norton (Cambridge: Cambridge UP, 1999) 77–87.

13. Quintillian, *The Institutio Oratoria*, trans. H. E. Butler, 4 vols. (London: Heinemann, 1920–22) Book 2, 4.1.63; Jonathan Culler, *The Pursuit of Signs: Semiotics, Literature, Deconstruction* (London: Routledge, 1981) 135.

14. James Winny, *A Preface to Donne* (London: Longman, 1970) 53–59; Thomas Docherty, *John Donne, Undone* (London: Methuen, 1986) 126–28.

15. John Donne, *The Complete English Poems,* ed. A. J. Smith (Harmondsworth: Penguin, 1971) 58, ll. 1–2.

16. Tilottama Rajan, "'Nothing sooner broke': Donne's *Songs and Sonets* as Self-Consuming Artefacts," *John Donne: Contemporary Critical Essays,* ed. Andrew Mousley (Basingstoke, Macmillan, 1999) 45–62; 57.

17. Acshah Guibbory, "'Oh, Let Mee Not Serve So': The Politics of Love in Donne's *Elegies,*" *English Literary History* 57 (1990): 811–33; 814; H. L. Meakin, *John Donne's Articulations of the Feminine* (Oxford: Clarendon P, 1998).

18. David Cunnington, "Donne's New Days," *Essays in Criticism* 54 (2004): 18–37; 24.

19. Linda Woodbridge, *Women and the English Renaissance: Literature and the Nature of Womankind, 1540–1620* (Brighton: Harvester, 1985).

20. John Carey, *John Donne: Life, Mind and Art* (London: Faber, 1981) 64–66.

21. D. Harris Willson, *King James VI and I* (London: Cape, 1956).

22. Barbara L. Estrin, *Laura: Uncovering Gender and Genre in Wyatt, Donne, and Marvell* (Durham: Duke UP, 1994).

23. *Elizabethan Sonnets,* ed. Maurice Evans (London: Dent, 1977) 179–80.

24. Cleanth Brooks, *The Well Wrought Urn: Studies in the Structure of Poetry,* Rev. ed. (London: Methuen, 1968).

25. Kevin Pask, *The Emergence of the English Author: Scripting the Life of the Poet in Early Modern England* (Cambridge: Cambridge UP, 1996), ch. 4.

26. Guibbory, "'Oh, Let Mee Not Serve So'" 828; Julia Walker, ed., *Dissing Elizabeth: Negative Representations of Gloriana* (Durham: Duke UP, 1998).

## READING LIST

Armstrong, Alan. "The Apprenticeship of John Donne: Ovid and the *Elegies." English Literary History* 44 (1977): 419–42.

Bald, R. C. *John Donne: A Life.* Oxford: Clarendon P, 1970.

Carey, John. *John Donne: Life, Mind and Art.* London: Faber, 1981.

Cunnington, David. "Donne's New Days." *Essays in Criticism* 54 (2004): 18–37.

Donne, John. *The Complete English Poems.* Ed. A. J. Smith. Harmondsworth: Penguin, 1971.

———. *Selected Prose.* Ed. Neil Rhodes. Harmondsworth: Penguin, 1987.

Guibbory, Achsah. "'Oh, Le Mee Not Serve So': The Politics of Love in Donne's *Elegies." English Literary History* 57 (1990): 811–33.

LaBranche, A. "'Blanda Elegeia': The Background to Donne's 'Elegies.'" *Modern Language Review* 61 (1966): 357–68.

Marotti, Arthur F. *John Donne, Coterie Poet.* Madison: U of Wisconsin P, 1986.

Mousley, Andrew, ed. *John Donne: Contemporary Critical Essays.* Basingstoke, Macmillan, 1999.

# 20

# Satire and the Politics of Town

*Andrew McRae*

An understandably neglected pamphlet published in 1613 by Richard Johnson makes a bold effort to apply satire to the project of urban reform. *Looke on Me, London* is presented on its title page as the work of "an honest Englishman, ripping up the Bowels of Mischiefe, lurking in thy sub-urbs and Precincts." As such, it parallels the investigations of the book's dedicatee, the lord mayor, Sir Thomas Middleton, who had made his own "discovery of abuses" by personally visiting the suburbs in order "to enquire after evil livers" and "root out iniquity" (iii). Underpinning both projects, of writer and civic governor, is a commitment to rendering corruption visible. To reveal hidden vice is to strip it of its subversive power; to give names to new crimes is to expose them properly to the gaze of authority. This fantasy of revelation informs the author's vision of a city in which houses devoted to immoral ends are clearly identified: "that upon the gate or dore of every tabling-house and bowling-alley might bee set a whip and a halter for a signe; then surely all unthrifts and their associates would be ashamed to come to those places, unless shame had utterly forsooke them" (13). House-signs are thus enlisted in a program of moral demarcation. If sinful places are to be allowed to exist, they must proclaim to the world their purpose and effects.

By the time he wrote, however, Johnson's vision of writing and reform was distinctly dated. In its perception of absolute and unproblematic moral categories, the text invokes a tradition of complaint literature, which predated the rash of verse and prose satire that emerged in the latter years of the sixteenth century.[1] By comparison, contemporary satire more commonly expressed profound skepticism regarding traditional discourses of moral revelation and legibility. Ben Jonson's satiric comedy *Bartholomew Fair,* for example, translates the narrative of a civic official uncovering corruption into a parodic register. Jonson's justice of the peace Adam Overdo, for all his confidence in his ability to discover "the yearly enormities" of the fair (2.1.40), is relentlessly exposed not only as fallible in his judgments, but also as personally implicated in the city's prevailing codes of mercantilism and self-interest. Like much of the best Renaissance satire, therefore, the play undermines claims to objectivity, and scrutinizes the processes through which individuals form judgments. Indeed, while a writer of complaint aimed to state what was perceived to be self-evidently true, like a magistrate or clergyman, the satirist might contest the very boundaries between virtue and vice. This helps us to appreciate Renaissance satire as inherently political: not in the sense that it might easily be labeled "conservative" or "radical," but rather in the sense that it is committed to defining lines of debate and division.

In the light of this governing perception of satire, this chapter considers the functions of satiric writing within the early modern town. Along with a number of other studies, it considers the urban environment, and especially that of London, as unsettling and confusing, presenting myriad challenges to traditional moral codes.[2] It focuses on a period of roughly ten years from the late 1580s, during which satire became a popular yet highly controversial genre. Ultimately the chapter centers attention on the verse satire that flourished in the latter years of the 1590s; however, it necessarily places these works within wider literary and cultural contexts, especially by glancing toward an important wave of prose pamphlets published in the late 1580s and early 1590s. The first section explores the relation between authors and authority, setting the anxieties expressed by one of the most eloquent literary critics of age, Gabriel Harvey, against the practices of satirists. The second section looks more closely at satire in the city, examining the sophisticated attention to signs in the work of John Donne.

## Authors and Authority

Literature of the Renaissance is often seen to be characterized by a reassessment of relations between authors and authority. In Robert Weimann's influential argument, for instance, "the claims on God-given legitimacy of secular and ecclesiastical institutions" at this time "were irretrievably undermined." Weimann positions the Renaissance as a transitional period, in which authors sought new kinds of authorization:

> In several fields of early modern culture, this shift in the grounding of validity culminated in a new sense of the relations of authority and representation. Because authority, including the authorization of discourse itself, was no longer given, as it were, before the writing and reading began, the act of representation was turned into a site on which authority could be negotiated, disputed, or reconstituted.[3]

Hence, while an author might once have justified his work by claiming to speak on behalf of the church or the state, and while his writing might as a result have been offered as a straightforward statement of orthodox values, in the Renaissance such claims were exposed to unprecedented scrutiny. And satire, perhaps more than any other literary mode, was informed by this cultural flux. It provided a forum for writers to test their relations with authority, and it equally became a target for those who were troubled by the changes.

The conservative scholar Gabriel Harvey is instructive in this context, as he was one of the earliest commentators on the "Invectives" and "Satyres" he saw proliferating in the 1580s and 1590s.[4] Although he was concerned specifically with particular prose pamphlets—such as those attacking the Elizabethan church hierarchy, published under the pseudonym Martin Marprelate, or those written by Harvey's long-term antagonist, the remarkable Thomas Nashe—his critique is much more general in its application. In his view, the rise of satire was a novel and troubling phenomenon, which undermined the proper relation between authors and authority. As Lorna Hutson has demonstrated, according to Harvey this relation was correctly circumscribed by structures of patronage, through which an author identified himself with a particular member of the elite. "By virtue of the patron's credit the author's words gain an authority beyond the dreams of oratory: they become the authentic words of the body politic." Conversely, without that association "the author was liable to be under suspicion of 'singularity,'" or the audacious articulation of "individualism."[5] Harvey was therefore alarmed by texts published anonymously, without a dedication, or with a parodic dedication. This flouting of convention would in fact become something of a feature of printed satires. Perhaps most notoriously, John Marston's contemptuously curt dedication "To his most esteemed and best beloved Self," pointedly isolates the author as a man in need of no further authority, reliant only on his capacity to sell his work within a literary marketplace.[6]

In such aggressively individualistic forms, Harvey feared, satire threatens to destabilize authority. In one passage he surveys those "Satyricall Spirites" for whom "scoffing, and girding is their daily bread," including among their number "Scoggin," "Rabelays" and "Kett" (36–37). The list tellingly conflates threats to structures of textual and political order. The bawdy *Scoggins Jests* stretched bounds of morality, while François Rabelais's notorious French prose romance *Gargantua and Pantagruel* combined a vibrantly indecorous style with strains of political and social critique. Meanwhile, the third author on the list, Robert Kett, put his name only to a petition.[7] He was a rebel, leader of a 1549 rebellion in Harvey's native East Anglia: and this, the logic of Harvey's list suggests, is where the individualistic flouting of convention will inevitably lead. Indeed Harvey's admonitory vision is nothing less than the disintegration of social and political order. If every "Martin Junior" (one of the pseudonyms adopted in the Marprelate tracts) or "Puny Pierce" (an allusion to one of Nashe's pseudonyms, Pierce Penniless) claims the status, through access to the press, of "a monarch in the kingdome of his owne humour," then "God-night all distinctions of persons, and all difference of estates" (58). When literature, and especially the printed page, becomes a vehicle for unauthorized expression, the field of textuality becomes (in Harvey's view, for the first time) truly politicized.

At the time that Harvey was writing, the clearest instance of textual controversy was provided by the Marprelate tracts. Elizabethan England had seen nothing like these scurrilous and subversive pamphlets, which seemed to threaten the foundations of order in church and state alike. Interestingly, Nashe himself contributed to the rebuttal of Marprelate, thus placing him (for once) on the same side as Harvey. But his success was achieved not by invoking authority, but rather by appropriating Martin's own strategies of satire and irony, ridiculing his opponent as pompous and unreliable.[8] For Harvey, this was yet further evidence of sociopolitical division; he speaks fearfully of "this Martinish and Counter-martinish age: wherein the Spirit of Contradiction reigneth, and everie one superaboundeth in his owne humor" (35). As he recognized, the Marprelate tracts fashioned a fresh model of printed polemic, combining earnest ecclesiastical discourse, humanist satiric tropes, and a strain of popular scurrility. Though written predominantly in prose, one pamphlet even slides at its close into crude verse:

> Either from Country or Court
> Master Martin Marprelate, will do you hurt.
>    Rime doggerel,
> Is good enough for bishops, I can tell;
>    And I do much marvel,
> If I have not given them such a spell,
>    As answer it how, they cannot tell.[9]

The poem revels in Harvey's "Spirit of contradiction," wilfully leveling distinctions between the bishops and the elusive Martin. Moreover, while Harvey encodes individualistic expression as threatening and anarchic, Martin elsewhere seeks more carefully to establish a legitimizing foundation for such speech-acts. In one marginal note he states that his antagonist, John Bridges, "shall never get me to swear against my conscience" (40). Subsequently, he echoes a radical proverb (also invoked by the clumsy rebels of Shakespeare's *The Tempest*): "Thought is free" (51). For all their evasive irony and populist humor, and despite the fact that the authorities could never ascribe the tracts to a particular author, it is fair to state that these pamphlets were involved in a crucial reassessment of the political values of individualism. A world of independent thought and conscience, toward which they insistently gesture, was precisely what Harvey feared.

While the Marprelate tracts were soon suppressed by state censorship, the rise of formal verse satire in the latter half of the 1590s extended this textual interrogation of issues of truth and authority. Significantly, much satire from these years actually retains a commitment to the revelation of truth and the protection of absolute moral values, thereby aligning the genre with a conservative and orthodox position. For Joseph Hall, for instance, satire assumes the status of a vocation:

> Envie waits on my backe, Truth on my side:
> Envie will be my Page, and Truth my Guide.
> Envie the margent holds, and Truth the line:
> Truth doth approve, but Envy doth repine.[10]

The personified figure of Truth legitimates his project; the "muse" of satire, in his poems, will "the ugly face of vice unmaske."[11] Yet this was never a simple or uncomplicated position, since satirists consistently admitted at once the limitations of their art and the fundamental difficulty of defining moral boundaries in their uncertain social and economic milieu. Like other Elizabethan satirists, Hall is repeatedly drawn to indices of instability. He writes:

> For thousands beene in every governall,
> That live by losse, and rise by others fall.
> What ever sickly sheepe so secret dies,
> But some foule Raven hath bespoke his eyes?
> What else makes *N.* when his lands are spent,
> Go shaking like a threedbare malecontent[?][12]

The naturalization of change in these lines concedes the possibility that human rises and falls, as opposed to a structure of hierarchy and social order, may somehow be removed from the reach of moral judgment. There is in fact a characteristic weariness to the passage, as Hall dispassionately surveys instances of social flux.[13] Moreover, Hall's social genealogy of the "threedbare malecontent" might be seen to reflect back on satire itself, a genre in which authors typically situate themselves as angry outsiders. A malcontent might be understood as a man who has been unsuccessful in the struggle of early modern urban life, who speaks with bitterness and vitriol as a result. He is therefore complicit in the world he criticizes, not a detached and disinterested observer.

Hall's contemporary John Marston, more than any other Elizabethan satirist, pursues the implications of this strain of skepticism. Crucially, whereas Hall continued to claim in his satire a degree of insight and objectivity, Marston effectively aligns himself with the malcontents of his age, conceding that "my selfe am not imaculate, / But many spots my minde doth vitiate." He is at best, he says, "a snaphaunce Satyrist" (a satirist, that is, in the form of a marauder or highwayman), forever removed from the honor and purity of "milk-white robes" and a "Censorian seate."[14] As others have argued of Marston, this approach is informed in part by a Calvinist theory of election, which suggested to some that all "depraved man can do is to despair of his own efforts towards virtue." The premise of moral satire is therefore profoundly shaken: "If men are good or evil as a result of the arbitrary act of God, they cannot be justly attacked for their vices or praised for their virtues."[15] Yet his work is also informed by an appreciation of the socioeconomic status of the author within an intensely commercialized urban environment. In one poem, Marston figures satirists beginning "To sette up shop"; in another, he reflects on the way that within print culture a poet cedes a critical measure of control over the interpretation of his work:

> But will you needs stay? am I forc'd to beare,
> The blasting breath of each lewd Censurer?
> Must naught but clothes, and images of men
> But sprightles truncks, be Judges of my pen?
> Nay then come all, I prostitute my Muse,
> For all the swarme of Idiots to abuse.[16]

The author, compromised at the outset by his own spotted mind, is figured as ultimately malleable to the interests and desires of others. To purchase his work is to claim the right to determine its meaning, just as hiring a prostitute gives the man, by the crude laws of the marketplace, the right to impress his will upon her.

The concerns expressed by Gabriel Harvey, amplified as they were in a wealth of prose and verse satire, demonstrate the insistent challenges posed by writing in this period. To return to the work of Weimann, we might identify in such texts the emergence of a "deeply divisive register of legitimation, one residing in the strength of personal beliefs and convictions, in the differentiating uses of knowledge, discussion, and a busier exchange of signs and meanings."[17] Hence Marprelate's appeal to freedom of thought; hence the willful destabilizing of textual conventions in Renaissance prose satire; and hence Marston's sophisticated appreciation of literature in the marketplace. Satirists at this time were consistently registering and analyzing the manifold changes of their world: and nowhere was their work more successful than when focused specifically on the city.

## Satire and the City

Richard Johnson's *Looke on Me, London,* for all of its outmoded commitment to satire as a vehicle of moral reform, is nonetheless a telling product of the city. For the late Elizabethan and early Jacobean years constituted a period of unsettling change in London, characterized by rapid population growth, unprecedented social and geographical mobility, the movement of commercial and industrial practices toward capitalist structures, and devastating outbreaks of dearth and plague. To many, the city was a phenomenon that stretched existing social and spatial categories; James I, for instance, admitted a nightmare vision in which "all the countrey is gotten into *London;* so as with time, *England* will onely be *London,* and the whole countrey be left waste." For him, as for many other commentators, the city eroded what James described simply as the "old fashion of *England.*"[18] While the function of satire within this context remains a wide field of critical enquiry, the discussion here will focus on the ways in which satire concerns itself with the surfaces of civic life. As will be seen, satirists consistently scrutinize the relation between appearances and substances, and worry further about the status of literature in the new urban environment. Satire was a literary mode fixated on—and also implicated in—the instability and malleability of signs in the city.

Early modern London was awash with signs, which contemporaries read with varying degrees of clarity and depth. In the city streets, for an age before Londoners had the benefit of civic mapping or house numbers, pictorial signboards provided basic aids for navigation. John Stow, whose Elizabethan *Survey of London* consistently asserts values of tradition and history, records numerous signboards, thereby acknowledging them as "a key resource in negotiating and deciphering the spaces of the city."[19] The social life of London, similarly, was dependent on one's ability to interpret signs. Codes of dress were still, in theory at least, governed by sumptuary laws, which defined in detail what types of clothes those at each level of society were entitled to wear. In the city's streets, therefore, social identities were supposed to be legible to all. But such a stable, essentializing approach to signs was besieged by the vicissitudes of change, particularly under the pressures of a nascent market culture. Despite Stow's commitment to tradition, success in the marketplace promised rather to rewrite structures of history and hierarchy, just as a successful merchant might purchase fresh clothes and a new house. In response to this threat, satirists seized upon the unreliability of signification. Everard Guilpin, for example, imagines "a new sherifes gate-posts, whose old faces / Are furbisht over to smoothe times disgraces."[20] Marston teases away futher at the relation between signs and substance—insides and outsides—when he suggests that in his contemporary environment, "every signe can brothelrie afford."[21]

The satirist's fascination with simulation helps to explain his preoccupation with women. Female use of dress and cosmetics, in particular, are recurrent topics in satires. One epigram invokes laws of trade in order to problematize easy assumptions between identity and appearance:

> Lucas on's Lady layes a foule objection,
> Saying she weareth not her owne complexion.
> But then her Ladyship may say he lyeth,
> Is't not her owne I pray you which she buyeth?[22]

As much as the poem seems to settle for an easy misogyny, it betrays nonetheless a nexus of anxieties centering on the determination of identity. Like so much contemporary discourse on social relations and the market, the passage hinges on the adjective "owne." For Lucas, the identity of his "Lady" (whether she be his wife or lover) should be legible to all men; for the woman, identity is instead malleable, like any other marketable commodity. The market, in which she claims full rights, enables her to evade or deceive the otherwise determining male gaze.

To the extent that the male gaze may be equated with an authorial gaze, especially for one of the most distinctly gendered of all literary modes, such acts of deception equally instill anxieties concerning the power of language. Marston explores these anxieties further in his speculation on a London woman's sexual desires:

Shal *Lucea* scorne her husbands luke-warme bed?
(Because her pleasure being hurried
In joulting Coach, with glassie instrument,
Doth farre exceede the *Paphian* blandishment)
Whilst I (like to some mute *Pythagoran*)
Halter my hate, and cease to curse and ban
Such brutish filth? (115)

Not only does Lucea prefer autoerotic sex with a dildo, she chooses to take this pleasure in a "joulting Coach": an image of sexual and economic control that pointedly inverts contemporary stereotypes of wealthy men pursuing sexual conquests over helpless women in this relatively new and private form of transport. The lines thus betray a sophisticated appreciation of the symbolic value of the penis. In the terms of modern gender theory, Lucea's pursuit of pleasure on her own, in a space that her economic power has commanded, undermines her husband's phallic control within the marriage. And for the poet, by extension, there is even more at stake. If Lucea chooses the inanimate "instrument" over her husband's "*Paphian* blandishment" (i.e., erotic flattery), she implicitly challenges myths of male (phallocentric) control over language itself. By analogy, even though the satirist may "curse and ban," he simultaneously concedes his inability to effect any significant reform. Like Lucea's husband, the satirist acknowledges a measure of impotence.

Satire is thus driven to reassess existing models of linguistic authority. Indeed the performative verbal dexterity that becomes characteristic of the mode in the 1590s might be read in part as a response to a sense that traditional myths of power were losing their hold. This peculiar cultural context, far from rendering satire irrelevant, underpins its distinctive character and voice. For Renaissance satirists, despite their furious indignation in the face of change, increasingly move away from a traditional role of marking accepted categories and boundaries and engage instead in struggles over their determination. Moreover, they acknowledge their limitations of vision and their complicity in the myriad power struggles of the early modern town and forge in response a freshly engaged mode of literature. Satire emerges as a mode committed to contesting signification. Rather than appealing insistently to the authority of certain absolute values, in the expectation that no reader could conceivably challenge them, satire engages in politicized acts of discrimination.[23]

At this stage it may be helpful to concentrate on one poet, and ultimately one poem. Donne is in some respects unrepresentative of Elizabethan satire, since he probably wrote earlier than any of the other major satirists, and circulated his five *Satyres* in manuscript among a relatively discrete body of readers, rather than committing the poems to the marketplace of print.[24] Yet he provides a valuable study of an author thinking his way through some of the implications of his chosen mode. In poems that are remarkably self-reflective, Donne weighs the value of different satiric traditions and works to situate satire afresh in his contemporary urban context. Several studies of the *Satyres* have focused on Donne's relative engagement with different classical models, especially those provided by the satires of Horace and Juvenal.[25] By comparison, the present reading of "Satyre I" aims to situate the poem in a broadly social and cultural, as opposed to a more traditionally literary, context. "Satyre I" is structured around the divergent responses to the city adopted by a scholar—who is, in most respects, an authorial figure—and a "fondling motley humorist" (l. 1). Crucially, the latter draws the scholar out of his study and into the city, where he is forced to consider the relation between abstract humanist values and the multitudinous corruptions of his world.

"Satyre I" thus takes the form of pedestrian satire, a type that would flourish through subsequent years. Such poems reassess the relation between the individual and civic space, in ways that challenge myths of order and community fostered by writers such as Stow. If a perambulation of the city for Stow serves as a rehearsal of history, situating the walker within an established and well-known space, the experiences of individuals in satires are more specific and unpredictable. They "represent city space through the encounter, through description, substantives, lists of consumer goods, street life with its enumerated pleasures and dangers."[26] Donne's representation of the city, as Karen Newman demonstrates, is socially selective; the speaker and his companion directly acknowledge only "men of sort, of parts, and qualities" (l. 105), while those of lower degree instead enter the poem in rhetorically mediated ways. Hence "[m]erchants, shopkeepers, and artisans appear only metonymically through the goods they trade," while male and female prostitutes are mentioned parenthetically to evidence the humorist's decadence.[27] But while this rhetorical evasiveness contrasts with the clutter of objects and people in Marston's satires—mirroring, in a sense, the speaker's inadequate efforts to partition himself from the city—it nonetheless creates a textual space within which the multiplicity of the city might be assessed.

Like so much Elizabethan verse satire, Donne's poem encompasses that multiplicity by amassing images of appearances and surfaces. Throughout, the satiric assault on the humorist centers on his eagerness to judge people by appearances: "skip[ping] forth now to greet / Every fine silken painted foole we meet" (ll. 71–72). Before the speaker is finally drawn from his study, he imagines the humorist being distracted in the city, and conceives a vow that the latter should not abandon him:

Not though a Captaine do come in thy way
Bright parcell gilt, with forty dead mens pay,
Nor though a briske perfum'd piert Courtier
Deigne with a nod, thy courtesie to answer,
Nor come a velvet Justice with a long
Great traine of blew coats, twelve, or fourteen strong,
Wilt thou grin or fawne on him, or prepare
A speech to court his beautious sonne and heire. (ll. 17–24)

The three social types in these lines are carefully chosen, representing three forms of authority on which a state should rest: military, political, and legal. The central point of the satire, however, lies in exposing the society's commitment to display at the expense of more fundamental human values. Hence the soldier effectively clothes himself in embezzled "dead mens pay," while the status of the "Justice" is established less by his mind than by the splendid livery of his retainers. The final couplet of this passage has bemused some critics, who have translated the overt homoeroticism into more modest terms.[28] Situated within the context of the humorist's devotion to surfaces, however, the couplet proffers a definitive image of emotional and sexual relations being governed by carefully managed appearances and the logic of the marketplace. The point is recalled in a subsequent image of

a cheape whore, that hath beene
Worne by as many severall men in sinne,
As are black feathers, or musk-colour hose. (ll. 53–55)

If sexual relations are subordinated to the imperatives of a consumer culture, the treasured structures of society collapse. Traditional indices of value, such as one's birth and behavior, are overlooked in favor of appearances and market values, whether of the "beautious sonne and heire" or the "cheape whore." As a result, the speaker notes, the whore can hardly "Name her childs right true father, 'mongst all those" (l. 56).

Yet the poem is still more searching in its representation of the speaker's struggle to identify clear and reliable moral absolutes. In one passage, ostensibly targeting the humorist's sexual mores, the speaker attempts to define ideals to set against his images of corruption:

Why should'st thou (that dost not onely approve,
But in ranke itchie lust, desire, and love
The nakednesse and barenesse to enjoy,
Of thy plumpe muddy whore, or prostitute boy)
Hate vertue, though shee be naked, and bare?
At birth, and death, our bodies naked are;
And till our Soules be unapparrelled
Of bodies, they from blisse are banished.
Mans first blest state was naked, when by sinne
Hee lost that, yet hee'was cloath'd but in beasts skin,
And in this course attire, which I now weare,
With God, and with the Muses I conferre. (ll. 37–48)

There is something naggingly persistent, even fretful, about these lines. The key term, "naked," appears to offer an unproblematic antithesis to the humorist's preoccupation with clothes; however, once it has prompted a morally unsatisfactory image of "thy plumpe muddy whore, or prostitute boy," the speaker reaches beyond the body and its temporal location, to the "unapparrelled" soul at the point of birth or death. This idea provides a kind of vanishing point, not only for the imagery of clothing, but equally for the satirist and his use of language. Disembodied "blisse" is a state necessarily timeless and silent. By contrast, as the poem moves away from this vision and back toward the demands of the world, the speaker acquires at once his "course attire" and the words with which he "conferre[s]." Though posited by the speaker as an image of someone as close as possible to a purified state, this invites recognition as merely another pose. Like the postures adopted by other social types on the city's streets, the speaker's stance represents a self-conscious positioning of the self in relation to codes of dress and speech. As other critics have also noted, the poem thus deconstructs the speaker's perception that the divergent attitudes toward the city evidenced by himself and the humorist might be categorized simply as right and wrong, moral and immoral. Instead, the poem betrays a sophisticated awareness that "the stark contrasts of satire obviously distorted their world."[29]

Read in this way, "Satyre I" also invites a degree of skepticism in the opening lines, in which the speaker situates himself within a context of Christian humanism. Of his study, in which he wishes to "lye" as though "coffin'd" (ll. 3–4), he claims:

Here are Gods conduits, grave Divines; and here
Natures Secretary, the Philosopher;
And jolly Statesmen, which teach how to tie
The sinewes of a cities mistique bodie;
Here gathering Chroniclers, and by them stand
Giddie fantastique Poëts of each land. (ll. 5–10)

While the speaker confidently proclaims this library "constant company" (l. 11), his perception of constancy is undermined by the terms of his praise. In a manner that is analogous to the lines on nakedness, with their effort to imagine a state beyond physicality, this passage originates in a vision of texts that may serve passively as "Gods conduits." Donne's famous third satire, on religious controversy, would explode this view of religious writing as a pernicious fantasy. Here, the subsequent lines, leading to the strikingly ambivalent representation of poets as "Giddie" and "fantastique," underscore the complicit status of writing in society. Moreover, while "the Philosopher" might confidently be identified as Aristotle, the "jolly Statesmen" are more mysterious, and their claims of knowledge are undermined by Donne's adjective. ("Jolly" at this time means "full of presumptuous pride" or "arrogant.")[30] Donne is therefore positioning his speaker—and, by extension, himself—at the heart of ongoing intellectual debates about knowledge and power, centering specifically on the nature of a city's corporate existence. These debates, involving continental writers such as Giovanni Botero and Justus Lipsius and endebted to the Roman historian Tacitus and the political theories of Niccolo Machiavelli, focused attention on the uncertain relation between morality and power. Such debates—like Renaissance satire itself—were involved in the formulation of new models and discourses of politics.[31]

Donne's poem therefore admits a tendency of language to transform apparently clear distinctions between good and bad into more arbitrary distinctions between differing interpretations of signs. This is not to say that the poem does not privilege one form of engagement with the city over another; clearly it does. But it is to say that the poem acknowledges, however anxiously, that the city breaks down moral absolutes and politicizes acts of writing. Written as it was in the mid-1590s—after Gabriel Harvey's anxious reflections on his age, yet immediately before the late Elizabethan outpouring of printed verse satires—the poem usefully clarifies the political status of satire. Though never easily classifiable according to modern political categories, satire at this time participated in a critical reassessment of statecraft and morality. It was engaged, that is, in the *politicization* of both town and nation.

## NOTES

I am grateful to Andrew Gordon and Nicholas McDowell for their comments on drafts of this essay.

1. See John Peter, *Complaint and Satire in Early English Literature* (Oxford: Clarendon P, 1956).

2. See esp. Lawrence Manley, *Literature and Culture in Early Modern London* (Cambridge: Cambridge UP, 1995); Douglas Bruster, *Drama and the Market in the Age of Shakespeare* (Cambridge: Cambridge UP, 1992); Steven Mullaney, *The Place of the Stage: License, Play, and Power in Renaissance England* (Chicago: U of Chicago U, 1988).

3. *Authority and Representation in Early Modern Discourse,* ed. David Hillman (Baltimore: Johns Hopkins UP, 1996) 5.
4. *Foure Letters and certaine Sonnets* (London, 1592) 15.
5. *Thomas Nashe in Context* (Oxford: Clarendon P, 1989) 199, 198.
6. Marston, *Poems,* ed. Arnold Davenport (Liverpool: Liverpool UP, 1961) 94.
7. Cf. Hutson, *Thomas Nashe* 200–01.
8. E.g., *An almond for a parrat* (London, 1589).
9. *Marprelate Tracts* (Leeds: Scolar, 1967) 121.
10. *Collected Poems,* ed. Arnold Davenport (Liverpool: Liverpool UP, 1949) 11.
11. *Collected Poems* 11.
12. *Collected Poems* 66.
13. See my discussion of Hall in *God Speed the Plough: The Representation of Agrarian England, 1500–1660* (Cambridge: Cambridge UP, 1996) 89–91.
14. *Poems* 72.
15. Arnold Davenport, "Introduction" to Marston, *Poems* 21.
16. *Poems* 97–98.
17. *Authority and Representation in Early Modern Discourse* 5.
18. *Political Writings,* ed. Johann P. Sommerville (Cambridge: Cambridge UP, 1994) 226.
19. Andrew Gordon, "'If my sign could speak': The Signboard and the Visual Culture of Early Modern London," *Early Theatre* 8 (2005): 35–52: 38.
20. *Skialetheia or A Shadowe of Truth, in Certaine Epigrams and Satyres,* ed. D. Allen Carroll (Chapel Hill: U North Carolina P, 1974) 70.
21. *Poems* 109.
22. Henry Parrot, *The Mastive* (London, 1615) B2v.
23. Cf. Manley's influential interpretation of Renaissance satire (*Literature and Culture in Early Modern London* 372–430).
24. *The Satires, Epigrams and Verse Letters,* ed. W. Milgate (Oxford: Clarendon P, 1967).
25. See esp. Heather Dubrow, "'No man is an island': Donne's Satires and Satiric Traditions," *Studies in English Literature 1500–1900* 19 (1979): 71–83; M. Thomas Hexter, *Kinde Pitty and Brave Scorn: John Donne's "Satyres"* (Durham: Duke UP, 1982).
26. Karen Newman, "Walking Capitals: Donne's First Satyre," *The Culture of Capital: Property, Cities, and Knowledge in Early Modern England,* ed. Henry S. Turner (New York: Routledge, 2002) 217.
27. Newman, "Walking Capitals" 208.
28. Newman, "Walking Capitals" 212.
29. Arthur Marotti, *John Donne: Coterie Poet* (Madison: U Wisconsin P, 1986) 38. Cf. Hexter, *Kinde Pitty* 18; Barbara L. Parker and J. Max Patrick, "Two Hollow Men: The Pretentious Wooer and the Wayward Bridegroom of Donne's 'Satyre I,'" *Seventeenth-Century News* 33 (1975) 13.
30. *Satires* 118.
31. See esp. Richard Tuck, *Philosophy and Government 1572–1651* (Cambridge: Cambridge UP, 1993).

# READING LIST

Griffin, Dustin. *Satire: A Critical Reintroduction.* Lexington: UP of Kentucky, 1994.
Hutson, Lorna. *Thomas Nashe in Context.* Oxford: Clarendon P, 1989.
Kernan, Alvin. *The Cankered Muse: Satire of the English Renaissance.* New Haven: Yale UP, 1959.

McRae, Andrew. *Literature, Satire and the Early Stuart State*. Cambridge: Cambridge UP, 2004.

Manley, Lawrence. *Literature and Culture in Early Modern London*. Cambridge: Cambridge UP, 1995.

Marotti, Arthur. *John Donne: Coterie Poet*. Madison: U of Wisconsin P, 1986.

Newman, Karen. "Walking Capitals: Donne's First Satyre." *The Culture of Capital: Property, Cities, and Knowledge in Early Modern England*. Ed. Henry S. Turner. New York: Routledge, 2002. 203–21.

Peter, John. *Complaint and Satire in Early English Literature*. Oxford: Clarendon P, 1956.

Selden, Raman. *English Verse Satire, 1590–1765*. London: Allen and Unwin, 1978.

# 21

# Donne's Religious Poetry
# and the Trauma of Grace

*Achsah Guibbory*

Donne's religious lyrics are deeply anxious. Obsessed with sin, their speakers struggle for faith and seek assurance of God's love while exploring the problem of salvation. Like most Christians, particularly since Augustine formulated the doctrine of "original sin," Donne felt he was born guilty, and like all Christians he was concerned with the salvation of his soul. But there is a depth to the anxieties expressed in the poems that must be understood not just in terms of Donne's own psychological makeup or as a general Christian condition but also in relation to the crisis over grace and salvation precipitated by the Protestant Reformation.

Donne's poetry reflects both intimate, personal concerns and public, cultural issues. His devotional poetry—passionate, witty, intelligent—moves us as it articulates a longing for personal redemption that transcends the boundaries of confessional differences and expresses the human desire to be delivered from imperfection and the painful conditions of this life. Yet issues particular to post-Reformation, early seventeenth-century England shape Donne's poetry.

With the Reformation, the church had split, divided between the Roman Catholic church and the reformed churches, in which there was far from complete agreement about all matters of worship and salvation (soteriology). The Reformation did not happen at once, but was an ongoing, contested process.[1] Generally, however, the Reformers taught that the individual Christian has (or should have) unmediated access to God and the Bible, or word of God; that human beings are saved by God's grace and not by their own works (or merit) or the intervention of intercessors; and that salvation requires faith not works. In contrast, the Roman church emphasized the necessity of good works as well as faith, the role of the church and the priests in salvation, and the importance of tradition (the church fathers and accumulated wisdom of the church) in formulating doctrine and interpreting the Bible. The Roman church insisted that the seven sacraments (Eucharist, baptism, confirmation, penance, extreme unction, matrimony, holy orders) are necessary conduits of salvation and claimed that the priest is an essential instrument of God's grace. In contrast, the Reformation reduced the sacraments from seven to two (baptism and communion) and declared the sacraments to be signs, not conduits, of grace, thereby also reducing the power of the priest.

The impact and effects of the Reformation are too complex to be summarized here. But if the Reformation was liberating (Luther described it as the deliverance of the church from its "Babylonian captivity"), it was also unsettling.[2] On the one hand, the Reformation provided assurance to believers that they did not have to depend on the church or priests for salvation, on their monetary contributions to the church, or their own inadequate efforts to live lives good enough to merit salvation. Salvation was now solely a matter of faith and God's grace, the worship of God was primarily internal and spiritual, and connection with God personal, centered in the individual. On the other, the Reformation could also produce a sense of loss and anxiety rather than assurance. God was no longer accessible through the sacraments. The priest and good works could no longer provide assurance of grace. God could not be apprehended in images or the crucifix, or the transubstantiated elements of the bread and wine that (the Roman church taught), with the priest's blessing, actually became the body and blood of Christ in the sacrament of communion. God's presence within, spiritually, was sufficient and reassuring for many Christians, but for others there was a sense of loss. In contrast with the corporeal spirituality of the Roman Catholic church, with its bodily ceremonies and ritual, according to reformed theology, God was materially absent. As Calvin wrote, explaining why Christ could not be physically present in the elements of the Eucharist, Christ after his resurrection "was received into heaven" to sit at his father's right hand, where his body will remain "till the last day."[3] Only then will he physically, materially return to the earth.

Whereas before the Reformation the Roman Catholic church had provided a universal community and dogma, there now was a challenge to its sovereign authority and its doctrine of salvation. The existence of more than one church, as well as the competing notions of salvation, could create the kind of "trauma of grace" that we will see expressed in Donne's poetry. Which is the true church? How can one be sure one is saved? How can one feel the presence of a God one can no longer materially apprehend in the church or its sacraments?

Donne's own situation made the trauma more particular and immediate. Born in 1572 into a family that boasted many Catholic martyrs (including Sir Thomas More, who was executed when he opposed Henry VIII's divorce) and raised as a Catholic, Donne "converted" to the (reformed) Church of England, was ordained as a priest in 1615, and became Dean of St. Paul's Cathedral in 1621, a position he retained until his death in 1631. We do not know when Donne converted, or whether he ever fully left behind his Catholic roots.[4] Yet the very fact of his "conversion" from Roman Catholicism to the English church might allow him to represent the crisis (and incompleteness?) of the Reformation, the anxieties and uncertainties it provoked.

Although perhaps best known for his love poetry, Donne wrote a considerable body of devotional verse expressing his spiritual longing for God. These poems include eighteen holy sonnets, "Goodfriday, 1613. Riding Westward," three "Hymns" to God or Christ, as well as "La Corona" (seven linked sonnets), "The Crosse," "A Litanie," and miscellaneous other poems.[5] The category of "religious verse" is slippery in the case of Donne, as there is considerable overlap between his "secular" and "sacred" poetry. Many of the *Songs and Sonets* and *Elegies,* as well as the two "Anniversaries" on the death of Elizabeth Drury, employ religious language and have a strong spiritual dimension. This essay, however, will focus on poetry that is explicitly, directly about or addressed to God.

Just as we do not know when Donne "converted" from Catholicism and became a member of the Church of England, we do not know when most of Donne's religious poems were written. They were not published in his lifetime. The titles tell us that "Goodfriday" was written in 1613, and the "Hymn to Christ, at the author's going into

Germany" in 1619. Most of the holy sonnets were probably written between 1608 and 1610, perhaps in 1609—a difficult period when Donne was living with his wife and growing family at Mitcham, ill, depressed, and without employment—although one scholar has suggested these sonnets may actually have been written in the 1590s.[6] Manuscript and internal evidence suggest that three holy sonnets ("Since she whom I lovd," "Show me dear Christ," and "Oh, to vex me") date from the period after Donne's ordination. The "Hymne to God my God, in my sicknesse" and "A Hymne to God the Father" were written either in 1623, when Donne was very ill, or during his final illness in March 1631. Because of the uncertainties of dating, we cannot trace a firm progression or narrative in the body of his religious verse as a whole.

Still, there is a common sensibility in his religious poetry, which wittily analyzes his imperfections, argues with God, and expresses an anxious, passionate desire for faith. For many of us, experience of life in a world filled with suffering, catastrophe, and war makes belief in a personal, benevolent God difficult. For Donne, too, faith did not come easily, though for different reasons. Although he never questions God's existence—that is the one certainty—his poetry expresses not a sense of God's presence, but rather the struggle for faith. The holy sonnet "Oh, to vex me" bitterly laments his habitual "Inconstancy" (l. 2), his disposition to "change in vowes, and in devotione" (l. 4), his alternation between "flattering" (l. 10) God, like a courtier, and quaking "with feare of his rod" (l. 11). The record of spiritual uncertainty, his poetry admits his spiritual imperfections as it voices a yearning to experience God's presence and saving "grace." Donne's anxiety may well have been constitutional, but surely it was intensified by the spiritual journey in which he left the Church of Rome and became a member and, eventually, an ordained priest in the reformed (Protestant) Church of England.

Christians in Donne's time, whether Protestant or Catholic, believed that salvation—the eternal fate of one's soul—was the most important issue in a person's life. In order to be saved one had to belong to the true church of God, the "bride" or "spouse" of God (according to the New Testament [e.g., *King James Bible* Eph. 5:22–28 and Rev. 21:9] and the Christian interpretation of the biblical Song of Songs), outside of which salvation was impossible. But there was more than one church. What was the true church, and where was it located? That was the issue Donne faced and explored in "Satire III," which probably was written in the mid-1590s. Although generically a satire, it is also a religious poem, expressing spiritual and political concerns that were intertwined in Donne's time.

Satirizing the material, secular concerns of his society and the lack of "devotion" to "our Mistresse faire Religion" (ll. 5–6), Donne urges, "Seeke true religion," only to immediately ask "O where?" (l. 43). He surveys the various options, drawing an analogy between choosing a church and choosing a woman to marry, as he portrays men who choose different churches for different reasons. Mirreus, thinking religion "unhous'd" (l. 44) in England, "Seekes her at Rome" (l. 45) (the Church of Rome) because she used to be there. Crants loves only the "plain, simple sullen, young" (l. 51) one at Geneva (Calvin's church). Graius takes the one at home (the Church of England) simply because it has been given to him by his "Guardian" (61). Phrygius "doth abhorre / All" (ll. 62–63) because he assumes they are all corrupt. The indiscriminate Graccus "loves all as one" (l. 65). Donne here goes through the options. Perhaps he is satirizing men who choose a church for the wrong reasons, but there is clearly a sense that none of the available options (Catholic, English, Calvinist) seem a suitable spouse—or at least that Donne has not yet discovered any of them to be the true "Mistresse" (l. 5), who as yet remains ideal—elusive, desired but not seen.

And so, Donne urges a continued search for religion. "Be busie to seeke her" (l. 74). It is necessary "worke"—the process arduous, uncertain, indirect.

> [. . .] doubt wisely; in strange way
> To stand inquiring right, is not to stray;
> To sleepe, or runne wrong, is: on a huge hill,
> Cragged, and steep, Truth stands, and hee that will
> Reach her, about must, and about must goe:
> And what the hills suddenness resists, winne so; [. . .] (ll. 77–82)

Donne's emphasis on the individual quest and relation with God accords with the Reformation emphasis on the individual. So, the poem seems to express a Protestant spirit. And yet, other aspects of the poem suggest a continuing, if covert, sympathy with his earlier Catholicism. He advises "aske thy father which is" "the right" (l. 71) "Religion" (l. 68) (in Donne's case, his father was Catholic); he urges his reader (and himself) not to let his "Soule be tyed / To mans lawes" (ll. 93–94), which in England would mean the anti-Catholic legislation passed under Elizabeth I. The issue of what constitutes the "true church," the "Mistresse" worthy of his devotion remains undecided at the end of the poem. The options available seem limited, and the search only beginning—perhaps never to be concluded in this lifetime. Worst of all, religion on earth seems contaminated by politics—by authorities religious (pope "Gregory," "Martin" Luther) and political ("Philip" [l. 96] of Spain, "Harry" [l. 97] VIII of England—or the unnamed Elizabeth I) that claim spiritual and religious power and exercise "force" (l. 70) in religious matters. As Donne well knew, early modern Europe had numerous victims—Catholic, Protestant, and Jewish—of religious persecution. The only mistress he remains devoted to is "truth"—not an institution, or the queen—and the final lines of the poem urge steadfast courage in the face of possible religious persecution and martyrdom. Though bodies may be destroyed by the "rage" of tyrants (l. 106), at least the "Soules" will not "perish" (l. 109).

"Satire III" poses the problem of finding the true church; it explores the imperfections of institutionalized religion and the dangers faced by those who would "Seeke" (l. 43) true religion, rather than bending to the force of earthly powers who unjustly claim God's "Power" (l. 103). Refusing the "idolatrie" (l. 102) of revering human power, Donne at the end of the poem turns from institutions to God. The individual's personal relation with God, with which "Satire III" concludes, is the center of his devotional poetry, especially the holy sonnets.

With the exception of the three late sonnets mentioned earlier, we do not know whether the holy sonnets were written after he had conformed to the Church of England, or were the expressions of a man still seeking the true church, existing in the space between the Roman and English churches. But what is striking in almost all his devotional poems (in contrast, say, to George Herbert's) is that Donne's speaker characteristically stands outside (or apart from) institutions or material churches, separate from any community, as he anxiously urges God to save him or tries to argue himself into assurance that he is, indeed, saved. In most of the holy sonnets, as the speaker meditates on his condition or imagines the moment of death or the end of the world, he is alone with his private thoughts and guilt. In the longer meditative poem, "Goodfriday, 1613," he is literally outside of the church, riding westward. In "Hymn to Christ, at the Author's last going into Germany," he represents himself as leaving England and "all whom I lov'd" (l. 10) there and traveling solitary toward God, even though we know that, actually, he was on his way to attend the Synod of Dort as one of the representatives of the English church.

Donne's holy sonnets are intimate, private meditations that express a sinfulness both personal and inherited from the fallen Adam. Drawing on the tradition of formal meditation practiced by Christians,[7] they take the form of the fourteen-line Italian Petrarchan sonnet, where the *volte,* or "turn," at line 9 aptly marks a rhetorical turn to God. He converts the sonnet (traditionally a form for love poetry) to sacred purpose, expressing an ardent longing for God that is compromised by his sense of sinfulness. Echoing not just Augustine's preoccupation with original sin but also Calvin's later insistence that the human being is, by nature and unaided by God's grace, totally depraved, Donne details his unworthiness. His "heart" is "iron," hardened with sin, resistant ("Thou has made me," l. 14). His "blacke Soule" is like a treasonous "pilgrim" or a "thiefe" ("Oh my blacke Soule," ll. 1, 2, 5). He feels "my sinnes abound" "above" the "numberless infinities" of people who have died before him ("At the round earths imagin'd corners," ll. 10, 3).

And yet, as he addresses God, he adopts a variety of postures that are not all subservient. In "As due by many titles," he "resignes" (l. 1) himself to God, first seemingly in humility, then in asserting that he belongs to God (as the "temple of thy Spirit," l. 8) and thus should be actively claimed by God, and finally in a plea to God to "chuse" him (l. 13). When he contemplates the apocalypse, he asks God to put it off so Donne will have time to be taught "how to repent" ("At the round earths imagin'd corners," l. 13). In "If poisonous minerals," he "dispute[s]" (l. 9) with God but then begs God to "drowne" the "memorie" of his "sinne" (l. 12). "This is my playes last scene" sets up a neat formula: at death, his body will "dwell" in earth (l. 10), his "sinnes" will "fall" to "hell" (ll. 11–12), and his "soule" will ascend to heaven (l. 9), all returning to their place of origin. Donne's final couplet concludes his logic, telling God: "Impute me righteous, thus purg'd of evil / For thus I leave the world, the flesh, and devill" (ll. 13–14).

Sometimes there is a question of tone: does he plead with or command God? Adapting erotic analogies, which had been used to describe God's relation with the believer ever since the Song of Songs was interpreted by Rabbi Akiva and by Christian exegetes as describing God's relation with his people or church, Donne flirts with blasphemy. He asks God to "ravish" him in order to make him "chast" ("Batter my heart, three person'd God," l. 14). Remaining at the center of his poems, irrepressible ego still intact, Donne is as clever, as witty in his address to God as he had been in his love poetry:

> [. . .] as in my idolatrie
> I said to all my profane mistresses,
> Beauty, of pitty, foulness onely is
> A signe of rigour: so I say to thee,
> To wicked spirits are horrid shapes assign'd,
> This beauteous forme assures [or "assumes"] a piteous minde. ("What if this
> present were the worlds last night" ll. 9–14)

But although Donne argues with God, his argument seems fruitless, for he seems to have no free will, no ability to do good or to help in his own salvation. His "Reason" is "captiv'd, and proves weake or untrue" ("Batter my heart" ll. 7–8). The speaker of Donne's poems is passive, helpless, "weigh[ed]" down by sin, which would drag him "to hell"; only God "like Adamant [can] draw mine iron heart" ("Thou has made me" ll. 8, 14). The "devil" "usurpe[s]" in him; so Donne asks God, "Why doth he steale, nay ravish that's thy right?" ("As due by many titles" ll. 9–10), challenging God to stand up for him. He represents himself as a pawn in the cosmic battle between God and Satan, which is, nevertheless, centered on him. Donne can, at best, "resigne" himself to God ("As due" l. 1), or wittily ask God to "forget" (his "sinnes") rather than "remember him" ("If poisonous minerals" ll. 13–14). But it is up to God to do the work:

I like an usurpt towne, to another due,
Labour to'admit you, but Oh, to no end,
[. . .]
Yet dearly'I love you, and would be lov'd faine,
But am betroth'd unto your enemie,
Divorce mee,'untie, or breake that knot againe,
Take mee to you, imprison mee, for I
Except you'enthrall mee, never shall be free,
Nor ever chast, except you ravish mee. ("Batter my heart" ll. 5–6, 9–14)

The witty, paradoxical, transgendered language of the poem places Donne in the conventionally "feminine" position of the town (to be taken) or the betrothed (expected to be chaste), as he expresses the insufficiency of his efforts, his anxious desire for God fully to possess him, to make it impossible for Donne to relapse into unfaithfulness. As things stand, he is betrothed (against his will?) to Satan, and his own "labour[s]" are to "no end." It is as if Donne's speaker is denying responsibility for his situation, which itself might be a sign of his sinfulness.

The holy sonnets thus represent a world in which human beings are, of themselves, thoroughly sinful, powerless to effect their salvation. Only by God's "leave" can he "looke" toward God and "rise againe" ("Thou hast made me" l. 10). God's grace is available to those who "repent" for their sins, "but who shall give thee that grace to beginne?," Donne asks, neatly expressing the catch-22 dilemma in which one cannot repent and get grace unless one already has it ("Oh my blacke Soule" ll. 9–10). Even repentance is not within the power of the individual. That sense of helplessness is part of the deep anxiety that runs through these poems about whether Donne will receive the grace that will save him, whether he is one of what Calvin called the "elect."[8]

Surely there were Catholics who were anxious about salvation, but the Reformation, with its "theology of grace," posed new problems even as it offered assurance that one would be saved by God, not by human means—including church institutions, traditions, or authorities. Catholicism had offered a kind of spiritual stability, as the sacraments (baptism, marriage, communion) were a "means" of grace. Good works too could help ensure your salvation. But reformation theology insisted that individuals were saved by faith and God's grace alone. Though it was reassuring that God would do the work, the dark side of the emphasis on God's grace was that you could do nothing to save yourself, that in a sense you were helpless, as all depended on God.

Calvinism made the situation even more complicated and anxious, for Calvin promoted the doctrine of "predestination"—God had predestined a limited number of people (the "elect") to be saved; the rest were the "reprobate" and would be damned. In the strict formulation of "double" predestination (which more moderate Calvinists did not necessarily subscribe to), God had predestined, even before they were born— perhaps even before Creation—both the number of people to be saved and the far greater number to be damned. Your good deeds could not save you. Only faith—and God's "free" (but unearnable) grace. But how could you get it if you didn't already have it?

This reformed, specifically Calvinist idea of predestination, salvation, and grace could comfort those who were convinced they were part of the elect, but it also could be deeply disturbing. Some theologians modified Calvinism to emphasize assurance and downplay predestination to damnation; the Dutch theologian Arminius, challenging Calvinist orthodoxy, insisted that human beings have "free will," that God's grace is "universal," potentially offered to all Christians, and that Christ died for "all," not some. The Synod of Dort was called for Protestants to consider the challenge Arminius posed to Calvin, and the Synod ended up affirming Calvinist theology. Still, Arminianism became a powerful counter to Calvinism in the English church during the 1620s, and there is evidence of Donne's attraction to its more inclusive theology in his later sermons, with their emphasis on God's "universal" grace and the importance of human actions. But Calvinism was the dominant theology of the Church of England until the death of King James I in 1625.[9] It was thus the theology of the church when Donne was considering conversion and when he joined it.

Donne's holy sonnets, with their sense of helplessness and total depravity, their anxiety about how to get God's grace and how to achieve a saving faith, seem to emerge from and represent a Calvinist world, although that does not necessarily mean Donne was a Calvinist.[10] Rather, we might see these poems as exploring what it might feel like for someone to live in a reformed, Calvinist world, where God might seem particularly distant if one did not feel God's presence within and could no longer access the divine through the church's institution and sacraments.

Emphasis on salvation only through faith and God's (unmeritable, unearnable) grace could produce anxiety, even what we would call depression, and what Robert Burton called "melancholy" in his *Anatomy of Melancholy.* Burton's comments in his discussion of "Religious Melancholy" about the "despair" of those who agonized about their salvation resonate with the sentiments expressed so powerfully in Donne's religious verse. "Continual meditation of Gods judgments troubles man," Burton remarked. "Papists" "terrify men's souls," but so do "our indiscreet pastors": "whilst in their ordinary sermons they speak so much of election, predestination, reprobation," "they still aggravate sin, thunder out God's judgments without respect, intempestively rail at and pronounce them damned"[11] (Part 3, sec. 4, memb.2, subs.3; 395, 397, 399–400).

Sometimes a sense of sinfulness and the uncertainty of salvation produce a state in the speaker that verges on despair. Despair might seem the opposite of pride, but actually it is a kind of pride for a person to believe that he is beyond God's power to rescue.

Knowing that he cannot save himself, convinced that he is the worst of all sinners, Donne worries that God might not take the necessary action.

> Except thou rise and for thine owne worke fight,
> Oh I shall soone despaire, when I doe see
> That thou lov'st mankind well, yet wilt not chuse me.
> And Satan hates mee, yet is loth to lose me. ("As due by many titles" ll. 11–14)

Even in the late "A Hymne to God the Father," Donne's confesses, "I have a sinne of feare, that when I'have spunne / My last thred, I shall perish on the shore" (ll. 13–14). Desperately needing assurance that he is chosen, that God loves him and will save him, Donne seeks external, material, sensible evidence of God's love for him. As in Donne's love poetry, the spirit is not enough. Love must "take a body," as he says in "Aire in Angels" (l. 10). Donne's poems persistently express an urgent desire for a sensible experience of connection with God—something he can feel in a bodily way. We see this in Donne's fondness for material, amorous images of his relation to God—his desire to be "divorced" from the devil, or the world, or "all whom I lovd and who lovd mee," so he can be married to God ("Hymne to Christ, at the Authors last going into Germany" l. 10)—and in his use of charged erotic language to image his relation with God. The pleas for marriage and ravishment—the longing for a consummated relation—suggest a painful sense of distance from God that is vividly expressed in "Goodfriday, 1613. Riding Westward," where the poem begins with Donne traveling westward into the future, away from Christ, whom he pictures in the east and the past, crucified—though by the end of the poem Donne rationalizes that he is really going the right way, that east and west will eventually meet. As he meditates on his wrongful path and on the crucifixion, he reinterprets his "turn[ing]" his "backe" (l. 37) on Christ, not as an insulting but a humble posture:

> I turne my backe to thee, but to receive
> Corrections, till thy mercies bid thee leave.
> O thinke mee worth thine anger, punish mee,
> Burne off my rusts, and my deformity,
> Restore thine Image, so much, by thy grace,
> That thou may'st know mee, and I'll turne my face. (ll. 37–42)

This is the expression of a person who feels intensely corrupt and unworthy and longs to sense the presence of God, even if only through painful affliction. It seems Donne can only be sure of God's presence if it is felt or experienced in the body. Affliction is the instrument of God; "anger" would at least show that God cares, that there is a personal connection. As he says in the "Hymne to God my God, in my sicknesse"—the poem that seems most confident of his salvation—"that he may raise the Lord throws down" (l. 30).

Donne's personal explorations of his spiritual life vividly represent post-Reformation dilemmas, not only in expressing the anxieties produced by Calvinism, but also in longing for a corporeal, material experience of an embodied God that had been implicit in theology and worship of the Roman Catholic church, but had been discredited by the Reformation, with its iconoclastic reformation of images, its redefinition of the sacraments as "signs" not agents of God's grace, and its abolition of saints and the intercessory power of priests.

Traces of these controversial, officially outlawed things appear in Donne's religious poems. "The Crosse" depicts images of the cross in the body, in flying birds, in maps, and other aspects of the material world (if not in the church); and it begins by criticizing whoever "from the picture would avert his eye" (l. 7), insisting: "From mee, no Pulpit, nor misgrounded law, / Nor scandal taken, shall this Crosse withdraw" (ll. 9–10). "Goodfriday, 1613" meditates on the crucified body of Christ, which could not be represented in Protestant churches. "The picture of Christ crucified" again appears in the holy sonnet, "What if this present were the worlds last night." There it dwells "in my heart" (if not a church), and he contemplates it, trying to discover assurance of whether he is saved or not, though the import of that picture in which "blood" fills Christ's "frowns" remains unclear at the end (does it reassure him of salvation? or does it suggest he'll be condemned to hell?).

In the holy sonnet written after his wife Ann More's death in August 1617 ("Since she whome I lovd"), Donne claims that while she was alive, she performed a kind of saintly or Catholic sacramental role for him. She was like a "streame" of God's grace that did "shew the head" (l. 6) or source and thus led him to God. Through her he has "found" God, who has "fed" his "thirst"; still a "holy thirsty dropsy melts mee yet" (ll. 7–8), leaving him unsatisfied, particularly as the beloved woman who embodied the divine is no longer on earth. Donne here expresses an unquenched desire (not just for God but for his dead wife), but also a worry that it is not appropriate—that God "feare[s] least I allow / My Love to Saints and Angels" (ll. 11–12)—that even the most worthy objects of love compete with God and lure us away, that only God should be loved.

Like the love poem "The Exstasie," Donne's religious verse reflects his sense that the spirit can only work or communicate through the body, and that this link has somehow become problematic. Donne complained in the "First Anniversary" on the death of Elizabeth Drury that the "commerce twixt heaven and earth" has been "Embarr'd, and all this traffique quite forgot" (ll. 399–400). For all the Calvinist preoccupations, we might see a residual "Catholic" mentality in the devotional poems. Desiring sensible evidence of God's interest in him, Donne in his religious poems represents a world where God seems remarkably distant, in contrast to George Herbert's lyrics, where God is given a voice and answers Herbert. The world of Donne's poems is the legacy of the Reformation, but it is not a world in which Donne's speaker seems comfortable. There is something missing—a strong sense of the actual presence of God.[12]

Even if Donne's religious poetry was written while he was "in" the Church of England, the speaker in them remains outside the confines of the church, in the space between existing churches, hoping for something more perfect. One of the late holy sonnets returns to the problem raised by "Satire III," as it asks,

Show me deare Christ, thy spouse, so bright and cleare,
What, is it she, which on the other shore
Goes richly painted? Or which rob'd and tore
Laments and mournes in Germany and here?
Sleepes she a thousand, then peepes up one yeare?
Is she selfe truth and errs? Now new, now'outwore?
Doth she,'and did she, and shall she evermore
On one, on seaven, or on no hill appeare? (ll. 1–8)

He questions whether any of the existing churches is really the bride of Christ referred to in Revelation. Rome, Geneva, England—even perhaps the Temple Mount or Dome of the Rock in the holy land—each religious site is imperfect. Donne rather suggestively asks Christ to "Betray" "thy spouse to our sights" (l. 11), concluding that she is "most trew, and pleasing to thee, then / When she'is embrac'd and open to most men" (ll. 3–14). We see here the desire for a unified Christendom that many of those disturbed by the divisiveness of the Reformation shared. We may also hear an echo of the Hebrew prophets' vision of a utopian time when all peoples/nations will be united in the worship of God. Despite his sense of separateness and anxiety, Donne deeply desires community, inclusiveness, and unity in a world where each church assumes salvation belongs only to them, where churches excommunicate each other and people kill for religion. Such churches cannot be the "mild Dove" (l. 12), the true spouse of God who is, paradoxically, most "true" (or chaste) when promiscuous or "open to most men"—though the qualifier "most" suggests a limit.

In his witty, imaginative, sometimes anguished religious verse, Donne has a distinctive place among the best English devotional poets, which include George Herbert in the next generation and Gerard Manley Hopkins more than two centuries later. Yet Donne differs from these, in part because his devotional poems draw on the wit and passion of his love poetry, and because Donne's religious poetry expresses spiritual crisis— his own, as well as the Reformation's. We hear so strongly in his devotional verse, in his addresses to God, in his efforts to woo a remote beloved, his desire for faith, and for assurance—not that there is a God, but that God is benevolent, gracious, a God of compassion and mercy rather than only judgment. We hear Donne's sense of isolation, but also his desire for an inclusive church, a time when people will not be persecuted or killed in the name of religion. Above all, we see in Donne's poetry faith and belief as a work in progress, a process, not something possessed once and for all. His eloquent expression of these truths and his desire for a personal relation with God reflect Reformation issues, but they also constitute perhaps the greatest, most powerful wrestling with faith in the canon of English lyric poetry. Such qualities make his poetry speak powerfully to people even now, no matter what their confessional identities or differences might be.

## NOTES

1. See Christopher Haigh, *English Reformations: Religion, Politics, and Society Under the Tudors* (Oxford: Clarendon P, 1993); and Anthony Milton, *Catholic and Reformed: The Roman and Protestant Churches in English Protestant Thought 1600–1640* (Cambridge: Cambridge UP, 1995).
2. Luther, *The Babylonian Captivity of the Church,* trans. A. T. W. Steinhaeuser, *Works,* (Philadelphia: A. J. Holman, 1916) vol. 2.
3. John Calvin, *Institutes of the Christian Religion,* trans. John Allen, 2 vols. (Philadelphia: Presbyterian Board of Publication, n. d.) 2: 552–53.
4. On Donne's life, see R. C. Bald, *John Donne: A Life* (New York: Oxford UP, 1970); and Dennis Flynn, *John Donne and the Ancient Catholic Nobility* (Bloomington: Indiana UP, 1995).
5. I have used Herbert J. C. Grierson's edition of *The Poems of John Donne* (London: Oxford UP, 1912) vol. 1.

6. Dennis Flynn, "'Awry and Squint': The Dating of Donne's Holy Sonnets, *John Donne Journal* 7 (1988): 35–46; 43.

7. Louis L. Martz, *The Poetry of Meditation* (New Haven: Yale UP, 1954), discusses the tradition of formal meditation.

8. See John Stachniewski, "John Donne: The Despair of the 'Holy Sonnets,'" *ELH* 48 (1981): 677–705.

9. Nicholas Tyacke, *Anti-Calvinists: The Rise of English Arminianism c. 1590–1640* (Oxford: Clarendon P, 1987); Peter Lake, "Calvinism and the English Church 1570–1635," *Past and Present* 114 (1987): 32–76; and Achsah Guibbory, "Donne's Religion: Montagu, Arminianism, and Donne's Sermons, 1624–1630," *English Literary Renaissance* 31 (2001): 412–39, suggest Donne's link with Arminianism. For an alternative argument aligning Donne with moderate Calvinism, see Jeanne Shami, *John Donne and Conformity in Crisis in the Late Jacobean Pulpit* (Cambridge: D.S. Brewer, 2003).

10. Taking issue with Stachniewski's linking of despair with Calvinism, Strier argues that the anxieties in the poem are not those of "the convinced Calvinist" but the expression of a person who "would like to be a convinced Calvinist but who is both unable to be so and unable to admit that he is unable to be so" (361). Young, rejecting theological labeling, sees Donne "trying out different versions of grace in order to arrive at a theologically moderate position" (*Doctrine* 8).

11. Robert Burton, *Anatomy of Melancholy,* ed. Holbrook Jackson (New York: Vintage, 1977), Part 3, sec. 4, memb.2, subs.3; 395, 397, 399–400.

12. R. V. Young discusses Donne's preoccupation "with the absent presence of he deity" in *Doctrine and Devotion in Seventeenth-Century Poetry: Studies in Donne, Herbert, Crashaw, and Vaughan* (Cambridge: D.S. Brewer, 2000) 81–106; 95.

## READING LIST

Friedman, Donald M. "Memory and the Art of Salvation in Donne's Good Friday Poem." *English Literary Renaissance* 3 (1973): 418–42.

Stachniewski, John. "John Donne: The Despair of the 'Holy Sonnets.'" *ELH* 48 (1981): 677–705.

Strier, Richard. "John Donne Awry and Squint: 'The Holy Sonnets,' 1608–1610." *Modern Philology* 86 (1989): 357–84.

Summers, Claude. "The Bride of the Apocalypse and the Quest for True Religion: Donne, Herbert, and Spenser." *"Bright Shootes of Everlastingnesse": The Seventeenth-Century Religious Lyric.* Ed. Claude Summers and Ted-Larry Pebworth. Columbia: U of Missouri P, 1987. 72–95.

Young, R. V. *Doctrine and Devotion in Seventeenth-Century Poetry: Studies in Donne, Herbert, Crashaw, and Vaughan.* Cambridge: D. S. Brewer. 2000.

———. "Donne's Holy Sonnets and the Theology of Grace." *"Bright Shootes of Everlastingnesse".* 20–39.

# 22

# Lanyer and the Poetry of Land and Devotion

## Helen Wilcox

The year 1611 was an extraordinary one for English literary history. During it, the Authorized (King James) Version of the Bible, a work that had an incalculable influence on English language and literature, was first published after eight years of preparatory work. Among the new plays on the public stage that year were Ben Jonson's *The Alchemist*, Beaumont and Fletcher's *A King and No King*, and *A Chaste Maid in Cheapside* by Thomas Middleton. At the royal Court, the year began with Jonson's masque *Oberon*, with scenery by Inigo Jones and music by Alfonso Ferrabosco, and later in the year, Shakespeare's *The Tempest* was performed to the privileged courtly audience at Whitehall. The lists of new books published in 1611 feature, among others, Chapman's magnificent verse translation of Homer's *Iliad* and the folio edition of Spenser's works. The year also saw the publication of John Donne's *An Anatomy of the World*, a poem commemorating the young Elizabeth Drury in a lament for the decay of the world and the unsettling effects of the "new philosophy."[1] Those who wanted to read about an expanding rather than a declining world could relish Thomas Coryate's *Crudities*, also published in 1611, which boasts travel stories from "France, Savoy, Italy, Rhetia commonly called the Grisons country, Helvetia alias Switzerland, some parts of High Germany and the Netherlands," all "dispersed to the nourishment of the travelling members of this Kingdome."[2] Amidst these colorful texts stands one other equally remarkable work of 1611: Aemilia Lanyer's *Salve Deus Rex Judaeorum*, the first book of poems in the history of English literature to have been written solely by a woman and published with her own name on its title page.

### "Mistris *AEmilia Lanyer*"

The manner in which this pioneering author was named in print immediately reveals several important aspects of her origins and status. She is described on the title page of her book as "Mistris *AEmilia Lanyer*, Wife to Captaine *Alfonso Lanyer* Servant to the Kings Majestie."[3] First, the emphasis on the fact that she is a "Wife" suggests that marriage was a defining factor in her social identity, as was the case with almost all early modern women. Second, the foreignness of her name identifies her as part of an immigrant community in London. Though her mother, Margaret Johnson, was English, her father, Baptista Bassano, was a musician from a Venetian family who worked at the Court of Queen Elizabeth. Aemilia herself, born in 1569, continued the family tradition by marrying another royal musician of foreign origin, the Huguenot Alfonso Lanyer, in 1592. Third, and perhaps most important, this printed construction of Lanyer for the benefit of her readers suggests an intense consciousness of social class and, in particular, class difference. Though not an aristocrat—she is simply "Mistris," a gentlewoman—Lanyer lays claim to royal connections through her husband, who as a musician and officer is a "Servant of the Kings Majestie." As we shall see, the necessity for an early modern writer of her class and gender to be supported by royalty (and other prominent Court figures) forms an integral part of Lanyer's writing.

In addition to the information about Aemilia Lanyer gleaned from her self-presentation on the title page of her book, there are two major sources from which we can establish her biography: the notebooks of the astrologer Simon Forman and a variety of legal documents.[4] From Forman's sometimes questionable and often self-serving jottings, we discover that Lanyer was brought up in Kent, probably being educated in the household of the Countess Dowager of Kent, to whom she also refers in a dedicatory poem as "the noble guide of my ungovern'd dayes" (18). This upbringing would certainly account for Lanyer's knowledge of classical and literary traditions, which was unusually extensive for a nonaristocratic and, as she described herself, "unlearned" woman (9). Forman also notes that the young Lanyer became the mistress of the much older Lord Chamberlain, Henry Cary, Lord Hunsdon, until she was hastily married to Lanyer when found to be pregnant. We gather from Forman's casebooks that, after the safe delivery of her son Henry in 1593, Lanyer suffered from difficult pregnancies and had several miscarriages, and consulted Forman for medical help. Unfortunately only one subsequent pregnancy led to a successful birth, but this child—her daughter Odillya, born in 1598—died aged only nine months. Lanyer also visited Forman for advice on her husband's future career, in the futile hope that he might be knighted in the king's service; meanwhile she apparently resisted Forman's own attempts to seduce her during their consultations. From the scattered legal evidence we learn that Lanyer had intermittent financial troubles, both before and after her husband's death in 1613, and that as a widow she ran a school in St. Giles in the Field from 1617 to 1619 for "the children of divers persons of worth and understandinge."[5] At the time of her death in 1645, Lanyer was a seventy-six-year-old grandmother of two, with no other written works to her name than the small book of poems published more than three decades earlier.

## *Salve Deus Rex Judaeorum*

What is the significance of the work of this early modern woman, living on the fringes of the Court and the English aristocracy, cultured in music and languages, ambitiously making her poetry public in her own lifetime but subsequently disappearing into obscurity?[6] This chapter attempts to answer that question by looking closely at Lanyer's poetry and placing it in appropriate historical and cultural contexts. Her work is best understood in relation to the discourses of her contemporary literary culture,[7] even if (or perhaps because) she wrote in active opposition to some of the basic assumptions of her time. *Salve Deus Rex Judaeorum* is a three-part work, and each section of this "triptych"[8] may be linked to the debates and concerns represented by other works published in 1611. The first part of the volume has been termed a "multiple-dedication scattershot at patronage":[9] nine substantial prefatory poems and two prose epistles, all addressed to individuals or groups of readers and exploring the language of praise with considerable skill. The fact that ten of these eleven dedicatory texts are addressed to women is, of course, radically distinctive,[10] but Lanyer was nevertheless like most other writers of her generation in needing the support of those who were richer or better placed than she was. Her participation in the rhetoric of patronage sets her in the very same early modern literary mold as Donne's *Anatomy* and Jonson's *Oberon,* works published or performed in 1611 under the auspices of important patrons.[11]

The second part of Lanyer's book, its centerpiece and title poem, is a narrative of the Passion of Christ: its title, "Salve Deus Rex Judaeorum" ["Hail God, King of the Jews"] refers to the inscription on the cross on which Jesus was crucified (Matt. 27:37). This poetic meditation is in fact a rewriting of the Gospel account of the crucifixion and resurrection of Christ. Although it is remarkably daring in its reconfiguration of the roles of men and women in the Passion, it is nevertheless in keeping with the humanist project of translating and reinterpreting classical and scriptural texts, of which Chapman's Homer and King James's Authorized Version, both 1611 publications, were also leading examples. Indeed, the entire *Salve Deus,* with its dedication to the queen and its insistence upon a woman's right to rewrite the scriptures "In other Phrases" (64), may be seen—as Achsah Guibbory has wisely suggested—in terms of "an oppositional alternative to the monumental biblical project of James."[12] Lanyer's volume closes with "The Description of Cooke-ham," an elegiac landscape poem that, in its exploration of natural beauty and the loss of Eden, takes up issues explored and challenged in Shakespeare's *The Tempest* as well as given practical shape in the newly settled English colonies in Virginia. As a work seeking patronage for its poetic voyage into Christian devotion and in search of an ideal land, *Salve Deus* may indeed be seen as expressive of its era.

The topic of womanhood, too, was in the air in 1611. Middleton's play from that year, for example, appeared to mock the very thought that there might be such a thing as a "chaste maid" in Cheapside while, at the other extreme, Donne idealized Elizabeth Drury in his *Anatomy of the World,* depicting not so much an individual as the idea of woman, the "first originall / Of all faire copies."[13] Lanyer's *Salve Deus* contributed to this ongoing intertextual and social debate: it is preoccupied with women in all its three sections. The dedicatory poems address women as specific individuals and patrons; "Salve Deus" is concerned with women as biblical figures and as models of devotion and virtue; "Cooke-ham" focuses on a community of women as true guardians of the land. It is also clear that Lanyer had a female readership in mind. Her first dedicatee is "the Queenes most Excellent Majestie" (3)—James's wife, Anne of Denmark—who presided over a female Court and whose prominence in the volume suggests the extent to which Lanyer wished to associate herself with that alternative world. Anne is constructed by Lanyer as the first of her muses, contemporary equivalents of the "nine Worthies" to whom "all faire mindes resort" (13). These nine dedicatees include prominent royal ladies—Anne's daughter, Princess Elizabeth, and the king's ill-fated cousin, Lady Arbella Stuart—as well as Lanyer's most eminent female predecessor as a sacred poet, Mary Sidney, the countess of Pembroke, whose translation of the Psalms makes "sweet harmony" which "might in eares of Angels ring" (27). There are also, not surprisingly, poems addressed to the women who seem to have given Lanyer access to education and aristocratic company, including the Countess Dowager of Kent and the volume's chief dedicatee, the Countess Dowager of Cumberland, along with her daughter, Lady Anne Clifford. As if to be on the safe side, Lanyer does not leave out any women: there is a poem "To all vertuous Ladies in generall" (12) and a final prefatory epistle "To the Vertuous Reader." This last group is predominantly envisaged as "all virtuous Ladies and Gentlewomen of this kingdome," though it is ultimately expanded in terms of gender and geography to encompass "all good Christians and honourable minded men" (48, 50). In the range of her anticipated readers, as well as in the radical scope of her poetic project, Lanyer was nothing if not ambitious.

## Poetry of Devotion

As she presented herself and her "blessed Booke" (41) to her readers, Lanyer was intensely conscious that this amounted to a phenomenon "seldome seene": "A Womans writing of divinest things" (3). She offered her work in biblical terms as "first fruits" (Exod. 23:16) but her poems were that rare harvest, the first fruits of "a womans wit" (11), given expression in defiance of the equally biblical injunction for a woman to "be in silence" (1 Tim. 2:12). Her wit is in evidence when she deals with precisely this paradox of being a woman and a poet of "divinest things." Addressing her own "lowely Muse" (62), she discovers that her weakness is in fact a strength:

> But yet the Weaker thou doest seeme to be
> In Sexe, or Sence, the more his Glory shines,
> That doth infuse such powerfull Grace in thee,
> To shew thy Love in these few humble Lines; (63)

All devotional poets require inspiration by divine grace, but when the poet is a woman, she argues, the transforming power of God is shown to be greater; thus, by implication, the aim of glorifying God is more amply fulfilled. Her achievement is God's: "his powre hath given me powre to write" (36). This statement, in her dedicatory poem to the countess of Suffolk, functions as both a token of modesty and a claim to divine authority at this preliminary stage of her work. At the other end of the volume, she rounds off her work with a similar sense of high vocation. In a short paragraph "To the doubtfull Reader" on the last page of her book, she explains that the title was given to her in a dream, confirming "that I was appointed to performe this Worke" (139). Lanyer knew that she was taking on a huge challenge in *Salve Deus*—her "Muse" was in danger of flying above its "appointed straine" (63)—and she sought all possible assistance, both human and divine.

The perspective on redemption taken by "Salve Deus" is made clear on the title page of Lanyer's "small volume" (48): she gives primary attention to "The Passion of Christ" but her focus is sharpened by the inclusion of subsections entitled "Eves Apologie in defence of Women," "The Teares of the Daughters of Jerusalem," and "The Salutation and Sorrow of the Virgine Marie" (1). What the title page does not announce, however, is that this female supporting cast in the drama of Good Friday is strengthened by a host of other biblical women, from Deborah and Judith to Pilate's wife, in a thoroughly feminized re-reading of the Bible. In addition, this substantial "meditation" (57) on the Passion is framed by extended passages of praise addressed, as the marginal notes make clear, to Lanyer's chief patron, Margaret Countess of Cumberland. Indeed, while the countess only receives a prose epistle in the dedicatory section of the volume, the long poem "Salve Deus" is itself Lanyer's "patronage poem to that beloved lady whom she served at Cookham Dean."[14] "The Description of Cooke-ham" tells us that is was the countess who encouraged Lanyer to write her book: "this worke of Grace" sprang from the "desires" of this "great Lady" (130). Lanyer's resulting poetic account of the Passion is set within a framework of address to the countess—"To thee great Countesse now I will applie / My Pen" (51)—and the events of Good Friday are reenacted in the poem as though they are taking place inside the countess's heart, which becomes a "holy shrine" (108). This sense of internal drama is in keeping with the tradition of private meditation on biblical history that was common in devotional and literary practice in the early modern period, but the heart or memory in which such scenes were composed was generally the poet's own.[15] In the case of Lanyer's "Salve Deus," it is the countess of Cumberland's heart that is said to contain Christ's "perfect picture" (108) drawn by the poet's pen. The countess's role in the poem is therefore almost comparable to the function of the Virgin Mary: she conveys the incarnate Christ to the world.[16]

## "Eves Apologie"

At the very center of "Salve Deus"—approached step by step via the poet, the countess, and Christ—is the passage labeled "Eves Apologie," an embedded piece of polemical exegesis set within the narrative of Christ's trial. Pontius Pilate's wife, who features in just one verse of the Bible (Matt. 27:19), bursts on the scene in Lanyer's poem and urges her husband not to condemn "him that must thy Saviour be" (84). The subsequent nine stanzas amount to an audacious reinterpretation of the biblical account of the Fall and have justly become the most famous passage of "Salve Deus." Their strategy is twofold. First, it is suggested that Adam should bear more of the blame for the original human disobedience to God:

> But surely *Adam* can not be excusde,
> Her fault though great, yet hee was most too blame;
> What Weaknesse offerd, Strength might have refusde,
> Being Lord of all, the greater was his shame:
> Although the Serpents craft had her abusde,
> Gods holy word ought all his actions frame,
>> For he was Lord and King of all the earth,
>> Before poor *Eve* had either life or breath. (85)

Accepting the status of women as coming second both in the sequence of creation and in the hierarchy of strength and weakness, Lanyer turns apparent disadvantage to good use as she suggests that the prior and stronger partner should logically bear the larger part of the blame for the Fall. The almost ironic "poor *Eve*" is a fine example of her control of tone here, even in the heat of this historic debate. Similarly, she wittily suggests that the very things that men now claim as their own were actually taken from Eve, who, if she erred, did so "for knowledge sake": men "boast of Knowledge," though Adam took it "From *Eves* faire hand, as from a learned Booke" (86).[17]

Lanyer's first strategy thus involves a daring rereading of the book of Genesis against the grain of centuries of exegesis. Her second depends upon an equally adventurous comparative reading of the Fall and the Passion, by which the accepted typological relationship between the Old and New Testaments is substantially altered. Instead of reading Mary as the second Eve who makes up for the sins of the first, and Christ as the second Adam who cancels out the sins of the first, Lanyer argues that the sin of the men who condemned Christ to death should be seen as greater than the sin of the woman who ate the forbidden fruit. As is typical of Lanyer's skilled use of the stanza form in "Salve Deus," she sums up the contrast in one of her devastating final rhyming couplets: "Her Weaknesse did the Serpents words obay; / But you in malice Gods deare Son betray" (86). The consequences of this reverse interpretation, if accepted, would be a liberation for women:

> Then let us have our Libertie againe,
> And challendge to your selves no Sov'raigntie;
> You came not in the world without our paine,
> Make that a barre against your crueltie;
> Your fault beeing greater, why should you disdaine
> Our being your equals, free from tyranny?
>     If one weake woman simply did offend,
>     This sinne of yours, hath no excuse, nor end. (87)

As this stanza makes clear, "Eves Apologie" moves from a rereading of two key events in the Bible to a call for religious and social equality for women. It is Lanyer's most outspoken and visionary moment.

It would be wrong, however, to imply that Lanyer's work is radical only in gender terms. It is true that her portrayal of Christ is as a deeply feminized saviour—patient (77), mild (81) and, above all, silent[18]—but he is also a monarch whose humble social circumstances are emphasized. Recalling the title of Beaumont and Fletcher's 1611 play, we might call Lanyer's Christ "a king and no king." He came to earth "Possessing worlds, yet seeming extreame poore," and he took the form of a "seeming Trades-mans sonne, of none attended, / Save of a few in povertie and need" (124). This concern with Christ's lowliness is part of the egalitarian ideal present throughout Lanyer's volume, by which no gender or class should exercise "tyranny" (87) over any other. As she asks in her dedicatory poem to Lady Anne Clifford,

> What difference was there when the world began?
> Was it not Virtue that distinguisht all?
> All but sprang from one woman and one man,
> Then how doth Gentry come to rise and fall? (42)

This rational questioning of the social system takes a more emotive form in "The Description of Cooke-ham" since it is clear that Lanyer herself has suffered as a result of "diffrence [. . .] in degree" (134). She laments the fact of being cast down "into so lowe a frame" that she cannot enjoy the daily company of "great friends" (134), "great" here implying high-born as well as good. In Lanyer's vision of the creation, expressed in her dedicatory poem to Anne Clifford, "God makes both even, the Cottage with the Throne" (42).

## Poetry of Land

Despite the optimism of Lanyer's multiple dedications to "great" women, her cottage rarely came close to the throne. There is an undertone of loss and exclusion throughout *Salve Deus* that reaches a climax in the final section of the book, "The Description of Cooke-ham." The poem depicts the crown estate of Cookham in Berkshire, the place of the countess of Cumberland's temporary retreat "from the Court to the Countrie" (58) where Lanyer appears to have spent some time in the company of the countess and her daughter Anne.[19] Since "Cooke-ham" was published five years earlier than Ben Jonson's "To Penshurst," and was probably also written before it, Lanyer's work is now generally credited as the first "country house poem" in English literature.[20] In the opening sequence of "Cooke-ham," the poem constructs what Jacqueline Pearson has called a "matriarchal utopia,"[21] a regained Eden full of pious learning and natural beauty:

> The House receiv'd all ornaments to grace it,
> And would indure no foulenesse to deface it.
> The Walkes put on their summer Liveries,
> And all things else did hold like similies. (131)

However, it is no accident that the poem's very first word is "Farewell"; the pastoral ideal of the *locus amoenus* (pleasant place) is viewed throughout from an elegiac perspective, suggesting that this Eden is about to witness another Fall. The women with whom Lanyer associates Cookham are not its owners but only short-term occupants of the estate. The place itself is already in "griefe [. . .] / At their departure" (135).

Unlike Jonson, whose poem "To Penshurst" celebrates the fact that the family of Sir Robert Sidney "dwells" in the ancient house,[22] the poet of "Cooke-ham" confronts absence and can only wistfully enjoy the "sweet Memorie" (135) of the women's presence. In contrast to the country house poems that followed it—not only Jonson's but also, among others, Carew's "To Saxeham" and Marvell's "Upon Appleton House"—the beauty of "Cooke-ham" is somber and melancholy. Its focus is on an almost biblical landscape:

> In these sweet woods how often did you walke,
> With Christ and his Apostles there to talke;
> Placing his holy Writ in some faire tree,
> To meditate what you therein did see. (133)

By the end of the poem, every "stately tree" is "bare and desolate" in the absence of the Clifford women, and "all greene things" have made "the earth their grave" (138). Where Lanyer emphasises in "Cooke-ham" the remembered virtues and sacred conversation of the temporary "Mistris of that Place," Jonson praises the generous hospitality and epicurean lifestyle of the Sidneys at Penshurst. Where Lanyer delights in the "hills, vales, and woods" of Cookham (133), her successors tend to pay more attention to the house at the center of the estate. As Kari Boyd McBride has noted,[23] the houses that interest Lanyer are those metaphorical places such as Anne Clifford's "faire breast" where the poet asserts that "true virtue then was hous'd" (134). The women honored by the country house poems of Jonson and his male colleagues are generally perceived as the virtuous bearers of the patriarchal lineage: Barbara Sidney, for example, was described in

"Penshurst" as "noble, fruitful, chaste," ensuring that her husband could call his children "his own."[24] The "Cooke-ham" women, in striking contrast, possess their own virtues and inhabit a world in which the only men are biblical or classical figures in the landscape. Lacking the sturdy line of inheritance confirmed in Jonson's "To Penshurst," however, the Clifford women of Lanyer's poem are shown to be vulnerable; at the close of the poem, their situation, both actual and metaphoric, was closer to exile than to paradise.

## "Without the Assistance of Man"

Lanyer's *Salve Deus* thus concludes, symbolically perhaps, with the removal of poet and patron from their fading landscape, while the poet's alter-ego, "Delightfull Eccho," who was "wonted to reply / To our last words," dies of sorrow (138). This is not quite Lanyer's last word, however. The poet appends a prose epilogue "To the doubtfull Reader," in which she assures us that she received the title of her book in a prophetic dream and thus felt called to carry out the task that she has just completed. It is as though her authorial self-confidence is in need of a boost even as she completes her work—and this would not be surprising, since her achievement was indeed extraordinary. She constructed a poetic work in which patronage, religion, and landscape were united by a proto-feminist concentration on women. After all, as she claims in her prefatory epistle "To the Vertuous Reader,"

> it pleased our Lord and Saviour Jesus Christ, without the assistance of man [. . .] to be begotten of a woman, borne of a woman, nourished of a woman, obedient to a woman; and that he healed woman [sic], pardoned women, comforted women; yea, even when he was in his greatest agonie and bloodie sweat, going to be crucified, and also in the last houre of his death, tooke care to dispose of a woman: after his resurrection, appeared first to a woman, sent a woman to declare his most glorious resurrection to the rest of his Disciples. (49–50)

Driven by this conviction of the central but neglected importance of women in the Gospel, Lanyer explores the role of female strengths and virtues from the first woman in the Garden of Eden to her own contemporaries in the garden at Cookham. As Elizabeth Hageman has commented, in Lanyer's work "nature and nature's God" both seem to "prefer qualities traditionally associated with femininity."[25]

We have seen that *Salve Deus Rex Judaeorum* has two recurring concerns that are illuminated by a woman-centered approach: land and devotion. The volume opens with a poem to Anne, "Renowned Empresse, and Great Britaines Queene" (3), the emblematic feminine expression of the land as nation. It closes with a detailed poetic glorification of a particular piece of land, the estate at Cookham, identified with a female trinity and a brief time when "Virtue then did rest" within them and its grounds. But the most important lands in *Salve Deus* are symbolic and biblical. In her poem to the queen, Lanyer asserts that Christ is her king and "in his kingdome onely rests my lands" (6), suggesting that the true land with which the poet is concerned is heaven. In her address to the "Mistris of my youth," the countess of Kent, she invokes her patron's "noble Virtues" as "the ground I write upon," punningly implying both the paper on which she writes and the earth on which her poem is built. In each case, the land is poetic and spiritual, comprising personal qualities and divinely inspired strengths. Most fundamental of all, the "ground" of "Salve Deus" and "Cooke-ham" is Eden, the paradisal land, lost, reinterpreted, and temporarily regained in the course of her small book.

The second unifying factor within the female-focused frame of *Salve Deus* is religious devotion. One of Lanyer's most frequently used words is "grace," the gift of God in the redemption brought about by Christ. In her patronage poems, she refers to her book as a "worke of grace" (36) that will draw the readers' attention to Christ and allow his "grace" to fill their souls (17). In "Salve Deus" she celebrates the innocent "grace" of Christ "disgrac'd with impure blame" for our sake at the crucifixion (99). Most memorably, the opening lines of "Cooke-ham" play expressively on this favourite word, which links the sacred and the feminine secular world:

> Farewell (sweet *Cooke-ham*) where I first obtain'd
> Grace from that Grace where perfit Grace remain'd. (130)

Patrick Cook has successfully demonstrated that "Cooke-ham" is a text with "polyphonic richness" and is as much a devotional poem as a panegyric to a country estate.[26] The three parts of *Salve Deus* are thus held together by religious concerns and, as Barbara Lewalski claims, "boldly reimagine and rewrite the fundamental Christian myths—Eden, the Passion, the Community of Saints—with women at their center."[27]

*Salve Deus* explores a further sense of devotion that is wider in scope yet remains linked with spiritual devotion. As Elaine Beilin splendidly puts it, *Salve Deus* is like a triptych not just because the book has three parts but because, like an altar painting, "the large central panel conveys the crucial doctrine" while "each side panel relates that divine image to the human landscape and to particular lives."[28] The female examples held up for respect and imitation by Lanyer in these "side panels" are figures of loyalty to God and to one another (as mothers, sisters and daughters, or members of Anne of Denmark's female Court), an idealized community of women who serve as temporal models of eternal values. Lanyer's work, based in part on her own devotion to these patrons, encourages further spiritual devotion by acting as a "Mirrour" of their virtues (41). This multiplicity of kinds of devotion anticipates Geoffrey Hill's twentieth-century sonnet "The Laurel Axe," in which the Platonic idea of England is expressed in terms of a declining country estate—Cookham, as it might be—"replete with complex fortunes that are gone." This "house of solitudes" recalls its past, and especially "all that devotion long since bought and sold."[29] Lanyer's work is about devotion in this fullest sense—bought and sold in patronage, but also holding together and purchasing "all," from community and service to land and souls.

At the heart of the English landscape in "Cooke-ham" stands the symbolic "faire tree" (136) which is a place of devotion to Christ (as an emblem of his cross) and a revisited paradisal tree of knowledge, where Lanyer, the early modern Eve, does indeed take learning from a "Booke" (86, 136). The tree is also a site of affectionate human devotion, being the place where Lanyer and Anne Clifford part "with a chaste, yet loving kisse" (137) before leaving Cookham to what Geoffrey Hill would call its "complex fortunes."[30] Finally, Lanyer's tree is, of course, an "Oake" (132), symbol of England, uniting devotion to God, friends, and land. Indeed, the more closely one reads *Salve Deus,* the more evident it becomes that the whole work is interlinked, forming one extended woman-centered meditation on land and devotion.

## "Cast Your Eyes upon This Little Booke"

Let us return to the question with which we began: what is the significance of Lanyer's "little Booke" (17) in literary history? As Marshall Grossman has asked, if Lanyer's work "had, in fact, no historical consequence, failed to *cause* anything at all, in what sense (if any) was it a literary historical event?"[31] The answer lies, in part, in approaching literary history itself from a different angle. Lanyer's work was a historical event because she did something new, creative, and ambitious, even if it was not immediately repeated or imitated; after all, "unique" and "original" are themselves major adjectives in a history of literature. Lanyer did not do what was expected of her. She possessed a gift for poetry but did not limit herself to private writing nor take the obvious route (as far as we know) of supplying lyrics to be set to music by her husband or his colleagues at the Court. Instead, she published and claimed her work without much conventional female modesty but with a sense of divine authorization and wrote in genres that she newly created or extended by her use of them. Her patronage poems constitute the first sustained use in English of the poetry of praise by a woman exclusively in honor of women.[32] Her narrative of the Passion of Christ in "Salve Deus" uniquely combines a familiar mode, as exemplified in Robert Southwell's *Saint Peters Complaynt,* with the praise of virtue and a proto-feminist polemical intent. "The Description of Cooke-ham," in its elegiac evocation of a time and place, inaugurated a new genre in English literature, the country house poem.

    As with any exciting work of literature, many questions remain unanswered and must be left for individual readers and future critics to decide. Do we do justice to Lanyer's uniqueness or do we diminish it by placing her too firmly in the context of other works from 1611? How useful is it to set her poetry in the sequence of women's writing from Mary Sidney to Anne Finch[33] or in the tradition of devotional poetry from Anne Lok to George Herbert?[34] What are we to make of the contradictions in Lanyer's work? She is a bold and assertive writer, yet she can at times, like the Echo in "Cooke-ham," withdraw into silence, reflecting others' voices or mirroring their virtues. As Judith Sherer Herz has observed, the "theological daring" of Lanyer's work is given urgency by the danger of her "potential disappearance from her own text (figuring her disappearance from literary history itself)."[35] Lanyer is also, paradoxically though understandably, deeply implicated in the culture of patronage and at the same time radically opposed to social inequality. As a result, does she really express solidarity with her privileged dedicatees (as far as courtesy and modesty permit) or does she feel herself under threat from them? There are also several biographical puzzles that remain unsolved and may well never be satisfactorily explained. For example, why did Lanyer publish only one book, and did she write anything else? To what extent did she move in the circles of Shakespeare, Jonson, Donne, and other male writers of her day? Finally, we will need to come to a critical judgment of her work, even if we prefer to regard her achievement in terms other than stylistic prowess or possible greatness. As Elaine Beilin has asked, is this a poet of "slender skill" (to use Lanyer's own phrase [9] in her dedicatory poem to the queen), or was she a "fit contemporary"[36] of the poets of the early seventeenth century whose works have long been accepted as part of English literary history?

    While letting these and other questions play in our minds, it is appropriate to give Lanyer herself the final comment. This poet of land and devotion, refiguring biblical and social history in terms of women's roles and Christ's qualities, modestly asks her readers to "grace this little Booke" (15). For, since her aim is devotion and not profit, "how can these poore lines goe unrespected?" (20).

## NOTES

1. Donne, *The Complete English Poems,* ed. C. A. Patrides (London: Dent, 1985) 335.
2. Coryate, *Coryats Crudities* (London, 1611) title page.
3. Lanyer, *The Poems of Aemilia Lanyer: Salve Deus Rex Judaeorum,* ed. Susanne Woods (New York: Oxford UP, 1993) 1.
4. See Susanne Woods, *Lanyer: A Renaissance Woman Poet* (NewYork: Oxford UP, 1999) 3–41.
5. Lanyer, *Poems* xxviii.
6. Ironically, Lanyer's work was only republished by the historian A. L. Rowse in the 1970s because of his (mistaken) assumption that she was the "dark lady" of Shakespeare's sonnets. See Rowse, *The Poems of Shakespeare's Dark Lady* (London: Jonathan Cape, 1976). *Salve Deus Rex Judaeorum* thus regained attention by accident, as a footnote to the history of the most famous male writer of the English Renaissance. This bizarre turn of events is a parable (or perhaps a parody) of the processes of women's literary history, both written and lived.
7. It is important not to continue the state of affairs noted with concern in 1997 by Judith Sherer Herz, who rightly observed that Lanyer remained "outside the literary history that is cataloguing and processing her." See Herz, "Aemilia Lanyer and the Pathos of Literary History," *Representing Women in Renaissance England,* ed. Claude J. Summers and Ted-Larry Pebworth (Columbia: U of Missouri P, 1997) 121–35; 123. Susanne Woods, in *Lanyer: A Renaissance Woman Poet* (New York: Oxford UP, 1999), has led the way in placing Lanyer more centrally in the history of early modern literature, setting *Salve Deus* alongside the works of her male contemporaries such as Shakespeare, Jonson, and Donne.
8. Elaine Beilin, *Redeeming Eve: Women Writers of the English Renaissance* (Princeton: Princeton UP, 1987) 206.
9. Debra Rienstra, "Dreaming Authorship: Aemilia Lanyer and the Countess of Pembroke," *Discovering and (Re)Covering the Seventeenth-Century Religious Lyric,* ed. Eugene R. Cunnar and Jeffrey Johnson (Pittsburgh: Duquesne UP, 2001) 80–103; 80.
10. See Barbara K. Lewalski, "Of God and Good Women: the Poems of Aemilia Lanyer," *Silent but for the Word: Tudor Women as Patrons, Translators and Writers of Religious Works,* ed. Margaret P. Hannay (Kent: Kent State UP, 1985) 203–24.
11. Since Donne had not met Elizabeth Drury, the anniversary of whose death was the occasion of his *Anatomy* (subsequently known as *The First Anniversarie*), it is assumed that he wrote it at the behest of her parents, Sir Robert and Lady Anne Drury (née Bacon). Jonson was honoring Prince Henry, son and heir of King James, in the title role of his masque *Oberon, the Fairy Prince.*
12. Guibbory, "The Gospel According to Aemilia: Women and the Sacred in Aemilia Lanyer's *Salve Deus Rex Judaeorum,"* *Sacred and Profane: Secular and Devotional Interplay in Early Modern British Literature,* ed. Helen Wilcox, Richard Todd, and Alasdair MacDonald (Amsterdam: Free UP, 1996) 105–26; 108.
13. Donne, *Poems* 336.
14. Louise Schleiner, *Tudor and Stuart Women Writers* (Bloomington: Indiana UP, 1994) 25.
15. See, for example, John Donne's poem, "Goodfriday, 1613. Riding Westward," in which Christ's crucifixion is made "present yet unto my memory" (Donne, *Poems* 456).
16. Lanyer's focus on the Virgin Mary in "Salve Deus" (95–100) has given rise to speculation on her possible Catholic leanings, though her upbringing was undoubtedly strictly Protestant

as her poem to the countess of Kent makes clear (19). It is likely that Lanyer also had Jewish connections through her father's Venetian family. For a summary of these complex religious affiliations, see Kari Boyd McBride, "Gender and Judaism in Meditations on the Passion: Middleton, Southwell, Lanyer, and Fletcher," Cunnar and Johnson, eds. 17–40; 31–32.

17. This female reclamation of knowledge lies at the heart of Lanyer's didactic vocation in *Salve Deus;* see Helen Wilcox, "'As from a learned Booke': Aemilia Lanyer's 'Eve's Apologie' and the Gendered Transmission of Knowledge," *Calliope's Classroom: Didactic Poetry from the Ancient Near East to the Western Renaissance,* ed. Annette Harder et al. (Leuven: Peeters, 2005) 293–313.

18. See Christina Luckyj, *"A Moving Rhetoricke": Gender and Silence in Early Modern England* (Manchester: Manchester UP, 2002) 128.

19. Since Lanyer identifies Lady Anne Clifford, the daughter of the dowager countess of Cumberland, as "To honourable *Dorset* now espows'd" (134), the poem must date from after Clifford's marriage to the earl of Dorset in 1609, though it probably refers to a slightly earlier period spent with the mother and daughter at Cookham. During that time the situation of the aristocratic women was actually very insecure, both legally and financially, as Clifford had been denied her Cumberland inheritance after her father's death in 1605. These difficulties dominate the early years of her extensive diaries; see *The Diaries of Lady Anne Clifford,* ed. D. J. H. Clifford (Stroud: Sutton, 1990).

20. A poem offering praise of a distinguished family in an idealized description of their house and land. For a useful anthology of the genre, see Alastair Fowler, ed., *The Country House Poem: A Cabinet of Seventeenth-Century Estate Poems and Related Items* (Edinburgh: Edinburgh UP, 1994). For a cultural history of the genre, see Kari Boyd McBride, *Country House Discourse in Early Modern England: A Cultural Study of Landscape and Legitimacy* (Aldershot: Ashgate, 2001).

21. Pearson, "'An Emblem of Themselves, in Plum or Pear': Poetry, the Female Body and the Country House," *Write or Be Written: Early Modern Women Poets and Cultural Constraints,* ed. Barbara Smith and Ursula Appelt (Aldershot: Ashgate, 2001) 87–104; 95.

22. Ben Jonson, *Poems,* ed. Ian Donaldson (London: Oxford UP, 1975) 91.

23. McBride, *Country House Discourse* 111.

24. Jonson, *Poems* 91.

25. Hageman, "Women's Poetry in Early Modern Britain," *Women and Literature in Britain, 1500–1700,* ed. Helen Wilcox (Cambridge: Cambridge UP, 1996) 190–208; 198.

26. Cook, "Aemilia Lanyer's 'Description of Cooke-ham' as Devotional Lyric," Cunnar and Johnson, eds. 104–18.

27. Lewalski, *Writing Women in Jacobean England* (Cambridge: Harvard UP, 1993) 241.

28. Beilin, *Redeeming Eve* 206.

29. Hill, *Tenebrae* (London: André Deutsch, 1978) 30.

30. Hill, *Tenebrae* 30.

31. Grossman, ed., *Aemilia Lanyer: Gender, Genre, and the Canon* (Lexington: UP of Kentucky, 1998) 128.

32. Beilen, *Redeeming Eve* 177.

33. See Helen Wilcox, "'First Fruits of a Woman's Wit': Authorial Self-Construction of English Renaissance Women Poets," Smith and Appelt, eds. 199–221; 202–04; and McBride, *Country House Discourse* 164–66.

34. See, for example, two discussions by Susanne Woods: *Lanyer* 182, and "Anne Lock and Aemilia Lanyer: A Tradition of Protestant Women Speaking," *Form and Reform in Renaissance England* ed. Amy Boesky and Mary Thomas Crane (Newark: U of Delaware P, 2000) 171–84.

35. Herz, "Pathos" 132.

36. Beilin, *Redeeming Eve* 207.

# READING LIST

Beilin, Elaine. *Redeeming Eve: Women Writers of the English Renaissance*. Princeton: Princeton UP, 1987.

Chedgzoy, Kate, Melanie Hansen, and Suzanne Trill, eds. *Voicing Women: Gender and Sexuality in Early Modern Writing*. Keele: Keele UP, 1996.

Clarke, Danielle, and Elizabeth Clarke, eds. *"This Double Voice": Gendered Writing in Early Modern England*. Basingstoke: Macmillan, 2000.

Cunnar, Eugene R., and Jeffrey Johnson, eds. *Discovering and (Re)Covering the Seventeenth-Century Religious Lyric*. Pittsburgh: Duquesne University Press, 2001.

Ezell, Margaret. *Writing Women's Literary History*. Baltimore: Johns Hopkins UP, 1993.

Grossman, Marshall, ed. *Aemilia Lanyer: Gender, Genre, and the Canon*. Lexington: UP of Kentucky, 1998.

Hannay, Margaret P., ed. *Silent but for the Word: Tudor Women as Patrons, Translators and Writers of Religious Works*. Kent: Kent State UP, 1985.

Herz, Judith Sherer. "Aemilia Lanyer and the Pathos of Literary History." *Representing Women in Renaissance England*. Ed. Claude J. Summers and Ted-Larry Pebworth. Columbia: U of Missouri P, 1997. 121–35.

Keeble, N. H., ed. *The Cultural Identity of Seventeenth-Century Woman: A Reader*. London: Routledge, 1994.

Lewalski, Barbara K. *Writing Women in Jacobean England*. Cambridge: Harvard UP, 1993.

McBride, Kari Boyd. *Country House Discourse in Early Modern England: A Cultural Study of Landscape and Legitimacy*. Aldershot: Ashgate, 2001.

Smith, Barbara, and Ursula Appelt, eds. *Write or Be Written: Early Modern Women Poets and Cultural Constraints*. Aldershot: Ashgate, 2001.

Wall, Wendy. *The Imprint of Gender: Authorship and Publication in the English Renaissance*. Ithaca: Cornell UP, 1993.

Wilcox, Helen, ed. *Women and Literature in Britain, 1500–1700*. Cambridge: Cambridge UP, 1996.

Woods, Susanne. *Lanyer: A Renaissance Woman Poet*. New York: Oxford UP, 1999.

# 23

# Jonson, King, and Court

## Julie Sanders

In the "Epithalamion" or marriage poem that Ben Jonson (?1572–1637) wrote for the marriage of Jerome Weston, son of the lord high treasurer, Richard Weston, first earl of Portland, to Lady Frances Stuart, daughter of the late duke of Lennox, Esme Stuart, at Roehampton Chapel on June 25, 1632, the poet-playwright declared: "All is a story of the king and queen!" (1.91).[1] Charles I and his French queen consort Henrietta Maria were both present at the wedding celebrations and had indeed been active in securing the match between these two high-profile Caroline families. This in itself explains the flattering references Jonson makes to their involvement in the nuptials and his decision to use the suggestive floral imagery of roses and lilies, symbolic of England and France, respectively, and therefore of the monarchs' own symbolic union. It is, however, one of the aims of this essay to ask to what extent Ben Jonson's poetic output, composed across the timespan of three highly distinct and important monarchical reigns—those of Elizabeth I (1558–1603), James VI and I and his queen consort Anna of Denmark (1603–1625), and Charles I and Henrietta Maria (1625–1642)—and frequently described as the work of a political conservative and supporter, albeit self-appointed reformer, of Court ideology, was always and only a "story of the king and queen." Outlining the ways in which the symbolic and actual domain of the Court proved a constant source both of attraction and repulsion for Jonson as a writer throughout his long career, the essay will interrogate his ambivalent representation of that locale in his poetry.

The first question we may wish to pose in this period is to what extent it is useful or even justifiable to talk of the "Court" as if it were a single, definable entity. The early modern Court can be linked to specific, symbolic spaces, most significantly the palace of Whitehall, and certainly that locale proved important in Jonson's career; many of the Court masques he was commissioned to write were performed there. Nevertheless, the Court had other important architectural locations including palaces such as Somerset House and Greenwich, "satellite royal households" as James Knowles has described them, and these spaces had particularly resonant associations with the queens consort of the Jacobean and Caroline reigns, with whom, as many scholars of the masque have indicated, Jonson was intimately associated.[2] In addition, when the Court went on summer progresses it consciously relocated itself at the country estates of various aristocratic hosts in the regions. Jonson wrote several provincial and country-house entertainments for visits of this kind, including the *Entertainment at Theobalds* (1607), *The King's Entertainment at Welbeck* (1633), and *Love's Welcome at Bolsover* (1634), and in the poem "To Sir Robert Wroth" he describes how Wroth's Enfield estates, with their excellent hunting opportunities, became a virtual Court by dint of the presence of the monarch. James VI and I was an avid exponent of the hunt, and, as Jonson informs Wroth, "for it makes thy house his court" (l. 24). In this respect, the Court could function as a highly mobile and fluid concept. In addition, the term "Court" had official meanings, signifying the bureaucratic structures that administered the daily business and operations of government. As an umbrella term it could refer to the directives and discussions of the Privy Council, the offices of the gentlemen and gentlewomen appointed to the royal bedchamber, and to the bevy of household officials and employees who maintained the huge machine of monarchy.[3] Last, the "Court" could constitute the different and often competing factions who assembled in these multivalent spaces in order to seek the monarchs' attentions and persuade the royal view to support their interests.

A close reading of Jonson's extensive poetic output reveals a writer in persistent dialogue with this last manifestation of the "Court." His *Epigrams* collection, self-consciously written in the style of the classical epigrammatist Martial, alternately praises individual courtiers and castigates Court corruption via stereotypical portraits of sycophancy and competition. For instance, while the epigram "To King James" declares him "best of kings" (l. 1), other poems in the collection describe the vanities of nameless courtiers, or "court-worms," who pursue the king's favor. The use of the impersonal pronoun is equally damning in "On Something That Walks Somewhere": "At court I met *it*, in clothes brave enough / To be a courtier" (ll. 1–2, my emphasis). Poems in subsequent collections such as *The Forest* and *The Underwood* (the significance of these titles will be considered later) continue the theme: in the latter's "An Epigram to a Friend, and Son," Jonson reflects on the current predominance of flattery at Court, suggesting that it offers "More subtle works and finer pieces far / Than knew the former ages" (ll. 22–23).

Certain Jonson poems are, however, clearly written to order for specific courtly occasions, such as the epithalamion with which this essay began, or the poems composed to mark royal birthdays and the anniversaries of respective monarchs' coronations. Jonson was well aware that incursions into the art of writing panegyric, the poetry of praise, needed to avoid the charge of empty flattery he had leveled against others. In the "Epigram to Our Great and Good K[ing] Charles on his Anniversary Day, 1629," included in *The Underwood,* he praises the monarch in the following terms:

> [. . .] when had Great Britain greater cause
>    Than now, to love the sovereign and the laws?
> When you that reign are her example grown,
>    And what are bounds to her, you make your own? (ll. 7–10)

The careful dating of this poem tells us much as readers about the ways in which Jonson sought to distinguish his particular brand of verse panegyric from cheap flattery. The year 1629 was a highly significant one in the context of the reign of Charles I. The monarch's former favorite, and object of much animosity and political grievance in the House of Commons, George Villiers, duke of Buckingham, had been assassinated in the previous year, raising hopes of greater accommodation between the king and his Parliament. These hopes had, however, collapsed in the face of the failure of the Petition of Right in the sessions of 1628 and 1629, which led to Parliament's dissolution and Charles's decision to embark on an eleven-year period without governments that has come to be known as the "Personal Rule." Jonson's poem is, then, a careful and considered intervention at that particular time, seeking both to smooth over the parliamentary tensions caused by heated discussion of the Petition of Right and to recognize the moral and ethical integrity of Charles's ongoing attempts to reform the financial operations and accounting procedures of the royal households and offices, whose excessive expenditure and internal corruption had become infamous.[4]

This is not abject flattery, but rather the deployment of poetry in an ethical and political enterprise. Throughout his career, Jonson undoubtedly assigned an ethical role to poetry. Modeling his public persona on that of the ancient Roman writer Horace, who served the Emperor Augustus, he fashioned for himself, as Kevin Sharpe and Peter Lake have termed it, the role of "counsellor of kings."[5] It is in this context that we can best understand the operations of panegyric in his poems. Rather than blind flattery, it is praise articulated with the purpose of moral and ethical reform, and which is, therefore, always hedged in by the shades and nuances of criticism and counsel.[6] As Martin Butler has argued, "In praising king or patron, the poet was representing him not as he was but as it was hoped that he would be."[7] Jonson envisaged the roles of poet and patron as mutually supportive.

Other verses in Jonson's poetic collections are, however, specific appeals for financial patronage from the monarch and several prominent courtiers. In one poem written in 1630, Jonson pleads with Charles I to increase the annual royal pension granted him by his father:

> Please your majesty to make
> Of your grace, for goodness' sake,
> Those your father's marks, your pounds. ("The Humble Petition of Poor Ben. To the Best of Monarchs, Masters, Men, King Charles" ll. 25–27)

The bid clearly proved successful, since Jonson acknowledges the monarch's generosity in a sonnet elsewhere in *The Underwood*, "An Epigram to the Household, 1630"—although this poem also chides the royal household for its tardiness in paying the sum ("Go now, deny his tierce!" l. 14).

It is typical of Jonson that having elsewhere recognized his refusal to participate in the contemporary fashion for love poetry and sonneteering—"Why I Write Not of Love" opens *The Forest* with a poignant and moving recognition of advancing age: "wonder not / That since, my numbers are so cold, / When Love is fled, and I grow old" (ll. 10–12), and "My Picture Left in Scotland" in *The Underwood* continues in a similar vein, reflecting on Jonson's "hundred of grey hairs," "mountain belly," and "rocky face" (ll. 14, 17)—he should then deploy the genre in a distinctly unromantic complaint about late payment. Ian Donaldson speculates that Jonson eschewed Petrarchan-inflected poetic modes because they tended to depict the poet "in various postures of abjection and servility, which had small appeal."[8] Whatever the truth, expectations are constantly tested and tried at the level of form, context, and meaning in Jonson's verse.

Intriguingly, the other significant venture Jonson makes into sonnet-writing is to praise the sonneteering of a female poet, Lady Mary Wroth, whose *Pamphilia to Amphilanthus* sequence had been published in 1621:

> I, that have been a lover, and could show it,
> Though not in these, in rhymes not wholly dumb,
> Since I exscribe your sonnets, am become
> A better lover, and much better poet. ("A Sonnet to the Noble Lady, the Lady Mary Wroth" ll. 1–4)

Jonson dedicated the published version of his play *The Alchemist* to Mary Wroth in 1611, and this generous recognition of the skills of a contemporary woman writer serves to query any easy critical assumptions about Jonson's misogyny. As Richard Helgerson has noted, with particular reference to *The Forest,* Jonson's poetry is frequently addressed to women.[9] Admittedly these addressees can all be identified as aristocratic, but they are invariably elite women who either wrote poetry or drama themselves or were involved in some form of artistic patronage. Jonson also demonstrates considerable empathy for those women alluded to in the context of other of his verses. During his career, he addressed multiple poems to Wroth; Queen Henrietta Maria; Elizabeth, countess of Rutland; and Lucy Russell, countess of Bedford, as well as writing single verses about Katherine, Lady Aubigny, Lady Covell, and Lady Katherine Ogle. He alluded to specific elite women in the context of poems such as "To Penshurst" and authored elegies and epitaphs on still more, including Elizabeth Chute; Jane Paulet, marchioness of Wiston; and several on Venetia Digby.

Critics have observed that a predominance of Jonson's poems of petition, those that refer explicitly to his financial needs, occur in the Caroline 1630s. The dire state of Jonson's finances is confirmed by a letter addressed to his most significant Caroline patron, William Cavendish, earl of Newcastle (himself the subject of several poems in *The Underwood*), in 1631. In this letter, the poet-playwright describes his condition of penury and want via the elaborate mechanism of describing a dream. In the dream, Jonson's pet fox speaks, informing him that his cellar is overrun with moles; the moles in turn come to signify the want that destroys households and families (a "want" is a species of mole, though Jonson clearly puns on the more material sense).[10]

If Richard Helgerson detects a more female-influenced or at least empathetic Jonson in *The Forest,* Annabel Patterson suggests that *The Underwood* evidences a greater sense of despair and political pragmatism on the poet's part. In this miscellany, she suggests Jonson is rewriting, or at the very least revising, the high hopes of the Horatian model of counsel and influence that sounded in his earlier Jacobean verse:

> in *Underwood* he constructed a [. . .] voice [. . .] for which there was no obvious precedent in classical lyric, one that allowed history to tell its own story in the connection between poems: a voice that whispered of careerism, of the limits of idealism, of necessity, of the impossibility of independence.[11]

Many accounts of Jonson's career suggest that his previously mentioned dependency on Court patronage in the Caroline era was a product of financial hardship, caused both by finding his style of drama and poetry less favored at Court (his masque commissions began to dry up after 1631) and a series of debilitating strokes. We can, however, hear this voice of dependency, and to a degree resignation, as early as 1623 in "An Epistle Answering to One That Asked to be Sealed of the Tribe of Ben" with his denial of interest in European politics—"What is't to me whether the French design / Be, or be not, to get the Valtelline?" (ll. 31–32)—and his reductive dismissal of the significance of his career as a Court masque writer in references to "Christmas clay" and "animated porcelain" (ll. 52, 53). Jonson compares himself unfavorably to his long-time masque collaborator and intense rival, Inigo Jones, who had, unlike him, been asked to assist with devising entertainments to receive the Spanish Infanta (these, of course, never took place since the Infanta failed to come to England following the spectacular collapse of the negotiations over her proposed marriage to the then Prince Charles):

> my fame to his not under-hears,
>    That guides the motions and directs the bears.
> But that's a blow by which in time I may
>    Lose all my credit with my Christmas clay
> And animated porcelain of the court. (ll. 49–53)

In this same poem, in a remarkable act of self-reflection, deploying the image of himself as vessel or container found elsewhere in his work, Jonson states:

> Well, with mine own frail pitcher, what to do
> I have decreed; keep it from waves and press,
>    Lest it be jostled, cracked, made naught, or less;
> Live to that point I will, for which I am man,
>    And dwell in my centre as I can,
> Still looking to, and ever loving, heaven. (ll. 56–61)

The importance to Jonson of the notion of "dwelling" is a subject to which we will return, but suffice to note here the idea of a centered self, a personal state of equilibrium that Jonson strove to achieve throughout his life and career. The calm acceptance of his situation is reinforced by his use of largely regular iambic pentameter lines and simple forthright monosyllables in this section of the poem. The notable exception comes at line 59, where the crucial term "man" is an eleventh syllable, creating a hypermetrical line, which links to the ensuing nine-syllable line with its declaration of the centered self in which Jonson aims to "dwell."

All of this helps to reveal a writer with a constantly evolving relationship throughout his life with the very idea of the Court, as well as its day-to-day operations. Jonson's personal biography provides some firm clues to the intricacies of this difficult relationship. A figure with origins in the city of London rather than at Court, he was persistently reminded throughout his career of his training as an apprentice bricklayer, and this despite his Westminster School education. His ambivalent, even contradictory, responses to the "Court" can be traced to these facts of his social status. As Leah Marcus notes: "Jonson lived most of his life in close proximity to the English court at Whitehall, and the court figures prominently in his writings. But physical proximity is not the same thing as access" (Marcus 30). By the late Jacobean period, Jonson held a position equivalent to that of poet laureate in the nineteenth century—from 1616 onward he was granted an annual pension by the king—but this position never entirely resolved his problematic relationship to the social and spatial domain of the Court.

During his lifetime, Jonson's poetry was published in the form of two major collections: *Epigrams,* poems written on various occasions from the Elizabethan 1590s through to the mid-Jacobean period, and *The Forest,* a collection of fifteen poems, including examples of the ode, epistle, song, complaint, and lyric forms. Both of these collections appeared in the 1616 folio edition of Jonson's *Works* which the writer himself saw through publication. In the early 1630s, Jonson appears to have been preparing a further collection of poems for publication, but this only appeared posthumously under the heading of *The Underwood* in the second folio of Jonson's work, prepared for the press by Sir Kenelm Digby. Most of the poems in *The Underwood* date from post-1616, with a few significant exceptions, including the "Ode to James, Earl of Desmond, Writ in Queen Elizabeth's Time, Since Lost, and Recovered." *Epigrams* constitutes a strange blend of poems of "praise and dispraise" (Donaldson 124). Certain significant individuals from the age are named and identified as the moral arbiters of the period; these include Jonson's former Westminster School tutor and Renaissance humanist William Camden—"All that I am in arts, all that I know" ("To William Camden" l. 2), again those forthright monosyllables declaring a truth at the center of the poem— and worthy courtiers such as Sir Thomas Roe: "He that is round within himself, and straight, / Need seek no other strength, no other height" ("To Sir Thomas Roe" ll. 3–4). Set against these paradigms of integrity and ethical behavior, however, we are offered their antitheses, as Donaldson catalogues, "generic figures [such as]—Court Worm, Old Colt, Groom Idiot, Hazard the Cheater, Sir Cod the Perfumed, Lieutenant Shift, Sir Voluptuous Beast" (Donaldson 124). These creations' proximity to characters in Jonson's public theater plays, figures including *The Alchemist*'s Sir Epicure Mammon or *The New Inn*'s Sir Glorious Tiptoe, is regularly noted. *Epigrams* appears therefore to embody the reforming zeal with regard to the Court already observed in Jonson's career.

With *The Forest* comes a shift toward what might be described as more obviously coterie concerns and an interest in the preservation of particular kinds of community. The circulation of poetry during the early modern period, both in manuscript and print forms, amongst particular elite groups, including those at the universities and the Inns of Court, and those defined by familial and dynastic groupings, has been carefully documented by Arthur Marotti.[12] While a poet like John Donne, with his emphasis on experimental poetry in both an erotic and a religious vein, is regularly distinguished from Jonson with his more conservative interest in formal and occasional verse—often delivered in a so-called plain style of regular rhyming couplets and simple syllabic constructions, examples of which we have already seen—the operation of coterie communities on the understanding and reception of both writers' poetry at this time links them with intersecting groups of patronage and interest.[13] Both Donne and Jonson, for example, write verse for and about Lucy Russell, countess of Bedford, and in his later Caroline drama Jonson would happily acknowledge the influence of Donne's work on his own, directly alluding to poems such as "The Calm."[14]

The title of *The Forest* alludes to the Latin term *Sylva*, which was commonly used to denote a poetic miscellany. The varied poetic range and form of the fifteen poems that make up this taut collection has already been mentioned. Ian Donaldson suggests that a number of the poems also offer a persuasive refutation to those critics who claim that Jonson was vehemently antimarriage. To support these claims, critics generally cite the satiric attacks on the institution to be found in Jonson's plays, including *Epicene* (1609) and *Bartholomew Fair* (1614) (132). Perhaps as part of its wider communal ethos, however, *The Forest* includes several poems that acknowledge the power of loving couples, such as the Aubignys. In a strategy akin to the deployment of structures of contrast and antithesis in *Epigrams,* Lady Katherine Aubigny is differentiated from other more profligate or vain wives:

> Let who will, follow fashions and attires;
>   Maintain their liegers forth; for foreign wires
> Melt down their husbands' land, to pour away

> On the close groom and page on New Year's Day
> And almost all days after [. . .]
> [. . .]
> Let 'em on powders, oils, and paintings spend [. . .]
> [. . .]
> You, madam, young have learned to shun these shelves,
>    Whereon the most of mankind wrack themselves. ("Epistle to Katherine, Lady
>    Aubigny" ll. 71–75, 77, 89–90)

Lady Aubigny pays her husband and lord "the pledges of chaste love" (l. 96). Similarly, in "To Penshurst," Jonson's pioneering country-house poem, the marriage of the estate owners, Sir Robert Sidney and Lady Lisle (Lady Mary Wroth's parents), is described as "noble, fruitful, chaste withal" (l. 90).

"To Penshurst" is perhaps the best known of all the poems in *The Forest* and possibly in Jonson's entire poetic canon. It is a work that helps us in identifying another crucial aspect of Jonson's writing: poetry invested in and inspired by specific places and locations. As George Parfitt notes, the "tendency to generalization and idealization is matched in Jonson's lyrics by a counter tendency to the specific and the local."[15] Parfitt's example of this tendency from *The Forest* is "To the Same (Song To Celia)," where the Catullus-derived theme of multiple kisses is given a highly English geographical grounding in the marshlands to be found on the borders of London:

> Till you equal with the store
> All the grass that Romney yields,
> Or the sands in Chelsea fields,
> Or the drops in silver Thames. (ll. 12–15)

Parallel geographical impulses can be identified in "To Penshurst." The poem has the obvious literal setting of the Sidney family estate in Kent, and all the models of courtly hospitality and artistic patronage that provides, and the same localizing impulse of "To the Same" can be registered in the way that Jonson melds references to quintessentially English beech and chestnut trees to the classical pastoral idiom of satyrs and groves.

The formal architecture and proportion of "To Penshurst" has been detailed and discussed by many critics.[16] The poem as a whole moves from an outside space, in the grounds of the Penshurst estate, into the walled garden where the trained fruit provides both food and beauty for the estate's guests, and finally into the interior of the house. It is a formal enactment of welcome. Opening with the negative example of so-called Jacobean prodigy houses built to display their owners' wealth and social ambition, all the things the "ancient pile" of Penshurst is defiantly "not," the poem closes on that all-important Jonsonian notion of centeredness and "dwelling":

> Now, Penshurst, they that will proportion thee
>    With other edifices, when they see
> Those proud, ambitious heaps, and nothing else,
>    May say, their lords have built, but thy lord dwells. (ll. 99–102)

"To Penshurst" functions in *The Forest,* then, in a role akin to the poems on Camden and Roe in *Epigrams:* as a model of how things should be. The unattainable perfection of the self-sufficient estate described by Jonson, one where fish jump into nets to be eaten and fruit reaches into hands to be picked, has troubled those critics who seek for tension beneath its glimmering surfaces. The rural idyll offered by "To Sir Robert Wroth," the poem addressed to Lady Mary Wroth's husband that follows "To Penshurst" in the collection, has been similarly deconstructed by readers who feel uncomfortable with the overt binary it establishes by means of Wroth's rejection of the vanities and vices of the Court and city in favor of his country estate (situated north of London between Enfield Chase and Waltham Forest):[17]

> How blest art thou canst love the country, Wroth,
> 	Whether by choice, or fate, or both;
> And, though so near the city and the court,
> 	Art ta'en with neither's vice nor sport. (ll. 1–4)

Historical research reveals that Wroth's estates were not without their tensions, made manifest in recent disputes over attempts to make the local river navigable for London trading boats—a policy that was bitterly opposed by locals defending common rights—and Wroth's father's related attempts to secure land and property held by lease from the crown.[18] Similarly this poem's overt rejection of the world of Court masques as the "short bravery of the night" (l. 10) sits awkwardly alongside Jonson's own forays into that realm—although as we have already seen he was not averse to biting that hand that fed him in his poetry—as well as the frequent participation in the same by Sir Robert's wife. Perhaps the lesson is rather that when reading Jonson's deceptively simple poetic surfaces—this poem is once again constructed of fairly regular rhyming couplets—we should remain alert to subtext and nuance.

Jonson's experimentation in the poetry of place is as varied as his depiction of the Court and its associated value systems. In *Epigrams,* for example, one poem offers a parodic version of the contemporary vogue for poetic and prose accounts of journeys (several examples are mentioned between lines 31 and 40). "On the Famous Voyage" is an account of the travels of human waste through the open sewer of London's Fleet Ditch.[19] This verse-journey prefigures the mock-heroic experimentations of Alexander Pope and others in the eighteenth century, but it would also have sat in contrast to a more serious Jonsonian attempt within the genre if the intended poem on his epic walk to Scotland in 1618 had survived. In the poem "An Execration upon Vulcan" in *The Underwood* Jonson claims this work was lost in the 1623 fire that ravaged his personal library and manuscript collection. We can only speculate as to what this poem—"my journey into Scotland sung" (l. 94)—would have contained, but it suggests a continuing interest in the instructive use of contrast and antithesis in the formation of his poetic collections.

As David Norbrook has observed, *The Forest,* for all its seeming critique of the Court and the prevalence of certain tendencies therein in poems such as "To Sir Robert Wroth," is not necessarily an anticourtly volume (Norbook 163).[20] The title suggests an ostensibly regal domain, an area of land protected by royal prerogative laws for the purposes of the hunt. Within the collection as a whole, then, we can see the same laws in operation that reinterpreted Wroth's estate as a temporary extension of the Court on the occasion of a royal visit. Jonson is negotiating a space within, rather than outside, the courtly domain and ethos. Nevertheless, for all its courtly implications, Jonson retains in *The Forest* the rights to both criticism and compliment that defined all his work, for the theater, the court masque, in prose, and in poetry.

All of these interests in Jonson's poetry complicate any oversimplistic understandings of his verse panegyric as bland propaganda in the service of the Court and its prevailing ideologies. As we have seen, the "Court" promulgated very different, even opposing, views during the course of Jonson's lifetime: the early Jacobean interest in the union of Scotland and England gives way, for example, to James's self-appointed role as European peacemaker in the early 1620s. The latter role is alluded to in *The Underwood* in "The Dedication of the King's New Cellar. To Bacchus," a poem clearly written in 1623 in the weeks of expectation before the collapse of the Spanish marriage negotiations: James is envisaged presiding over the feast of the garter on April 23:

> Be it he hold communion
> In great Saint George's union,
> Or gratulates the passage
> Of some well-wrought embassage,
> Whereby he may knit sure up
> The wishèd peace of Europe. (ll. 43–48)

This was followed in turn by the later Caroline emphasis on Neoplatonism-inflected images of marriage, peace, and harmony during the Personal Rule. These differences of emphasis give rise to very different poetic modes and registers in the work of Jonson and his contemporaries.

*The Underwood* is the verse collection Jonson appears to have been amassing in the final decade of his literary career. As Ian Donaldson has noted, it is marked by a concern with money and indebtedness and includes several poems to aristocrats who we know were important patrons to Jonson at this time (135). William Cavendish is perhaps the most significant of these—in one epigram Jonson almost wishes himself into the position of the horse ridden by this noble master: "I began to wish myself a horse" ("An Epigram to William, Earl of Newcastle" l. 12)—and if we think about this particular aristocrat's relationship to the Caroline Court of the 1630s, when the majority of the poems in *The Underwood* appear to have been composed, our story of Jonson's relationship to the Court in his poetry comes full circle. Commenting on Jonson's establishment of figures such as Camden and Roe as moral arbiters in his first poetic collection, *Epigrams,* George Parfitt makes the astute observation that:

> As a whole [Jonson's] work is courtly in that the ethics he supports are often seen as embodied in persons of the court. But it is interesting that Jonson tends to admire people who are more than courtiers—administrators and others active in society at large. (Parfitt 30)

Cavendish was just such a figure: an aristocrat who had a complicated relationship to the Whitehall center of the Caroline Court; one who established his own model estates in his Nottinghamshire and Derbyshire domains; and a literary and artistic patron, who himself wrote poetry and plays of some significance. At the end of his life, for all the critical suggestions of his failing reputation and influence, Jonson was still working in proximity to the Court and yet he remained suspicious of, and alert to, the potential problems and inequities of the ideologies and policies of that complex institutional and social grouping. The story of Jonson's poetry, rather than being simply one "of the king and queen," is, it seems, a very complicated one indeed.

## NOTES

1. The edition of Jonson's poems used throughout is Ian Donaldson, ed., *Ben Jonson* (Oxford: Oxford UP, 1985). All further references to this edition are contained parenthetically in the essay.

2. James Knowles, "'Tied / To Rules of Flattery'? Court Drama and the Masque," *A Companion to English Renaissance Literature and Culture,* ed. Michael Hattaway (Oxford: Blackwell, 2000) 525–44; 530. See also Clare McManus, *Women on the Renaissance Stage* (Manchester: Manchester UP, 2002).

3. For an impressively detailed version of this argument, see Leah Marcus, "Jonson and the Court," *The Cambridge Companion to Ben Jonson,* ed. Richard Harp and Stanley Stewart (Cambridge: Cambridge UP, 2000) 30–42; 30.

4. Martin Butler has persuasively argued that Jonson's public theater play of the same year, *The New Inn,* should be seen in the context of the debates over the Petition of Right and the atmosphere of renewed optimism in the wake of Buckingham's assassination: "Late Jonson," *The Politics of Tragicomedy: Shakespeare and After,* ed. Gordon McMullan and Jonathan Hope (London: Routledge, 1992) 166–88.

5. Kevin Sharpe and Peter Lake, eds., *Culture and Politics in Early Stuart England* (Basingstoke: Macmillan, 1994) 12.

6. For the seminal discussion of this idea, see Kevin Sharpe, *Criticism and Compliment: The Politics of Literature in the England of Charles I* (Cambridge: Cambridge UP, 1987).

7. Martin Butler, "Ben Jonson and the Limits of Courtly Panegyric," in Sharpe and Lake 91–115; 92.

8. Ian Donaldson, "Jonson's Poetry," in Harp and Stewart 119–39; 133.

9. Richard Helgerson, "Ben Jonson," *The Cambridge Companion to English Poetry: Donne to Jonson,* ed. Thomas N. Corns (Cambridge: Cambridge UP, 1993) 148–70; 159; Barbara Smith, *The Women of Ben Jonson's Poetry* (Aldershot: Scolar P, 1995).

10. Jonson to the Earl of Newcastle, December 20, 1631. Cited in Ian Donaldson, *Jonson's Magic Houses* (Oxford: Clarendon, 1997) 87.

11. Annabel Patterson, *Censorship and Interpretation: The Conditions of Writing and Reading in Early Modern England* (Madison: U of Wisconsin P, 1984) 139.

12. Arthur F. Marotti, *Manuscript, Print, and the English Renaissance Lyric* (Ithaca: Cornell UP, 1995).

13. See Robin Robbins, "Poets, Friends and Patrons: Donne and His Circle, Ben and His Tribe," in Hattaway 419–41.

14. Ben Jonson, *The New Inn,* ed. Michael Hattaway (Manchester: Manchester UP, 1984) 4.4.253.

15. George Parfitt, *English Poetry of the Seventeenth Century* (London: Longman, 1992) 28.

16. Don E. Wayne, *Penshurst: The Semiotics of Place and the Poetics of History* (Madison: U of Wisconsin P, 1984).

17. Gary Waller, *The Sidney Family Romance: Mary Wroth, William Herbert and the Early Modern Construction of Gender* (Detroit: Wayne State UP, 1993) 117.

18. Martin Elsky, "Microhistory and Cultural Geography: Ben Jonson's 'To Sir Robert Wroth' and the Absorption of Local Community in the Commonwealth," *Renaissance Quarterly* 53 (2000): 500–28.

19. For a detailed reading of this poem, see Bruce Boehrer, *The Fury of Men's Gulletts: Ben Jonson and the Digestive Canal* (Philadelphia: U of Penn P, 1997) 161–66; Andrew McRae, "'On the Famous Voyage': Ben Jonson and Civic Space," *Literature, Mapping, and the Politics of Space in Early Modern Britain*, ed. Andrew Gordon and Bernhard Klein (Cambridge: Cambridge UP, 2001) 181–203.

20. David Norbrook, *Poetry and Politics in the English Renaissance*. 2d ed. (Oxford: Oxford UP, 2002) 163.

## READING LIST

Boehrer, Bruce. *The Fury of Men's Gullets: Ben Jonson and the Digestive Canal.* Philadelphia: U of Pennsylvania P, 1997.

Butler, Martin. "Ben Jonson and the Limits of Courtly Panegyric." *Culture and Politics in Early Stuart England.* Ed. Kevin Sharpe and Peter Lake. Basingstoke: Macmillan, 1994. 91–115.

Elsky, Martin. "Microhistory and Cultural Geography: Ben Jonson's 'To Sir Robert Wroth' and the Absorption of Local Community in the Commonwealth." *Renaissance Quarterly* 53 (2000): 500–28.

Harp, Richard, and Stanley Stewart, eds. *The Cambridge Companion to Ben Jonson.* Cambridge: Cambridge UP, 2000.

Hattaway, Michael, ed. *A Companion to English Renaissance Literature and Culture.* Oxford: Blackwell, 2000.

Helgerson, Richard. "Ben Jonson." *The Cambridge Companion to English Poetry: Donne to Marvell.* Ed. Thomas N. Corns. Cambridge: Cambridge UP, 1993. 148–70.

McRae, Andrew. "'On the Famous Voyage': Ben Jonson and Civic Space." *Literature, Mapping, and the Politics of Space in Early Modern Britain.* Ed. Andrew Gordon and Bernhard Klein. Cambridge: Cambridge UP, 2001. 181–203.

Marotti, Arthur F. *Manuscript, Print, and the English Renaissance Lyric.* Ithaca: Cornell UP, 1995.

Norbrook, David. *Poetry and Politics in the English Renaissance.* 2d ed. Oxford: Oxford UP, 2002.

Parfitt, George. *English Poetry of the Seventeenth Century.* London: Longman, 1992.

Patterson, Annabel. *Censorship and Interpretation: The Conditions of Writing and Reading in Early Modern England.* Madison: U of Wisconsin P, 1989.

Sharpe, Kevin. *Criticism and Compliment: The Politics of Literature in the England of Charles I.* Cambridge: Cambridge UP, 1987.

Waller, Gary. *The Sidney Family Romance: Mary Wroth, William Herbert and the Early Modern Construction of Gender.* Detroit: Wayne State UP, 1993.

Wayne, Don E. *Penshurst: The Semiotics of Place and the Poetics of History.* Madison: U of Wisconsin P, 1984.

# 24

# George Herbert, God, and King

## Michael Schoenfeldt

George Herbert is a religious poet for readers who hate religious poetry, and for those who love it. He achieves in his devotional verse a rare spiritual authenticity that appeals to devout readers of all religious persuasions, as well as to readers with no ostensible religious inclinations. This is a remarkable accomplishment, particularly since religious language is so prone to sound shrill, fulsome, righteous, or cringing. Herbert's poetry dodges these pitfalls and achieves an uncommon atmosphere of sincerity, in large part by modeling speech to God on speech to social superiors. Herbert's poetry, that is, exhibits a remarkably social relationship to God, sometimes imagining God as a king the speaker is trying to please, sometimes as a friend with whom the speaker shares a vexed if ardent relationship.

Herbert spent most of his creative life writing to one form of authority or another. In this regard, his life was a remarkable preparation for his verse. In his hands, prayers to God and supplications to earthly power both participate in an artful language of courtship. Whether writing to an earthly lord or the Lord, to King James or heaven's King, Herbert allows the strategies of courtly utterance to mingle with the spiritual aspirations of prayer. Herbert was particularly well poised by circumstances to appreciate the nuances of religious and courtly language. He was the younger son of an important, aristocratic family. His elder brother, Edward lord Herbert of Cherbury, served as ambassador to France. His younger brother Henry became master of the revels, in charge of court entertainment. His mother, Magdalen Herbert, was famous for her intelligence and beauty; her funeral sermon was preached by John Donne.

It would have been difficult not to experience the seductions of political ambition in such a family, and Herbert was certainly not immune. His youthful letters to his stepfather Sir John Danvers exude excitement at his growing academic success, as the world of power and position opened up to him. In these letters, Herbert talks in detail about "working the heads" of the university community in his efforts to win the position of university orator, a job that asked its holder to address in Latin all the dignitaries that visited the university. As such, the position combined the arts of the courtier with the skills of a scholar. Herbert tells Danvers that the oratorship is "the finest place in the University," since the orator "writes all the University Letters, makes all the Orations, be it to King Prince or whatever comes to the University," and argues that "this dignity, hath no such earthiness in it, but it may very well be joined with Heaven."[1] His efforts at working the heads won him the job, and Herbert had every reason to think that a spectacular political career awaited him, since the two previous orators had moved from this position to become secretaries of state.

But Herbert did not make that transition, for reasons that are still unclear. Herbert's good friend Nicholas Ferrar suggests in his preface to the first edition of *The Temple* that it was a deliberate choice: "Quitting both his deserts and all the opportunities that he had for worldly preferment, he betook himself to Sanctuaries and Temple of God, choosing rather to serve at Gods Altar, then to seek the honour of State-employments" (*Works* 3). Ferrar asserts that Herbert deliberately abandons state service for divine service. Circumstances, however, suggest a more complicated relationship between these two forms of subordination. One cause may well be a profoundly impolitic oration Herbert gives praising peace at a moment when the nation was ready for war with Spain; it is likely in these politically capricious times that such a politically incorrect utterance would have closed some doors of advancement. In this oration, given in 1623 to a nation eager for war with Spain, Herbert asserts that

> peace is to be preferred to war; for without peace, all life is a storm and the world a desert. In peace, sons bury their father—in war, fathers their sons; in peace, the sick are made whole—in war, even the whole perish; in peace there is safety in the fields—in war, not even within walls.[2]

In addition to this bold declaration of the catastrophic desolation of war, Herbert also castigates those "effeminate Caesars" who "feed themselves daily as if their bodies would not pass at some time into the elements, but into cakes and sweetmeats," and reminds his royal audience that "in that last dissolution there is no distinction of people or prince. [. . .] The vapours from slaves exhaled into the clouds will produce equally loud thunder with the vapours from kings" (Grosart 411). We will never know for sure if Herbert's career assumed a downward trajectory as a result of this bold and occasionally grisly utterance. But we do know that it is his last oration, despite the fact that he retains the position of orator for the next five years. We also know that Herbert was not ordained priest until 1630, seven years later, after which time he had only three short, busy years, marred by almost permanent illness, in which to serve God and church before his death. An old idea about Herbert suggests that all of his religious poetry was written in these last three years. But that is not an idea that this essay will endorse. Rather, I hope to show that Herbert struggled in his poetry, as well as his political career, to arrange the marriage of "earthiness" and "Heaven," that is, to wed his spiritual urges and his political aspirations. The progeny, his sacred verse, exhibits a deliberate assimilation of gritty reality to the most ethereal religious goals.

Like Jesus' parables, Herbert's religious poetry is actively involved in a process of translating into the terms of this world a spiritual message designed to challenge the values of this world. His single volume of posthumously published poetry, *The Temple,* begins with a long poem on proper behavior in and out of church, *The Church-porch,* and concludes with a long prophetic poem following the historical trajectory of the true church to the new world, *The Church-Militant.* In between are the poems for which Herbert is best known—177 of the most emotionally intense and formally accomplished devotional lyrics since the Davidic Psalms. Throughout *The Temple,* Herbert's volume of sacred verse, God's kingship is marked not only by the rarefied pleasures of the Renaissance Court but also of the extreme agonies of the Christian cross. "The Sacrifice," a monologue spoken by the suffering Christ, explores the excruciating political ironies whereby the King of Kings is subject to the scorn of his subjects. In "The Thanksgiving," Herbert's God is the "King of grief," a "King of wounds" (ll. 1, 3). The rule of this monarch is grounded not in pleasure but in suffering. In "Redemption," Herbert's God is a landlord who grants the suits of his tenants even before they ask. In "Unkindnesse," the speaker compares his relationship with God to that of human companionship: "I would not use a friend, as I use Thee" (l. 5). God, he argues, is a greater benefactor than any terrestrial companion could ever be, and yet is treated worse than "my foes" (l. 25). The speaker of "The Odour, 2 Cor. 2. 15" addresses God as "My Master," and longs to be welcomed in turn as "my servant" (ll. 1, 11–12). In the final sublime lyric of *The Temple,* "Love (III)," Herbert's God is a lord who serves his servants, and who feeds his creation with the meat of his own body: "You must sit down, sayes, Love, and taste my meat: / So I did sit and eat" (ll. 17–18). The book traces a complex and uneven trajectory from the profound physical and social suffering of Jesus in "The Sacrifice" to the gracious, sensual feast of love in "Love (III)."

Herbert's reputation is largely that of a poet of sweetness and light, and these are two of his favorite words, but we need to remember that he writes five poems entitled "Affliction" and only three entitled "Love." In the first "Affliction" poem, Herbert invites us to read the poem autobiographically, carefully mapping his experience of a capricious "King" of "pleasures" onto the curve of Herbert's own life (l. 13). He remakes his troubled political career as spiritual autobiography. The poem exemplifies how Herbert can in his poetry at once arraign the apparent injustice of God and indict the spiritual narrowness of his particular speakers. The poem opens with a careful record of the seductive pleasures that ensue from his monarch's initial favor: "When first thou didst entice to thee my heart, / I though the service brave" (ll. 1–2). The speaker describes himself as "argu'd into hopes"; "my thoughts" he proclaims, "reserved / No place for grief or fear" (ll. 15–16). The implicit passivity of the speaker amid this experience of bliss clears the way for a series of bitter accusations when the pleasures wane:

At first thou gav'st me milk and sweetnesse;
    I had my wish and way:
My dayes were straw'd with flow'rs and happinesse;
    There was no moneth but May.
But with my yeares sorrow did twist and grow,
And made a partie unawares for wo. ("Affliction [I]" ll. 19–24)

The suffering is then described with an intensity at least equal to the language depicting pleasure; Herbert imagines suffering so extensive it consumes every fiber of his being:

My flesh began unto my soul in pain,
    Sicknesses cleave my bones;
Consuming agues dwell in ev'ry vein,
    And tune my breath to grones.
Sorrow was all my soul; I scarce believed,
Till grief did tell me roundly, that I lived. ("Affliction [I]" ll. 25–30)

The pangs of acute suffering become the only proof of life.

In those few moments when health returns, moreover, the speaker is punished with other afflictions:

When I got health, thou took'st away my life,
    And more; for my friends die. ("Affliction [I]" ll. 31–32)

The speaker grows progressively accusatory of his monarch, reproaching him for seducing him with pleasures and then torturing him physically with sickness and emotionally with grief. The affliction of the title is total; the speaker is not even allowed the meager comfort of consistent suffering:

> Yet lest perchance I should too happie be
>  In my unhappinesse,
> Turning my purge to food, thou throwest me
>  Into more sicknesses.
> Thus doth thy power crosse-bias me, not making
> Thine own gift good, yet me from my wayes taking. ("Affliction [I]" ll. 49–54)

The speaker imagines that his deity uses him as in a game of bowls, even putting spin on him (the meaning of "crosse-bias") to keep him from going in the direction he wills.

Yet the term "crosse-bias" also underscores the central symbol of Christian suffering and salvation—the cross. The final stanza allows the full force of the speaker's resentment against this apparently very bad employment situation to emerge. The speaker initially tries to achieve a Stoic, uncomplaining response to his terrible treatment: "Yet, though thou troublest me, I must be meek; / In weaknesse must be stout" (ll. 61–62). But the rebellion that has been percolating through the poem's various complaints interrupts this effort to sustain philosophic calm in the face of suffering: "Well, I will change the service, and go seek / Some other master out" (ll. 63–64). In the moment of greatest rebellion, though, the speaker realizes that his monarch is the only king worth serving; he subsequently recoils into submission, asking only that his God grant him a relationship of authentic ardor: "Ah my deare God! Though I am clean forgot, / Let me not love thee, if I love thee not" (ll. 65–66). The accusations do not completely evacuate the terms of his submission—"I am clean forgot" can mean either that he has forgotten himself or that his monarch has forgotten him—but the passionate bond of sincere love renders irrelevant the issues of justice on which the speaker has based his long lament. If his monarch is indeed the figure who suffered the horrible death of crucifixion at the hands of his creatures, the poem suggests, what right has one of those creatures to complain about his comparatively benign afflictions?

"Affliction (I)" demonstrates the refreshing boldness and ardent intimacy of Herbert's addresses to God. One of Herbert's many admirers, the seventeenth-century nonconformist preacher Richard Baxter, describes well the profound immediacy that Herbert attains in his religious verse: "Herbert speaks to God like one that really believeth a God, and whose business in the world is most with God. Heart-work and Heaven work make up his Books."[3] What Baxter admires here is the spiritual legitimacy and emotional precision of Herbert's poetry, the way it stages and anatomizes a gamut of passions from joy to despair to rebellion to repentance.

Herbert is a great poet of rebellion, in large part because his rebellions never feel contrived, even though a recoil into submission is invariably their outcome. Part of the power of "Affliction (I)," and of so many Herbert poems, depends on a developing distinction between Herbert the poet and Herbert the putative speaker of the poem. Whereas Herbert the speaker of "Affliction (I)" continually confuses terrestrial service to a monarch with devotion to the heavenly king, Herbert the poet of course never does. Indeed, one of the ways in which this poem works is through a kind of self-directed irony; the speaker's misguided expectations of material reward, and his self-exculpating effort to translate his monarch's gracious gifts into seductive allurements, reveal the deep limitations of human comprehension of the complex patterns of divine grace. By staging the well-intended foibles of such speakers, Herbert's verse achieves a kind of endearing humility.

Herbert may have learned something about the charms of artful modesty at Court. But he probably learned something about its literary effects through studying the wittily self-deprecating poetry of his kinsman Sir Philip Sidney. Indeed, in the poem "Jordan (II)" Herbert was directly to parody one of Sidney's most self-effacing lyrics. In *Astrophel and Stella* 1 Sidney had mocked his own efforts to express authentic emotion in verse: "Loving in truth, and faine in verse my love to show." The effort becomes progressively frantic, until finally his muse intervenes to mock his misguided efforts: "Biting my trewand pen, beating my self for spite, / Foole said my Muse to me, looke in thy heart and write."[4] Herbert in the conclusion to "Jordan (II)" stages a similar moment of floundering between sincerity and artifice to a rather different end:

> As flames do work and winde, when they ascend,
> So did I weave my self into the sense.
> But while I bustled, I might heare a friend
> Whisper, *How wide is all this long pretence!*
> *There is in love a sweenesse readie penn'd:*
> *Copie out onely that, and save expense.* ("Jordan [II]" ll. 13–18)

Rather than Sidney's Muse, the speaker's divine "friend" intervenes (or does he? the verb is deliberately tentative) to suggest that bustling self-display may not be the best way to perform divine praise. Indeed, in the first "Jordan" poem, Herbert's speaker had wanted to identify himself not with those who value the artifice of "fictions onely and false hair" but with those "Who plainly say, *My God, My King*" (ll. 1, 15). But the plea for a simple poetry collapses on its own complex scaffolding; as we have seen in our reading of "Affliction (I)," "My God, My King" cannot be a specimen of plain speech.

Herbert was one of the most effective English poets at exploring in artful verse the immense difficulty of using human art to showcase God's power. John Donne, by contrast, for all of his remarkable poetic effects, never uses verse to ask if it might be an apt medium for his message. But Herbert asks this question several times, and makes some of his finest poems out of the provisional answers he supplies. He in fact remains divided throughout *The Temple* between his devout wish to give God his best artistic efforts and his awareness of the sinful self-display lurking in such purportedly devout desires. It is difficult to reconcile the mimetic compositional model proposed at the conclusion of "Jordan (II)"—copying out to save expense—with Herbert's promise in "Praise (II)" that "with my utmost art / I will sing thee" (ll. 9–10) or with Herbert's observation in "The Forerunners" that "my God must have my best, ev'n all I had" (l. 18). In "A true Hymne," the speaker argues that the phrase "*My joy my life, my crown*" can, "If truly said, [. . .] take part / Among the best in art," suggesting that what really matters is the sincerity of the utterance, not its aesthetic embellishments (ll. 1, 7–8).

Similarly, in "The Forerunners," Herbert says of the purposefully prosaic phrase *"Thou art still my God"* that God "will be pleased with that dittie; / And if I please him, I write fine and wittie" (ll. 10–12). In these intentionally clunky, cloying lines, in a poem that contemplates the loss of poetic power through age, Herbert pushes to its endpoint the principle that pleasing God rather than writing well is ultimately what matters. If this really is true, then repeating the phrase "thou art still my God" over and over is an act of equal value to the most highly wrought utterance.

Yet Herbert never relinquishes the pursuit of aesthetic accomplishment, although he frequently explores how it chafes against his overt goal of divine praise. Rather, he uses highly wrought lyrics to gesture toward the goal of simplicity and plainness. Indeed, Herbert has a fuller and more inventive sense of the resources of lyric form than any previous writer in English. In a variety of ingenious ways, he manages to make form an integral conceptual part of the poem. The poems of *The Temple* constitute a virtual anthology of the possibilities of formal innovation in the period. Herbert regularly uses rhyme to indicate a sense of spiritual harmony, and a lack of rhyme to designate devotional torpor. In the poem "Deniall," for example, Herbert uses a jagged left margin and the failure of the last line of each stanza to rhyme to suggest the dashed expectations the poem describes:

> When my devotions could not pierce
>   Thy silent eares;
> Then was my heart broken, as was my verse:
>   My breast was full of fears
>     And disorder:
>
> My bent thoughts, like a brittle bow,
>   Did flie asunder:
> Each took his way; some would to pleasures go,
>   Some to the warres and thunder
>     Of alarms. ("Deniall" ll. 1–10)

The poem boldly depicts a kind of internal fracture but also includes a remarkable challenge to the justice of its divine audience: "O that thou shouldst give dust a tongue / To cry to thee, / And then not hear it crying!" (ll. 16–18). But the last stanza, the speaker finds his heart-felt wish to be heard is granted even as it is uttered:

> O cheer and tune my heartlesse breast,
>   Deferre not time:
> That so thy favours granting my request,
>   They and my minde may chime,
>     And mend my ryme. ("Deniall" ll. 26–30)

In this, poem, Herbert at once indicates the way that spiritual suffering resists formal expression and demonstrates the manner in which aesthetic order can represent spiritual harmony.

Herbert's remarkable poem of spiritual rebellion, "The Collar," takes this aesthetic principle linking aesthetic and spiritual order as far as it would go for the next three hundred years of literary history. This poem, which begins brilliantly in a violent gesture of

pent-up frustration, approaches what the twentieth century would term free verse in its
studiedly uneven metrics and distended rhymes:

> I struck the board, and cry'd, No more.
>     I will abroad.
> What? Shall I ever sign and pine?
> My lines and life are free; free as the rode,
>     Loose as the winde, as large as store.
>         Shall I be still in suit?
>     Have I no harvest but a thorn
>     To let me bloud, and not restore
> What I have lost with cordiall fruit?
>         Sure there was wine
> Before my sighs did drie it: there was corn
>     Before my tears did drown it.
> Is the yeare onely lost to me?
>     Have I no bayes to crown it?
> No flowers, no garlands gay? All blasted?
>     All wasted? ("The Collar" ll. 1–16)

This poem, which was a favorite of Robert Oppenheimer's (the guiding force behind the
atom bomb), manages a remarkable glimmer of abstruse order amid apparent chaos.
As Joseph Summers suggests, the poem offers "a formalized picture of chaos."[5] Indeed,
every line in the poem rhymes, although some rhymes are separated by as much as
eighteen lines. As the poem grows progressively more frantic, the speaker works himself into a full-fledged rebellion against such unprofitable service, when suddenly a
calm voice intervenes to restore order to the poem and the speaker:

> But as I rav'd and grew more fierce and wilde
>     At every word,
> Me thoughts I heard one calling, *Child!*
>     And I reply'd, *My Lord.* ("The Collar" ll. 33–36)

As in "Jordan (II)," a voice that emerges somewhere between divinity and interiority intervenes to comment critically on the behavior of a bustling human; as in "Deniall," a
poem of formal disorder resolves itself with metrical relief in its conclusion. Fascinat-
ingly, though, "word" and "Lord" are slant rather than exact rhymes, as if the energies
of rebellion have not yet been fully dissipated in the poem's sedate yet sublime conclusion. Rather, they are absorbed in the gracious combination of judgment (you are behaving like a child) and acceptance (you are a child of mine) suffusing the single word
("child") whispered by the divine voice, and the complex blend of deference and affection present in the human response ("my lord"). Unlike "Affliction (I)" which directly
addresses a silent divine audience, "The Collar" is a soliloquy overheard, and interrupted, by God. Eminently faithful to the experience of unfaithfulness, the poem is remarkable for the ferocity of its rebellion and the authenticity of its submission. It does
this in large part by finding the perfect formal vehicle for each action.

Herbert, though, could also use formal composition to depict his ideal of spiritual
order. In "The Altar," the first lyric confronting the reader of the central section of

*The Temple,* Herbert fashions a poem whose shape is designed to advertise the abilities of its human maker:

A broken ALTAR, Lord, thy servant reares,
Made of a heart, and cemented with teares:
  Whose parts are as thy hand did fram'
  No workmans tool hath touch'd the same.
      A   HEART   alone
      Is   such   a   stone,
      As   nothing   but
      Thy pow'r doth cut.
      Wherefore each part
      Of  my  hard  heart
      Meets in this frame,
      To praise thy Name:
  That, if I chance to hold my peace,
  These stones to praise thee may not cease.
O let thy blessed SACRIFICE be mine,
And sanctifie this ALTAR to be thine.

Tellingly, though, the poem not only represents the place in a church where sacrifices to God are rendered but also assumes the form of a giant capital "I." Self-sacrifice, Herbert suggests, invariably occurs in the same medium as self-display.

In "Easter-wings," by contrast, Herbert uses varied line lengths to delineate the alternate current of enrichment and impoverishment that powers both Christian history and the individual Christian's experience:

Lord, who createdst man in wealth and store,
  Though foolishly he lost the same,
    Decaying more and more,
      Till he became
        Most poore:
        With thee
      O let me rise
    As larks, harmoniously,
  And sing this day they victories:
Then shall the fall further the flight in me.

  My tender age in sorrow did beginne:
  And still with sicknesses and shame
    Thou didst so punish sinne,
      That I became
        Most thinne.
        With thee
      Let me combine
    And feel this day thy victorie:
  For, if I imp my wing on thine,
Affliction shall advance the flight in me.

The curious shape may be intended to represent wings; but more significantly, Herbert laminates the expansion and contraction that produces flight onto the patterns of Christian existence, so that the spiritual necessity of alternating "affliction" and "wealth" can be made visible.

Herbert not only produces fresh and original lyric shapes in poetry, but can also take a conventional form and invigorate it through formal ingenuity. He writes a poem on the mysterious speech which is prayer—"Prayer (I)"—but in the process composes a sonnet that traverses the universe, and human history, without using an active verb:

> Prayer the Churches banquet, Angels age,
>> God breath in man returning to his birth,
>> The soul in paraphrase, heart in pilgrimage,
> The Christian plummet sounding heav'n and earth;
> Engine against th'Almightie, sinners towre,
>> Reversed thunder, Christ-side-piercing spear,
>> The six-daies world transposing in an houre,
> A kinde of tune, which all things heare and fear;
> Softnesse, and peace, and joy, and love, and blisse,
>> Exalted Manna, gladnesse of the best,
>> Heaven in ordinarie, man well drest
> The milkie way, the bird of Paradise,
>> Church-bels beyond the starres heard, the souls bloud,
>> The land of spices; something understood.

Brilliantly layering phrase upon phrase, the poem describes prayer as a mysterious blend of violence, sensuality, condescension, and comprehension. The poem's remarkable accomplishment of having plumbed the temporal and spatial coordinates of the universe without a transitive verb dramatizes the remarkable intuition posited in the poem's last two words.

The sonnet "Redemption" works very differently, aspiring to narrate the central spiritual shift of human history in just fourteen lines. The poem tells the story of a tenant who feels his rent is too high, and seeks out his landlord for renegotiation:

> Having been tenant long to a rich Lord,
>> Not thriving, I resolved to be bold,
>> And make a suit unto him, to afford
> A new small-rented lease, and cancel th'old.
> In heaven at his manour I him sought:
>> They told me there, that he was lately gone
>> About some land, which he had dearly bought
> Long since on earth, to take possession.
> I straight return'd, and knowing his great birth,
>> Sought him accordingly in great resorts;
>> In cities, theatres, gardens, parks, and courts:
> At length I heard a ragged noise and mirth
>> Of theeves and murderers: there I him espied,
>> Who straight, *Your suit is granted*, said, & died.

The poem manages to explain the mysterious movement from the Old Testament to the New in terms drawn from the gritty materials of terrestrial human experience. Remarkably, the audacious speaker never even gets to ask for a new lease, as his petition is granted before it is made. His profound misunderstandings of his "rich Lord"—looking for him in "great resorts" rather than amid "theeves and murderers"—signal the myriad ways that Christian salvation resists human comprehension. "Redemption," being bought back from slavery, is in this poem achieved completely free of human merit or desire; it is granted by the gracious last will and testament of the dying savior.

As is clear in "Redemption," Herbert's titles are critical to understanding his poems; only through the title are we able to identify the full religious significance of this wonderful parable. Herbert in fact makes the titles of his poems a more central part of his poetry than any previous poet in English.[6] The poem "The Collar" provides another marvelous example of Herbert's cleverness with titles. The title is a four-part pun that designates at once the clerical collar, an item of constriction, the "caller" who speaks in the last four lines, and "choler," the humoral fluid thought to cause anger. Herbert's poem "The Pulley," named after a device for raising things by pulling downward, never mentions its titular source but allows that source to structure and explain the poem:

> When God at first made man,
> Having a glasse of blessings standing by;
> Let us (said he) poure on him all we can:
> Let the worlds riches, which dispersed lie,
>     Contract into a span.
>
> So strength first made a way;
> Then beautie flow'd, then wisdome, honour, pleasure:
> When almost all was out, God made a stay,
> Perceiving that alone of all his treasure
>     Rest in the bottome lay.
>
> For if I should (said he)
> Bestow this jewell also on my creature,
> He would adore my gifts in stead of me,
> And rest in Nature, not the God of Nature:
>     So both should losers be.
>
> Yet let him keep the rest,
> But keep them with repining restlesnesse:
> Let him be rich and wearie, that at least,
> If goodnesse leade him not, yet wearinesse
>     May tosse him to my breast.

This charming parable, which Christianizes the story of Pandora's box in order to explain humanity's abiding spiritual agitation, demonstrates that even God's refusal of certain gifts is a kind of beneficence, just as a pulley transforms downward pull into upward lift. The proliferating puns on "rest," meaning both "repose" and "whatever is left," demonstrate a mutually necessary link between divine munificence and human discontent. Had God granted humans the gift of repose, Herbert suggests, they would ultimately be the poorer because they would never turn to God.

Herbert's abiding concern with form extends to the shape of the larger collection. *The Temple* is one of the most carefully constructed volumes of poetry published in its day. It is scrupulously structured as a book that guides and shapes a reader's experience. After a "Dedication" to God, the volume begins with a long poem of advice on behavior in the world and in church—"The Church-porch." This is followed by "Superliminare," a poem welcoming the reader to "approach and taste / The churches mysticall repast" (ll. 3–4). A group of poems ensue that talk loudly to each other in their effort to position the human worshiper in relation to Jesus' sacrifice—"The Altar," "The Sacrifice," "The Thanksgiving," "The Reprisall." In the second of two sonnets extolling "The H. Scriptures," Herbert praises the remarkable cross-referential unity of the Bible: "This verse marks that, and both do make a motion / Unto a third, that ten leaves off doth lie" (ll. 5–6). In his collection of sacred verse, Herbert aspired to produce a similar form of tacit organization. The volume concludes deliberately with poems pointing to the four last things—"Death," "Doomsday," "Judgment," "Heaven." Remarkably, though, the last lyric in *The Temple,* and the last poem except for the long prophetic "Church-Militant," is the sublime "Love (III)."

Herbert's sense of formal closure is attested by the fact that he concludes his volume of lyric verse with this remarkable poem—"Love (III)." The French mystic Simone Weil termed it "le plus beau poéme du monde."[7] If there is a more beautiful poem, I don't know it. The poem gently folds the soul's reception of the Eucharist into heaven's reception of the soul, adumbrating both spiritual levels of meaning via a stunningly mundane and primal experience. The speaker enters this poem like a dusty traveler; divine love is literally incarnated as the Lord of Hosts, welcoming reluctant humanity with ravishing courtesy to a feast of its own flesh:

> Love bade me welcome: yet my soul drew back,
>     Guiltie of dust and sinne.
> But quick-ey'd Love, observing me grow slack
>     From my first entrance in,
> Drew nearer to me, sweetly questioning,
>     If I lack'd any thing.
>
> A guest, I answer'd, worthy to be here:
>     Love said, You shall be he.
> I the unkinde, ungratefull? Ah my deare,
>     I cannot look on thee.
> Love took my hand, and smiling did reply,
>     Who made the eyes but I?
>
> Truth Lord, but I have marr'd them: let my shame
>     Go where it doth deserve.
> And know you not, sayes Love, who bore the blame?
>     My deare, then I will serve.
> You must sit down, sayes Love, and taste my meat:
>     So I did sit and eat.

Although sentenced to "repining restlessness" in "The Pulley," humanity is here commanded to "sit and eat," as if the long-sought rest and much-hungered-for nourishment pursued throughout *The Temple* were finally to be granted.

A gentle eroticism, moreover, suffuses the encounter, rendering the sensuality of love incarnate in the most rudimentary of terms. Since the age of sixteen, when he sent two sonnets to his mother, Herbert had been concerned with the relationship between sacred and secular love. In those poems he castigates secular love poets for praising "that, which one day Worms may chance refuse" rather than God (*Works* 206). But in "Love (III)" the differences between sacred and secular love dissolve in a work of consummate eroticism. "Love" is addressed both as "Lord" and "My dear," and progressively closes the distance between the speaker and the host, moving from welcome to hand-taking to entering the body as food. No greater intimacy is possible. The most quotidian of encounters is expressed in the simplest of lexicons, and yet the result is a confrontation with the deepest mysteries of incarnate love.

For all of its courtly splendor and aesthetic accomplishment, then, Herbert's poetry is also marked by a fastidious attention to the everyday and the mundane. In *The Country Parson,* the manual of conduct for rural clergy that Herbert was working on when he died, he described how "things of ordinary use are not only to serve in the way of drudgery, but to be washed and cleansed and serve for lights even of heavenly truths" (*Works* 257). In the poem "The Elixir," Herbert identifies this activity as the effort to make "drudgerie divine" (l. 18). Charles Taylor has characterized the "affirmation of everyday life as more than profane, as itself hallowed and in no way second class" as central to the revolution that was Protestantism.[8] Herbert's poetry is one of the first fruits of this revolutionary idea that everyday life might be made spiritually sanctified and dramatically enthralling.

There is in Herbert a fruitful and unresolved tension between the courtly and the quotidian, between prized elegance and purposeful plainness. The title of the poem "Sion" puns on "sighing," the aspirant cry of inarticulate grief, and Mount Zion, the hill in Jersusalem on which the Jews built the Temple. Herbert pointedly contrasts the construction of magnificent edifices with the inglorious utterance of authentic emotion:

Lord, with what glorie wast thou serv'd of old,
When Solomons temple stood and flourished!
    Where most things were of purest gold;
    The wood was all embellished
With flowers and carvings, mystically and rare:
All show'd the builders, crav'd the seers care.

Yet all this glorie, all this pomp and state
Did not affect thee much, was not thy aim;
    Something there was, that sow'd debate:
    Wherefore thou quitt'st thy ancient claim:
And now thy Architecture meets with sinne;
For all thy frame and fabrick is within.

There thou art struggling with a peevish heart,
Which sometimes crosseth thee, thou sometimes it:
   The fight is hard on either part.
   Great God doth fight, he doth submit.
All Solomons sea of brasse and world of stone
Is not so deare to thee as one good grone. ("Sion" ll. 1–18)

Wistful nostalgia for the glorious modes of Old Testament architecture gives way to a Christian interior design composed of spiritual struggle and intense emotion. Herbert suggests that the Christian God prefers one moment of garbled emotional authenticity to the most elaborate and costly temple imaginable. He explains this in part by recourse to the physics of the two modes of worship: where temples are ponderous and heavy, groans are

   quick, and full of wings,
And all their motions upward be:
And ever as they mount, like larks they sing;
   The note is sad, yet musick for a King. ("Sion" ll. 21–24)

Herbert's remarkable lyric accomplishment is the construction of his own temple of devotion, in which he manages to render the most mundane matters of mortal existence into music and forms fit for a terrestrial, or a heavenly, king.

## NOTES

1. *Works of George Herbert,* ed. F. E. Hutchinson (Oxford: Clarendon P, 1941) 369–70. All subsequent references to Herbert's works are from this edition unless otherwise indicated.
2. *Complete Works in Verse and Prose of George Herbert,* ed. A. B. Grosart, 3 vols. (London, 1874) 3.403–04.
3. Richard Baxter, *Poetical Fragments: Heart Imployment with God and It Self* (London, 1681), "The Epistle To The Reader," sigs A7–A7v; qtd. in Robert H. Ray, *The Herbert Allusion Book: Allusions to George Herbert in the Seventeenth Century, Studies in Philology* 83 (1986): 131–32.
4. Sir Philip Sidney, *Astrophil and Stella* 1, qtd. from *The Penguin Book of Renaissance Verse,* ed. David Norbrook (Harmonsworth: Penguin, 1992) 199–200.
5. Joseph Summers, *George Herbert: His Religion and Art* (Cambridge: Harvard UP, 1954) 90. On Robert Oppenheimer's admiration for Herbert, and for "The Collar" in particular (he considered having it read at his funeral), see Freeman Dyson, *Disturbing the Universe* (New York: Harper and Row, 1979) 81–83.
6. See Anne Ferry, *The Art of Naming* (Chicago: U of Chicago P, 1988).
7. Cited in Jean Mambrino, "Simone Weil et George Herbert," *Etudes* 340 (1974): 250.
8. Charles Taylor, *Sources of the Self: The Making of the Modern Identity* (Cambridge: Harvard UP, 1989), 218.

## READING LIST

Bloch, Chana. *Spelling the Word: George Herbert and the Bible.* Berkeley: U of California P, 1985.

Fish, Stanley. *The Living Temple: George Herbert and Catechizing.* Berkeley: U of California P, 1978.

Lewalski, Barbara Kiefer. *Protestant Poetics and the Seventeenth-Century Religious Lyric.* Princeton: Princeton UP, 1979.

Malcolmson, Cristina. *Heart-Work: George Herbert and the Protestant Ethic.* Stanford: Stanford UP, 1999.

Martz, Louis L. *The Poetry of Meditation: A Study in English Religious Literature of the Seventeenth Century.* Rev. ed. New Haven: Yale UP, 1962.

Schoenfeldt, Michael. *Prayer and Power: George Herbert and Renaissance Courtship.* Chicago: U of Chicago P, 1991.

Stein, Arnold. *George Herbert's Lyrics.* Baltimore: Johns Hopkins UP, 1968.

Strier, Richard. *Love Known: Theology and Experience in George Herbert's Poetry.* Chicago: U of Chicago P, 1983.

Summers, Joseph. *George Herbert: His Religion and Art.* Cambridge: Harvard UP, 1954.

Tuve, Rosemond. *A Reading of George Herbert.* Chicago: U of Chicago P, 1952.

Vendler, Helen. *The Poetry of George Herbert.* Cambridge: Harvard UP, 1975.

# 25

# Crashaw and Religious Bias in the Literary Canon

## Lowell Gallagher

Richard Crashaw's place in the canon of English devotional poetry is secure, but a quick glance at critical literature on the poet will tell you that Crashaw's poems also appear to be a guilty pleasure. As the proverb says, "No good deed goes unpunished." So, too, praise of Crashaw's iridescent imagery and keen spiritual instinct often goes hand in glove with consternation (or secret amusement) at the poems' apparent lapses in decorum. Take, for example, the headnote on Crashaw in the sixth edition of *The Norton Anthology of English Literature* (1993). While he earns admiration for his "consuming religious passion," Crashaw nonetheless stands for "phantasmagoria, a blurring together of erotic and spiritual, tortured and ecstatic, infantile and sadistic themes" (1389). Crashaw's poems, we are told, all too often indulge in a taste for the "grotesque" and the "perverse" (1389). This essay spells out the underlying reasons for Crashaw's ambivalent reception.

The *Norton*'s judgment points up the special challenge Crashaw's poetry presents to readers. You will find both beauty and strangeness in Crashaw's lines (as in most seventeenth-century poetry), but when you turn to studies on Crashaw for help in appreciating the poet's manner of combining the beautiful and the strange, you are likely to find something of a puzzle. Analytical guidelines are often laced with disapproving terms largely left unexplained. The lesson to be learned from the *Norton*—a typical example—is not that the anthology gets Crashaw wrong in some absolute sense, but rather that its seeming blindness to the promptings for its use of provocative language does nothing to help readers understand how the casual use of expressions like "grotesque" and "perverse," not to mention the corresponding note of mingled contempt and condescension, is itself a learned response in Crashaw criticism. To grasp Crashaw's accomplishment and better understand his place in the canon, we need to take stock of the ways in which critical responses to Crashaw became entangled in the vexed history of religious antagonism in English literary tradition.

Crashaw lived in exciting times, times of religious, social, and literary ferment, and his poems reflect this turbulence. Before looking at a sample of poems, however, I want to consider how two biographical details came to provide the interpretive key to his poetry. The son of a noted Puritan preacher, Crashaw had converted to Roman Catholicism near the end of his life, probably in 1645. And he had died, four years later, in Loreto, Italy, the pilgrimage site renowned throughout the Catholic (or "Romanist") world for the miraculous shrine maintained there by the Jesuits, the Santa Casa, legendary house of the Virgin's birth and Annunciation. Two working premises of cultural history explain why these events might hold more than merely biographical interest: (1) the formation of literary canons is closely allied to the project of nation-building; and (2) the Tudor-Stuart period marked the beginning of an unstinting collective ambition to secure the dual function of the English literary canon, as material sign of a fundamentally, if not exclusively, English Protestant polity, and as a visibly Protestant resource for the edification of national character. From such a vantage point, Crashaw's conversion and exile were not likely to be taken neutrally.

Signs of anti-Catholic bias toward Crashaw, however, did not appear overnight. For several decades after his death in 1649, his poetry was held in high esteem: he was the "other Herbert."[1] By the end of the seventeenth century, seven editions of his poetry had appeared, and an important eighteenth-century anthology, Robert Anderson's *Complete Edition of the Poets of Great Britain,* even declared Crashaw's preeminence over Herbert. Crashaw, wrote Anderson, was "infinitely superior [. . .] in sublimity and imagination" (Roberts 7). Similarly appreciative gestures can be found in the several Crashaw editions and commentaries published in the Romantic and Victorian eras, so much so that the collaborative interests of nineteenth-century readers and editors may fairly be said to have validated Crashaw's passport into the canon.

Let's take a closer look. Alexander B. Grosart's critical edition (1872) sounded an already well-rehearsed note when it found in Crashaw's "imaginative sensuousness" an instinct "so emotional as almost always to tremble into feeling" (Roberts 12). Nor was it a stretch for Crashaw to be considered a Romantic poet *manqué,* particularly in view of the alluring blend of metrical ingenuity and lush imagery to be found, and enjoyed, in poems like "Musicks Duell," with its clever verbal echoes of a musical contest between nightingale and lutenist. Yet to name Crashaw the "Christian Shelley," as George Gilfillan did in his mid-century edition, betrayed the suspicion that the poet apt to "tremble into feeling" was also somehow *out of place,* both in the canon of seventeenth-century poetry and, more broadly, on the map of the dominant culture in which Crashaw lived and wrote (Roberts 12). When William Hazlitt in 1820 found incriminating evidence in Crashaw's poetry of a man who had been "fascinated by the glittering bait of Popery," and when, in the same year, the critic Henry Southern found it necessary to temper his praise of Crashaw's technical skill and devotional fervor with the withering comment that many poems were disfigured by imagery "so gaudy and flowery, as to be disgusting to the simpler taste of a good protestant," both critics were giving testimony to the growing ambivalence with which the concluding events of Crashaw's life were received by the arbiters of mainstream critical taste (Roberts 10). Crashaw's conversion to "popery" had not simply left "some little blemish upon his holiness," as an eighteenth-century biographical dictionary reported (Roberts 8). It had also provided the rationale for judging his poetry defective.

Warning up ahead: the archive of Crashaw criticism has hallucinogenic properties. It is hard to tell which impression comes first: that the poems' extravagances can be accounted for by being treated as symptoms of the poet's tendency toward a "Catholic" and "gaudy" sensibility—a tendency supposedly confirmed by Crashaw's eventual conversion—or that English models of poetic decorum carry an ingrained anti-Catholic bias that works like a color gel applied to a camera lens, inducing spontaneous perception of Crashaw's "grotesque" and "perverse" style. In the same vein, Crashaw's perceived virtues—for starters, his arresting depictions of devotional rapture or ecstasy—seem genetically linked to his seeming deficiencies. High on the list: the lack of Donne's intellectual rigor and a fondness for outlandish imagery hard to find in Herbert. In the words of a recent diagnostic, "the extent to which religious prejudice influenced literary judgments about Crashaw's poetry in the nineteenth century—and continues to shape critical opinion—cannot be overestimated" (Roberts 10).

That said, specialized Crashaw studies in the twentieth century have encouraged scholars to consider more openly how religious bias (and other kinds, too) may have promoted distorted and reductive views of the often fluid connections between national, religious, and literary cultures in Crashaw's day. Recent anthologies show signs of the inroads made by the effort to resist pigeonholing judgments. The revised seventh edition of the *Norton* offers on the whole a more balanced and nuanced picture of Crashaw's life and work than the earlier edition, but you still have to navigate carefully, because mixed signals remain. For example, it is good to be reminded of Crashaw's nearly lifelong identification with the Anglican establishment, including his education at Pembroke College, Cambridge (a world more "High Church" than Puritan), and the fellowship he held at nearby Peterhouse (a college profoundly marked by the Romanist-leaning spirituality of the patriarch of the Anglican establishment, William Laud).[2] Not least, Crashaw's vocation to the Anglican priesthood is also duly noted. Curiously, though, the description fails to mention the dovetailing of Anglican and Romanist devotional practices during Crashaw's lifetime. Imagine yourself in the chapel at Peterhouse, surrounded by religious paintings of saints and the Virgin Mary, stained-glass windows, carved angels, crucifixes with effigies of the body of Jesus. All delirious trappings of popery—from a Puritan perspective. In sum, the material texture of Crashaw's world testifies to a neighborly relation between Anglican and Romanist confessions, borne out by shared attachment to the devotional objects and rituals of the pre-Reformation church.[3]

Nevertheless, the revised *Norton* rehearses the commonplace that Crashaw's "attraction to Roman Catholicism was a natural expression of his temperament," while it also endorses an even older proposal, going back to the seventeenth century: "without the catalyst of the Civil War he might not have converted" (1629). The latter conjecture acknowledges the political sway of the Puritan faction—and the demise of conservative Anglicanism—at the outbreak of the Civil War, in the years immediately preceding Crashaw's conversion. Yet the parts of the picture don't quite add up. While the anthology distances itself from the default attitude of suspicion toward all things "popish," shadowed ambivalence toward Crashaw's Catholicism remains, in the sense that his Catholicism is treated, in one breath, as a "natural" trait and as something approaching a forced choice, deeply contingent on the mechanics of a political endgame. Imagine Crashaw's different confessional identities, his devotional habits, his Englishness, and his aesthetic sensibility as colored areas on a map. You would see a floating archipelago.

If the history of the critical reception of Crashaw teaches us anything, it is that one of the distinct challenges of reading Crashaw's poetry comes from observing its migratory flight between fixed and fluid notions of confessional identity, poetic craft, and literary reputation. The revised *Norton* is therefore right, I think, to call Crashaw a poet of exile, though the point is apt in more ways than the anthology recognizes. The *Norton* uses the word to refer to the upheavals of the Civil War, which led to a chain of exiles: the retreat of Queen Henrietta Maria, wife of Charles I, and her Court to Paris; Crashaw's brief refuge there after the parliamentary Puritans' uprooting of the Laudian community at Cambridge; and then, with time running out, the months of quasi-nomadic wandering before his appointment to the post of canon (a priest in residence) at the Cathedral of the Santa Casa in Loreto. Perhaps Crashaw himself appreciated the irony of having found a home, finally, next to an edifice hallowed for its miraculous flight, or exodus, under angels' wings from Palestine to the Adriatic coast.

If there is irony here, there is also a pattern that only hindsight reveals. The arc of Crashaw's life and poetic career spells out surprising kinships between themes of exodus, exile, and ecstasy—all words to describe the experience of being out of place. While on fellowship at Peterhouse, for example, he found a spiritual home at Little Gidding, the Anglican hermitage most often associated in literary history with George Herbert. From his pulpit at Little St. Mary's Church, near Peterhouse, Crashaw delivered sermons reputed to have "ravished more like Poems [. . .] scattering not so much Sentences as Ecstasies."[4] And he wrote poems whose subject matter and technical range defy restrictive notions of what it might mean to be at once English and Protestant: Marian devotions, Eucharistic songs, imitations of innovative Spanish and Italian poets, suave meditations on biblical saints (Mary Magdalene) as well as modern—and Catholic—ones (Teresa of Avila).

Instead of resisting the view that Crashaw cuts a strangely exilic figure in the literary canon, then, we should embrace it. The next task is to consider how some of the key critical concepts in Crashaw scholarship can also be nudged out of place—made to work against the grain of the partisan and reductive uses to which they have been put. I want to focus on two terms that have regularly framed modern discussions of Crashaw's historical context and poetic style: "Counter Reformation" and "baroque." The first term generally refers to the multilateral program of reform in the Roman Catholic world, which was supervised by the Council of Trent in the decades following the Protestant Reformation. The oppositional cast to the term "Counter Reformation" has encouraged a narrow view of the Tridentine spirit, seeing it as an essentially militant reaction to the widespread changes introduced by the Reformation into the rhythms of Christian thought and practice. This view tends to discount the ways in which the Counter Reformation belonged to an ongoing process of innovation and conservation which began before the Reformation, in the late medieval world. This view also encourages the received impression of the Tridentine world's repressive and bureaucratically meddlesome climate. As it happens, you don't have to look far. Think of the Roman Inquisition's coercive actions against heretics and the Vatican's implementation of the notorious Index of Forbidden Books, which dictated restrictive supervision of book publication in matters pertaining to questions of faith and biblical interpretation, as well as to new forms of knowledge that might challenge the authority of scripture. Galileo's condemnation by the Inquisition in 1633 would not be your first line of defense against the argument that Trent was animated by a powerfully reactionary spirit.

But to view matters from this perspective alone distorts the larger picture. The council itself was not a bureaucratic monolith. Its sessions, conducted sporadically over close to twenty years (1545–63), were disrupted by social and political upheavals (plague as well as recurrent conflicts with the imperialist maneuvers of the Hapsburgs). Moreover, no master plan guided the council's reforms.[5] In the course of its sessions, numerous traditional doctrines were reinforced (especially concerning belief in the presence of God in the Eucharist and in the mutually participatory role of human will and divine providence in the justification of souls). Significant expansion of the infrastructure of the church helped create an institutional edifice that was as much a network of interactive regions, under the supervision of bishops, as a centralized disciplinary regime. New religious orders that arose in the space of a few decades before and after the council's sessions produced several different models of pastoral as well as missionary practice, spiritual edification, and educational reform, for Catholic laity and clergy alike. (The spectrum included Jesuits, Capuchins, Discalced Carmelites, Ursulines, and Oratorians, to name but a few.) Though vernacular Bibles were discouraged, Tridentine reforms actively promoted the publication of catechisms and a wide range of devotional protocols. The rhythms of piety after Trent were indeed re-formed by the widespread use of new meditative manuals (like the Jesuit Ignatius Loyola's *Spiritual Exercises*) as well as established ones (Thomas à Kempis' *Imitation of Christ*); by the revitalized practice of the Rosary and observance of traditional feast days like Corpus Christi; and by the promotion of devotional reading of saints' lives, Marian veneration, and pilgrimages to Marian shrines, like Loreto.

The practices just mentioned were also part of an ambitious program to rehabilitate the devotional use of images, in clear opposition to the iconoclasm that had taken root in the Protestant world.[6] In the decades after Trent, numerous manuals of instruction for the devotional use of images and sacramental objects issued from Catholic presses. The adversarial and polemical edge exhibited by many of these texts, however, is hard to distinguish from the tactics used in Protestant accounts of the spiritual danger of idolatrous images. And no wonder. The debate over images across the Protestant-Catholic divide spoke to a shared conviction that there could be only one "true church" and to a shared ambition to isolate contaminating agents. Differences were keenly felt, but both sides spoke the same language, and that language found its moorings in the Old Testament story of rival brothers: Jacob and Esau, sons of Rebecca and Isaac (Gen. 27–36). So, too, the story of the divided Christian church (Reformation/Counter Reformation) was filled with episodes of territorial skirmishes, not simply because of declared antagonisms between rival churches (typically in matters of theological doctrine and institutional organization), but because of shifting zones of resemblance and proximity (notably in the practice of piety).

It is important to recognize, then, that the term "Counter Reformation" presents only one side of the reformist impulse in the Catholic world. In recent years, many church historians have taken up the term proposed by John W. O'Malley—"early modern Catholicism"—not as a wholesale substitute for the earlier name, but as a corrective complement that avoids reductive and polemical connotations.[7] It may be even more useful to speak of "early modern *Catholicisms*." This is not to suggest that Roman Catholicism after Trent gave rise to multiple denominations or communities of faith, as in Protestantism. Rather, the plural noun emphasizes the several ways that Catholicism was being practiced, under the canopy of doctrinal uniformity. As already noted, the practice of piety, in particular, encompassed elements that also crossed the Protestant-Catholic divide. Thinking of "Catholicisms" as a word with relatively porous boundaries helps us understand how there might be no worrisome contradiction in the evidence that the widespread popularity of a Jesuit book of meditations—the Ignatian *Exercises*—was due to the manual's use in Protestant as well as Catholic households. So, too, the colorful ambiance of Crashaw's chapel at Peterhouse does not indicate crypto-Romanism. Instead, it testifies to a strain within the Anglican establishment that sought to repossess aspects of Catholic spirituality, and the gesture was one part inheritance, one part theft: this was the legacy of Jacob, the younger son of Isaac, seeking the blessings of the past. Further, Crashaw's journey from Cambridge to Loreto demonstrates the degree to which diverse facets of confessional identity—devotional, pragmatic, doctrinal, political—belonged to a living practice acutely responsive to contrasting aspects of the Christian drama. No single element could be made to stand for a static conception of a unified whole. The same could be said for Crashaw's poetry.

The word that best describes the dynamic energy in Crashaw's poetry is "baroque." The term, it must be said, has had a vexed history as a critical concept. The revised *Norton* suggests some of the reasons for this. Baroque usefully summarizes the "poetics of the Catholic Counter-Reformation" and refers in particular to the post-Tridentine world's enthusiastic development of the late medieval taste for "sensuous metaphors" to represent "spiritual themes and objects" (1629). Critical ambivalence toward the concept may owe more than it would care to admit to residual religious prejudice against "Catholic" devices. Be that as it may, baroque sensibility is deliberately provocative because of its drive to "transcend the limits of each genre or medium" (1629). One consequence of this impulse is that the concept has become vulnerable to the charge of being too vague to serve as a reliable analytical tool. Anything considered "over the top" can be slurred simply be being called "baroque."

In at least one respect, however, the apparent fuzziness of the term can enhance rather than limit understanding of Crashaw's poetic project. Whether used to refer to poetry, painting, or sculpture, "baroque" typically stands for dazzling and arresting spectacle, achieved through virtuoso displays of paradox, catachresis (mixed metaphor), and *chiaroscuro* (light and shadow) effects. An illuminating comparison of baroque sensibility and the more sedate values associated with classical taste appeared in Marshall Brown's 1982 account of one of the landmark discussions of the baroque, Heinrich Wölfflin's *Principles of Art History* (1932). According to Brown, Wölfflin's own study actually does what it describes. In fact, it cannot help doing so, for what Wölfflin sees is that "history is always moving toward the baroque and away from the classic," and that, accordingly, *"every artwork is both classic and baroque,* classic in its essence and baroque in its existence, classic in its formal perfection and baroque in its expressivity."[8] Though it may appear to liquidate meaningful distinctions between historical periods and aesthetic categories, Brown's formula in fact acknowledges the complex relation between artworks and their historical setting. "Classic" and "baroque" attributes do not function here as stable categories, but instead as responsive sounding devices, designed to gauge permutations in the relation between a given work and the conditions shaping its production as well as its reception. Implicitly, Brown's formula also enjoins us to see the work of art not as an inert object, but instead as an ongoing event, whose meaning is expressed through the ways in which its stylistic traits stand over and against its historical frame, like a moving silhouette. Such an event exists in a partly unmoored—exilic, if you will—relation not only to its historical location, but also to itself, in the sense that the work creates, without fully determining, the conditions for its possible meanings.

Crashaw's case illustrates Brown's point. Habits of religious prejudice aside, the uncertain critical reception of Crashaw owes more than a little to the volatile energy that saturates his poems and defies easy judgment. Consider, in this light, modern scholarship's attempt to rehabilitate one of Crashaw's most infamous poems, "The Weeper," a rapturous meditation on Mary Magdalene's penitential tears. The poem has often been judged an embarrassing miscalculation—the 1993 *Norton* calls it "ludicrous" (1389)— in part because of the meandering (and presumably self-indulgent) course the speaker pursues in imagining the spiritual attributes of the tears. One of the early rescue efforts, by Marc F. Bertonasco, demonstrates how the poem's organization takes its cue from the meditative instructions written by the Savoyard Counter-Reformation saint Francis de Sales (1567–1622).[9] As it happens, Salesian meditation pursued a loosely associative itinerary that differed significantly from the more regimented protocol in the Ignatian *Exercises,* though both played an important role in the enlistment of affects or emotions in post-Tridentine spirituality. Bertonasco's study reminds us that cultural context (which includes the question of literary influence) is not a homogeneous field of obeyed norms but a site of diverse and even conflicted vectors of experience. The more pertinent lesson, however, is that careful inspection of Crashaw's cultural context does not necessarily eliminate the shock effect of Crashaw's poetry. This is so because the poems' unsettling traits are not simply illusions produced by prejudicial or anachronistic frames of reference. Such traits are generated by the poems themselves—more precisely, by the reverberation that takes place between the poems' formal models (e.g., the Salesian background to "The Weeper") and their uniquely expressive torque. Discovering the Salesian element (among others) in "The Weeper" does not cancel the poem's wayward appearance. Rather, it deepens and complicates one's awareness of Crashaw's investment in drawing his readers into the exodic journey toward penitential rapture and dispossession.

To ask whether such investment is more Romanist than Anglican is a short-sighted question because it tends to discount the poems' declamatory power. By this I mean that, with few exceptions, the poems' status as gestures of solicitation eclipses their status as vessels of encoded meaning. Accordingly, their impact—whether disorienting or pleasurable, or both—cannot be entirely explained by referring to matters of dogmatic confessional identity, or by seeking a normative model of poetic decorum. But the poems' impact does have a lot to do with their promotion of a distinctly religious, as well as aesthetic, sensibility that may fairly be called baroque, without being owned by either Romanist or Anglican denominations.

Broadly speaking, the baroque temperament reinvented the grammar of redemption laid out by the medieval scholastics. Inherited Aristotelian schemes of thought—the language of categories, cosmological hierarchies (the so-called Great Chain of Being), and principles of logic—were embraced, but in the embrace they were transfigured by a sense of the propulsive currents of divine love radiating through the universe.[10] To paraphrase Heather Asals's insight, one of the fundamental questions in medieval and Renaissance metaphysics was whether divine Being was a noun or a participle (i.e., a verbal adjective). The baroque answer was not simply that Being was participial (i.e., action-filled), but that its charisma suffused the created realm in an eroticized superabundance that outstripped rationalist modes of speculation.[11] This view helps explain the unbounded wealth of the baroque imagination in combining emotive, erotic, and rational modes of communicating with others (including God).

Crashaw's poetry bears powerful witness to the post-Tridentine era's interest in exploring the "participial-participating" nature of both divine Being and human existence (Asals 38). Consider, again, "The Weeper." The opening question ("Is she a

Flaming Fountain, or a Weeping Fire?") takes the reader into a scene of continuously dilating, disorienting movement: a flush of participles. As the poem unfolds, it becomes clear that the poem's project is not to stabilize the perturbation, but to intensify it. "The Weeper" depicts the Magdalene's penitential drama (and the speaker's response to it) as a transformative event that nearly exceeds the representational resources of language. In this regard, the poem's multiplied images of liquidity suggest more than rhetorical exuberance on the topic of tears. Language itself is brought to the melting point, where contractual relations between parts of speech and between words and things are unloosed. As suggested earlier, the technique is not without precedent (mystical as well as meditative models can be detected). The poem's strangeness, however, comes from the impression it gives of both consuming a transmitted legacy and verging on unthought regions of experience.

Simply put, "The Weeper" conveys the radical sensibility of Crashaw's poetic voice. The radical element, however, has less to do with any violation of devotional or literary norms than with the imaginative energy the poem invests in recapturing the ecstatic spirit found at the root of Christian tradition, in the letters of St. Paul. The Magdalene's grief cannot be separated from joy and spiritual regeneration: all of these are part of an intensely felt experience of a world transfigured by divine grace and love. As with "The Weeper," so, too, with the majority of Crashaw's poems, which do not dwell on the troubled condition of fallen humanity or on the soul's search for signs of redemption. In this regard, Crashaw's range is narrower than, say, John Donne's or George Herbert's. Yet the power of his poems, taken collectively, comes from the sheer wealth of invention with which they depict Paul's affirmation of a world already redeemed by Christ's death and resurrection, and poised to acquire decisive, "imperishable" form "at the last trumpet" (1 Cor. 15:51–52). In other words, Crashaw's virtuoso technique shapes poetic forms that enact Paul's spiritual conviction that "the present form of this world is passing away," and doing so "in the twinkling of an eye" (1 Cor. 7:31, 15:52).

What would it be like to inhabit such a world? Crashaw's poetry answers this question not simply by drawing on a wide range of devotional practices (e.g., meditations on Christ's crucified body and prayers to the saints) but by demonstrating how immersion in such practices brings about a *deformation* that is also a *reformation* of familiar ways of seeing things. One of Crashaw's most famous poems, "The Flaming Heart," offers a good example of what I mean. The poem is the last of three Crashaw wrote to commemorate one of the greatest saints of the Catholic Reformation, the Spanish mystic Teresa of Avila, who was canonized in 1622. In one respect, "The Flaming Heart" touches a nerve. It presents a rapt description of an engraved portrait of Teresa in ecstasy, corresponding to images found in many contemporary editions of the saint's life. The poem could easily be taken as an endorsement of the Council of Trent's advocacy of the devotional use of images, in opposition to the iconoclasm associated with the reformed churches. And endorsement it is, though this feature alone, for reasons already mentioned, hardly offers a reliable index to Crashaw's confessional identity. What it does offer is a reformation of a devotional object. More precisely, it teaches "Well meaning readers" (l. 1) how to recognize the spiritual value of such objects without falling into the idolatrous habit of attributing miraculous powers to material things.

This purpose accounts for the poem's basic two-part structure. The first part (ll. 1–74) describes the essential elements of the saint's most memorable ecstatic experience, in which an angel pierced her heart with a flaming dart. Instead of producing verbal equivalents of the scene's elements (saint, seraphim, heart, and dart) as they are "usually expressed" in visual media, the description follows two sets of compositional instructions. First, the speaker urges readers of the poem and its accompanying engraving to see through appearances by making a "well-plac't and wise mistake": "You must transpose the picture quite, / And spell it wrong to read it right: / Read HIM for her, and her for him; / And call the SAINT the SERAPHIM" (ll. 8–12). Literal or objective readings, the speaker suggests, simply fail to grasp the spiritual energies shaping the life of the soul. To clarify the point, the speaker addresses the painter (ll. 13–74), chiding him for failing to grasp the spiritual truth of the saint's mystical experience. In Pauline terms, the painter emphasizes the "letter" at the expense of the "spirit" of the saint's writings, and so misguidedly presents Teresa as a merely passive recipient of divine gifts administered by the seraphim. Following his own advice to readers, the speaker transposes the picture, setting virtually all the elements in fluid motion, blurring the distinctions between saint and seraphim, so that the poem is able to show what the picture does not. What the poem shows is a continuum of grace-filled experience in which Teresa's capacity to love—the fullness of her heart—finds expression in a mystical wound that surpasses the wounding power given to the seraphim. Teresa's heart is indeed more than "seraphicall," because it is both recipient and channel of the fullest expression of divine love in Christian thought: the incarnation and redemptive suffering of God's son. As the speaker puts it, "Love's passives are his activ'st part. / The wounded is the wounding heart" (ll. 73–74).

Teresa's heart holds the attention of the speaker for the rest of the poem (ll. 75–108). The speaker's fascination with the heart's paradoxical attributes (passive and active, wounded and wounding) generates an unusually powerful depiction of the mutual participation of divine creator and created world in promoting the domain of grace through the work of love. Teresa's heart appears as ardent witness to the redemptive wounds of the crucified Christ, as exemplary memory of the martyrs' heroic imitation of Christ's suffering, and as catalyst for the wounding and regenerative action of grace on the speaker's "carcasse of a hard, cold hart" (l. 86). Imperceptibly, the speaker's meditation takes on the characteristics of the wounded heart it describes. As meditation gives way to rapturous prayer, a cascade of parallel lines replicates the wounding action of the fiery dart on the saint's heart ("By all thy dowr of LIGHTS and FIRES; / By all the eagle in thee, all the dove" [ll. 94–105]). The poem ends with the speaker's supplication to be granted the gift of mystical self-annihilation, yet the propulsive energy informing the poem at large, and especially the prayer sequence just mentioned, suggests that the desired experience is not a distant prospect but an event already underway in the poem. "The Flaming Heart" embodies the process through which both speaker and "well-meaning readers" are drawn into the company of saint and seraphim—in spiritual terms, into the life of grace.

Perhaps the question to be asked of Crashaw's poetic language is not whether it goes too far, but whether it could have gone even further had he lived to write more. The poems surveyed here, at any rate, demonstrate how Crashaw's poetry is driven by an impulse to repeat and explore the apostle Paul's ecstatic affirmation of a "new creation" (*kainos ktisis*) won through conversion to the Christic revelation (Gal. 6:15).[12] From this perspective, Crashaw's language signals a flash point at which the medieval scholastics' dream of divine Being as a category of timeless and unchanging essence awakens to the call of a messianic promise. In other words, Crashaw's poems are unsettling because they open onto a scene of radical exposure to an End-time in which human beings and the Christian mystery of the Word made Flesh enter into an ongoing relation of "mutual answerability and co-creation."[13] To read Crashaw's poetry is also to be exposed—to a degree not found elsewhere in the canon—to a language that incarnates as much as it gives witness to a world reborn, in gestures rapturous and bruising at the same time. It is not for nothing that a contemporary of Crashaw's heard in his poems the "Language of the Angels."[14]

## NOTES

1. Lorraine M. Roberts and John R. Roberts, "Crashavian Criticism: A Brief Interpretive History," *New Perspectives on the Life and Art of Richard Crashaw*, ed. John R. Roberts (Columbia: U of Missouri P, 1990) 3. My summary of Crashaw's critical reception is indebted to this account.

2. William Laud (1573–1645), archbishop of Canterbury between 1633 and 1645, was associated with the anti-Puritan and High Church conservatism of the Anglican establishment. A series of political contretemps led to his arrest and execution for high treason in 1645.

3. See Graham Parry, *Seventeenth-Century Poetry: The Social Context* (London: Hutchinson, 1985) 129–31.

4. From a memoir by David Lloyd, "Mr. Richard Crashaw," cited in *The Poems of Richard Crashaw*, ed. L. C. Martin (Oxford: Oxford UP, 1957) 416.

5. See Robert Bireley, *The Refashioning of Catholicism, 1450–1700: A Reassessment of the Counter Reformation* (Washington, D.C.: Catholic U of America P, 1999).

6. An English translation of the relevant degrees, pronounced at the twenty-fifth session (1563), is in *The Canons and Decrees of the Council of Trent*, trans. H. J. Schroeder, O. P. (1941; rpt. Rockford, Ill.: TAN Books, 1978) 214–17.

7. John W. O'Malley, *Trent and All That: Renaming Catholicism in the Early Modern Era* (Cambridge, MA: Harvard UP, 2000).

8. Marshall Brown, "The Classic Is the Baroque: On the Principle of Wölfflin's Art History," *Critical Inquiry* 9 (1982): 401. Emphasis in text.

9. Marc F. Bertonasco, *Crashaw and the Baroque* (U of Alabama P, 1971).

10. See Anthony Raspa, *The Emotive Image: Jesuit Poetics in the English Renaissance* (Fort Worth, Texas: Texas Christian UP, 1983).

11. Heather Asals, "Crashaw's Participles and the 'Chiaroscuro' of Ontological Language," *Essays on Richard Crashaw*, ed. Robert M. Cooper, Salzburg Studies in English Literature (Salzburg: Institut für Anglistik und Amerikanistik, 1979) 35–49. Asals downplays the baroque element in Crashaw's poetics. An insightful account of the homoerotic implications of Crashaw's language is in Richard Rambuss, *Closet Devotions* (Durham: Duke UP, 1998).

12. The dominant vernacular translations in Crashaw's day (Rheims New Testament and King James Version) used the cognate expression "new creature."

13. Richard Kearney, *The God Who May Be: A Hermeneutics of Religion* (Bloomington: Indiana UP, 2001) 30.

14. "Preface to the Reader," *The Complete Poetry of Richard Crashaw*, ed. George Walton Williams (New York: New York UP, 1972) 650.

# READING LIST

Asals, Heather. "Crashaw's Participles and the 'Chiaroscuro' of Ontological Language." *Essays on Richard Crashaw.* Ed. Robert M. Cooper. Salzburg Studies in English Literature. Salzburg: Institut für Anglistik und Amerikanistik, 1979. 35–49.

Bertonasco, Marc. *Crashaw and the Baroque.* University: U of Alabama P, 1971.

Cunnar, Eugene R. "Opening the Religious Lyric: Crashaw's Ritual, Liminal, and Visual Wounds." *New Perspectives on the Seventeenth-Century English Religious Lyric.* Ed. John R. Roberts. Columbia: U of Missouri P, 1994. 237–67.

Marotti, Arthur, ed. *Catholicism and Anti-Catholicism in Early Modern English Texts.* New York: St. Martin's P, 1999.

Martz, Louis L. *The Poetry of Meditation: A Study of English Religious Literature of the Seventeenth Century.* 1962; New Haven: Yale UP, 1969.

Mullett, Michael. *The Catholic Reformation.* London: Routledge, 1999.

O'Malley, John W. *Trent and All That: Renaming Catholicism in the Early Modern Era.* Cambridge, MA: Harvard UP, 2000.

Rambuss, Richard. *Closet Devotions.* Durham: Duke UP, 1998.

Roberts, John R., ed. *New Perspectives on the Life and Art of Richard Crashaw.* U of Missouri P, 1990.

Shell, Alison. *Catholicism, Controversy, and the English Literary Imagination, 1558–1660.* Cambridge: Cambridge UP, 1999.

Wallerstein, Ruth. *Richard Crashaw: A Study in Style and Poetic Development.* 1935; Madison: U of Wisconsin P, 1959.

Young, R. V. *Doctrine and Devotion in Seventeenth-Century Poetry: Studies in Donne, Herbert, Crashaw, and Vaughan.* Rochester, NY: D. S. Brewer, 2000.

# 26

# Cavalier Poetry and Civil War

## *Laura Lunger Knoppers*

In the spring of 1639, King Charles I led an expedition against the Scots, who had re-sisted the imposition of the Book of Common Prayer and English Episcopal polity. An abnormally cold spring and inadequate supplies brought hardships and discontent: soldiers suffered from dysentery and pleurisy, and even some officers had to sleep outside without tents. On June 18, 1639, the Articles of Pacification at Berwick ended the so-called Bishops War without an actual battle.

Among those who followed the king on this ill-planned and ill-prepared expedition were three Court poets: Thomas Carew, John Suckling, and Richard Lovelace. Suckling volunteered in flamboyant style, outfitting at great expense a troop of one hundred young men with white doublets and scarlet breeches and coats. An early letter reveals a certain swagger: "So (Sir) you may now imagine us walking up and down the banks of *Tweed* like the Tower-Lyons in their Cages, leaving the people to think what we would do if we were let loose."[1] Yet on the dubious terms of the Peace of Berwick, the disillu-sioned young courtier wrote: "Posterity must tell this miracle, That there went an Army from the South, of which there was not one man lost, nor any man taken prisoner but the King" ("To an Unknown Correspondent" 147).

Richard Lovelace served in the regiment of George Goring and like Suckling was displeased with the preemptive peace treaty, writing "Now the *Peace* is made at the Foes rate"; yet he turned readily enough from fellowship in arms to fellowship in drink: "In ev'ry hand a Cup be found, / That from all Hearts a health may sound / To *Goring*! to *Goring*! see't goe round."[2] Returning from the Scottish borders to reside with the earl of Kent and his lady at Wrest Park, the third courtier-poet, Thomas Carew, praised "the temperate ayre of *Wrest* / Where I no more with raging stormes opprest, / Weare the cold nights out by the bankes of Tweed" and celebrated the "hospitalitie" threatened by reminders of rebellion and war.[3]

Carew, Lovelace, and Suckling—courtiers, poets, and soldiers, marked by loyalty to their king—have been commonly grouped together by literary historians as "Cavalier poets."[4] Of these, however, only Suckling self-identified as a cavalier, approvingly quoting one of his commanding officers as saying "that wee were Cavaleirs [sic] that studied not the cause but came for honor and love to the king" ("Letter to the Earl of Middlesex" 145). And while Carew and Suckling were linked by contemporaries for their wit, the term "Cavalier poetry" is of much later vintage. In fact in the 1640s, "cavalier" was predominately used (as with its opposite, puritan or roundhead) as a term of abuse. We begin, then, by asking: what precisely were the contemporary meanings of cavalier? How useful is the term "cavalier" in considering the poetry of Lovelace, Suckling, and Carew?

## Contemporary Uses of "Cavalier"

Stereotypes of the cavalier are seen in a flurry of polemical pamphlets in 1642, the year of the outbreak of civil war in England. Opposed to the "puritan" supporters of Parliament, the "cavaliers" who fought for their king are characterized as whoring, drinking, plundering, and swearing. *The Debauched Cavalleer* (1642) comments on the current debasement of the term: "The word *Cavallier* used amongst us here in England, is derived from the Italian word *Cavallero,* which signifies an Horse-rider [. . . and] from the French word, *Chevalier,* which signifies an horseman."[5] But while the name itself is honorable, signifying "a Knight, a Souldier, or a golden horseman," these "unworthy miscreants have made the very name a reproach" (3). Similarly, "A brief Character of a Cavalier" denigrates cavalier loyalty and love alike: "He loves his King as he doth his Whore, expressing to both a feigned fidelity, onely to satisfie his unlawfull appetites, which being done, he regards both alike."[6]

*The Wicked Resolution of the Cavaliers* (1642) even more sensationally depicts a cavalier world of profanity, murder, plunder, and rape. A loutish speaker rouses one of his "Dammee Companions": "My brave companion and Cavalier, let us drink couragiously, that we may kill the Divell and all his regiments of roundheads. I need not instruct thee friend in cutting of throats, for thou and I have been formerly theeves and cutters on the high way."[7] Boasting of their having "all of us seven deadly sins, besides damnable swearing" (1), the speaker envisions raping the London goldsmiths' wives, making their husbands "loving quiet complete cuckolds, Cavalier-cuckolds, as we have often done in the countrey" (3).

Nonetheless, like Suckling's commander, others embraced or treated positively the name of cavalier. Satirist John Taylor contrasts the "noble cavalier" with the quarrelsome "caviller" (here used for puritan or roundhead): "The *Cavalier* is a Gentleman, a Commander on Horsebacke. The *Caviller* is a Rascall, whether he swim, go, or ride; the *Cavalier* dares fight and be valiant, obey Law, and serve for his Soveraigne, his Countrey, for the true Religion established, for the Lawes, for the Subjects Liberty, for the Rights and Priviledges of Parliaments, and for the peace, conservation, and tranquillity of all these he will spend his best blood, and life too."[8]

These uses of cavalier usefully remind us that the poetry of Carew, Suckling, and especially Lovelace is marked by loyalty to the king and willingness to take up arms on his behalf. Of the three, only Lovelace lived into and through the civil wars. But the poetry of Carew and Suckling, composed and circulated in manuscript during the peace of the 1630s, was published in vastly different personal and political circumstances in the 1640s; and Lovelace wrote his verses in direct response to the civil wars, regicide, and republic. As Thomas Corns has aptly commented, the 1640s transformed courtiers into cavaliers.[9]

Hence, we can ask about all three poets: how is Cavalier poetry born out of the circumstances and conditions of civil war? What kind of political statement do the love lyrics—as well as the lyrics celebrating friendship, hospitality, retirement, wine, and song—make in these new, changed circumstances? Most important, how do these three poets transpose earlier Elizabethan love poetry and, in particular, the wit and formulae of Petrarchism, to England's specific political circumstances and to their own professional predicaments? In this latter bold and innovative transposition of earlier motifs and styles to the English civil wars, Carew, Lovelace, and Suckling offer their most distinctive contribution.

## England and Civil War

The confrontation in Scotland with which we began forced King Charles to call Parliament after an eleven-year hiatus. Disputes between the king and both the Short Parliament of 1639 and the Long Parliament of 1640 escalated into faction, acrimony, and civil war. After military defeat and botched attempts at compromise and treaties, Parliament was "purged" by force of arms under Colonel Thomas Pride, and the king—tried and condemned by a specially formed High Court of Justice—was executed by beheading outside of the Banqueting House at Whitehall on January 30, 1649. The regicide, supported and carried out by a small military minority, sent shock waves across not only England but all of Europe. Royalists fled into exile, faced the rigors of imprisonment, or were forced to "compound," to admit their guilt and pay high fines to retain their property. Four years of rule by a Council of State were followed by the installation of a Protectorate under Oliver Cromwell in December 1653. For royalists, the civil war years and the republic that followed were times of hardship, impoverishment, and exile.

Yet as we examine the poetry of Carew, Suckling, and Lovelace, we will see that cavalier verse was produced not despite but because of the conditions of civil war, regicide, and republic. The upheaval of military action and defeat and the dispersion of the Court provided an impetus for publication: highly polished courtly verses that had previously circulated only in manuscript were put into print, evoking a lost courtly milieu and offering a provocative alternative to "puritan" moralism. Prefaces and arrangement of verses foregrounded loyalty to the king; and relations between poet and mistress, poet and friend, poet and king were paralleled or intertwined. The apparent escapism of cavalier poetry—its advocacy of retirement, fellowship, loyalty, women, wine, and song—in fact played an oppositional role in the English republic, helping to keep a royalist ethos alive until the restoration of monarchy occurred in actuality in May 1660.

## Thomas Carew and the Committed Petrarchan Subject

Thomas Carew was born in Kent in 1595, studied at Oxford, and entered the Middle Temple at the Inns of Court, presumably with intent to enter the legal profession. Probably owing to the financial difficulties of his father, Carew took service abroad under Sir Dudley Carleton, in Venice and then in the Hague, but he was discreetly cashiered in 1616 after the discovery of some written aspersions on the character of Sir Dudley and his wife. Carew's distraught father sent several letters pleading on his behalf, albeit also commenting with some temper that "Ever since his departure from your lordship he hathe lingered heere with me, myspendeng his tyme, and now lieth here syck with me of a new [venereal] disease com in amongest us, by the which I pray God that he may be chastised to amend his lyfe here or els to take hym awaye to his mercye" (Dunlap xxvii).

Yet, despite the apparent ruin of his fortunes and health, Carew was soon appearing at the Jacobean Court. By 1630, the witty courtier and poet was in high favor with Charles I and had been named Gentleman of the King's Privy Chamber Extraordinary and appointed Sewer in Ordinary to his Majesty (in charge of official dining arrangements). Carew's elaborate and largely flattering Court masque, *Coelum Britannicum,* was performed at Whitehall in 1634. His service to the king, as we have seen, extended to military service in Scotland in spring 1639, whereupon he soon fell ill. Carew died shortly thereafter, most likely of syphilis.

Published posthumously in 1640, *Poems by Thomas Carew* is clearly marked as royalist. The title page indicates that his songs were set to music by Henry Lawes of the King's Chapel. Carew's poetry, then, offered a glimpse into the privileged inner circles of the Caroline Court: first when that Court was under threat and later when it was dispersed and the king was dead. While his verses show a generic diversity—epitaphs, occasional verse, country house poems, and love poems—most frequent and distinctive are lyrics that play with the devotional language of the Petrarchan lover: seducing, cajoling, pleading, remonstrating, and speciously reasoning with a mistress. But Carew's poems to the king use similarly devotional language with no humorous twist, and these scattered verses, along with the framework of title page and frontispiece, make clear that the volume is not an escapist reverie but a royalist intervention into a changed political and cultural world: before and after January 1649.

Like the Petrarchan lover, the speaker in many of Carew's highly polished amatory lyrics alternatively burns and freezes; he is tossed on a stormy sea and is smitten by the darts or lightning cast by the scornful eyes of his mistress. Out of keeping with the spring season that renews all else, his mistress carries "*June* in her eyes, in her heart *January*" ("The Spring" 3). And, unlike the gods themselves, "shee disdaines the spotlesse sacrifice / Of a pure heart that at her altar lyes" ("A Cruell Mistris" 8). As a smitten but witty lover, Carew's speaker meditates hyperbolically on such topics as a fly landing upon his mistress—"She did from hand to bosome skip, / And from her breath, her cheeke, and lip, / Suckt all the incense, and the spice, / And grew a bird of Paradise" ("A flye that flew into my Mistris her eye" 38).

Bur Carew also tempers the idealism of the Petrarchan lover with the wit of the courtly gallant. In "A divine Mistris," praise for his mistress ends not with a summing up of her eyes, hair, teeth, lips, and bosom, but with a witty twist: "Shee hath too much divinity for mee, / You Gods teach her some more humanitie" (7). And elsewhere the speaker sounds a realistic, if still playful note: "Know *Celia,* (since thou art so proud,) / 'Twas I that gave thee thy renowne," concluding (after more scolding): "Let fooles thy mystique formes adore, / I'le know thee in thy mortall state: / Wise Poets that wrap't Truth in tales, / Knew her themselves, through all her vailes" ("Ingratefull beauty threatned" 17–18).

In other poems, metaphors drawn from the Petrarchan tradition are amassed for erotic, libertine purposes. In Carew's well-known "A Rapture," a cascade of metaphors—the mistress's body as gold, ivory, lawn, virgin treasure, a garden of cherries, apples, a vale of lilies, a grove of eglantine, and a sea of milk; and the lover as a roving bee in paradise, an invading ocean, and a ship—are marshaled in the service of an astonishingly explicit eroticism:

Yet my tall Pine, shall in the *Cyprian* straight
Ride safe at Anchor, and unlade her fraight:

My Rudder, with thy bold hand, like a tryde,
And skilfull Pilot, thou shalt steere and guide
My Bark into Love's channell, where it shall
Dance, as the bounding waves doe rise or fall. (51)

Highly crafted, polished, and witty, Carew's amorous verses offer a glimpse of a Caroline gallant and the kind of courtly play that by 1640 was under siege from an ascendant Puritan moralism and by the second edition of 1651 nostalgically evoked a Court that was no more.

Carew's interspersed poems to the royal family make the political import of the volume even more clear. These poems express loyalty to the king and queen, lament the loss of a princess or the sickness of the king, and praise the Caroline peace of the 1630s. The speaker takes up a devotional stance toward the monarchical object: but unlike Carew's witty play with Petrarchan stances in his love lyrics, there is here no playful irony, no undercutting. Rather, the adulation is straightforward in such poems as "To the King at his Entrance into *Saxham*":

SIR,
    Ere you passe this threshold, stay,
And give your creature leave to pay
Those pious rites, which unto you,
As to our houshold Gods, are due. (30)

Like the faithful lover, the king's subjects offer sacrifice: each breast is "like a flaming Altar, drest / With zealous fires, which from pure hearts / Love mixt with loyaltie imparts" (30); they hope for nothing but the "gracious favour" (31) of the king. Here and elsewhere the religiously framed devotion shown to the Petrarchan mistress is transferred to the king, but never with the knowing wink: "I'le know thee in thy mortall state."

On the surface, Carew's Petrarchism is absolutely conventional, a belated reiteration of Sir Philip Sidney's formulas from *Astrophil and Stella* back in the 1580s and 1590s. But what changes Carew's poetry and gives it its historic originality is the deployment of conventional Petrarchism in the new circumstances of the English civil wars. Carew's love lyrics attest to a clash of cultures that led to and fueled military conflict. And his poems of praise to the king become increasingly resonant with the breakdown of the world that they embrace. Courtly love lyrics and devotion to the king alike are both threatened and transformed by civil war, military defeat, and regicide.

## Sir John Suckling and the Pose of Cavalier

Sir John Suckling was born in Middlesex in 1609, matriculated at Trinity College, Cambridge, and, like Carew, held a position at court. Contemporary John Aubrey provides a colorful description of the courtier-poet:

> He was the greatest gallant of his time, and the greatest gamester, both for bowling and cards, so that no shop-keeper would trust him for *6d.*, as today, for instance, he might, by winning, be worth 200 *li.*, the next day he might not be worth half so much, or perhaps be sometimes *minus nihilo.*[10]

Suckling exemplifies the dashing, devil-may-care cavalier. He inherited and lost a large fortune, primarily through gambling. He seems to have had two main romantic attachments, first to his cousin Mary Cranfield and then to Mary Bulkeley. He also pursued an unsuccessful courtship of heiress Anne Willoughby, presumably for her fortune, which ended in a fight with another suitor, John Digby (in which Suckling was well cudgeled), and in an even more ignominious attempt at revenge (in which one of Suckling's men was killed).

Nonetheless, Suckling cut a dashing figure at Court. His play *Aglaura* was produced at Court in 1637 and put on at Blackfriars Theatre (at his own expense) in 1638, followed by publication in folio. He participated (extravagantly, we have seen) in the first Bishops War, as well as in Charles's second expedition to Scotland. After Scotland, Suckling continued actively to support the king's cause. He served as a member of the Long Parliament in 1640. He was also involved, more dangerously, in the so-called Army plot to free the earl of Strafford just before his attainder and execution; when the plot was exposed, Suckling fled to France and was condemned in absentia for high treason. He died in Paris, in poverty and likely by his own hand, in 1641.

Suckling was very much a public figure: the subject of some twenty early attacks in anti-royalist pamphlets and doggerel verse as well as fulsome eulogies after his death. When Humphrey Moseley brought out Suckling's epigrams, songs, sonnets, occasional verse, and letters as *Fragmenta Aurea* in July 1646, the connections with the Caroline Court were made clear.[11] In his poetry, as in his life, Suckling constructed a series of poses, inverting Petrarchan clichés in the voice of a witty, urbane, irreverent, and cynical courtier, albeit also speaking as a humble servant devoted to his king. An early portrait by Sir Anthony Van Dyck showed a courtly Suckling posed with a volume of Shakespeare, open to *Hamlet*. Suckling also humorously wrote himself into some of his own poems, as, for instance, a gallant who fails to appear at a contest of wits before Apollo ("The Wits" or "A Sessions of the Poets" 71–76). But, as we shall see, the pose of cavalier, devoted with life and love to the king, was one that eventually went tragically beyond Suckling's own script.

Many of Suckling's speakers unmask Petrarchan clichés of unrequited love. One well-known "Song" begins rather plaintively:

Why so pale and wan fond Lover?
  Prithee why so pale?
Will, when looking well can't move her,
  Looking ill prevaile?
Prithee why so pale? (64)

The language is simple (primarily monosyllabic) and sweet. Yet the speaker concludes with a scornful dismissal: "If of her selfe shee will not Love, / Nothing can make her, / The Devill take her" (64). In another verse, Suckling speculates on the sparse rewards that may be found in the afterlife for lovers scorned in this world—"Some Bayes (perchance) or Myrtle bough"—concluding with a witty turn: "And if that be the onely odds, / (As who can tell) ye kinder Gods, / Give me the Woman here" ("Sonnet III" 50). The metrical variation with the opening spondee ("Give me") highlights the humorous inversion of expectation: as the pragmatic lover has no desire to wait until the afterlife for a dubious reward.

Most notorious are a series of poems depicting love as an appetite, linked with various forms of consumption and eating. "Against Fruition [I]" offers a series of memorable similes:

Women enjoy'd (what s'ere before th'ave been)
Are like Romances read, or sights once seen:
Fruition's dull, and spoils the Play much more
Than if one read or knew the plot before;
'Tis expectation makes a blessing dear:
It were not heaven, if we knew what it were. (37–38)

In this verse the earlier demand for immediate gratification ("Give me the Woman here") is cynically reversed: consummating love will spoil it. An equally plain-spoken speaker of "Sonnet II" asserts: "'Tis not the meat, but 'tis the appetite / makes eating a delight," going on to compare the lover with a watch that simply needs to be wound up "No matter by what hand or trick" (48–49). The blunt language recalls Shakespeare's "expense of spirit in a waste of shame," and it seems designed to reveal honest sentiment. But in fact this anti-Petrarchism is as carefully crafted and posed as the more idealistic language of Sidney's love-struck Astrophil.

Yet although Suckling is known for his cynicism and calculated wit, the poem given premier place in the 1646 volume is an adulatory poem to the king:

Awake (great Sir) the Sun shines heer,
    Gives all Your Subjects a New-yeer,
    Onely we stay till You appear,
For thus by us Your Power is understood:
He may make fair days, You must make them good.
        Awake, awake,
        and take
Such Presents as poor men can make,
They can adde little unto blisse
        who cannot wish. ("On New-years day 1640. To the King" 84–85).

Again, the language is simple and direct: in this case, not to convey cynicism or realism, but sincerity in service of the king. Like Carew's, Suckling's verses to the king and royal family eschew irony in a position echoing that of Petrarchan lover. Like the lover, he imagines the bliss associated with an objection of devotion: in this case the idealized monarch.

Suckling's contributions to the king—"Such Presents as poor men can make"—in the end went well beyond the genteel offerings of courtly verse. Aubrey gives a more detailed and poignant account of the miseries of his final act: "he went into France, where after some time being come to the bottome of his fund that was left, reflecting on the miserable and despicable condition he should be reduced to, having nothing left to maintaine him he (having a convenience for that purpose, lyeing at an apothecaries house, in Paris) tooke poyson, which killed him miserably with vomiting. He was buryed in the Protestants church-yard" (*Brief Lives* 9).

Like Carew, Suckling returns to the Petrarchan pose of the late sixteenth century. But he both undercuts and deploys such conventions to attest to loyalty to his king; and, when published, his artful poses offer a counternarrative to military defeat and parliamentary judgment. Although Suckling was an inveterate poser, the role of cavalier was scripted not only by his own loyalty to the king but also by the tumultuous events of his time. And, in the end, it was a role for which he sacrificed not only fortune but life.

## Richard Lovelace: Paradox, Idealism, and Disillusionment

Richard Lovelace was born to an influential Kentish family and educated at Charterhouse and Oxford. Having served in Charles's expedition against the Scots, Lovelace continued to be active for the king; his presentation of a royalist petition to the House of Commons on behalf of his native Kent in 1642 resulted in his imprisonment in the Gatehouse, Westminster. Lovelace did not actively fight in the English civil wars, perhaps as a condition of his release from prison, but he contributed arms and horses to the royalist side and later fought under the French king Louis XIV on the Continent and was wounded at the siege of Dunkirk in 1646. Back in England, in June 1648, Lovelace was again imprisoned after a general round-up of royalists, in Peterhouse, Aldersgate. While in prison, he apparently worked on his volume of poems, although it was delayed in publication and did not appear until May 1649. After the execution of the king, Lovelace was set at liberty but he had reputedly squandered his fortune in the royalist cause and spent the last decade of his life in poverty. He died in 1658, and, the following year, his brother published his remaining verses in *Lucasta: Posthume Poems*.

Unlike Carew and Suckling, then, Lovelace lived through the civil war years, and his verses register a direct impact. His *Lucasta* was licensed for publication in 1648 in the brief period of hope between military defeat and the execution of the king; when the volume appeared in 1649, the king was dead. His second volume of poems was written during the republic, when hopes for a restoration of the monarchy (which did in fact occur in May 1660) were all but lost. Lovelace's life and verse show the quintessential positive "cavalier" combination of love and honor, loyalty to one's king, friendship, and retirement in a dark age. But the poems also show the immense strain of years of defeat and poverty. While the early verses are chivalric and romantic, idealistic toward love and life, and transforming Petrarchan paradox to assert inner freedom, the later poems use such paradox to dissect and lament, to reject both Oliver Cromwell's England and the poet's own earlier idealism.

*Lucasta: Epodes, Odes, Sonnets, Songs, &c* appeared with prefatory verses (including one by Andrew Marvell) that praised Lovelace's combination of martial and poetic prowess. Most striking throughout are the lyrics that combine love and war. The exquisite "To Lucasta, Going to the Warres" turns on a central paradox: that the speaker's apparent inconstancy guarantees his constancy:

Tell me not (Sweet) I am unkinde,
    That from the Nunnerie
Of thy chaste breast, and quiet minde,
    To Warre and Armes I flie.

True; a new Mistresse now I chase,
    The first Foe in the Field;
And with a stronger Faith imbrace
    A Sword, a Horse, a Shield.

Yet this Inconstancy is such,
   As you too shall adore;
I could not love thee (Deare) so much,
   Lov'd I not Honour more. (18)

Lovelace's poem is typically "cavalier" in its high-minded merging of loyalty to mistress and king. Its clear, simple diction lucidly embodies idealistic sentiments and indeed the language that turns away from the actual brutalities of civil war. "Honour" remains undefined but resonant, evocative of loyalty, virtue, and courage. As Corns has noted (214), the poem is marked by studied archaism, evoking the knighthood of old, and it perhaps also recalls the renewal of the ceremonies of the Order of the Garter by Charles I and his chivalric equestrian portraits by Sir Anthony Van Dyck. The speaker is a chevalier, the honorable knight of a chaste mistress: this is the positive side of the cavalier image, eloquently wrought and defiant.

In other lyrics, Lovelace plays with a second paradox: the attainment of freedom in and through bondage. The polished lyric, "To Althea, From Prison," moves through four parallel stanzas to show how self-chosen bonds give the speaker freedom, even while he is literally in prison and in manacles. In the opening stanza, images of imprisonment are transposed to the lovers:

When Love with unconfined wings
   Hovers within my Gates;
And my divine *Althea* brings
   To whisper at the Grates:
When I lye tangled in her haire,
   And fetterd to her eye;
The *Gods* that wanton in the Aire,
   Know no such Liberty. (78)

The poem again works by paradox: a series of willing confinements attest to true liberty. Here the divinity of the mistress works not to make her unattainable but to transport the speaker from actual to metaphorical (love) bondage: he is "tangled" in Althea's hair and "fetterd" to her eye. Subsequent stanzas continue boldly to transpose the language of bondage: heads "bound" with roses, hearts with loyal flames. Rather than focus on—or even acknowledge—the disease, filth, and discomfort of the Gatehouse in which he is immured, the speaker focuses on willing bondage, singing like "committed" (encaged and devoted) linnets of the "sweetnes, Mercy, Majesty, / And glories of my KING" (79).

The final stanza of "To Althea, From Prison" moves beyond liberating comparisons in the natural world to a moving repudiation of the speaker's bondage:

Stone Walls do not a Prison make,
   Nor I'ron bars a Cage;
Mindes innocent and quiet take
   That for an Hermitage.
If I have freedome in my Love,
   And in my soule am free;
Angels alone, that sore above,
   Injoy such Liberty. (79)

The speaker finds freedom in bondage, choosing to celebrate in defeat. Cold physical realities (stone, iron) transmute to the cloistered silence of a religious hermitage. The lyric to Althea asserts eloquently that defeat of body is not defeat of mind: the cavalier spirit remains free.

"The Grasse-hopper. To my Noble Friend, Mr. Charles Cotton," another lovely and well-known lyric, similarly asserts the power of commitment and fellowship in a dark season. The allusive and poignant verse follows the fate of the grasshopper, mediating between the Anacreontic celebration of the grasshopper king and the Aesopian fable of the careless grasshopper and the industrious ant. Carefree and merry, the grasshopper revels in summer—"The Joyes of Earth and Ayre are thine intire"—only to be struck down by the coming of winter:

> Poore verdant foole! and now green Ice! thy Joys
>   Large and as lasting, as thy Peirch of Grasse,
> Bid us lay in 'gainst Winter, Raine, and poize
>   Their flouds, with an o'reflowing glasse. (39)

The diction of the poem is strikingly apt: "verdant foole" and "green Ice" are original and poignant, yet unsentimental terms. In the miniature world of the grasshopper, Lovelave captures the fleeting hopes and pleasures of the loyal subject. Rich and allusive, the poem's depiction of the grasshopper cut off by the frosts of winter would have been even more resonant after January 1649.

While some have seen "The Grasse-hopper" as escapist, the very retreat into fellowship and wine indicates defiance of the current regime and rejection of the judgment on the king. The speaker will learn from the grasshopper to protect himself against the winter of the year and of monarchy, turning to friendship and fellowship:

> Thou best of *Men* and *Friends*! we will create
>   A Genuine Summer in each others breast;
> And spite of this cold Time and frosen Fate
>   Thaw us a warme seate to our rest. (39)

Lovelace effectively employs the rhetorical figures of cold time and frozen fate to show (as with the prison poems) the transformative power of inner freedom and commitment.

After a decade of poverty, Lovelace's *Lucasta: Posthume Poems* (1659) is a dark and bitter volume, reflecting national and personal loss. An early poem, "Lucasta laughing," presents a moribund and nightmarish world:

> Heark how she laughs aloud,
>     Although the world put on its shrowd;
> Wept at by the fantastick Crowd,
>     Who cry, One drop let fall
> From her, might save the Universal Ball.
>     She laughs again
>     At our ridiculous pain;
> And at our merry misery
>     She laughs until she cry. (122)

Here again we see paradoxes, once deployed in conventional love poetry, but now dark and ironic. Oxymorons capture the sense of the world turned upside down by war and regicide: "ridiculous pain" and "merry misery"—the ironic conjunction of laughter and death ("shrowd"), laughter and tears.

Similarly, the movements of the new Spanish dance or saraband in "A loose Saraband" sound, if somewhat more frenetically, the earlier note of women, wine, and song: "When once we twining marry / Mad Love with wilde Canary" (139). But the tone quickly darkens: "See all the World how't staggers, / More ugly drunk then we, / As if far gone in daggers, / And blood it seem'd to be" (140). The harsh consonant sounds and blunt terms—"staggers," "ugly drunk" —contrast with the melodic smoothness of the earlier verse. From an earlier speaker who professes, "I could not love thee (Deare) so much, / Lov'd I not Honour more," we move to a bleak cynicism aimed equally at honor in love and war:

> Now, is there such a Trifle
>     As Honour, the fools Gyant?
> What is there left to rifle,
>     When Wine makes all parts plyant?
> Let others Glory follow,
> In their false riches wallow,
> And with their grief be merry;
> Leave me Love and Sherry. (141)

Again, Lovelace's unusual diction and rhyming surprises the reader into recognition of the futility, even the foolishness, of honor: it is a mere "Trifle," and the effects of "Love and Sherry" leave idealized notions of the chaste mistress or long-suffering suitor far behind.

Similarly, the moral and political lessons drawn from the natural world, the world of little creatures, considerably darken in the second volume of *Lucasta*. Although "The Ant" begins with a sympathetic tone, the overindustrious, puritanical creature soon provokes the speaker's anger and scorn:

> Look up then miserable Ant, and spie
>     Thy fatal foes, for breaking of her Law,
> Hov'ring above thee, Madam, *Margaret Pie,*
>     And her fierce Servant, Meagre, Sir *John Daw:*
> Thy Self and Storehouse now they do store up,
>     And thy whole Harvest too within their Crop. (135)

The vision of the ant about to be consumed by the jackdaw and magpie produces not a useful moral lesson for the speaker—as in the earlier grasshopper poem—but a nightmarish vision of a world in which all are devoured. Likewise, in "A Fly caught in a Cobweb," the fly struggles vainly to free itself, while its "all belly'd foe" lies waiting to consume it (155). The fly evokes the debased royalist condition under the compromising conditions of the Cromwellian regime, "Trapp'd basely in a slimy frame; / And free of Air, thou art become / Slave to the spawn of Mud and Lome" (156). The speaker's sympathy for the emblematic animal world—the "verdant foole" and "green Ice" of the merry but ill-fated grasshopper—mutates into reproach and loathing.

In the second *Lucasta,* then, Lovelace returns to paradox: seen earlier in Petrarchan lovers who starve and surfeit, freeze and burn, live and die in the favor or scorn of a mistress. But now we see not (as the first volume of *Lucasta*) the brilliant liberating paradoxes of freedom in bondage, nor the "sweet" wit of Carew, nor the cynical humor of Suckling, but paradox as a weapon to embody and eviscerate the absurdities of the post-regicide world.

What conclusions can we draw, then, about these three poets (Thomas Carew, Sir John Suckling, and Richard Lovelace) under the central rubric of cavalier poetry and civil war? The term "cavalier poetry," often undefined and loosely applied by modern scholars, must be used carefully. But the stereotype of the cavalier and the circumstances of civil war can significantly sharpen our sense of the meaning and cultural resonance of the poetry of the period. These three poets do show differences in tone, subject, and style. But also marking their work are persistent themes: love, honor, fellowship, the good life, war. A keen wit can be seen in all three: the juxtaposition of unlike entities, and the use of paradox and oxymoron for humor or praise, satire or elegy.

All three poets thus ably revise conventions of earlier Elizabethan poetry: boldly reworking the stance of Petrarchan lover to profess romantic devotion to king and country. Courtiers in the 1630s, these three poets enjoyed what Carew termed the "peace and plenty, which the blessed hand / Of our good King gives this obdurate Land" (75). But that "obduracy" would result in factionalism, civil war, and regicide. And in the 1640s and 1650s, Carew, Suckling, and Lovelace lived—and died—cavaliers.

## NOTES

1. Suckling, "To an Unknown Correspondent," *The Works of Sir John Suckling. Vol. 1: The Non-Dramatic Works,* ed. Thomas Clayton (Oxford: Clarendon P, 1971) 144.
2. Lovelace, "Sonnet. To Generall *Goring,* after the pacification at *Berwicke,*" *The Poems of Richard Lovelace,* ed. C. H. Wilkinson (Oxford: Clarendon P, 1930) 81.
3. Carew, "To my friend *G.N.* from *Wrest,*" *The Poems of Thomas Carew,* ed. Rhodes Dunlap (Oxford: Clarendon P, 1949) 86–87.
4. Although Robert Herrick is often included in scholarly discussions of cavalier poetry, he was not in the Court, nor did he serve militarily with Charles I. For these reasons, I have not included him in this essay which proposes a precise, more historically grounded definition of cavalier.
5. *The Debauched Cavalleer: Or the English Midianite* (London, 1642) 2–3.
6. "A brief Character of a Cavalier of these Times," *A New Mercury Called Mercurius Problematicus* (London, 1644) Sig. A4r.
7. *The Wicked Resolution of the Cavaliers, Declaring their Malice and Hatred to the Parliament, the Commonwealth, and Especially the City of London* (London, 1642) 1.
8. John Taylor, *The Noble Cavalier Caracterised, and a Rebellious Caviller Cauterised* (Oxford, 1643) 1.
9. Thomas N. Corns, "Thomas Carew, Sir John Suckling, and Richard Lovelace," *The Cambridge Companion to English Poetry: Donne to Marvell,* ed. Thomas N. Corns (Cambridge: Cambridge UP, 1993) 200.
10. Aubrey, *Brief Lives and Other Selected Writings,* ed. Anthony Powell (London: Cresset, 1949) 59.

11. In the 1640s and 1650s, Moseley published a great deal of royalist literature, including the 1651 edition of Carew's poems. See John Curtis Reed, "Humphrey Moseley, Publisher," *Oxford Bibliographical Society Proceedings and Papers* 2, pt.1 (1927–30): 57–142.

## READING LIST

Aubrey, John. *Brief Lives and Other Selected Writings*. Ed. Anthony Powell. London: The Cresset P, 1949.

Bruce, Donald. "The War Poets of 1639: Carew, Suckling and Lovelace." *Contemporary Review* (1991): 309–14.

Corns, Thomas N. "Thomas Carew, Sir John Suckling, and Richard Lovelace." *The Cambridge Companion to English Poetry: Donne to Marvell*. Ed. Thomas N. Corns. Cambridge: Cambridge UP, 1993.

————. *Uncloistered Virtue: English Political Literature, 1640–1660*. Oxford: Clarendon P, 1992.

King, Bruce. "Green Ice and a Breast of Proof." *College English* 26,7 no. 7 (1965): 511–15.

Loxley, James. *Royalism and Poetry in the English Civil Wars: The Drawn Sword*. Basingstoke: Macmillan, 1997.

Miner, Earl. *The Cavalier Mode from Jonson to Cotton*. Princeton: Princeton UP, 1971.

Parker, Michael P. "'All are not born (Sir) to the Bay': 'Jack' Suckling, 'Tom' Carew, and the Making of a Poet." *English Literary Renaissance* 12 (1982): 341–68.

Post, Jonathan. *English Lyric Poetry: The Early Seventeenth Century*. London: Routledge, 1999.

Potter, Lois. *Secret Rites and Secret Writing: Royalist Literature, 1641–1660*. Cambridge: Cambridge UP, 1989.

Smith, Nigel. *Literature and Revolution in England, 1640–1660*. New Haven: Yale UP, 1994.

Wilcher, Robert. *The Writing of Royalism, 1628–1660*. Cambridge: Cambridge UP, 2001.

# 27

# Marvell and Pastoral

## *Thomas Healy*

In 1660 John Evelyn, diarist, traveler, horticulturist, and garden designer, wrote to Sir Thomas Browne:

> We do endeavour to shew how the aire and genius of Gardens worke upon humane Spirits to-wards virtue and Sanctitie, I meane in a remote preparatory and instrumentall working: How Caves, Grotts, Mounds and other like irregular ornaments of Gardens do contribute to con-templative and Philosophical Enthusiasms.[1]

Evelyn's remarks illustrate a dilemma that besets the early modern age's pursuit of the pastoral. Nature in its most perfect state is believed both to entice mankind toward social accord and to draw us toward divinity, a harmony founded on unaf-fected rural simplicity. Yet, this simple proposition is established on a series of apparent contradictions. The natural model being celebrated is one that is "irregu-lar," a wilderness containing grottos and caves, not an environment arranged according to formal structures. As this period perceived proper human and heavenly social organizations as highly regulated, the ideal natural world seems at variance with these. To add further complication, Evelyn envisages human action as required to help this idyllic landscape come into being. The grottos and other garden "orna-ments" are not preexistent but created by the gardener to encourage philosophical contemplation: the natural ideal seems dependent on the human agent to bring it to perfection. There is, at best, a reciprocity between humanity and nature: the "Philosophical Enthusiasms" that persuade the gardener to fashion a model land-scape are then further encouraged by that created landscape, an apparent "green thought in a green shade" that helps elevate humanity toward greater social and spiritual perfection.[2] Yet, the deceitful fiction this involves is evident. Evelyn proposes that "the aire and genius" of the garden that works on the human agent is "preparatory" to his or her contemplations; this environment is imagined as prior to human action not the consequence of it.

For the seventeenth century, such dilemmas around achieving a true pastoral mode were further reinforced because the human agent's capacity to become a true gardener was perceived as insecure. The Christian tradition teaches that when Adam and Eve dis-obeyed God's ordinance not to eat the fruit of the tree of knowledge in Eden, they and the rest of created nature had fallen, losing their perfection and harmony with both the natural and the divine world. Employing a philosophical model known as the Great Chain of Being, a commonplace assumption of Marvell's age was that all creation was connected in an orderly hierarchy. Because humanity was seen as the highest worldly link in this chain, when mankind's tie to the divine was severed through sin, all nature "below" mankind was also separated. But through divine grace and mankind's salvation in Christ, humanity, or some part of it, had been given the opportunity of restoring a link to the divine. In many respects, how this restoration might be accomplished became the central quest within European intellectual traditions until the late nineteenth century.

John Evelyn and those who shared his passion for Nature accepted that some vestiges of an unfallen edenic environment remained potentially observable in the contemporary natural world, as, indeed, similar remnants of former glory remained discoverable in mankind. It was these aspects of Nature that needed to be harnessed to create the surroundings that would promote human perfection. The classical world, too, provided models, as the pastoral norms of Greek and Roman antiquity readily coalesced with the Christian. The classical world had also celebrated a previous golden age when Nature was simple and free: "The Golden Age was first, a time that cherished / Of its own will, justice and right; no law."[3] This now lost world was one without urban space, when mankind and nature lived in a harmony that provided what was needed for life without labor: "The years went by in peace. And Earth, untroubled/ Unharried by hoe or plowshare, brought forth all / That man had need for, and those men were happy" (*Metamorphoses* 1.104–06).

Evelyn may now be celebrated as a fountainhead of a garden design movement that sought to translate Virgilian and other classical pastoral ideas to the English countryside, but there is a much longer English tradition of realizing both classical and Christian pastoral ideals in poetry. Not requiring the actual land and financial resources necessary to transform a physical landscape, the pastoral could be realized much more readily in verse. The zenith of this poetic tradition that spliced together classical and Christian concepts to celebrate a golden paradise world, the consequences of it lost, and its potential rediscovery are developed in arguably the most important piece of seventeenth-century English writing: John Milton's *Paradise Lost*. Yet Milton and Andrew Marvell, his younger contemporary and friend, were both highly conscious that the poet as much as the gardener was the product of a fallen world. Though the poet could present himself as inspired, even by God, the very language used to formulate a pastoral vision was open to misuse and misconstruction because it emerged out of humanity's decayed condition. Consequently, poets and their readers were aware that there was a danger that they might actually be celebrating an ideal that was a consequence of human error, constructing an illusionary perfect world that did not "worke upon humane Spirits towards virtue and Sanctitie" but which actually furthered human vice.

Within the pastoral idyll of Milton's Eden, one of the most preeminent "fruits" of Paradise is that produced by the Tree of Knowledge, whose taste brings death and the loss of Eden to mankind because God forbids its consumption. Yet, when Adam and Eve initially glut themselves eating from this tree, they believe that the knowledge they have gained is not only greater than what they previously possessed but that their understanding of their new condition is based on reason, the highest quality of human thinking. They seem to imagine themselves gaining in the "Philosophical Enthusiasms" that Evelyn celebrates as a consequence of enjoying his perfect garden. Adam's first words to Eve after biting the apple reveal how quickly a rhetorically evasive language masquerading as candor asserts itself in his discourse, one that previously has been open and unaffected. Language in the fallen world will be no secure vehicle to discover truth. Adam's praise of Eve's provision of the apple is based around words—exact, elegant, sapience, judicious—commonly used to confirm an activity's propriety or reasonableness:

Eve, now I see thou art exact of taste,
And elegant, of sapience no small part,
Since to each meaning savour we apply,
And palate call judicious; I thee praise
Yield to thee, so well this day thou has purveyed.[4]

Adam imagines the fruit he has tasted aids his judgment: it "savours" his understanding, literally providing an agreeable taste; ironically, given savor's linguistic proximity to both the French *savoir* (know) and the English saviour, it is also imagined to provide him with greater security and knowledge. He appreciates the Tree of Knowledge's fruit in terms that are almost a textbook fulfillment of pastoral values: the apple provides "of itself" (it requires no human labor) and is an easy way to happiness, sustenance, and freedom. In his intoxicated fallen condition, Adam has wholly mistaken that its consequences for him are the very opposite of these things. Yet, as Milton makes clear, it is not the fruit that is inherently endowed with a poison. Its catastrophic effects rest with human action; it is Adam's disobedience of God's command that generates mankind's fall.

For the seventeenth century, therefore, there is constantly a double aspect to the pastoral. Ideal nature has in reality been lost and must be "re-created" by gardeners, poets, and painters. Yet, such human agents are themselves imperfect fallen creatures who can never be completely certain of the truth of their vision. Further, even if the pastoral can be realized—in print, paint or in "real" gardens—there is the danger that its effect upon its witnesses may be other than is intended because its observers may not have the intellectual grasp, spiritual resources, or aesthetic sensibilities to interpret it correctly, even though they may be convinced they have done so. This double quality of poetic pastoral experience—a vision of a natural ideal that seems realizable in verse, yet one that also remains constantly elusive and uncertain—rests at the center of Marvell's landscape poetry. He offers a vision of the natural world that is regularly invaded by external disruption (*Upon Appleton House, The Nymph Complaining of the Death of Her Fawn*), or by our realization that his poetic narrators may be voyeuristically tarnishing the perfections they celebrate ("The Picture of Little T.C. in a Prospect of Flowers") or that what might seem a pastoral ideal may, in fact, be a false image of one ("The Garden"). What is striking about Marvell's use of the pastoral is how deliberately unsuccessful it is in sustaining "Philosophical Enthusiasms" that "worke upon humane Spirits towards virtue and Sanctitie."

Marvell's ambivalence toward pastoral is observable in both his seemingly simplest lyrics as well as his more complex works. Take for instance this example from his short "The Mower to the Glow-worms."

Ye glow-worms, whose officious flame
To wand'ring mowers shows the way,
That in the night have lost their aim,
And after foolish fires do stray;

Your courteous lights in vain you waste,
Since Juliana here is come,

For she my mind hath so displaced
That I shall never find my home. (ll. 9–16)

The mower, a lowly rustic figure who cuts hay, celebrates the glow-worms whose light Nature provides to guide his companions home and prevent them from ending up in swamps—Smith's edition clarifies that the "foolish fires" are *ignis fatuus,* the phosphorescent light seen above marshy ground (*Poems* 143). Yet, as the mower acknowledges, Nature proves to be an ineffective guide as he disregards its assistance. The brighter light of Juliana (whose name recalls both the heat and intense light of July but also the imperial conqueror Julius Caesar who the month is named after) "displaces" the mower. This word has ironic implications here since in Marvell's time "displace" was commonly used in relation to persons of high rank who lost an office or position of dignity. The supposedly humble mower has apparently become so mentally blinded by the superior Juliana that his very identity is disturbed. This commonplace pastoral character, whose lyric ostensibly addresses the glow-worms as a positive force, reveals their futility—and by implication Nature's—in offering him guidance. The mower is aware that he is pursuing a destructive "foolish fire" in Juliana but does so regardless.

Social elitism is not a quality that the pastoral ethos is meant to celebrate, rather the reverse. That a mower conceives himself socially "placed" at all shows that this character has in some sense never accepted his identity as a lowly rustic. Similarly, characterizing the glow-worms' lights as "courteous" proposes that the mower is aspiring to the values of the socially refined Court, as much as employing the word to redirect these values to uncultivated nature. But Marvell's irony here is wider than the particular circumstance of a rustic who presents himself vanquished by Juliana in inflated terms that parallel how an earlier nobility might have been conquered by Caesar. A familiar but paradoxical feature of pastoral is that while it is peopled with figures from a world of rural simplicity, notably shepherds, they often tend to possess the accomplishments of the socially refined. As John Creaser points out, Marvell's pastoral occupies a verse "where everything knows it place: every line is end-stopped, every couplet is closed."[5] Since the Middle Ages pastoral had particularly appealed to the aristocracy: the creation of country idylls was something only the rich could indulge with the resources of large estates. As Christopher Marlowe's influential Elizabethan lyric "The Passionate Shepherd to His Love" exemplifies, the litany of gifts and activities the shepherd uses to entice his beloved and that ostensibly are readily provided by Nature also present an industry of arts and craft matched with a richness of materials gathered from around the globe that only the affluent might procure in actuality.

Marvell's pastoral is keenly aware of how the leisured classes use wealth to create environments supposedly unsullied by worldly pursuits. In the "The Garden" the narrator offers a vision of quiet and repose in a garden in contrast to political, mercantile, and social engagements. The narrator has a whole range of plants and trees to content him, in contrast to humanity's vain worldly pursuits:

What wonderous life is this I lead!
Ripe apples drop about my head;
The luscious clusters of the vine
Upon my mouth do crush their wine;

> The nectarene, and curious peach,
> Into my hands themselves do reach. (ll. 33–38)

This may appear a straightforward fulfillment of the pastoral ideal, with nature offering its bounty without the necessity of human labor. But the strategic adjective "curious" signals that this is just as likely a fabricated garden idyll that implies more than Marvell merely employing commonplace poetic convention. The Mediterranean origins of classical pastoral poetry meant that traditionally this region's horticulture stocked the poems, even when later northern poets celebrated the "golden worlds" of environments whose climates did not encourage the fruits and fauna of the south. In much pastoral poetry this is not problematic; the presence of exotic plants serves to emphasize the wondrous purity of the model landscape. But "curious"—meaning unusual and rare as well as delicate—recalls that peaches, as nectarines and melons, are not easily grown in England. They are possible to nurture if attended to carefully, grown against walls or under glass, but consequently they are found only in gardens that are fastidiously cultivated—well-designed spaces that inevitably were only the prerogative of the wealthy. Who are we to assume Marvell's narrator in "The Garden" is and how genuinely natural, as opposed to a man-made artifice, is his garden?

> How well the skilful gard'ner drew
> Of flow'rs and herbs this dial new;
> Where from above the milder sun
> Does through a fragrant zodiac run;
> And, as it works, th'industrious bee
> Computes its time as well as we.
> How could such sweet and wholesome hours
> Be reckoned but with herbs and flow'rs! ("The Garden" ll. 65–72)

There are at least two distinct ways of interpreting who the "skilful gard'ner" might be, a decision for readers that has enormous consequences for negotiating Marvell's pastoral vision. Conventionally, many critics have seen him as God, the master architect of the universe (*Poems* 154–55, 159). In this case, "The Garden" appears to be praising a temperate harmonious natural order, one it suggests the narrator has rejoined in contrast to a man-made world that abides by artificial conventions such as the human measurement of time. In another respect, though, the narrator may be praising his very earthly gardener who has constructed an ornamental floral clock, positioning herbs and flowers to form an elaborate sundial. The bee, ironically, therefore, appears to be accounting for its hours in the same way as humans do as it collects nectar from this artifice, moving (presumably clockwise) through the dial. Nature, in other words, has become subject to human design.

If the poem's gardener is understood as an actual gardener, then, far from being a natural philosopher who has restored a link with the divine order, the narrator emerges as a decadent figure who fails to recognize that his garden is an artful pretence of the pastoral, one built on the labor of others. Rather than a genuine natural refuge that opposes man-made environments, this garden is their epitome, a place predicated on the wealth human pursuits generate: contemplation in solitude is an expensive commodity. In Marvell's "The Mower against Gardens," the mower narrator castigates "Luxurious man, to bring his vice in use,/ did after him the world seduce" (ll. 1–2), complaining about how gardeners stock their enclosed spaces with exotic plants either created artificially through grafting different stocks together or by importing them from the four corners of the globe. He contrasts the "sweet fields" that lie forgotten against the artfulness of man-made fountains and grottoes, suggesting that where such gardens display imported statuary of gods and goddesses, in the neglected fields the genuine deities dwell forgotten: humanity seems to prefer pretense to authenticity (esp. ll. 31–40). The mower's attack might be read as a critical castigation of "The Garden."

At various stages in the "The Garden," Marvell directs a gentle irony at his narrator. For instance, he is an astonishingly naive and inexact reader of Ovid, proposing that Apollo and Pan pursued Daphne and Syrinx because they anticipated their metamorphoses into a laurel and a reed rather than this change occurring as a consequence of these nymphs escaping the gods' attempted rape of them. The "wondrous life" of the narrator starts to appear potentially in the manner of the lethargic poet who Marvell's *An Horatian Ode Upon Cromwell's Return from Ireland* proposes "in the shadows sing / His numbers languishing"—a figure who is chastised in contrast to the energy of the active warrior Cromwell.[6]

If Marvell's narrator starts to seem unreliable, a figure who parodies the genuine pastoral, this has consequences for the poem's most celebrated lines:

Meanwhile the mind, from pleasure less,
Withdraws into its happiness;
The mind, that ocean where each kind
Does straight its own resemblance find;
Yet it creates, transcending these,
Far other worlds and other seas;
Annihilating all that's made
To a green thought in a green shade. ("The Garden" ll. 41–48)

During the nineteenth century, Marvell became known as the "laureate of grass and greenery" and these lines have been cited as the principal example of how he anticipated the Romantic movement's celebration of Nature as leading to spiritual insight.[7] In 1892, E. K. Chambers, for example, was decidedly Wordsworthian in celebrating what he saw as Marvell's "real passion [. . .] for nature [. . .] the great spiritual influence which deepens and widens life for us" (Story Donno 269). Though usually in less inflated language, this critical sense of Marvell as a conventional, if exceptionally gifted, pastoral poet still dominates many current readers' views today. There appears to be a lyrical Marvell and a political Marvell, figures who infrequently meet in many critical accounts, with those at the forefront of the current wave of Marvell's rehabilitation as a major seventeenth-century political figure tending to characterize his pastoral poetry as marginal to his main concerns.[8]

This supposed division between what might be termed Marvell's public and private poetry is less marked than the critical tradition indicates. As demonstrated, it is certainly possible to envisage a satiric reading of "The Garden," its poetic narrator an illustration of misemployed philosophy: the "green thought in a green shade" not signaling elevated thoughts but idle complacent "languishing." Given Marvell's parliamentary sympathies both during the English Civil War and after, and royalist poets' particular celebration of retirement in the late 1640s and 1650s, Marvell's apparent praise of retreat in "The

Garden" might be seen as a parodic ridiculing of the opposition's poetics, a common feature of the period.[9] This use of pastoral is designed to look superficially attractive but with further exploration is revealed as empty artifice, questioning the integrity of the social and political positions from which it ostensibly emerges.

It would be reductive, however, merely to claim that Marvell is actually a type of antipastoral wolf masquerading as a pastoral lamb. As we have seen with Milton's Adam in *Paradise Lost,* the human experience of eating from Eden's Tree of Knowledge is to become intoxicated by its fruit, imagining a heightened sensibility when the reality is the loss of easy communication with the divine. But while, in many respects, Marvell's narrator in "The Garden" might be potentially witnessed as a type of overstimulated Adam, Marvell is characteristically less directive than Milton in establishing the temperaments of his poetic narrators. *Paradise Lost* relies on its readers knowing Scripture. Because the consequence of humanity's fall was understood as indisputable fact in Milton's age, it is assumed we recognize that Adam is self-deceiving in thinking that Eve has "well [. . .] purveyed" in giving him the apple. Marvell is far less clear about his narrator's experience in "The Garden" or in most of his other poetry because he is deliberately playful about the type of poetic voice that is operating in his work. It is rare with Marvell's poems that we can be confident about their narrators' integrities—how serious, ironic, or farcical they should be understood to be. Indeed, it is frequently the case that all these elements may appear present: even a clownish messenger may deliver a serious message. Marvell's poetics repeatedly challenge readers' security about whether they are reading accurately or whether they have failed to grasp a poem's tone correctly and, consequently, are likely misconstruing its arguments.

"The mind, that ocean where each kind / Does straight its own resemblance find": as some of the best recent critics of Marvell have noted there is a strikingly narcissistic aspect to much of his poetry.[10] While it is possible to read the narrator's experience in "The Garden" as either a vehicle to a higher knowledge or, conversely, as an excise in self-indulgence, Marvell's poem raises an important issue about how human creativity may operate. If the mind is an ocean where, despite its expanse, each "kind" (not only each species of plant and animal but also human social classes, as well as other classifications such as literary genres) readily discovers its own resemblance, are all further acts of creativity similar exercises in self-reproduction? Are the other worlds and seas the mind potentially can create not genuinely transcendent but familiar arenas where, once again, each "kind" seeks to locate its own likeness? It is notable that many of Marvell's lyric exercises are in dialogue form: the presence of different ways of witnessing the world is a feature found throughout his poetry. A striking feature of Marvell's verse is this sense of varying simultaneous alternate possibilities being present in it, with a reader often left uncertain about what the poet's—as opposed to the narrator's—precise vision actually is. His employment of pastoral offers no clear assurance that Marvell perceived turning to Nature as a legitimate vehicle to fathom human experience or whether his inclination was to witness it more as a retreat away from genuine inquiry into a self-regarding fancy.

The relation between pastoral and the world outside its idealized domain was an issue that Renaissance writing regularly addressed. In Ben Jonson's influential "To Penshurst," for instance, the poet celebrates the harmonious estate of the Sidney family. Jonson proposes that even King James and Prince Charles delight to visit Penshurst because it is more faultlessly governed than the realm outside, bringing attention to the imperfections that exist beyond the estate's boundaries.[11] Considering the growth of retirement poetry in the seventeenth century, James Turner observes that while such magic estates could be created in verse, the reality was a land racked by bad harvests, poverty, and oppression (Turner 1). The period was also uncertain about whether a retreat to the *locus amoenus,* "the pleasant place," was a morally defensible strategy to pursue. For example, in both Sir Philip Sidney's *Arcadia* and Edmund Spenser's *The Faerie Queene,* two of the most influential English literary texts read during the seventeenth century, the concept of pastoral retreat is presented ambivalently and often portrayed as an abandonment of civic duties. The pastoral may often offer a refuge against a hostile external environment but it can also become a place of inactivity that enables both external and internal vice to thrive and ultimately to threaten the pastoral's supposedly golden world. Marvell did not need Milton's *Areopagitica* to remind him of the dangers "of fugitive and cloistered vertue, unexercised and unbreath'd."[12]

In his *Horatian Ode,* Marvell favors the active life outside the garden above a composed life within in it. Cromwell moves from his "private garden, where / he lived reservèd and austere" to where he "Could by industrious valour climb / To ruin the great work of time": not a presumptuous assault on a legitimate order, but a reclaiming of a corrupt world (ll. 29–34). Yet, as we have seen, Marvell is rarely a poet who offers a single perspective on issues and this is the case with his complex considerations of how pastoral relates to an ostensibly harsher world outside it.

In "The Nymph Complaining for the Death of her Fawn" the poem begins with a sad intrusion by the world outside the nymph's enclosure into her pastoral sphere: "The wanton troopers riding by / Have shot my fawn and it will die" (l.1–2). But this poem rapidly becomes something more challenging than a naive lament for the destruction of the innocent by external predators. The reference to troopers is almost certainly to the cavalry of the English Civil War, though they could be either parliamentarian or royalist troops. As the poem establishes, however, the fawn has been a gift, a ruse to beguile the nymph's virginity. It was a present from Sylvio, a fellow inhabitant of her domain, but one who eventually grew "wild" and left the nymph with a "smart" (ll. 25–36). Given that some of the contemporary meanings of "wanton" were cruel and undisciplined, it would seem that in shooting the fawn the troopers have enacted a similar assault to Sylvio's: the nymph's pastoral environment is not as innocent as might first seem. Indeed, as the poem develops, the nymph recalls how in her private garden, so overgrown it has become "a little wilderness" (l. 74), she and the fawn enacted a baroque fantasy of mock bleeding and mock fatality, a play of sex and death in red and white that links even this inner retreat to Sylvio and the troopers' wildness / wantonness (ll. 71–92). The nymph experiences the fawn's death as a prelude for her own (and we should recall that a Renaissance commonplace is to perceive sex as a "little death": dying also suggests orgasm). But this fictional mortality provides her with an opportunity to imagine herself becoming the subject for enduring elaborate statuary, another opportunity for Marvell to employ a type of mock-Ovidian metamorphosis. Perversely, the nymph desires to abandon her being to become the luxurious object the mower castigated in his assault on artificial gardens, where statuary takes the place of genuine deities. Her final address to the dead fawn seem equally directed to herself, a craving for appearance over reality, less a plea for a genuine restoration of lost virginity than for its façade: "For I would have thine image be / White as I can, though not as thee" (121–22). Marvell's poem seems closer in spirit to the social dilemmas and posturing explored some half a century later in Pope's *Rape of the Lock* than to the familiar seventeenth-century motif of *"Et in Arcadia Ego"*—where pastoral denizens discover their rural idyll does not prevent death.[13]

In the fashion of the narrator of "The Garden," the nymph's narcissist self-involvement pays scant regard to the world beyond her enclosure. As with most of Marvell's poetry, this lyric is impossible to date precisely, though "troopers" is not recorded before 1640 at the start of the Civil War. But regardless whether this poem was written during the Civil War period or in the nearly two decades that Marvell lived after those events, it is striking that the nymph is portrayed as apparently utterly oblivious about the troopers' destructive disposition. In a historical context where the trauma of civil conflict had touched all parts of the British Isles with actual loss, her childlike failure to recognize that "wanton troopers" hardly require a logical rationale to shoot a fawn seems breathtaking in its ingenuousness. This exposes the totality of her egocentric self-absorption rather than acting as a revelation of her purer innocence. The nymph's pastoral enclosure appears a place to indulge in decadent vanity instead of a *locus* to further enlightened spiritual and moral values.

A similar uneasy quality often seems to haunt the sanctuary provided by the wood in Marvell's longest and most sustained poetic engagement with pastoral, *Upon Apple-ton House, To My Lord Fairfax*. The narrator in this poem, too, is capable of adopting attitudes that threaten the integrity of his vision: "Thus languishing with ease, I toss / On pallets swoll'n of velvet moss" (ll. 593–94). His self-presentation as a figure who, conferring with the birds and trees, has "read in Nature's mystic book" can give the impression of an exercise in fantastic delusion more than authentic illumination:

> What Rome, Greece, Palestine, ere said
> I in this light mosaic read.
> Thrice happy he who, not mistook,
> Hath read in Nature's mystic book. (ll. 581–84)

As Marvell intimates, there is a possibility of mistaking the reading of Nature's book, a prospect the narrator does not seemingly entertain for himself but which others witnessing him may not share: his "light mosaic" can appear insubstantial rather than enlightening.

Although the narrator of *Upon Appleton House* shares qualities that make him a candidate of Marvellian satire in the manner of the mower, the narrator of "The Garden," or the nymph of "The Nymph Complaining for the Death of her Fawn," this lengthy poem develops a more profound meditation on the relation of pastoral to the actual world of mid-seventeenth-century England. As Derek Hirst and Stephen Zwicker have conclusively established, the poem is an occasional one.[14] In the summer of 1651, after resigning his commission as commander of Parliament's army a year earlier, Thomas Lord Fairfax had retired to his Yorkshire estate at Nun Appleton with Marvell in attendance as tutor to his daughter Maria. Fairfax's resignation has been occasioned by Parliament's decision to invade Scotland, a former ally against Charles I, to prevent the executed king's son, Charles Stuart, winning Scottish Presbyterian support to his cause and invading England. Fairfax felt such an invasion unjustified and, more generally, had shown unease about the Parliament's regicide. His decision allowed Oliver Cromwell to gain supreme command over the army. But despite initial English victories over the Scots, it was not until after the battle of Worcester in September 1651 that a Scottish threat to England was over. Further, the summer of 1651 witnessed the culmination of the millenarian reformist movement within the parliamentary army. With this faction's concerns often focused on the right to own property and the poor's access to common land, this was an internal dissension that England's leaders perceived as a threat to social order. In one of the poem's episodes that depicts a flood that turns Nun Appleton's environment topsy-turvy (ll. 457–80), *Upon Appleton House* portrays this anxiety, recording the Leveller's desires for common land for their cattle as allowing the landscape to be "pinched yet nearer by the beast" rather than being enriched (ll. 449–54). The Leveller threat to Fairfax's estate was real during the summer of 1651, with riots against the enclosure of land nearby (Hirst and Zwicker 252–53). Despite the poem's setting among fruitful fields and protective woods, it portrays a landscape that might at any moment be invaded. Fairfax's decision to resign his command of the army had meant the State's loss of his leadership in opposing a potential foreign threat but also in controlling a rebellious element within it:

> Oh thou, that dear and happy isle
> The garden of the world ere while,
> Thou Paradise of four seas,
> Which heaven planted us to please,
> But, to exclude the world, did guard
> With wat'ry if not flaming sword;
> What luckless apple did we taste,
> To make us mortal, and thee waste?
> [. . .]
> And yet there walks one on the sod
> Who, had it pleased him and God,
> Might once have made our gardens spring
> Fresh as his own and flourishing. (*Upon Appleton House* ll. 321–28, 345–48)

Marvell's presentation of Britain as a now lost Eden is vague about when the island's paradise state was abandoned, though the contemporary resonance of the country as "wasted" was inescapable in 1651. What is abundantly clear is that it proposes that Fairfax might have re-created a national garden with the same integrity as his own estate. His retirement has prevented this. The poem suggests that this decision rests with Fairfax's cultivation of "conscience," a heavenly plant that composes the "crowns" of heavenly saints (ll. 353–60). *Upon Appleton House* carefully does not address directly the context underlying Fairfax's exercise of conscience; yet, as the previous lines illustrate, Marvell intimates his uncertainty about Fairfax's decision. While acknowledging that Fairfax's action "pleased" God, the emphasis on the choice being principally Fairfax's may imply the poet is doing no more than conceding that these events necessarily conform with divine providence as all actions in some sense do. The poem is neither unequivocally stating that the former lord general's retirement to his estates gained divine admiration, nor that it was in accord with England's interest.

With Marvell in Fairfax's employ and sharing his retirement at Nun Appleton, the poet is not in a position to attack the former general's decision. But equally, it would misconstrue *Upon Appleton House* to read it as unambiguously supporting Fairfax's strategy. Marvell negotiates a potentially awkward stance by making his narrator full of confidence about the perfections of the estate and of the advantages it offers to philosophize within it pastoral enclosures, while at the same time constantly raising doubts about the narrator's reliability as he is confronted by events he can only awkwardly explain:

> How safe, methinks, and strong, behind
> These trees have I encamped my mind;
> [. . .] where the world no certain shot
> Can make, or me it toucheth not.
> But I on it securely play,
> And gall its horseman all the day. (ll. 601–08)

Despite celebrating his safety at Nun Appleton, the narrator's experience of the estate is of the world's intrusion into it, often mocking his attempts to characterize its events according to conventional pastoral models (e.g., the strange interruption of Thestylis who sarcastically answers the narrator at ll. 393–408). *Appleton House*'s conclusion sums up this unsettling combination of the narrator's evocation of an environment apparently both droll and threatening: the salmon-fishers placing their leather coracles on their heads making them appear as tortoises, "rational amphibii," and their similarity to the encroaching "dark hemisphere" that indicates the poem's audience should take shelter inside. What might appear a pastorally convoluted manner for describing a benign end to a day as readily seems to indicate a menacing global finality.

As *Upon Appleton House* acknowledges: "'Tis not, what once it was, the world; / But a rude heap together hurled" (ll. 761–62). Yet, though Fairfax's estate contains the necessary imperfections of fallen nature, it is "in more decent order tamed," and, as a result, is heaven's centre on earth and, significantly, "Paradise's only map" (ll. 766–68). As Donald Friedman has noted, one of the central issues for mid-seventeenth-century England was around a redefinition of sovereignty and where it resided.[15] The "lesser world" (l. 765) of Fairfax's estate becomes an illustration of England. While Marvell celebrates its order and government, its shaping of a place where humanity might regain some perspective of the divine world that has been lost, Appleton House nevertheless remains vulnerable. Marvell recognizes a paradox in celebrating Fairfax for possessing moral qualities that have enabled him to create this supposedly ideal environment but ones that, in provoking his retirement from public life, have also generated the conditions that further his estate's exposure to external assault.

There appears to be something almost intrinsic about Nun Appleton's pastoral space and the qualities it promotes that render it in someway defenseless. Further, because it does not offer the clarity of vision that pastoral should possess, Marvell exposes the estate's limitations as an ideal spot to provoke effective "Philosophical Enthusiasms." Ultimately, he seems to question its authenticity as a paradigm of an ideally designed environment. For Marvell, pastoral may offer humanity either a map of Paradise or a map that leads us toward Paradise, but such maps are at the mercy of imperfect interpreters.

After the restoration of the monarchy in 1660, John Evelyn and his followers in the emergent landscape movement particularly celebrated Virgilian pastoral because one of its features is the possibility of recurrence. Just as the Emperor Augustus had brought about a *Pax Romana* after the scars of Roman civil war, so England might not only restore earlier glories but also create a similar greater Augustan golden age (Chambers, *Planters* 23). As we have seen, Marvell's sense of pastoral revival is much less certain. Nature may potentially offer a means of renewal in its ideal enclosures, but just as humanity failed to remain in harmony with the perfected landscape in our first possession of Eden, for Marvell, even paradise regained may sadly be merely a prelude to a further paradise lost.

## NOTES

1. John Evelyn, Letter of January 28, 1660, Christ Church, Oxford MS39a. Cited in Douglas D. C. Chambers, *The Planters of the English Landscape Garden: Botany, Trees and the Georgics* (New Haven: Yale UP, 1993) 3.

2. Andrew Marvell, "The Garden" 48, *The Poems of Andrew Marvell,* ed. Nigel Smith (Harlow, Essex: Pearson Education Ltd, 2003) 158. All citations from Marvell's poetry from this edition.

3. Ovid, *Metamorphoses* 1.88–98, trans. Rolfe Humphries (Bloomington: Indiana UP, 1955) 5.

4. John Milton, *Paradise Lost,* Book 9.1017–21, ed. Alastair Fowler (London: Longman, 1971) 497.

5. John Creaser, "'As one scap't strangely from Captivity': Marvell and Existential Liberty," *Marvell and Liberty,* ed. Warren Chernaik and Martin Dzelzainis (Basingstoke: Macmillan, 1999) 146.

6. Blair Worden notes how "languishing" was a common parliamentary critique of royalist aesthetics: "Andrew Marvell, Oliver Cromwell and *The Horatian Ode,*" *The Politics of Discourse: The Literature and History of Seventeenth-Century English,* ed. Kevin Sharpe and Steven N. Zwicker (Berkeley: University of California P, 1987) 167.

7. Elizabeth Story Donno, ed., *Andrew Marvell: The Critical Heritage* (London: Routledge and Kegan Paul, 1978) 1.

8. See Annabel Patterson, "Andrew Marvell and the Revolution," *The Cambridge Companion to Writing of the English Revolution,* ed. N. H. Keeble (Cambridge: Cambridge UP, 2001) 107.

9. For an overview of the period's landscape poetry, see James Turner, *The Politics of Landscape: Rural Scenery and Society in English Poetry 1630–1660* (Cambridge, MA: Harvard UP, 1979). For contrasts between republican and royalist work, see David Norbrook *Writing the English Republic: Poetry, Rhetoric and Politics, 1627–1660* (Cambridge: Cambridge UP, 1999). For Civil War parody, see Margaret Anne Doody, *The Daring Muse: Augustan Poetry Reconsidered* (Cambridge: Cambridge UP, 1985) 30–56.

10. Jonathan Goldberg, "Marvell's Nymph and the Echo of Voice," *Voice Terminal Echo: Postmodernism and English Renaissance Texts* (London: Methuen, 1986) 14–32; Paul Hammond, "Marvell's Sexuality," *The Seventeenth Century* 11 (1996): 87–123.

11. For Jonson and Marvell, see my "Dark All Without It Knits: Vision and Authority in Marvell's *Upon Appleton House,*" *Literature and the English Civil War,* ed. Thomas Healy and Jonathan Sawday (Cambridge: Cambridge UP, 1990) 181–82.

12. See Douglas D. C. Chambers, "'To the Abyss': Gothic as a Metaphor for the Argument About Art and Nature in *Upon Appleton House,*" *On the Celebrated and Neglected Poems of Andrew Marvell,* ed. Claude J. Summers and Ted-Larry Pebworth (Columbia: U of Missouri P, 1992) 139–53.

13. Panofsky demonstrates that the *"ego"* of *et in arcadia ego* (I too am in Arcadia) is often Death announcing his presence. See Erwin Panofsky, *"Et in Arcadia Ego:* Poussin and the Elegiac Tradition," *Meaning in the Visual Arts: Papers in and on Art History* (Garden City, NY: Doubleday Anchor Books, 1955) 295–320.
14. Derek Hirst and Steven Zwicker, "High Summer at Nun Appleton, 1651: Andrew Marvell and Lord Fairfax's Occasions," *The Historical Journal* 36 (1993): 247–69.
15. Donald M. Friedman, "Rude Heaps and Decent Order," in *Marvell and Liberty* 124.

## READING LIST

Colie, Rosalie. *"My Echoing Song": Andrew Marvell's Poetry of Criticism.* Princeton: Princeton UP, 1970.
Crewe, Jonathan. "The Garden State: Marvell's Poetics of Enclosure." *Enclosure Acts: Sexuality, Property and Culture in Early Modern England.* Ed. Richard Burt and John Michael Archer. Ithaca: Cornell UP, 1994. 270–89.
Friedman, Donald. *Marvell's Pastoral Art.* London: Routledge and Kegan Paul, 1970.
Healy, Thomas Healy, ed. *Andrew Marvell.* Longman Critical Reader, Harlow, Essex: Addison Wesley Longman 1998.
Marcus, Leah S. *The Politics of Mirth: Jonson, Herrick, Milton, Marvell, and the Defense of Old Holiday Pastimes.* Chicago: U of Chicago P, 1986.
Williams, Raymond. *The Country and the City.* London: Oxford UP, 1973.
Zwicker, Stephen. *Lines of Authority: Politics and English Literary Culture, 1649–1689.* Ithaca: Cornell UP, 1994.

# 28

# Milton, the Nativity Ode, the Companion Poems, and *Lycidas*

*Barbara K. Lewalski*

No writer before Milton fashioned himself quite so self-consciously as an author, and he began to do so even in his early poems. Born in 1608 to a family that was staunchly Protestant, bourgeois, and cultured, Milton was profoundly grateful to his father, a scrivener (notary and money-lender) by profession and a musician and composer by avocation, for fostering his deep commitment to learning and poetry. He had private tutors at home in many languages (Latin, Greek, Hebrew, Italian, French), attended one of the finest private schools in England (St. Pauls), and earned a B.A. and then an M.A. at Cambridge University (Christ's College) over the course of seven years (1625–32). He then spent six additional years at his father's house in a self-designed intensive program of reading and study in philosophy, theology, the ancient and modern languages and their literatures, science, history, and much else, and finished his education with an extended "grand tour" in France, Italy, and Switzerland. He probably went to the University with the serious intention of preparing to take orders in the church, the most likely vocation for a young man of his scholarly and religious propensities. But he rapidly became more and more disenchanted with the English church that was moving, as he thought, away from Reformation ideals and back toward Rome, and more and more persuaded that poetry was his true vocation.[1]

Nevertheless, when civil war became imminent in 1641 he set his poetic ambitions aside for a time, thinking himself called by God to write treatises and polemic tracts that would advance reformation in church and state. After the execution of King Charles I in 1649, he served as Latin Secretary for the republic and for the Protector Oliver Cromwell. But he also thought such life experiences vital to his poetic aspirations, since one who would write major poetry must do so out of the values and virtues he has cultivated within himself:

> I was confirm'd in this opinion, that he who would not be frustrate of his hope to write well hereafter in laudable things, ought him selfe to be a true Poem, that is, a composition, and patterne of the best and honorablest things; not presuming to sing high praises of heroick men, or famous Cities, unless he have in himselfe the experience and the practice of all that which is praise-worthy.[2]

For twenty years he was deeply involved with the major intellectual and political issues of his time, developing and arguing passionately for increasingly radical positions: very broad religious toleration, divorce for incompatibility, a press unfettered by licensing regulations (*Areopagitica*), intellectual freedom, separation of church and state, popular sovereignty, justification of revolution and regicide, republicanism, and also several heterodox theological ideas, including antitrinitarianism. After the restoration of King Charles II brought about the defeat of the causes he had served, the now blind poet wrote his three greatest poems, *Paradise Lost, Paradise Regained,* and *Samson Agonistes.*

Milton's major early poems are the product of his years at university and his studious retirement at home (1625–38). Like most collegiate poets, Milton wrote much of his undergraduate poetry in Latin—still the universal language—but his rise well above the flood of imitative Latin verse the age produced. During his graduate years and after he turned chiefly to the vernacular, writing Petrarchan sonnets in Italian and in English some epitaphs and lovely lyrics, the masque popularly called *Comus,* and the four masterpieces treated here. At first, as fledgeling poets customarily do, Milton tried on a number of styles, drawing chiefly on Spenser and Shakespeare among English poets and also on classical and continental poets (Homer, Virgil, Ovid, Tasso, DuBartas, and many more). But he did not look to his popular near-contemporaries, John Donne and the Cavalier lyric poets. More than any other English poet, Milton brought to bear upon his poetry—early and late—the whole weight of his literary and intellectual heritage.

In the nativity ode, *L'Allegro,* and *Lycidas,* Milton makes extensive use of pastoral elements, consciously imitating Virgil's (and Spenser's) conception of the poet's proper progress from the "lower" pastoral kinds to epic. In the Renaissance, pastoral was often used to present an image of innocence, recalling the classical Golden Age and the biblical Eden. The usual setting is an ideal landscape (the so-called *locus amoenus*) replete with the loveliness of spring—rolling hills, green grasses, grazing sheep, soft breezes, cool winds, murmuring springs. The activities of pastoral are love and song: the highest value is *otium,* contentment, carelessness.[3] Its opposite is *neg / otium,* business—implying the values of war, civic and political action, ambition, glory (the values of epic). Pastoral had become a way of exploring the relation of humans and nature, of art and nature, and of the poet and his world. It typically depicts humankind in harmony with a nature that reflects and responds to human emotions and circumstances. Milton makes strikingly original uses of the pastoral mode.

As an aspiring poet, Milton had to determine how to situate himself in the culture wars that intensified during the 1630s. One sign of his divergence from contemporary cultural norms is the fact that throughout his university career his muse entirely ignored the various royal and courtly occasions celebrated by other university poets—the death and funeral of James I, the coronation and wedding of Charles I, the visits of Charles and Buckingham to the university, the births and deaths of royal children. Unlike Donne and Herbert, this serious-minded young bourgeois poet seems never to have thought about courtiership; though not yet an antiroyalist, he showed no inclination to look to the Court for patronage or imaginative stimulus. Also, some of his early writing bears an overt or covert political charge—vehemently anti-Catholic, anti-Laudian, critical of Stuart religious repression, supportive of Protestant militancy in Europe, prophetic—a politics that aligns him with reformist and oppositional views. We can sometimes glimpse in the student Milton the Puritan revolutionary in the making, and also the inspired bard. By contrast with his contemporaries, Milton began even as a young poet to construct himself as a new kind of author, one who commands all the resources of learning and art but links them to radical politics, reformist poetics, and the inherently revolutionary power of prophecy.

Milton's first great poem, "On the Morning of Christs Nativity," was composed in 1629, some months after he took his B.A. degree. In a verse letter to his dearest friend,

Charles Diodati, Milton comments on his high poetic aspirations and on this ode as the first major realization of them, underscoring its reach toward prophetic poetry (ll. 81–86).[4] Terming it his gift "for the birthday of Christ" written at daybreak on Christmas morning, he no doubt saw special significance in its composition just after his own important twenty-first birthday (December 9, 1629). This early poem already displays qualities that remain constants in Milton's poetry: allusiveness, revisionism, mixture of genres, stunning originality, cosmic scope, prophetic voice. It is a remarkable achievement in conception and craft for this twenty-one-year old, as well as a crucial gesture of self-definition, self-presentation, and dedication as a poet.

Each stanza of the four stanza Proem contains six lines of iambic pentameter and a concluding alexandrine (a six foot line); the rhyme scheme is ababbcc. This rhyme royal stanza is a gesture to Chaucer and Spenser's *Faerie Queene*. The speaker presents the nativity event as both past and now reenacted in his present moment. He is humble and at the same time audacious. By locating himself among Bethlehem's shepherds as a pastoral poet, he proposes in the chronology of the nativity event that his muse arrive with his "humble ode" (pastorals are normally written in a simple style) before the Magi come with their more ostentatious gifts: gold, frankincense and myrrh: "O run, prevent them"; that is, come before them. Behind this identification is Virgil's Fourth Eclogue, more elevated in style than most pastorals since it celebrates (probably) the birth of the Roman consul Pollio's son, taking that birth to begin a return to the Golden Age.[5] Milton's poem revises Virgil, celebrating the true Messiah who alone can restore the Golden Age, at the Millennium. But he also associates his poem with the angels' hymns at the nativity, describing it as a "hymn or solemn strain," and himself as an inspired prophet like Isaiah, whose lips were purified by a burning coal held to them by an angel: "And join thy voice unto the angel choir, / From out his secret altar touched with hallowed fire" (27–28).[6] With these lines Milton formally assumes the role of prophet-poet.

The verse form of the "Hymn" proper is apparently Mlton's own invention: eight-line stanzas with lines of varying lengths (6-6-10-6-6-10-8-12), culminating in a stately alexandrine and employing an intricate, interlaced rhyme scheme (aabccbdd). There are many Spenserian elements: the music of the names and places; allegorical personifications such as Earth and Sun portrayed as lovers and the green-robed, "meek-eyed Peace"; and Spenserian onomatopoeia (figures in which the sound imitates the sense): the old serpent "Swinges the scaly horror of his folded tail" (172), and at the Last Judgment "The wakeful trump of doom must thunder through the deep" (156). This literary hymn is very different from liturgical or congregational hymns meant for singing in religious services and different also from the several sixteenth and seventeenth-century nativity poems in a private, metaphysical vein, such as Robert Southwell's "Burning Babe" or George Herbert's "Christmas."[7] It has a grand theme: not simply the nativity story but the uneasy encounter of the natural order with this supernatural event, and the meaning of the Incarnation for humankind, nature, and the entire cosmos. It also inaugurates a poetic technique characteristic of Milton, in which a particular event is made to encompass all time and space and history: here the poet continually shifts his focus from the morning of Christ's nativity back to Creation and forward to Doomsday, and, in cinematographic fashion, from the particular locale, the Bethlehem scenes, to the widest cosmic perspective.

The poem begins with the manger scene, then moves quickly to the cosmos as Nature, first personified as a wanton harlot, the paramour of the Sun, attempts unsuccessfully to hide her "guilty front with innocent Snow." Marred by the fall of humankind, Nature has been unfaithful to her true lover, the Son/Sun of God. Now the awestruck natural order responds as if to the Second Coming, not the first, as the supernatural order seems ready to supplant the natural: the stars will not take flight and the sun hesitates to appear, supposing himself made superfluous now that a greater Sun/Son has brought Light to the world. The poet is led by Nature's responses to imagine that the Millennium is almost at hand.

Suddenly the focus shifts to a local, distinctly pastoral, scene—"The shepherds on the lawn, / Or ere the point of dawn, / Sat simply chatting in a rustic row"—and then promptly moves out again to the cosmos, as the heavenly music of the angelic choirs announces Christ's nativity. The poet imagines that he hears that choir sounding in harmony with the music of the spheres, describing that music in wonderfully evocative lines:

> Ring out ye crystal spheares,
> Once bless our human ears,
> (If ye have power to touch our senses so)
> And let your silver chime
> Move in melodious time,
> And let the base of heav'n's deep organ blow,
> And with your ninefold harmony
> Make up full consort to th'angelic symphony.
> For if such holy song
> Enwrap our fancy long,
> Time will run back, and fetch the age of gold. ("Nativity Ode" 125–35)

By this music Nature is again "almost won / To think her part was done, / And that her reign had here its last fulfilling." And the poet's imagination is carried back to the Creation and forward to the Millennium where that music was before and will again be heard, so he too supposes that the Golden Age is imminent. He imagines that the "Base of heav'n's deep organ"—Earth, which has been out of tune since the fall—might blow again, and that the other qualities from Psalm 85—Truth, Justice, and Mercy—are coming to join Peace, already descended.[8] Then in another stunning shift of perspective he is abruptly recalled to the nativity moment—"But wisest Fate says no" (149)—and remembers all that must happen before the end: the babe just born must live out his entire history of passion and suffering and must come again as judge in all the terror of the Last Judgment before the millennial Golden Age can come.

The last section focuses on the immediate effects of the nativity, beginning with the "old Dragon" bound and then describing the flight of all the pagan deities from all their dark places throughout the earth. They are differentiated in terms of their relative degrees of darkness and evil—from the utter blackness of Moloch on whose alters infants were burned to the shadowy but lovely "yellow-skirted *Fayes*" (205–36). In this section the pagan gods, understood literally, are seen to be conquered by Christ, but Christ is himself is figured in this poem as the "mighty *Pan*" (the name means "All") come to live among the shepherds (89–90) and as an infant Hercules strangling in his cradle the giant serpent Satan and all his monster crew (227–28). The complex interplay of pagan myth and Christian story often confuses modern readers but it is entirely characteristic of Milton and many Renaissance writers, who take some classical myths as types (foreshadowings) of aspects of the Christian story.

This section had contemporary political resonance. Reproving speculation that the Millennium is imminent, Milton suggests by the length of his catalogue of idols how long and difficult will be the process that must preceed it: ridding humankind of all its idols, lovely as well as hideous. Also, by dramatizing the silencing of Apollo's oracles at Christ's birth, Milton sets Christ's power against what Apollo the Sun-God had come to symbolize as a prominent emblem of Renaissance popes and also of the Stuart kings, James I and Charles I.[9] Many images in Milton's descriptions of the pagan gods (173–220)—"consecrated earth, "service quaint," sable-stoléd sorcerers," "Heaven's queen and mother both" (suggesting the cult of the Virgin)—make this long passage register Puritan anxiety in 1629 over the "popish idolatry" fostered by Bishop and soon-to-be Archbishop William Laud. Milton's poem locates the restored Golden Age at the Millennium, which will arrive only after idols old and new have been cast out.

The final stanza shifts the perspective back to the Bethlehem scene and the "courtly stable." That oxymoron, juxtaposing opposites, is emblematic of the poem itself: it is a pastoral ode/hymn, a humble yet exalted treatment of the great paradox of the Incarnation.

The graceful, urbane companion poems, *L'Allegro* and *Il Penseroso,* climax Milton's university years. They explore the ideal pleasures appropriate to contrasting lifestyles—"heart-easing Mirth," and "divinest Melancholy"—that a poet might choose, or might choose at different times, or in sequence.[10] In one of his academic orations, *Prolusion VII,* Milton indicates that he spent the summer of 1631 in some delightful village that greatly stimulated his intellectual and poetic growth—probably Hammersmith, the "country place" that his father moved to permanently at about this time.[11] *L'Allegro* and *Il Penseroso* were most likely the poetic fruits of that summer. These poems might appear to turn aside from the lofty purposes of the *"Nativity Ode,"* but Milton took quite seriously the linkage they treat so delightfully between choice of lifestyle and the kind of poetry produced.

Both poems are modeled on the classical hymn; the speakers with their Italian names—L'Allegro, the happy man, Il Penseroso, the melancholy man—celebrate their chosen allegorical deities, the Grace Euphrosone (Youthful Mirth) and Melancholy. The poems begin with an exorcism or banishment of the opposing deity, then invite the figure celebrated, then celebrate her ancestry and allegorical companions, then describe the activities of her followers, and finally ask to be admitted to her company.[12] The first five sections of the two poems are closely paralleled, save that those in *Il Penseroso* are a little longer and *Il Penseroso's* eight-line coda has no parallel in *L'Allegro.*

Stylistically, these poems turn away from Spenser. *L'Allegro* especially shows the influence of Ben Jonson's lyrics—his clarity, delicacy, and grace—and also the Shakespeare of *Midsummer Night's Dream* and *Romeo and Juliet.* The final couplet of each poem echoes and answers the question posed in Marlowe's pastoral seduction poem, "The Passionate Shepherd to His Love." Metrically and rhythmically these poems are a *tour de force.* Both begin with a ten-line prelude, with alternating lines of six and ten syllables and an intricate rhyme pattern. For the rest, both use octosyllabic couplets. Milton is now so skillful with metrics that from the same verse form he can produce very different tonal effects. In *L'Allegro* the quick short vowels, the monosyllables, the liquid consonants, and the frequent trochaic rhythms trip over the tongue in an imitation of youthful frolic:

> Haste thee nymph, and bring with thee
> Jest and youthful Jollity,
> Quips and Cranks, and wanton Wiles,
> Nods, and Becks, and wreathed Smiles. (*L'Allegro* ll. 25–28)

In *Il Penseroso* polysyllables, clusters of consonants, and long vowels (echoing "o" sounds especially) produce a deliberate and somber tone:

> Come pensive nun, devout and pure,
> Sober, steadfast, and demure,
> All in a robe of darkest grain,
> Flowing with majestic train. (*Il Penseroso* ll. 31–34)

*L'Allegro* is a praise of youthful mirth, innocent joy, lighthearted pleasure, freedom from care. The prologue banishes this speaker's conception of melancholy, "loathed Melancholy," the disease caused by an imbalance of black bile and associated with depression and madness. Then the speaker invites and praises Mirth, the youthful Grace *Euphrosone*. Setting aside the usual myth of origin deriving her from Bacchus and Venus (suggesting wanton sensuality and excess), he appeals to a Neoplatonic myth (the one depicted in Botticelli's *Primavera*) deriving her from purer sources evocative of springtime: Zephyr, the West Wind, and Aurora, the Dawn. Her associates are Jests, Sports, and Laughter, and her special companion and defining quality is "The mountain nymph, sweet Liberty" (l. 36). The sociable daytime pleasures of Mirth's devoté are presented in a series of delightful pastoral scenes that mix classical shepherds and shepherdesses—Corydon, Thyrsis, Phyllis—with the sights and sounds, the sunshine holidays, and the folk-tales of rural England. Then the speaker turns from pastoral to depict in briefer compass the nocturnal pleasures L'Allegro seeks in "Towered cities": festivals, knightly jousts, court masques, stage comedies.

*Il Penseroso* celebrates Melancholy, seen by this speaker as the scholarly, saturnine temperament that seeks solitude, study, and religious contemplation.[13] Again, a ten-line prologue banishes this speaker's conception of Mirth as "vain deluding joys." He then invites and praises Melancholy: she is sage and holy with a majestic stateliness and a rapt soul; her visage is saintly and black, "staid Wisdoms hue"—something like the figure in Albrecht Durer's famous engraving *Melancholia*—and her parents are Saturn and Saturn's daughter, Vesta. Her companions are calm Peace and Quiet, Spare Fast, and Silence; and her chief associate and defining characteristic is "The Cherub Contemplation" (54). Reversing *L'Allegro,* this poem describes at greatest length the nocturnal pleasures of Melancholy's man—philosophical studies and "gorgeous tragedy" in the theater. During the day Il Penseroso hides from the Sun, enjoying "twilight groves," "shadows brown," and sleep filled with mysterious dreams.

Milton contrasts and evaluates these modes of life as imagined ideals. Some readers have seen surprising affinities with the Cavalier poets in L'Allegro's pastoralism and his attendance at masques and stage plays, and surprising affinities with Roman

Catholic or Laudian ritual in Il Penseroso's fondness for the architecture, art, and organ music of cathedrals, and his final retreat to a hermitage.[14] But Milton, I suggest, uses these images to define and evaluate lifestyles in terms of literary modes, and to reclaim genres and art forms from debased to valid uses. He does not, here or elsewhere, repudiate pastoral, stage plays, or masques because he thinks Cavaliers and the Stuart Court have turned them to licentious or debased uses, or church music and art because he thinks Laudians use them in the service of idolatry. Rather, these poems reclaim such art for innocent delight.

*L'Allegro's* essence, youthful mirth, is displayed chiefly in the activities and values of the pastoral mode and in literary genres harmonious with it: rural folk and faery tales of Queen Mab and Goblin, court masques and pageants, Jonson's "learned" comedy, and romantic comedies in which "sweetest Shakespeare, Fancy's child / Warble[s] his native wood-notes wild" (ll. 133–34). L'Allegro enjoys and perhaps voices love songs in the Greek Lydian mode, describing those soothing (or as Plato thought, enervating) songs in wonderfully mimetic lines:

> And ever against eating cares,
> Lap me in soft Lydian Aires,
> Married to immortal verse
> Such as the meeting soul may pierce
> In notes, with many a winding bout
> Of linkéd sweetness long drawn out,
> With wanton heed, and giddy cunning,
> The melting voice through mazes running;
> Untwisting all the chains that tie
> The hidden soul of harmony.
> That Orpheus' self may heave his head
> From golden slumber on a bed
> Of heaped Elysian flow'rs, and hear
> Such strains as would have won the ear
> Of Pluto, to have quite set free
> His half-regained Eurydice. (*L'Allegro* ll. 135–50)

This music wakens a still-drowsy Orpheus, the figure of the poet, promising, but only in the subjunctive mood, a song that would have power over Pluto. Though not tainted, Lydian song and the life of Mirth seem to be limited, as the conditional terms of the final couplet also indicate: "These delights, if thou canst give,/ Mirth with thee, I mean to live."

In *Il Penseroso* the activities, pleasures, and values of a solitary scholar-errant are rendered chiefly in a medievalizing romance mode. This speaker wanders through a mysterious gothic landscape with a melancholy nightingale, a "high lonely tow'r," a drowsy bellman, a cathedral cloister with "high embowed roof," storied stained glass windows, "dim religious light," a "pealing organ," and a "full voiced choir" participating in "service high," and a hermitage with mossy cells. Melancholy's devoté enjoys the esoteric philosophy of Plato and Hermes Trismegistus, romances like Chaucer's unfinished *Squire's Tale* for their marvels and allegory, Greek tragedies about Thebes and Troy by Aeschylus and Euripides, and bardic hymns like that of Orpheus, which, unlike in *L'Allegro,* is here described in wholly positive terms: it "made Hell grant what Love did seek" (108). Finally, Il Penseroso hears Church music and hymnody that produce ecstasy and vision:

> There let the pealing organ blow
>   To the full-voiced choir below,
>     In service high, and anthems clear,
>   As may with sweetness, through mine ear,
>     Dissolve me into ecstasies,
> And bring all Heav'n before mine eyes. (*Il Penseroso* ll. 161–66)

The title personages of both poems are drawn with some playfulness, as ideal but exaggerated types, representing two kinds of art and life. Yet I think Milton sets them in a sequential relation and implies a progression.[15] This is suggested by comparing the literary genres L'Allegro enjoys to the higher kinds Il Penseroso delights in: L'Allegro's folk tales to Il Penseroso's allegorical romances, comedy to tragedy, Lydian airs to Christian hymns. More important, the eight-line coda of *Il Penseroso* disrupts the poems' parallelism by opening to the future:

> And may at last my weary age
>   Find out some peaceful hermitage,
>     The hairy gown and mossy cell,
>   Where I may sit and rightly spell,
>     Of every star that heav'n doth show,
> And every herb that sips the dew;
>     Till old experience do attain
> To something like prophetic strain. (*Il Penseroso* ll. 167–74)

Clearly Milton does not plan a monastic retreat for himself or hold it forth as an ideal, but he makes those medievalizing romance images figure his aspiration to prophetic poetry. *L'Allegro* portrays the lifestyle of youth as a cyclic round, beginning with Mirth's man awakening from sleep and ending with the drowsing Orpheus. In *Il Penseroso,* age has its place: Melancholy's devoté begins with evening and ends with a waking ecstatic vision of heaven, all embracing knowledge of nature, and prophecy. In this reading the companion poems present a natural progression from *L'Allegro* to the higher life of *Il Penseroso,* which can lead, after the ripening of "long experience," to "something like Prophetic strain"—the creation of prophetic poetry.

*Lycidas* is the *chef d'oeuvre* of Milton's early poetry and arguably the finest funeral elegy in the English language. The grief, shock, and terror called forth by the fact of human mortality, especially by the death of those we care about, have prompted poetic responses from classical to modern times. In this elegy Milton confronts and works through his most profound personal concerns: about vocation, about early death, about belatedness and unfulfillment, about the worth of poetry. He also incorporates reformist politics: the dangers posed by a corrupt clergy, the menace of the Roman church, the call to prophecy. The opening phrase, "Yet once more," places this poem in the group of funeral poems Milton had hitherto written (mostly in Latin), in the long series of pastoral funeral elegies stretching back to the Greek poet Theocritus, and in a collection of biblical warnings and apocalyptic prophecies beginning with those words.[16]

The headnote calls attention to the particular circumstance prompting this funeral elegy: "In this monody the author bewails a learned friend, unfortunately drowned in his passage from Chester on the Irish Seas, 1637." That friend was his college associate Edward King: a memorial volume for him by his Cambridge associates, *Justa Edouardo King naufrago*, appeared early in 1638, containing in Part I twenty-three Latin and Greek poems and in Part II thirteen English poems. *Lycidas* was placed last, as the longest and most impressive contribution. The year 1637 gave Milton ample cause to confront the harsh facts of human mortality: his mother died in April and there were several deaths from plague in his village, Horton. Milton's deepest feelings are clearly engaged in *Lycidas* but not by personal grief, as King was not a close friend. However, his life situation nearly resembled Milton's own. They had shared youthful pleasures and poetic beginnings at Cambridge, and King continued a scholarly life as a fellow of Christ's College, wrote poetry, and served the church as an ordained minister. Confronting a world in which King, three years his junior, could be cut off at age twenty-five with his aspirations, talents, and promise unfulfilled, Milton was driven to call into agonizing question the value of undertaking the arduous vocations of poet and minister. The opening lines establish Lycidas/King and the Miltonic speaker as virtual *alter egos:* since Lycidas was cut off before his time the Miltonic "uncouth swain" must sing a funeral elegy before his poetic gifts are ripe, shattering with "forc'd fingers rude" (l. 4) the unripe laurel and myrtle leaves, time-honored symbols of poetic accomplishment. And so might another poet soon be called upon to do similar honors to a Milton cut off before his talents have been realized. The death of Lycidas seems to demonstrate the uselessness of exceptional talent, lofty ambition, and noble ideals, to show human life and nature alike given over to meaningless chaos. These universal concerns take on special resonance in 1637, in a crisis-ridden nation soon to face Civil War.

The headnote also identifies this poem as a monody, a funeral song by a single singer,[17] though in fact other speakers are quoted in the poem and the coda introduces yet another poetic voice. In 1645 Milton added a final sentence to the headnote, pointing to the poem's prophecy, now fulfilled, of "the ruin of our corrupted clergy then in their height." In the throes of a war in which reformation of the church is a central issue, Milton calls special attention to his own "prophetic" prescience in foretelling this fall. The poem incorporates the expected topics of funeral elegy: praise, lament, and consolation.[18] The verse is chiefly iambic pentameter with occasional short lines, a very irregular rhyme scheme, and verse paragraphs of irregular length: this metrical form intensifies tensions, denies surface smoothness, and prevents facile resolutions. Virtually every line echoes other pastoral elegies by classical, neo-Latin, and vernacular Renaissance poets: Theocritus, Virgil, Petrarch, Mantuan, Spenser, and very many more.[19] Yet no previous, or I think subsequent, funeral poem has the scope, dimension, poignancy, and power of *Lycidas;* it is, paradoxically, at once the most derivative and most original of elegies.

Milton's choice of the pastoral mode—by then out-of-fashion for funeral elegies— enabled him to call upon the rich symbolic resonances Renaissance pastoral had come to embody. Recalling the harmony of nature and humankind in the Golden Age, pastoral elegy traditionally portrays the course of human life and death in harmony with the rhythms of nature and seasonal change: spring (youth), summer (maturity), autumn (fruition and harvest in age), and winter (death). In classical tradition the shepherd is the poet, and pastoral is a way of exploring the relation of art and nature. In biblical tradition the shepherd is pastor of his flock, like Christ the Good Shepherd. He may also be a prophet like Moses, Isaiah, or David, all of them called to that role from tending sheep. Moreover, pastoral allowed for political comment and satire, as in Virgil's Eclogue I, Sidney's *Arcadia,* and Spenser's *Shepheardes Calender.*

As Milton treats the usual topics of pastoral funeral elegy, he evokes the pastoral vision again and again, then dramatizes its collapse. The dead poet and the living mourner are first presented in a poignantly nostalgic scene as youthful companion shepherds singing and tending sheep in a *locus amoenus*—an idealized Cambridge University characterized by pastoral *otium,* in which nature, humankind, and poetic ambition seem to be secure, unthreatened by the fact or even the thought of mortality. Lycidas's death shatters this idyll, revealing in nature as in human life not the orderly seasonal processes that pastoral assumes, but rather the wanton destruction of youth and beauty: the blighted rosebud, the taintworm destroying the weanling sheep, and frostbitten flowers in early spring.

In the poem's first central panel the swain identifies passionately with the plight of the lost poet: the nymphs do not protect their bards, who may be subject to the savagery and mindless violence symbolized in the myth of Orpheus. So often invoked as the type of poets, Orpheus's song had power to charm the very sticks and stones, but he here figures the poet's extreme peril. Even his mother, the Muse Calliope, could not save Orpheus from a horrific death, torn limb from limb by the Maenads who embody the dark forces of savagery that can so easily overcome the fragile civilizing arts. If poetic talent, labor, and the noble desire for fame can be so early and so easily snuffed out, why not live a life of ease and pleasure: why not "sport with Amaryllis in the shade, / Or with the tangles of Neaera's hair?" instead of devoting "laborious days" to "the thankless Muse?" (ll. 66–72). The swain's bitter disillusion is rendered in graphic, appalling metaphors of the "blind Fury" and the "thin-spun life":

> Fame is the spur that the clear spirit doth raise
> (That last infirmity of noble mind)
> To scorn delights, and live laborious days;
> But the fair guerdon when we hope to find,
> And think to burst out into sudden blaze,
> Comes the blind Fury with th'abhorred shears,
> And slits the thin-spun life. (*Lycidas* ll. 70–76)

The speaker does not see beyond the horror of Orpheus's death and dismemberment, but the Orpheus myth also carries an intimation of resurrection, in that Apollo, father of the Muses, guided his head to Lesbos, bringing that island the gift of poetry. The implication is that Lycidas's talent may somehow survive his watery death, and so appropriately it is Apollo who disrupts the pastoral mode, offering another perspective in a "higher [epic] strain." Figuring God in the aspect of true critic, Apollo assures the living swain and the dead Lycidas of fame in the Platonic sense—not praise of the masses but of the best: the "perfect witnes of all-judging Jove" (82) promises enduring fame in Heaven.

This consolation, however partial, encourages the swain to recall the oaten flute of pastoral. He turns to a usual topic of pastoral elegy, questioning the nymphs, the muses, and the classical gods as to why they did not prevent this death. But their denial of all responsibility places this death outside the order of nature and pastoral, as does the fact that Milton avoids all reference to the rock that actually caused the shipwreck. The only conclusion is: "It was that fatal and perfidious bark / Built in th'eclipse, and rigged with curses dark, / That sunk so low that sacred head of thine" (100–02). Those lines reverberate with menacing connotations, but the primary metaphor suggests sailing on the sea of life in the frail bark of the human body, subject to mortality because of the fall of man. That, the metaphor implies, is why Lycidas died, and why pastoral assumptions cannot deal with it.

The poem's second central panel considers the impact of death on the ministry and the society it serves. It begins with a procession of mourners appropriately associated with water—Camus, God of the River Cam flowing by Cambridge University, and St. Peter as "Pilot of the *Galilean* Lake." Lycidas/King was minister as well as poet, and Milton was beginning to imagine an analogous role for himself, that of prophet/teacher. The value of such a role is also called into question by King's early death, since Milton constructs King as a sorely needed, worthy exception to the general greed and ignorance of the clergy—a last chance at reformation.[20] St. Peter, in his role as chief pastor of Christ's Church, launches into a long and fiercely satirical denunciation of the Laudian church and clergy that entirely suppresses the pastoral music. His scornful paradox, "Blind mouths," brilliantly exposes the ignorance, ambition, and greediness of those bad shepherds who seek only to feed their bellies, leaving their hungry sheep unfed (untaught), "swoll'n with wind," and subject to the ravages of the Roman Catholic "grim Wolf" raging freely in the Caroline Court.[21]

> Blind mouths! that scarce themselves know how to hold
>     A sheep-hook, or have learnt aught else the least
>     That to the faithful herdmans art belongs!
>     What recks it them? What need they? They are sped;
>     And when they list, their lean and flashy songs
>     Grate on their scrannel pipes of wretched straw;
>     The hungry sheep look up, and are not fed,
>     But swoll'n with wind, and the rank mist they draw,
>     Rot inwardly, and foul contagion spread:
>     Besides what the grim Wolf with privy paw
>     Daily devours apace, and nothing said. (*Lycidas* ll. 119–29)

That denunciation further emphasizes the apparent meaninglessness of Lycidas's death: where is the justice that takes the good and leaves the wicked?[22] Yet Peter's invective voicing God's wrath and promising imminent Divine retribution supplies a kind of consolation—an apocalyptic prophesy that some formidable if ambiguous "two-handed engine" stands ready "at the door" to smite the guilty and cleanse the church.[23]

Now the swain again recalls pastoral—the river Alpheus and the Sicilian muse were frightened away by Peter's diatribe—and produces a pastoral flower passage echoing numerous others but surpassed by none in its delicacy and nostalgic loveliness. He imagines Lycidas's funeral bier heaped with the flowers into which heroes of classical myth were often transformed, providing for them a kind of immortality in nature. We still find that flowers at funerals offer some consolation by bringing nature's beauties to honor the human dead. But in this case the consolation collapses with the swain's bitter realization that it is based on "false surmise" (153). Lycidas's body is not here to receive the tribute of nature's loveliest flowers but instead is weltering in the sea, subject to the horrors of the monstrous deep. Pastoral consolations based on sympathy and harmony between humankind and nature will not finally serve. The fallen world presents horrors:

> Ay me! whilst thee the shores, and sounding seas
> 　Wash far away, where'er thy bones are hurled,
> Whether beyond the stormy Hebrides,
> Where thou perhaps under the whelming tide
> Visit'st the bottom of the monstrous world. (*Lycidas* ll. 154–58)

From this nadir the movement from inadequate or false to true consolation begins, catching up earlier intimations of resurrection in the myths of Orpheus, Hyacinth, Amaranthus, and Peter. The tone modulates from horror to hope, from the violence of "bones hurled" to the peace of "Sleep'st by the fable of Bellerus old" (l. 160). The swain now sees St. Michael's Mount off the Cornish coast where Lycidas drowned as an image of heavenly protection (warding against Spain), and finds similar import in the myth of the poet Arion saved by dolphins (a type of Jonah). The line, "Weep no more, woeful shepherds, weep no more" (l. 165) echoes the opening line and marks a clear turn to consolation. Nature provides a symbol of resurrection from the sea as the sun sinks into the ocean at night and rises from it at dawn—a type of the divine Son who walked the waves and through whose power St. Peter, and now Lycidas, were "sunk low, but mounted high" (l. 172). At length the swain envisions a heavenly pastoral scene in which Lycidas enjoys true *otium* beside heavenly streams, with both his vocational roles preserved. As poet he now participates in the "unexpressive nuptial song" (l. 176) of the Lamb and the harmonies of heaven. As pastor he is now the "Genius of the shore" (l. 182), a guide, perhaps by means of his exemplary story immortalized in Milton's poem, to all who wander in the "perilous flood" of human life.[24] Pastoral is now caught up in the higher mode of prophetic vision: though painfully inadequate to the fallen human condition, it has its true locus in heaven.

The new voice introduced in the eight-line coda may be the most surprising feature of this always surprising poem. We now discover that a more mature poetic self has been voicing the "uncouth" swain's monody; and he now places in wider perspective the swain's movement from despair to affirmation of life:

> Thus sang the uncouth swain to th'oaks and rills,
> While the still Morn went out with sandals gray;
> He touch'd the tender stops of various quills,
> With eager thought warbling his Doric lay:
> And now the sun had stretch'd out all the hills,
> And now was dropped into the western bay;
> At last he rose, and twitched his mantle blue:
> Tomorrow to fresh woods and pastures new. (*Lycidas* ll. 186–93)

Having had his vision of the perfected pastoral in heaven, the swain is restored to hope and direction through the example of Lycidas/King, and can now take up his several pastoral roles in this world—seen now as fallen but also redeemed. He retains his blue shepherd's mantle and (as poet) continues to warble his pastoral Doric lay. Blue is also the color of Aaron's priestly robes (Exod. 28:31), intimating that, like Lycidas, the swain will continue some kind of ministry in the church. Twitching that mantle, he assumes poetry's prophetic/ teaching role—like an Elisha receiving the mantle of prophecy from an Elijah taken up to heaven.[25] Reprising the daily cycle of pastoral— forth at dawn, home at evening—the coda points to the promise of new adventures, personal and literary, for the Miltonic swain: the next stage of life and poetry and national reformation.

Milton published these and several other poems late in 1645, in a volume titled *Poems of Mr. John Milton.* He placed his English lyrics first, beginning with the nativity ode, in which he dedicated himself as a poet-prophet, and ending with *Lycidas,* with its formal rededication: "Tomorrow to fresh woods and pastures new." Then comes his reformed masque, commonly known as *Comus,* and as a separate part, his Latin and Greek poems presented as juvenalia. This volume is an exercise in self-fashioning and self-presentation to the world. It is seen by some as a bid for respectability, in which Milton sought to distance himself from his recent polemics and to associate his book with contemporary Cavalier collections.[26] But while the bookseller's prefatory matter invites such a reading, Milton's title-page epigraph from Virgil's Eclogue VII presents him instead as predestined bard (*vati [. . .] futuro*),[27] explicitly refusing the "Cavalier" construction. In the volume as a whole Milton presents himself as a new kind of reformist poet, one who has command of several languages and all the resources of high culture, but who distinguishes himself sharply from Cavalier lyricists, court masque writers, and Anglican devotional poets. His poems are designed to reclaim and reform genres they dominate; and he also claims a poetic mode shunned by the cavaliers, prophecy. Milton evidently saw his 1645 *Poems* as a worthy alternative to the cavalier collections: a volume of learned, delightful, reformed poems that would advance the project he formally proposed in *The Reason of Church Government* (1642)—to help transform English culture through good art (*YP* I: 819).

## NOTES

1. For further biography and criticism relating to these and later years, see Barbara K. Lewalski, *The Life of John Milton: A Critical Biography,* Rev. ed. (Oxford: Blackwell, 2003).
2. From *An Apology Against a Pamphlet* (1642), *Complete Prose Works of John Milton,* ed. Don M. Wolfe et al. 8 vols. (New Haven: Yale UP, 1953–82) 2: 890. Cited hereafter as *YP,* by volume and page number.
3. See Paul Alpers, *What Is Pastoral?* (Chicago: U of Chicago P, 1996).
4. "Elegy VI," *John Milton: The Complete Poems,* ed. John Leonard (London: Penguin, 1998) 535–40. All references to Milton's poetry in the text are by line number to this edition.
5. Milton draws upon the centuries-old Christian tradition identifying Virgil's Fourth or "Messianic" Eclogue as an unconscious prophecy of the birth of Christ.

6. Isaiah 6:6–7.

7. Milton's poem looks back to the Homeric hymns and Pindaric odes and to their Renaissance imitators, including Spenser's "Fowre Hymnes." See Phillip Rollinson, "Milton's Nativity Ode and the Decorum of Genre," *Milton Studies* 7 (1975): 165–84; and Stella Revard, *Milton and the Tangles of Neaera's Hair: The Making of the 1645 Poems* (Columbia: U of Missouri P, 1997) 64–90.

8. The descent of the green-robed, meek-eyed Peace in the third stanza refers to the legend that at Christ's birth there was peace throughout the world. It also alludes to Psalm 85:10, part of the liturgy for Christmas, "Mercy and truth are met together; righteousness and peace have kissed each other." In stanza 15 the other three qualities are imagined as returning when the Golden Age is fully restored.

9. Revard, *Tangles of Neaera's Hair* 66–87.

10. There are no close analogues for these companion poems, though anthologies sometimes printed together contrasting poems by different authors, e.g., John Fletcher's "Hence all you vain Delights" spoken by Melancholy, and William Strode's poem "Against Melancholy."

11. *YP* I, 289. Though *Prolusion VII* cannot be dated with certainty, most critics place it in 1631–32.

12. Rosemond Tuve, *Images and Themes in Five Poems by Milton* (Cambridge, Mass.: Harvard UP, 1957) 15–36. The poems also incorporate elements of other literary kinds: the academic debate, the Theocritan pastoral idyll of the ideal day and its festivals, the Theophrastian prose "character" with such titles as "The Happy Man" and "The Melancholy Man," and encomia in poetry and prose.

13. See Robert Burton's contemporary account, *The Anatomy of Melancholy* (London, 1621); and Raymond Klibansky, Erwin Panofsky, and Fritz Saxl, *Saturn and Melancholy* (New York: Basic Books, 1964).

14. See Annabel Patterson, " 'Forc'd fingers': Milton's Early Poems and Ideological Constraint," *The Muses Common-Weale,* ed. Claude Summers and Ted-Larry Pebworth (Columbia: U of Missouri P, 1988) 9–22.

15. For a different reading see, e.g., Stanley Fish, "What It's Like to Read *L'Allegro* and *Il Penseroso,*" *Milton Studies* 7 (1975): 77–99.

16. Hebrews 12:26–27 reads, "Yet once more I shake not the earth only, but also heaven./ And this word, Yet once more, signifieth the removing of those things that are shaken, as of things that are made, that those things which cannot be shaken may remain." See Joseph A. Wittreich, Jr., *Visionary Poetics: Milton's Tradition and His Legacy* (San Marino: Huntington Library, 1979) 137–53.

17. [George] Puttenham, *The Arte of English Poesie* (London, 1589) 39, identifies two varieties of funeral song: "*Epicedia* if they were sung by many, and *Monodia* if they were uttered by one alone."

18. The funeral elegy and its parts are discussed in O. B. Hardison, *The Enduring Monument* (Chapel Hill: U of North Carolina P, 1962); and Ellen Lambert, *Placing Sorrow: A Study of the Pastoral Elegy Convention from Theocritus to Milton* (Chapel Hill: U of North Carolina P, 1975).

19. See *A Variorum Commentary on the Poems of John Milton,* vol. II.2, ed. A. S. P. Woodhouse and Douglas Bush (New York: Columbia UP, 1972) 544–734, for allusions and a resumé of criticism; also Revard, *Tangles of Nearea's Hair* 179–90.

20. In fact, King's poems display royalist and Laudian sentiments; Milton deals with King's politics by entirely eliding them.

21. Cedric Brown, "Milton and the Idolatrous Consort," *Criticism* 35 (1993): 429–30, notes that the wolf's predations point especially to a string of notorious female converts in the circle of the Roman Catholic queen, Henrietta Maria.
22. Peter's tirade and King's death resonate with the passage in Isaiah 56:10–57:1 warning of blind watchmen, greedy and drunken shepherds, and the righteous man "taken away from the evil to come"—often seen to predict impending national disaster.
23. See *Variorum* II.2: 686–704 for a survey of interpretations of this image, the poem's most-debated crux.
24. Or, he is perhaps mythologized as a classical Genius of a place, the Irish Sea, protecting English Protestants who cross it to conquer and colonize the rebellious Catholic Irish. See Lawrence Lipking, "The Genius of the Shore," *PMLA* 111 (1995): 205–21.
25. Wittreich, *Visionary Poetics* 142–43. Cf. 2 Kings 2:14–15.
26. See, e.g., Louis L. Martz, *Poet of Exile: A Study of Milton's Poetry* (New Haven: Yale UP, 1980) 31–59; and Thomas Corns, "Milton's Quest for Respectability," *Modern Language Review* 77 (1982): 769–79.
27. Ll. 27–28. See C. W. R. D. Moseley, *The Poetic Birth: Milton's Poems of 1645* (Aldershot: Scolar P, 1991) 82.

## READING LIST

Alpers, Paul. *What Is Pastoral?* Chicago: U of Chicago P, 1996.

Corns, Thomas. "Milton's Quest for Respectability." *Modern Language Review* 77 (1982): 769–79.

Fish, Stanley. "What It's Like to Read *L'Allegro* and *Il Penseroso*." *Milton Studies* 7 (1975): 77–99.

Hardison, O. B. *The Enduring Monument*. Chapel Hill: U of North Carolina P, 1962.

Lambert, Ellen. *Placing Sorrow: A Study of the Pastoral Elegy Convention from Theocritus to Milton*. Chapel Hill: U of North Carolina P, 1976.

Lewalski, Barbara K. *The Life of John Milton: A Critical Biography*. Rev. ed. Oxford: Blackwell, 2003.

Martz, Louis L. *Poet of Exile: A Study of Milton's Poetry*. New Haven: Yale UP, 1980.

Moseley, C. W. R. D. *The Poetic Birth: Milton's Poems of 1645*. Aldershot: Scolar P, 1991.

Patrides, C. A. *Milton's Lycidas: The Tradition and the Poem*. Rev. ed. Columbia: U of Missouri P, 1983.

Patterson, Annabel. "'Forc'd fingers': Milton's Early Poems and Ideological Constraint." *The Muses Common-Weale*. Ed. Claude Summers and Ted-Larry Pebworth. Columbia: U of Missouri P, 1988. 9–22.

Revard, Stella. *Milton and the Tangles of Neaera's Hair: The Making of the 1645 Poems*. Columbia: U of Missouri P, 1997.

Rollinson, Phillip. "Milton's Nativity Ode and the Decorum of Genre," *Milton Studies* 7 (1975): 165–84.

Tuve, Rosemond. *Images and Themes in Five Poems by Milton*. Cambridge, Mass.: Harvard UP, 1957.

Vendler, Helen. "Milton's *L'Allegro*." *Coming of Age as a Poet: Milton, Keats, Eliot, Plath*. Cambridge, MA: Harvard UP, 2003.

Wittreich, Joseph A., Jr. *Visionary Poetics: Milton's Tradition and His Legacy*. San Marino: Huntington Library, 1979.

# Notes on Contributors

**Catherine Bates** is reader in English Renaissance literature at the University of Warwick. Publications include *The Rhetoric of Courtship* (1992), *Play in a Godless World* (1999), and an edition of Sidney's poems (1994).

**Patrick Cheney** is professor of English and comparative literature at The Pennsylvania State University. Most recently, he is the author of *Shakespeare, National Poet-Playwright* (2004), *Shakespeare's Literary Authorship: Books, Poetry, and Theatre* (2007), and editor of *The Cambridge Companion to Shakespeare's Poetry* (2006).

**Danielle Clarke** is senior lecturer in English at University College Dublin. Publications include *The Politics of Early Modern Women's Writing* (2001) and an edition of *Three Renaissance Women Poets: Isabella Whitney, Aemilia Lanyer and Mary Sidney* (2000). She is currently working on relationships between gender and discourse in the early modern period.

**Lynn Enterline** is professor of English at Vanderbilt University. She is author of *The Rhetoric of the Body from Ovid to Shakespeare* (2000) and *The Tears of Narcissus: Melancholia and Masculinity in Early Modern Writing* (2005); She has published articles on Ovid, Petrarch, Shakespeare, Webster, Marvell, Milton, and problems in literary and feminist theory in *The Oxford Companion to Shakespeare* (2004), *Shakespeare Quarterly*, *Shakespeare Studies*, and *The Yale Journal of Criticism*. At present, she is writing *Shakespeare's Schoolroom*, a book about what Shakespeare's depictions of character and emotion have to tell us about the Latin grammar school's discursive and material practices.

**Lowell Gallagher** is associate professor of English at the University of California, Los Angeles. He is the author *Medusa's Gaze: Casuistry and Conscience in the Renaissance* (1991) and articles on early modern English Catholicism, postmodern ethics, and hermeneutic theory. Recent publications include "Balloons and Guillotines: Francis Poulenc's Ethics of Mutilation," in *Recherches Semiotiques / Semiotic Inquiry* 23 (2003), and "Waiting for Gobbo," in *Spiritual Shakespeares*, ed. Ewan Fernie (2005).

**Jonathan Goldberg** is Arts and Sciences Distinguished Professor of English at Emory University. His most recent book is *Tempest in the Caribbean* (2004).

**Achsah Guibbory** is now professor of English at Barnard College, Columbia University, after many years at the University of Illinois. In addition to having published many essays on Donne and other seventeenth-century writers, she is the author of *The Map of Time* (1986) and *Ceremony and Community from Herbert to* Milton (1998) and editor of *The Cambridge Companion to John Donne* (2005).

**Andrew Hadfield** is professor and head of the department of English at the University of Sussex. He is the author of a number of books on Renaissance literature, including *Edmund Spenser's Irish Experience: Wilde Fruit and Salvage Soil* (1997) and *Shakespeare and Republicanism* (2005). He is the editor, with Raymond Gillespie, of *The Oxford History of the Irish Book, Vol. III: The Irish Book in English, 1550–1800* (2005).

**Elizabeth D. Harvey** is associate professor of English and director of graduate studies at the University of Toronto. She is the author of *Ventriloquized Voices: Feminist Theory and Renaissance Texts* (1992) and, most recently, editor of *Sensible Flesh: On Touch in Early Modern Culture* (2003) and coeditor, with Theresa Krier, of *Luce Irigaray and Premodern Culture* (2004).

**Thomas Healy** is professor of Renaissance studies at Birkbeck College, University of London. He is the author of three books on Renaissance writers and editor of the *Arnold Anthology of British and Irish Literature in English* (1997).

**Peter C. Herman** is professor of English and comparative literature at San Diego State University. He has published two books, *Destabilizing Milton: "Paradise Lost" and the Poetics of Incertitude* (2005) and *Squitter-wits and Muse-haters: Sidney, Spenser, Milton and Renaissance Antipoetic Sentiment* (1996), as well as edited a number of anthologies, including *Approaches to Teaching Milton's Shorter Poetry and Prose* (forthcoming), *Historicizing Theory* (2004), and *Reading Monarchs Writing: The Poetry of Henry VIII, Mary, Queen of Scots, Elizabeth I, and James VI/I* (2002). His essays have appeared in such journals as *Renaissance Quarterly*, *SEL*, and *Criticism*.

**William J. Kennedy** is professor of comparative literature at Cornell University. On the topic of Renaissance poetry, he has published *Authorizing Petrarch* (1994) and *The Site of Petrarchism: Early Modern National Sentiment in Italy, France, and England* (2003).

**John N. King** is Distinguished University Professor and Humanities Distinguished Professor of English and Religious Studies at The Ohio State University. Most recently, he is the author of *Milton and Religious Controversy: Satire and Polemic in* Paradise Lost (2000) and *Foxe's* Book of Martyrs *and Early Modern Print Culture* (2006) and editor of *Voices of the English Reformation: A Sourcebook* (2004).

**Laura Lunger Knoppers** is professor of English at Pennsylvania State University. Most recently, she is author of *Constructing Cromwell: Ceremony, Portrait, and Print* (2000) and editor, with Joan Landes, of *Monstrous Bodies/Political Monstrosities in Early Modern Europe* (2004).

**Barbara K. Lewalski** is William R. Kenan Professor of History and Literature and of English Literature at Harvard University. Her recent books include *The Life of John Milton: A Critical Biography* (2000, rev. 2003) and *Writing Women in Jacobean England, 1603–1624* (1993). She also edits the seventeenth-century section of *The Norton Anthology of English Literature*.

**Steven May** retired in 2004 as professor of English at Georgetown College. With William A. Ringler, Jr., he compiled *Elizabethan Poetry: A Bibliography and First-Line Index of English Verse, 1559–1603* (2004). He is also the editor of *Queen Elizabeth I: Selected Works* (2004).

**Arthur F. Marotti** is professor of English at Wayne State University. He is the author of the recently published *Religious Ideology and Cultural Fantasy: Catholic and Anti-Catholic Discourses in Early Modern England* (2005) as well as *Manuscript, Print, and the English Renaissance Lyric* (1995) and *John Donne, Coterie Poet* (1986).

**Andrew McRae** is professor of Renaissance studies at the University of Exeter. He is the author of *God Speed the Plough: The Representation of Agrarian England* (1996) and *Literature, Satire and the Early Stuart State* (2004) and coeditor of the electronically published "Early Stuart Libels: An Edition of Poetry from Manuscript Sources."

**Naomi J. Miller** is professor of English and women's studies at Smith College. The author and editor of two books on Mary Wroth, she is coeditor, with Naomi Yavneh, of *Maternal Measures: Figuring Caregiving in the Early Modern World* (2000), and editor of *Reimagining Shakespeare for Children and Young Adults* (2003).

**William A. Oram** is Helen Means professor of English at Smith College. He is the coordinating editor of the *Yale Edition of the Shorter Poems of Edmund Spenser* (1989) and the author of *Edmund Spenser* (1997) and articles on Spenser, Milton, and other Renaissance writers.

**Sasha Roberts** is lecturer in English at the University of Kent. Her publications include *Women Reading Shakespeare 1660–1900* (1997), *Writers and Their Work: Romeo and Juliet* (1998), and *Reading Shakespeare's Poems in Early Modern England* (2003).

**Julie Sanders** is professor of English literature and drama at the University of Nottingham. She has published several books and articles on Ben Jonson and Caroline drama and is the author, most recently, of *Adaptation and Appropriation* (2006).

**Michael Schoenfeldt** is professor of English at the University of Michigan. Most recently, he is the author of *Bodies and Selves in Early Modern England: Physiology and Inwardness in Spenser, Shakespeare, Herbert, and Milton* (Cambridge: Cambridge University Press, 1999) and editor of the *Blackwell Companion to Shakespeare's Sonnets* (2006).

**Alan Sinfield** is a professor in the department of English at the University of Sussex and teaches on the M.A. program "Sexual Dissidence and Cultural Change." His publications include *Cultural Politics—Queer Reading* (2d ed., 2005) and *On Sexuality and Power* (2004). He is completing a new book: *Unfinished Business: Authority and Sexuality in Shakespeare and His Contemporaries.*

**Garrett A. Sullivan, Jr.,** is professor of English at Pennsylvania State University. He is the author of *The Drama of Landscape: Land, Property, and Social Relations on the Early Modern Stage* (1998) and *Memory and Forgetting in English Renaissance Drama: Shakespeare, Marlowe, Webster* (2005).

**Bart van Es** is a fellow and university lecturer at St. Catherine's College, Oxford. He is the author of *Spenser's Forms of History* (2002) and editor of *A Critical Companion to Spenser Studies* (2006).

**John Watkins** is professor of English and medieval studies at the University of Minnesota. He is the author of *The Specter of Dido: Spenser and Virgilian Epic* (1995),

*Representing Elizabeth in Stuart England: Literature, History, Sovereignty* (2002), and numerous articles on medieval and Renaissance literature.

**Helen Wilcox** is professor of English at the University of Wales, Bangor. She has published widely on early modern English literature and is the editor of *Women and Literature in Britain, 1500–1700* (1996) and *The English Poems of George Herbert* (2007).

**Susanne Woods** is provost and professor of English at Wheaton College in Massachusetts. Her books include *Natural Emphasis: The Development of English Versification* (1985) and *Lanyer: A Renaissance Woman Poet* (1999).

# Index